Elgar Encyclopedia of Environmental Crime

ELGAR ENCYCLOPEDIAS IN THE SOCIAL SCIENCES

Elgar Encyclopedias in the Social Sciences serve as the definitive reference works to their fields. Each *Encyclopedia* is overseen by an editor internationally recognised as a leading name within the field, and contains a multitude of entries written by key scholars, providing an accessible and condensed overview of the key topics within a given subject area. Volumes in the series are commissioned across the breadth of the social sciences, and cover areas including, but not limited to, Political Science, Sociology, Human Geography, Development Studies, Social Policy, Public Management and Public Policy. Individual entries present a concise and logical overview of a given subject, together with a list of references for further study. Each *Encyclopedia* will serve as an invaluable resource for practitioners, academics, and students, and should form an essential part of any research journey.

Elgar Encyclopedia of Environmental Crime

Edited by

Rob White

Emeritus Distinguished Professor of Criminology, School of Social Sciences, University of Tasmania, Australia

ELGAR ENCYCLOPEDIAS IN THE SOCIAL SCIENCES

Edward Elgar PUBLISHING

Cheltenham, UK • Northampton, MA, USA

Published by
Edward Elgar Publishing Limited
The Lypiatts
15 Lansdown Road
Cheltenham
Glos GL50 2JA
UK

Edward Elgar Publishing, Inc.
William Pratt House
9 Dewey Court
Northampton
Massachusetts 01060
USA

A catalogue record for this book
is available from the British Library

Library of Congress Control Number: 2024951132

This book is available electronically in the **Elgar**online
Sociology, Social Policy and Education subject collection
https://doi.org/10.4337/9781803923833

MIX
Paper | Supporting responsible forestry
FSC® C013604

ISBN 978 1 80392 382 6 (cased)
ISBN 978 1 80392 383 3 (eBook)

Printed and bound by CPI Group (UK) Ltd, Croydon, CR0 4YY

Contents

Contributors

Sharareh Abtahi, Qom State University, Iran

Michelle Anagnostou, University of Waterloo, Canada

Inés Arroyo-Quiroz, Centro Regional de Investigaciones Multidisciplinarias, UNAM, Mexico

Alexander Baird, Deakin University, Australia

Ash Barnes, University of Tasmania, Australia

Stoyan Barrett, Independent Researcher, Durham, United Kingdom

Lieselot Bisschop, Erasmus University Rotterdam, the Netherlands

Matthew Box, University of New England, Australia

Marília De Nardin Budó, Law Department, Federal University of Santa Catarina, Brazil

Michelangelo Casali, Department of Oncology and Hemato-oncology, University of Milano, Italy

Melanie Flynn, Liverpool Hope University, United Kingdom

Ekaterina Gladkova, Northumbria University, United Kingdom

David R. Goyes, University of Oslo, Norway

Aalayna R. Green, Department of Natural Resources & the Environment, Cornell University, USA

Mark Hamilton, Thomas Moore Law School, Australian Catholic University, Australia

Alistair Harkness, University of New England, Australia

Monica Pons Hernandez, Universitat Rovira i Virgili, Spain

Chelsea Hickman, University of Tasmania, Australia

Annette Hübschle, Global Risk Governance Programme, Faculty of Law, University of Cape Town, South Africa

Melissa Jarrell Ozymy, The University of Nevada, Reno, United States

Jack A. Lampkin, York St John University, United Kingdom

Alexandra Lebron, Florida International University, United States

Joel Maddock-James, York St John University, United Kingdom

Kyle Mulrooney, University of New England, Australia

Lorenzo Natali, School of Law, University of Milano-Bicocca, Italy

Angus Nurse, Anglia Ruskin University, United Kingdom

Delon Omrow, Ontario Tech University, Canada

Abby Muricho Onencan, Erasmus University Rotterdam, the Netherlands

Joshua Ozymy, The University of Nevada, Reno, United States

Cassie Pedersen, Federation University, Australia

Gary R. Potter, Lancaster University, United Kingdom

Brandon Rochester, York St John University, United Kingdom

Lily Rubino, University of Cambridge, United Kingdom

Michael Smith, Griffith University, Australia

Ragnhild Sollund, University of Oslo, Norway

Nigel South, University of Essex, United Kingdom

Toine Spapens, University of Tilburg, the Netherlands

Peter Stoett, Faculty of Social Science & Humanities, Ontario Tech University, Canada

Noriyoshi Takemura, Toin University of Yokohama, Japan

Daan van Uhm, Utrecht University, the Netherlands

Karin van Wingerde, Erasmus University Rotterdam, the Netherlands

Sammie Verbeek, Erasmus University Rotterdam, the Netherlands

Reece Walters, Deakin University, Australia

Rob White, University of Tasmania, Australia

1. Thinking about environmental crime

Introduction

This entry provides a general introduction to the study and analysis of environmental crime. It observes that the notion of 'environmental crime' is far from simple. To demonstrate its complexities, the entry discusses its conceptual variations with respect to legality, harm, seriousness, justice and sustainability. Fundamentally, how we think about environmental crime has implications for how we measure it, explain it, understand its consequences, and respond to it.

The Encyclopedia as a whole examines many dimensions of environmental crime – its nature and dynamics, its victims and perpetrators, and state and community responses to it. A wide range of topics are covered in the book. These have been grouped to reflect overarching themes:

- Theories, concepts and approaches
- Crimes of extraction
- Crimes of contamination
- Crimes of use and modification
- Environmental injustice and victimisation
- Offenders and perpetrators
- Combatting environmental crime

Superficially, while the term 'environmental crime' seems simple and straightforward, the entries in this encyclopedia demonstrate the complexities of environmental crime as a concrete phenomenon. Moreover, as discussed in this first entry, the *concept* of environmental crime is itself contentious, complicated and contested. One of the hallmarks of green criminology, as a pivotal way in which to examine and interpret environmental harm, is the adoption of a critical perspective on environment-related issues (Brisman & South, 2021; White, 2022). This also applies to how we define and respond to the idea of environmental crime.

Legality

From a strictly legal perspective, environmental crime is what the law says it is (Situ & Emmons, 2000). That is, if an activity or omission affecting the environment (including e.g., ecosystems, rivers, non-human animals and plants) is listed in legislation as a serious offence (generally due to the degree of harm it causes), then transgression of that law may be accompanied by criminal proceedings.

A defining characteristic of environmental crime is that many of the activities legally defined as criminal are, under normal circumstances, simply treated as ordinary activities (Bricknell, 2010). The prefix 'illegal' is thus placed on activities that otherwise would be considered legitimate: for instance, illegal fishing; illegal logging; illegal mining; illegal trade in wildlife; illegal pollution; and illegal land clearing.

The types of activities usually included under the umbrella of environmental crime include resource offences and pollution offences. *Resource offences* typically deal with extraction from the environment. These include, for example, illegally taking fish from the sea, minerals from the earth and trees from the forest. It also includes altering or changing aspects of the natural world, such as through illegal land clearance. *Pollution offences* include the illegal introduction of contaminates into air, water and land, with the result that the environment is defiled and degraded in some way.

The fact that many environmental crimes encapsulate activities that are in other circumstances legal complicates their status, study of them, and their prevention (Bisschop, 2015; Ruggiero & South, 2013; van Uhm, 2016; Wyatt, 2022). For instance, the interplay between legal and illegal means that illegal waste mixed in with legal waste becomes harder to detect and prosecute. Likewise, the legal trade in wildlife creates difficulties when it comes to identifying which individuals and species are on prohibited lists, especially if the bird, lizard or plant closely resembles a legally traded specimen. Similarly, most pollution, for example from factories and power plants, is regulated but perfectly legal. The issue is one of allowable levels, not prohibition as such. Thus, examination of pollution crimes needs to be undertaken in the context of regulatory frameworks and measurement capacities. The crime is determined by transgression of standards and thresholds; it does not reside in the activity itself.

Harm

A critical green perspective also looks at environmental crime from a harm perspective

(Brisman & South, 2021; Gacek & Jochelson, 2022; White, 2022). This usually refers to the *ecological impact* of human activities, not simply whether they are legal or not. For example, environmentally harmful activities include deforestation (not just illegal logging), carbon emissions (the contribution to climate change), destruction of habitat (not just illegal mining), and threats to biodiversity (not just wildlife trafficking).

Central to understanding the social construction of activities as state-sanctioned environmental crime is examination of who wields the power to legally define what is 'wrong' and 'harmful'. Who defines what is criminal is ultimately determined by the balance of political forces in a society. That is, defining environmental crime is shaped by specific sectional interests and power dynamics.

This is important insofar as powerful elites, economic and political, determine the contours of environmental and criminal laws in ways that generally privilege their interests. These specific sectoral interests may be related to the state. For example, laws that allow fracking and mineral and oil exploration may generate revenue for state coffers that government leaders find attractive, regardless of environmental costs. Corporations that profit from resource extraction, contamination and modification will influence lawmakers to protect and secure their interests. Thus, there is a close connection between what is officially sanctioned as environmental crime and what is not, and whose interests are ultimately served in protective legislation.

A harm perspective offers an alternative vision of 'right' and 'wrong'. Less important is what the law says. What really matters is whether and how activities affect the environment. For example, the construction of dams, and substitution of vegetation (such as corn crops) in geographical areas formerly populated by other types of plants (for example, tropical and temperate forests), may cause great ecological harm and disruption. Assessments of potential and substantive harms form a key component in this kind of analysis.

Harm also provides a lens into how victimhood and victimisation are socially constructed. The law defines who or what is a victim (or that requires a duty of care) in given circumstances. Largely, humans are the ones legally defined as victims of environmental crime, who may suffer economic damage, threats to livelihood, and risks to their health and well-being because of certain harms (e.g., air pollution and illnesses). Again, critical green criminology wishes to extend the notion of victimhood to include the non-human regardless of legality (Flynn & Hall, 2017; Maher, Beirne & Pierpoint, 2017). Environmental entities such as rivers, mountains, plants and non-human animals thus may be victimised regardless of legal status. From this perspective, both humans and the non-human count when it comes to assessing risk, threat and harm.

Seriousness

How humans interact with the environment always has an impact of some kind. The question, therefore, is how best to view this interaction and how best to regulate human behaviour in ways that minimise harm (White, 2023).

Some harms can be considered *malum in se* – that is, serious in their own right; so serious in fact that they require immediate prevention and prohibition. The poisoning and contamination of freshwater, for example, may be considered harmful to the extent that it warrants community intervention because of the gravity of the harm, especially if the main consumers are residents. The main issue here is to 'eradicate the problem' (usually framed in terms of the banning of specific substances or activities). The intent of the law is the prevention and abolition of harmful practices, as seen for example in the application of public interest law in India to stop polluting industries from destroying sites of national significance (Mehta, 2009). However, determinations of risk, threat and harm are generally contentious politically (e.g., what level of arsenic in water is 'safe' from the point of view of human consumption) and require scientific as well as other kinds of knowledge assessments (e.g., application of Indigenous modes of knowing, feeling and valuing).

A lesser form of harm is those activities considered *malum prohibitum* – that is, harm that is an offence because it relates to rule-breaking, not because it is intrinsically bad. For example, contamination of water from a factory may be allowable up to certain defined limits, after which it is considered harmful and an offence. It thus becomes a formal transgression when it surpasses pre-determined legal limits and standards. Fishing over the allowable quota, for instance, is considered illegal. However, it is not the fishing activity itself which is deemed to be the problem, but over-fishing as defined in relevant licensing provisions and fishing laws. Within this framework, it is the illegal aspects of ordinary legitimate practices that are problematic.

State interventions around environmental crime tend to reflect the latter approach to harm. Very few activities affecting the environment are considered bad in themselves. Rather, there is a scale of harmfulness that is reflected in state responses to certain activities. This is generally reflected in the continuum of sanctions that range from administrative measures (such as issuing a fine for trespass or fishing out of season) and civil measures (such as injunctions to stop specific activities (such as land clearance and cutting down of trees) through to criminal sanctions (such as, at its most harsh, the use of imprisonment). This continuum represents official conceptions of and legally defined measures of seriousness of harm, and the sanctions vary within each sphere of state intervention, with criminal sanctions usually the most punishing.

The differences (and tensions) between conceptions of harm as *malum in se* and *malum prohibitum* are evident in public debates on whether to ban and prohibit specific activities (such as trade in wildlife, transportation of hazardous waste) or permitting but regulating specific activities (such as public entry into national parks and marine parks in accordance with use rules). Critics of international laws such as the Convention on the International Trade in Endangered Species of Wild Fauna and Flora (CITES), for example, argue that such laws facilitate harmful behaviour against non-animals and plants rather than protecting species from further exploitation (Sollund, 2019). For critics, this is a matter of empathy and justice.

Justice

In discussing environmental crime and justice, three philosophical perspectives are of relevance (Brisman & South, 2018; Halsey & White, 1998). An anthropocentric worldview tends to put human needs and human rights at the centre. Harm is judged in relation to these rather than through reference to the requirements of the non-human entity such as river, forest or kangaroo. The environment is basically viewed as a resource for humans.

By contrast, a biocentric viewpoint tends to equate all species as being equal in status and value. Accordingly, harm is gauged in terms of any human action that diminishes or destroys another part of the ecosystem, including other species and the ecosystem itself. Humans may be conceived as being of no greater importance or value than any other part of the biosphere.

An ecocentric perspective sees nature as having value in and of itself, and humans are viewed not only as part of the web of life but as having a vital and leading role in both the destruction and preservation of the natural environment. Harm, in this conception, has both social and ecological dimensions since it is construed as both a social phenomenon (affecting different groups of humans in different ways) and an ecological phenomenon (affecting local habitats, ecosystems, birds and animals as well as humans).

Translated into an eco-justice three-pronged framework, these kinds of ideas offer different points of focus and action (White, 2013, 2022). *Environmental justice* deals with humans and their access to and use of the environment. Recent work around environmental justice, for example, has looked at how racial discrimination is embedded in environmental inequalities (such as access to clean water), and how European colonialism has ravaged the lands, knowledge and cultures of people geographically distant from the original homeland (through the imposition of foreign rule, the capitalist mode of production and Western knowledge systems). Harm, here, is basically harm associated with the exploitation of natural resources perpetrated against human population groups on the basis of race, ethnicity, geography, and language and culture.

Species justice refers to the notion that non-human animals and plants have specific rights and status that, while still generally unrecognised in law, ought to be protected and cherished. Speciesism is the term used to describe the discriminatory treatment of non-human animals. The protection of biodiversity, including plants and animals, is also an expression of species justice. Harm, here, generally refers to threats to the well-being and viability of species at the individual level, the group level and the species level.

A wider systems perspective underpins the notion of *ecological justice*. This refers to human behaviour as it affects specific ecosystems and indeed the Earth as a whole. Justice is sometimes framed in the language of the 'rights of nature', an effort to extend formal legal rights to specific rivers, mountains, regions and species. Harm, here, is viewed as that which impinges upon the capacity of environmental entities to 'be' and to 'do' as nature allows and intended. Disruption and destruction of ecological systems constitutes one of the major harms on the planet today.

These dimensions of eco-justice are reflected in the actions of local and global environmental activist groups. There are movements for justice in relation to non-human animals, communities suffering from environmental disaster and calamity, and to protect forests, rivers and ecosystems both specific and general.

Sustainability

The nature–human relationship features diverse kinds of respect, interaction, utility and morality. An ecocentric perspective emphasises the intrinsic value of nature as well as the necessity for humans to live in nature by using that which is provided by nature. There is a mutual reciprocity at play (Goyes, 2019).

Harm can also be defined, negatively, in terms of loss or diminishment. A key concept here is sustainability, where this refers to notions of ongoing ecological and environmental balance over time (Merchant, 2005; Al-Damkhi et al., 2009). A loss of environmental resources or biological diversity can thus be construed as harmful if 'sustainability' is the yardstick by which harm is measured.

However, much of the nature–human relationship globally is dominated by the capitalist mode of production, a system that prioritises profit over ecology and economic over environmental benefit. This system is anthropocentric to its core. But more than this, it is based on the exploitation of both the human and the non-human – via wage slavery, expropriation of traditional lands, invasion, natural resource extraction and generation of widespread pollution, contamination and waste. Harming people and places are ingrained in the commodity production (and consumption) process, as evident for example, in the pollution and waste, sickness and mortality, associated with the fast fashion industry. Global studies of environmental crimes and harms attest to the reach of such ideologies and practices (Arroyo-Quiroz & Wyatt, 2018; Goyes, 2023; Goyes et al., 2017; Sollund, Stefes & Germani, 2016; Wong, 2019; Zabyelina & van Uhm, 2020).

The lack of sustainability is one of the hallmarks of dominant systems of production worldwide. Yet, an ecocentric cosmology (vision of the universe) and ontology (ways of being) have demonstrated in practice that sustainable ways to live in and with nature are possible (Goyes, 2019). This is evident from analysis of the pre-colonial days of Indigenous communities, where some groups lived for tens of thousands of years in what might be considered harsh and unforgiving physical environments (e.g., deserts, tundra). Rather than substantive harm being a feature of such philosophies and societies, the emphasis was and continues to be on nurturing and preserving the integrity of the totality of nature, humans included. Importantly, among the leaders in the movements against exploitation and for a re-balancing of the dominant nature–human relations are women (Milne et al., 2023). The themes of healing and renewal feature in discourses that emphasise sustainability rather than exploitation, exclusion and inequality.

Conclusion

As this entry has demonstrated, there is no one definition or singular understanding of environmental crime. Rather, there are various ways in which to conceptualise it, each of which has consequences for social action around environmental crime. The specific manner in which one thinks about and interprets harms affecting the environment also has implications for how we measure and respond to it. Legal definitions inform much of the international and national reporting of environmental crimes. Yet, wider definitions of harm, justice and sustainability also alert us to the serious harms occurring outside of mainstream legal frameworks. Thus, environmental crime is a contested term, one that inevitably reflects varying emphasis on and understandings of legality, morality and ecology.

ROB WHITE

ROB WHITE

Further reading

Arroyo-Quiroz, A. & Wyatt, T. (eds) (2018) *Green Crime in Mexico: A Collection of Case Studies*. Basingstoke: Palgrave Macmillan.

Goyes, D. (ed.) (2023) *Green Crime in the Global South: Essays on Southern Green Criminology*. Basingstoke: Palgrave Macmillan.

Mesko, G., Dimitrijevic, D. & Fields, C. (eds) (2010) *Understanding and Managing Threats to the Environment in South Eastern Europe*. Dordrecht: Springer.

Sollund, R., Stefes, C. & Germani, A. (eds) (2016) *Fighting Environmental Crime in Europe and Beyond*. Basingstoke: Palgrave Macmillan.

United Nations Office on Drugs and Crime (2024) *World Wildlife Crime Report 2024: Trafficking in Protected Species*. Vienna: UNODC.

White, R. (ed.) (2009) *Environmental Crime: A Reader*. London: Willan/Routledge.

Wong, R. (2019) *The Illegal Wildlife Trade in China: Understanding the Distribution Networks*. Basingstoke: Palgrave Macmillan.

Wyatt, T. (2022) *Wildlife Trafficking: A Deconstruction of the Crime, the Victims, and the Offenders*. Basingstoke: Palgrave Macmillan.

Zabyelina, Y. & van Uhm, D. (eds) (2020) *Illegal Mining: Organized Crime, Corruption and Ecocide in a Resource-Scarce World*. Basingstoke: Palgrave Macmillan.

References

Al-Damkhi, A., Khuraibet, A., Abdul-Wahab, S. & Al-Attar, F. (2009) 'Toward Defining the Concept of Environmental Crime on the Basis of Sustainability', *Environmental Practice*, 11(2): 115–124.

Arroyo-Quiroz, A. & Wyatt, T. (eds) (2018) *Green Crime in Mexico: A Collection of Case Studies*. Basingstoke: Palgrave Macmillan.

Bisschop, L. (2015) *Governance of the Illegal Trade in E-Waste and Tropical Timber: Case Studies on Transnational Environmental Crime*. Farnham, UK: Ashgate.

Bricknell, S. (2010) Environmental Crime in Australia. AIC Reports Research and Public Policy Series 109. Canberra: Australian Institute of Criminology.

Brisman, A. & South, N. (2018) 'Green Criminology and Environmental Crimes and Harms', *Sociology Compass*, 13(1): e12650. https://doi.org/10.1111/soc4.12650

Brisman, A. & South, N. (eds) (2021) *The Routledge Handbook of Green Criminology*. Abingdon: Routledge.

Flynn, M. & Hall, M. (2017) 'The Case for a Victimology of Nonhuman Animal Harms', *Contemporary Justice Review*, 20(3): 299–318.

Gacek, J. & Jochelson, R. (eds) (2022) *Green Criminology and the Law*. Basingstoke: Palgrave Macmillan.

Goyes, D. (2019) *Southern Green Criminology: A Science to End Ecological Discrimination*. Bingley, UK: Emerald Publishing.

Goyes, D. (ed.) (2023) *Green Crime in the Global South: Essays on Southern Green Criminology*. Basingstoke: Palgrave Macmillan.

Goyes, D., Mol, H., Brisman, A. & South, N. (2017) *Environmental Crime in Latin America: The Theft of Nature and the Poisoning of the Land*. Basingstoke: Palgrave Macmillan.

Halsey, M. & White, R. (1998) 'Crime, Ecophilosophy and Environmental Harm', *Theoretical Criminology*, 2(3): 345–372.

Maher, J., Beirne, P. & Pierpoint, H. (eds) (2017) *The Palgrave International Handbook of Animal Abuse Studies*. Basingstoke: Palgrave Macmillan.

Mehta, M. (2009) *In the Public Interest: Landmark Judgment and Orders of the Supreme Court of India on Environmental and Human Rights*, vols 1–3. New Delhi: Prakriti Publications.

Merchant, C. (2005) *Radical Ecology: The Search for a Liveable World*. New York: Routledge.

Milne, E., Davies, P., Heydon, J., Peggs, K. & Wyatt, T. (eds) (2023) *Gendering Green Criminology*. Bristol: Bristol University Press.

Ruggiero, V. & South, N. (2013) 'Toxic State–Corporate Crimes, Neo-liberalism and Green Criminology: The Hazards and Legacies of the Oil, Chemical and Mineral Industries', *International Journal for Crime, Justice and Social Democracy*, 2(2): 12–26.

Situ, Y. & Emmons, D. (2000) *Environmental Crime: The Criminal Justice Systems' Role in Protecting the Environment*. Thousand Oaks, CA: Sage.

Sollund, R. (2019) *The Crimes of Wildlife Trafficking: Issues of Justice, Legality and Morality*. Abingdon: Routledge.

Sollund, R., Stefes, C. & Germani, A. (eds) (2016) *Fighting Environmental Crime in Europe and Beyond*. Basingstoke: Palgrave Macmillan.

van Uhm, D. (2016) *The Illegal Wildlife Trade: Inside the World of Poachers, Smugglers and Traders*. London: Springer.

White, R. (2013) *Environmental Harm: An Eco-Justice Perspective*. Bristol: Policy Press.

White, R. (2022) *Theorising Green Criminology: Selected Essays*. Abingdon: Routledge.

White, R. (2023) *Advanced Introduction to Applied Green Criminology*. Cheltenham, UK

and Northampton, MA, USA: Edward Elgar Publishing.
Wong, R. (2019) *The Illegal Wildlife Trade in China: Understanding the Distribution Networks.* Basingstoke: Palgrave Macmillan.
Wyatt, T. (2022) *Wildlife Trafficking: A Deconstruction of the Crime, the Victims, and the Offenders.* Basingstoke: Palgrave Macmillan.
Zabyelina, Y. & van Uhm, D. (eds) (2020) *Illegal Mining: Organized Crime, Corruption and Ecocide in a Resource-Scarce World.* Basingstoke: Palgrave Macmillan.

Rob White

PART I

THEORIES, CONCEPTS AND APPROACHES

2. Astro-green criminology and environmental harms

Introduction

Astro-green criminology is an emerging area of green criminology founded by Noriyoshi Takemura in 2019. Since then, a small but growing body of work has amassed, addressing issues relating to outer space and anthropogenic environmental harm, some of which has been dubbed 'space criminology' (Lampkin and White, 2023). So far, this work has largely focussed on orbital space debris, space mining, and emissions pollutions. In 2021, Lampkin provided the first definition of astro-green criminology and thereby laid the foundations for further study. While additional astro-green issues have since been considered, there are still many outer space issues yet to be addressed from within this perspective. This entry deliberates these problems, while at the same time emphasising the importance of astro-green criminological research as humans enter a new – private and commercially driven – space race, that looks set to cause many terrestrial and extra-terrestrial environmental harms in the coming decades.

Defining astro-green criminology

The term *astro-green criminology* (AGC) is used to describe an area of study pertaining to environmental harms connected with outer space. As such, the broad remit of astro-green criminological study is twofold. On the one hand, it is employed to describe the study of human activities that have an environmental impact off-Earth, such as the creation of planetary orbital debris or the mining of rare Earth elements on celestial bodies. On the other hand, astro-green criminological enquiry includes the study of environmental harms related to outer space activity and exploration that occur on-Earth, such as the ecological harms associated with space industry supply chains and rocket launchings. This entry will define AGC and explore the significance of this new field of academic enquiry including how it developed and the plans for future research.

Professor Noriyoshi Takemura of the Toin University of Yokohama, Japan, first coined the term astro-green criminology in his pioneering article entitled 'Astro-Green Criminology: A New Perspective Against Space Capitalism'. In this publication, Takemura (2019) is critical of contemporary anthropogenic interactions with outer space, analysing them from a zemiological perspective (one centred on harm) suggesting that outer space should be a wilderness to protect, rather than a frontier to exploit.

Although Takemura laid the foundations of AGC, highlighting several important areas of study (such as space mining and Earth orbital debris), it was Lampkin who provided the first definition of the subject in an article published in *Astropolitics: The International Journal of Space Politics and Policy*. Here, Lampkin (2021: 242) defined AGC as:

> the theoretical and practical study of space-related environmental harms and crimes that are facilitated by human actions. These harms can be Earth-based, atmospheric, or extra-terrestrial and may create human victims, non-human victims, and ecological victims both on Earth and in outer space.

This first definition of AGC was kept intentionally broad for two main reasons. First, the scope of environmentally harmful activity that has, and most likely will, occur in outer space is extremely diverse. For instance, anthropogenic harm can range from *micro issues* such as ecological harm in the immediate vicinity of rocket launch sites on Earth, to *macro issues* in terms of the contamination of celestial bodies with space junk and rocket propellants that exist many millions of miles away (such as on Earth's Moon or the planet Mars).

Second, the selective use of the terms 'Earth-based', 'atmospheric', and 'extra-terrestrial' accommodates both the wide array of issues that are encompassed within astro-green criminological study as well as the varied and distant locations where environmental harms can occur. The definition of AGC alludes to the numerous areas of study that are encompassed within the discipline (Lampkin, 2021).

Areas of study

Five key issues represent the main focus of an astro-green criminology (Lampkin, 2021: 243). These are:

(1) orbital space debris;
(2) space mining;
(3) emissions pollutions associated with space travel and exploration;
(4) the protection of space heritage sites; and
(5) the future uses of outer space, such as for extra-terrestrial colonisation and space tourism ventures.

Each of these aspects has an associated *environmental* element, whether that be related to the extraction of resources, or the harmful emissions produced through rocket launching.

Ultimately, what constitutes the 'environment' is of great significance to an area of study that claims to consider *environmental* harm – hence the 'green' element of AGC. Perhaps surprisingly, what composes the 'environment' off-Earth is in fact a contested area in itself. Consequently, it is important to outline some of the key arguments relating to exo-environments (that is, off-Earth spaces), because this is important to the future remit and study of AGC. Ultimately, there are arguments for and against considering outer space as an 'environment' (Reiman, 2009) and some of these arguments will be debated in the following paragraphs, starting with conceptualisations of outer space *as* an environment.

First, outer space contains planets that orbit the sun, including our own planet, the Earth. Although there is no conclusive evidence that complex life exists on other planets (or indeed, on other celestial bodies including moons, dwarf planets, asteroids, comets and so forth) as it does on Earth, primitive or microbial life may be present, and more complex life may have existed elsewhere in the past.

Scientific exploration activities have already confirmed the presence of water at the poles of Mars and Earth's Moon in the form of water ice, and this is likely to exist elsewhere in our own solar system. Even Mercury, the closest planet to the sun, contains water or water ice in deep craters that are permanently in the shadows, shielded from extreme temperatures and solar radiation (Schörghofer et al., 2021). Water in a place so close to the sun was historically thought to be impossible, but recent scientific explorations of such areas have revealed this is not the case. Therefore, due to the presence of water off-Earth, it is both reasonable and practical to think of such places as being an 'environment', just the same way that we consider lakes, oceans, rivers, and arctic locales as 'environments' on Earth.

It is also useful to think of outer space as an environment because it is arguably a closed system. The universe is so infinitely vast that it is nearly impossible to physically travel out of our own solar system, let alone transport ourselves to other star systems or galaxies, at least for the foreseeable future. For context, it takes roughly eight months of space travel to reach the (relatively nearby) planet of Mars with current technology (Carroll, 2009). These vast distances mean the remit of human expansion and colonisation off-Earth is limited to a finite number of other 'environments'; hence outer space can be seen, for now, as a closed system. This also means there is a finite number of accessible resources that our solar system environment can provide (Elvis and Milligan, 2019).

Finally, many have argued that there is intrinsic value in outer space matter (Peters, 2019; Reiman, 2009; Takemura, 2019). This perspective views extra-terrestrial spaces as so unique that they should remain untouched and undisturbed by humans. This ties in well with the concepts of *Earth jurisprudence* (Berry, 1999), *space jurisprudence* (Loder, 2018), and *general* or *universal jurisprudence* (Taylor, 1909, in Lampkin and Wyatt, 2022) which view Earth and outer space as interrelated places, rather than being distinct from each other. Such interconnectedness means that environmental protection is in the best interests of not only natural environments and ecologies, but also the human species as a whole. As Tan (2000: 146) explains 'just as we are beginning to view human interaction with the atmosphere, oceans, and other biological species as an integrated ecosystem (on Earth), this same environmental paradigm should be extended to outer space to encompass a holistic stellar-ecosystem'.

If outer space environments are acknowledged as having worth and status in their own right, then preventing harm to such environments becomes a major concern. However, the obvious criticism of proponent claims around the need for exo-environmental harm prevention is that such protective mechanisms have so far failed to prevent terrestrial environmental harms and therefore have limited value. Accordingly, some have argued that anthropogenic exploration of outer space should be avoided at all costs in order to, as Takemura (2019: 13) puts it, 'prevent us making the same mistakes in space as we have on Earth'.

There are, however, also several reasons for perceiving outer space as not being an 'environment' at all. A central idea is that there has been so little life found in outer space that celestial bodies are incapable of supporting any meaningful life and, therefore, there is no harm that can come from exploiting such places. Furthermore, outer space may contain elements that, if exploited, could offer solutions to Earth-environmental problems (such as energy creation and finite terrestrial natural resources) (Christensen et al., 2019). Therefore, protecting what are essentially barren and lifeless wildernesses may prevent humans from fulfilling their own terrestrial wants and needs.

A second argument against viewing outer space as an 'environment' follows a similar train of thought in that, if humans are considered to be the only complex life forms in the solar system, galaxy, or even universe, then they are the only ones with interests worth protecting, and therefore, ultimately, the only entities that matter (Chon-Torres et al., 2024). As a result of this anthropocentric perspective, some view outer space as a frontier to exploit for the benefit and advancement of human civilisation, the only known intelligent society (Lenard, 2001). As such, there would be no harm to any other intelligent life forms if outer space is exploited for human wants and needs.

Astro-green criminology was born out of the radical, critical criminological perspective of 'green criminology' which encompasses the study of environmental harms and crimes broadly conceived (discussed in more detail in the next section). As such, green criminologists largely advocate for environmentally protective solutions to anthropogenic activity that inhibit or limit environmental harms in the best interests of humans, non-humans and the natural world (all of whom rely on the Earth environment to survive and thrive). Astro-green criminologists have thus far also aligned with this protective mindset in the best interest of exo-environments, humans, and future generations who may also wish to use outer space.

Situating astro-green criminology

Criminology has historically focussed on the theoretical and practical study of criminal behaviours. This includes those human actions that violate the criminal law and are thus subjected to criminal sanctions. Conversely, zemiology is the study of harmful behaviours, irrespective of whether they constitute 'criminal' actions (Boukli and Kotzé, 2018; Canning and Tombs, 2021). The study of social harm was born out of the perceived failure of criminologists to study occurrences that were harmful yet lawful. Green criminologists straddle the boundary between harm and crime by researching environmentally harmful activities that are both legal and illegal. For green criminologists, environmental harm is a more purposeful and just object of study, rather than the narrow conception of crime (Nurse, 2015; White and Heckenberg, 2014). The main rationale for this is that what constitutes a crime varies over time, whereas harmful behaviour is more straightforward and consistent (Hopkins-Burke, 2018; Lampkin, 2020).

Astro-green criminology aligns with this green criminology tradition, that is, the study of astro-green harms and crimes. This is particularly important for AGC because there is no binding law applicable to outer space activities, so the term 'astro-criminology' would not sufficiently cover all the harmful behaviours that are not criminal. Consequently, focussing only on 'crime' would omit a large number of environmentally destructive practices and behaviours both on and off Earth.

The most influential 'law' pertaining to outer space is the Outer Space Treaty enacted at the height of the Cold War in 1967. This put limits on several anthropogenic actions in outer space, such as the national appropriation of celestial bodies. However, the Outer Space Treaty does not consider environmental issues, and not all states are party to the treaty. Even those that have signed the agreement are not specifically punished for actions that contravene it. As such, it is currently virtually impossible to commit a crime in outer space and, therefore, orthodox notions of criminology would not consider off-Earth behaviours. However, this situation is showing recent signs of change. Lampkin and White (2023) explain how some nation states are now implementing domestic laws that apply to their citizens when in outer space. 'For instance, in 2022 the Canadian parliament passed an amendment to the nation's Criminal Code to allow for the prosecution of crimes committed on the Moon. This follows previous legislation that extended its jurisdiction over criminal acts committed by *Canadian* astronauts during space travel to the International Space Station' (Lampkin and White, 2023: 4, emphasis in original).

Acknowledging these issues, a broader version of 'space criminology' has been developed that includes human actions in, or connected to, outer space, and that considers issues beyond purely environmental ones. Lampkin and White (2023) published the first book on *space criminology* which covers traditional 'astro-green' criminological issues (like space junk, space mining, and orbital debris), while also acknowledging other harmful and criminal behaviours of a non-environmental nature. This includes issues that connect with traditional criminological enquiry such as crimes of the powerful, inter-personal crimes, and illicit trade in space objects and materials. Space criminology thus offers an encompassing area of study that incorporates both green and non-green harm and crime issues.

Space criminology builds upon the foundations laid by astro-green criminological endeavours. Importantly, both AGC and space criminology, like the more established discipline of *green* criminology, are perhaps best imagined, to take from South (1998), as *perspectives* rather than rigid unitary theories. As such, the broad remit and conceptualisations of green, astro-green, and space criminologies enables academics and space practitioners to utilise whichever umbrella concept best fulfils the requirements of their research. While some may criticise such openness as being 'too broad' and lacking focus (Adakawa and Janardhana, 2022: 8), it can be suggested that criminology should be an open, interdisciplinary and collaborative venture that encourages researchers to tackle difficult and wide-ranging questions and projects. A broad criminological approach to the study of space harms would facilitate this kind of inclusive and constructive research environment, and this is undeniably a principal aim of space criminology.

Future research in astro-green criminology

At the time of writing there have only been a handful of publications that could be considered as contributing to an astro-green criminological perspective and understanding. These texts include foundational AGC publications (Lampkin, 2021; Takemura, 2019), a focus on space criminology (Eski and Lampkin, 2024; Lampkin and White, 2023; Sachdeva, 2023), space mining (Lampkin and McClanahan, 2024), orbital debris and space junk (Lampkin and South, Entry 23 in this encyclopedia), emissions pollutions (Lampkin and Carpio-Domínguez, 2024), and space heritage protection (Lampkin and Wyatt, 2022; Lampkin, 2020).

There are many areas that remain relatively unexplored from an astro-green criminological approach. These include issues surrounding the environmental and atmospheric impacts of space tourism, the environmental impacts of new and emerging space projects (such as NASA's Gateway Lunar Orbiter, set for launch in 2024), and the environmental impacts of space warfare. Additionally, there is scope for researchers to utilise AGC as a lens to research celestial colonisation, the impacts of spaceports, outposts and fuel stations, and the best usages of outer space environments. It is clear, then, that there are a number of issues related to outer space that require criminological and zemiological attention.

Indeed, there are likely to be expansions into space in the coming decades that may be harmful, but that we currently know little about. For instance, Elon Musk's SpaceX have ambitions to land humans on Mars as soon as 2024 (Cantu and Lunsford, 2022) but at least by 2030, and Jeff Bezos' Blue Origin are working towards the implementation of off-Earth space settlements, possibly in Earth orbit, but probably on the moon (Athanasopoulos, 2019). Ultimately, astro-green criminology provides a useful foundation and framework that allows scholars to research environmentally harmful human actions related to outer space activities and explorations. There are many avenues for further research of a theoretical (i.e., philosophical notions regarding any intrinsic value of outer space) and practical nature (i.e., measuring the ecological impacts of rocket launching emissions on local environments and populations).

Conclusion

To summarise, astro-green criminology is an open and inclusive perspective that broadly involves the theoretical and practical study of anthropogenic actions and behaviours that result in terrestrial and/or extra-terrestrial environmental harm. The key areas of astro-green criminological study include the environmental effects of current or imminent environmentally harmful activities (such as space mining, space junk, and emissions pollutions). Yet, there is much more to consider, plan for, and protect as humans move beyond the Earth into the further reaches of the solar system.

Now is the right time to be considering astro-environmental harm since we are at the dawn of a new era of private and commercial space exploration. AGC provides an intellectual place for critical scholars to research and conceptualise harmful anthropogenic space issues, and hopefully to influence policy and legislation in ways that prevent space harm and protect extra-terrestrial environments.

JACK A. LAMPKIN AND NORIYOSHI TAKEMURA

Further reading

Eski, Y. (2023) *A Criminology of the Human Species: Setting an Unsettling Tone*. Cham: Springer Nature Switzerland.

Rothe, D.L. and Collins, V.E. (2023) 'Planetary Geopolitics, Space Weaponization and Environmental Harms', *The British Journal of Criminology*, 63(6): 1523–1538.

Takemura, N. (2019) 'Astro-Green Criminology: A New Perspective Against Space Capitalism', *Toin University of Yokohama Research Bulletin*, 40: 7–16.

Takemura, N. (2022) 'Extraterrestrial Super Intelligence and Energy-and-Resource Control in the Star, Galaxy, and Universe: Prospect of Ultimate Astro-Green Criminology', *Toin University of Yokohama Research Bulletin*, 47: 27–37.

References

Adakawa, M.I. and Janardhana, G.R. (2022) *Information on Environmental Pollution and International Student Community: A Challenge for Using Science and Technology in Stabilizing Ecosystem in the 21st Century* [Online]. Available at: https://tinyurl.com/4h33deht (Accessed: 14th December 2022).

Athanasopoulos, H.K. (2019) 'The Moon Village and Space 4.0: The "Open Concept" as a New Way of Doing Space?', *Space Policy*, 49: 101323.

Berry, T. (1999) *The Great Work: Our Way into the Future*. New York: Three Rivers Press.

Boukli, A. and Kotzé, J. (eds) (2018) *Zemiology: Reconnecting Crime and Social Harm*. London: Springer.

Canning, V. and Tombs, S. (2021) *From Social Harm to Zemiology: A Critical Introduction*. Abingdon: Routledge.

Cantu, K. and Lunsford, R.B. (2022) 'Space Travel Privatization by SpaceX', *Review of Business and Finance Studies*, 13(1): 79–92.

Carroll, M. (2009) *The Seventh Landing: Going Back to the Moon, This Time to Stay*. New York: Springer.

Chon-Torres, O.A., Chela-Flores, J., Dunér, D., Persson, E., Milligan, T., Martínez-Frías, J., Losch, A., Pryor, A. and Murga-Moreno, C.A. (2024) 'Astrobiocentrism: Reflections on Challenges in the Transition to a Vision of Life and Humanity in Space', *International Journal of Astrobiology*, 23: e6.

Christensen, I., Lange, I., Sowers, G., Abbud-Madrid, A. and Bazilian, M.D. (2019) 'New Policies Needed to Advance Space Mining', *Issues in Science and Technology*, 35(2): 26–30.

Elvis, M. and Milligan, T. (2019) 'How Much of the Solar System Should We Leave as Wilderness?', *Acta Astronautica*, 162: 574–580.

Eski, Y. and Lampkin, J.A. (eds) (2024) *Crime, Criminal Justice and Ethics in Outer Space: International Perspectives*. Abingdon: Routledge.

Hopkins-Burke, R. (2018) *An Introduction to Criminological Theory*. Abingdon: Routledge.

Lampkin, J.A. (2020) *Uniting Green Criminology and Earth Jurisprudence*. Abingdon: Routledge.

Lampkin, J.A. (2021) 'Mapping the Terrain of an Astro-Green Criminology: A Case for Extending the Green Criminological Lens Outside of Planet Earth', *Astropolitics: The International Journal of Space Politics and Policy*, 18(3): 238–259.

Lampkin, J.A. and Carpio-Domínguez, J.L. (2024) 'Atmospheric Justice: Analysing Pollution Caused by the Global Airline and Space Exploration Industries'. In: Eski, Y. and Lampkin, J.A. (eds) *Crime, Criminal Justice and Ethics in Outer Space: International Perspectives*. Abingdon: Routledge.

Lampkin, J.A. and McClanahan, W. (2024) 'Astronomical Withdrawals: A Green Criminological Examination of Extreme Energy

Mining on Extraterrestrial Objects', *Crime, Law and Social Change*, 81: 365–384.

Lampkin, J.A. and White, R. (2023) *Space Criminology*. Basingstoke: Palgrave Macmillan.

Lampkin, J.A. and Wyatt, T. (2022) 'Widening the Scope of "Earth" Jurisprudence and "Green" Criminology? Towards Preserving Extra-Terrestrial Heritage Sites on Celestial Bodies'. In: Gacek, J. and Jochelson, R. (eds) *Green Criminology and the Law*. Cham: Palgrave Macmillan.

Lenard, R.X. (2001) 'Societal Imperatives and the Need for Space Nuclear Power and Propulsion Systems', *Space Policy*, 17(4): 285–289.

Loder, R.E. (2018) 'Asteroid Mining: Ecological Jurisprudence Beyond Earth', *Virginia Environmental Law Journal*, 36(3): 275–317.

Nurse, A. (2015) *Policing Wildlife: Perspectives on the Enforcement of Wildlife Legislation*. Basingstoke: Palgrave Macmillan.

Peters, T. (2019) 'Does Extraterrestrial Life Have Intrinsic Value? An Exploration in Responsibility Ethics', *International Journal of Astrobiology*, 18(4): 304–310.

Reiman, S. (2009) 'Is Space an Environment?', *Space Policy*, 25(2): 81–87.

Sachdeva, G.S. (2023) *Crimes in Outer Space: Perspectives from Law and Justice*. Singapore: Springer Nature.

Schörghofer, N., Benna, M., Berezhnoy, A.A., Greenhagen, B., Jones, B.M., Li, S., Orlando, T.M., Prem, P., Tucker, O.J. and Wöhler, C. (2021) 'Water Group Exospheres and Surface Interactions on the Moon, Mercury, and Ceres', *Space Science Reviews*, 217(6): 1–35.

South, N. (1998) 'A Green Field for Criminology? A Proposal for a Perspective', *Theoretical Criminology*, 2(2): 211–233.

Takemura, N. (2019) 'Astro-Green Criminology: A New Perspective Against Space Capitalism', *Toin University of Yokohama Research Bulletin*, 40: 7–16.

Tan, D. (2000) 'Towards a New Regime for the Protection of Outer Space as the Province of All Mankind', *Yale Journal of International Law*, 25: 145–194.

Taylor, H. (1909) 'The Science of Jurisprudence', *Harvard Law Review*, 22(4): 241–249.

White, R. and Heckenberg, D. (2014) *Green Criminology: An Introduction to the Study of Environmental Harm*. Abingdon: Routledge.

3. Colonialism and environmental violence

Introduction

Even when humans started causing the extinction of animal species 50,000 years ago (Harari, 2011), the global mass degradation and destruction of nature for the benefit of some human groups and at the cost of others only began with the colonisation of the Americas. European colonisers arrived in the 'New Continent' at the dawn of the fifteenth century. They plundered the natural riches of the invaded territories, exploited the original inhabitants as a labour force, and altered Indigenous cosmovisions. Beyond these 'material' consequences, colonisation left long-lasting legacies that keep producing environmental violence. Through the consolidation of modernity, capitalism, and a highly unequal world-system, colonialism set the bases for a global system of inequality and environmental violence that lives on today. Since the colonisation of the Americas, nature became a resource to exploit rather than a home to protect, living beings were instrumentally categorised in a hierarchy of value, and colonised territories became dependent on and prone to predation by colonising powers. Colonialism and environmental violence are inextricably intertwined.

Colonialism and environmental violence

Colonialism is the direct physical occupation of a territory originally inhabited by other human groups (Goyes, 2023b; Mahoney, 2012). It is intrinsically violent as it, through force, subdues human communities and defaces their social systems to impose new ways of living and being that are beneficial to the invaders. Colonialism's primary goal is to plunder natural riches (Goyes, 2023a) – a goal partly achieved by using nature as a weapon (Abad Castelos, 2023). The effects of colonial invasions extend beyond what happens during physical occupation; colonial invasions, through the establishment of systems of social control that perpetuate dependency, set the bases for further plundering (Furtado, 1956; Quijano, 1971). Colonialism is thus motivated by a thirst for environmental resources, executed through environmental violence, and results in further environmental destruction. It is not possible to study colonialism without attending to environmental violence and not possible to understand environmental destruction without understanding the dynamics of colonialism.

European colonisers and American original inhabitants met at the dawn of the fifteenth century in the first major colonial encounter. While civilisations had clashed before, the conquest of the 'New World' rippled like never before in the history of humanity. The European takeover of the Americas (or *Abda Yala*, as some of the native inhabitants call the territory) had material and symbolic effects of such magnitude that they set the bases for a system that has sustained large-scale and systematic environmental violence and destruction worldwide up to today.

The Spaniards arrived in the Americas in 1492. They were immediately attracted by the shiny jewellery worn by the locals and their 'enormous treasures of gold ornaments' (Koning, 1993: 25). Upon seeing gold, a 'lust for gold, lust for silver' possessed the invaders (Galeano, 1997: 1). They used the army, Catholic missions, and administrative authorities to take over lands, dominate the original inhabitants of the continent, and plunder the natural riches (Goyes et al., 2021b). Compelled by the desire to extract steadily more minerals and natural riches, the colonisers penetrated Abda Yala to its deepest regions, leaving behind a trail of destruction and dispossession (Robertson, 2005).

The colonisers developed and perfected their technologies of subjugation during the conquest of the Americas – but soon thereafter they transferred their methods to other regions of the world. In 1497, Vasco da Gama built a market in Goa (on the west coast of India) and used it as the base camp to invade Asia, the world's largest continent. From Goa, the Portuguese expanded, razing religious and cultural sites, and achieving the colonisation of the Persian Gulf (Zaffaroni, 2022). Then, aroused by their lust for spices and a geopolitical interest to accumulate more wealth, they launched a larger campaign to seize further portions of the continent (LePoer, 1987). Colonialism in Asia was less absolute than in the Americas because Europeans did not gain control over the entire continent and their institutions 'had to coexist (then and now) with existing local instituted knowledge, local languages, belief systems and forms of life' (Mignolo & Walsh, 2018: 125). But the colonised locations were exploited intensively.

In Africa, a full-fledged colonial campaign started only in the mid-seventeenth century, almost two centuries after operations in the Americas and Asia. But when the colonisation of Africa started, it was more pronounced than anywhere in the world (Arowolo, 2022). The Dutch initiated the colonisation of Cape Town in 1652 (Zaffaroni, 2022) and soon after they were joined by other European nations. The popularity of colonial campaigns among Europeans led to the 'Scramble for Africa', in which European powers arbitrarily divided the continent. The colonial invasion 'clearly defined and shaped the role of Africa in global economic relations and world politics till today' (Arowolo, 2022: 1).

The first major colonial encounter started in the Americas and was later replicated in Africa and Asia, becoming a global colonial campaign that would shape the social and natural worlds until today. The first major colonial encounter brought about three direct, immediately visible consequences and three indirect, subtle, long-term transformations – all of which had consequences for nature.

Immediate consequences of colonisation

The first direct consequence of the colonial encounter in the Americas was genocide. The colonisers reduced the Indigenous population, 'who totalled no less than 70 million when the foreign conquerors appeared on the horizon' to 3.5 million 'half a century later' (Galeano, 1997: 38). The diseases brought by the Europeans contributed to the killings (Koch et al., 2019), and the exploitation of Indigenous people as a labour force was a major driver of deaths (Mignolo & Walsh, 2018). The Indigenous peoples who survived were cornered and their lands were taken and despoiled (Goyes, 2023a; Goyes & South, 2021).

Second, the colonisers transformed the natural landscape, opening 'new whole regions for immigrant settlement and exploitation' (Goyes 2023c: 92), extracted minerals and plants, and replaced fauna and flora with their own by imposing 'crops and livestock pre-adapted to American environments' (Goyes 2023c: 92). Crosby (2004) coined this phenomenon as 'ecological imperialism'. The Americas, and later other continents in the global South, became adjacent gardens reshaped to fill the desires of the colonisers.

Third, together with the genocide of many Indigenous peoples, the colonisers erased from the world millennia-old environmental ontologies or ways of relating with nature (Goyes, 2023c). The environmental ontologies wiped out were comprised of universes of symbols and stories that put humans in a close spiritual relationship with nature, inspiring protective behaviours (Goyes et al., 2021a).

Genocide of the protectors of nature, superimposition of crops and livestock on native ecosystems, and the erasure of Indigenous environmental ontologies entailed large-scale social and ecological destruction. Yet, it is the long-term transformations brought about by colonisation that have produced the most environmental violence.

Long-term consequences of colonisation

Further impacts of colonisation only became perceivable two centuries after the invasion of the Americas. These impacts are simultaneously embodied in corporeal elements and every aspect of global social life; yet hidden to the uninformed naked eye. Modernity (including racialisation), capitalism, and an unequal world-system are not only the subtle consequences of colonisation; they are those with the deepest consequences for society and nature.

Modernity and racialisation

The colonisers, seeking to plunder the riches of the Americas and exploit the Indigenous peoples and African slaves as a labour force, classified humans from superior to inferior – a strategy that enabled colonisers to 'legitimately' abuse non-Europeans (Quijano, 2000, 2007). The hierarchy that the colonisers created encompassed biological features and cognitive capacities and placed West European anatomies and ways of learning on top. The hierarchy had a strong racialising component: 'if modernity is a set of fictional narratives that justified and legitimized the actions of those who told the story and built institutions that made the story credible, then *race* is one of its conceptual fictions, effective fictions nonetheless' (Mignolo & Walsh, 2018: 182).

The practice of organising humans in a hierarchy had three underpinning messages: (1) that the world, natural and human, can be categorised from most valuable to least; (2) that the human and natural worlds – a dichotomy created by the colonisers – can be not only categorised but also instrumentally organised to maximise the fruits of its exploitation, leading to human progress and development; and, (3) that Western Europeans, and their superior cognitive capacities, can lead humanity to progress. These messages spread through the world, via globalised colonialism, and have shaped international relations since the first major colonial encounter until today, in what we call 'modernity'.

Modernity views progress as a unitary path that leads to human fulfilment (Vattimo, 1990, 1998) and is characterised by the pursuit, more than the achievement, of rationalisation, precision and efficiency, as well as by its thirst for (universal) improvement following an instrumental logic (Bauman, 2000). Modernity, Bauman (p. 18) wrote,

> prompts us to view society as an object of administration, as a collection of so many 'problems' to be solved, as 'nature' to be 'controlled', 'mastered', and 'improved' or 'remade' as a legitimate target for 'social engineering' and in general a garden to be designed and kept in the planned shape by force (the gardening posture divides vegetation into 'cultured plants' to be taken care of, and weeds to be exterminated).

The instrumental modern logic, developed alongside colonisation, sees ecosystems and most living beings (including a big portion of humanity) as resources useful in the progress and fulfilment of 'humanity' (Goyes, 2019; Goyes & Sollund, 2018). Seeing nature, including humans, as instruments for a bigger goal is a core cultural pillar of the current mass destruction of the planet (Brisman & South, 2014).

Capitalism

Decolonial theorist Aníbal Quijano (1992) traces the definitive establishment of capitalism as the default production mode back to the colonisation of the Americas. As Mignolo (2011: 21) explains, 'both [colonialism and capitalism] are constitutive of what is generally understood by Western civilisation'. The colonisation of the Americas created 'vast opportunities for land appropriation/expropriation', which enabled the expansion of production. It also created a 'new pattern of management of labour' that, exploiting the colonial classification of humans, allowed it to manipulate the production systems minimising costs and increasing profit. Finally, colonialism began to establish 'a truly planetary commerce—unknown until then' (Mignolo & Walsh, 2018: 183), where commodity trade was expanded. In sum, colonisation made possible a mode of production 'centred and managed according to the interests of the holder of capital' (Mignolo & Walsh, 2018: 183). The possibilities that colonisation opened led to current capitalism, a system characterised by the constant expansion of production in order to increase profit, the manipulation of production systems to create surplus profits, and the unlimited expansion of capital (Stretesky et al., 2014).

Colonisers also created a system of cultural representations that provided legitimated capitalism. As Mignolo explains, 'capitalism is not merely an economic structure; it involves the subjectivities and belief systems that go with it, without which it couldn't be sustained' (Mignolo, 2011: 21) The conquerors created, among others, international laws that 'legitimized imperial appropriation and expropriation of land' and the 'imperial slave trade and exploitation of labor to produce commodities for the emerging global market' (Mignolo, 2011: 21).

Finally, colonialism not only made capitalism possible; capitalism keeps functioning thanks to colonial practices. The colonial expropriation of lands across the world to increase the wealth and power of a few, which Harvey (2003) denominates as *accumulation by dispossession*, permits capitalism to reach new regions and expand its commodities and wealth.

Capitalism is thus a key driver of environmental destruction. As Stretesky and colleagues (2014) explain, capitalism has two main interactions with nature: extractions, to obtain the materials necessary for production; and additions, to dispose of the waste from production processes and discarded used commodities. Both interactions alter ecosystems and when added contribute to the current environmental crises. Capitalism and colonialism, an inextricable dyad, advance environmental violence through the commodification of lands and ecosystems.

World-system

The plundering of lands and the enslaving of original inhabitants in the Americas, Africa, and parts of Asia gave the colonisers a privileged position in the world. They acquired supreme economic power from the riches they stole across the world. Colonisers gained political power by imposing rules on other cultures. Colonisers endowed themselves as the ultimate knowledge creators and accumulated epistemological power. By dictating how the world should be seen, sensed, and appreciated, they amassed cultural power (Goyes, 2023b). Using the supreme capital gained in these four categories – economic, political, epistemological, and cultural – colonisers kept augmenting their power in a self-reinforcing logic. Colonisers invested the superior power to keep plundering the world in a seemingly never-ending spiral of environmental violence.

Colonisers, to maintain and augment their power, have defined the international legal instruments that regulate human interactions with nature, imposed environmental practices on the colonised, and situated the colonised in a situation of dependency (Goyes, 2023b). As Alberto Acosta (1994; see also Escobar, 1995) explained, funding for development, given by the colonisers to the colonised, usually leads to an 'eternal debt'. Economic help comes with such high interest and political conditions that the colonised will never be able to repay. Instead, the colonisers force the colonised to pay back through raw materials – fuelling the further destruction of nature.

Economic, political, epistemological, and cultural power unequally distributed between colonisers and colonised give shape to the contemporary world-system. Wallerstein (2004) conceptualised this global structure as split into two: 'core' countries that have semi-monopolies over financial and knowledge institutions, media and communication systems, technologies, and weapons of mass destruction (see also Amin, 1997); and 'peripheral' countries that generate raw materials and supply an 'unqualified labour force'. The core–periphery divide is self-reinforcing as the core continuously accumulates more power to exploit the periphery. The core achieves economic growth and heightened living standards at the cost of 'the social imbalances, political tensions, and poverty' (Gutiérrez, 1974: 51; Furtado, 1956; Prebisch, 1963), and one might add environmental violence, in the periphery.

The dependence that a highly unequal world-system creates allows colonisers to benefit from ecologically unequal exchanges. In the global flows of commodities, the market price for the products sold by the colonised is significantly lower than the human and land labour embodied in them. Meanwhile, the price of the processed commodities sold by the colonisers is significantly higher than the labour invested in them (Honborg, 1998). As Dorninger et al. (2021: 3) explains, 'countries rich in economic, technological, or military power are more likely to gain access to resources (materials, energy, land, and labor) that are relevant to achieve economic growth and to build technological infrastructure'. The thirst for development, increased accumulation, and a position of advantage lead colonisers to increasingly plunder more natural resources from the colonised, thereby producing mass environmental destruction.

Terminology

Colonialism, modernity, capitalism, and an unequal world-system are mutually constitutive. The four are based on, and accelerate, the destruction of nature worldwide. Yet, colonialism has different ways of advancing. The following are key concepts to understand the ways of colonialism:

Coloniality

The colonisations of the Americas brought about a set of social representations that sustain modernity, capitalism, and the world-system. Aníbal Quijano (2000, 2007) gathers these representations under the term of 'coloniality', or the preference to consider valid only what follows the modern European way of knowledge creation. Coloniality is pervasive of every social and individual space. It directs how people, in colonial and colonised locations, are and behave. It structures social interactions, also with nature. It trickles down 'framing subjectivities, education, ways of eating, health, and destroyed conviviality' (Mignolo & Walsh, 2018: 108); and is 'engraved in global social structures' (Goyes, 2023b: 15).

Internal colonialism

Colonialism often creates, coexists with, and is fuelled by hierarchised relations among inhabitants of the colonised regions. Mondaca (2017: 37) defines internal colonialism as a 'structure of social relations of domination and exploitation among heterogeneous cultural groups within a single state'. Internal colonialism is driven, partly, by the offspring of the colonisers who, although born and raised in colonised locations, prolong the exploitation of their countrypeople. But also, members of native communities can be agents of internal colonialism when they are co-opted by their colonisers. Internal colonialism is then the exploitation of the racialised and colonised at the hands of the racialised and colonised – all in the service of the original colonisers.

Neocolonialism

While colonialism is the physically violent occupation of a territory – a phenomenon most associated with previous centuries – the contemporary world most often witnesses neocolonialism, the 'de facto occupation of a country via land grabs after the country has gained independence from its coloniser' (Goyes, 2023b: 10). Through land grabs, neocolonisers impose colonial ways of interacting with nature (Goyes & South, 2016).

Imperialism

Imperialism is the indirect control of nations, not primarily by physical occupation but through economic and political manipulation (Goyes, 2023c). Using their superior economic, political, epistemological, and cultural power, colonisers – new and old – can influence and direct the macro-dynamics of colonised states. The coups supported by the US in the 1960s and 1970s, and the manipulation of elections in the 2010s and 2020s, as well as the imposition of particular international legal frameworks (e.g., free trade agreements), are all acts of imperialism (Goyes, 2017).

Ecological discrimination

Specifically located in the realm of environmental interactions, ecological discrimination is 'the systematic negative differentiation and oppression of some human groups, non-human animals, and ecosystems, based on modern instrumental ideas about how to treat and relate to the natural environment' (Goyes, 2019: 15). Ecological discrimination is the application of coloniality to environmental issues, and the resulting exploitation of a large portion of beings.

Environmental violence and environmental crime

Orthodox criminology understands *crime* as those behaviours that breach the penal law (Johansen, 2021). Yet, almost six decades ago, Schwendinger and Schwendinger (1970) drew attention to the problem of relying only on the penal law to determine what is a crime and what is not (at the time, racism and imperialism were not defined as crimes). Afterwards, Pearce (1976), Davies et al. (1999) and Passas (2005) highlighted that not being punished by the criminal law does not mean that an action or omission is not harmful or undesirable. The law, skewed to protect the interests of the powerful, can symbolically hide and legitimise the acts that harm society and nature the most (Baratta, 2004; Lynch & Michalowski, 2010). Some green criminologists (e.g., Sollund, 2015, 2019), relying on a critical view of the criminal justice system, have called to apply the label of crime to acts that are lawful but cause environmental degradation and victimisation. While orthodox criminology understands environmental crime only as those included in the penal code, critical green criminology understands as crime all acts and omissions that victimise humans, non-humans, and the environment.

The soul of a harm perspective, however, calls not only to expand the array of researched phenomena beyond the purview of the penal code, but also to take distance from the logics of the criminal justice system itself. Even invoking the crime nomenclature can lead to beliefs that the criminal justice system offers *the* solution to deep social problems through the use of its technologies (Canning & Tombs, 2021; Hillyard et al., 2004). But the criminal justice system, beyond its selectivity (Vegh Weis, 2018) and vacuous responses (Mathiesen, 2006) to social issues, has historically been a tool of colonialism. The colonial use of criminal justice systems to plunder natural riches ranges from the sixteenth- and seventeenth-century ad hoc courts established by the Spaniards to judge Indigenous people for not extracting enough resources from nature, to the current use of the penal law to prosecute 'illegal' exploitation of resources while allowing the most destructive large-scale exploitation of nature by corporations. There are deep links between 'the exploitation of nature by colonizers, former and current, the creation of social systems [including the criminal justice system] to legitimize such plundering, and the extensive harms inflicted on Indigenous inhabitants, their lands, and their ecosystems' (Goyes, 2023a: 413).

Decolonial thought, which tries to undo the consequences of colonialism (Quijano, 2007) or delink knowledge from 'epistemic assumptions common to all the areas of knowledge established in the Western world' (Mignolo & Walsh, 2018: 106), thinks in terms of *environmental violence* rather than of *environmental crime*. To avoid reproducing colonial categories but still convey the devastating environmental effects of colonialism, decolonial work therefore uses the term *environmental violence*: the systemic harm that stems from most human interactions with nature when they are guided by the modern, capitalist, colonial way of being.

Conclusion

While decolonial theory and praxis demonstrate the links between colonialism, modernity, capitalism, and an unequal world-system with global mass environmental destruction, other theories try to delink colonialism from current environmental destruction and instead blame the colonised countries and peoples (e.g., Auty, 1993). As Mignolo & Walsh (2018: 107) describe, however, 'while for some [the colonisation of the Americas] was a moment of salvation and civilisation, for others it was the beginning of the historical crimes justified by the narratives of modernity – salvation, progress, development'. Decolonial theory and praxis accept the contributions Western civilisation and modernity have made to humanity, but also emphasise and highlight their intrinsic human and environmental violence.

DAVID R. GOYES

Further reading

Escobar, A. (1995). *Encountering Development: The Making and Unmaking of the Third World*. Princeton University Press.

Galeano, E. (1971). *Open Veins of Latin America*. Monthly Review Press.

Goyes, D. R. (2019). *Southern Green Criminology: A Science to End Ecological Discrimination*. Emerald.

Goyes, D. R. (Ed.). (2023). *Green Crime in the Global South*. Palgrave Macmillan.

Mignolo, W., & Walsh, C. (2018). *On Decoloniality: Concepts, Analytics, Praxis*. Duke University Press.

References

Abad Castelos, M. (2023). Towards a holistic consideration of crimes against nature committed in times of armed conflict: A critical approach to the case of Iraq. *International Journal for Crime, Justice and Social Democracy, 12*(3), 77–92. doi:10.5204/ijcjsd.2707.

Acosta, A. (1994). *La Deuda Eterna: Una Historia de la Deuda Externa Ecuatoriana* [*The Eternal Debt: A History of the Ecuadorian External Debt*]. Libresa.

Amin, S. (1997). *Capitalism in the Age of Globalization: The Management of Contemporary Society*. Zed Books.

Arowolo, D. E. (2022). Dancing on a knife-edge: European colonisation of Africa and Nigeria's cultural crisis. *African Identities*, 1–17. https://doi.org/10.1080/14725843.2022.2040422

Auty, R. M. (1993). *Sustaining Development in Mineral Economies: The Resource Curse Thesis*. Routledge.

Baratta, A. (2004). *Criminología Crítica y Crítica al Derecho Penal* [*Critical Criminology and Critique to Penal Law*]. Siglo Veintiuno Editores.

Bauman, Z. (2000). *Modernity and the Holocaust*. Cornell.

Brisman, A., & South, N. (2014). *Green Cultural Criminology: Constructions of Environmental Harm, Consumerism, and Resistance to Ecocide*. Routledge.

Canning, V., & S. Tombs (2021). *From Social Harm to Zemiology: A Critical Introduction*. Routledge.

Crosby, A. W. (2004). *Ecological Imperialism: The Biological Expansion of Europe 900–1900*. Cambridge University Press.

Davies, P., Francis, P., & Jupp, V. (Eds.). (1999). *Invisible Crimes: Their Victims and their Regulation*. St. Martin's Press.

Dorninger, C., Hornborg, A., Abson, D. J., van Wehrden, H., Schaffartzik, A., Giljum, S., Engler, J. O., Feller, R. L., Hubacek, K., & Wieland, H. (2021). Global patterns of ecologically unequal exchange: Implications for sustainability in the 21st century. *Ecological Economics*, *179*, 106824.

Escobar, A. (1995). *Encountering Development: The Making and Unmaking of the Third World*. Princeton University Press.

Furtado, C. (1956). *Uma economia dependente* [*A Dependent Economy*]. Ministério da Educação e Cultura.

Galeano, E. (1997). *Open Veins of Latin America*. Monthly Review Press (first ed., 1971).

Goyes, D. R. (2017). Corporate lobbying and criminalization. *Crime, Law & Social Change*, *69*, 401–419.

Goyes, D. R. (2019). *Southern Green Criminology: A Science to End Ecological Discrimination*. Emerald.

Goyes, D. R. (2023a). First, they took the land: Decolonizing nature to decolonize society. In C. Cunneen, A. Deckert, A. Porter, J. Tauri, & R. Webb (Eds.), *The Routledge International Handbook on Decolonizing Justice* (pp. 413–422). Routledge.

Goyes, D. R. (2023b). Southern green criminology: Fundamental concepts. In D. R. Goyes (Ed.), *Green Crime in the Global South: Essays on Southern Green Criminology* (pp. 1–30). Palgrave Macmillan.

Goyes, D. R. (2023c). Latin American green criminology. *Justice, Power and Resistance*, *6*(1), 90–107.

Goyes, D. R., & Sollund, R. (2018). Animal abuse, biotechnology and species justice. *Theoretical Criminology*, *22*(3), 363–383. https://doi.org/10.1177/1362480618787179

Goyes, D. R., & South, N. (2016). Land-grabs, bio-piracy and the inversion of justice in Colombia. *British Journal of Criminology*, *56*(3), 558–577. https://doi.org/10.1093/bjc/azv082

Goyes, D. R., & South, N. (2021). Indigenous worlds and criminological exclusion: A call to reorientate the criminological compass. *International Journal for Crime, Justice and Social Democracy*, *10*(3), 115–128. https://doi.org/10.5204/ijcjsd.1983

Goyes, D. R., Abaibira, M. A., Baicué, P., Cuchimba, A., Ñeñetofe, D. T. R., Sollund, R., South, N., & Wyatt, T. (2021a). Southern green cultural criminology and environmental crime prevention: Representations of nature within four Colombian Indigenous communities. *Critical Criminology*, *29*(3), 469–485. https://doi.org/10.1007/s10612-021-09582-0.

Goyes, D. R., South, N., Abaibira, M. A., Baicué, P., Cuchimba, A., & Ñeñetofe, D. T. R. (2021b). Genocide and ecocide in four Colombian Indigenous communities: The erosion of a way of life and memory. *The British Journal of Criminology*, *61*(4), 965–984. https://doi.org/10.1093/bjc/azaa109.

Gutiérrez, G. (1974). *A Theology of Liberation*. SCM Press.

Harari, Y. N. (2011). *Sapiens: A Brief History of Humankind*. Penguin.

Harvey, D. (2003). *The New Imperialism*. Oxford University Press.

Hillyard, P., Pantazis, C., Thombs, S., & Gordon, D. (Eds.) (2004). *Beyond Criminology: Taking Harm Seriously*. Pluto Press & Fernwood Publishing.

Honborg, A. (1998). Towards an ecological theory of unequal exchange: Articulating world system theory and ecological economics. *Ecological Economics*, *25*(1), 127–136.

Johansen, N. (2021). Bruddet med samfunsskontrakten: Om forskjellen mellom gullalderen og den kritiske tradisjonen innenfor kriminologi og rettsosiologi [The breach of the social contract: The difference between the golden age and the critical tradition in criminology and sociology of law]. *Tidsskrift for samfunnsforskning* [*Journal of Social Research*], *62*(2), 176–191.

Koch, A., Brierley, C., Maslin, M., & Lewis, S. (2019). European colonization of the Americas killed 10 percent of world population and caused global cooling. *The Conversation*. Retrieved 2 June 2024 from https://www.pri.org/stories/2019-01-31/european-colonization-americas-killed-10-percent-world-population-and-caused

Koning, H. (1993). *Conquest of America: How the Indian Nations Lost Their Continent*. Monthly Review Press.

LePoer, B. L. (1987). *Thailand: A Country Study*. GPO.

Lynch, M. J., & Michalowski, R. (2010). *Primer in Radical Criminology*. Lynne Rienner Publishers.

Mahoney, J. (2012). *Colonialism and Postcolonial Development: Spanish America in Comparative Perspective*. Cambridge University Press.

Mathiesen, T. (2006). *Prison on Trial*. Winchester.

Mignolo, W. (2011). Decolonizing Western epistemology / Building decolonial epistemologies. Decolonizing Epistemologies: Latina/o Theology and Philosophy, Transdisciplinary Theological Colloquia (FUP). Retrieved 20 September 2023 from https://doi.org/10.5422/fordham/9780823241354.003.0002

Mignolo, W., & Walsh, C. (2018). *On Decoloniality. Concepts, Analytics, Praxis*. Duke University Press.

Mondaca, E. (2017). The archipelago of Chiloé and the uncertain contours of its future: Coloniality, new extractivism and political-social re-vindication of existence. In D. R. Goyes, H. Mol, A. Brisman, & N. South (Eds.), *Environmental Crime in Latin America: The*

Theft of Nature and the Poisoning of the Land (pp. 31–56). Palgrave Macmillan.

Passas, N. (2005). Lawful but awful: 'Legal corporate crimes'. *The Journal of Socio-Economics, 34*, 771–786.

Pearce, F. (1976). *Crimes of the Powerful*. Pluto Press.

Prebisch, R. (1963). *Hacia una dinámica del desarrollo latinoamericano* [*Towards a Dynamic of Latin American Development*]. Fondo de Cultura Económica.

Quijano, A. (1971). *Nationalism and Capitalism in Peru: A Study in Neo-imperialism*. Monthly Review Press.

Quijano, A. (1992). Colonialidad y modernidad/racionalidad [Coloniality and modernity/rationality]. *Perú Indígena, 13*(29), 11–20.

Quijano, A. (2000). Coloniality of power, Eurocentrism, and Latin America. *Nepantla: Views from South, 1*(3), 533–580.

Quijano, A. (2007). Coloniality and modernity/rationality. *Cultural Studies, 21*(2–3), 168–178.

Robertson, L. (2005). *Conquest by Law: How the Discovery of America Dispossessed Indigenous Peoples of their Lands*. Oxford University Press.

Schwendinger, H., & Schwendinger, J. (1970). Defenders of order or guardians of human rights? *Issues in Criminology, 5*(2), 123–157.

Sollund, R. (2015). Introduction: Critical green criminology – an agenda for change. In R. Sollund (Ed.), *Green Harms and Crimes: Critical Criminology in a Changing World* (pp. 1–26). Ashgate.

Sollund, R. (2019). *The Crimes of Wildlife Trafficking: Issues of Justice, Legality and Morality*. Routledge.

Stretesky, P. B., Long, M. A., & Lynch, M. J. (2014). *The Treadmill of Crime: Political Economy and Green Criminology*. Routledge.

Vattimo, G. (1990). *La sociedad transparente [The Transparent Society]*. Ediciones Paidós.

Vattimo, G. (1998). *El fin de la modernidad, nihilismo y hermenéutica en la cultura posmoderna [The End of Modernity, Nihilism and Hermeneutics in the Postmodern Culture]*. Gedisa.

Vegh Weis, V. (2018). *Marxism and Criminology: A History of Criminal Selectivity*. Haymarket Books.

Wallerstein, I. (2004). *World-Systems Analysis: An Introduction*. Duke University Press.

Zaffaroni, E. R. (2022). *Colonialismo y Derechos Humanos: Apuntes para una historia criminal del mundo* [*Colonialism and Human Rights: Notes for a Criminal History of the World*]. Penguin.

4. Conservation justice

Introduction

Conservation justice encompasses the notion that conservation, which leverages on the human aspect of human–environment relationships, must account for societal marginalisations and ensure the fair treatment and meaningful involvement of people regardless of race, ethnicity, class, national origin, gender, and sexuality in any conservation effort. This perspective wishes to reckon with the legacies, as well as modern practice, of colonialism, imperialism, and capitalism which obstruct justice-oriented solutions from being at the forefront of conservation efforts. Conservation justice is a verb as it is a noun, meaning that enacting justice-oriented solutions within conservation is an active process that requires intentional input from and with local and Indigenous communities. Broadly, conservation justice reflects more equitable and righteous approaches to conservation which values people as well as their intersecting identities.

The contours of conservation justice

Conservation justice is an emerging term in conservation circles (see Martin et al., 2016; Ferketic, Latimer, & Silander Jr., 2010). However, the idea of justice-influenced conservation has been discussed at length, particularly within the environmental crime sector (see Wolf, 2011; White, 2007), and it stems from the environmental justice movement (Bullard, 1993; Mohai, Pellow, & Roberts, 2009). The term conservation justice can be illuminated in the light of two allied phrases: 'just conservation' and 'justice *and* conservation'. The first, 'just conservation' indicates that there is an element of conservation that is practised to limit the amount of inequity that results from that conservation project. The second concept, 'justice *and* conservation', predicates itself on the notion that trust and justice must occur in tandem to produce viable, as well as equitable, environmental change (see Whyte, 2020; Turner et al., 2016; Young et al., 2016). Trust is ultimately connected to different forms of power and justice, which directly effects the outcomes of conservation interventions (Saif, Keane, & Staddon, 2022). These two strands of thought ultimately culminate in the idea of *conservation justice*, which is defined here as encompassing the notion that conservation must account for societal marginalisation and ensure the fair treatment and meaningful involvement of all people in any conservation effort.

Conservation justice emerged as a connection between environmental justice and conservation social science. Environmental justice refers to the equitable and fair distribution of environmental harms and benefits amongst all communities, regardless of their identity (London et al., 2011). The connection between environmental justice and conservation has largely been centred around conservation policy (Ulibarri, Figueroa, & Grant, 2022; Wang & Lo, 2022); protected areas (Loos, 2021; Bontempi et al., 2023); governance (Haenn, 2012; Dawson et al., 2023); and community engagement (Bourgeois et al., 2023; Wiens et al., 2024). Similar in some respects to the notion of environmental justice, conservation justice emphasises the right of local communities to fair treatment and meaningful involvement within conservation policy and practice (Ferketic, Latimer, & Silander Jr., 2010). When we consider justice within the conservation sector, it is necessary to expand on the preconceived notions pertaining to the prioritisation of non-human life over human life (e.g., species protection and national parks), and the prioritisation of the ideals and values of the Global North over those of the Global South (e.g., preservation and conservation for specific use-purposes that benefit non-local populations). Conservation-related marginalisation can further exacerbate existing social inequalities. Poverty, gender-based violence, environmental degradation, and racism, for example, all contribute to an individual's likelihood to be negatively impacted by some types of conservation intervention (e.g., Koot, Büscher, & Thakholi, 2022; Ma et al., 2019; Doubleday, 2020).

By contrast, conservation justice asserts that justice-oriented solutions should be prioritised in any conservation effort and advocates an approach to conservation that centres the human component of human–environment relationships. It is argued that integrating justice principles as they pertain to alleviating social inequalities can serve to make a more equitable, justice-oriented conservation. Conservation justice thus warrants a targeted approach that centres on increasing equity and empowerment for local and Indigenous peoples, with the expectation that just, equitable conservation could lead to greater socio-ecological benefits (see Dawson et al., 2021). Justice within conservation is heavily contested (Martin et al., 2013). This is primarily due to the distinct roles that colonialism, patriarchy, and imperialism play in who is allowed to benefit from conservation, and who is not. Conservation benefits are often restricted for the people who inhabit these conserved ecosystems or share space with the species of conservation interest. This translates into a disproportionate level of harm being inflicted on marginalised peoples and communities, thus resulting in a perpetuation of social injustice as a result of conservation efforts. A more fluid application of justice-oriented practices that acknowledges both the needs of the environment and the people who inhabit it is needed.

Framing conservation within an environmental justice framework provides a spotlight on the dimensions of social inequity that are perpetuated for the sake of conservation-related interests (Martin, Akol, & Gross-Kamp, 2015). Just conservation, one which conserves the needs of people as well as the needs of the environment, can produce a form of conservation which is more sustainable (e.g., Fielding, 2022; Karki & Adhikari, 2015), equitable (e.g., Bennett et al., 2021; Dawson et al., 2021), inclusive (e.g., Rai et al., 2021; Bailey, Morales, & Newberry, 2020) and empowering (e.g., Petriello et al., 2021; Noe & Kangalawe, 2015). Considering conservation justice as a measure of how conservation and environmental justice can be practised in tandem allows for a more holistic and comprehensive approach to conservation. Practising and implementing conservation justice is twofold: the first centres on addressing the potential breaches of equity affecting the people who share the conserved environment and its non-human inhabitants, and the second focuses on the justice-oriented socio-ecological impacts of the conservation project. In essence, conservation justice seeks to counter the dimensions of conservation which view marginalised communities as a disposable expense for biodiversity conservation while simultaneously allowing for the emotional, physical, and spiritual needs of the community to be addressed in tandem with the needs of biodiversity conservation.

Addressing conservation justice is a task which involves the intertwining of multiple systems of restoration, resolution, and reconciliation which are reflective of socio-ecological relationships. The utilisation of just conservation practices is dependent on a clear understanding and incorporation of Indigenous lives, livelihoods, and interests into the process. Conservation justice thus requires an intentional restructuring of the ways in which conservation is largely being practised today. Justice and conservation can intersect, and should intersect, but it has to be done intentionally.

Intersectionality

Intersectionality is central to the conservation justice mandate of social inclusion. This dimension of evaluating race, gender, and class in tandem follows the theory of *intersectionality* as first coined by Kimberlé Crenshaw in 1989 (Cooper, 2015). As described and defined by Collins and Bilge (2016: 1):

> Intersectionality investigates how intersecting power relations influence social relations across diverse societies as well as individual experiences in everyday life. As an analytic tool, intersectionality views categories of race, class, gender, sexuality, class, nation, ability, ethnicity, and age – among others – as interrelated and mutually shaping one another. Intersectionality is a way of understanding and explaining complexity in the world, in people, and in human experiences.

Intersectionality has been used in Black feminist theory to conceptualise the relationship between systems of oppression and how these are reinforced through power hierarchies and privilege (Carastathis, 2014), specifically from the perspective of Black women. Intersectionality has been drawn upon to address the lack of attention given to the intersections of racism and patriarchy by contemporary feminist and antiracist discourse (Crenshaw & Bonis, 2005). The usage of intersectionality within the environmental and conservation sector has also gained traction in recent years (see Apostolopoulou et al., 2021; Lynch & Turner, 2021). However, its contemporary use in conservation science and practice warrants deeper investigation.

Consideration of the intersectional dimensions of conservation science and practice forces us to reckon with the legacies of injustice that uniquely affect multiply marginalised peoples. These multiply marginalised populations sit at the intersection of societal injustices (e.g., race and gender), and ecological or environmental injustice (e.g., living in an area of poor water quality). For example, Pandya (2022) found that women's engagement with an ecotourism venture in India's Corbett Tiger Reserve was influenced by their individual intersections of caste and class.

Specific identities, as well as their intersections, greatly shape how an individual is impacted by conservation, thus warranting deeper understanding of the linkage between intersectionality and conservation science and practice. This understanding can contribute to how we assess whether conservation is being practised in a way that is just or what steps must be taken in order for conservation justice to be achieved. Further, intersectionality can allow for a deeper understanding of the human dimension of conservation-related injustices. Specifically, intersectionality can allow for greater insight into the ways peoples' intersecting identities impact their relationships with, and how they are affected by, conservation science and practice.

Conservation injustice

The contestation of conservation-oriented justice protocols for the peoples impacted by conservation *injustice, and especially Indigenous peoples*, warrants much further investigation than has hitherto been the case. What classifies as a conservation injustice, and how these injustices occur and are measured, requires close scrutiny. For instance, conservation injustices manifest in a myriad of ways, namely through the displacement of Indigenous peoples for the establishment of protected areas (Sinthumule, 2018; Redford & Fearn, 2007); the murder of environmental defenders (Zeng, Twang, & Carrasco, 2022; Le Tran et al., 2020); and the criminalisation of Indigenous peoples in protected areas (e.g., Fanari, 2022). These examples illustrate the instances in which conservation has a negative impact on the lives of people who inhabit areas of conservation interest. There are also discriminatory prosecution practices which disproportionately affect socially marginalised people and communities. For example, Paudel, Potter, and Phelps (2019) found that of those imprisoned for illegal wildlife trade offences in Nepalese prisons, 56% were poor and 75% were from Indigenous communities. This has a profound impact in both social as well as ecological contexts. Settler colonialism, for instance, has an ecological dimension which works to explicitly undermine Indigenous peoples' social resilience as self-determining entities (Whyte, 2018). These instances of socio-ecological injustice as they pertain to conservation can have long-lasting impacts that transcend generations and ecosystems. Conservation injustice occurs when the well-being of local and/or Indigenous communities is jeopardised in favour of Western-dominated notions of conservation implementation.

The intersecting identities of individuals lay the foundation for acts of conservation injustice to be committed against and have enormous impacts on marginalised peoples, particularly those identities pertaining to race, gender, and class. In the environmental justice literature, environmental inequities (e.g., access to fresh water) often reinforce social inequities (e.g., poverty and capacity to work). These types of inequities are a byproduct of structural inequality and are further exacerbated through denying land access and creating unjust working conditions for people who live in or near areas of conservation interest (Thakholi & Büscher, 2021). When we consider the dimensions of injustice that arise with a conservation initiative, we have to understand the ways in which conservation contributes to these legacies of inequity. However, although conservation has historically pushed injustices onto local and Indigenous communities, it is not a necessary requirement for conservation to be done effectively. That is, injustice and conservation do not have to be synonymous. Accordingly, conservation planning should, for example, emphasise the essential role of Indigenous peoples and Indigenous livelihoods in biodiversity protection, preservation, and longevity.

Translating conservation justice into practice

Globally, the application of conservation justice into conservation practice is limited in scope. Nonetheless, the utilisation of environmental justice practices is gaining traction in the broader conservation literature (e.g., Saif, Keane, & Staddon, 2022; Guibrunet et al., 2021; Malin et al., 2019) and has proven effective in addressing the dynamics of power and control which are embedded within Western conservation practices (e.g., Boillat et al., 2018; Dahlberg, Rohde, & Sandell, 2010). From an international perspective, we can now begin to assess how conservation justice manifests itself both socially and ecologically, and how justice can be a foundational component of conservation. Emphasising care and justice can generate better, more long-lasting positive effects that are socially and ecologically sustainable. Investigation into the use of justice within community-based conservation practices, as well as in human–wildlife conflict-related conservation programmes, can provide insight into what has been successful and what requires improvement.

For instance, one of the most pressing issues in conservation management is the exclusion of local and Indigenous people from the decision-making process. If not handled with care, conservation can continue to perpetuate the forefathers' colonialistic, capitalist, and imperialist ideals (see Kashwan et al., 2021; Rudd et al., 2021). A different approach to conservation management, which centres on the experiences, values, and cultural practices of local and Indigenous people, is needed. Intersections between conservation and social justice action and policy require intentional intervention which greatly reduces the infliction of injustice or inequality onto local and/or Indigenous peoples. Critical analysis of conservation reveals the leverage that disproportionate power relations have in setting the foundations of practice and implementation, with socially unequal and unjust consequences (Hart, 2014). In response, Lopes et al. (2021) propose a Just Aquatic Governance framework that delves into the alignment of the social interests of Amazonian locals and conservation priorities. This framework draws on the environmental justice pillars of recognition, procedure, and distribution in order to ensure equitable access to governance and security (Lopes et al., 2021). The framework illustrates the need for justice-oriented conservation to concern itself with the wants and needs of the community while simultaneously supporting conservation goals. It is imperative, however, that the needs of one do not become dependent on the success of the other. In Australia, for example, a new dilemma has emerged at the intersection of conservation and Indigenous social justice which is slowly making Indigenous social justice dependent on the success of conservation initiatives (Moorcroft, 2016). Insofar as this is the case, it illustrates how conservation and social justice can start to undermine the prerogatives of local and Indigenous peoples, in essence making their justice dependent on the success of conservation initiatives. It is thus critical to evaluate the outcomes of conservation justice initiatives to account for the intersectional dimensions of social marginalisation, and how conservation can exacerbate or alleviate those dimensions.

Just conservation decision-making processes are a crucial component for achieving both social and ecological goals (Ruano-Chamorro, Gurney, & Cinner, 2021). However, the difficulties associated with decision-making processes, namely participation and ethical engagement, rest on the need to intentionally engage and appease multiple stakeholder groups. Ferketic, Latimer, and Silander Jr. (2010) investigated the application of conservation justice within an urban conservation project in Cape Town, South Africa. Through semi-structured interviews with members of communities who were affected or interested in the conservation project, they found that conservation projects could provide tangible benefits to all stakeholder groups, despite apparent differences in need and perspective (Ferketic, Latimer, & Silander Jr., 2010).

While community-based conservation has been considered a way of practising equitable conservation, there are instances where not everyone's voice is heard in management decisions. For example, Schnegg and Kiaka (2018) conducted both an ethnography and survey interviews with 20 communities in Namibia regarding the use of community based natural resource management (CBNRM) strategies. The Namibia system for CBNRM started as a means of addressing the growing wildlife populations and instances of human–wildlife interactions (see Khumalo & Young, 2015; O'Connell-Rodwell et al., 2000). A large component of Namibia's economy comes from wildlife tourism, which means that there is added pressure on local communities to share their space with sometimes troublesome or dangerous wildlife. Because of this, CBNRM is a crucial component of Namibia's conservation management strategies. Schnegg and Kiaka (2018) found that, overall, there was huge improvement in CBNRM because of the wildlife and water policies, but also an increase in economic impoverishment within the adjacent communities. These results indicated that there was little community collaboration in the implementation of wildlife policies within the conservancy. The study provided insight into the trade-offs between conservation management and economic development, specifically how this trade-off has an impact on local communities. It provided evidence that the voices, opinions, and interests of communities are typically taken for granted within conservation management decisions. This dimension illustrates the necessity for greater attention to the disparities between intent and practice, and what that means for local and Indigenous peoples in conservation management decisions.

Conclusion

Globally, conservation justice, both in theory and in practice, warrants an approach which seeks to effectively and intentionally address social inequities and potential conservation-related exacerbation of these inequities. One of the most prominent ways of practising just conservation is through the use of community-based conservation projects. Community-based conservation promotes the idea that long-lasting conservation success requires engagement with, and providing benefits for, local communities (Brooks, Waylen, & Mulder, 2013). This is one of the foundations of conservation justice.

AALAYNA R. GREEN

Further reading

Artelle, K. A., Zurba, M., Bhattacharyya, J., Chan, D. E., Brown, K., Housty, J., & Moola, F. (2019). Supporting resurgent Indigenous-led governance: A nascent mechanism for just and effective conservation. *Biological Conservation, 240*, 108284.

Dawson, N., Coolsaet, B., Sterling, E., Loveridge, R., Nicole, D., Wongbusarakum, S., Sangha, K., Scherl, L., Phan, H. P., Zafra-Calvo, N., & Lavey, W. (2021). The role of Indigenous peoples and local communities in effective and equitable conservation. *Ecology and Society, 26*(3), 19.

Ferketic, J. S., Latimer, A. M., & Silander Jr., J. A. (2010). Conservation justice in metropolitan Cape Town: A study at the Macassar Dunes Conservation Area. *Biological Conservation, 143*(5), 1168–1174.

Hernandez, J. (2022). *Fresh banana leaves: Healing Indigenous landscapes through Indigenous science.* North Atlantic Books.

Kashwan, P. (2017). *Democracy in the woods: Environmental conservation and social justice in India, Tanzania, and Mexico.* Oxford University Press.

Martin, A., Akol, A., & Gross-Camp, N. (2015). Towards an explicit justice framing of the social impacts of conservation. *Conservation & Society, 13*(2), 166–178.

Martin, A., Coolsaet, B., Corbera, E., Dawson, N. M., Fraser, J. A., Lehmann, I., & Rodriguez, I. (2016). Justice and conservation: The need to incorporate recognition. *Biological Conservation, 197*, 254–261.

Massarella, K., Nygren, A., Fletcher, R., Büscher, B., Kiwango, W. A., Komi, S., … & Percequillo, A. R. (2021). Transformation beyond conservation: How critical social science can contribute to a radical new agenda in biodiversity conservation. *Current Opinion in Environmental Sustainability, 49*, 79–87.

Mollett, S., & Kepe, T. (Eds.). (2018). *Land rights, biodiversity conservation and justice: Rethinking parks and people*. Routledge. https://doi.org/10.4324/9781315439488.

Rudd, L. F., Allred, S., Bright Ross, J. G., Hare, D., Nkomo, M. N., Shanker, K., … & Dávalos, A. (2021). Overcoming racism in the twin spheres of conservation science and practice. *Proceedings of the Royal Society B, 288*(1962), 20211871.

Saif, O., Keane, A., & Staddon, S. (2022). Making a case for the consideration of trust, justice, and power in conservation relationships. *Conservation Biology, 36*(4), e13903.

Tan, K. (2021). Just conservation: The question of justice in global wildlife conservation. *Philosophy Compass, 16*(2), e12720.

Taylor, D. E. (2016). *The rise of the American conservation movement: Power, privilege, and environmental protection.* Duke University Press.

Vucetich, J. A., Burnham, D., Macdonald, E. A., Bruskotter, J. T., Marchini, S., Zimmermann, A., & Macdonald, D. W. (2018). Just conservation: What is it and should we pursue it? *Biological Conservation, 221*, 23–33.

References

Apostolopoulou, E., Chatzimentor, A., Maestre-Andrés, S., Requena-i-Mora, M., Pizarro, A., & Bormpoudakis, D. (2021). Reviewing 15 years of research on neoliberal conservation: Towards a decolonial, interdisci-

plinary, intersectional and community-engaged research agenda. *Geoforum*, *124*, 236–256.
Bailey, K., Morales, N., & Newberry, M. (2020). Inclusive conservation requires amplifying experiences of diverse scientists. *Nature Ecology & Evolution*, *4*(1), 1294–1295.
Bennett, N. J., Katz, L., Yadao-Evans, W., Ahmadiyya, G. N., Atkinson, S., Ban, N. C., … & Wilhelm, A. (2021). Advancing social equity in and through marine conservation. *Frontiers in Marine Science*, *8*, 711538.
Boillat, S., Gerber, J. D., Oberlack, C., Zaehringer, J. G., Ifejika Speranza, C., & Rist, S. (2018). Distant interactions, power, and environmental justice in protected area governance: A telecoupling perspective. *Sustainability*, *10*(11), 3954.
Bontempi, A., Venturi, P., Del Bene, D., Scheidel, A., Zaldo-Aubanell, Q., & Zaragoza, R. M. (2023). Conflict and conservation: On the role of protected areas for environmental justice. *Global Environmental Change*, *82*, 102740.
Bourgeois, R., Guerbois, C., Giva, N., Mugabe, P., Mukamuri, B., Fynn, R., Daré, W. S., Motsholapheko, M., Nare, L., Delay, E., & Ducrot, R. (2023). Using anticipation to unveil drivers of local livelihoods in Transfrontier Conservation Areas: A call for more environmental justice. *People and Nature*, *5*(2), 726–741.
Brooks, J., Waylen, K. A., & Mulder, M. B. (2013). Assessing community-based conservation projects: A systematic review and multilevel analysis of attitudinal, behavioral, ecological, and economic outcomes. *Environmental Evidence*, *2*, 2.
Bullard, R. D. (1993). Anatomy of environmental racism and the environmental justice movement. In R. D. Bullard (Ed.), *Confronting environmental racism: Voices from the grassroots* (pp. 15–39). South End Press.
Carastathis, A. (2014). The concept of intersectionality in feminist theory. *Philosophy Compass*, *9*(5), 304–314.
Collins, P. H., & Bilge, S. (2016). *Intersectionality – Key concepts*. Polity Press.
Cooper, B. (2015). Intersectionality. In L. Disch & M. Hawkesworth (Eds.), *The Oxford handbook of feminist theory* (pp. 385–406). Oxford University Press.
Crenshaw, K. W., & Bonis, O. (2005). Cartographies des marges: intersectionnalité, politique de l'identité et violences contre les femmes de couleur. *Cahiers du genre*, *39*(2), 51–82.
Dahlberg, A., Rohde, R., & Sandell, K. (2010). National parks and environmental justice: Comparing access rights and ideological legacies in three countries. *Conservation and Society*, *8*(3), 209–224.
Dawson, N., Carvalho, W. D., Bezerra, J. S., Todeschini, F., Tabarelli, M., & Mustin, K. (2023). Protected areas and the neglected contribution of Indigenous peoples and local communities: Struggles for environmental justice in the Caatinga dry forest. *People and Nature*, *5*(6), 1739–1755.
Dawson, N., Coolsaet, B., Sterling, E., Loveridge, R., Nicole, D., Wongbusarakum, S., Sangha, K., Scherl, L., Phan, H. P., Zafra-Calvo, N., & Lavey, W. (2021). The role of Indigenous peoples and local communities in effective and equitable conservation. *Ecology and Society*, *26*(3), 19.
Doubleday, K. F. (2020). Tigers and 'good Indian wives': Feminist political ecology exposing the gender-based violence of human–wildlife conflict in Rajasthan, India. *Annals of the American Association of Geographers*, *110*(5), 1521–1539.
Fanari, E. (2022). Struggles for just conservation: An analysis of India's biodiversity conservation conflicts. *Journal of Political Ecology*, *28*(1), 1051–1081.
Ferketic, J. S., Latimer, A. M., & Silander Jr., J. A. (2010). Conservation justice in metropolitan Cape Town: A study at the Macassar Dunes Conservation Area. *Biological Conservation*, *143*(5), 1168–1174.
Fielding, R. (2022). Whalers in 'a post-whaling world': Sustainable conservation of marine mammals and sustainable development of whaling communities: With a case study from the Eastern Caribbean. *Sustainability*, *14*(14), 8782. doi:https://doi.org/10.3390/su14148782.
Guibrunet, L., Gerritsen, P. R. W., Sierra-Huelsz, J. A., Flores-Díaz, A. C., García-Frapolli, E., García-Serrano, E., Pascual, U., & Balvanera, P. (2021). Beyond participation: How to achieve the recognition of local communities' value-systems in conservation? Some insights from Mexico. *People and Nature*, *3*(3), 528–541.
Haenn, N. (2012). Risking environmental justice: Culture, conservation and governance at Calakmul, Mexico. In S. E. Eckstein & T. P. Wickham-Crowley (Eds.), *Struggles for social rights in Latin America* (pp. 81–102). Routledge.
Hart, C. R. (2014). The role of environmental justice in biodiversity conservation: Investigating experiences of communities near Kruger National Park, South Africa. *Dalhousie Journal of Interdisciplinary Management*, *10*(1).
Karki, M., & Adhikari, J. R. (2015). Integrating Indigenous, local and modern knowledge for sustainable conservation and management of forest ecosystems in Nepal. *Forestry Nepal: Gateway to Forestry Information in Nepal.*
Kashwan, P., Duffy, R. V., Massé, F., Asiyanbi, A. P., & Marijnen, E. (2021). From racialized neocolonial global conservation to an inclusive and regenerative conservation. *Environment:*

Science and Policy for Sustainable Development, 63(4), 4–19.

Khumalo, K. E., & Young, L. A. (2015). Women, human–wildlife conflict, and CBNRM: Hidden impacts and vulnerabilities in Kwandu Conservancy, Namibia. *Conservation & Society, 13*(2), 232–243.

Koot, S., Büscher, B., & Thakholi, L. (2022). The new green apartheid? Race, capital and logics of enclosure in South Africa's wildlife economy. *Environmental Planning E: Nature and Space, 7*(1), 123–140.

Le Tran, D., Martinez-Alier, J., Navas, G., & Mingorria, S. (2020). Gendered geographies of violence: A multiple case study analysis of murdered women environmental defenders. *Journal of Political Ecology, 27*(1), 1189–1212.

London, L., Joshi, T. K., Cairncross, E., & Claudio, L. (2011). Environmental justice: An international perspective. *Encyclopedia of Environmental Health*, 441–448.

Loos, J. (2021). Reconciling conservation and development in protected areas in the Global South. *Basic and Applied Ecology, 54*, 108–118.

Lopes, P. F. M., de Freitas, C. T., Hallwass, G., Silvano, R. A. M., Begossi, A., & Campos-Silva, J. V. (2021). Just aquatic governance: The Amazon basin as fertile ground for aligning participatory conservation with social justice. *Aquatic Conservation: Marine and Freshwater Ecosystems, 31*(5), 1190–1205. https://doi.org/10.1002/aqc.3586

Lynch, M., & Turner, S. (2021). Rocking the boat: Intersectional resistance to marine conservation policies in Wakatobi National Park, Indonesia. *Gender, Place & Culture*. doi:10.1080/0966369X.2021.1971630

Ma, B., Cai, Z., Zheng, J., & Wen, Y. (2019). Conservation, ecotourism, poverty, and income inequality: A case study of nature reserves in Qinling, China. *World Development, 115*, 236–244.

Malin, S. A., Ryder, S., & Lyra, M. G. (2019). Environmental justice and natural resource extraction: Intersections of power, equity and access. *Environmental Sociology, 5*(2), 109–116.

Martin, A., Coolsaet, B., Corbera, E., Dawson, N. M., Fraser, J. A., Lehmann, I., & Rodriguez, I. (2016). Justice and conservation: The need to incorporate recognition. *Biological Conservation, 197*, 254–261.

Martin, A., Akol, A., & Gross-Camp, N. (2015). Towards an explicit justice framing of the social impacts of conservation. *Conservation & Society, 13*(2), 166–178.

Martin, A., McGuire, S., & Sullivan, S. (2013). Global environmental justice and biodiversity conservation. *The Geographical Journal, 179*(2), 122–131.

Mohai, P., Pellow, D., & Roberts, J. T. (2009). Environmental justice. *Annual Review of Environment and Resources, 34*, 405–430.

Moorcroft, H. (2016). Paradigms, paradoxes and a propitious niche: Conservation and Indigenous social justice policy in Australia. *Local Environment, 21*(5), 591–614.

Noe, C., & Kangalawe, R. Y. (2015). Wildlife protection, community participation in conservation, and (dis)empowerment in southern Tanzania. *Conservation and Society, 13*(3), 244–253.

O'Connell-Rodwell, C. E., Rodwell, T., Rice, M., & Hart, L. A. (2000). Living with the modern conservation paradigm: Can agricultural communities co-exist with elephants? A five-year case study in east Caprivi, Namibia. *Biological Conservation, 93*(3), 381–391.

Pandya, R. (2022). An intersectional approach to neoliberal environmentality: Women's engagement with ecotourism at Corbett Tiger Reserve, India. *Environment and Planning E: Nature and Space*, 25148486221082469.

Paudel, K., Potter, G. R., & Phelps, J. (2019). Conservation enforcement: Insights from people incarcerated for wildlife crimes in Nepal. *Conservation Science and Practice, 2*(2). https://doi.org/10.1111/csp2.137

Petriello, M. A., Redmore, L., Sène-Harper, A., & Katju, D. (2021). Terms of empowerment: Of conservation or communities? *Oryx, 55*(2), 255–261.

Rai, N. D., Devy, S., Ganesh, T., Ganesan, R., Setty, S. R., Hiremath, A. J., Khaling, S., & Rajan, P. D. (2021). Beyond fortress conservation: The long-term integrations of natural and social science research for an inclusive conservation practice in India. *Biological Conservation, 254*, 108888.

Redford, K. H., & Fearn, E. (Eds.). (2007). *Protected areas and human displacement: A conservation perspective* (Vol. 29). Wildlife Conservation Society.

Ruano-Chamorro, C., Gurney, G. G., & Cinner, J. E. (2021). Advancing procedural justice in conservation. *Conservation Letters, 15*(3), e12861.

Rudd, L. F., Allred, S., Bright Ross, J. G., Hare, D., Nkomo, M. N., Shanker, K., Allen, T., Biggs, D., Dickman, A., Dunaway, M., Ghosh, R., González, N. T., Kepe, T., Mbizah, M. M., Middleton, S. L., Oommen, M. A., Paudel, K., Sillero-Zubiri, C., & Dávalos, A. (2021). Overcoming racism in the twin spheres of conservation science and practice. *Proceedings of the Royal Society B, 288*(1962), 20211871.

Saif, O., Keane, A., & Staddon, S. (2022). Making a case for the consideration of trust, justice, and power in conservation relationships. *Conservation Biology*, *36*(4), e13903.

Schnegg, M., & Kiaka, R. D. (2018). Subsidized elephants: Community-based resource governance and environmental (in)justice in Namibia. *Geoforum*, *93*, 105–115.

Sinthumule, N. I. (2018). Conservation, displacement and social injustice at the South African section of Greater Mapungubwe Transfrontier. *Development and Society*, *47*(2), 261–284.

Thakholi, L., & Büscher, B. (2021). Conserving inequality: How private conservation and property developers 'fix' spatial injustice in South Africa. *Environment and Planning E: Nature and Space*, 25148486211066388.

Turner, R. A., Addison, J., Arias, A., Bergseth, B. J., Marshall, N. A., Morrison, T. H., & Tobin, R. C. (2016). Trust, confidence, and equity affect the legitimacy of natural resource governance. *Ecology and Society*, *21*(3), 18.

Ulibarri, N., Figueroa, O. P., & Grant, A. (2022). Barriers and opportunities to incorporating environmental justice in the National Environmental Policy Act. *Environmental Impact Assessment Review*, *97*, 106880.

Wang, X., & Lo, K. (2022). Pastoralism and conservation: The politics and notions of environmental justice under the grazing ban policy in Inner Mongolia, China. *Political Geography*, *99*, 102779.

White, R. (2007). Green criminology and the pursuit of social and ecological justice. In P. Beirne & N. South (Eds.), *Issues in green criminology* (pp. 32–54). Routledge.

Whyte, K. (2020). Too late for Indigenous climate justice: Ecological and relational tipping points. *Wiley Interdisciplinary Reviews: Climate Change*, *11*(1), e603.

Whyte, K. (2018). Settler colonialism, ecology, and environmental injustice. *Environment and Society*, *9*(1), 125–144.

Wiens, K., Groulx, M., Booth, A., & Lemieux, C. J. (2024). The lemmings dilemma: An examination of environmental justice, volunteerism, and the pursuit of empowerment in biodiversity conservation organizations in Canada. *Environmental Justice.*

Wolf, B. (2011). 'Green-collar crime': Environmental crime and justice in the sociological perspective. *Sociology Compass*, *5*(7), 499–511.

Young, J. C., Searle, K., Butler, A., Simmons, P., Watt, A. D., & Jordan, A. (2016). The role of trust in the resolution of conservation conflicts. *Biological Conservation*, *195*, 196–202.

Zeng, Y., Twang, F., & Carrasco, L. R. (2022). Threats to land and environmental defenders in nature's last strongholds. *Ambio*, *51*(1), 269–279.

5. Ecocide

Introduction

There are multiple definitions of the term ecocide in circulation, and there is considerable debate over whether it can, dependent on the definition employed, be classified as a crime. Literally, ecocide refers to the murder of the environment (or, more precisely, the prefix *eco* is from the Greek *oikos*, which means home; ecology is the science of understanding the interacting parts of the home; thus, ecocide is the process of destroying it). The most obvious way to destroy the environment is to attack it directly, which has been done throughout history during military campaigns as part of deliberate strategy aimed at harming enemy forces and, very importantly, civilians.

However, ecocide has been defined differently over several decades. It can be viewed in a strict (minimalist) sense as the deliberate destruction of natural resources, including biota, for military purposes; or in a much broader sense (maximalist) as the gradual destruction of the biosphere due to the collective, cumulative impact of human activities. Between these two extremes are many other efforts to arrive at an operational definition that can be used in courts by prosecutors, including perhaps international criminal courts. Once used mostly to describe a military act, it is now much more commonly used to describe purposeful human behaviour that harms the environment, regardless of the motivation. This distinction between a hard and soft definition, or a minimalist and maximalist one (see Stoett, 2000), has become overshadowed by an effort to codify the latter on a global scale that could affect the jurisdiction of the International Criminal Court and other judicial bodies.

Once viewed largely as the acts of governments and their military apparatus, the popular conception (if not a universal legal one) has also expanded to include the acts of corporations and, even, individuals. However, we are some way off from reaching a point of consensus on this significant step. A recent panel of experts has arrived at what seems to be a fairly widely acceptable definition (Stop Ecocide International, 2023), but moving from there to criminalising the ecocidal behaviour this definition describes will be a difficult journey.

The grass suffers most

A well-cited African proverb suggests that when elephants fight, anything below or near them suffers the consequences. This is certainly the case with the natural environment (biota in particular) when military conflict takes place. History is replete with examples of the deliberate, strategic destruction of local ecosystems during military conflict (Stoett, 2000). But it was the American "Operation Ranch Hand" and other efforts in Vietnam that brought global and legal attention to ecocide as an approach to warfare (Weisberg, 1970). Indeed, the inaugural volume of the *Bulletin of Peace Proposals* featured a groundbreaking article by Richard Falk drawing attention to the effects of ecocide as a consequence of environmental warfare, and an appreciable body of literature followed suit (Falk, 1973).

Barry Weisberg's edited book arrived even earlier, in 1970, and included chapters by Jean Paul Sartre, Orville Schell, Arthur Westing (who would go on to produce an astounding array of articles on the environmental impacts of war; e.g., Westing, 1974), Noam Chomsky, and others. Weisberg defined ecocide as:

> the premeditated assault of a nation and its resources against the individuals, culture and biological fabric of another country and its environs ... To understand the destruction of Indochina as ecocide requires that we come to understand that the ecosystem of Southeast Asia is an organic fabric in which all living things are tied together by an infinite number of interdependent strands. (Weisberg, 1970: 4)

This is a lovely definition that foreshadows a much broader conception of purposeful or even indirect violence against nature, and conservation biology would certainly affirm the "organic fabric" perspective in a short time.

The use of the term to connote deliberate environmental destruction gave rise to the *Convention on the Prohibition of Military or Any Other Hostile Use of Environmental Modification Techniques* (known as ENMOD), and the Additional Protocol I to the 1949 Geneva Conventions, both in 1977. Seen within the context of the Cold War and heightened concern about nuclear

Armageddon, these diplomatic advances were more about reducing the chances of World War III than they were about strengthening international environmental law or expanding conceptions of crime. And it is painfully self-evident that no international legal barriers, from the ENMOD to the International Criminal Court (ICC) and beyond, have had a substantive impact when it comes to restraining the willingness of armies to inflict environmental damage in warfare (as recent actions by Russia in Ukraine strongly suggest).

Importantly, this definition of ecocide can be slightly stretched to include not just acts of war, but military preparation as well (Stoett, 2000). This gets us closer to attaching ecocide to acts rooted as much in negligence of environmental consideration, as to deliberate destruction for strategic gain. The environmental damage caused by the testing and weapons development during the Cold War arms race was in fact colossal, especially on the Soviet Union side. Military installations are notorious for leaving unwanted toxic waste behind. The biggest single polluter on Earth remains the Pentagon, which contributes more greenhouse gases to the atmosphere than the vast majority of countries combined. Jet fuel alone is a remarkable contribution: the new single-piloted F-35 burns about 5,600 litres per hour of flight (to put this in perspective, a Boeing 747, which can carry upwards of 500 passengers, burns around 14,500). Indeed, no one knows what the real ecological footprint of major military powers is: classified information, partial reporting, concealed training exercises, and other unreported events make public carbon accounting impossible.

Article 8(2)(b)(iv) of the Rome Statute of the International Criminal Court, adopted in 1998 and in force in 2002, declares it a war crime to "intentionally launch an attack in the knowledge that such attack will cause incidental loss of life or injury to civilians or damage to civilian objects or widespread, long-term and severe damage to the natural environment which would be clearly excessive in relation to the concrete and direct overall military advantage anticipated" (see Palarczyk, 2023). And pillaging natural resources during war has been treated as an international crime as well, at the ICC and elsewhere. Former ICC Prosecutor Fatou Bensouda did express the desire to see the ICC's jurisdiction expanded to include environmental crimes in peacetime and released an Office Policy Paper to this effect, though it was, arguably, aimed as much at curbing the modern practice of "land grabbing" as anything else. But the mere fact that there is ongoing discussion about expanding the remit of the ICC so it can approach ecocide as non-military environmental destruction is testament to not only how serious the twin ecological threats of climate change and biodiversity loss are, but to the elasticity of the term "ecocide" today.

Broadening out

Polly Higgins was a tireless campaigner for this conceptual development, though green criminology had already taken solid footsteps in this direction. In 2010 she submitted a suggestion to the UN Law Commission to define it as "the extensive damage to, destruction of or loss of ecosystem(s) of a given territory, whether by human agency or by other causes, to such an extent that peaceful enjoyment by the inhabitants of that territory has been severely diminished" (see Higgins, 2010; Higgins, Short, and South, 2013). In this view, ecocide should be seen as the fifth Crime against Peace, and it should not take a military conflict to allow prosecution to take place.

This is part of a broader story of the term being applied to more and more things (similar to the trajectory of the term *genocide* which was once applied only to the Holocaust, then to other cases of mass murder, then to a wide array of human rights abuses and oppressive acts). As early as 1971, Clifton Fadiman and Jean White published a book titled *Ecocide ... And Thoughts Toward Survival*; in the introduction Harvey Wheeler wrote that the "message of our day is ecocide, the environment being murdered by mankind" (Fadiman and White, 1971); he meant it went beyond what the United States was doing in Vietnam and applied to all the industrialised world. In law journals, in 1993 Lynn Berat suggested "geocide" should be viewed as a crime under international law (Berat, 1993); Mark Allan Gray published a piece on the "international crime of ecocide" a few years later (Gray, 1996; see also Feshback and Friendly, 1992, for an important condemnatory text on the environmental impact of economic policies in the Soviet Union).

It can be sensibly argued that what Nigel South referred to as the "ecocidal tendencies of late modernity" (South, 2013), exhibited in perfectly legal but wantonly destructive acts of resource extraction, agricultural and industrial pollution, and the wide array of contributions to climate change made across the globe on a daily basis, formed the normative background in which the development of green criminology took place. Others have discussed ecoviolence as a term that denotes harm against the environment that stems from the super-exploitation of humans by humans, or the reverse: the violent harm to humans that causes harm to nature (Stoett and Omrow, 2021). The idea that ecocide is an apt term to describe so much of what goes on every day (Agnew refers to the "ordinary acts" that contribute to ecocide: Agnew, 2020) might be too much for those deeply wed to the liberal teleology of continuous progress through economic growth and technological progress, but will make perfect sense to those who have suffered the most during these historical and contemporary processes, such as indigenous peoples on every continent touched by colonialism.

Towards a contemporary applicable definition

Judges at the 2016–2017 Citizens' Monsanto Tribunal were "of the view that the time is ripe for proposing to set up the new legal concept of Ecocide and to integrate it in a future amended version of the Rome Statute" (International Monsanto Tribunal, 2017: 47). As international environmental legal expert Valerie Cabanes suggests, this take on the concept implies that "strict liability is not only established by malicious intent can but also be knowledge of the consequences of the individual or legal entity's action" (Cabanes, 2023: 236). To put it differently, strict liability may be applied to more severe risks and harms, given the seriousness of the harm, in which case *mens rea* (the mental element) is less important than *actus reus* (the act itself), although subjective factors are nonetheless taken into consideration as part of sentencing deliberations. Thus, if widespread destruction and damage does occur, this should trigger prosecution and conviction regardless of the mental element.

Similarly, the End Ecocide on Earth movement defined ecocide as "severe damage to any part or system of the global commons, or to Earth's ecological system" (Cabanes, 2023: 237). More recently, the Stop Ecocide International group (with Swedish encouragement) convened a panel of experts who arrived at the following definition, which was well covered in global media and widely disseminated on social media:

> unlawful or wanton acts committed with knowledge that there is a substantial likelihood of severe and either widespread or long-term damage to the environment being caused by these acts. (Stop Ecocide International, 2023)

This is a clever definition which escapes the vice-like grip of intentionality as a determinative factor, includes legal acts (though they must be "wanton", meaning "with reckless disregard for damage which would be clearly excessive in relation to the social and economic benefits anticipated"), and employs language used in the ENMOD, Rome Statute, and elsewhere to refer to the damage caused, but avoids the necessity of *both* widespread and long-term damage (one of either is enough to trigger the charge of ecocide, though of course they most often do go together).

While it seems unlikely that the Rome Statute will be refurbished with this new addition as a fifth crime against the peace and security of humanity under the present circumstances, it is certainly not out of the question – if the political constellations of stars align in several influential places at once. Public outrage may indeed push the needle here. As the ravages of natural resource exploitation continue, and the impacts of climate change, biodiversity loss, pollution, and other Earth system threats compound, we inch closer to the universal criminalisation embedded in this conception of ecocide. Green criminologists, undeterred by existing legal mechanisms, have been pushing this conception of environmental harm as a topic for sociological investigation for many years now (see e.g., White, 2023).

Negligence has also emerged as a key theme, one that links the minimalist and maximalist definitions discussed in this brief entry. If military commanders can be charged with ecocide because they neglected to consider the environmental impact of their actions on a battlefield, then surely corporate executives can be subject to the same scrutiny in the future. And although one can argue that ecocide is built right into the fabric of centuries-old patterns of imperialism, colonialism, and epistemic violence, the question of negligence perhaps rings as loudly today as ever, when rising sea levels pose an existential threat to small island states and we are in the midst of a great extinction event. Is the refusal to engage in serious climate change mitigation policy a crime? And equally interesting: what are the limits of complicity in such a crime – politicians, corporate executives, consumers of luxury goods, investors, workers, public educators – when does our own participation in the economic activities driving global environmental change assume the spectre of criminality?

Conclusion

Though ecocide was once thought of as a deliberate military act or strategy (and with good reason), the use of the term has changed over time. The central conceptualisation that has emerged on ecocide may be summarised as follows: the knowledge of the deleterious impact of many forms of what were once dismissed as solely economic activities implies that people who know better should do better. Intent will always be a problematic demand, but it does seem as though we have slipped into the realm of prior knowledge as a sufficient factor. Negligence then becomes an active crime in areas where it was previously dismissed with a small fine or warning.

Are we nearing the point where we will see serious criminal prosecution based on a non-war-related act of sustained environmental destruction? The wild rights law movement seems convinced this is the case (see Cullinan, 2011). Indeed, people will employ the concept to support their own cause, from their own perspective, and there is nothing inherently wrong with that; but the time for more clarity in international courts and the conceptualisation of environmental crime has surely come.

PETER STOETT

Further reading

Falk, R. (1973) Environmental warfare and ecocide. *Bulletin of Peace Proposals* 4: 1–17.
Higgins, P. (2010) *Eradicating Ecocide*. Shepheard Walwyn.
Mégret, F. (2011) The problem of an international criminal law of the environment. *Columbia Journal of Environmental Law* 36(2): 195–236.
Stop Ecocide International (2023) Website. https://www.stopecocide.earth/what-is-ecocide
Weinstein, T. (2005) Prosecuting attacks that destroy the environment: Environmental crimes or humanitarian atrocities. *Georgetown International Environmental Law Review* 17(4): 697–714.
White, R. (2023) Conceptions of ecocide and challenges for social transformation. *Current Issues in Criminal Justice* 35(3): 312–323. doi:10.1080/10345329.2023.2203272
Zierler, D. (2011) *The Invention of Ecocide: Agent Orange, Vietnam, and the Scientists Who Changed the Way We Think about the Environment*. University of Georgia Press.

References

Agnew, R. (2020) The ordinary acts that contribute to ecocide: A criminological analysis. In N. South and A. Brisman, eds., *Routledge International Handbook of Green Criminology* (pp. 52–67). Routledge.
Berat, L. (1993) Defending the right to a healthy environment: Toward a crime of geocide in international law. *Boston University International Law Journal* 11: 327–348.
Cabanes, V. (2023) Rights of nature: A new perspective in law. In S. Lamalle and P. Stoett, eds., *Rights and Representations of Nature* (pp. 233–258). Cambridge University Press.
Cullinan, C. (2011) *Wild Law: A Manifesto for Earth Justice* (2nd ed.). Chelsea Green.
Fadiman, C., and White, J., eds. (1971) *Ecocide ... and Thoughts Toward Survival*. James Feel and Associates.
Falk, R. (1973) Environmental warfare and ecocide. *Bulletin of Peace Proposals* 4: 1–17.
Feshbach, M., and Friendly, A. (1992) *Ecocide in the USSR: Health and Nature under Siege*. Basic Books.
Gray, M. A. (1996) The international crime of ecocide. *California Western International Law Journal* 26(2): 215–272.
Higgins, P. (2010) *Eradicating Ecocide*. Shepheard Walwyn.
Higgins, P., Short, D., and South, N. (2013) Protecting the planet: A proposal for a law of

ecocide. *Crime, Law Social and Change* 59: 251–266.
International Monsanto Tribunal. (2017) Advisory Opinion. The Hague, 18 April.
Palarczyk, D. (2023) Ecocide before the ICC: Simplicity is better than an elaborate embellishment. *Criminal Law Forum* 34: 147–207.
South, N. (2013) The ecocidal tendencies of late modernity: Transnational crime, social exclusion, victims and rights. In R. White, ed., *Global Environmental Harm: Criminological Perspectives* (pp. 246–266). Willan.
Stoett, P. (2000) Environmental degradation: Ecocide. In P. Stoett, *Human and Global Security: An Exploration of Terms*. University of Toronto Press.
Stoett, P., and Omrow, D. (2021) *Spheres of Transnational Ecoviolence: Environmental Crime, Human Security, and Justice*. Palgrave Macmillan.
Stop Ecocide International (2023) Website. https://www.stopecocide.earth/what-is-ecocide
Weisberg, B. (1970). *Ecocide in Indochina*. Canfield Press.
Westing, A. (1974) Proscription of ecocide. *Science and Public Affairs* 30(1): 24–27.
White, R. (2023) Conceptions of ecocide and challenges for social transformation. *Current Issues in Criminal Justice* 35(3): 312–323. doi:10.1080/10345329.2023.2203272

PETER STOETT

6. Economics and environmental harm

Introduction

The question of responsibility is a recurring theme in debates about our current environmental and ecological crisis. Responsibility of all kinds is often invoked in relation to the environmental 'value–action gap'. This refers to the collective cognitive dissonance of continuing environmentally harmful production and consumption practices despite the global awakening in environmental consciousness that the existential threat of climate change has fostered. Some environmental campaigners believe that 'personal responsibility' and 'ethical consumerism' are smokescreens preventing people from seeing and addressing the real material drivers of global warming, thus allowing institutional actors to continue 'business as usual'. In contrast there are the 'pragmatists' who contend that consumption-orientated environmental activism is the only recourse for effective action since production only ever ultimately serves final consumption. This entry reviews this intellectual debate by summarising the key social, political and economic dividing lines and evaluating whether responsibility can be equally distributed according to a 'chain' logic of causality, or if this hinders realistic assessment of agency and power relations in modern capitalist societies when it comes to environmental harm.

Responsibility and environmental sustainability

'Just 100 companies are responsible for 71% of global emissions' is a familiar claim in discussions and debates about the causes of the current climate catastrophe. This is in reference to the widely shared 'Carbon Majors Report', a piece of research carried out by the Carbon Majors Database (CMD) in 2017 that mapped how the distribution of *industrial* greenhouse gas (GHG) emissions is concentrated globally (Griffin and Heede, 2017). The report makes for damning reading. Environmental campaigners in particular will be familiar with at least some of the investor-owned companies that make this list: ExxonMobil; Shell; BP; Chevron; and Gazprom, for example. Likewise, it will come as no surprise that a firm like Shell, the multinational oil and gas company which in 2018 spent $55 million on 'climate branding' yet since then has dedicated just 1% of its long-term investments to sources of low-carbon energy like wind and solar, should make it into the climate black book. Returning to the original claim – that 100 companies are answerable for nearly three-quarters of the carbon emissions that have rendered the future of human civilisation at risk – we can use this framing as a point of departure to explore the economic drivers of environmental and ecological harm and the responsibility it bears on various actors. It particularly raises questions about the role of and relationship between production and consumption, since the question then often becomes: does the individual matter if only 100 companies are responsible for 71% of CO_2 emissions? This question is reviewed below.

To flesh out the differences in perspective laid out above, we can recall Slavoj Žižek's (2009) playful critique of what he calls *cultural capitalism.* In typically glib fashion, Žižek jokes how recycling our Coca-Cola cans provides the necessary disavowal for belonging to a heating planet, where structural transformation of the economy is permanently sidelined in favour of 'ethical' consumer behaviour. Put simply, it is up to consumers, acting with their wallets, to save the environment from catastrophe. As long as we shift to paper straws, for example, we can carry on consuming with impunity, engaging in business as usual. George Monbiot (2021) describes this so-called ethical consumerism as simply 'micro-consumerist bollocks' (MCB). MCB often manifests itself in pronouncements from within the political and media classes, which have a tendency to deflect attention from addressing the energy-intensive mode of production that has historically benefitted those particular classes economically.

To offer one example of such political tactics in regard to the environmental crisis, during a televised debate on the BBC between Conservative politicians Rishi Sunak and Liz Truss in July 2022 as they vowed to become the next prime minister of the United Kingdom, a question was put to both candidates by presenter Sophie Raworth. Raworth began by pointing to the record temperatures the country had experienced only a week prior to the debate. This was followed by the question, 'What three things should people change in their lives to help tackle climate change faster?' The move from discussing the global existential threat of global warming to placing the onus on consumer responsibility was virtually seamless and was met with similarly hollow responses from both candidates. Sunak in particular chose to frame his answer specifically around his own household consumption, pointing to how he 'take[s] advice from [his] two young daughters who are the experts on this in [their] household', and stressing the importance of recycling, even if it comes with the additional burden of 'need[ing] lots of bins'.

This debate, its framing, delivery of the question, and responses, personifies what Maniates (2001) argued over two decades ago with respect to the manner in which environmental issues are individualised and depoliticised. It reflects a broader ideological ambition from within the history of the conservative political tradition to promote 'personal responsibility' above all other forms of duty (Kuypers et al., 2003: 12; Lepistö, 2021), often with the implication that adverse experiences of life are the fault of individual shortcomings rather than the negative externalities of our social and economic system. Critics of this perspective argue that there is a stultification of meaningful action on the environment every time we narrow the horizon to strictly supply-side reforms (i.e., the conditions under which goods and services are supplied and consumed). This shifts attention away from what matters: how we produce and who produces the emissions.

Institutional responsibility and environmental sustainability

What might be the issue with the claim that 'just 100 companies are responsible for 71% of global emissions' both on its own terms and when it is cited in debates about the economic causes of climate breakdown? Perhaps the first thing to mention is that the statistic covers carbon emissions dating back all the way to the beginning of the Industrial Revolution. This might alter the emphasis of the original claim, knowing that we are not referring simply to current emissions but *historically* speaking, carbon that has previously been emitted. There are limits to this counterclaim, however, since evidently the problem is not limited to emissions that have already been released but also includes the influence the polluting companies continue to have on world markets. As Bigger and Carton (2020: 647–8) point out, 'many of these companies continue to form a structurally important pillar of financial markets, so a rapid move to decarbonization has significant ramifications for the portfolios of investors, not to mention the fortunes of politicians in fossil fuel producing and consuming countries'. In other words, the financial imperatives to continue fossil fuel extraction remain, as do the state buy-ins that underpin them.

The question of extraction is also relevant to how seriously we should take the charge that corporations bear an institutional responsibility that well exceeds that of any individual. Straightforwardly, the extraction of fossil fuels is done in the service of the production of commodities, itself guided by the effective demand of buyers. Production would be rendered entirely meaningless without consumption. This supply-side logic – in keeping with 'Say's Law' – the idea that supply necessarily creates its own demand – has led the likes of Eikenberry (2021) to argue that 'consumption-based accounting' should in fact be the priority:

> For before we shrug in defeat, we might pause to clarify, what are these 100 companies, and just what are they alone doing that is so damaging? Well, they are fossil fuel producers at the primary level of extraction, that is, coal, oil, and natural gas producers. The number two villain, for example, is the state-owned Saudi oil company Aramco, but it is certainly not pumping oil for its own sake, but for export to consumers around the world. Shall I really burn away hundreds of gallons of gasoline a year in my vehicle, but protest my innocence that the Saudis who dared sell to me are to blame? More broadly, it is the consumption of fossil fuels that is the direct driver of global warming, and, while fossil extraction is clearly a necessary step in the causal chain, to blame this alone ignores the simple fact that fossil producers do not act in a vacuum.

Eikenberry and other like-minded scholars (Larsen and Hertwich, 2009) suggest that it is individuals, or more accurately *households*, that frequently create the demand for fossil fuel extraction (Mitchell, 2012; Ivanova et al., 2016) – they are the ones using the fuel to heat their homes and run their cars.

Does this mean that it is actually the anti-extractivists (those who demand fossil fuels be left in the ground) who are reductionist if their arguments are leveraged in a manner that (wilfully or not) discourages worthwhile steps that consumers can and should take? After all it is true that production does not occur in a vacuum, and this does somewhat complicate the earlier claim about emitter responsibility.

Certainly, there have been questions about the feasibility of a campaign slogan like 'Just Stop Oil', for example. One critique of this is that oil is not just an energy source, but a chemical 'feedstock' also – the literal raw material of commodity production itself. As Hanieh (2021: 27) reminds us, the petrochemical revolution that occurred during and after the Second World War was based on the *synthetisation* of petroleum, such that 'from the 1950s onwards, a wide array of naturally derived substances – wood, glass, paper, natural rubber, natural fertilizers, soaps, cotton, wool and metals – were systematically displaced by plastics, synthetic fibres, detergents and other petroleum-based chemicals'. In other words, the production of the commodities we consume daily has become derivative of the production of energy. There are very few sustainable substitutes, although researchers have recently discovered a fungus that could eventually serve as an alternative to plastic (Pylkkänen et al., 2023). For now, though, if consumer goods of all shapes and sizes are laced with oil, then supply-side climate activists might contend that the demand for fossil fuels is implicated directly in their consumption, thereby feeding into one of the fundamental pillars of the 'degrowth' argument: to consume less. The invisibility of petrochemicals in the climate debate must therefore be accounted for, if only to further complicate the notion that just 100 companies are responsible for 71% of global emissions. Without a sustainable replacement, one might arrive at the conclusion that these things cannot simply 'stop' until demand for them does.

Ethical consumerism and the culture industry

One thing for certain is that over-consumption linked to petrochemicals makes the case for ethical consumerism more persuasive if the implication is that consumers can act responsibly to dictate the direction of production and therefore negate the destructive forms of extraction inflicting irreversible harm on the planet. Sociologists suggest there are limits to this perspective, however, in that it relies on a particular understanding of the relationship between production and consumption that attaches a great deal of weight not only to how consumers can steer production in the short and long term, but also how effective demand is configured in the first place (Shwom and Lorenzen, 2012). Indeed, social theorists (Gould et al., 2004; Dietz, 2015; White, 2018) like to point out that the notion that companies produce according to a causal chain such that the buck can hardly stop with them (since producers do not act in a vacuum) omits a critical detail from its analysis. Namely how, materially and ideologically, our systems of production have historically generated particular *wants, needs and desires* that ensure their steady and unremitting reproduction.

We need look no further than Horkheimer and Adorno's analysis of the 'culture industry' to reaffirm this intervention. In *Dialectic of Enlightenment* (2002: 95), they challenge the notion that the culture industry – the monopolising conditions of modern capitalism which create homogeneous, standardised forms of entertainment culture for the masses to passively consume – is merely a mirror of the newfound demands of the masses:

> Interested parties like to explain the culture industry in technological terms. Its millions of participants, they argue, demand reproduction processes which inevitably lead to the use of standard products to meet the needs at countless locations. The technical antithesis between few production centers and widely dispersed reception necessitates organisation and planning by those in control. The standardised forms, it is claimed, were originally derived from the needs of the consumers: that is what they accepted with so little resistance. In reality, a cycle of manipulation and retroactive need is unifying the system ever more tightly. What is not mentioned is that the basis of which technology is gaining power over society is the power of those whose economic position in society is strongest. Technical rationality today is the rationality of domination. It is the compulsive character of a society alienated from itself.

Horkheimer and Adorno were at pains to point out the existence and function of mass deception in modern capitalist society working beneath the surface level to radically alter consciousness and control cognition. The pair claimed to have unearthed a self-reproducing 'technical rationality' that precipitates an endless cycle of manipulation and socially constructed desire which can never be properly traced back to its source, thereby giving the outward impression that consumers are acting with an agency and autonomy all of their own.

Because this consumerist subjectivity is in fact a *pseudo* subjectivity, it could prove difficult to assign it foremost responsibility for something like the continued consumption of fossil fuels on a heating planet. This is because the want for the commodities attached to fossil fuel use is the upshot of a particular set of social relations under capitalism which mass consumerism itself has emerged from. Actually existing consumption, in other words, is driven by the machinations of the culture industry, where '[e]ach single manifestation of the culture industry inescapably reproduces human beings as what the whole has made them' (Horkheimer and Adorno, 2002: 100). The Frankfurt School were working off a tendency that Marx (1938: 47–8) theorised in *Capital: Volume One* termed 'commodity fetishism', which was used to describe how a 'definite social relation between men ... assumes, in their eyes, the fantastic form of a relation between things'. What Marx meant by this was that we encounter and experience the world through commodities, assigning a symbolic value to them that abstracts the object from its physical embodiment as a product of our labour. Therefore consumption, being socially embedded in the way we relate to one another and delinked from its basis in human exertion, inevitably becomes something to be desired and expanded, regardless of its actual *use value*.

Living through the global developments to capitalist production after the Second World War, these theorists are likely to have viewed this as an accurate reflection of the relationship between production and consumption because of major new cultural developments. As Hanieh (2021: 46) notes by referring to the 1960 classic, *The Waste Makers*, the influx of new and easily reproducible synthetic goods during the post-war period met with the obstacles of limited market size and the restricted needs of the post-war consumer. This, in turn, initiated the spectacular expansion of another 'new' industry: advertising. Corporate mergers resulted in global advertising 'mega-agencies' (O'Barr, 2005) that inculcated the mass consumer with 'plausible excuses for buying more of each product than might in earlier years have seemed rational or prudent' (Packard, 1960: 37). The way to end the 'general glut' of goods, in other words, was to produce gluttons, with the 'ever-accelerating quantities of waste, inbuilt obsolescence and the ubiquitous spread of disposability [now] hallmarks of capitalist production' (Hanieh, 2021: 46). The signs, systems and imagery of advertising thus assumed a much greater role in the growth dynamics of accumulation as they accelerated consumption through the manipulation of desires, the promotion of new lifestyles (Harvey, 1989: 287) and the incorporation of certain types of consumption into unconscious routines (White, 2018: 104).

Advanced by the credit system and the market-conscious service sector, consumerism constituted a strategic attempt to increase the rate of *unproductive demand* so as to mitigate the problems of over-accumulation (Wright, 1978: 144). Seen in this context, one where 'cultural infantilisation' serves the specific function of promoting false needs and excess to secure the realisation of capital and prevent adults from facing the true consequences of their present actions (White, 2018: 104), one might ascertain that consumption is downstream of production in a structural sense, and that, in the case of environmental harm, it may be reasonable to ascribe responsibility to institutional actors (Dietz, 2015: 338).

Chain or treadmill

These twentieth-century developments problematise the assumptions of Say's Law by suggesting that *supply does not necessarily create its own demand* (Harvey, 2018: 194), and that there in fact might not be general unity between supply and demand that could legitimately refract the emphasis of environmental harm onto consumers in the first instance. This goes to the heart of the question of how critical the role of the individual is if only 100 companies are responsible for 71% of CO_2 emissions, since it demonstrates limitations in conceptualising the issue as causal relationships of a chain-like structure. If it is a chain, then power and agency across its various linkages are not equally distributed. Therefore, the way consumers are implicated in the scorching of the Earth is not without significant convolutions. Such is why environmental sociologists often propose that we would be better served to think of the economy as a *treadmill.*

The 'treadmill of production' (ToP) theory developed by Schnaiberg (1980) and later advanced by Stretesky, Long and Lynch (2014) makes the case that humans have devised an economic system in capitalism that is altering the organisation of the Earth's ecological system by artificially disrupting the speed of naturally occurring entropy processes for the purpose of endless capital accumulation. The search for profit dictates the constant expansion of production without limits and the commodification (transforming use value into exchange value) of elements that would formally have been 'free' (White, 2018: 101). Foster (2000: 156) terms this capitalism's 'metabolic rift', borrowed from Marx's (1938: 333, 348) underappreciated writing on ecology, to describe how the 'blind desire for profit' had 'exhausted the soil' and created an unsustainable and 'irreparable rift'. Writing with Magdoff in *What Every Environmentalist Needs to Know About Capitalism* (2011: 43), Foster suggests that no amount of profit, no amount of wealth, and, crucially to this particular debate, no amount of consumption is either enough or too much. Thus, in ToP theory, the primary cause of ecological disorganisation in the modern world is capitalism itself (Stretesky et al., 2014: 22), built into its very logic and dynamics.

The checks and balances that might halt capitalism's ecological death drive are negated by the stakes that groups and individuals have in the very system that threatens their continued existence. Indeed, the current economic system requires the constant participation of its various actors in order for them to renew and survive. A worker's buy-in, for example, comes as a consequence of capitalism's structural precondition to leave an individual destitute if they do not sell their labour in exchange for a wage. Likewise, the state is inclined to support the expansion of production as a means to promote 'growth' and reproduce itself through tax revenues for social security purposes. What we have then is a social structure that functions as the driving force behind ecological disorganisation (Stretesky et al., 2014: 35). There is undoubtably an agency here, but it might not be in the ethical consumerist sense. Rather, for ToP theorists, agency is rooted in the interests of participants in the production process, which continues to be tethered to the interests of capital. This basic premise led Gould et al. (2004: 301), who also helped to popularise the ToP theory of environment harm, to surmise that mainstream economics alone is incapable of diagnosing our current crisis:

> To place consumption decisions first in our analyses would obscure the power relations embedded in the political economy. Henry Ford's famous 'consumer choice' comes to mind: He told the public they could purchase any colour Model T they wished 'as long as it's black!' 'Consumer behavior' studies contain few theories about the power underlying them. Obscuring the distribution of economic and political power serves the discipline of neo-classical economics quite well in its status quo reinforcement functions. It violates the critical analytical and empirical requirements of sociology, however. A key dimension of the exercise of power is the ability to influence, if not dictate, the choices of those less powerful [citation omitted]. Individual choices to not consume products generated by powerful actors involve an underlying power struggle between highly unequal contenders.

Ultimately, critical analysis of economy, production and consumption must address the questions of power and interests. That is, environmental harm stems from the self-interested decisions of corporate and state elites about what and how to produce/consume, in accordance with the growth imperatives of the global capitalist system.

Conclusion

Diagnosing our current environmental and ecological crisis must also account for who controls the economic levers, as well as for the fact that as much as production does not occur in a vacuum, neither does the consumption that it is linked to. In the context of the fossil fuel industries, those who control energy supplies also dominate politically and socially (White, 2018: 102). This is certainly not to suggest that the cause for ethical consumerism should be abandoned or that one should disregard one's own carbon footprint.

Rather, it is to argue that combatting the *real helplessness* that renders the individual powerless, stupefied and repressed (Gunderson, 2023) in the face of climate Armageddon, requires bringing the treadmill of production to a grinding halt. This political task is a vital precondition to forging sustainable solutions to the economic chaos and destruction of the moment.

Joel Maddock-James

Further reading

Blake, J. (1999). Overcoming the 'value–action gap' in environmental policy: Tensions between national policy and local experience. *Local Environment*, *4*(3), 257–278.

Cuomo, C. J. (2011). Climate change, vulnerability, and responsibility. *Hypatia*, *26*(4), 690–714.

Curran, D. (2017). The treadmill of production and the positional economy of consumption. *Canadian Review of Sociology/Revue canadienne de sociologie*, *54*(1), 28–47.

Debord, G. (1983). *The Society of the Spectacle*. Detroit: Black & Red.

Foster, J. B. (1993). The limits of environmentalism without class: Lessons from the ancient forest struggle of the Pacific Northwest. *Capitalism Nature Socialism*, *4*(1), 11–41.

Foster, J. B., and Clark, B. (2018). Marx and alienated speciesism. *Monthly Review*, *70*(7), 1–20.

Hickel, J. (2018). The hope at the heart of the Apocalyptic Climate Change Report. *Foreign Policy*, *18*.

Macdonald, B. J. (2011). Marx and the human/animal dialectic. In J. Grant and V. Jungkunz (eds.), *Political Theory and the Animal/Human Relationship* (pp. 23–48). Albany, NY: State University of New York Press.

Stuart, D., Gunderson, R., and Petersen, B. (2020). Overconsumption as ideology: Implications for addressing global climate change. *Nature and Culture*, *15*(2), 199–223.

Wells, V. K., Ponting, C. A., and Peattie, K. (2011). Behaviour and climate change: Consumer perceptions of responsibility. *Journal of Marketing Management*, *27*(7–8), 808–833.

References

Bigger, P., and Carton, W. (2020). Finance and climate change. In J. Knox-Hayes and D. Wojcik (eds.), *The Routledge Handbook of Financial Geography* (pp. 646–666). Abingdon: Routledge.

Dietz, T. (2015). Environmental value. In T. Brosch and D. Sander (eds.), *Handbook of Value: Perspectives from Economics, Neuroscience, Philosophy, Psychology and Sociology* (pp. 329–349). Oxford: Oxford University Press.

Eikenberry, S. (2021). Yes, 100 companies are 'responsible' for 71% of global warming emissions: So what? *EnvironMath!* Available at: http://environmath.org/2020/12/01/yes-100-companies-are-responsible-for-71-of-global-warming-emissions-so-what/

Foster, J. B. (2000). *Marx's Ecology: Materialism and Nature*. New York: New York University Press.

Gould, K. A., Pellow, D. N., and Schnaiberg, A. (2004). Interrogating the treadmill of production: Everything you wanted to know about the treadmill but were afraid to ask. *Organization & Environment*, *17*(3), 296–316.

Griffin, P., and Heede, C. R. (2017). The Carbon Majors Database. *CDP Carbon Majors Report 2017*, 14.

Gunderson, R. (2023). Powerless, stupefied, and repressed actors cannot challenge climate change: Real helplessness as a barrier between environmental concern and action. *Journal for the Theory of Social Behaviour*, *53*(2), 271–295.

Hanieh, A. (2021). Petrochemical empire: The geo-politics of fossil-fuelled production. *New Left Review*, July–August, *130*, 25–51.

Harvey, D. (1989). *The Condition of Postmodernity*. Oxford: Blackwell Press.

Harvey, D. (2018). *The Limits to Capital*. London: Verso.

Horkheimer, M., and Adorno, T. W. (2002). *Dialectic of Enlightenment*. G. Noeri (ed.), E. Jephcott (trans). Stanford: Stanford University Press.

Ivanova, D., Stadler, K., Steen-Olsen, K., Wood, R., Vita, G., Tukker, A., and Hertwich, E. G. (2016). Environmental impact assessment of household consumption. *Journal of Industrial Ecology*, *20*(3), 526–536.

Kuypers, J. A., Hitchner, M., Irwin, J., and Wilson, A. (2003). Compassionate conservatism: The rhetorical reconstruction of conservative rhetoric. *American Communication Journal*, *6*(4), 1–27.

Larsen, H. N., and Hertwich, E. G. (2009). The case for consumption-based accounting of greenhouse gas emissions to promote local climate action. *Environmental Science & Policy*, *12*(7), 791–798.

Lepistö, A. (2021). *The Rise of Common-Sense Conservatism: The American Right and the Reinvention of the Scottish Enlightenment*. Chicago: University of Chicago Press.

Magdoff, F., and Foster, J. B. (2011). *What Every Environmentalist Needs to Know about Capitalism: A Citizen's Guide to Capitalism and the Environment*. New York: New York University Press.

Maniates, M. F. (2001). Individualization: Plant a tree, buy a bike, save the world? *Global Environmental Politics*, *1*(3), 31–52.

Marx, K. (1938). *Capital: A Critique of Political Economy, Volume One*. London: Penguin.

Mitchell, R. B. (2012). Technology is not enough: Climate change, population, affluence, and consumption. *The Journal of Environment & Development*, *21*(1), 24–27.

Monbiot, G. (2021). Capitalism is killing the planet – it's time to stop buying into our own destruction. *The Guardian*. Available at: https://www.theguardian.com/environment/2021/oct/30/capitalism-is-killing-the-planet-its-time-to-stop-buying-into-our-own-destruction

O'Barr, W. M. (2005). A brief history of advertising in America. *Advertising & Society Review*, *11*(1).

Packard, V. (1960). *The Waste Makers*. New York: Pelican.

Pylkkänen, R., Werner, D., Bishoyi, A., Weil, D., Scoppola, E., Wagermaier, W., and Mohammadi, P. (2023). The complex structure of *Fomes fomentarius* represents an architectural design for high-performance ultralightweight materials. *Science Advances*, *9*(8), 1–13.

Schnaiberg, A. (1980). *The Environment: From Surplus to Scarcity*. New York: Oxford University Press.

Shwom, R., and Lorenzen, J. A. (2012). Changing household consumption to address climate change: Social scientific insights and challenges. *Wiley Interdisciplinary Reviews: Climate Change*, *3*(5), 379–395.

Stretesky, P. B., Long, M. A., and Lynch, M. J. (2014). *The Treadmill of Crime: Political Economy and Green Criminology*. London: Routledge.

White, R. (2018). *Climate Change Criminology*. Bristol: Policy Press.

Wright, O. E. (1978). *Class, Crisis and the State*. London: Verso.

Žižek, S. (2009). First as tragedy, then as farce. *RSA Animate*. Available at: https://www.thersa.org/globalassets/pdfs/blogs/rsa-lecture-slovoj-zizek-transcript.pdf

7. Feminist political ecology of wildlife crime

Introduction

Feminist political ecology of wildlife crime refers to the use of a feminist approach to evaluate the ways in which gender, as well as other aspects of identity, influence how an individual engages with and is affected by wildlife crimes. As a result of socially constructed gendered norms, as well as expectations for how gender is performed, wildlife crime has been assessed almost entirely through a heteronormative masculine lens, with little emphasis on the broader gender dimensions of wildlife crime activity, prevention, and impact. Attributing wildlife crime, as well as analysing crime and basing criminal procedure, on a heteronormative and masculinised scale is detrimental to the species and individuals affected and involved in wildlife crime. A feminist political ecology of wildlife crime can serve as a measure to ensure that the intersections between gender, race, and class are adequately considered in wildlife crime analysis and prevention strategies.

Gendered dimensions of wildlife crime

A feminist political ecology of wildlife crime allows a deeper investigation into the gendered dimensions of wildlife crime which accounts for how gendered power and control socio-dynamics affect wildlife-related crimes. Wildlife crime is the illegal trade in wild animals and wild animal products (i.e., ivory, furs) (Wilson-Wilde, 2010). Some examples of wildlife crime include wildlife trafficking (i.e., Wyatt, 2021; Agu & Gore, 2020); illegal hunting or poaching (i.e., Massé, Givá, & Lunstrum, 2021; Kahler & Gore, 2012); and the unauthorised trade in federally protected species (i.e., Pires & Moreto, 2016; Wyatt, 2009). Wildlife crime can have an effect on communities both directly (e.g., the spread of zoonotic diseases) and indirectly (e.g., biodiversity loss over time), thus warranting intervention strategies that centre the experiences, voices, and attitudes of community members. Much of wildlife crime research has been focused on the effectiveness of policy implementation (Haas & Ferreira, 2018; Bennett et al., 2006); how the crime is being committed (van Vliet et al., 2019); where the crimes are occurring (Kurland et al., 2017; Wyatt et al., 2017); and the species affected by wildlife crime (Ripple et al., 2016; Cowlishaw, Mendelson, & Rowcliffe, 2005). One area that requires further investigation and commentary, however, relates to the fact that women are disproportionately involved and impacted by wildlife crimes, whether directly or indirectly (Kahler & Rinkus, 2021).

A feminist political ecology of wildlife crime thus views gender as a key focus, although this is increasingly viewed through an intersectional lens, one that recognises the unique positionality of women beyond and inclusive of their gender, that considers

> … gender as a critical variable in shaping resource access and control, interacting with class, caste, race, culture and ethnicity to shape processes of ecological change, the struggle of men and women to sustain ecologically viable livelihoods and the prospects of any community for sustainable development. (Rocheleau, Thomas-Slayter, & Wangari, 1996)

The application of feminist political ecology to wildlife crime brings issues of power, gender, and patriarchy to the forefront of both criminology and biodiversity conservation studies. Contesting the expectation of masculine heteronormativity, a feminist political ecology of wildlife crime challenges the assumption that wildlife crime is solely a masculinised activity. The gendered expectations associated with who commits wildlife crime-related offences, and who is impacted by them, are challenged insofar as a feminist assessment of wildlife crime allows for deeper insight into the ways that power, patriarchy, sexuality, and gender impact how wildlife crime is conducted (Sollund, 2017; Gore & Agu, 2022; Milne et al., 2023). These social dimensions often include the intersecting dynamics of race and ethnicity (Büscher, 2016; Marguiles, Wong, & Duffy, 2019), sexuality (Burnett & Milani, 2017; Davé & Gupta, 2024), and class (Duffy et al., 2016; Anagnostou et al., 2021), which shape how people engage with wildlife crime.

Feminist political ecology

Feminist political ecology is a perspective incorporating the insights of feminism, ecology, economics, and politics, as well as the associated analyses of gendered power relationships (Rocheleau, Thomas-Slayter, & Wangari, 1996). Within feminist political ecology, gender (along with class relations and race, among other social dimensions), is considered a crucial theoretical lens for understanding conservation, insofar as it also directly pertains to one's access to, control over, and knowledge of natural resources (Sundberg, 2017). The perspective also serves as a counter to the political ecology tendency to gloss over gendered and patriarchal struggles at both local and global scales (Mollett, 2017; Sollund, 2019). Feminist political ecology broadens political ecology to consider gender as a category and women as a group (Rocheleau, 1995). Rao (2020) summarises feminist political ecology as being comprised of:

> (a) an intersectional analysis of human–nature relations; (b) a multi-scalar analysis of power differentials and the way these translate into embodied experiences of environmental degradation and dispossession; and (c) an analysis of knowledge production and decision-making processes that shape environmental governance. (p. 272)

However, critics argue that feminist political ecology has an explicit absence of attention to race despite preaching an intersectional agenda (see Mollett & Faría, 2013). Particularly, dimensions and aspects of race, such as caste, ethnicity, regional ethnic nationalism, racialisation, and racism, affect the relationship between gender and the environment in profound ways (Mollett & Faría, 2013) Accordingly, Mollett and Faría (2013) further posit that feminist political ecology would benefit from an expansion of gender, described as a "messier notion of 'gender'", which encapsulates the racialised and colonial dimensions of how one experiences gender. Mollett (2017) argues that greater attention to race could lead to a more critical analysis of natural resource control, distribution, and access that could also result in more gender-aware conservation development, policy, and planning strategies.

Acknowledging this, it is necessary to expand upon ideas of feminist political ecology and its shortcomings when it comes to conceptions of gender outside the white Western frame of consciousness. Due to the shaping processes of gender and race (and class), it is also necessary to recognise how colonial legacies of racism and patriarchy shape power inequities between the Global North and the Global South (Mollett & Faría, 2013). These critiques warrant an application of a race-aware *and* gender-aware approach to feminist political ecology so as to more adequately assess how interlocking systems of oppression and identity shape human–environment relationships (e.g., Thomas, 2020; Thompson, 2016). Distributions of class power and divergent class interests are also fundamentally intertwined with the material realities associated with the gender–race nexus. There are clear social divisions between and amongst women related to their position within the various social hierarchies.

For those intrinsically disadvantaged by dominant social arrangements and social structures, it is a truism that social marginalisation shapes how people engage with and are affected by conservation (see James et al., 2021; Chaudhury & Colla, 2020). This can be attributed to, for example, the lack of access to natural spaces (Satcher, 2022; Taylor, González, & Razani, 2021) or lacking a sense of belonging in natural spaces (e.g., Roberts & Henderson, 1997). These dimensions, which form the foundation of human–environment relationships, as well as potential experiences with the environment, are a crucial part of understanding how social insecurities can be exacerbated by environmental degradation (e.g., Cannon, 2020; Norgaard, Reed, & Bacon, 2018). Feminist political ecology, which accounts for how individual lives are shaped by both society and the environment, can introduce an intersectional approach to evaluating human–environment relationships across many groups. Cementing an anti-racist agenda within feminist political ecology is a necessary part of this process, especially if we are to account for the differing human–environment relationships disenfranchised women have within a colonial, imperialistic, and capitalist society. This necessitates an integrated approach to human–environment relationships, one that is culturally sensitive and inclusive.

Gendered dimensions of wildlife crime

Prior to the feminist revolution within criminology, women were often omitted from criminal analysis as their deviance was not considered worthy of scrutiny (Estrada, Nilsson, & Pettersson, 2019). This omission has tended to carry over into the area of environmental crime insofar as, for example, the role of women within wildlife crime has almost exclusively been as victims or as secondary characters such as wives or caretakers (Hübschle, 2014). It is nonetheless necessary to consider how crime is experienced differently depending on an individual's intersecting identities, and how gendered experiences introduce different barriers and access into the wildlife crime sector (Andrew & Agu, 2022). Some dimensions of women's criminal involvement do present as being similar to men's, namely securing economic advancement or opportunity, as women's engagement in wildlife crime can be incentivised by the need for income supplementation (Banjade, Adhikari, & Oh, 2020), protein (Babatunde et al., 2020), empowerment (Nana, 2022), or cultural use (Davis et al., 2020). Through a literature review of women's involvement in wildlife trafficking in Africa, Agu and Gore (2020) found that women can take on the roles of consumers, enablers, poachers, smugglers, and sellers. LeBreton et al. (2006) found that women were two times more likely to engage in the butchering of bushmeat than men, an activity which also makes women more likely to contract zoonotic infectious diseases (Subramanian, 2012). Women also overwhelmingly depend on bushmeat trafficking as a source of income, with one study of 249 individuals claiming bushmeat trading as their primary occupation, finding that 84.3% of those individuals were women (Edderai & Dame, 2006). These examples suggest that women are engaging with wildlife crime in ways that are outside the usual gender normative expectation.

It is also necessary to evaluate the ways that women's roles are *complementary* to those of men. For example, a qualitative analysis conducted by Lowassa, Tadie, and Fischer (2012) found that women in communities in Ethiopia and Tanzania utilised verbal and non-verbal actions which could encourage or discourage male hunting activities. Often women will hold support roles within men's hunting groups, where women drive the animals into nets or beat the animals after they've been shot or snared (Schulte-Herbrüggen et al., 2013). Nijman (2019) noted that labourers in Indonesian commercial shell workshops were predominantly women who were often in charge of tending the shops and selling the shells that the men had harvested. This idea that women are co-offenders sees women as having the ability to engage in criminal activity as well as sharing similar motivations to their male counterparts. Nonetheless, since they are not perceived as the dominating offenders, they are less likely to receive harsh punishment for their actions (Barlow & Weare, 2018).

As these studies illustrate, gender in non-Western countries often transcends the non-Indigenous Western binary conceptions of femininity and masculinity in practice, given the active engagement of women in wildlife crime (Costello, 2020). It is notable that conservation as a whole tends to adhere to the binary expression of gender, which is already limited in scope (e.g., Liévano-Latorre et al., 2020) with limited investigation into non-hetero or non-masculine involvement. This is reflected in the limited investigation into the role of sex, sexuality, and gender beyond the binary in wildlife crime spaces. Oftentimes, the sample size for non-male participants is so small that they are excluded from the analysis (e.g., Ostermann-Miyashita et al., 2022) or their numbers are too low to garner a reliable conclusion on behaviour (e.g., Barboza et al., 2016). This absence of gendered representation may be caused by a lack of public identification of women by researchers due to cultural, societal, or familial constraints (e.g., Ahmadia et al., 2021). There is a distinct need for these "invisible" and "powerless" actors within conservation and wildlife crime to receive further investigation for a more encompassing approach to prevention strategies and policies (Meissner & Gonçalves, 2022). For instance, Sollund's (2020) study on reptile-related crimes argues that classifying reptile crime as a masculine industry does not lead to any definitive conclusion on why women are less likely to be involved in reptile crime than men. Kahler and Rinkus (2021: 836) suggest that "future research should consider how power and patriarchy influence the involvement of men and women in wildlife crime, and the impacts of wildlife crime, and responses and interventions, on gender relations".

Preventing wildlife crime

Attesting to the effect feminist political ecology has had on wildlife crime globally, we can notably see its application in addressing wildlife trafficking and poaching. For instance, a study conducted in the Mozambican borderlands adjacent to the Kruger National Park in South Africa utilised feminist political ecology to assess the rhino poaching economy (Massé, Givá, & Lunstrum, 2021). The authors found that the dual effects of patriarchy and gendered norms were reflected in both the motivations for men to pursue poaching despite the associated risks, and in increasing the vulnerabilities of women to poverty and exploitation due to the loss of their husbands (Massé, Givá, & Lunstrum, 2021). The study allowed for these elements of wildlife crime, which are commonly obscured, to come to light and this in turn can greatly influence wildlife crime prevention strategies and conservation policy. Furthermore, within wildlife trafficking, there are often trends related to gender and the specialisation of species being trafficked. Green et al. (2024), for example, found that besides the actual hunting of the animal, the trade in the Dwarf Crocodile (*Osteolaemus tetraspis*) within the urban bushmeat trade in the Republic of Congo, was entirely dominated by women. Feminist political ecology in these contexts revealed a dimension to wildlife crime that was dependent on the gender of the individuals committing the offence.

Conclusion

Contextualising the use of feminist political ecology globally allows for insight into the application of the approach as a tool for addressing the biases and gendered dimensions that arise within the wildlife crime sector. At the international level, the dimensions of culture, nationality, and gender, as well as their intersections, can have a profound impact on crime prevention and assessment (Mayer, 2020). Evaluating intersecting components of individual identities can illuminate dimensions of wildlife crime that could be key to preventing the crime from occurring in the first place. For example, the hidden costs of wildlife crime, including those associated with increased instances of human–wildlife conflict, are linked to broader issues relating to the dynamics of highly patriarchal societies (Doubleday, 2020).

Future research within this space is needed to gain a better sense of global differences in gendered norms and how they impact individuals' engagement with wildlife crime. Wildlife crime studies must dismantle the academic and practical barriers that are preventing further investigation into non-masculine roles within wildlife crime activities. Addressing gender issues could potentially lead to a decrease in wildlife crime activities. Further, the feminist political ecology of wildlife crime could contribute not only to a broader understanding of an illicit industry, but it could also allow insight into how to more successfully implement wildlife crime intervention and policy.

AALAYNA R. GREEN

Further reading

Agu, H. U., & Gore, M. L. (Eds.). (2022). *Women and Wildlife Trafficking: Participants, Perpetrators and Victims.* Routledge.

Agu, H., Andrew, C., & Gore, M. L. (2020). Cracking glass ceilings in conservation crime? An expert elicitation of women in wildlife trafficking. Available at https://ssrn.com/abstract=3667145 or http://dx.doi.org/10.2139/ssrn.3667145

Doubleday, K. F. (2020). Tigers and "Good Indian Wives": Feminist political ecology exposing the gender-based violence of human–wildlife conflict in Rajasthan, India. *Annals of the American Association of Geographers, 110*(5), 1521–1539.

Kahler, J. S., & Rinkus, M. A. (2021). Women and wildlife crime: Hidden offenders, protectors and victims. *Oryx, 55*(6), 835–843.

Lau, J. D. (2020). Three lessons for gender equity in biodiversity conservation. *Conservation Biology, 34*(6), 1589–1591.

Massé, F., Givá, N., & Lunstrum, E. (2021). A feminist political ecology of wildlife crime: The gendered dimensions of poaching economy and its impacts in Southern Africa. *Geoforum, 126*, 205–214.

Mollett, S., & Faría, C. (2013). Messing with gender in feminist political ecology. *Geoforum, 45*, 116–125.

Mollett, S., Vaz-Jones, L., & Delicado-Moratalla, L. (2020). Feminist political ecologies: Race, bodies and the human. In A. Datta, P. Hopkins, L. Johnston, E. Olson, & J. M. Silva (Eds.),

Routledge Handbook of Gender and Feminist Geographies (pp. 271–284). Routledge.

Rocheleau, D., Thomas-Slayter, B., & Wangari, E. (1996). A feminist political ecology perspective. In D. Rocheleau, B. Thomas-Slayter, & E. Wangari (Eds.), *Feminist Political Ecology: Global Issues and Local Experiences* (pp. 3–26). Routledge.

Sollund, R. (2020). Wildlife crime: A crime of hegemonic masculinity? *Social Sciences*, *9*(6), 93.

References

Agu, H. U., & Gore, M. L. (2020). Women in wildlife trafficking in Africa: A synthesis of literature. *Global Ecology and Conservation, 23*, e01166.

Ahmadia, G. N., Cheng, S. H., Andradi-Brown, D. A., Baez, S. K., Barnes, M. D., Bennett, N. J., … & Wosu, A. (2021). Limited progress in improving gender and geographic representation in coral reef science. *Frontiers in Marine Science*, *8*, 731037.

Anagnostou, M., Moreto, W. D., Garner, C. J., & Doberstein, B. (2021). Poverty, pandemics, and wildlife crime. *Conservation and Society*, *19*(4), 294–306.

Andrew, C., & Agu, H. U. (2022). Using a feminist political ecology lens to explore the gendered dimensions of wildlife trafficking literature. In H. U. Agu & M. L. Gore (Eds.), *Women and Wildlife Trafficking: Participants, Perpetrators and Victims* (pp. 11–26). Routledge.

Babatunde, T. O., Babatunde, O. O., Babatunde, K. O., Aduloju, A. R., Okeleke, S. O., & Ekaun, A. A. (2020). Roles of women in bushmeat trade in Oluyole Local Government Area of Oyo State. *The Pacific Journal of Science and Technology*, *21*(2), 371–378.

Banjade, M., Adhikari, P., & Oh, H. (2020). Illegal wildlife trade in local markets of Feuang and Mad districts of Vientiane Province, Lao People's Democratic Republic. *Journal of Asia-Pacific Biodiversity*, *13*(4), 511–517.

Barboza, R. R. D., Lopes, S. F., Souto, W. M. S., Fernandes-Ferreira, H., & Alves, R. R. N. (2016). The role of game mammals as bushmeat in the Caatinga, northeast Brazil. *Ecology & Society*, *21*(2), 2.

Barlow, C., & Weare, S. (2018). Women as co-offenders: Pathways into crime and offending motivations. *Howard Journal of Criminal Justice*, *58*(1), 86–103.

Bennett, E. L., Blencowe, E., Brandon, K., Brown, D., Burn, R. W., Cowlishaw, G., Davies, G., Dublin, H., Fa, J. E., Milner-Gulland, E. J., Robinson, J. G., Rowcliffe, J. M., Underwood, F. M., & Wilkie, D. S. (2006). Hunting for consensus: Reconciling bushmeat harvest, conservation, and development policy in West and Central Africa. *Conservation Biology*, *21*(3), 884–887.

Burnett, S., & Milani, T. M. (2017). Fatal masculinities: A queer look at green violence. *ACME: An International Journal for Critical Geographers*, *16*(3), 548–575.

Büscher, B. (2016). "Rhino poaching is out of control!": Violence, race and the politics of hysteria in online conservation. *Environment and Planning A*, *48*(5), 979–998.

Cannon, C. (2020). Examining rural environmental injustice: An analysis of ruralness, class, race, and gender on the presence of landfills across the United States. *Journal of Rural and Community Development*, *15*(1), 89–114.

Chaudhury, A., & Colla, S. (2020). Next steps in dismantling discrimination: Lessons from ecology and conservation science. *Conservation Letters*, *14*(2), e12774.

Costello, C. G. (2020). Beyond binary sex and gender ideology. In N. Boero & K. Mason (Eds.), *The Oxford Handbook of the Sociology of Body and Embodiment* (pp. 199–220). Oxford University Press.

Cowlishaw, G., Mendelson, S., & Rowcliffe, J. M. (2005). Evidence for post-depletion sustainability in a mature bushmeat market. *Journal of Applied Ecology*, *42*(3), 460–468.

Davé, N. N., & Gupta, A. H. (2024). The homoxenoerotics of elephant crime and captivity in India. In C. Taylor (Ed.), *The Routledge Companion to Gender and Animals* (pp. 399–410). Routledge.

Davis, E. O., Gibson, M., Lim, T., & Glikman, J. A. (2020). Bear bile use at the intersection of maternal health in Cambodia. *Journal of Ethnobiology and Ethnomedicine*, *16*(1), 28.

Doubleday, K. F. (2020). Tigers and "Good Indian Wives": Feminist political ecology exposing the gender-based violence of human–wildlife conflict in Rajasthan, India. *Annals of the American Association of Geographers*, *110*(5), 1521–1539.

Duffy, R., St. John, F. A., Büscher, B., & Brockington, D. (2016). Toward a new understanding of the links between poverty and illegal wildlife hunting. *Conservation Biology*, *30*(1), 14–22.

Edderai, D., & Dame, M. (2006). Species protection, the changing informal economy, and the politics of access to the bushmeat trade in the Democratic Republic of Congo. *Conservation Biology*, *20*(4), 1262–1271.

Estrada, F., Nilsson, A., & Pettersson, T. (2019). The female offender: A century of registered crime and daily press reporting on women's crime. *Nordic Journal of Criminology*, *20*(2), 138–156.

Gore, M. L., & Agu, H. U. (2022). The roles of women in wildlife trafficking are mostly unknown, but not unknowable. In H. U. Agu

& M. L. Gore (Eds.), *Women and Wildlife Trafficking* (pp. 1–10). Routledge.
Green, A. R., Plowman, C., Mwinyihali, R., Wieland, M., & Gore, M. L. (2024). Women and urban wildmeat trafficking in the Republic of Congo. *Biological Conservation, 293*, 110587.
Haas, T. C., & Ferreira, S. M. (2018). Finding politically feasible conservation policies: The case of wildlife trafficking. *Ecological Applications, 28*(2), 473–494.
Hübschle, A. (2014). Of bogus hunters, queenpins and mules: The varied roles of women in transnational organized crime in Southern Africa. *Trends in Organized Crime, 17*(1–2), 31–51.
James, R., Gibbs, B., Whitford, L., Leisher, C., Konia, R., & Butt, N. (2021). Conservation and natural resource management: Where are all the women? *Oryx, 55*(6), 860–867.
Kahler, J. S., & Gore, M. L. (2012). Beyond the cooking pot and pocketbook: Factors influencing noncompliance with wildlife poaching rules. *International Journal of Comparative and Applied Criminal Justice, 36*(2), 103–120.
Kahler, J. S., & Rinkus, M. A. (2021) Women and wildlife crime: Hidden offenders, protectors and victims. *Oryx, 55*(6), 835–843.
Kurland, J., Pires, S. F., McFann, S. C., & Moreto, W. D. (2017). Wildlife crime: A conceptual integration, literature review, and methodological critique. *Crime Science, 6*, 4.
LeBreton, M., Prosser, A. T., Tamoufe, U., Sateren, W., Mpoudi-Ngole, E., Diffo, J. L. D., Burke, D. S., & Wolfe, N. D. (2006). Patterns of bushmeat hunting and perceptions of disease risk among central African communities. *Animal Conservation, 9*(4), 357–363.
Liévano-Latorre, L. F., da Silva, R. A., Vieira, R. R. S., Resende, F. M., Ribeiro, B. R., Borges, F. J. A., Sales, L., & Loyola, R. (2020). Pervasive gender bias in editorial boards of biodiversity conservation journals. *Biological Conservation, 251*, 108767.
Lowassa, A., Tadie, D., & Fischer, A. (2012). On the role of women in bushmeat hunting: Insights from Tanzania and Ethiopia. *Journal of Rural Studies, 28*(4), 622–630.
Marguiles, J. D., Wong, R. W., & Duffy, R. (2019). The imaginary "Asian super consumer": A critique of demand reduction campaigns for the illegal wildlife trade. *Geoforum, 107*, 216–219.
Massé, F., Givá, N., & Lunstrum, E. (2021). A feminist political ecology of wildlife crime: The gendered dimensions of poaching economy and its impacts in Southern Africa. *Geoforum, 126*, 205–214.
Mayer, C. H. (2020). Failures in wildlife crime eradication and strategies forward. In E. Vanderheiden & C. H. Mayer (Eds.), *Mistakes, Errors and Failures across Cultures* (pp. 495–512). Springer.
Meissner, R., & Gonçalves, D. P. (2022). Considering the "Other" in wildlife crime mitigation: A South African strategy case study. *Acta Criminologica: African Journal of Criminology & Victimology, 34*(2), 103–122.
Milne, E., Davies, P., Heydon, J., Peggs, K., & Wyatt, T. (2023). Why gendering green criminology matters. In E. Milne, P. Davies, J. Heydon, K. Peggs, & T. Wyatt (Eds.), *Gendering Green Criminology* (pp. 1–14). Bristol University Press.
Mollett, S. (2017). Gender's critical edge: Feminist political ecology, postcolonial intersectionality, and the coupling of race and gender. In S. MacGregor (Ed.), *Routledge Handbook of Gender and Environment* (pp. 146–158). Routledge.
Mollett, S., & Faría, C. (2013). Messing with gender in feminist political ecology. *Geoforum, 45*, 116–125.
Nana, E. D. (2022). Women, wildlife crime, and sustainable livelihoods in Cameroon. In H. U. Agu & M. L. Gore (Eds.), *Women and Wildlife Trafficking: Participants, Perpetrators and Victims* (pp. 72–86). Routledge.
Nijman, V. (2019). Souvenirs, shells, and the illegal wildlife trade. *Journal of Ethnobiology, 39*(2), 282–296.
Norgaard, K. M., Reed, R., & Bacon, J. M. (2018). How environmental decline restructures indigenous gender practices: What happens to Karuk masculinity when there are no fish? *Sociology of Race and Ethnicity, 4*(1), 98–113.
Ostermann-Miyashita, E. F., König, H. J., Pernat, N., Bellingrath-Kimura, S. D., Hibler, S., & Kiffner, C. (2022). Knowledge of returning wildlife species and willingness to participate in citizen science projects among wildlife park visitors in Germany. *People and Nature, 4*(1), 1–15.
Pires, S. F., & Moreto, W. D. (2016). The illegal wildlife trade. *Oxford Handbooks Online.*
Rao, M. (2020). Gender and the urban commons in India: An overview of scientific literature and the relevance of a feminist political ecology perspective. *International Quarterly for Asian Studies (IQAS), 52*(1–2), 261–276.
Ripple, W. J., Abernethy, K., Betts, M. G., Chapron, G., Dirzo, R., Galetti, M., Levi, T., Lindsey, P. A., Macdonald, D. W., Machovina, B., Newsome, T. M., Peres, C. A., Wallach, A. D., Wolf, C., & Young, H. (2016). Bushmeat hunting and extinction risk to the world's mammals. *Royal Society Open Science, 3*(10), 160498.
Roberts, N. S., & Henderson, K. A. (1997). Women of color in the outdoors: Culture and meanings. *Journal of Experiential Education, 20*(3), 134–142.
Rocheleau, D. (1995). Gender and biodiversity: A feminist political ecology perspective. *IDS Bulletin, 26*(1), 9–16.
Rocheleau, D., Thomas-Slayter, B., & Wangari, E. (1996). A feminist political ecology perspec-

tive. In D. Rocheleau, B. Thomas-Slayter, & E. Wangari (Eds.), *Feminist Political Ecology: Global Issues and Local Experiences* (pp. 3–26). Routledge.

Satcher, L. A. (2022). Multiply-deserted areas: Environmental racism and food, pharmacy, and greenspace access in the Urban South. *Environmental Sociology*, 1–13.

Schulte-Herbrüggen, B., Cowlishaw, G., Homewood, K., & Rowcliffe, J. M. (2013). The importance of bushmeat in the livelihoods of West African cash-crop farmers living in a faunally-depleted landscape. *PLoS One*, *8*(8), e72807.

Sollund, R. (2020). Wildlife crime: A crime of hegemonic masculinity? *Social Sciences*, *9*(6), 93.

Sollund, R. A. (2019). *The Crimes of Wildlife trafficking: Issues of Justice, Legality and Morality*. Routledge.

Sollund, R. (2017). Doing green, critical criminology with an auto-ethnographic, feminist approach. *Critical Criminology*, *25*(2), 245–260.

Subramanian, M. (2012). Zoonotic disease risk and the bushmeat trade: Assessing awareness among hunters and traders in Sierra Leone. *EcoHealth*, *9*(4), 471–482.

Sundberg, J. (2017). Feminist political ecology. In *International Encyclopedia of Geography: People, the Earth, Environment and Technology*, 1–12. Wiley.

Taylor, K. D., González, J. G., & Razani, N. (2021). Justice in access to the outdoors. *Parks Stewardship Forum*, *37*(1), 23–33.

Thomas, M. O. (2020). Intersectional ecocultural identity in family stories. In T. Milstein & J. Castro-Sotomayor (Eds.), *Routledge Handbook of Ecocultural Identity* (pp. 119–130). Routledge.

Thompson, J. A. (2016). Intersectionality and water: How social relations intersect with ecological difference. *Gender, Place & Culture*, *23*(9), 1286–1301.

van Vliet, N., Muhindo, J., Nyumu, J. K., & Nasi, R. (2019). From the forest to the disk: A comprehensive study of the wildmeat value chain in Yangambi, Democratic Republic of Congo. *Frontiers in Ecology & Evolution*, *7*, 132.

Wilson-Wilde, L. (2010). Wildlife crime: A global problem. *Forensic Science, Medicine, and Pathology*, *6*(3), 221–222.

Wyatt, T. (2021). *Wildlife Trafficking: A Deconstruction of the Crime, Victims and Offenders*. Springer Nature.

Wyatt, T. (2009). Exploring the organization of Russia Far East's illegal wildlife trade: Two case studies of the illegal fur and illegal falcon trades. *Global Crime*, *10*(1–2), 144–154.

Wyatt, T., Johnson, K., Hunter, L., George, R., & Gunter, R. (2017). Corruption and wildlife trafficking: Three case studies involving Asia. *Asian Journal of Criminology*, *13*(1), 35–55.

AALAYNA R. GREEN

8. Environmental harm

Introduction

Environmental harm is the injury and degradation of the natural environment through use, misuse and poor management. It captures harm arising from environmental crime, such as crimes of extraction, contamination, use and modification. It also captures activities which harm the environment, but which are sanctioned; so-called 'lawful but awful' activity, such as transport emissions, greenhouse gas emissions arising from coal-fired electricity production, and the use of natural resources. Such lawful but awful activity is the trade-off between environmental preservation and technological/societal/financial progress. Important when considering environmental harm are the victims of, and those who cause, such harm, and the very nature of the harm across space and time.

Environmental harm is an umbrella term that captures the 'wide variety of injuries and degradations linked to the use, misuse and poor management of the "natural environment"' (White and Heckenberg 2014: 301) and is the central focus of 'green criminology'. Environmental harm can come from activities which are deemed criminal by the law, for example crimes of extraction (wildlife poaching, illegal land clearing, water theft), crimes of contamination (pollution, illegal dumping), and crimes of use and modification (animal abuse, biodiversity threats, wildlife markets). Importantly, environmental harm can come from sanctioned activity, such as the pollution coming from transport, greenhouse gas emissions arising from coal-fired electricity production, and use of natural resources.

Central to any discussion of environmental harm are considerations of the victims of such harm. Victimhood is one aspect which differentiates environmental harm from the harm that can occur from more traditional, or mainstream (for want of a better word) crime. Also central are those who cause environmental harm. Whilst many think of 'offenders' as seedy characters lurking in the dark, those who cause environmental harm are very diverse and have motives which go beyond the malicious. Finally, central to any discussion of environmental harm is the nature of the harm caused, including effects across space and time. While some environmental harm is localised to a specific location, other environmental harm may permeate a geographically large area and indeed may affect the whole world. Likewise, environmental harm may be transient, but it may also be world changing and catastrophic.

Having introduced environmental harm, the remainder of this entry will flesh out some central features. Namely:

- the *illegal v legal harm* distinction and its importance to environmental harm;
- the *victims* of environmental harm;
- *those who cause* environmental harm and their motives; and
- the *nature* of environmental harm across space and time.

These are the vital issues surrounding harms pertaining to the environment.

The illegal versus legal harm distinction

Environmental harm can come from both illegal (criminal) activity, but also lawful (sanctioned) activity. One of the unique features of this aspect is the fact that there is a fine line between criminal and sanctioned activity, with the dividing line being one of degree (quantity and quality), rather than there being a fundamental difference between the two. For example, a person may get a licence, permit, consent, or authority to pollute, clear native vegetation, take wildlife, etc. Operate within the confines of that licence, permit, consent, or authority, then there is no infraction of the law; the activity is lawful. Operate outside, or without, a licence, permit, consent, or authority, then there is an infraction of the law; the activity is criminal. However, even though the criminal activity and the lawful activity may be qualitatively or quantitatively different, they are not different in a fundamental sense where one could positively identify the difference in terms of the nature of the activity. Importantly, for the study of environmental harm, the legal/illegal dichotomy does not mean that legal activity does not harm the environment whereas illegal activity does. Indeed, both 'illegal and legal activities harm the environment' (Hamilton 2021: 2), and for this reason are central to the study of environmental harm. Additionally, for this reason, lawful activity (i.e., sanctioned activity) has been referred to as 'the lawful but awful' (Passas 2005). It is lawful in that it is sanctioned, but it is awful because of the harm to the environment it causes.

The reason why sanctioned environmental harm is permitted is that '[t]he reality of our age is that much of the economy is based on the exploitation of natural resources' (Skinnider 2013: 3). Indeed, the very characterisation of the environment as a 'natural resource' signifies a preponderance towards exploitation. An 'ecological-economic trade-off' is reached where environmental preservation gives way to technological/societal/financial progress (Lampkin and Wyatt 2019). That is, for society to progress it needs to use the environment, be that burning of coal for electricity, the clearing of forest for homes and farms, the killing of wildlife for food, etc. Naturally, it is open to debate in the face of environmental degradation and the looming catastrophe that is climate change (considered a failure of capitalism), whether the correct trade-off has been achieved. Indeed, some would positively say that the trade-off balance has not been achieved in a sustainable way and that we must change our lifestyles to better protect the environment and avoid pending catastrophe, through, for example, a move away from fossil fuels to renewable energy, adoption of a vegan diet, and the returning of land to the environment.

Victims of environmental harm

The victims of environmental harm can be diverse. Broadly speaking there are four categories of victims of environmental harm (Hamilton 2021: 214). First, there are human victims comprising currently living humans and future generations of humans (that is, those unborn). Considering a water pollution incident, individuals who become sick because of the pollution in the river are considered victims. Their sickness may be a result of, for example, swimming or wake boarding at the time of the incident, or subsequently from eating the fish they caught in the river. Similarly, if individuals have their recreational pursuits interrupted because of the pollution, swimming, wake boarding, fishing, for example, they are victims of that environmental harm. If the environment that has been harmed 'does not recover and is passed onto the next generation in a worse state then the current generation inherited it' (Hamilton 2021: 214), then that future generation is a victim of environmental harm through the concept of intergenerational (in) equity (Preston 2011: 143; for an overview of the concept of intergenerational equity see Anstee-Wedderburn 2014).

Second, the environment and its constituent parts are victims of environmental harm. For example, in a water pollution incident, '[t]he body of water (e.g. river) which has been degraded by the pollutants' is a victim; '[t]he fish harmed and killed that lived in the river' are victims; and '[t]he river gulls (birds) harmed and killed that lived on the river' are victims (Hamilton 2021: 214). While the traditional terminology is to refer to such victims as 'non-human', more recently the phrase 'more-than-human' has been adopted 'to signify a positionality actively aiming to be non-anthropocentric' (Forsyth et al. 2021: 20). That is, not to view the environment as a 'natural resource' for human exploitation but rather something that is valuable in and of itself.

Third, 'communities (both Indigenous and non-Indigenous)' are victims of environmental harm (Hamilton 2021: 214). Communities are victims by dint of the degradation of a community asset, for example a river in a water pollution incident. Indigenous communities are victims if some connection with the environment is impacted, such as the Māori (Indigenous New Zealanders) sacredness of water, or Aboriginal (Indigenous Australians) connection to Country. In terms of climate change, the concept of community moves from a discrete geographical location to towns (such as Fairbourne in Wales where retreat from sea-level rise will see the town lost to the sea; Cunnington Wynn 2022; Hamilton 2022), regions (such as those lost to sea-level rise in the Pacific) and the developing world unable to mitigate and adapt to the challenges of climate change.

Fourth, commercial operators may be the victim of environmental harm. Take for example a river pollution incident, 'a farm located downstream of the pollution point that can no longer draw water from the river to irrigate its crops' is considered a victim (Hamilton 2021: 214). 'Another example is a kayaking business that is no longer able to take people on guided tours of the river' (Hamilton 2021: 214).

Victimhood is *universal* yet *particular*. Take climate change harm as an example.

MARK HAMILTON

The harm is universal in that global warming affects everyone around the world. It is also particular in that some people and communities are disproportionately affected by climate change due to inequality, geography, and historical injustices (for example, the Pacific Islands and Bangladesh). Essentially, environmental victimhood is not socially, ecologically or species neutral in regard to who is harmed, why and to what extent. As has been pointed out elsewhere,

> it is the poorer countries and poorer communities who will suffer the most from climate change (in terms of flood, drought, crop failure, sea level rise, coastal inundation, and forced migration) and who, because they are economically and technologically poor, will have the least opportunity to mitigate and adapt. Conversely, developed nations, and the middle and upper classes within those countries, will have the financial and technological resources to mitigate and adapt to those climate changes most effectively. To add to this injustice is the acknowledgement that the greatest contributors to climate change are those countries and citizens which have the greatest capacity to mitigate and adapt to the problems climate change will cause. (Hamilton 2021: 242)

Those who cause environmental harm

When considering crime, it is natural to talk in terms of 'perpetrators' or 'offenders'; however, such expressions are not apt when considering environmental harm, because as discussed earlier only part of that harm is caused by environmental crime. The balance is caused through sanctioned activity. Hence, it is preferrable to talk in terms of 'those who cause environmental harm'.

As part of Hamilton's (2019) PhD research, he explored criminal law prosecutions in New South Wales, Australia, between 2000 and 31 August 2017; namely water pollution offences under the Protection of the Environment Operations Act 1997 (NSW) ('POEO Act'), s 120, and breach of environment protection licence (POEO Act, s 64). That study found that 92.51% of offenders were organisational offenders consisting of corporations (79.14%) and government entities, such as local council and utility providers (13.37%), with 7.49% being individuals (Hamilton 2019: Figure 5). In terms of the motivation behind environmental offending, the majority of offending was accidental (59.18%), about a quarter was intentional (24.49%) and 16.33% was negligent (Hamilton 2019: Figure 3; based on 98 breach of environment protection licence (POEO Act, s 64) offences in New South Wales, Australia, between 2000 and 31 August 2017).

In terms of those causing environmental harm from lawful but awful activities, they range from the obvious – fossil fuel energy producers, large transport networks, broadscale native vegetation clearing for residential communities and farming, seafood production, all of which are sanctioned under licence, permit, consent, or authority. However, the not so obvious drivers of environmental harm are you and I, through our reliance on fossil fuel for electricity and petrol, our consumer throw-away lifestyles, high meat diets, and technology dependency; indeed, what could be called 'ordinary acts' (Agnew 2020). All of this of course is bound up with the 'ecological-economic trade-off' (Lampkin and Wyatt 2019) that was discussed earlier, and therefore individual 'blame' is somewhat tempered by the reality in which we live.

Nature of environmental harm across space and time

Another way in which to analyse the nature of environmental harm is to consider its spatial and temporal dimensions.

Space

Some environmental harm is localised to a specific geographical area, other environmental harm may arise in one location but manifest in another, while some environmental harm may be so pervasive that it has worldwide impact. A water pollution incident may be localised to a specific section of a river near the pollution point. So, for example, there may be some aquatic and bird life harmed and the water quality in that location of the river may be altered for a period of time. A similar incident may result in more of the river being polluted with downstream aquatic and bird life affected, and even downstream users of the river affected. A larger river pollution incident may lead to pollution of bays and oceans into which the river runs.

Other environmental harm may be transnational in that it originates in one country, but the environmental harm is felt or transferred to another country. This can be by accident, or it can be by design. As an example of 'accidental' environmental harm transference, consider that 'the Rhine, the Meuse and other European rivers that run through more than one country were heavily polluted with all sorts of waste, a process which started upstream and affected countries downstream' (Spapens and Huisman 2016: 27). While the pollution may have been deliberate, it was not a deliberate attempt to 'ship-off' the harm to another country, unlike the example of e-waste.

The illegal transport and 'dumping' of e-waste sees the transference of environmental harm from the developed world to the developing world. Such transference is by 'design' because of the deliberate decision of the developed world to ship-off its environmental fallout from discarded e-waste. One case study involves the illegal transportation of e-waste from the Port of Antwerp (Belgium, EU) to Ghana, Africa (Bisschop and Vande Walle 2013). Once in Ghana, the e-waste is either dismantled, burnt or dumped, which can cause environmental harm: 'the impact of the hazardous components upon ecosystems', climate change through the release of greenhouse gases through burning the waste, human impacts resulting from the dismantling of the waste, often without protective equipment (Bisschop and Vande Walle 2013: 40). Such transference is seen as a way of reducing the dissonance felt by producers and consumers of such products: '[e]xporting the waste is a way to externalise the harm and create a distance between producers and consumers, on the one hand, and those affected by the dumping or recycling of the products, on the other hand' (Bisschop and Vande Walle 2013: 38).

Other environmental harm has the potential to impact the whole world. Climate change is the most obvious example. Despite the worldwide impact, one of the greatest ironies and indeed injustices of climate change, is that the causes are not worldwide, and the impacts are not equally felt worldwide. The causes of climate change are predominantly first world (developed nations), whereas the worst impacts are felt by the third world (developing nations) who are finding it difficult because of a lack of finance and technology to mitigate and adapt to climate change.

Time

There are two central considerations when discussing the temporal aspect of environmental harm. First, how long environmental harm lasts. That is, will the effects persist temporarily or for a long time. Second, what is the lead-in time to the manifestation of environmental harm. That is, some environmental harm may manifest immediately, whereas other types of environmental harm may have a long lead-in time and hence may not manifest until some distant time in the future. Naturally, there is a relationship between these two considerations. Some environmental harm may manifest immediately, but the harm disappears just as quickly. Some environmental harm may manifest immediately, and yet the harm lingers for many years or perhaps forever. Other environmental harm may not manifest for many years in the future, with the harm disappearing quickly, or alternately the harm lingers for many years after manifestation.

Some environmental harm will take time to manifest. One example is the harm from the illegal dumping of asbestos. Used widely, particularly between the 1950s and 1980s, asbestos is a building product. It came in a variety of forms, but which had in common the presence of fibrous crystals. The material is generally stable until broken at which stage the microscopic fibrous crystals are released into the air. If those fibrous crystals enter human lungs, it can cause various diseases of the lungs and lead to death. The maturation time of ill effects after inhalation is indeterminate and may be upward of 30 years, if at all. For this reason, the success of the prosecution for the dumping of asbestos turns on the act of dumping itself and not the manifestation of harm. Actual causing of environmental harm (remembering its wide definition and diversity of victims), and the potential for such harm, is considered in sentencing. Once the harm is manifest the symptoms will depend on the individual case. For some people the harm may be short-lived yet catastrophic in that it kills quite quickly once it has developed. For others, the harm may be longer lasting, and they may live for many years with the disease(s) of the lungs asbestos can cause.

Other illegal dumping may have a more immediate effect on the environment, such as marine pollution. Oil spills, for example, may manifest in almost immediate environmental harm, especially to aquatic and bird life, with differential lasting effects. It has been opined that 'in most cases, environmental recovery is relatively swift and is complete within 2–10 years' (Kingston 2002: 53). However, the environmental harm may linger for years to come. For example, in some cases '[o]il contamination may persist in the marine environment for many years after an oil spill and, in exceptional cases such as salt marshes and mangrove swamps, the effects may be measurable for decades after the event' (Kingston 2002: 53). On 24 March 1989, the *Exxon Valdez* spilled 260,000 barrels of crude oil (42 million litres; 10.8 million gallons) in Prince William Sound, Alaska. Less than five months after the spill, 30,000 dead birds comprising 90 different species were retrieved from the polluted area (Piatt et al. 1990: 387). Extrapolating from those numbers of dead birds recovered and 'aerial and ship-based surveys for populations at risk' it was estimated that the total number of dead birds numbered between 100,000 and 300,000 (Piatt et al. 1990: 387). In terms of longer-term environmental harm, 'for some species, such as harlequin ducks and sea otters, chronic oil spill effects persisted for at least two decades and were a larger influence on population dynamics over the long term than acute effects of the spill' (Esler et al. 2018: 36). Conversely, 'killer whales, suffered population declines due to acute spill effects that have not been resolved despite lack of chronic direct effects, representing a novel pathway of long-term injury' (Esler et al. 2018: 36).

Conclusion

The scale and scope of environmental harm today is unprecedented. The Intergovernmental Science-Policy Platform on Biodiversity and Ecosystem Services ('IPBES') (2019: 12) estimates 'that around 1 million species already face extinction, many within decades, unless action is taken to reduce the intensity of drivers of biodiversity loss'. Not surprisingly, '[c]limate change is a direct driver that is increasingly exacerbating the impact of other drivers on nature and human well-being' (IPBES 2019: 13). But biodiversity loss and climate change are not the only drivers of environmental harm, 'pollution, as well as invasive alien species, are increasing, with negative impacts for nature' (IPBES 2019: 13). Despite the scale and scope of environmental harm, to date existing legal and criminal justice responses have been woefully inadequate in stemming the tide of environmental destruction, degradation and damage. Indeed, '[e]conomic incentives have generally favoured expanding economic activity, and often environmental harm, over conservation or restoration' (IPBES 2019: 14). A paradigm shift in how one views the environment is needed. Perhaps ecocentrism is the much-needed paradigm shift. 'Ecocentrism refers to an approach to law and crime that is environment-centred rather than solely human-centred. Put simply, ecocentrism views the environment as having value for its own sake apart from any instrumental or utilitarian value to humans' (White 2022: 62; see also White 2017a; 2017b).

Mark Hamilton

Further reading

Gacek, J., & Jochelson, R. (Eds) (2002). *Green Criminology and the Law*. Cham: Palgrave Macmillan.

Hall, M., Maher, J., Nurse, A., Potter, G., South, S., & Wyatt, T. (Eds) (2017). *Greening Criminology in the 21st Century: Contemporary Debates and Future Directions in the Study of Environmental Harm*. Abingdon and New York: Routledge.

Lynch, M. J., Long, M. A., & Stretesky, P. B. (2019). *Green Criminology and Green Theories of Justice: An Introduction to a Political Economic View of Eco-justice*. Cham: Palgrave Macmillan.

Spapens, T., White, R., & Huisman, W. (Eds) (2014). *Environmental Crime and its Victims: Perspectives within Green Criminology*. Farnham, UK: Ashgate.

Spapens, T., White, R., & Huisman, W. (Eds) (2016). *Environmental Crime in Transnational Context: Global Issues in Green Criminology*. Abingdon: Routledge.

Walters, R., Solomon Westerhuis, D., & Wyatt, T. (Eds) (2013). *Emerging Issues in Green Criminology: Exploring Power, Justice and Harm*. Basingstoke: Palgrave Macmillan.

White, R. (2014). *Environmental Harm: An Eco-justice Perspective*. Bristol: Policy Press.

White, R., & Heckenberg, D. (2014). *Green Criminology: An Introduction to the Study of Environmental Harm*. Abingdon: Routledge.

References

Agnew, R. (2020). The Ordinary Acts that Contribute to Ecocide: A Criminological Analysis. In A. Brisman & N. South (Eds),

Routledge International Handbook of Green Criminology (pp. 52–67). Abingdon: Routledge.
Anstee-Wedderburn, J. (2014). Giving a Voice to Future Generations: Intergenerational Equity, Representations of Generations to Come, and the Challenge of Planetary Rights. *Australian Journal of Environmental Law 1*(1), 37–70.
Bisschop, L., & Vande Walle, G. (2013). Environmental Victimisation and Conflict Resolution: A Case Study of e-Waste. In T. Wyatt, R. Walters, & D. Westerhuis (Eds), *Emerging Issues in Green Criminology: Exploring Power, Justice and Harm* (pp. 34–54). Basingstoke: Palgrave Macmillan.
Cunnington Wynn, L. (2022). 'The Fight for Fairbourne': A Welsh Study of Environmental Harm and its Victims. *Criminological Encounters 5*(1), 35–51.
Esler, D., Ballachey, B. E., Matkin, C., Cushing, D., Kaler, R., Bodkin, J., Monson, D., Esslinger, G., & Kloecker, K. (2018). Timelines and Mechanisms of Wildlife Population Recovery Following the *Exxon Valdez* Oil Spill. *Deep-Sea Research Part II 147*, 36–42.
Forsyth, M., Cleland, D., Tepper, F., Hollingworth, D., Soares, M., Nairn, A., & Wilkinson, C. (2021). A Future Agenda for Environmental Restorative Justice? *The International Journal of Restorative Justice 4*(1), 17–40.
Hamilton, M. (2019). *Restorative Justice Conferencing in Response to Pollution Offending: A Vehicle for the Achievement of Justice as Meaningful Involvement* (PhD Dissertation, University of New South Wales).
Hamilton, M. (2021). *Environmental Crime and Restorative Justice: Justice as Meaningful Involvement.* Cham: Palgrave Macmillan.
Hamilton, M. (2022). 'The Fight for Fairbourne': Climate Change and its Impacts on Sea Level Rise. A Commentary by Mark Hamilton. *Criminological Encounters 5*(1), 210–214.
Intergovernmental Science-Policy Platform on Biodiversity and Ecosystem Services (IPBES). (2019). *The Global Assessment Report on Biodiversity and Ecosystem Services: Summary for Policymakers*. Bonn, Germany: IPBES Secretariat.
Kingston, P. F. (2002). Long-Term Environmental Impact of Oil Spills. *Spill Science & Technology Bulletin 7*(1–2), 53–61.
Lampkin, J., & Wyatt, T. 2019. Utilising Principles of Earth Jurisprudence to Prevent Environmental Harm: Applying a Case Study of Unconventional Hydraulic Fracturing for Shale Gas in the United Kingdom. *Critical Criminology 28*(3), 501–516.
Passas, N. (2005). Lawful but Awful: 'Legal Corporate Crimes'. *Journal of Socio-Economics 34*(6), 771–786.
Piatt, J. F., Lensink, C. J., Butler, W., Kendziorek, M., & Nysewander, D. R. (1990). Immediate Impact of the 'Exxon Valdez' Oil Spill on Marine Birds. *The Auk 107*(2), 387–397.
Preston, Hon Justice B. J. (2011). The Use of Restorative Justice for Environmental Crime. *Criminal Law Journal 35*(3), 136–153.
Protection of the Environment Operations Act 1997 (NSW).
Skinnider, E. (2013). *Effect, Issues and Challenges for Victims of Crimes that Have a Significant Impact on the Environment.* Vancouver: International Centre for Criminal Law Reform and Criminal Justice Policy.
Spapens, T., & Huisman, H. (2016). Tackling Cross-Border Environmental Crime: A 'Wicked Problem'. In T. Spapens, R. White, & W. Huisman (Eds), *Environmental Crime in Transnational Context: Global Issues in Green Enforcement and Criminology* (pp. 27–42). Abingdon: Routledge.
White, R. (2017a). *The Sentencing of Environmental Offences Involving Non-Human Environmental Entities in the NSW Land and Environment Court.* (Master of Laws Thesis, University of Tasmania).
White, R. (2017b). Reparative Justice, Environmental Crime and Penalties for the Powerful. *Crime, Law and Social Change 67*(2), 117–132.
White, R. (2022). Environmental Crime, Ecological Expertise and Specialist Environment Courts. In J. Gacek & R. Jochelson (Eds), *Green Criminology and the Law* (pp. 61–84). Cham: Palgrave Macmillan.
White, R., & Heckenberg, D. (2014). *Green Criminology: An Introduction to the Study of Environmental Harm*. Abingdon: Routledge.

MARK HAMILTON

9. Gender and environmental crime

Introduction

This entry discusses the role and impact of gender with respect to environmental crimes and harms. Particular attention is given to the status and position of women in the context of environmental change and disaster, as well as their experiences as victims and survivors of environmental harm. Recurring themes include violence against women and children, and the gendered nature of threats to environmental and personal security. This entry also considers the agency of women as both activists defending the environment and significant players in the commission of environmental crimes. Issues of gender inequality are central to understanding differences between women and men in regard to the dynamics, impacts, and consequences of environmental crime.

Gender

Gender relates to the situated and historical social construction of sexual differences or the ways in which human beings are categorised and socialised according to the social organisation of sexual difference within social-cultural groups. Gender refers to the roles, behaviours, activities, and attributes that a given society at a given time considers appropriate for men and women. Gender is part of the broader socio-cultural context, including class, race, poverty level, ethnic group, sexual orientation, and age. In most societies there are differences and inequalities between women and men in responsibilities assigned, activities undertaken, access to and control over resources, as well as opportunities for decision-making (International Union for Conservation of Nature (IUCN), 2018). The gendered condition of men and women leads to relational power differences (Segato, 2014), being the patriarchy, the historical system of social inequality, violence, subordination, and injustice that organises people, power, social spaces, activities, resources, and relations according to political hierarchies in favour of the male gender. It includes processes of alienation, destruction, degradation, oppression, injustice, violence, and the symbolic distribution of space and power (Lagarde, 2015). For instance, certain social groups or individuals are more likely to be harmed by or suffer risks associated with environmental crimes than others, inequalities and violence being part of the equation.

Environmental crimes have different impacts on the lives of women and children compared with men. Gender inequality is one of the main challenges to creating a clean, safe, and healthy environment for all. Yet the role of gender in crimes that affect the environment is still poorly understood (United Nations Office on Drugs and Crime (UNODC), 2024). Gender analysis is important to examine systematically the differences in gender roles, activities, needs, opportunities, and rights/entitlements – querying how those differences are created and sustained, and for what purposes (Seager, 2021). Gender analysis unpacks how those differences affect outcomes in daily life, or in specific activities and projects. Gender analyses examine the relationships between women and men, their access to and control of resources, and the constraints they face relative to each other (Seager, 2021).

Gender inequality and environmental harms

Gender inequality affects women on a global scale in an untold number of ways, but environmental crime serves as a particularly stark lens through which to examine and understand the extent to which gender disparity continues to pervade society (Dakeyne, 2024). International and regional legal instruments and reports recognise that biodiversity loss and the effects of climate change, for instance, have different impacts on women and men due to their distinct roles, responsibilities, and relationships with natural resources. A reported 80 per cent of people displaced by climate change are women, and women make up more than 40 per cent of the agricultural labour force and are responsible for 60–80 per cent of global food production. This makes them especially vulnerable to environmental disasters, as their livelihoods and social expectations are directly affected. Emergency shelters and camps become fertile ground for the trafficking and exploitation of women and children. In many regions, forced child marriages have been reported, as family incomes from agriculture are depleted following an environmental crisis (Ngum and Barooah, 2023).

Around the world, environmental crime and degradation and increased competition over scarce resources are exacerbating gender-based violence. Gender-based violence is an umbrella term for any harmful act (e.g., physical, verbal, sexual, psychological, and socio-economic) that is perpetrated against a person's will and that is based on socially ascribed (gender) differences between females and males (IUCN, 2018). The nature and extent of specific types of gender-based violence vary across cultures, countries, and regions and examples include sexual violence, including sexual exploitation/abuse and forced prostitution; domestic violence; trafficking; forced/early marriage; harmful traditional practices; honour killings; and widow inheritance (IUCN, 2018). Gender-based violence affects the security and well-being of nations, communities, and individuals, violating human rights, jeopardising development goals, and contributing to cycles of vulnerability at all levels. Rooted in discriminatory gender norms and laws and shrouded in impunity, gender-based violence occurs as a means of control, subjugation, and exploitation that further reinforces gender inequality (Castañeda Camey et al., 2021).

Gender-based violence and gender inequality are pervasive across all environmental contexts. National and customary laws, societal gender norms, and traditional gender roles often dictate who can access and control natural resources, which frequently results in the marginalisation of women compared to men and increases the vulnerabilities women can face in relation to violence (Castañeda Camey et al., 2021). Around the world, women who act as environmental defenders and activists against the destruction or degradation of their land, natural richness, and communities are often targeted with violence (Dakeyne, 2024). There is therefore a need to understand the resilience strategies of women who are emerging as environmental defenders against criminal groups, land grabbing, deforestation, biodiversity loss, and soil and water contamination because of extractive industries and agribusiness.

The UNODC 2023 Global Homicide Study highlighted that environmental defenders face considerable risks of being killed for their activism to protect natural resources. The research also shows that women environmental defenders face different threats than their male counterparts – for instance, it is more likely that they will be threatened with sexual violence or harm to their children (UNODC, 2024). In this regard, the 2021 Special Issue by IUCN on the stories and voices of environmental defenders across the globe and the UNODC 2023 Global Homicide Study highlighted that women environmental defenders face considerable risks of being killed for their activism to protect natural resources and in certain circumstances women even face specific threats compared with their male counterparts. Indeed, women defenders are more at risk of suffering certain forms of violence and other violations, prejudice, exclusion, and repudiation than their male counterparts, ranging from verbal abuse based on their sex to sexual abuse and rape (Luna et al., 2021). A potent example is the sexual abuse that has been observed in the illegal fishing industry across south-east Asia and southern and eastern Africa, which includes 'fish for sex' arrangements whereby fishermen withhold the sale of fish to women (who are largely responsible for securing food for their families) if they refuse to engage in sex (Dakeyne, 2024).

The extractivist model of 'development' women confront thrives on the large-scale exploitation of resources (e.g., land, water, and minerals) to drive profits for elite and private interests, at the expense of local and Indigenous communities. Increasingly, the violence used to impose the model of 'development' and suppress resistance has thrust women into the dangerous role of defenders of their lands, ways of life, and life itself (Carlsen and Mazwarira, 2021). For example, the illegal logging, charcoal and mining industries across certain countries like the Democratic Republic of Congo, Colombia and Peru are associated with sex trafficking, with women and girls brought into mining and logging camps for the benefit of labourers (Dakeyne, 2024; van Uhm, 2023). Women land defenders have developed a strong critique of this model through their own experience. Rural and Indigenous women depend directly on the land and its resources to sustain their families and their communities. Their relationship to land and territory encompasses not only dependence on the land for physical sustenance, but also an attachment to the territory for personal and community identity, traditional knowledge, spiritual connection and cultural continuity. When the land comes under attack, women also come under attack, and they are often the first to defend against land grabs, displacement and environmental destruction (Carlsen and Mazwarira, 2021).

Environmental crime also drives the climate crisis and it is widely agreed that climate change is not gender neutral, instead, exacerbating and amplifying existing gender inequalities. There are physiological as well as sociological reasons for this: in many regions of the world, women depend more on natural resources, which environmental crime depletes (Dakeyne, 2024). In many low- and lower-middle-income countries, women bear a disproportionate responsibility for securing natural resources to support their families. This includes things like water, fuel, and food, and when these resources are jeopardised by environmental crime, climate change, or extreme weather conditions caused and driven by environmental crime, it is women who are put under greater pressure to secure them (Dakeyne, 2024). This includes requiring them to walk longer distances to fetch water when local sources dry up, often putting them at greater risk of sexual violence *en route*; requiring girls to drop out of school to help their mothers – or be married off early to reduce the number of mouths that need to be fed (child marriage is considered an act of gender-based violence) – even inducing them to sell organs to organ traffickers in a desperate attempt to support their families, as has been observed in refugee camps following extreme weather events (Dakeyne, 2024).

Physiologically, women also suffer the effects of climate change and extreme weather conditions more than men. More women than men die from extreme heat, for reasons including differences in how they sweat, their ratio of body surface area to mass, their cardiovascular systems, and – sociologically – their greater propensity to be physically active in the home and to live alone. Extreme heat is also linked to the increased incidence of stillbirth and diseases (e.g., Zika virus, malaria, and dengue fever), which can cause poor maternal and neonatal outcomes (Dakeyne, 2024). The relatively higher amount of body fat on women as opposed to men also means that they retain toxic chemicals (stored in fat deposits) in their bodies for longer, so chemical run-off and air and water pollution from environmental crime activities like illegal mining, waste dumping, or the use of illegal pesticides affects them to a greater extent than it does men. Furthermore, the rapid physiological changes that women may undergo at certain stages of their lives, like pregnancy, lactation, and menopause, tend to increase their vulnerability to health damage from toxic chemicals (Dakeyne, 2024).

Threats to human security

A helpful conceptual framework for examining green victims and eco-violence is the lens of human security: economic; food; health; environment; personal; community; and political (Cao and Wyatt, 2016 cited in Stoett and Omrow, 2021). In terms of gender and environmental crimes, we can relate to environmental and personal security. Environmental security would be the loss of access to a healthy ecosystem, safety from natural disasters and access to basic resources such as water and land, loss to future generations of the right to a stable environment via climate change and other anthropogenic environmental changes (Stoett and Omrow, 2021). Aspects of victimisation on personal security include the inability to progress in personal development; gender discrimination and sexualised violence often accompanied by organised crime; increases in anxiety; enslavement or forced labour and child labour (like most of the estimated 250 million children trapped in bonded labour who toil on farms that lack both decent facilities for workers as well as environmental protection); and the loss of physical safety due to agential and structural violence (Stoett and Omrow, 2021). Agential violence occurs when deliberate harm is caused to ecosystems, and structural violence when oppressed people suffer disproportionately when environmental conditions worsen by indirect change. For instance, the plight of colonised Indigenous peoples has been marked by both agential and structural violence on a global scale (Stoett and Omrow, 2021).

To examine environmental crime, victimisation, and gender further, we could also look at the aspect of political security, understood as the loss of freedom from State oppression and abuses of basic human rights; imprisonment and other forms of abject cruelty by the State; as well as propaganda efforts to encourage discrimination against certain groups, State-sponsored terrorism of environmental stewards and activists, and State–cartel and State–corporate collusion in committing eco-violence (Stoett and Omrow, 2021). In addition to being disproportionately affected by environmental crimes and climate change, women are severely under-represented when it comes to environmental policy and protection, in line with a general lack of representation in, and active exclusion from, policymaking and decision-making processes globally (Dakeyne, 2024).

Women's role in wildlife related crimes

Recent studies which integrate diverse perspectives and analyses to advance the conversation about women's roles, particularly in wildlife trafficking (e.g., Seager, 2021; Agu and Gore, 2022), point out that female gender differentiation, gender inequality, and gender norms anchor and shape wildlife trafficking at diverse points throughout production and value chains. Women and men participate differently in all domains of illegal wildlife trade, from poaching through to consumption, and in policymaking. The costs and benefits of poaching, trafficking, and consuming wildlife are different for men and women, as are the costs and benefits of curbing or ending illegal wildlife trade. Access to resources, control over those resources, attitudes about them, and decisions about what resources to use are different for men and for women. Men and women typically hold different attitudes about animals, human–wildlife conflict, the value of protected areas, and commitments to conservation. The extent to which this 'matters' in terms of illegal wildlife trade involvement needs serious investigation (Seager, 2021).

It is observed that women can be involved in crimes through a diverse array of roles, such as defenders, influencers, offenders, beneficiaries, observers, supporters, partners, leaders, agents of change, among others (Agu and Gore, 2022). As defenders, formal law enforcement female authorities such as police, rangers, or customs officials work across multiple jurisdictions to both respond to wildlife trafficking events and prevent the crime from happening, although there are other types of wildlife trafficking defenders besides law enforcement authorities; informal guardians often function at the community level and use non-technical tools such as relationships with local communities (Agu and Gore, 2022). Influencers, in turn, can be individuals linking to wildlife trafficking via a range of relationships, connections, and networks. In this sense, women may influence individuals or groups of people involved in wildlife trafficking and this influence can be both positive and negative; family members, religious figures, educators, friends, and romantic partners may all be influencers, as can be female social media influencers (Agu and Gore, 2022).

Offenders, considered the main wrongdoers, are among the most important stakeholders in wildlife trafficking. However, research on the role of women as perpetrators of crime has been limited (Agu and Gore, 2022). In regard to this, there is active participation by women in the harvest, transport, distribution, sale, and consumption of wildlife parts. Women can be supporters (i.e., subordinate to the leading traffickers either under threat or 'voluntarily'), partners (i.e., women who have a relationship with a man and cooperate with him), and madams (i.e., offenders who play a central role, lead criminal organisations) (Agu and Gore, 2022). Delineating types of offenders may inform targeted interventions or education and outreach and deeper understanding about the motivations and intentions of offenders can advance insight about offender behaviour (Agu and Gore, 2022). Overall, however, the wheels of wildlife trafficking are greased by astonishing levels of sexual exploitation and violence. Sexual exploitation, prostitution of women, and sex trafficking facilitate personal and commercial illegal wildlife trade transactions on local to global scales. For example, commercial-scale illegal logging of rare timber in Madagascar, unlike animal poaching, is usually characterised by an influx of large numbers of temporary male workers, who establish medium-to-long-term encampments in the forests or swell the population of previously small, isolated villages and towns. In this regard, an investigation revealed the staggering gendered social costs of the incursions of large numbers of mostly young men: rape; prostitution; sexually transmitted diseases; and unwanted pregnancies (Seager, 2021). Reports of sexual exploitation of women come additionally from Peru and South Sudan; the poaching economy of Kafue National Park in Zambia; illegal wildlife trade and traditional Chinese medicine enterprises in Uganda; and hotspots for prostitution and illegal wildlife trade in Myanmar, among other examples (Seager, 2021).

INÉS ARROYO-QUIROZ

Integrating gender analysis and equality into wildlife trafficking work offers high-level rewards both in regard to understanding and crime prevention. Because wildlife trafficking takes place in a world that is thoroughly defined by gender differentiation, the actors, practices, impacts, pressures, and outcomes of wildlife trafficking – as well as efforts to curb or eradicate it – too are 'gendered'. Bringing gender analysis into wildlife trafficking work improves the likelihood of conservation success, and it can be a catalyst for challenging social inequalities (Seager, 2021). Gender analysis will not solve the problems of the unsustainable and violence-infused trade in wildlife, but it can contribute to solutions by engaging a wider-angle understanding of problems, approaches, and policies not offered elsewhere (Seager, 2021).

Highlighting the importance of gender

There is a well-known sex bias in crime; however, research on the roles of women is still limited and there are clear gaps in knowledge that remain. Recently, a first volume in green criminology devoted to gender (Milne et al., 2023) presents compelling evidence attesting to the gender patterning, and gendered nature, of green crimes and environmental harms. The book illustrates the gendered impacts of these problems and the gendered nature of harm and victimisation caused and experienced in different contexts and in different parts of the globe. Moreover, it examines the gendered nature of resistance and aftermath recovery, thus offering an informed critical understanding and appreciation of how to ameliorate the harms currently being experienced (Milne et al., 2023). This edited collection, from a diverse range of disciplines, contributes to our understanding of these important intersections by addressing questions such as:

- How can feminism and a critical gender approach engage meaningfully with environmental harm? Why should those interested in environmental harm also be concerned with gender?
- In what ways can a gender-focused lens provide greater insight into the nature and impact of gendered harms?

Among the theoretical and empirical explorations are topics such as gender and the perpetrators of environmental harm; gender and victims of environmental harm; eco-feminism and justice; feminist approaches to environmental harm; interactions between gender and environmental harms; the gendered nature of structural violence and environmental harm; gender, environmental catastrophe, resilience, and recovery; and gender, intersectionality, and species.

Fundamentally, the recent global discourse on environmental protection and conservation promotes 'gender mainstreaming' of environmental policies and frameworks at national, regional, and international levels. In December 2022, for example, at the 15th Conference of the Parties (CoP15) to the UN Convention on Biological Diversity, representatives of 188 countries adopted the Kunming–Montreal Global Biodiversity Framework for action, setting four goals to be reached by 2050 and 23 targets to be achieved by 2030. The framework is recognised as a significant step in protecting biodiversity, using a human rights approach to tackle human-induced biodiversity loss and climate change. Target 23 of the Global Biodiversity Framework focuses on gender equality, which is a step forward from the previous Aichi targets set by the UN Convention on Biological Diversity for 2011–2020. The post-2020 Global Biodiversity Framework includes a gender action plan to increase gender-disaggregated baseline data on conservation, use and ownership of land resources, and participation in decision-making processes.

In a similar vein, the UN Framework Convention on Climate Change and the United Nations' 2030 Agenda for Sustainable Development (United Nations, 2015) seek to realise the human rights of all, to achieve gender equality and the empowerment of all women and girls and foster peaceful, just, and inclusive societies free from fear and violence (Ngum and Barooah, 2023). These thematic approaches extend to regional agreements, such as the African Union Gender Policy, the Regional Action Plan on Women's Access to Land and Forest Resources in Latin America and the Caribbean, and the Asia-Pacific Forestry Sector Outlook Study, all of which promote the integration of gender considerations into programmes and policies, including decisions related to the environment (Ngum and Barooah, 2023).

Feminist social justice

The 3Rs tripartite model (i.e., representation, recognition, and redistribution) of engendered social justice aims to help assess participatory parity (Fraser, 2000, 2007, 2009).

- *Representation* implies self-determination or to affirm as a political subject with shared power, civil rights, and political rights.
- *Recognition* implies considering, recognising, and affirming an individual or collective subject as a socio-cultural agent beyond essentialisms.
- *Redistribution* implies restructuring the political economy, overcoming exploitation by social class, and equal sharing of social burdens and benefits.

Fraser's feminist social justice perspective incorporates systems of social structures, institutions, and symbolism in an integrated manner, in which each dimension co-creates the other, and change entails systemic transformation; despite advances (e.g., a higher number of women represented at different levels of policy or development of multilateral and State institutional frameworks), important challenges remain unless all dimensions are addressed (Arroyo-Quiroz, Castro-Salazar, and Serrano-Oswald, 2022).

For instance, although higher female representation in positions at all levels is a historical and important advance, having women in key positions where they can make or enforce laws or direct environmental protection agencies does not translate into gender equality automatically; it is also important to include political representation as a transversal axis in supporting green and social justice. In another example, if feminist social justice does not focus on the importance of relational fair treatment and only women or only men have well-being, society as a whole will not progress and equality will not be achieved. Societal change involves changing conceptions and the practice of a feminist and green social justice, which incorporates the socio-cultural, economic, and political dimensions of recognition, representation, and redistribution. Altogether, these create a framework that envisages a more just society that is better able to commit itself transversally to values of sustainability and equality (Arroyo-Quiroz, Castro-Salazar, and Serrano-Oswald, 2022).

Conclusion

Gender equality will be achieved when women and men, and girls and boys, have equal rights, life prospects, and opportunities, and the power to shape their own lives and contribute to society (Seager, 2021). Equality between the sexes is a question of a fair and equitable distribution of power, influence, and resources in everyday life and in society. Equality does not mean that women and men will become the same, but that rights, responsibilities, and opportunities will not depend on whether people are born male or female. Gender equality implies that the interests, needs, and priorities of both women and men should be taken into consideration, recognising the diversity of different groups of women and men. A gender equal society would also be equitable, which in turn refers to fairness and the need for differential treatment to achieve a fair outcome in an unequal society (Seager, 2021).

Without romanticising women and considering their intra-generic diversity, womanism will not lead to the depatriarchalisation of society automatically, although it is a crucial step forward. For effective and sustainable interventions to prevent, mitigate, or counteract environmental crimes, it is important to consider the anthropocentric-capitalist social representations of nature and property based on patriarchal culture, as sex-gender political economy and ecology evolve through identities and cultural processes (Arroyo-Quiroz, Castro-Salazar, and Serrano-Oswald, 2022). From a green and gender social justice perspective, it is important to recognise the way in which patriarchal sex-gender systems generate forms of oppression that affect women, men, and non-human animals, and the planet, to include alternative critical perspectives, dialogues, and narratives and to look specifically at the ways in which patriarchal anthropocentric civilisation models have generated multiple forms of harm. This does not mean that we should consider a women-only or a human-only perspective, and it does not encompass a totalitarian and static perspective that puts all human beings, all women, and all men in the same group. Instead, it enables processes of deconstruction and transformation of oppressive social representations and the construction of alternative ways of understanding identities and cultures (Arroyo-Quiroz, Castro-Salazar, and Serrano-Oswald, 2022).

INÉS ARROYO-QUIROZ

Being fair and eradicating violence is a critical invitation to look at ourselves and to understand how patriarchal forms based on violence and oppression cut across the way we have treated and continue to treat each other (intra-species), which in turn extends to our inter-species and inter-spaces relations (Arroyo-Quiroz, Castro-Salazar, and Serrano-Oswald, 2022). Study, for example, the case of the devastation of sea otters in the American north-west in the 18th to 21st centuries from the perspective of ecoglobal history and criminology (Souto Mantecón and Arroyo-Quiroz, 2022). Humans have become increasingly aware of our systemic interconnection with and dependence on other non-human life forms and the entire planet. The moral imperative behind fair treatment and respect for all humans can certainly be extended to all other forms of life, which justifies the extension of social justice to green justice.

Inés Arroyo-Quiroz

Further reading

Castañeda Camey, I., Sabater, L., Owren, C., and Boyer, A. E. (2021). *Gender-based violence and environment linkages: Summary for policy makers*. Wen, J. (ed.). IUCN. Available at: https://portals.iucn.org/library/sites/library/files/documents/2020-002-En-Summ.pdf

ECLAC (2020). Building a new future: Transformative recovery with equality and sustainability. Economic Commission for Latin America and the Caribbean (LC/SES.38/3-P/Rev.1), Santiago. Available at: https://repositorio.cepal.org/server/api/core/bitstreams/a033b848-0f8e-436a-8f2b-cb95ab6c894f/content

Hicks, J. (2021). The role of gender in serious and organised/transnational crime. K4D Helpdesk Report 984. Brighton, UK: Institute of Development Studies. Available at: https://opendocs.ids.ac.uk/opendocs/bitstream/handle/20.500.12413/16554/984_Gender_and_Serious_Organised_Crime.pdf?sequence=1&isAllowed=y

IUCN (2020). Gender-based violence and the environment. IUCN Issues Brief, September 2020. Available at: https://iucn.org/sites/default/files/2022 03/gbv_issues_brief_september_2020_final.pdf

Kramer, R., and Hart, E. (2020). Reducing corruption's impact on natural resources: How does a gender lens help? Targeting Natural Resource Corruption. WWF. Available at: https://www.worldwildlife.org/pages/tnrc-introductory-overview-reducing-corruption-s-impact-on-natural-resources-how-does-a-gender-lens-help.

Ngum, F., and Barooah, R. (2023). Impact of biodiversity loss and environmental crime on women from rural and Indigenous communities: Evidence from Ecuador, Mexico, Cameroon and Indonesia. The Global Initiative Against Transnational Organized Crime. Available at: https://resiliencefund.globalinitiative.net/wp-content/uploads/2023/10/Faith-Ngum-Radha-Barooah-Impact-of-biodiversity-loss-and-environmental-crime-on-women-from-rural-and-indigenous-communities-GI-TOC-October-2023.v3.pdf

Ramos, A., Le Billon, P., Seagle, C., Madzwamuse, M., Walker Painemilla, K., Petriv, I., and Jauregui, L. (eds.) (2021). Policy matters, special issue 22, volumes I–III. Gland, Switzerland: IUCN. Available at: https://www.iucn.org/news/commission-environmental-economic-and-social-policy/202109/stories-and-voices-environmental-defenders-across-globe-special-issue-policy-matters

Weeden, A.-M. (2023). Understanding the female wildlife offender: Lessons from the case files. *Nature, Guns and Money*. Royal United Services Institute for Defence and Security Studies (RUSI). Available at: https://rusi.org/networks/shoc/nature-guns-money/understanding-female-wildlife-offender-lessons-case-files

Other resources

Bisschop, L. (2023). In September 2022, the seminar 'Environmental Crime & Gender' organised by green criminologists from around the world took place in Malaga, Spain with the aim of exploring the varied intersections of environmental crime and gender within the criminological community, pushing green criminological scholarship further by bridging (sub)disciplinary boundaries and inspiring new research and collaborations. Key aspects of presentations on gendered dynamics of environmental crime. Available at: https://www.eur.nl/en/news/gendered-dynamics-environmental-crime

Webinar Recording on Gender and Environmental Crime (2023). Explores emerging evidence on gender's role in environmental crime and its impacts, and how understanding this may help shape the societal response. Chaired by: Anne-Marie Weeden. Speakers: Dr Helen U. Agu, Dr Meredith L. Gore, and Dr Francis Masse. Royal United Services Institute. Available at:

https://rusi.org/research-event-recordings/recording-gender-and-environmental-crime

References

Agu, H., and Gore, M. (eds.) (2022). *Women and Wildlife Trafficking: Participants, Perpetrators and Victims*. Routledge.

Arroyo-Quiroz, I., Castro-Salazar, I., and Serrano-Oswald, S. E. (2022). Using a feminist and green social justice perspective to better understand governance of wildlife trafficking in Mexico. In H. Agu and M. Gore (eds.), *Women and Wildlife Trafficking: Participants, Perpetrators and Victims* (pp. 44–58). Routledge.

Carlsen, L., and Mazwarira, A. (2021). Women defenders of land and territory: Challenging extractive 'development'. In A. Ramos, P. Le Billon, C. Seagle, M. Madzwamuse, K. Walker Painemilla, I. Petriv, and L. Jauregui (eds.), *Policy Matters*, special issue on environmental defenders 22, volume III. Gland, Switzerland: IUCN.

Castañeda Camey, I., Sabater, L., Owren, C. and Boyer, A. E. (2021). *Gender-Based Violence and Environment Linkages: Summary for Policymakers*. Wen, J. (ed.). IUCN.

Dakeyne, O. (2024). International Women's Day: The disproportionate impact of environmental crime on women. Insight, Themis. Available at: https://www.wearethemis.com/uk/about/blog/international-women-s-day-the-disproportionate-impact-of-environmental-crime-on-women/.

Fraser, N. (2000). Rethinking recognition. *New Left Review* 3: 107–120.

Fraser, N. (2007). Transnationalizing the public sphere: On the legitimacy and efficacy of public opinion in a post-Westphalian world. *Theory Culture & Society* 24: 7–30.

Fraser, N. (2009). *Scales of Justice: Reimagining Political Space in a Globalizing World.* Columbia University Press.

IUCN (2018). Gender equality and women's empowerment policy: Mainstreaming gender-responsiveness within the IUCN programme of work. Available at: https://www.iucn.org/sites/default/files/2022–05/iucn-policy-on-gender-equity-and-equality-october-2018-english-only.pdf.

Lagarde, M. (2015). *Los Cautiverios de las Mujeres: Madresposas, Monjas, Putas y Locas*. Ed. Siglo XXI.

Luna, M., Sabater, L., Castañeda, I., and Owrend, C. (2021). The urgency of addressing gender-based violence against women environmental human rights defenders. In A. Ramos, P. Le Billon, C. Seagle, M. Madzwamuse, K. Walker Painemilla, I. Petriv, and L. Jauregui (eds.), *Policy Matters*, special issue on environmental defenders 22, volume III. IUCN.

Milne, E., Davies, P., Heydon, J., Peggs, K., and Wyatt, T. (eds.) (2023). *Gendering Green Criminology*. Bristol University Press.

Ngum, F., and Barooah, R. (2023). Impact of biodiversity loss and environmental crime on women from rural and Indigenous communities: Evidence from Ecuador, Mexico, Cameroon and Indonesia. The Global Initiative Against Transnational Organized Crime.

Seager, J. (2021). *Gender and Illegal Wildlife Trade: Overlooked and Underestimated.* WWF.

Segato, R. L. (2014). *Las nuevas formas de la guerra y el cuerpo de las mujeres*. Editorial Pez.

Souto Mantecón, M., and Arroyo-Quiroz, I. (2022). La devastación de las nutrias marinas en el noroeste americano: una mirada desde la historia y la criminología ecoglobales (siglos XVIII al XXI). In M. Souto Mantecón and D. Kent Carrasco (eds.), *Miradas globales desde América Latina: estudio histórico más allá de lo nacional* (pp. 89–114). Instituto Mora. Available at: https://mora.repositorioinstitucional.mx/jspui/handle/1018/580

Stoett, P., and Omrow, D. A. (2021). *Spheres of Transnational Ecoviolence: Environmental Crime, Human Security, and Justice*. Palgrave Macmillan.

United Nations (2015). Transforming Our World: The 2030 Agenda for Sustainable Development. A/RES/70/1. Available at: https://sdgs.un.org/sites/default/files/publications/21252030%20Agenda%20for%20Sustainable%20Development%20web.pdf.

UNODC (2024). Interview with UNODC researcher Tanya Wyatt about gendered dimensions of crimes that affect the environment. UNODC. Available at: https://www.unodc.org/unodc/en/frontpage/2024/February/gender-and-crimes-that-affect-the-environment_-why-it-matters.html.

van Uhm, D. (2023). *Organized Environmental Crime: Black Markets in Gold, Wildlife, and Timber*. Bloomsbury.

INÉS ARROYO-QUIROZ

10. News framing of environmental crime

Introduction

Vietnam is known as both a consumer and transit hub for the illegal wildlife trade (IWT) and is the leading market nation for rhino horn poached from Africa, particularly South Africa. At global IWT conferences global elites have promoted the framing of IWT as a criminal issue rather than a conservation issue (Masse et al. 2020). Furthermore, the Vietnamese government has adopted the definition of IWT as a serious crime under the UNODC. The trade is routinely presented in popular digital newspapers in Vietnam as a serious transnational crime committed by organised criminal networks. Moreover, the enforcement of the trade is framed as Vietnam is fighting it with tough law enforcement in compliance with its international commitments under the Convention on International Trade in Endangered Species (CITES). In addition to enforcement and legal frameworks, behaviour change campaigns aiming to reduce demand are important to fight the rhino horn trade (Smith 2022).

Much of the reporting and framing of the rhino horn trade as a serious crime stems from Vietnamese official media releases and media conferences. However, local and international ENGOs and other international sources also act as important sources of information for Vietnamese journalists. Hence there is an interplay of frames stemming from local and supranational sources, creating a transnational public sphere in the news media of this small Southeast Asian country. Lack of enforcement is the third frame that encapsulates the reporting of the criminal aspects of the rhino horn trade.

Newspaper articles about the rhino horn trade in Vietnamese online newspapers are a key source of information about the trade for the Vietnamese public and political officials as well as international stakeholders. Hence news framing plays a strong role in how the trade is understood and responded to publicly and politically in this Southeast Asian country. Media criminology and green cultural criminology are valuable research frameworks in understanding the rhino horn trade and may be useful to understand government policy responses to other environmental crimes.

Media framing

Framing analysis is central to media criminology. The concept of 'framing' refers to the ways in which certain aspects of a story will be highlighted and signposted as important while others will be downplayed. In essence, frames serve as 'the *organizing principles* that are socially *shared* and *persistent* over time, that work *symbolically* to meaningfully *structure* the social world' (Reese 2001: 11, emphasis in original). In other words, how themes are emphasised and organised entails specific ways of discussing a problem and the kinds of discourses that will follow.

Framing devices include headlines, subheads, photos, photo captions, leads, source selection, quote selection and so on. Thus, they involve news angles, sources, language choice, visual images, and statistics or crime data (Clifford and White 2017). For example, depending on how it is framed, illegal drug use may be portrayed as a 'public health issue' or a 'criminal justice issue'.

The challenge is to understand not only how crime and justice are framed within media (content), but why they are framed in particular ways (context) and what the potential implications are of these framing practices (as framing effects), including what harms might be inadvertently produced and what opportunities there are to counter conventional media frames (consequence) (Clifford and White 2017). This challenge applies to the present study – that is, how best to understand and interpret media framing of the rhino horn trade in Vietnam.

The serious crime frame

The rhino horn trade is framed in the Vietnamese news media as a serious crime through a variety of interpretive packages. The frame is communicated directly when journalists literally state that it is a serious crime, or that it is run by organised criminal networks (or chains or wires) on a large transnational scale. The networks are sometimes portrayed as family based or as a kind of mafia through Hollywood popular culture references. The serious crime framing is often achieved through words that suggest the organised criminal networks are sophisticated.

The serious criminal nature of the trade is also presented in the news as a potential security threat. Journalists sometimes convey the seriousness of the security threat by comparing the trade to other serious transnational organised crimes, such as drug, weapon or human trafficking. The newspapers also refer to the involvement of corrupt low-level customs or police officials.

A key way that journalists suggest the involvement of organised criminal networks is through the depiction of various roles in a smuggling chain. For example, the use of the word 'boss' in the news is indicative of an organisation. News articles that describe a seizure at an airport in which sophisticated concealment methods were used to avoid detection and the arrested courier or mule had received rhino horns from a person in Africa to deliver to a contact in Vietnam, are also indicative of two more people cooperating. Hence a level of organisation is depicted rather than simply an individual acting alone. These criminal networks are also portrayed as ruthless, exploitative or cruel. These depictions of the networks' character contribute to an interpretation of the rhino horn trade as a serious crime. This emphasis is particularly highlighted in articles when the rhino horn trade is converged with the trade in bushmeat and tigers that occurs at the land-based border between Laos and Vietnam. Through images and cultural nuances, the IWT bosses are depicted as cruel ruthless criminals. Such a convergence is regularly reported in Vietnamese digital newspapers with a reputation for investigative reporting.

International elites and CITES officials have promoted the framing of IWT as a serious criminal issue rather than a conservation issue at a series of global IWT conferences and CITES conferences. In 2010, the International Consortium on Combating Wildlife Crime (ICCWC), in which CITES partners with INTERPOL, the United Nations Office on Drugs and Crime, the World Bank, and the World Customs Organization, was established with this intent. These framing efforts have been aimed at getting enforcement agencies worldwide to take IWT more seriously. A possible result of these efforts is that serious crime frames now dominate in reports of the rhino horn trade in the Vietnamese news media.

The compliance frame

News stories about the rhino horn trade in the Vietnamese media tend to feature a combination of serious crime and compliance framing. The state, in conjunction with the news media, frame policy, policy implementation and instances of Vietnam enforcing laws against the rhino horn trade as Vietnam complying with its CITES obligations. For example, government officials are quoted in news stories declaring Vietnam's determination and commitment to comply with CITES. Vietnam had previously come under strong criticism from CITES for not complying with its provisions intended to protect endangered and threatened species.

As a part of its CITES obligations, Vietnam self-reports to CITES yearly on compliance. The compliance frame in the Vietnamese news media echoes the CITES criteria in terms of enforcement, coordination and cooperation, and the legal frameworks of those self-reports. This includes rhino horn seizures, arrests, prosecutions and sentencings and information on coordinated local investigations and instances of international cooperation. The news media also depict compliance throughout Vietnam as involving the taking of a tough approach to the rhino horn trade with a tough legal framework including jail sentences of more than five years, and by describing their customs officials as hard-working, skilled officers.

A tough law and order approach is a well-established trope in the Vietnamese state-run media. Photographs of offenders in handcuffs, flanked by police and posed with contraband tend to suggest a tough punitive system. The photographs of rhino horn couriers and kingpins display similar compositions. Paragraphs that list a number of Vietnamese investigative enforcement agencies coordinating and paragraphs that describe clever work by customs officers to arrest sophisticated criminals suggest Vietnam has strong security measures. Furthermore, the War on the Rhino Horn Trade frame echoes the controversial War on Drugs and War on Crime frames that were politically expedient in the United States decades ago, even though these frames were associated with major social problems, including abuses of state power. While Vietnam has a history of security and harsh treatment of criminals, it may have adopted this particular War on Crime rhetoric from international stakeholders. In summary, the Vietnamese state-run news media frames enforcement of laws against the rhino horn trade as compliance activity.

Lack of enforcement frame

Most of the national news media portray Vietnam as effectively fighting the rhino horn trade; however, some stories suggest that it could do better. When this occurs, Vietnamese journalists tend to enact the lack of enforcement frame through suggestion or inference. The use of metaphor, tropes and cultural nuance is common in the enactment of this frame. For example, investigative stories that link the rhino horn trade with the trade in bushmeat and tigers along the Lao border suggest that policing along the border is lacking. Furthermore, some stories suggest that corruption may be a factor. In the case of international sources and ENGOs, diplomatic language is employed, usually along the lines that Vietnam has improved but needs to do better or that, in general, globally more needs to be done to address wildlife trafficking.

Securitisation creeps into the Vietnamese media

Securitisation is a news frame that is beginning to appear in stories of the rhino horn trade in the Vietnamese newspapers. Securitisation is communication in which certain crimes are depicted as so serious that they require extraordinary enforcement and security measures such as militarised responses. The crimes and criminal networks are presented as threats to national security.

Securitisation in the Vietnamese news media has occurred through the association of the rhino trade with a militarised response, particularly through the visual means of images of armed soldiers guarding rhinos and rhino horns. There is concern that both conservation and IWT are being securitised worldwide which may be seen as placing conservation issues into the hands of enforcement elites (Duffy 2021; Cao and Wyatt 2016; Floyd 2015). National newspapers thus carry photos of armed soldiers guarding rhino horn thereby enacting the securitisation frame. In addition, some newspapers have featured photographic essays of armed African soldiers guarding rhinos, in Africa and reports of militarised anti-poaching units in Africa.

The criminality framing of the rhino horn trade in the Vietnamese press can be traced to the influence of international elites. A series of four global IWT conferences organised by Great Britain were instrumental in shifting the rhino horn trade from a conservation issue to a criminal and security issue. The third conference in the series was held in Hanoi. It symbolically marked not only Vietnam's commitment and determination to fight the trade, but through a publicity event on the side of the conference – the Ivory Burn and Rhino Horn Crush – the conference marked a shift to criminal framing in the Vietnamese media. Images of the ivory and rhino horn being destroyed under the gaze of armed guards and international elites were published widely across Vietnamese national news, announcing the conference. Images of fire engulfing stacks of rhino horn and ivory signified Vietnam's tough approach.

The serious crime and compliance framing of wildlife issues in the Vietnamese press indicates that Vietnam has a level of commitment to fight the rhino horn trade and suggests the importance of pressure of international elites in promoting criminal framing and the dominance of Vietnamese government officials as sources of information. The lack of enforcement frame in conjunction with inferences of corruption in the news on the rhino horn trade suggest that ENGOs play a significant role in Vietnam's green public sphere, in league with sympathetic Vietnamese journalists who possess politico-cultural dexterity born through professional experience in navigating Vietnam's authoritarian media system.

Conclusion

Several implications arise from the dominance of the serious crime and compliance frames of the rhino horn trade in Vietnam. One is that it tends to place great emphasis on coercive state intervention in ways that legitimise armed responses to the illegal wildlife trade. By contrast, such issues are rarely considered through a conservation frame or one that puts community engagement at the centre of image and analysis. The dominant framing implies the preference for and approval of a top-down approach to wildlife trafficking, one in which ordinary persons and communities are absent. An emphasis on criminal networks further entrenches the idea of 'good' versus 'evil' in ways that obfuscate complex social contexts and thereby privilege adoption of coercive force over and above more nuanced community-level approaches.

MICHAEL SMITH

Further reading

Floyd, R., 2015. Environmental security and the case against rethinking criminology as 'security-ology'. *Criminology and Criminal Justice*, 15(3), 277–282.

Masse, F., Dickinson, H., Margulies, J., Joanny, L., Lappe-Osthege, T. and Duffy, R., 2020. Conservation and crime convergence? Situating the 2018 London Illegal Wildlife Trade Conference. *Journal of Political Ecology*, 27(1), 23–42.

Scanlon, J. E., 2016. Remarks on the destruction of confiscated elephant ivory and rhino horn in Hanoi, Viet Nam. https://cites.org/eng/CITES_SG_remarks_destruction_ivory_rhino_horn_vietnam_12112016

Sumrall, K. A., 2009. *Confronting Illegal Wildlife Trade in Vietnam: The Experience of Education for Nature-Vietnam* (Unpublished Doctoral dissertation, University of Michigan).

UNTOC – United Nations Convention against Transnational Organised Crime and the Protocols Thereto. https://www.unodc.org/unodc/en/organized-crime/intro/UNTOC.html

Wellsmith, M., 2011. Wildlife crime: The problems of enforcement. *European Journal on Criminal Policy and Research*, 17(2), 125–148.

Wyatt, T., 2014. Assessing the partner and media engagement with the International Consortium on Combating Wildlife Crime. In R. White, M. Kluin and T. Spapens (eds) *Environmental Crime and its Victims: Perspectives within Green Criminology* (pp. 277–291). Ashgate Publishing.

References

Cao, A. N. and Wyatt, T., 2016. The conceptual compatibility between green criminology and human security: A proposed interdisciplinary framework for examinations into green victimisation. *Critical Criminology*, 24, 413–430.

Clifford, K. and White, R. 2017. *Media and Crime: Content, Context and Consequence*. Oxford University Press.

Duffy, R., 2021. Crime, security, and illegal wildlife trade: Political ecologies of international conservation, *Global Environmental Politics*, 1–22.

Floyd, R., 2015. Environmental security and the case against rethinking criminology as 'security-ology'. *Criminology and Criminal Justice*, 15(3), 277–282.

Masse, F., Dickinson, H., Margulies, J., Joanny, L., Lappe-Osthege, T. and Duffy, R., 2020. Conservation and crime convergence? Situating the 2018 London Illegal Wildlife Trade Conference. *Journal of Political Ecology*, 27(1), 23–42.

Reese, S., 2001. Prologue – Framing public life: A bridging model for media research. In S. Reese, O. Gandy and A. Grant (eds), *Framing Public Life: Perspectives on Media and Our Understanding of the Social World* (pp. 7–32). Lawrence Erlbaum Associates.

Smith, M. S., 2022. You better believe it: Rhino horns are a bloody risky business. In E. Freedman, S. S. Hiles and D. B. Sachsman (eds), *Communicating Endangered Species* (pp. 116–134). Routledge.

11. Rights of nature and wild law

Introduction

There is a growing social movement advocating for the rights of nature and there are now a significant number of success stories where environmental rights have been enshrined in domestic legislation and the constitutions of sovereign nations. Such rights are an example of wild law, that is, laws that put the Earth at the centre of law-making, rather than human wants and needs. Wild laws, though, are not always embodied by rights of nature. Other legislation, case law or constitutional amendments that give priority to the natural world over the human world are considered to represent the philosophy of Earth jurisprudence (rather than human jurisprudence). This entry explains what is meant by the terms 'rights of nature', 'wild law', 'Earth jurisprudence' and 'ecocentrism', summarising key debates in these areas, and offering ideas for the advance of the academic study of wild law in the future.

The term *Rights of Nature* refers to both the legal and philosophical privileges of nature (that being 'the environment' in its broadest sense, inclusive of humans, non-humans, and natural ecosystems regardless of sentience). It also refers to a growing global socio-environmental movement towards protecting the natural world through the medium of environmental rights. Concurrently, *Wild Laws* are laws constructed by humans but according to the principles of the philosophy of *Earth Jurisprudence*. *Ecocentrism* refers to the valuing of nature for its own sake (White, 2024), valuing their interests as morally and philosophically important (Medlock and White, 2022). This entry will define these terms, and explore their meaning, significance and development in the context of environmental harms and crimes.

Human rights, natural rights and environmental rights

Whilst the idea of natural rights and human rights can be traced back to eighteenth-century revolutions in France and the United States, it was not until the United Nations (UN) Charter of 1945 and the 1948 UN Universal Declaration of Human Rights that human rights came into fruition at an international law and, subsequently, domestic law level (Freeman, 2022). The timing of the Charter and Declaration is important as they followed atrocities committed at the human-to-human level in World War II, and the global human community was finally in widespread agreement that people's basic rights needed to be recognised in order to survive and thrive.

Ultimately, human rights and natural rights are inextricably intertwined. *Human* rights are 'reasonable demands for personal security and basic well-being' (Messer, 1993: 222), entitlements that are deemed necessary to live humanely. In essence, allowing and ensuring basic human rights is considered (at least by the UN initially, and many others since) the right thing to do morally.

Natural rights in legal philosophy have a very similar meaning, namely that natural rights are 'rights (entitlements) held simply by virtue of being a person (human being)', such as, for example, the right to be free from slavery (Donnelly, 1982: 391). This is a basic explanation of natural rights, although there is disagreement as to whether natural rights exist, as some argue that such rights are simply a human construct with no intrinsic reality (for critique see Hart, 1955 and MacDonald, 1946).

If human rights, then, refer to the personal security, well-being and survival of *Homo sapiens* (as discussed above), then environmental rights refer to entitlements applied and afforded to the natural world. Therefore, whilst the concept of *natural rights* is historically aligned to debates around human needs, the term *rights of nature* is very different, and applies to the survival needs of the whole Earth community including humans, non-humans, and naturally occurring ecosystems that sustain life. As such, the term *rights of nature* refers to the idea that 'nature has legal rights and accepting these rights as part of our (human) legal systems' (Pecharroman, 2018: 1).

In just the same way that human rights have been enshrined into law in different guises around the world (such as the UK's enactment of the Human Rights Act 1998), the rights of nature have also been written into law in different respects around the world through human-made laws, albeit to a significantly lesser extent than human rights. The adoption of the rights of nature into law can be described as a form of *wild law*.

Rights of nature and wild law

In some places around the world, different aspects of nature have been afforded legal significance and standing. For instance, in New Zealand, the Whanganui River is considered to have legal personhood (Pecharroman, 2018). Similarly, the Ecuadorian constitution recognises the rights of Mother Earth or *Pacha Mama* (Espinosa, 2019), and in the period 2010–2012, Bolivia enacted two pieces of domestic legislation recognising the rights of Mother Earth (Calzadilla and Kotzé, 2018). New Zealand, Ecuador and Bolivia are three high-profile examples of humans awarding legal status and significance to the natural world through human-made law in anthropogenic legal systems. These are examples of the institutionalisation of wild laws.

However, it is important to recognise that wild laws are not just specific and concrete. They can also be seen to have a metaphorical component. Laws pertaining to the natural world are *wildly* different from all other human-made laws because they put the natural world at the forefront of law-making, rather than human wants and needs (Lampkin, 2020). The rights of nature exist in a small number of high-profile examples, as cited above. However, some scholars in the academic disciplines of environmental ethics, wild law, green criminology, and Earth jurisprudence have argued that the failure of humans to recognise and afford rights to nature on a greater scale is a reflection of powerful state–corporate relationships that exist to exploit the natural world, and that do so through entirely legal means (rather than laws existing to protect the natural world) (Lampkin and Wyatt, 2019). Thus, many laws actively allow and encourage environmental degradation and destruction, which in part is due to the absence of meaningful, domestic and international environmental laws and rights, and the failure of authorities to prosecute environmental protection laws that do exist. For instance, oil and gas companies around the world are permitted, through various domestic and international laws, to extract natural resources using methods guaranteed to create environmental harm, such as unconventional hydraulic fracturing for shale gas (Lampkin, 2018), or mountain-top removal mining to expose coal stores (Long et al., 2012).

Full discussion of the absence of wild law, the failure to institutionalise wild laws effectively, and the presence of legal systems that facilitate environmental destruction is beyond the scope of this entry. What is clear, though, is that powerful state–corporate relationships exist that both prevent the creation of wild law, and severely restrict the policing and prosecution of what wild law does exit (Stretesky et al., 2014).

Possibly as a response to the ineffectiveness of wild laws (environmental harm does still occur at great levels in Ecuador and Bolivia, for instance), some scholars have argued that wild law does not just encompass laws aiming to protect the natural world, but that it is informed by the philosophy of Earth jurisprudence (Lampkin, 2020; Lampkin and Wyatt 2022). This legal philosophy is an approach to law-making where the whole Earth community is considered and prioritised, rather than solely anthropogenic or human-centred wants and needs (as is the case in most human-made law). It is this philosophy of *Earth* jurisprudence (rather than *human* jurisprudence) that will now be considered.

Earth jurisprudence

It has been argued that nature intrinsically has rights, and that nature is inclusive of the whole Earth community. This approach is known as Earth jurisprudence, widely recognised to have been developed by Thomas Berry. Whilst Berry did not expressly use the term *Earth jurisprudence* in his seminal book *The Great Work* (1999), his ideas are widely accepted as encompassing a philosophy of Earth jurisprudence. According to Cullinan (2011: 13) Earth jurisprudence is:

> A philosophy of law and human governance that is based on the idea that humans are only one part of a wider community of beings and that the welfare of each member of that community is dependent on the welfare of the earth as a whole. From this perspective, human societies will only flourish if they regulate themselves as part of this wider earth community and do so in a way that is consistent with the fundamental laws or principles that govern how the universe functions.

There are subtle differences between the terms wild law, Earth jurisprudence, and the rights of nature. As Cullinan (2011) observes, Earth jurisprudence is a philosophy of law that places the environment (rather than humans) at the forefront. In a slightly different respect, wild laws are 'laws made by humans but constructed according to the principles of the philosophy of earth jurisprudence' (Lampkin, 2020: 30). Consequently, wild laws can be seen as the *product* of an Earth jurisprudential approach to law-making.

In a similar regard, legislation reflecting the rights of nature can be seen as forms of wild law concerned with protecting the natural world through rights akin to human rights. However, not all wild laws are concerned with rights for nature. For instance, while the rights of nature were enshrined in the Ecuadorian constitution in 2008 (an example of the rights of nature embodying wild law), the UK's Climate Change Act 2008 (which can be interpreted as a form of wild law concerned with environmental protection) set long-term limits for UK emission outputs, without enshrining in the legislation anything about the rights of nature.

Critiquing wild law and the rights of nature

The academic sub-disciplines of wild law and Earth jurisprudence can be seen as radical offshoots of the more established and human-orientated academic discipline of law. It is 'radical' because in the philosophy of Earth jurisprudence, the whole Earth community is considered as part of law-making (and not just humans and their wants and needs). Furthermore, proponents of Earth jurisprudence view it as not just an approach to law-making that should be employed in the environmental law sector, but to *all* law-making.

Bell (2003) recognised that implementing Earth jurisprudence and wild law in a global legal system concerned almost entirely with human interests would have huge and widespread implications and is therefore problematic. He suggested that there would need to be a transitionary period between human jurisprudence and Earth jurisprudence and that this would take time. Whilst there has been significant legal innovation since Berry (1999) and Bell (2003), as mentioned above (Ecuador, Bolivia, New Zealand), it is undeniable that no modern, contemporary legal system operates on the basis of Earth-centred jurisprudence. In fact, questions remain over whether Earth jurisprudence could ever properly materialise due to the difficulty of representing nature and non-human animals in a human-centred court. This means that wild law and Earth jurisprudence risk remaining 'trapped in a realm of ideas' (Schillmoller and Pelizzon, 2013: 14). These are ideas already explored by White's (2018) work on ecocentrism. He suggests that criminal law must have both anthropocentric and ecocentric dimensions, since the protagonists are human even if the victims are non-human. Therefore, the human element cannot be removed, as people are required to make laws. As many laws do in some way impact the natural world, the ecocentric dimension is always present. It is to what extent the natural world is considered which ultimately determines whether a law is 'wild' or not. Where the duty of care for the non-human world is thoughtfully considered and implemented within the legal doctrine, this would be considered a heightened application of ecocentrism (White, 2018). However, where the natural world is not fully considered or protected within the law, that law can be considered anthropocentric, or enacted without an ecocentric vision.

In terms of the rights of nature, these are also flawed in practice. Just as human rights have not stopped millions of humans from being denied those rights every day (think of slavery, torture, right to life, all occurring ubiquitously across societies and cultures over space and time), so too is nature consistently denied the right to be, exist, flourish, and thrive on a daily basis. Whilst the rights of nature may go some way to limiting or reducing environmental harm, it is unlikely to ever eradicate such harms completely. This is summed up in Bell's (2003: 75–76) explanation of the term 'human jurisprudence' which he suggests to be 'a system of laws designed to recognize the pre-eminence of the human species. Far from protecting the Earth and other species in their own right, our human jurisprudence systems have continually protected the rights of humans over and against the rights of non-humans.'

It can also be argued that wild laws and rights of nature are, in practice, usually a human response to environmental wrongdoing that has already occurred. In essence, they are a reaction to environmental harms rather than being a wholly precautionary endeavour. In the case of New Zealand's Whanganui River, for example, legal personhood came as a result of exploitation and pollution of the river (Argyrou and Hummels, 2019). Whilst this case is often cited in rights of nature literature, it is perhaps more accurately a triumph of the indigenisation of environmental laws and rights. The close cultural connection that the Māori people have to the Whanganui River was a major factor in drafting the Te Awa Tupua (Whanganui River Claims Settlement) Act 2017 which gave legal personhood to the river (Argyrou and Hummels, 2019). However, it took a 140-year legal battle and a great deal of pollution and environmental degradation before legal personhood was established.

Conclusion

The philosophy of nature having rights akin to human rights is a global social movement. This movement is gaining traction, and more wild laws and environmental rights are making their way into legislation around the world. These developments could be vitally important in terms of environmental protection and the prevention of ecological harm, based on the history and impact of social movements worldwide. For instance, the suffragette movement of the early twentieth century paved the way for subsequent women's rights and many women, particularly in the Western world, now enjoy the same rights as their male counterparts (such as the right to vote). Similarly, the gay rights movements have led to legislative changes in various legal systems around the world. For example, in 2014 the UK passed the landmark Marriage (Same Sex Couples) Act which enabled persons of the same sex to marry, rather than simply engage in a civil partnership. Perhaps then, in the not-too-distant future, the natural world will see more rights afforded to it, as a result of social movement pressure.

A limitation to wild laws so far is that they are often a reaction to environmental harm that has already occurred rather than proactive in nature. Another emerging issue is the application of the rights of nature and Earth jurisprudence in off-Earth locales. For instance, while space exploration and technical ability have increased rapidly since the beginning of the Cold War, there is virtually no environmental law pertaining to outer space. This is because extra-terrestrial spaces (such as Earth orbit, the Moon, Mars, asteroids, and meteorites) are not 'owned' by any country or jurisdiction in the same way that land has been appropriated by nations on planet Earth. The challenges of Earth jurisprudence are therefore not restricted to what happens on the planet itself. The rights of nature and wild law are generally seen to apply to 'the environment'. How this is institutionalised around the globe as well as beyond has enormous significance for the human and the non-human now and into the future.

JACK A. LAMPKIN

Further reading

Burdon, P.D. (2013) 'The Earth Community and Ecological Jurisprudence,' *Oñati Socio-Legal Series*, 3(5): 815–837.
Burdon, P.D. (2010) 'Wild Law: The Philosophy of Earth Jurisprudence,' *Alternative Law Journal*, 35(2): 62–65.
Humphreys, D. (2017) 'Rights of Pachamama: The Emergence of an Earth Jurisprudence in the Americas,' *Journal of International Relations and Development*, 20(3): 459–484.
Koons, J.E. (2012) 'At the Tipping Point: Defining an Earth Jurisprudence for Social and Ecological Justice,' *Loyola Law Review*, 58: 349–390.
Maloney, M. and Siemen, P. (2015) 'Responding to the Great Work: The Role of Earth Jurisprudence and Wild Law in the 21st Century,' *Earth Jurisprudence and Environmental Justice Journal*, 5: 6–22.
Medlock, F. and White, R. (2022) 'Ecocide, Ecocentrism and Social Obligation,' *Erasmus Law Review*, 15: 142–155.
Murray, J. (2015) 'Earth Jurisprudence, Wild Law, Emergent Law: The Emerging Field of Ecology and Law – Part 2,' *Liverpool Law Review*, 36: 105–122.
Shelton, D. (1991) 'Human Rights, Environmental Rights, and the Right to Environment,' *Stanford Journal of International Law*, 28: 103–138.
Turner, S.J. (2013) 'Factors in the Development of a Global Substantive Environmental Right,' *Oñati Socio-Legal Series*, 3(5): 893–907.
White, R. (2018) 'Green Victimology and Non-Human Victims,' *International Review of Victimology*, 24(2): 239–255.
Woods, K. (2006) 'What Does the Language of Human Rights Bring to Campaigns for Environmental Justice?' *Environmental Politics*, 15(4): 572–591.

References

Argyrou, A. and Hummels, H. (2019) 'Legal Personality and Economic Livelihood of the Whanganui River: A Call for Community

Entrepreneurship,' *Water International*, 44(6–7): 752–768.
Bell, M. (2003) 'Thomas Berry and an Earth Jurisprudence,' *The Trumpeter: Journal of Ecosophy*, 19(1): 69–96.
Berry, T. (1999) *The Great Work: Our Way into the Future*. New York: Three Rivers Press.
Calzadilla, P.V. and Kotzé, L.J. (2018) 'Living in Harmony with Nature? A Critical Appraisal of the Rights of Mother Earth in Bolivia,' *Transnational Environmental Law*, 7(3): 397–424.
Cullinan, C. (2011) A History of Wild Law. In: Burdon, P.D. (ed.), *Exploring Wild Law: The Philosophy of Earth Jurisprudence* (pp. 12–23). Mile End, Australia: Wakefield Press.
Donnelly, J. (1982) 'Human Rights as Natural Rights,' *Human Rights Quarterly*, 4: 391–405.
Espinosa, C. (2019) 'Interpretive Affinities: The Constitutionalization of Rights of Nature, Pacha Mama, in Ecuador,' *Journal of Environmental Policy & Planning*, 21(5): 608–622.
Freeman, M. (2022) *Human Rights* (4th ed.). Cambridge: Polity Press.
Hart, H.L.A. (1955) 'Are There Any Natural Rights?' *The Philosophical Review*, 64(2): 175–191.
Lampkin, J.A. (2020) *Uniting Green Criminology and Earth Jurisprudence*. Abingdon: Routledge.
Lampkin, J.A. (2018) *Will Unconventional, Horizontal, Hydraulic Fracturing for Shale Gas Production Purposes Create Environmental Harm in the United Kingdom?* (PhD Thesis, University of Lincoln, UK).
Lampkin, J.A. and Wyatt, T. (2022) Widening the Scope of 'Earth' Jurisprudence and 'Green' Criminology? Towards Preserving Extra-Terrestrial Heritage Sites on Celestial Bodies. In: Gacek, J. and Jochelson, R. (eds), *Green Criminology and the Law* (pp. 309–330). Cham: Palgrave Macmillan.
Lampkin, J.A. and Wyatt, T. (2019) 'Utilising Principles of Earth Jurisprudence to Prevent Environmental Harm: Applying a Case Study of Unconventional Hydraulic Fracturing for Shale Gas in the United Kingdom,' *Critical Criminology*, 1–16.
Long, M.A., Stretesky, P.B., Lynch, M.J. and Fenwick, E. (2012) 'Crime in the Coal Industry: Implications for Green Criminology and Treadmill of Production,' *Organization & Environment*, 25(3), 328–346.
MacDonald, M. (1946) 'Natural Rights,' *Proceedings of the Aristotelian Society*, 47(1946–1947): 225–250.
Medlock, F. and White, R. (2022) 'Ecocide, Ecocentrism and Social Obligation,' *Erasmus Law Review*, 15: 142–155.
Messer, E. (1993) 'Anthropology and Human Rights,' *Annual Review of Anthropology*, 22(1): 221–249.
Pecharroman, L.C. (2018) 'Rights of Nature: Rivers That Can Stand in Court,' *Resources*, 7(1): 1–14.
Schillmoller, A. and Pelizzon, A. (2013) 'Mapping the Terrain of Earth Jurisprudence: Landscape, Thresholds and Horizons,' *Environment and Earth Law Journal*, 3: 1–32.
Stretesky, P.B., Long, M.A. and Lynch, M.J. (2014) *The Treadmill of Crime: Political Economy and Green Criminology*. New York: Routledge.
White, R. (2024) 'Ecocentrism, Harm and Morality in Environmental Crime Proceedings,' *NK Neue Kriminalpolitik*, 36(1): 4–21.
White, R. (2018) 'Ecocentrism and Criminal Justice,' *Theoretical Criminology*, 22(3): 342–362.

12. Speciesism

Introduction

Speciesism entails more than mere individual prejudice against non-human animals based on their species classification. It is prejudice and injustice "within material institutions, discursive regimes, and embodied affects" (Weitzenfeld and Joy, 2014: 20). To explore the emergence of speciesism within criminology, this entry will do three things. The first section will encompass an exploration of the definition of speciesism, with an accompanying examination of the main arguments and areas of study. The second section will discuss the descending historical discourses that have resulted in the propagation of speciesist attitudes. Finally, the entry will discuss the recent emergence of a *non-speciesist criminology*.

Defining speciesism

Although the term "speciesism" was coined in 1970 by the English psychologist Richard Ryder, it was popularised by Peter Singer, who is often considered the father of the contemporary animal liberation movement. In his seminal work, *Animal Liberation*, Singer (1975: 6) defines speciesism as a "prejudice or attitude of bias in favour of the interests of members of one's own species and against those of members of other species". According to Singer (1995), this prejudice is analogous to other prejudices, such as racism or sexism. Just like racism or sexism, this prejudice holds no logical grounds: "we cannot claim that biological commonality entitles us to superior status over those who are not members of our species" (Singer, 2009: 572), in the same way that we cannot claim that ethnic commonality entitles us to superior status in comparison to other ethnicities (Singer, 1995). To Singer (1995), moral worth is determined by the ability to have preferences and to feel pain – it is not determined by one's ability to act rationally or to communicate verbally. Therefore, speciesism, according to Singer (1995), is a morally incoherent and inconsistent position as it justifies the exploitation of non-human animals on fallacious criteria – on a species criterion – which is demonstrably abhorrent when applied to differentiating moral worth between humans based on a group's differences and cognitive ability (Singer, 1995).

Nonetheless, this is an over-simplified definition of speciesism (Horta and Albersmeier, 2020). Within social psychology, for example, there are two primary forms of speciesism; "anthropocentric speciesism" and "pet speciesism" (Caviola and Capraro, 2020: 1080). This bifurcation suggests that not only do we privilege humans and discriminate against all non-human animals, but it also further suggests that we attribute more moral consideration to non-human animals that we classify as companions (Caviola and Capraro, 2020). Explaining this, Joy (2011) suggests that we categorise animals depending on whether we consider them as being edible or inedible, with those considered as edible being excluded from the moral circle. Those that we consider companions are awarded more ethical worth (Amiot, Lépine and Zaky, 2019). There are various other categories that determine moral worth, such as whether we consider animals as pests, predators or prey (Amiot, Lépine and Zaky, 2019). Moreover, as White (2013) has suggested, non-human animals are often categorised first by whether they are wild or domesticated, and second according to their value relative to human needs. However, space does not permit a thorough elucidation of all the various socially constructed boundaries that non-human animals are judged on. It is, however, the edible/inedible differentiation that manifests one of the largest forms of interspecies injustice that exists in the modern world – the industrialised production of non-human animal consumables (Joy, 2011).

This process of moral worth assessment is predicated on an array of socio-ideological factors and cognitive processes (Weitzenfeld and Joy, 2014). For this reason, Weitzenfeld and Joy (2014) go further in their definition by including what constitutes and reinforces speciesism. They define speciesism as "a composite of interspecies injustices within material institutions, discursive regimes, and embodied affects" (Weitzenfeld and Joy, 2014: 20). This definition suggests that speciesism is an unjustified prejudice based on species membership, as Peter Singer (1995) saw it to be. However, their definition goes further, by describing how speciesism is informed and perpetuated by certain historical discourses, political-economic ideologies, and cognitive mechanisms. It is essential, therefore, to take a holistic approach and consider how socio-cognitive mechanisms coalesce to produce and uphold speciesism

(Weitzenfeld and Joy, 2014: 20). Accordingly, this entry will elucidate the sociohistorical and cognitive ingredients that manifest speciesist attitudes. For further insights into how speciesist attitudes are perpetuated by political-economic ideologies – namely the paradigm of neoliberal capitalism – please refer to the recommended further reading at the end of this entry.

History of speciesist discourse

Speciesist myths regarding non-human animal minds have maintained considerable potency within the contemporary Western world. These myths, which have to a large extent resulted in the mistreatment, under-valuing and exploitation of non-human animals, have been embedded in Western society through the influence of several key historical discourses. They continue to lie at the heart of modern justifications for the differential treatment of species, thus highlighting their continued influence in shaping beliefs.

In Western philosophy, for instance, Aristotle's works have led to the proliferation of speciesist beliefs (Sias, 2015). Although in his view of the soul Aristotle believed there to be "considerable similarity between animals and humans", he concomitantly believed that the *telos* of non-human animals – their ultimate purpose – was to be used for human ends (Grumett, 2019: 327). This is because non-human animals lacked *logos* – the capacity for rationality (Sias, 2015). Thereafter, his view constructed a trichotomous hierarchy, with plants existing for the sake of non-human animals, and non-human animals for the sake of humans (Mesaroş, 2014; Sias, 2015). Although "it was not necessarily Aristotle's denial of animal mind [alone] that led to centuries of extreme similar positions" (Mesaroş, 2014: 192), his philosophy undeniably influenced the Christian Church's doctrine and an array of descendant scholars.

Although the Church's speciesist theology was already entrenched due to the "great divide" initiated by the book of Genesis (Merskin, 2021: 129), Aristotle's influence in the development of the "great chain of being" (Marino, 2010: 132) has been a constant source of legitimation for the differential treatment of non-human animals. For example, in his discovery of Aristotle's works, St Thomas Aquinas embroidered "the philosophers" ideas into Christianity (Lovejoy, 1936; Scott and Coester, 2015; Vieru, 2010). Through this integration, he came to three key conclusions: (1) reason determines moral worth (Scott and Coester, 2015); (2) non-human animals lack this capacity; and (3) "the imperfect are for the perfect" (Sias, 2015: 22). This meant that the Church, who canonised Aquinas in 1323 (Vieru, 2010), further developed its already anthropocentric ethic, on the view that humans can use non-human animals to their ends due to their lack of *logos* (Scott and Coester, 2015). Because of the Church's hegemony, the demarcation between (hu)man and beast became solidified within colloquial discourse and resulted in the legitimised plight of non-human animals (Merskin, 2021; Sias, 2015). Nonetheless, "Christianity alone is [not fully] responsible" (Sias, 2015: 23); thinkers within scientific disciplines were also heavily influential in the propagation of speciesism (Merskin, 2021).

For instance, René Descartes, in his philosophy of the dualistic separation between the mind and body, incorporated speciesism into "500 years of science" (Merskin, 2021: 130). In his dualism, Descartes reinforced the notion that non-human animals lacked cognitive interiors. Influenced by Christian doctrine (Singer, 1995), Descartes believed that the mind was a soul-like substance, possessed solely by humans, who could use reason and produce speech (Blackmore, 2017). Just like Aristotle and Aquinas before him (Hosford, 2010), Descartes' "reasoning criterion" (Dennett, 1993: 449) thereby classified non-human animals as "unfeeling autonoma" (Blackmore, 2017: 120) who lacked consciousness. Despite some prevailing beliefs that non-human animals are "subjective agents" (Hosford, 2010: 534), the belief of non-human animals as autonoma has always dominated and been used as a justification for their exploitation (Buller and Morris, 2003). For instance, animal experimentation increased in the aftermath of Descartes' dualistic discourse (Petetta and Ciccocioppo, 2021) and people often appeal to non-human animals' cognitive and emotional deficiencies to justify meat eating and factory farming (Krings, Dhont and Salmen, 2021). In fact, the "Cartesian mechanisation perspective" largely enabled the industrialisation of non-human animal agriculture and has thus vastly extended the plight of non-human animals (van Uhm, 2015: 575). Ergo, "Descartes's metaphysics achieved the hyper-separation of human mind from the 'mechanism' of nature" (Hawkins, 1998: 162), by broadcasting the belief that non-human animals are inert beings and thereby indifferent to instrumentalisation (Smit, 2014).

Writing in 1986, Michael Giannelli suggested that despite the Darwinian and Copernican revolutions, humans "still believed as if we were the 'Special Darlings' of the Universe" (Giannelli, 1986: 157). This was particularly true within the field of psychology, which had its origins "in Judeo-Christian culture" (Giannelli, 1986: 109), whereby humans occupy the peak of the preordained pedestal. At the time, psychology was dominated by *behaviourism*, pioneered by Skinner (1904–1990). This school of thought operated under a "black box" epistemology, believing there is "no need to speculate about the inner workings" of non-human animals (Giannelli, 1986: 113). Behaviourism can therefore be recognised as "a modern, camouflaged version of Cartesianism", whereby non-human animals are perceived to be mere "beast machines" and indifferent to instrumentalisation (Probucka, 2007: 267). Despite behaviourism falling out of fashion, its neo-Cartesian belief system still operates within contemporary laboratories, where across just 37 countries in 2015, there were 41.8 million experiments conducted using animals (Petetta and Ciccocioppo, 2021). This ideology is also still fashionable amongst the contemporary public, who seem to be largely sceptical of non-human animal consciousness (Leach et al., 2023). Therefore, behaviourism is a modern manifestation of speciesist discourse which, along with all the other discourses, has culminated in the persistence of and justifications for contemporary speciesist practices.

These historical social discourses, when taken together, have eradicated the perceived experiential capacities of non-human animals, generating an entire culture defined by speciesist beliefs. Although this is indeed the case, it is important to keep in mind that additional cognitive and political-economic factors also form critical elements in the composition of the assemblage which manifests, propagates, and legitimises speciesist beliefs and practices. As will be shown, these speciesist beliefs – although apparently inconsistent with a progressive and critical schema – are largely ingrained into the critical social sciences even where these social sciences are based ostensibly on radical and harm-based approaches (Beirne, 1999).

Speciesism within criminology

The field of criminology has had a long history of reflecting and maintaining a legalistic approach towards its scope of inquiry (Henry and Lanier, 2001). This has long delimited the field to research agendas focusing solely on criminalised harms whilst concomitantly diverting attention away from other harms, defined as "legal", that often contain far larger levels of injury (Hillyard and Tombs, 2007; 2017). The legalistic approach positioned the field within a "behavioural paradigm" (Kramer, 1985: 472); a narrow legalistic lens concerned mainly with individualistic harms and intentions, with individualistic and piecemeal responses to such issues (Hillyard and Tombs, 2017). Harm associated with corporations, by contrast, had gone unremarked and undertheorised (Hillyard and Tombs, 2017; Henry and Lanier, 2001; Przemienicki, 2017). So, too, had harms involving non-human animals.

However, the emergence of critical criminology paved the way for the advent of social harm approaches (Hillyard and Tombs, 2007; Pemberton, 2015). These harm-based orientations were to include non-speciesist considerations by the late 1990s (Sollund, 2021). This non-speciesist perspective (Beirne, 1999) was situated within green criminology, which focused on crimes and harms pertaining to the natural world and its inhabitants (Taylor and Fitzgerald, 2018; White and Heckenberg, 2014). Nonetheless, the plight of non-human animals has continued to be largely ignored even within this domain, and even the inclusion of non-human animals under the green criminology umbrella is a contested issue (Griffin and Griffin, 2021; Stretesky, Long and Lynch, 2014). Although attention has grown within this arena (Beirne, 1999; Spencer and Fitzgerald, 2015), it is marginal and primarily focuses on wild animals and the co-occurrence of animal abuse and interpersonal human violence. Studies on issues concerning non-human animals within criminology (Taylor and Fitzgerald, 2018) and in textbooks (Girgen, 2020) show that little regard is being given to the situation of non-human animals, especially with respect to those harms that emanate within and because of animal agriculture. Thus, although criminology has increased its breadth and become more critical, it is still a widely anthropocentric and speciesist field, which fails to take seriously the plight of non-human animals, particularly within the context of food production.

Advancement of non-speciesist study has nonetheless been achieved. The progression towards a non-speciesist criminology owes itself largely to the widening moral influence of writers such as Peter Singer, Tom Regan, and Gary Francione, along with the social movements that such theorists have inspired or reflected. Additionally, the cognitive behavioural sciences have also played a large role by empirically dismantling the human—animal divide by verifying that non-human animals are subjective agents (Sollund, 2021). However, the antithesis to these progressions still dominates. This is illustrated by the billions of non-human animals who are subject to reproductive injustice, mutilation, and slaughter each year, practices that are routinely justified through anthropocentric appeals that privilege human interests over the non-human (Weitzenfeld and Joy, 2014). To combat this hegemony and to alleviate the plight of non-human animals, it is imperative to decipher the causes of speciesist attitudes and then work towards utilising this knowledge to then prevent and dismantle it (Beirne, 2009). Only when non-human animals are considered to have moral importance, through the breaking down of (in)difference, can all forms of prejudice begin to be eroded (Costello and Hodson, 2014).

Discourses and dualisms

In recent decades, criminology has undergone a theoretical metamorphosis by voyaging beyond its anachronistic and anthropocentric remit of only studying harms prohibited by the state. Yet, an array of sociohistorical discourses have been highly influential in perpetuating the diminished status of non-human animals through the construction of a human/animal dichotomous dualism. Although such discourses have lost their incontestability, they still dominate commonplace justifications for animal exploitation.

Sociocultural discourses from the past and present, which are permeated through a variety of mediums, work to create a dualistic dichotomy between humans and animals, which justifies their exploitation. This is the "social matrix", underpinned by a coalition of speciesist institutions and myth makers that work to maintain the speciesist status quo (Joy, 2011). This social matrix is accompanied by an "internal matrix", that consists of cognitive mechanisms which categorise non-human animals into groups with different levels of moral worth – such as the categories of edible and inedible (Joy, 2011: 131). Moreover, the internal matrix is also comprised of mystification tactics that objectify, deindividualise, and dementalise non-human animals, which subsequently reduces their moral worth (Bastian et al., 2012).

However, while categorisation is natural, the association of moral value to classifications is mediated by culture and is thus "not hard-wired" (Harris and Fiske, 2009: 221). This can be demonstrated by a simple examination of the differences between cultures or age groups. For example, it has been shown that children are far less speciesist than adults (McGuire, Palmer and Faber, 2023), which is attributed to their lack of socialisation into speciesist customs. Insofar as this is the case, preventing speciesist practices needs to begin by challenging the learned human—animal divide. This can be accomplished to some extent by increasing empathy and humanising non-human animals, which in turn can be progressed through socialising future generation with sentiocentric norms and values (Amiot and Bastian, 2017; Costello and Hodson, 2010; 2014; Pedersen, 2004; Thomas and Beirne, 2002).

Conclusion

The development of a non-speciesist criminology continues apace with new concepts being used to describe animal killing – "theriocide" (Beirne, 2014) – and important critiques of wildlife trafficking emerging that focus on issues of animal rights, empathy, and the ontological status of non-human animals (Sollund, 2019). A critical step within the social sciences more generally is to embed into the curriculum the study of speciesism, the nature of prejudice, and consideration of the consequential externalities and harms of such belief systems (Pedersen, 2004). For criminology, practitioners, policymakers and researchers need to grapple with the complex ethical issues surrounding speciesism, taking into account diverse understandings of non-human animals as well as how historical and social context shapes contemporary relations between humans and non-human animals.

BRANDON ROCHESTER

Further reading

Caviola, L., Everett, J. A. C. and Faber, N. S. (2019) The moral standing of animals: Towards a psychology of speciesism. *Journal of Personality and Social Psychology*, 116(6), 1011–1029. https://doi.org/10.1037/pspp0000182 [accessed 9 February 2023].

Clark, B. and Wilson, T. D. (2020) The capitalist commodification of animals: A brief introduction. In B. Clark and T. D. Wilson (eds.), *The Capitalist Commodification of Animals*. Emerald Publishing, pp. 1–5.

Gunderson, R. (2011) From cattle to capital: Exchange value, animal commodification, and barbarism. *Critical Sociology*, 39(2), 259–275. https://journals.sagepub.com/doi/pdf/10.1177/0896920511421031 [accessed 30 May 2021].

Krings, V. C., Dhont, K. and Salmen, A. (2021) The moral divide between high- and low-status animals: The role of human supremacy beliefs. *Anthrozoös*, 34(6), 787–802. https://www.tandfonline.com/doi/full/10.1080/08927936.2021.1926712#:~:text=People%20endorsing%20stronger%20beliefs%20in,animals%20than%20about%20companion%20animals [accessed 15 February 2023].

Salmen, A. and Dhont, K. (2023) Animalizing women and feminizing (vegan) men: The psychological intersections of sexism, speciesism, meat, and masculinity. *Social and Personality Psychology Compass*, 17(2), 1–14. https://kar.kent.ac.uk/99276/3/Salmen%20-%20Animalizing%20women%20and%20feminizing%20vegan%20men%20-%20PPDF.pdf [accessed 20 February 2023].

Stibbe, A. (2001) Language, power and the social coconstruction of animals. *Society and Animals*, 9(2), 145–161. https://brill.com/view/journals/soan/9/2/article-p145_3.xml?language=en [accessed 28 March 2021].

Stuart, D. and Gunderson, R. (2018) Nonhuman animals as fictitious commodities: Exploitation and consequences in industrial agriculture. *Society & Animals*, 29(3), 291–310. https://philpapers.org/rec/STUNAA [accessed 3 April 2022].

White, R. (2012) Capitalism and the commodification of animals: The need for critical vegan praxis, aanimated by anarchism! In D. Nibert (ed.), *Animal Oppression and Capitalism*. ABC-CLIO, pp. 270–294.

References

Amiot, C. and Bastian, B. (2017) Solidarity with animals: Assessing a relevant dimension of social identification with animals. *PLoS ONE*, 12(1), 1–26. https://doi.org/10.1371/journal.pone.0168184 [accessed 14 February 2023].

Amiot, C., Lépine, O. and Zaky, J. (2019) Compartmentalization of animals: Toward an understanding of how we create cognitive distinctions between animals and their implications. *Analyses of Social Issues and Public Policy*, 19(1), 150–176. https://spssi.onlinelibrary.wiley.com/doi/epdf/10.1111/asap.12177 [accessed 1 December 2022].

Bastian, B., Loughnan, S., Haslam, N. and Radke, H. R. M. (2012) Don't mind meat? The denial of mind to animals used for human consumption. *Personality and Social Psychology Bulletin*, 38(2), 247–256. https://journals.sagepub.com/doi/pdf/10.1177/0146167211424291?casa_token=sXkPOQsLKW8AAAAA:FaeK_xaFwrFSi8oi_3kcm9cRaCP4jKtdmW01cMzt2Xt-iCphGLSwtZjYfynIUU4rqyEqxkMfKEmU [accessed 20 February 2023].

Beirne, P. (1999) For a nonspeciesist criminology: Animal abuse as an object of study. *Criminology*, 37 117–148. https://doi.org/10.1111/j.1745–9125.1999.tb00481.x [accessed 1 February 2023].

Beirne, P. (2009) *Confronting Animal Abuse Law, Criminology, and Human–Animal Relationships*. Rowman & Littlefield.

Beirne, P. (2014) Theriocide: Naming animal killing, *International Journal for Crime, Justice and Social Democracy*, 4(3), 50–67.

Blackmore, S. (2017) *Consciousness: A Very Short Introduction* (2nd ed.). Oxford University Press.

Buller, H. and Morris, C. (2003) Farm animal welfare: A new repertoire of nature–society relations or modernism re-embedded? *Sociologia Ruralis*, 43(3), 216–237. https://onlinelibrary.wiley.com/doi/abs/10.1111/1467-9523.00242 [accessed 5 February 2023].

Caviola, L. and Capraro, V. (2020) Liking but devaluing animals: Emotional and deliberative paths to speciesism. *Social Psychological and Personality Science*, 11(8), 1080–1088. https://journals.sagepub.com/doi/pdf/10.1177/1948550619893959?casa_token=gujFK0l0rSEAAAAA:5jVG2hRiJrkkA5-LlRfHPmOD3G15RN7wPskwEj1W_CpI0u4GaBlTpxQZk6yYWEXdv1GCoYhmwWVs [accessed 5 February 2023].

Costello, K. and Hodson, G. (2010). Exploring the roots of dehumanization: The role of animal–human similarity in promoting immigrant humanization. *Group Processes and Intergroup Relations*, 13, 3–22. https://psycnet.apa.org/

record/2010-08923-008 [accessed 13 February 2023].
Costello, K. and Hodson, G. (2014) Explaining dehumanization among children: The interspecies model of prejudice. *British Journal of Social Psychology*, 53(1), 175–197. https://bpspsychub.onlinelibrary.wiley.com/doi/10.1111/bjso.12016 [accessed 4 January 2022].
Dennett, D. C. (1993) *Consciousness Explained.* Penguin.
Giannelli, M. A. (1986) Three blind mice, see how they run: A critique of behavioral research with animals. In M.W. Fox and L. D. Mickley (eds.), *Advances in Animal Welfare Science*. The Humane Society of the United States, pp. 109–164.
Girgen, J. (2020) Neglecting nonhuman animals: A content analysis of introductory criminal justice and criminology textbooks. *Society and Animals*, 1, 1–20. https://www.semanticscholar.org/paper/Neglecting-Nonhuman-Animals%3A-A-Content-Analysis-of-Girgen/aa8765c5caabc64524d28c855a80f95583475e9d [accessed 2 February 2023].
Griffin, N. S. and Griffin, N. (2021) Beyond meat? Taking violence against non-human animals seriously as a form of social harm. In P. Davies, P. Leighton and T. Wyatt (eds.), *The Palgrave Handbook of Social Harm*. Palgrave Macmillan, pp. 281–310.
Grumett, D. (2019) Aristotle's ethics and farm animal welfare. *Journal of Agricultural and Environmental Ethics*, 32, 321–333. https://doi.org/10.1007/s10806-019-09776-1 [accessed 4 February 2023].
Harris, L. T. and Fiske, S. T. (2009) Social neuroscience evidence for dehumanised perception. *European Review of Social Psychology*, 20(1), 192–231. https://doi.org/10.1080/10463280902954988 [accessed 10 February 2023].
Hawkins, R. Z. (1998) Ecofeminism and non-humans: Continuity, difference, dualism, and domination. *Hypatia*, 13(1), 158–197. https://www.jstor.org/stable/3810611 [accessed 20 February 2022].
Henry, S. and Lanier, M. M. (2001) *What Is Crime? Controversies Over the Nature of Crime and What to Do About it*. Rowman & Littlefield.
Hillyard, P. and Tombs, S. (2007) From "crime" to social harm*? Crime, Law and Social Change*, 48(1–2), 9–25. https://link.springer.com/article/10.1007/s10611-007-9079-z [accessed 3 January 2023].
Hillyard, P. and Tombs, S. (2017) Social harm and zemiology. In A. Liebling, S. Maruna and L. McAra (eds.), *The Oxford Handbook of Criminology* (6th ed) Oxford University Press, pp. 284–305.
Horta, O. and Albersmeier, F. (2020) Defining speciesism. *Philosophy Compass*, 15(11), 1–9. https://compass.onlinelibrary.wiley.com/doi/epdf/10.1111/phc3.12708 [accessed 5 February 2023].
Hosford, D. (2010) Uneasy anthropocentrism: Cartesianism and the ethics of species differentiation in seventeenth-century France. *JAC*, 30(3–4), 515–538. https://www.jstor.org/stable/pdf/20866963.pdf?refreqid=excelsior%3A28f1ddff100fadd0de30b1fe460167d3&ab_segments=&origin=&initiator=&acceptTC=1 [accessed 3 February 2022].
Joy, M. (2011) *Why We Love Dogs, Eat Pigs, and Wear Cows: An Introduction to Carnism*. Conari Press.
Kramer, R. C. (1985) Defining the concept of crime: A humanistic perspective. *The Journal of Sociology & Social Welfare*, 12(3), 469–487. https://scholarworks.wmich.edu/jssw/vol12/iss3/4 [accessed 30 November 2022].
Krings, V. C., Dhont, K. and Salmen, A. (2021) The moral divide between high- and low-status animals: The role of human supremacy beliefs. *Anthrozoös*, 34(6), 787–802. https://www.tandfonline.com/doi/full/10.1080/08927936.2021.1926712#:~:text=People%20endorsing%20stronger%20beliefs%20in,animals%20than%20about%20companion%20animals [accessed 15 February 2023].
Leach, S., Kitchin, A. P., Sutton, R. M. and Dhont, K. (2023) Speciesism in everyday language. *British Journal of Social Psychology*, 62(1), 486–502. https://doi.org/10.1111/bjso.12561 [accessed 22 February 2023].
Lovejoy, A. (1936) *The Great Chain of Being: A Study of the History of an Idea*. Harvard University Press.
Marino, L. (2010) Sentience. In M. D. Breed and J. Moore (eds.), *Encyclopedia of Animal Behavior*. Academic Press, pp. 132–138.
McGuire, L., Palmer, S. B. and Faber, N. S. (2023) The development of speciesism: Age-related differences in the moral view of animals. *Social Psychological and Personality Science*, 14(2), 228–237. https://doi.org/10.1177/19485506221086182 [accessed 10 February 2023].
Merskin, D. (2021) Species traitor? Foundations and tensions in human/animal scholarship and advocacy. In N. Khaazal and N. Almiron (eds.), *Like an Animal: Critical Animal Studies Approaches to Borders, Displacement, and Othering*. Brill, pp. 125–160.
Mesaroș, C. (2014) Aristotle and animal mind. *Procedia – Social and Behavioral Sciences*, 163, 185–192.
Pedersen, H. (2004) Schools, speciesism, and hidden curricula: The role of critical pedagogy for humane education futures. *Journal of Futures Studies*, 8(4), 1–14. https://jfsdigital

.org/wp-content/uploads/2014/07/84-A01.pdf [accessed 8 February 2023].

Pemberton, S. (2015) *Harmful Societies: Understanding Social Harm*. Policy Press.

Petetta, F. and Ciccocioppo, R. (2021) Public perception of laboratory animal testing: Historical, philosophical, and ethical view. *Addiction Biology*, 26(6), 1–8. https://onlinelibrary.wiley.com/doi/epdf/10.1111/adb.12991 [accessed 5 February 2023].

Probucka, D. (2007) The negative impact of scientific ideology on education about the moral status of animals. *Kwartalnik Pedagogiczny*, 2(244), 261–269. https://www.ceeol.com/search/article-detail?id=561419 [accessed 5 February 2023].

Przemieniecki, C. J. (2017) Social construction of crime. In C. J. Schreck (ed.), *The Encyclopedia of Juvenile Delinquency and Justice*. John Wiley & Sons, pp. 1–4.

Scott, C. D. and Coester, Y. M. (2015) Rewriting Aquinas' animal ethics: The primacy of reason in the determination of moral status. *South African Journal of Philosophy*, 34(3), 289–303. https://www.tandfonline.com/doi/abs/10.1080/02580136.2015.1055450?casa_token=VpKanYELWzAAAAAA:dFP_JOtwgo9i_nG-YUUD-WmvvfTWGOWfuPSzK0dp562ZXf9rdgBw7IiDBas86GC2yAFu31sHw7JTKA [accessed 5 February 2023].

Sias, J. J. (2015) Ancient animal ethics: The earliest arguments for the ethical consideration of nonhuman animals. *The Downtown Review*, 2(1), 1–26. https://engagedscholarship.csuohio.edu/cgi/viewcontent.cgi?article=1021&context=tdr [accessed 31 January 2023].

Singer, P. (1975) *Animal Liberation: A New Ethics for Our Treatment of Animals*. HarperCollins.

Singer, P. (1995) *Animal Liberation* (2nd ed.). Pimlico.

Singer, P. (2009) Speciesism and moral status. *Metaphilosophy*, 40(3–4), 567–581. https://www.jstor.org/stable/pdf/24439802.pdf?casa_token=qqJJgVZUtJ4AAAAA:Hj_pGgQlooGwtjDRGJNpqWak7HJFygKG0_9-e_UnRaGhIerO2u-pqKYeyPxj6VWmtV0HFZV7v9jkYxmWYRoAsGit8gadDLShbDWHVqAok0_TNhO7jgU [accessed 1 February 2023].

Smit, H. (2014) Dualism, monism and evolutionary psychology. In H. Smit (ed.), *The Social Evolution of Human Nature*. Cambridge University Press, pp. 101–122.

Sollund, R. (2019) *The Crimes of Wildlife Trafficking: Issues of Justice, Legality and Morality*. Routledge.

Sollund, R. (2021) Green criminology: Its foundation in critical criminology and the way forward. *The Howard Journal of Crime and Justice*, 60(3), 304–322. https://doi.org/10.1111/hojo.12421. [accessed 8 February 2023].

Spencer, D. C. and Fitzgerald, A. (2015) Criminology and animality: Stupidity and the anthropological machine. *Contemporary Justice Review*, 18(4), 407–420. https://www.tandfonline.com/doi/abs/10.1080/10282580.2015.1093685?journalCode=gcjr20 [accessed 20 January 2023].

Stretesky, P., Long, M. A. and Lynch, M. J. (2014) *The Treadmill of Crime: Political Economy and Green Criminology*. Routledge.

Taylor, N. and Fitzgerald, A. (2018) Understanding animal (ab)use: Green criminological contributions, missed opportunities and a way forward. *Theoretical Criminology*, 22(3), 402–425. https://journals.sagepub.com/doi/pdf/10.1177/1362480618787173?casa_token=IygGyFNWKpkAAAAA:F0YN96SL7jM2TD3K1NeiZdUgahnYEQMHw8qs_cRdomN6iH5VR0g38KgCXOQYOxPOYEpXJR-Qi_yM [accessed 1 February 2023].

Thomas, S. C. and Beirne, P. (2002) Humane education and humanistic philosophy: Toward a new curriculum. *The Journal of Humanistic Counseling, Education and Development*, 41(2), 119–123. https://onlinelibrary.wiley.com/doi/epdf/10.1002/j.2164-490X.2002.tb00142.x?saml_referrer [accessed 11 March 2023].

van Uhm, D. (2015) Towards moral principles regarding non-human animals: A ggreen criminological perspective. In F. de Jong (ed.), *Overarching Views of Crime and Deviancy*. Eleven International, pp. 565–588.

Vieru, S. (2010) Aristotle's influence on the Natural Law Theory of St Thomas Aquinas. *The Western Australian Jurist*, 1, 115–122. https://www.murdoch.edu.au/School-of-Law/_document/WA-jurist-documents/WAJ_Vol1_2010_Simona-Vieru---Aristotle-and-Aquinas.pdf [accessed 3 February 2023].

Weitzenfeld, A. and Joy, M. (2014) An overview of anthropocentrism, humanism, and speciesism in critical animal theory. *Counterpoints*, 448, 3–27. https://www.jstor.org/stable/pdf/42982375.pdf?refreqid=excelsior%3A28a14496627bb5cae5a1c597a939a74b&ab_segments=%2Cfe-placement-accordion&origin=&initiator= [accessed 3 February 2023].

White, R. (2013) Species justice and harm to animals. In R. White (ed.), *Environmental Harm: An Eco-justice Perspective*. Policy Press, pp. 111–145.

White, R. and Heckenberg, D. (2014) *Green Criminology: An Introduction to the Study of Environmental Harm*. Routledge.

BRANDON ROCHESTER

PART II

CRIMES OF EXTRACTION

13. Illegal hunting and shooting

Introduction

Illegal hunting/shooting (and poaching) involves the illegal killing or taking of wildlife. It is a phenomenon which, amongst an array of impacts, has driven some species towards extinction, and can take many forms depending on its location and target. This entry provides a definition of illegal hunting/shooting, placing it within the wider gambit of environmental crimes, and overviews the phenomenon and those involved. The notion of hunters possessing a social licence and their overall motivations are considered, along with consideration of preventive and enforcement measures. Such criminal behaviour is oftentimes difficult to detect and enforce owing to the remoteness of where the offending frequently occurs, and thus there is a lack of both formal and informal guardianship. The entry concludes with a discussion of measures used to promote legal hunting.

Defining the issues

The terms 'illegal hunting' and 'poaching' are often used as synonyms in the extant literature, with the definition involving two key elements: (i) the killing/taking of wildlife; and (ii) the action being illegal (Duffy et al., 2016; Eliason, 2003; Treves et al., 2017). As with many environmental crimes, it is the breaking of regulations in the taking (or killing) of wildlife which constitutes the crime not the taking per se. However, there is some deviation in this general definition. For instance, von Essen et al. (2014: 632) include 'the taking of wildlife and wildlife resources' whilst Agan et al. (2021) use the wider term 'non-permitted' rather than illegal, acknowledging the grey areas involved in this activity and its governance.

Examples of illegal 'hunting' include the killing of animals without a licence and/or on property where it is prohibited. Illegal 'shooting' includes such behaviours as shooting at inappropriate targets and using incorrect ammunition. While these are often distinct behaviours or actions, illegal shooting often occurs within the context of illegal hunting insofar as the perpetrators and the places are generally the same.

Legitimate hunters (referring here to those who are licensed and obeying rules) see their pursuit as an ethical activity which requires skill, effort, time, money and preparation. They may argue that animals are respected and are hunted for the purpose of recreation and/or putting food 'on the table', an activity to be shared with friends and family. Hunting game animals is considered by hunters as a fair fight because they are hard to hunt due to their good senses. Indeed, certain hunters perceive what they do as not simply a hobby or even driven by self-sustenance but rather as one of eco-management. There exists, anecdotally, significant disdain by legal hunters for those acting illegally, because of the threat posed to their 'social licence to hunt', and thus prefer illegal actions to be referred to as 'shooting' to differentiate from regulated conduct (Delibes-Mateos et al., 2013).

There is a significant dark figure of crime when it comes to illegal hunting. These crimes take place in environments that are sparsely populated and thus often have nothing in the way of formal or informal guardianship. There also exists the notion of 'cryptic poaching', whereby illegal hunters destroy evidence of their activity in order to conceal their crimes (Santiago-Ávila et al., 2020).

Social licence to hunt

While hunting pre-dates *Homo sapiens*, its early practice was undertaken in the context of hunter-gatherer societies wherein the lifestyle and survival of humans relied on hunting and fishing animals (National Geographic, n.d.). Fast forwarding, as agricultural practices developed nearly 12,000 years ago, humans became less reliant on hunting out of necessity. However, hunting did not disappear but is practised for sport, social connection and connection to culture, sustenance and economic opportunity, among others. Access to land and resources for hunting has long been an important part of the social history of many rural communities in economic, social and cultural terms, dating back to the seventeenth century with the beginnings of enclosure in Europe.

Hunting can have significant impacts on the environment. As such, there often exists a high degree of tension which can be crudely juxtaposed as between those engaged in hunting and those opposed to it, with the former proclaiming legitimacy for their actions. Duncan et al. (2018: 318) state that a 'Social Licence to Operate (SLO) is an intangible, unwritten and non-legally binding social contract' which has been used in reference to the mining and minerals industry, farming, forest management, and more recently, animal-based industries. The essence of a social licence is that it is 'applied to a practice whose practitioners seek legitimacy due to the perception that those practices or actions cause environmental and/or social harms' (Duncan et al., 2018: 318). Access to and control of natural resources for the purposes of hunting has been a significant developing issue of recent times (Sonne et al., 2019; von Essen et al., 2014). For instance, the social licence to hunt may be in competition with political sensibilities around conservation and modern sensibilities around animal welfare. In Africa, the issues may pertain to exploitation by the wealthy at the expense and exclusion of traditional communities in which the practice of hunting may be culturally embedded (Duffy et al., 2016). Different contexts mean that hunting is problematised differently according to local developments, histories and social inequalities.

Around the globe, this has led to conflict, particularly where the interests of First Nations people are infringed. An example of this phenomenon comes from Sweden where action has been taken by the Swedish government to protect wolves (von Essen & Allen, 2017). In response to tighter regulation, hunters have claimed victimhood as a form of political resistance, arguing that their social licence to hunt wolves has been infringed upon and, subsequently, their livelihood has been threatened. The notion of being 'subjects of injustice', accompanied by a declining trust in government and regulatory authority, may be used by hunters to normalise and negate their illegal hunting of wolves, and in essence, is a reaction to perceived persecution of their lifestyles and livelihood (von Essen & Allen, 2017). Similar views exist in Australia where illegal hunting is justified by some perpetrators, particularly those in rural communities, as they see conservation rules as being politically motivated rather than being based on notions of conservation (Adams, 2014).

Ultimately, there are three competing social licences at play: (i) landowners and occupiers' rights regarding their land; (ii) the ability to exercise long-standing traditional hunting practices of rural communities; and (iii) cultural practices of First Nations communities. Such perceptions of a social licence among these groups appear to 'permit' what would otherwise be an illegal act.

Hunter motivations

There is a propensity among some of those involved in illegal hunting to deny either their involvement or acknowledge that their activity is criminal (von Essen et al., 2014). This has been looked upon with some scepticism by conservation officers, who tend to view the actions of illegal hunters as motivated by a sense of entitlement or as fulfilling a traditional right or furtherance of their social licence.

Such fulfilling of traditional rights has seen illegal hunting being classified as a 'folk crime'. As White (2016) notes, folk crimes are activities that are considered 'legitimate' by individuals or cultural insiders, according to local customs and traditions that may supersede the law. These claims can be seen as part of a 'neutralisation technique', similar to denial, where the offender attempts to justify their actions both internally and externally (Eliason, 2003). Agan et al. (2021) highlight that the folk nature of illegal hunting can be enhanced and supported by political interventions – for example, proposals to increase the permitted grounds for shooting protected animals – whilst Sonne et al. (2019) highlight the role played by wider opinion formers including the media in contributing to the discourse on the topic.

Closely associated with the folk nature of illegal hunting is the notion of defiance and furtherance of a political agenda (Agan et al., 2021; Sonne et al., 2019). In many respects, this is a reaction to an 'Other' – an outside authority imposing restriction on hunters' lifestyles with a perception of lack of procedural fairness leading to marginalisation, following a trajectory of radicalisation driving them towards a subcultural grouping of like-minded people (von Essen et al., 2014). Fear and conflict generally relate to the same concern regarding the target of the illegal hunting: that it poses a threat either to the individual directly or to their wider interests. For hunters this particularly concerns the competition which a protected species may pose for their target (such as deer, fish) whilst other hunters see a direct threat to the 'rural lifestyle' and particularly to agricultural production (such as crops) (Atkinson et al., 2008; Balmori, 2019; Person & Russell, 2008). It is also interesting, but not surprising, to note that such conflicts are more common where agricultural land and nature reserves intersect.

Types of offending

Offending varies, but reasons typically nominated for criminal conduct include a disregard for the law and consequences, doing it for fun, doing it for money, and the presence of drugs and alcohol.

Specific types of offending include hunting without a required licence; hunting prohibited species; hunting outside legal times and seasons; hunting in prohibited areas; illegal 'spotlighting' (using spotlights mounted on vehicles to shoot at night, often deer and in public spaces); animal cruelty offences (such as maiming but not killing an animal; using under-calibre firearms); trespass on private property and inappropriate use of vehicles; threats to human life through the inappropriate discharge of firearms; construction of illegal structures; not adhering to bag limits; for ducks, quail and so on using illegal methods to get birds to flight; and shooting without consent on private property (including at buildings, livestock, bee hives).

An analysis by the authors of press media articles in Victoria, Australia (unpublished research report), found an array of other complaints of illegal conduct: shooters blocking remote roads while they hunt; heavily armed hunters indiscriminately opening fire across private land after pulling their vehicles over on country roads; vandalism of property, such as damaging fences, padlocks and chains, and shooting at buildings; stealing from sheds; failing to extinguish campfires; destroying fields with their vehicles; farmers receiving death threats for standing up to the shooters after late-night experiences of gunfire; farmers losing livestock as a consequence of being shot by shooters; deer carcasses being dumped in waterways; heads being removed for trophies and carcasses left in camping grounds; and native animals, including emus and wombats, being shot.

Environmental impacts

There is scant contemporary and publicly available empirical information about the harms brought about by illegal hunting/shooting, such as damage to environments, harm to animals (native and livestock) and harm to people and property. Anecdotally, though, unauthorised access to public (such as crown land) and private (such as farms) rural property by illegal hunters/shooters can create social and economic harms to individual residents and rural communities, and to the rural sector more generally by way of bio-security threats (SSAA, 2023).

The types of harms associated with illegal hunting can to some degree be illustrated by examination of specific forms of legal hunting. For example, although much more regulated than deer or pig hunting, an environmental concern revolves around duck shooting, which can result in threatened birds being targeted, bag limits exceeded, pollution by lead shot of waterways, and associated littering. The shooting of feral horses, donkeys, camels and other 'feral' animals in Australia also raises issues over collateral damage due to rotting carcases, potential spread of disease, lead in the soil and forests, and potentially wrong identification of species.

Prevention and/or regulation of illegal hunting

Illegal hunting is driven by different motivations and there is no one single type of offender. From a communal perspective, some illegal hunting might be considered an unjust continuation of exclusionary colonial policies. Other sorts of hunting are linked to traditional ways of using natural resources that go back hundreds and possibly thousands of years. Criminological analyses of poaching and illegal killing of animals point to significant variation in contexts, cultures and causes when it comes to illegal hunting (Nurse, 2013; White, 2013).

Owing to the folk nature of some types of illegal hunting, greater enforcement is not necessarily seen as the most appropriate response, and it can sometimes be counterproductive. For instance, conservation officers report that some people who contact 'report a poacher' hotlines used variously in the United States were more concerned with 'thinning out the competition', particularly at their favourite fishing spot, than actually reporting illegal activity (Vazquez, 2018).

There are generally three alternatives to enforcement: (i) economic incentives; (ii) education; and (iii) changing culture/norms.

A response to the effects of carnivores on agricultural production has been to pay compensation for any livestock taken. A programme in Sweden pays farmers for a verified presence of breeding wolves rather than paying compensation: not only does this negate the conflict but also co-opts farmers into the wider conservation effort (Carter et al., 2017).

Education of hunters is an important aspect of prevention, particularly regarding hunting regulations and their need. This is seen as reducing not only the denial but also some of the folk crime aspects related to lack of legitimacy (Balmori, 2019; Boertje et al., 2019). Education can be aimed at achieving cultural change by 'nudging' hunting culture towards greater acceptance of conservation and a repudiation of those who wilfully breach. However, such cultural change can be difficult as illegal hunting is generally a learnt behaviour from a person's inner circle of close family and friends. To overcome these issues, the hunting and wider rural community need to be engaged as key stakeholders in the development of any regulatory regime rather than having it imposed (Carter et al., 2017; Eliason, 2004).

In practice, a problem-oriented approach to crime prevention is necessary owing to the variety of targets and methods involved in illegal hunting. This is imperative as such offending is related to immediate social contexts such as, for instance, exotic consumer products for a new and growing middle class in China, traditional hunting practices in Greece, community and commercial collusion in the taking of lobster in Canadian waters, and supplementing income in Bolivia (Sutton et al., 2024).

One approach is 'market reduction' which, whilst traditionally applied to burglary, may also be applied to illegal hunting (Schneider, 2012). The intention is to disrupt the market by identifying specific features which are open to intervention. This includes, for example, identifying the precise wildlife targeted; the characteristics of those who hunt, transport and purchase; the routine patterns of those involved, including hunters, handlers of illegal hunting by-products and consumers; and capable guardians, including conservationists, rangers, police and communities. Other variables that warrant consideration include mating seasons, country of origin, and methods of processing – all of which shape the illegal activity and, subsequently, the problem-oriented approach to prevention.

Enforcement strategies

Successful operations to prevent the illegal hunting of wildlife are intelligence-led, primarily based upon tip-offs from the local community (Vazquez, 2018). Given the rural context in which hunting takes place, local knowledge is vital as it enables the early warning signs of illegal hunting to be detected and communicated to authorities. The empowering of local communities and the harnessing of their knowledge is also an important way of engaging local people with conservation measures and developing local 'social licence' for such measures, including with Indigenous peoples. For instance, in Haulien County, Taiwan, a three-way engagement strategy has been adopted with input sought from Indigenous leaders, conservation groups and scholars (Forestry Bureau, 2019). In essence, this is the application of community policing where the values of a local community are prioritised (Drew & Prenzler, 2015).

Such enforcement operations have also involved law enforcement agencies working with local communities, building connections with local partners (including hunters), and addressing their needs relating to illegal hunting. In some cases, anti-hunting and conservation groups are actively involved in gathering evidence of illegal behaviour. This has led to successful prosecutions, particularly in the United Kingdom, where police are seen by some as reluctant to act (Egret, 2021). For example, such groups have deployed technology such as drones to monitor the activities of hunters (Lallanilla, 2013; Mandal, 2020).

Electronic surveillance is used as an intelligence gathering tool to inform preventive strategies, notably at main entry points to conservation areas (Dougherty, 2022). This is used as both a preventive tool when its presence and monitoring are known, and as a post-event forensic tool by investigators. There have also been some innovative uses of aerial surveillance (helicopters and drones) as well as the use of 'passive integrated transponder' (PIT) tags and DNA sampling to mark wildlife in problem areas. For example, Ceres Tag (a smart animal ear-tag), which can monitor animal location and health, has been deployed on animals such as rhinoceroses to combat poaching and aid in conservation efforts.

The use of DNA sampling has been particularly useful in developing a family tree to identify the source of harvested endangered species to determine whether it had been lawfully obtained (Cullingham, 2020). Traditional situational crime prevention techniques can be adapted by functionaries in regulating hunting to achieve significantly beneficial outcomes. However, this is dependent upon a well-trained and resourced law enforcement capacity (U.S. Fish & Wildlife Service, n.d.; World Wildlife Fund, n.d.). For laws to be effective there needs to be an associated strong enforcement capacity and such laws needed to be fit for purpose, with an effective balance between penalties, regulation and enforcement powers (*Poaching: Illegal Hunting*, n.d.).

Although not a panacea, penalties need to be set at a level where they deter illegal activity by removing its economic basis: fines should not be at a level where they can be viewed as 'just a cost of doing business'. Laws should also be structured to eliminate possible loopholes. For instance, the RSPCA (UK) in its review of anti-fox hunting laws in the United Kingdom has recommended the inclusion of an offence of 'recklessly hunting' to overcome the need to prove that an illegal hunter was purposefully hunting (RSPCA (UK), n.d.).

Inter-jurisdictional cooperation is an important aspect of combatting illegal hunting. This has been through supra-national bodies such as the European Union and the secretariat of treaties. In the United States, an interesting intra-national collaboration between states, known as the Interstate Wildlife Violator Compact (IWVC), sees mutual recognition of sanctions across the network so that violators of hunting laws cannot move their operations from one state to another (Animal Legal Defence Fund, 2022; Tompkins, 2010). Ultimately, if a hunter has had their hunting privileges suspended, or they have not paid an infringement notice, their hunting privileges are automatically suspended in their home state and they cannot obtain a hunting-related licence in any other state which is a member of IWVC. The success of this programme can be seen in the way ranch owners in Texas wanted 'professional' licences exempt from the compact when that state proposed to join.

Promotion of legal hunting

Hunting in many countries is seen as part of the agrarian 'folk nature' of national identity, and thus is actively promoted. This can result in conflict with the environmental focus of conservation, which is looked upon with scepticism by hunting-supportive groups. For instance, over 20 states within the United States have a hunter access programme (Newhouse, 2016). The aim of these programmes is to increase accessible land, not only for hunting but also for other outdoor activities such as angling, viewing, and bushwalking. The origin of these programmes was to facilitate public access to traditionally 'landlocked' public forests that had been designated as safe havens of conservation (Swearingen, 2015). However, the access programs have since morphed into more extensive facilitation of public access and engagement in a wider range of activities in these formerly protected spaces. At the centre of much of this, is hunting.

The hunting-related programmes range from posting the contact details of landowners receptive to giving permission to access (Alberta in Canada) (My Wild Alberta, 2021) through to walk-in access which may require either signing in with the landowner (Montana and Oklahoma) or general access (Kansas and Oklahoma) (Oklahoma Department of Wildlife Conservation, n.d.). With these arrangements, the state-based game hunting regulator acquires a limited lease from the landowner: in return for that lease, the landowner is generally paid a fee and indemnified for non-malicious acts. The payment will vary depending on the amount and quality of habitat and the activities permitted: these range between a few dollars to USD20 per acre (Oklahoma Department of Wildlife Conservation, n.d.). Some programmes, such as the Controlled Hunter Access Program in South Dakota, pay per hunter given access (South Dakota Game Fish & Parks, n.d.). These payments are generally funded as a proportion of hunting licences and federal grants funded through excise on hunting equipment, which can be seen as a conflict with the protection of native and protected species. The landowner can also receive other benefits such as a free 'sportsman' licence (Montana), assistance from state biologists for conservation plans (Washington State), through to patrols by game wardens (Pennsylvania).

MATTHEW BOX, KYLE MULROONEY AND ALISTAIR HARKNESS

Depending on the programme, the landowner can retain control over the numbers and type of access given. The benefit for the hunter is not only gaining consistent free access to private land but also a direct benefit from the fees which they pay. Furthermore, such benefits can build acceptance of wider conservation measures. Nevertheless, the promotion of increased hunting activities can have an overall negative impact on the environment, not only threatening the targets and 'accidental kills' of the hunting activities but also secondary activities such as erosion, littering and fire starting.

Conclusion

Illegal hunting is often hidden, but nevertheless harmful. For instance, we can consider harms to farmers upon whose land such offending might occur, as well as other individuals and species who might be threatened. In many instances, illegal hunting is a class of perceived customary rights against regulations imposed by central government leading it to being regarded as an agrarian folk crime. Increasingly, though, an array of crime prevention and law enforcement measures are being deployed locally throughout many jurisdictions to disrupt and deter these behaviours as well as build community support for conservation and legitimate hunting practices.

MATTHEW BOX, KYLE MULROONEY AND ALISTAIR HARKNESS

Further reading

Duncan, E., Graham, R. & McManus, P. (2018). 'No one has even seen... smelt... or sensed a social licence': Animal geographies and social licence to operate. *Geoforum*, *96*, 318–327. https://doi.org/10.1016/j.geoforum.2018.08.020

Pohja-Mykrä, M. (2016). Illegal hunting as rural defiance. In J.F. Donnermeyer (Ed.). *The Routledge international handbook of rural criminology* (pp. 329–338). Routledge.

von Essen, E. & Nurse, A. (2016). Illegal hunting special issue. *Crime, Law and Social Change*, *67*, 377–382. https://doi.org/10.1007/s10611-016-9676-9

von Essen, E. Hansen, H.P., Nordström Källström, H., Peterson, M.N. & Peterson, T.R. (2014). Deconstructing the poaching phenomenon: A review of typologies for understanding illegal hunting. *British Journal of Criminology*, *54*(4), 632–651. https://doi.org/10.1093/bjc/azuO22

White, R. (2016). Re-conceptualising folk crime in rural contexts. In J.F. Donnermeyer (Ed.). *The Routledge international handbook of rural criminology* (pp. 299–308). Routledge.

References

Adams, M. (2014). Caught in the net of life and time. *Meanjin*, *73*(2), 74–81.

Agan, S.W., Treves, A. & Willey, L.L. (2021). Estimating poaching risk for the critically endangered wild red wolf (*Canis rufus*). *PLoS One*, *16*(5), e0244261. https://doi.org/10.1371/journal.pone.0244261

Animal Legal Defence Fund. (2022). *Preventing convicted wildlife poachers from hunting in Massachusetts (Massachusetts)*. https://aldf.org/project/preventing-convicted-wildlife-poachers-from-hunting-in-massachusetts-massachusetts/.

Atkinson, S., Demaster, D.P. & Calkins, D.G. (2008). Anthropogenic causes of the western Steller sea lion *Eumetopias jubatus* population decline and their threat to recover. *Mammal Review*, *38*(1), 1–18.

Balmori, A. (2019). Endangered bird mortality by gunshots: Still a current problem. *Biodiversity and Conservation*, *28*(10), 2555–2564. https://doi.org/10.1007/s10531–019–01778–9.

Boertje, R.D., Frye, G.G. & Young, D.D. (2019). Lifetime sex-specific moose mortality during an intentional population reduction. *The Journal of Wildlife Management*, *84*(1), 6–19. https://doi.org/10.1002/jwmg.21782

Carter, N.H., Lopez-Bao, J.V., Bruskotter, J.T., Gore, M., Chapron, G., Johnson, A., Epstein, Y., Shrestha, M., Frank, J., Ohrens, O. & Treves, A. (2017). A conceptual framework for understanding illegal killing of large carnivores. *Ambio*, *46*(3), 251–264. https://doi.org/10.1007/s13280–016–0852-z.

Cullingham, C. (2020). *How genetic testing is helping scientists save animals from disease and illegal hunting*. https://theconversation.com/how-genetic-testing-is-helping-scientists-save-animals-from-disease-and-illegal-hunting-129676

Delibes-Mateos, M., Diaz-Fernández, S., Ferreras, P., Viñuela, J. & Arroyo, B. (2013). The role of economic and social factors driving predator control in small-game estates in central Spain. *Ecology and Society*, *18*(2). https://doi.org/10.5751/es-05367–180228

Dougherty, C. (2022). *7 ways to deal with deer-hunting neighbors*. https://www.deeranddeerhunting.com/content/articles/7-ways-to-deal-with-deer-hunting-neighbors

Drew, J. & Prenzler, T. (2015). *Contemporary police practice*. Oxford University Press.

Duffy, R., St John, F.A., Buscher, B. & Brockington, D. (2016). Toward a new understanding of the links between poverty and illegal wildlife hunting. *Conservation Biology*, *30*(1), 14–22. https://doi.org/10.1111/cobi.12622

Duncan, E., Graham, R. & McManus, P. (2018). 'No one has even seen... smelt... or sensed a social licence': Animal geographies and social licence to operate. *Geoforum*, *96*, 318–327. https://doi.org/10.1016/j.geoforum.2018.08.020

Egret, E. (2021). *The 'ongoing blatant illegal hunting' of stags is still happening now*. https://www.thecanary.co/opinion/2021/11/30/the-ongoing-blatant-illegal-hunting-of-stags-is-still-happening-now/.

Eliason, S.L. (2003). Illegal hunting and angling: The neutralization of wildlife law violations. *Society & Animals*, *11*(3), 225–243.

Eliason, S.L. (2004). Accounts of wildlife law violators: Motivations and rationalizations. *Human Dimensions of Wildlife*, *9*(2), 119–131. https://doi.org/10.1080/10871200490441775

Forestry Bureau. (2019). *Preventing wildlife from accidentally falling into traps: Government will strengthen the check for illegal hunting gear and seek effective management*. https://www.forest.gov.tw/EN/forest-news/0064114

Lallanilla, M. (2013). *Drones keep watchful eye on illegal hunting*. https://www.livescience.com/28122-drones-illegal-hunting.html

Mandal, P. (2020). *Prevention and detection of offences under the Wildlife Protection Act*. https://blog.ipleaders.in/prevention-detection-offences-wildlife-protection-act/

My Wild Alberta. (2021). *Land access*. https://mywildalberta.ca/hunting/land-access.aspx

National Geographic. (n.d.). *Hunter-gatherer culture*. https://education.nationalgeographic.org/resource/hunter-gatherer-culture/

Newhouse, R. (2016). *How to ask permission to hunt private land*. https://www.onxmaps.com/hunt/blog/how-to-ask-landowner-permission-the-right-way

Nurse, A. (2013). Sport and trophy hunting. In A. Nurse (Ed.) *Animal harm: Perspectives on why people harm and kill animals* (pp. 155–168). Routledge.

Oklahoma Department of Wildlife Conservation. (n.d.). *Oklahoma Land Access Program*. https://www.wildlifedepartment.com/sites/default/files/OLAP_Flyer_052021.pdf

Person, D. & Russell, A. (2008). Correlates of mortality in an exploited wolf population. *Journal of Wildlife Management*, *72*(7), 1540–1549. https://doi.org/10.2193/2007–520.

Poaching: Illegal Hunting. (n.d.). https://www.teenink.com/hot_topics/environment/article/4416/Poaching-Illegal-Hunting/

RSPCA (UK). (n.d.). *Fox hunting*. https://www.rspca.org.uk/getinvolved/campaign/hunting

Santiago-Ávila, F.J., Chappell, R.J. & Treves, A. (2020). Liberalizing the killing of endangered wolves was associated with more disappearances of collared individuals in Wisconsin, USA. *Scientific Reports*, *10*(1), 13881. https://doi.org/10.1038/s41598-020-70837-x

Schneider, J. (2012) *Sold into extinction: The global trade in endangered species*. Praeger.

Sonne, C., Hansen, H.P., Alstrup, A.K.O., Olsen, K., Jensen, T.H., Haugaard, L. & Sunde, P. (2019). Discussion: Illegal kills of protected wolves call for public reasoning. *Science of the Total Environment*, *665*, 617–619. https://doi.org/10.1016/j.scitotenv.2019.01.432

South Dakota Game Fish & Parks. (n.d.). *Hunting areas*. https://gfp.sd.gov/hunting-areas/

SSAA (Sporting Shooters Association of Australia). (2023, 9 August). *Protecting the lands we hunt – practising biosecurity hygiene*. Sport Shooters Association of Australia. Retrieved from https://www.ssaa.org.au/?ss_news=protecting-the-lands-we-hunt-practising-biosecurity-hygiene

Sutton, A., Cherney, A., White, A. & Clancey, G. (2024). *Crime prevention: Principles, perspectives and practices* (3rd edn). Cambridge University Press.

Swearingen, M. (2015). *Private property blocks access to public lands*. https://www.hcn.org/issues/47.2/this-land-is-their-land

Tompkins, S. (2010). *Stricter rules help prevent illegal hunting*. https://www.chron.com/sports/article/Tompkins-Stricter-rules-help-prevent-illegal-1603391.php

Treves, A., Artelle, K.A., Darimont, C.T. & Parsons, D.R. (2017). Mismeasured mortality: Correcting estimates of wolf poaching in the United States. *Journal of Mammalogy*, *98*(5), 1256–1264. https://doi.org/10.1093/jmammal/gyx052

U.S. Fish & Wildlife Service. (n.d.). *Law enforcement*. https://www.fws.gov/refuge/audubon/what-we-do/law-enforcement

Vazquez, T. (2018). *It's illegal to hunt alligators outside of hunting season without a permit – but it happens*. https://www.floridatoday.com/story/news/2018/06/22/illegally-hunted-gators-can-largely-go-unseen-experts-say/718236002/

von Essen, E. & Allen, M. (2017). The implications of victimhood identity: The case of 'persecution' of Swedish hunters. *International Journal for Crime, Justice and Social Democracy*, *6*(2), 78–94. https://doi.org/10.5204/ijcjsd.v6i2.353

von Essen, E., Hansen, H.P., Nordström Källström, H., Peterson, M.N. & Peterson, T.R. (2014). Deconstructing the poaching phenomenon: A review of typologies for understanding illegal hunting. *British Journal of Criminology*, *54*(4), 632–651. https://doi.org/10.1093/bjc/azu022

White, R. (2013). *Global environmental harm: Criminological perspectives*. Routledge.

White, R. (2016). Re-conceptualising folk crime in rural contexts. In J.F. Donnermeyer (Ed.).

The Routledge international handbook of rural criminology (pp. 299–308). Routledge.
World Wildlife Fund. (n.d.). *What is poaching: The illegal wildlife trade explained.* https://www.worldwildlife.org/threats/illegal-wildlife-trade

14. Illegal mining

Introduction

Precious metals and minerals have fascinated humankind since the beginning of time. From the fabulous search for El Dorado in Latin America in the sixteenth century, to the gold rush in the United States in the nineteenth century, the symbolic value of minerals and metals has influenced the world across cultures and civilisations.

In recent decades, illegal mining has become an attractive business for organised criminal groups, armed groups and mining companies due to the high value and low risks (Le Billon, 2012; van Uhm, 2023). From Latin American drug cartels to African militias, the rising global scarcity of natural resources has made illegal mining and trafficking in mined commodities an attractive criminal enterprise (Zabyelina & van Uhm, 2020a). Illegal mining and trade in minerals and metals has become one of the most lucrative environmental crimes and is estimated to generate USD12–48 billion in profits every year (UNEP & Interpol, 2016).

Illegal mining is often associated with other criminal activities such as forced labour, human trafficking, drugs trafficking, money laundering, arms trafficking and corruption (GFI, 2017; Global Initiative against Transnational Organized Crime, 2016; UNEP & Interpol, 2016). Moreover, illegal mining has devastating effects on the environment, ecosystems and non-human communities due to deforestation, land degradation, loss of biodiversity and pollution (Cortés-McPherson, 2020; White, 2020). This entry will discuss illegal and informal mining, the actors involved, and the environmental and social harms of the mining activities.

Illegal and informal mining

There is no universally accepted definition of illegal mining, but the term may refer to mining activity that is: (a) carried out by a person, natural or legal, or a group of people without complying with the requirements of applicable laws or administrative regulations that govern these activities; or (b) carried out in areas where the exercise of such activities is prohibited or using prohibited equipment, devices or chemicals (UNODC, 2023a). Several economic crimes can be linked to illegal mining, including forging licences, permits and inspections, tax evasion, fraud, as well as corruption. Illegal mining can occur on the surface and underground, in closed mines, abandoned mines or operating mines, and can take place in protected areas, in natural parks, at historical sites and on Indigenous lands (Zabyelina & van Uhm, 2020b).

There is considerable variation between legal and illegal mining. For example, artisanal and small-scale mining refers to formal or informal mining operations with predominantly simplified forms of exploration, extraction, processing and transportation. It denotes a broad range of mining-related activities performed by individuals, groups and cooperatives operating without formal oversight but not necessarily in contravention of existing legislation (Lahiri-Dutt, 2018; UNICRI, 2016). Several forms of artisanal and small-scale mining are synonymous with informal mining: it is illegal from the standpoint of formal law but legitimate in the eyes of informal miners and is sometimes seen as a transitional phase between illegal and legal mining (Bernet Kempers, 2020).

Large-scale mining refers to mining that is mainly conducted by mining companies and requires large investment and a high level of mechanisation. The structure of the global mining industry is heavily skewed towards a handful of major players that control most of the world's active mining production sites (Rodríguez-Novoa & Holley, 2023). Large-scale mining companies often mine at large sites and usually stay until the mineral or metal is completely excavated (UNODC, 2023a). Illegal mining can occur in the informal and small-scale artisanal mining as well as large-scale mining settings, in particular when organised crime or armed groups take control of the mining businesses, which illustrates the complex relationship between legal, illegal and informal mining (Wagner & Hunter, 2020).

Actors

The high profits associated with illegal mining make the industry attractive to offenders ranging from small-scale miners and organised crime groups to armed groups and state-facilitated corporate crime groups (Zabyelina & van Uhm, 2020a). Increasingly, organised crime groups and armed groups that are involved in illegal mining are associated with other criminal activities such as forced labour, human trafficking, trafficking in firearms, drugs trafficking, money laundering and corruption (UNODC, 2023a). For example, when gold prices increased fourfold between 2002 and 2012 (Seccatore et al., 2014; Tubb, 2015), crime groups began to play a bigger role in illegal gold mining, seeing it as a new lucrative business to run (van Uhm, 2020; Wagner & Hunter, 2020). They started to control access to mining sites, determining who could work, where, and when. In their territorial strongholds, they invested in machinery and imported their own people to work in the mines. Examples of the involvement of organised crime include the Gulf Clan cartel (Clan del Golfo) in gold mining in Colombia (van Uhm, 2020, 2023), the drugs cartel Knights Templar (Los Caballeros Templarios) in iron ore in Mexico (Carbajal Glass, 2020), Ukrainian organised crime involved in coal (Zabyelina & Markovska, 2019), and sand mining by Italian organised crime (Rege & Lavorgna, 2017).

In order to adapt to changing socio-economic and ecological circumstances, organised crime has diversified into illegal mining (Albanese, 2020; van Uhm, 2023). For example, in Colombia, Mexico and Peru, the transition from coca cultivation to illegal gold mining has been reported, influenced by the relatively stable and high price of gold (UNODC, 2023b; Wagner & Hunter, 2020). Organised crime groups usually launder illegal gold with the help of local officials, or well-known international gold companies – a classic example of the legal–illegal interface (Tubb, 2015). For example, transport of minerals and metals by helicopters can be arranged by legitimate companies that collaborate with organised crime members. One of the advantages created by forming alliances between organised crime groups and legitimate enterprises is that, in contrast to drugs like cocaine, minerals and metals are not by definition illegal, which makes it difficult for law enforcement officials to distinguish legal from illegal (UNODC, 2023a; Zabyelina & van Uhm, 2020a).

Furthermore, illegal mining can escalate and sustain violent conflicts, with the sale of illegally extracted minerals and metals being an important source of revenue for militias, warlords and other armed groups. The nexus between the illegal mining and armed conflict has been a concern for the international community for several decades. The extraction and sale of so-called 'blood diamonds' and, more recently, 'blood gold' is known to have sponsored non-state armed groups in different parts of the world, most devastatingly in African nations (Brisman et al., 2016; Le Billon, 2012; van Uhm et al., 2022). For example, the term 'conflict mineral' was used to describe the financing of violent rebel forces in Angola and Sierra Leone in the late 1990s. Consequently, the Kimberley Process Certification Scheme (KPCS) was established with the goal to prevent 'conflict diamonds' from entering the mainstream rough diamond market. Although the KPCS has had an impact on reducing the opportunity for illegal trade in conflict diamonds, the problem of conflict minerals is still prevalent (Siegel, 2009, 2020). For example, in the eastern edge of the Congo basin, in the Democratic Republic of the Congo (DRC), illegal mining of critical minerals, including cobalt, tantalum, tin, and tungsten, is linked to militias, such as the FDLR, M23, and Mai-Mai, fuelling the ongoing conflict (van Uhm, 2024).

Environmental and social harms

The global destruction of pristine rainforests, mass extinction of species, and pollution of the ecosphere by mining activities present a grave threat to humankind (Brisman & South, 2020; Lynch & Stretesky, 2014; White, 2011). The natural resources linked to the land are often an important reason to substantiate actions of dispossession, forced displacement and land grabbing driven by the desire to control land and expand power (Goyes et al., 2021; van Uhm & Grigore, 2021). The problem of illegal mining is most damaging in politically unstable, economically depressed regions, where organised crime groups, armed groups and corporations contribute to environmentally unsustainable mining practices (Bedford et al., 2020). The global economic and ecological asymmetries that influence the plundering of metals and minerals in the Global South, driven by the demand from the Global North, have tremendous social and environmental consequences, of which the most notable are large-scale land acquisitions, displacement of (Indigenous) communities, and extensive destruction of the natural environment (Bernet Kempers, 2020; Espin, 2020; Ferring & Hausermann, 2019; White, 2020).

From an eco-justice perspective, environmental destruction brought by organised crime groups, corporations and armed groups results in tremendous consequences for the environment. For instance, the heavy machinery and toxic substances, such as mercury and cyanide, used to extract the gold affect the natural environments and their ecosystem functions, by polluting the ground and water and destroying the rainforests, which are essential to the animals and plants as well as Indigenous lives and cultures (Banchirigah, 2008; White, 2020). Beyond its negative environmental impact, the explosive growth of illegal mining has stimulated other crimes. In many locations around the world, the diminishing supply and increasing demand for rare metals and minerals, combined with the quest for new sources of illicit revenue by criminal groups, has been strongly linked to trafficking in persons and other gross human rights abuses (Cortés-McPherson, 2020; Hilson, 2010). It is also closely associated with child labour, severe threats to workers' health and safety, and sex trafficking (Calys-Tagoe et al., 2017). Sexual exploitation and illegal mining are often intertwined, mainly because of the demand for sex in male-populated mining camps and settlements. For example, several Peruvian anti-trafficking groups reported on the presence of over 400 bars in Madre de Dios where child sexual exploitation takes place, with girls working as many as 13 hours a day (Cortés-McPherson, 2020). The mining industry also relies on children working in terrible conditions (Hilson, 2010).

Illegal mining as ecocide

Large-scale environmental destruction brought by organised crime groups, armed groups and corporations is akin to the crime of ecocide – the extensive damage to, destruction or loss of ecosystem(s) of a given territory to such an extent that peaceful enjoyment by the inhabitants of that territory is severely diminished (Higgins et al., 2013). Since many mining operations result in both human and environmental rights violations and the damage to the natural environmental takes decades to recover, this illustrates how forms of illegal mining could be considered as ecocidal acts (van Uhm, 2022). However, many such environmentally harmful activities are not criminalised (yet), even though the harm is overarching. The economic interests of powerful actors, whether states, corporations or landowners, have long hampered the effective criminalisation of environmental harms by illegal mining. For example, governments may work closely with the industry to preserve and protect the social and economic structures underlying the illegal mining (Zabyelina & van Uhm, 2020a). Despite the transnational and intergenerational character of illegal mining activities that are seriously harmful to the environment – including large-scale pollution, deforestation and defaunation – such activities have only recently been considered to be criminal or at least seriously harmful.

Such exploitation is generally strongly rooted in anthropocentric and materialistic worldviews, a 'precept of reason' that normalises over-exploitation, driven by the consumer society with few standards and much temptation (Bauman, 2001). In particular, the rampant economic growth of the Global North ensures harm to the natural environment, especially in the Global South (Goyes, 2019; van Uhm, 2023). Therefore, there is a substantial need for a more ecocentric approach to streamline the regulatory and enforcement chain in the policy cycle. By maintaining the natural balance and the integrity of non-human entities, humans are socially and ethically responsible for respecting the value of ecosystems and their living creatures (Halsey & White, 1998). The protection of the environment is not only about a specific nature-related interest, but also about the systemic preservation of the commons of nature, which are essential for the life conditions of humans and flora and fauna. By rejecting the dominant anthropocentric perspective within law and policymaking and acknowledging the dialectical relationship between humans and nature, ecocide may function as an ecocentric crime, the wrongfulness of which cannot be excused on the basis of any perceived socio-economic benefits (van Uhm & Ryngaert, 2023).

The criminalisation of illegal mining, however, should not deter officials from engaging in constructive dialogue with informal miners; otherwise, these miners will seek justice by embracing alternative forms of governance, such as that offered by organised crime groups (Bernet Kempers, 2020). It is common for state officials to treat informal miners as trespassers or even outright criminals whereas, conversely, informal miners often see the State's monopoly over natural resources or its granting of exclusive mining rights to large private businesses as depriving them of access to their land and thus their livelihood (Zabyelina and van Uhm, 2020a).

Conclusion

Illegal mining has become a crime of concern for the international community because of the involvement of organised crime groups, armed groups and corporate crime groups and the serious environmental harms associated with it. The demand for minerals and metals used in the transition to green energy has been forecast to increase. Due to the blurred line between illegal, informal and legal mining, it is increasingly associated with criminal organisations, armed groups and corporate crime groups as well as a source of livelihood for artisanal and small-scale miners. Moreover, illegal mining of minerals and metals is often accompanied by serious human rights abuses and other serious crimes, including forced labour, human trafficking, trafficking in firearms, drugs trafficking, money laundering and corruption. The lives of local communities – human and non-human – are thereby devastated and diminished. This negatively impacts peace, stability, security, development, governance, the rule of law, the economy and the environment locally and globally.

DAAN VAN UHM

Further reading

Brisman, A., South, N., & White, R. (eds) (2016). *Environmental Crime and Social Conflict: Contemporary and Emerging Issues*. Routledge.

Le Billon, P. (2012). *Wars of Plunder: Conflicts, Profits and the Politics of Resources*. Columbia University Press.

Siegel, D. (2009). *The Mazzel Ritual: Culture, Customs and Crime in the Diamond Trade*. Springer.

van Uhm, D. P. (2023). *Organized Environmental Crime: Black Markets in Gold, Wildlife, and Timber*. Bloomsbury.

Zabyelina, Y., & van Uhm, D. P. (eds) (2020). *Illegal Mining: Organized Crime, Corruption, and Ecocide in a Resource-Scarce World*. Palgrave Macmillan.

References

Albanese, J. S. (2020). Why Organized Crime Seeks New Criminal Markets. In Y. Zabyelina & D. van Uhm (eds), *Illegal Mining* (pp. 31–42). Springer. https://doi.org/10.1007/978–3-030–46327–4_2.

Banchirigah, S. M. (2008). Challenges with Eradicating Illegal Mining in Ghana: A Perspective from the Grassroots. *Resources Policy*, 33(1), 29–38.

Bauman, Z. (2001). Excess: An Obituary. *Parallax*, 7(1), 85–91.

Bedford, L., McGillivray, L., & Walters, R. (2020). Ecologically Unequal Exchange, Transnational Mining, and Resistance: A Political Ecology Contribution to Green Criminology. *Critical Criminology*, 28(3), 481–499. https://doi.org/10.1007/s10612–019–09464–6.

Bernet Kempers, E. (2020). Between Informality and Organized Crime: Criminalization of Small-Scale Mining in the Peruvian Rainforest. In Y. Zabyelina & D. van Uhm (eds), *Illegal Mining* (pp. 273–298). Springer. https://doi.org/10.1007/978-3-030–46327–4_10.

Brisman, A., & South, N. (2020). *Routledge International Handbook of Green Criminology*. Routledge.

Brisman, A., South, N., & White, R. (eds) (2016). *Environmental Crime and Social Conflict* Routledge. https://doi.org/10.4324/9781315580012

Calys-Tagoe, B. N. L., Clarke, E., Robins, T., & Basu, N. (2017). A Comparison of Licensed and Un-Licensed Artisanal and Small-Scale Gold Miners (ASGM) in Terms of Socio-Demographics, Work Profiles, and Injury Rates. *BMC Public Health*, 17(1), 862. https://doi.org/10.1186/s12889–017–4876–5.

Carbajal Glass, F. (2020). Where the Metal Meets the Flesh: Organized Crime, Violence, and the Illicit Iron Ore Economy in Mexico's Michoacán State. In Y. Zabyelina & D. van Uhm (eds), *Illegal Mining* (pp. 147–183). Springer. https://doi.org/10.1007/978–3-030–46327–4_6.

Cortés-McPherson, D. (2020). Digging into the Mining Subculture: The Dynamics of Trafficking in Persons in the Artisanal and Small-Scale Gold Mining of Peru's Madre de Dios. In Y. Zabyelina & D. van Uhm (eds), *Illegal Mining* (pp. 359–386). Springer. https://doi.org/10.1007/978-3-030–46327–4_13.

Espin, J. (2020). The Prevention of Green Crimes in Artisanal and Small-Scale Gold Mining in Peru: Translating Laws into Practice. In Y. Zabyelina & D. van Uhm (eds), *Illegal Mining* (pp. 469–496). Springer. https://doi.org/10.1007/978-3-030–46327–4_17.

Ferring, D., & Hausermann, H. (2019). The Political Ecology of Landscape Change, Malaria, and Cumulative Vulnerability in Central Ghana's Gold Mining Country. *Annals of the American Association of Geographers*,

109(4), 1074–1091. https://doi.org/10.1080/24694452.2018.1535885
GFI. (2017). *Transnational Crime and the Developing World*.
Global Initiative against Transnational Organized Crime. (2016). *Organized Crime and Illegally Mined Gold in Latin America*.
Goyes, D. R. (2019). *Southern Green Criminology: A Science to End Ecological Discrimination*. Emerald Publishing. https://doi.org/10.1108/9781787692299
Goyes, D. R., South, N., Abaibira, M. A., Baicué, P., Cuchimba, A., & Ñeñetofe, D. T. R. (2021). Genocide and Ecocide in Four Colombian Indigenous Communities: The Erosion of a Way of Life and Memory. *The British Journal of Criminology*, 61(4), 965–984. https://doi.org/10.1093/bjc/azaa109
Halsey, M., & White, R. (1998). Crime, Ecophilosophy and Environmental Harm. *Theoretical Criminology*, 2(3), 345–371. https://doi.org/10.1177/1362480698002003003
Higgins, P., Short, D., & South, N. (2013). Protecting the Planet: A Proposal for a Law of Ecocide. *Crime, Law and Social Change*, 59(3), 251–266. https://doi.org/10.1007/s10611-013-9413-6
Hilson, G. (2010). Child Labour in African Artisanal Mining Communities: Experiences from Northern Ghana. *Development and Change*, 41(3), 445–473. https://doi.org/10.1111/j.1467-7660.2010.01646.x.
Lahiri-Dutt, K. (2018). Reframing the Debate on Informal Mining. In K. Lahiri-Dutt (ed.), *Between the Plough and the Pick: Informal, Artisanal and Small-scale Mining in the Contemporary World* (pp. 1–28). ANU Press. https://doi.org/10.22459/BPP.03.2018.01.
Le Billon, P. (2012). *Wars of Plunder: Conflicts, Profits and the Politics of Resources*. Columbia University Press.
Lynch, M. J., & Stretesky, P. B. (2014). *Exploring Green Criminology: Toward a Green Criminological Revolution*. Ashgate.
Rege, A., & Lavorgna, A. (2017). Organization, Operations, and Success of Environmental Organized Crime in Italy and India: A Comparative Analysis. *European Journal of Criminology*, 14(2), 160–182. https://doi.org/10.1177/1477370816649627
Rodríguez-Novoa, F., & Holley, E. (2023). Coexistence Between Large-scale Mining (LSM) and Artisanal and Small-Scale Mining (ASM) in Perú and Colombia. *Resources Policy*, 80, 103162. https://doi.org/10.1016/j.resourpol.2022.103162.
Seccatore, J., Veiga, M., Origliasso, C., Marin, T., & De Tomi, G. (2014). An Estimation of the Artisanal Small-scale Production of Gold in the World. *Science of The Total Environment*, 496, 662–667. https://doi.org/10.1016/j.scitotenv.2014.05.003
Siegel, D. (2009). *The Mazzel Ritual: Culture, Customs and Crime in the Diamond Trade*. Springer.
Siegel, D. (2020). Diamond Mining, Organized Crime, and Corruption. In Y. Zabyelina & D. van Uhm (eds), *Illegal Mining* (pp. 185–203). Springer. https://doi.org/10.1007/978-3-030-46327-4_7.
Tubb, D. (2015). Muddy Decisions: Gold in the Chocó, Colombia. *The Extractive Industries and Society*, 2(4), 722–733. https://doi.org/10.1016/j.exis.2015.08.008
UNEP & Interpol. (2016). *The Rise of Environmental Crime: A Growing Threat to Natural Resources Peace, Development and Security*.
UNICRI. (2016). *Strengthening the Security and Integrity of the Precious Metals Supply Chain*.
UNODC. (2023a). *Responding to Illegal Mining and Trafficking in Metals and Minerals*.
UNODC. (2023b). *World Drug Report 2023*.
van Uhm, D. P. (2020). The Diversification of Organized Crime into Gold Mining: Domination, Crime Convergence, and Ecocide in Darién, Colombia. In Y. Zabyelina & D. van Uhm (eds), *Illegal Mining: Organized Crime, Corruption, and Ecocide in a Resource-Scarce World* (pp. 105–146). Palgrave Macmillan. https://doi.org/10.1007/978-3-030-46327-4_5.
van Uhm, D. P. (2022). Atrocity Crimes and Ecocide: Interrelations between Armed Conflict, Violence, and Harm to the Environment. In B. Holá, H. N. Nzitatira, & M. Weerdesteijn (eds), *The Oxford Handbook of Atrocity Crimes* (pp. 511–534). Oxford University Press. https://doi.org/10.1093/oxfordhb/9780190915629.013.22
van Uhm, D. P. (2023). *Organized Environmental Crime: Black Markets in Gold, Wildlife, and Timber*. Bloomsbury.
van Uhm, D.P. (2024). Transnational environmental crime. In S.L. Smith & I. Sahramäki (eds) *Research Handbook on Environmental Crimes and Criminal Enforcement*. Edward Elgar Publishing.
van Uhm, D. P., & Grigore, A. G. (2021). Indigenous People, Organized Crime and Natural Resources: Borders, Incentives and Relations. *Critical Criminology*, 29(3), 487–503. https://doi.org/10.1007/s10612-021-09585-x
van Uhm, D. P., & Ryngaert, C. M. J. (2023). Criminalising ecocide. In M. Luchtman, F. de Jong, F. Kristen, K. Ligeti, J. Lindeman, S. Tosza, R. Widdershoven & D. Zaitch (eds), *Of Swords and Shields: Due Process and Crime Control in Times of Globalization – Liber amicorum prof. dr. J.A.E. Vervaele*. Eleven 2023.
van Uhm, D. P., Tjoonk, M. M., & Bakole, E. Y. (2022). Organized Forest Crimes: Charcoal and Timber Trade in the Democratic Republic of

the Congo. In Y. Zabyelina & K. L. Thachuk (eds), *The Private Sector and Organized Crime* (pp. 149–162). Routledge.

Wagner, L., & Hunter, M. (2020). Links Between Artisanal and Small-Scale Gold Mining and Organized Crime in Latin America and Africa. In Y. Zabyelina & D. van Uhm (eds), *Illegal Mining* (pp. 77–104). Springer. https://doi.org/10.1007/978-3-030-46327-4_4.

White, R. (2011). *Transnational Environmental Crime: Toward an Eco-global Criminology*. Willan.

White, R. (2020). Eco-Justice and Destructive Mining in Australia: Lessons from the New South Wales Land and Environmental Court. In Y. Zabyelina & D. van Uhm (eds), *Illegal Mining* (pp. 529–558). Springer. https://doi.org/10.1007/978-3-030-46327-4_19.

Zabyelina, Y., & Markovska, A. (2019). Ukraine: Organised Crime, Politics and Frozen Conflicts. In F. Allum & S. Gilmour (eds), *Handbook of Organised Crime and Politics* (pp. 105–118). Edward Elgar Publishing. https://doi.org/10.4337/9781786434579.00016.

Zabyelina, Y., & van Uhm, D. P. (eds) (2020a). *Illegal Mining: Organized Crime, Corruption, and Ecocide in a Resource-Scarce World*. Palgrave Macmillan. https://doi.org/10.1007/978-3-030-46327-4.

Zabyelina, Y., & van Uhm, D. P. (2020b). The New Eldorado: Organized Crime, Informal Mining, and the Global Scarcity of Metals and Minerals. In Y. Zabyelina & D. van Uhm (eds), *Illegal Mining: Organized Crime, Corruption, and Ecocide in a Resource-Scarce World* (pp. 3–30). Palgrave Macmillan. https://doi.org/10.1007/978-3-030-46327-4_1.

15. Illegal, unreported and unregulated fishing

Introduction

Illegal, unreported, and unregulated (IUU) fishing is a transnational environmental crime that has a global scope. IUU fishing is one of the most severe environmental crimes worldwide, with close to 90 per cent of fisheries fully exploited or overexploited. IUU fishing is carried out by several intertwined legal and illegal actors. Among the perpetrators engaging in this practice are established organised crime groups, legal commercial fishers, and corrupt public officials, all driven by the high economic incentives and small disincentives attached to this crime. Moreover, through the use of illegal gear, predatory fishing techniques increasing by-catch, and the depletion of fish stocks, this practice harms humans, non-human animals, and environments alike. This entry presents the concept of IUU fishing and provides an overview of the main aspects surrounding this issue.

Illegal, unreported, and unregulated fishing is the concept used to capture a diverse range of illicit and quasi-licit fishing activities (FAO n.d.; Liddick 2014). Even though the use of the term IUU fishing has been criticised for undermining small-scale fisheries (see Song et al. 2020) or for its flaws as a legal concept (see de Coning 2016; Rosello 2017), it is widely accepted to refer to the crimes of the fishing sector.

- Illegal fishing refers to the fishing activity in contravention of the laws of the fishery, either under the jurisdiction of a coastal State or the regulations of regional fisheries management organisations (RFMOs) – for example, it can include fishing without a licence or in violation of the licence (Liddick 2014; FAO n.d.).
- Unreported fishing refers to fishing that is unreported or misreported to the national authority or the RFMO (Liddick 2014; FAO n.d.).
- Unregulated fishing refers to fishing conducted by vessels without nationality or flying a flag of a State not party to the regional organisation governing this particular fishing region or species (Liddick 2014; European Commission 2021).

IUU fishing is estimated to amass losses between US$10–23 billion annually (Agnew et al. 2009; European Commission 2021; Pew Charitable Trusts 2017). According to the Intergovernmental Science-Policy Platform on Biodiversity and Ecosystem Services (IPBES) (2019), in 2011, IUU fishing represented up to one-third of the world's reported catch; and it is estimated that more than 1,800 pounds of wild-caught fish are lost to IUU fishing every second (see Pew Charitable Trusts 2017). IUU fishing affects all types and dimensions of fisheries and occurs in high seas and continental waters globally (FAO n.d.; IPBES 2019). It involves a variety of actors, including organised crime groups, legal commercial fishing companies, and corrupt officials (Liddick 2014) and entails a vast range of harm to humans, non-human animals, and environments alike. With almost 90 per cent of the world's fisheries fully exploited or overexploited, IUU fishing is one of the most serious environmental crimes globally (Liddick 2014; Marteache et al. 2021).

The global scale of IUU fishing

It is widely agreed that IUU fishing is global in scope. According to Marteache et al. (2021), almost all fishing waters globally are affected by IUU fishing. However, it does not affect all regions to the same extent. As the authors explain, highly biodiverse areas with poor governance and corruption are more affected by IUU fishing (see Marteache et al. 2021). For example, an area especially affected by this crime is the East Central Atlantic, most notably in West African states (Agnew et al. 2009). Also, on the Pacific Russian coast, in Kamchatka, IUU fishing is so embedded that it generates an 'economy within an economy' that employs tens of thousands of illicit workers (Dronova and Spiridonow 2008: 33); and the Indonesian archipelago is also a hotspot for IUU fishing (Liddick 2014).

Nevertheless, IUU fishing is also framed as a transnational crime (Liddick 2014; de Coning 2016). As Liddick (2014) argues, the globalisation process facilitates and enables IUU fishing. For instance, most of the illegal fishing perpetrated in the South African Development Community (SADC) region is carried out by distant water fishing Nations (DWFNs) like Spain, China, Taiwan, or Russia (Liddick 2014). Moreover, a significant problem embedded in the globalisation process contributing to IUU fishing is the exploitation of flags of convenience and ports of convenience.

On the one hand, the flags of convenience system is a legal practice related to fishing vessel registration where the various actors engaging in IUU fishing exploit the asymmetries among countries to fish under the flag that is more convenient to their illicit activity (Liddick 2014). In this vein, according to the United Nations Office on Drugs and Crime (UNODC) (2011: 134), flag States, or Flags of Convenience, 'are targeted by corporate entities and unscrupulous fishing operators because they are amongst others unlikely to investigate and prosecute criminal activities'. Thus, some vessels engage in flag-hopping several times a year to avoid surveillance, and corrupt governments of flag States gain millions of dollars selling their flags to foreign vessels (UNODC 2011).

On the other hand, the existence of ports of convenience also facilitates IUU fishing. Ports of convenience are those with few or no standards or procedures in place to guarantee that only fish that has been legally caught is landed or transhipped (Palma et al. 2010). Thus, the uneven application of port controls also facilitates IUU fishing. In this case, IUU fishing vessels can simply move from port to port and target those with loose regulations. The so-called ports of convenience provide an essential service to IUU fishing vessels, supplying fuel and allowing the landing or shipping of illegally caught fish (UNODC 2011). Liddick (2014) and Petrossian et al. (2015), highlight, among others, the case of Las Palmas de Gran Canaria in Spain as an example of a port of convenience. According to the authors, the main port of entry for fish from West Africa into Europe is Las Palmas de Gran Canaria. From there, fish can be transported anywhere in the European Union without further verification of their legality or place of capture, making it simple to launder illegally caught fish into the market.

Actors involved in IUU fishing

A wide range of perpetrators engage in IUU fishing. First, IUU fishing is a crime perpetrated, among others, by legal fishers and private commercial enterprises (see Liddick 2014; UNODC 2020). For example, the UNODC (2020) describes how legal fishers might under-report their fishing quota to divert the unreported fishing towards the black market, and Liddick (2014: 294) explains that Japanese and Russian IUU salmon fishers record their catch of 'lucrative sockeye, chinook, and coho salmon as less valuable pink and chum salmon'. Liddick (2014) also highlights how commercial vessels from the EU and the Middle East, taking advantage of the lack of governance, overfish tuna, lobster, and shark in Somali waters, and how vessels from China, Russia, and Japan similarly exploit Angola's waters. Overall, IUU fishing is often perpetrated by legitimate companies willing to decimate fish stock and local communities for economic gain (Liddick 2014).

Transnational criminal organisations are also involved in IUU fishing (see UNODC 2011; Liddick 2014; Martínez and Ibáñez-Alonso 2021). As Wyatt (2013) describes, organised crime groups intervene in the trafficking of wildlife, from poaching to smuggling, when the profit in the black market is high, which happens, for example, with eels (see UNODC 2020). Hence, as reported by the UNODC (2020), there is evidence suggesting that to traffic European eels, organised crime groups have developed sophisticated trafficking networks to poach and smuggle the eels from Europe to Asia. Also, Martínez and Ibáñez-Alonso (2021) highlight the involvement of Mexican organised crime groups in totoaba maw poaching and smuggling, and Warchol and Harrington (2016) expose the involvement of organised criminal groups in South Africa's illegal abalone trade.

The great profits related to some targeted IUU fishing species provide the basis for the involvement of corrupt public officials in facilitating illegal and unsustainable fishing practices. For example, van Uhm and Siegel (2016) and Musing et al. (2019) explain how poachers are often protected by the police. In this vein, van Uhm and Siegel (2016) explain how, in 1996, a fishing boat was intercepted by coastguards in Dagestan while transferring poached sturgeon to trucks. When the coastguard tried to stop the activity, corrupt water police opened fire and the trucks got away. To sum up, in IUU fishing legal and illegal actors are intertwined, with considerable movement across the upper and underworld driven by significant economic gain and minimal disincentives.

Harms associated with IUU fishing

The harms associated with fishing are not limited to IUU fishing (White 2008; 2013). As White (2008: 241) observes, 'fishing – both legal and illegal – is associated with a wide range of potentially harmful activity'. For example, aquaculture, a practice associated with legal fishing, causes harm. While acknowledging that there are harms associated with legal fishing, the focus here is how IUU fishing harms humans, non-human species, and environments.

Traditionally, fishing-related harms have been explored from an anthropocentric perspective where the emphasis is on harms to humans. In the context of IUU fishing, these harms pertain to economic, social, and environmental factors (Stefanus and Vervaele 2021). For instance, developing coastal countries are disproportionately affected by IUU fishing (Petrossian 2015). Thus, already vulnerable local communities that depend upon nearby species and ecosystems for their livelihood are being severely impacted (see Wyatt 2013). This is a consequence of the combination of legal but harmful overconsumption and illegal fishing. As mentioned, 33 per cent of marine fish stocks are overfished, 60 per cent are maximally sustainably fished, and only 7 per cent are underfished, threatening food security globally (see Liddick 2014).

A harms approach, based on notions of eco-justice, also considers non-human species and ecosystems as victims of IUU fishing in addition to humans (White 2013; Wyatt 2013). In this vein, as IPBES (2019) reports, fishing has had the most impact on biodiversity in marine systems that include target species, by-catch species, and vulnerable habitats. As described by Marteache et al. (2021), IUU fishing targets large predatory species, like tuna, which not only impacts the populations of the species but also ecosystem dynamics. Similarly, the overfishing of small species, like anchovies, has been linked to population shifts of bottlenose dolphins in the Mediterranean Sea (Petrossian and Marteache 2018). Moreover, illegal fishing vessels frequently use destructive fishing techniques like bottom trawling, blast fishing, and dredging that severely harm vital aspects of marine ecosystems such as coral reefs or seagrass beds (FAO n.d.). Thus, IUU fishing harms ecosystem health and biodiversity due to a wide range of impactful activities.

Furthermore, IUU fishing harms the individual fish that are being fished. Whether fish feel pain or not has been an ongoing debate for the last few decades (Braithwaite 2010), with some authors denying that fish can feel pain (see Key 2016), while others argue the opposite (see Braithwaite 2010). IUU fishing harms the individuals that have been caught and are victims of this trade and traffic. As Sollund (2019) claims, individual non-human animals receive little protection; instead, their value is only reflected in terms of species endangerment. However, as Wyatt et al. (2021) argue, trading wildlife, either legally or illegally, also threatens the welfare of the traded animals. According to White (2008; 2013), species linked to economic activity, such as fish species, tend to be disregarded as victims and their welfare overlooked. Similarly, Hutchinson et al. (2022) claim that fish receive less attention than other species considered to be more charismatic, such as megafauna like rhinoceros and tigers. These aspects, being economically valuable and being less charismatic than other species, make exploitation and disregard of rights and welfare more likely (see White 2013; Hutchinson et al. 2022). This raises important ethical issues about the nature of speciesism and the dynamics of the nature–human relationship more generally.

Conclusion

Overall, IUU fishing is global in scope and constitutes a transnational environmental crime. As discussed in this entry, the actors engaging in this crime take advantage of the globalisation process by exploiting the asymmetries between the state flags and the port controls, choosing those that are more convenient for carrying out their nefarious activities. They also use illegal gear and predatory techniques. All of this is driven by the potential for economic gain. In this process, humans, non-human animals, and the environment suffer considerable harms with long-lasting effects and consequences.

MONICA PONS HERNANDEZ

MONICA PONS HERNANDEZ

Further reading

EUROPOL (2022) *Environmental Crime in the Age of Climate Change*. Available at: https://www.europol.europa.eu/publications-events/publications/environmental-crime-in-age-of-climate-change-2022-threat-assessment (accessed: 29 June 2022).

Helyar, S. J., Lloyd, H. A. D., Bruyn, M., Leake, J., Bennett, N., and Carvalho, G. R. (2014) 'Fish product mislabeling: failings of traceability in the production chain and implications for illegal, unreported, and unregulated (IUU) fishing', *PLoS ONE*, 9(6), e98691.

Le Gallic, B. and Cox, A. (2006) 'An economic analysis of illegal, unreported, and unregulated (IUU) fishing: key drivers and possible solutions', *Marine Policy*, 30, 689–695.

Lee, J. (2019) 'Subsidies for illegal activities? – Reframing IUU fishing from the law enforcement perspective', *Journal of International Economic Law*, 22, 417–438.

Leroy, A., Galletti, F., and Chaboud, C. (2016) 'The EU restrictive trade measures against IUU fishing', *Marine Policy*, 64, 82–90.

Marteache, N., Viollaz, J., and Petrossian, G. A. (2015) 'Factors influencing the choice of a safe haven for offloading illegally caught fish: a comparative analysis of developed and developing economies', *Crime Science*, 4(32), 1–13.

Martinez, I. A. and Martinez, E. R. (2018) 'Trafficking of totoaba maw', in I. Arroyo-Quiroz and T. Wyatt (eds.) *Green Crime in Mexico: A Collection of Case Studies*. Palgrave Macmillan, pp. 149–170.

Petrossian, G. A. (2015) 'Preventing illegal, unreported and unregulated (IUU) fishing: a situational approach', *Biological Conservation*, 189, 39–48.

Petrossian, G. A. (2019) *The Last Fish Swimming: The Global Crime of Illegal Fishing*. Bloomsbury Publishing.

Petrossian, G. A. and Clarke, R. V. (2014) 'Explaining and controlling illegal commercial fishing: an application of the CRAVED theft model', *The British Journal of Criminology*, 54(1), 73–90.

Soyer, B., Leloudas, G., and Miller, D. (2018) 'Tackling IUU fishing: developing a holistic legal response', *Transnational Environmental Law*, 7(1), 139–163.

UNODC (2016) *Caviar: The Seafood Industry*. Available at: https://www.unodc.org/documents/data-and-analysis/wildlife/WLC16_Chapter_9.pdf (accessed: 20 June 2022).

Wyatt, T., Friedman, K., and Hutchinson, A. (2021) 'Are fish wild?', *Liverpool Law Review*, 42, 485–492.

References

Agnew, D. J., Pearce, J., Pramod, G., Peatman, T., Watson, R., Beddington, J. R., and Pitcher, T. J. (2009) 'Estimating the worldwide extent of illegal fishing', *PLoS ONE*, 4(2), e4570.

Braithwaite, V. A. (2010) *Do Fish Feel Pain?* Oxford University Press.

de Coning, E. (2016) 'Fisheries crime', in L. Elliott and W. H. Schaedla (eds.) *Handbook of Transnational Environmental Crime*. Edward Elgar Publishing, pp. 146–167.

Dronova, N. A. and Spiridonow, V. A. (2008) *Illegal, Unreported, and Unregulated Pacific Salmon Fishing in Kamchatka*. Available at: https://portals.iucn.org/library/sites/library/files/documents/Traf-109.pdf (accessed: 18 June 2022).

European Commission (2021) *Factsheet: Tackling Illegal, Unreported and Unregulated (IUU) Fishing*. Available at: https://ec.europa.eu/oceans-and-fisheries/fisheries/rules/illegal-fishing_en (accessed: 6 June 2022).

FAO (n.d.) *Illegal, Unreported and Unregulated (IUU) Fishing: What Is IUU Fishing?* Available at: https://www.fao.org/iuu-fishing/background/what-is-iuu-fishing/en/ (accessed: 30 May 2022).

Hutchinson, A., Stephens-Griffin, N., and Wyatt, T. (2022) 'Speciesism and the wildlife trade: who gets listed, downlisted and uplisted in CITES?', *International Journal for Crime, Justice and Social Democracy*, 11(2), 191–209.

IPBES (2019) *The Global Assessment Report on Biodiversity and Ecosystem Services: Summary for Policymakers*. Available at: https://ipbes.net/system/files/2021-06/2020%20IPBES%20GLOBAL%20REPORT%28FIRST%20PART%29_V3_SINGLE.pdf (accessed: 31 May 2022).

Key, B. (2016) 'Why fish do not feel pain', *Animal Sentience*, 3(1). doi:10.51291/2377-7478.1011.

Liddick, D. (2014) 'The dimensions of a transnational crime problem: the case of IUU fishing', *Trends in Organised Crime*, 17, 290–312.

Marteache, N., Sosnowski, M. C., and Petrossian, G. A. (2021) 'A review of responses to IUU fishing around the world through the lens of situational crime prevention', in J. Blaustein, K. Fitz-Gibbon, N. W. Pino, and R. White (eds.) *The Emerald Handbook of Crime, Justice and Sustainable Development*. Emerald Publishing Limited, pp. 485–512.

Martínez, I. A. and Ibáñez-Alonso, A. (2021) 'Mexican organized crime and the illegal trade in totoaba maw', *Trends in Organized Crime*, 24, 526–546.

Musing, L., Harris, L., Williams, A., Parry-Jones, R., van Uhm, D., and Wyatt, T. (2019) *Corruption and Wildlife Crime: A Focus on Caviar Trade*. TRAFFIC, WWF, U4, ACRC, Utrecht University, and Northumbria University report.

Palma, M. A., Tsamenyi, M., and Edeson, W. (2010) *Promoting Sustainable Fisheries: The International Legal and Policy Framework to*

Combat Illegal, Unreported and Unregulated Fishing. Brill.

Petrossian, G. A. (2015) 'Preventing illegal, unreported and unregulated (IUU) fishing: a situational approach', *Biological Conservation*, 189, 39–48.

Petrossian, G. A. and Marteache, N. (2018) 'Environmental criminological perspectives on illegal, unreported and unregulated fishing', in W. Moreto (ed.) *Wildlife Crime: From Theory to Practice*. Princeton University Press, pp. 38–61.

Petrossian, G. A., Marteache, N., and Viollaz, J. (2015) 'Where do "undocumented" fish land? An empirical assessment of port characteristics for IUU fishing', *European Journal on Criminal Policy and Research*, 21, 337–351.

Pew Charitable Trusts (2017) *How to End Illegal Fishing: From Coastal Waters to the High Seas, Criminals Are Robbing the Oceans and Hurting Economies*. Available at: https://www.pewtrusts.org/en/research-and-analysis/issue-briefs/2017/12/how-to-end-illegal-fishing (accessed: 17 June 2022).

Rosello, M. (2017) 'Cooperation and unregulated fishing: interactions between customary international law, and the European Union IUU fishing regulation', *Marine Policy*, 84, 306–312.

Sollund, R. (2019) 'Wildlife management, species injustice and ecocide in the Anthropocene', *Critical Criminology*. doi:10.1007/s10612-019-09469-1.

Song, A. M., Scholtens, J., Barclay, K., Bush, S. R., Fabinyi, M., Adhuri, D. S., and Haughton, M. (2020) 'Collateral damage? Small-scale fisheries in the global fight against IUU fishing', *Fish and Fisheries*, 21, 831–843.

Stefanus, A. A. and Vervaele, J. A. E. (2021) 'Fishy business: regulatory and enforcement challenges of transnational organised IUU fishing crimes', *Trends in Organised Crime*, 24, 581–604.

UNODC (2011) *Transnational Organized Crime in the Fishing Industry*. Available at: https://www.unodc.org/documents/human-trafficking/Issue_Paper_-_TOC_in_the_Fishing_Industry.pdf (accessed: 20 June 2022).

UNODC (2020) *European Glass Eels*. Available at: https://www.unodc.org/documents/data-and-analysis/wildlife/2020/WWLC20_Chapter_7_Eels.pdf (accessed: 9 August 2020).

van Uhm, D. and Siegel, D. (2016) 'The illegal trade in black caviar', *Trends in Organized Crime*, 19, 67–87.

Warchol, G. and Harrington, M. (2016) 'Exploring the dynamics of South Africa's illegal abalone trade via routine activities theory', *Trends in Organised Crime*, 19, 21–41.

White, R. (2008) *Crimes Against Nature: Environmental Criminology and Ecological Justice*. Willan Publishing.

White, R. (2013) *Environmental Harm: An Eco-justice Perspective*. Policy Press.

Wyatt, T. (2013) *Wildlife Trafficking: A Deconstruction of the Crime, the Victims, and the Offenders*. Palgrave Macmillan.

Wyatt, T., Maher, J., Allen, D., Clarke, N., and Rook, D. (2021) 'The welfare of wildlife: an interdisciplinary analysis of harm in the legal and illegal wildlife trades and possible ways forward', *Crime, Law and Social Change*. doi:10.1007/s10611-021-09984-9

MONICA PONS HERNANDEZ

16. Poaching

Introduction

Often referred to as the illegal shooting or capture of game, fish or plants, and the trafficking of rare and iconic wildlife, poaching is a component of wildlife trafficking (i.e., illegal trade in wildlife) and is evolving every day. From the extant literature on wildlife crime, poaching is generally viewed as the illegal practice of entering another's property to hunt or steal game without permission (Kahler and Gore, 2012, Harrison et al., 2015). In fact, not all wildlife trade is illegal: many species of wild plants and animals are caught and harvested and then sold legitimately as food, pets, ornamental plants, tourist ornaments and 'folk medicine' – traditional Chinese medicine (TCM), for example. However, when the wildlife trade is illegal and unsustainable, it threatens some species' long-term viability, pushing them to the brink of extinction.

Illegal wildlife poaching has grown into an international problem, threatening the planet's ecological balance and ecotourism. Despite the flurry of conservation efforts such as debt-for-nature swaps (DNS), debt-for-climate swaps and the creation of conservation areas, numerous animals continue to be at risk due to a glaring lack of capacity and sufficient resources to protect them from poachers.

Types of poaching

There are two types of poaching: subsistence and commercial. Subsistence poaching is practised by poor households, whereas commercial poaching is practised by wealthy people working in collaboration with local communities (Ntuli and Muchapondwa, 2017). The former is mostly conducted when wildlife is occupying buffer zones and communal lands, while the latter is usually done for sport or commercial profit, enhancing an ever-growing black market.

Subsistence poaching is entrenched in a long tapestry of cultural activities and is often passed on from generation to generation (Hübschle, 2017; Wyatt et al., 2020). This type of poaching also stems from human–wildlife conflicts wherein animals are poached in an effort to circumvent crop damage (e.g., trampling of crops by elephant herds). Interestingly, larger communities experience more subsistence poaching and, oftentimes, poaching is not generally viewed as an offence because it involves 'less valuable' species such as impalas, kudus, water bucks, inyalas, rabbits, birds, etc. In Mozambique and Zimbabwe, for instance, some park authorities and police condone such activities, turning a 'blind eye' as evidenced by either insignificant penalties or lack of punishment for subsistence poaching or repeat offenders (Ntuli et al., 2021).

Hübschle (2017) reveals that commercial poaching in select African countries, on the other hand, is an act of social defiance and symbolic protest at local management practices, as communities try to supplement household income and nutrition or, because of cultural or traditional beliefs, continue to harvest wildlife even if it is no longer legal to do so. These social dynamics mean that simple definitions of poaching tend to be informed by ethnocentrism and shaped by colonial histories. For instance, Duffy and Humphreys (2016) contend that colonial authorities in various parts of the world would often outlaw the techniques used by communities to meet their subsistence needs. While European sport hunters were portrayed as conservationists, Indigenous hunting methods were portrayed as cruel. Human–wildlife conflict and poaching, then, can be viewed as retaliatory behaviour against colonial legacies because some communities have historically been denied access to wildlife, prompting scholars like Mavhunga (2014) to propose the decriminalisation of poaching. The author argues that the criminalisation of poaching disproportionately impacts African hunting and that wildlife conservation regimes should be leveraging hunters (and their knowledge) as allies in the march towards sustainability in wildlife conservation. Following this line of argument, links between poverty and poaching must be highlighted. For Duffy and Humphreys (2016), theoretically minded conservationists must understand motivations for poaching within a wider context, and explore intergenerational poverty as not just material deprivation, but as disempowerment and a lack of voice, preventing certain communities from developing, and sustaining, life paths.

Regulation and intervention

Large-scale commercial poaching is a big business, comprised of dangerous international networks, and is similar to that of the illegal drugs and arms trade insofar as the same international criminal gangs who smuggle weapons and drugs are often involved in poaching. This places the act of poaching in the same category as drug and weapons smuggling.

In 2014, the London Conference on the Illegal Wildlife Trade presented a high-level commitment from various global leaders to tackle illegal poaching through poverty-alleviation and alternative income-generating options such as community development, job creation and the disbursement of revenue from wildlife tourism schemes. Another policy option is the increased use of force to offer protection to endangered species. Beginning in the mid 2000s, militarised forms of anti-poaching have highlighted the relationship between the military and conservation sectors and the integration of conservation efforts into national security agendas. The human security angle is also present in this approach; for example, the Thin Green Line is an organisation that campaigns on behalf of park rangers killed or wounded on duty by poachers. With approximately 1,000 rangers killed worldwide since 2000, the growing inclination towards militarised counter-poaching seems to be the norm in many countries, but also has its detractors. The enhanced militarisation of conservation has been dubbed 'green violence' and 'green militarisation' because state actors and private operators employ deadly force, perpetuating cycles of escalation which compromise human security (Duffy and Humphreys, 2016).

The United Nations Office on Drugs and Crime (UNODC) identifies various actors involved in poaching: those who hunt for consumption or local sale for comparatively small profits; local intermediaries who transport wildlife products for onward trafficking; organised commercial poachers; international intermediaries; and manufacturers and retailers in destination markets. With respect to international law and norm-generating instruments, the Convention on International Trade in Endangered Species of Wild Fauna and Flora (CITES) is a multilateral treaty that governs the international trade in animals and plants that are endangered by trade. The treaty is ratified by 183 countries, and establishes species-specific restrictions dedicated to preserving species sustainability. Other international organisations which lend support to regulating the illegal trade of wildlife include the International Criminal Police Organization (INTERPOL), the International Consortium on Combating Wildlife Crime, UNODC, and the Wildlife Enforcement Network, all of which uphold the tenets of CITES by connecting authorities, law enforcement entities, and other actors focused on combatting wildlife crime.

The African Union (AU) is also instrumental in addressing transnational poaching, facilitating regional interactions and partnerships between non-governmental organisations, individual states, and international governmental organisations like the United Nations and NGOs like TRAFFIC. The AU serves as a forum for coordinating collaborative efforts to offer alternate pathways for development, and providing a means to address corruption within Africa. With the economic development of Africa being one of the strategic priorities of the AU, the organisation promotes development in rural areas and adopts policies that attempt to reduce the ability of illegal organisations to recruit new poachers (Birdwell, 2022).

A 2021 report by the Congressional Research Service, a public policy research institute of the United States Congress, revealed that large-bodied animal species – some of which are crucial to the functioning of natural ecosystems as well as local and national economies – are also disproportionately impacted by wildlife poaching (Fang et al., 2017). African elephants and rhinoceroses are two large-bodied animal species considered threatened or endangered under international conventions. Other rare and endangered species include lions, mountain gorillas, pangolins, certain tortoises, and cheetahs. The majority of these species are poached for their body parts and often support transnational criminal and militant groups, weakening the rule of law and contributing to the spread of zoonotic diseases. Poaching has increased since the COVID-19 pandemic restrictions went into effect around the world, prompting new efforts to maintain Earth's biodiversity and its diverse ecosystem services.

DELON OMROW

Theoretical frameworks

There are several theoretical approaches to understanding poaching: social exchange theory; game theory; environmental criminology theories (such as rational crime theory and routine activities theory); behavioural economics; and various social-ecological systems (SESs) frameworks (Ntuli et al., 2021).

Social exchange theory posits that the study of social behaviour between two parties entails a cost–benefit analysis to determine risks and benefits. Maximising benefits and minimising costs are the overall purposes of the exchange and, therefore, various actors calculate the potential benefits and costs of social relationships and act in accordance with their calculation (Homans, 1958). *Game theory* is a framework for conceiving social situations among competing players. When applied to poaching, the theory predicts the areas where poaching may take place, drawing upon earlier poaching incidents and the interaction between poachers and defenders. *Rational choice theory*, in the main, describes criminal activity as the result of outcomes of rational decision-making processes (Clark, 1990). Carter et al. (2017) suggest that an abundance of rare and iconic species in an area can induce illegal poaching activities because of the sheer economic opportunities it creates for local community members. Similar to social exchange theory, various actors calculate the costs and benefits of committing a crime, and the perceived costs and benefits are influenced by local, national and international policy interventions. Under the framework of rationality, rational choice theory posits that criminal behaviour will be committed if the benefits outweigh the costs of committing a crime.

It is helpful to analyse whether these theories are focused on the offender or the offence and the implications of this for practice and prevention. Theories that focus on reducing the opportunity of poaching include situational crime prevention (SCP), problem-oriented policing (POP), and routine activity theory (RAT). Carter et al. (2017) explore normative approaches and their utility in understanding poaching. For instance, *normative approaches* try to understand the role of norms and values in justifying illegal poaching. Modern approaches to theorising poaching employ Ostrom's (2007) social-ecological systems (SESs). Consider, for a moment, Ntuli et al. (2021) and their utilisation of SESs to understand community-based natural resource management (CBNRM). The theory identifies eight dimensions that are linked together in a three-tier system. The third tier is comprised of the external environment – namely, economic, political and social forces, but also complex ecosystems such as rivers and woodlands. The second tier features resource systems such as a trans-frontier conservation area (TFCA), resource units (wildlife), local communities and tourists, and overall governance systems such as institutions and rules governing the park. Lastly, the first tier refers to the action domain where the aforementioned dimensions interact to produce outcomes which are either desirable or undesirable depending on whether it is below, above or at the social optimum level.

The above theoretical frameworks have produced some general observations about poaching, especially considering the intersectional identities of various actors. For example, Kahler et al. (2013) conclude that young men are more likely to poach than older men, and women, particularly older women, exhibit pro-conservation behaviour. Social exchange theory, routine activities theory and social-ecological systems frameworks reveal that poaching is very risky and has a very high opportunity cost in terms of effort or the likelihood of being caught. From an intersectional lens, the opportunity cost of forgone agricultural activities is very high for older men with families to feed; this cost is even higher for women because of their responsibilities at home and their reputation if caught engaging in illegal activities. Interestingly, Hübschle (2017) notes that young men are risk-loving and invest plenty of time and effort in poaching when profitable.

Challenges and innovations

In order to prescribe measures to assess (and reduce) the risk of poaching, in-depth knowledge of the poachers' behaviour is required. Recording such behaviour is challenging, however, for many reasons: wildlife crime datasets lack specificity and are extremely imbalanced; data are unreliable due to the difficulty of detecting well-hidden poaching signs in forests and jungles; historical poaching records are not collected thoroughly, resulting in biased datasets; and poaching trends and landscape features vary from one protected area to another. Knowledge is also limited because poaching is a sensitive activity for select communities and to fully understand their motivation, we would need to unpack the harmful impact of colonialism and its links to institutional policies which inform contemporary wildlife policy. As such, universal predictive models cannot be created and utilised across the globe (Xu et al., 2020).

In a related vein, the distinction between subsistence and commercial poaching is much more nuanced than originally imagined: the characteristics of subsistence poachers are relatively unknown as a result of a constellation of factors – chief among these are the presence of poor institutions and corrupt park officials. Some studies reveal that there is less poaching in communities where local people trust each other, respect institutions, perceive that the management of the park is good, and view wildlife as an asset. When there is a lack of trust among resource users, there is an over-exploitation of wildlife because of competition (Ntuli et al., 2021). Nevertheless, poaching remains under-researched and with such fragmented data, myriad questions remain unanswered, such as: (i) what are the factors driving subsistence poaching behaviour in local communities? (ii) What are the characteristics of individuals who are likely to violate hunting rules? And (iii) what measures can be instituted to counter the drivers of subsistence poaching?

One emerging trend in anti-poaching efforts is Conservation International's embrace of gender equity as a pillar of equitable and effective practice. Lau (2020) suggests that deeper engagement with feminist theory and feminist political ecology advances biodiversity conservation, bringing attention to power dynamics, intersectionality and subjectivity. The COVID-19 pandemic saw increased wildlife poaching across the globe, and its impacts have disproportionately affected women in developing countries. For instance, in Africa, an alarming increase in bushmeat harvest and wildlife trafficking has been directly linked to COVID-19-related lockdowns, decreased food availability and damaged economies as a result of stagnated tourism.

Many anti-poaching organisations have subsequently been formed, including a squad of vegan, women rangers in Zimbabwe's national parks. According to Mavhunga (2022), this intersectional approach to conservation allows those most impacted by the pandemic and poaching – namely, racialised women – to exercise agency, leading to a renewed sense of empowerment. In Zimbabwe, as people lost their jobs, they immediately turned to hunting animals for food and other sources of income. Working alongside the International Anti-Poaching Foundation, women have joined a group known as Akashinga – or the 'Brave Ones' – to stave off the threats of poaching. Young women are taught about animal behaviour and how to handle certain endangered species. Volunteers are well armed, and if they encounter poachers, they detain them, and turn them over to the police for prosecution. The Akashinga project was created by Damien Mander, an Australian national and an Iraq war veteran. Mander started a pilot project with 16 women who were tasked with protecting 90,000 acres. Over time, 240 staff joined the effort and as of 2021, Akashinga now has eight reserves that are patrolled. By 2026, 1,000 staff will be hired and trained in anti-poaching law enforcement. Feminist theory and feminist political ecology, it is argued, can alter the power dynamics of poaching and empower women to protect their livelihoods as well as endangered species.

Another fascinating trend in anti-poaching campaigns is the use of emerging technology. Birdwell (2022) suggests that over the last decade, a technological arms race between conservationists, law enforcement, national governments, and the international community against poachers has reached its apex. At the turn of the twenty-first century, poachers had begun to make use of sophisticated weaponry and technologies such as global positioning systems (GPS), night-vision goggles and even helicopters (Duffy and Humphreys, 2016). In response, a suite of innovative technologies such as drones and digital monitoring have been leveraged to better protect endangered animals from being illegally poached and placed into the black market. For example, researchers from the Indian Institute of Technology Madras and Harvard University have developed a novel machine learning algorithm named 'CombSGPO' (Combined Security Game Policy Optimization) that can be used to tackle poaching. Specifically, the research team argues that algorithms can provide a good strategy to protect wildlife because they handle resource allocation and strategise patrolling after the extent of resources available has been identified (Goswami, 2022). The algorithm utilises data on the animal population in select areas and assumes that poachers in the vicinity are aware of the patrolling being done at various sites.

The use of the algorithm was motivated by the need to engage in strategic resource allocation in so-called 'hot-spots' to prevent illegal activities such as wildlife poaching, illegal logging and illegal fishing. Human patrollers (forest rangers) and surveillance drones have object detectors mounted on them for animals and poachers and perform strategic signalling. This algorithm then utilises a game theory-based model and a 'Stackelberg Security Game Model', which is linked to drones that have been used by Air Shepherd, a foundation that deploys drones to stop elephant and rhino poaching in Africa. There is tremendous scope in the application of algorithms to deter illegal poaching, as this new technology can be applied in domains such as security, search and rescue, and aerial mapping for agriculture. The research teams from the Indian Institute of Technology Madras and Harvard University are also experimenting with sample-efficient multi-agent reinforcement learning, since data collection remains a challenge in real-world poaching scenarios. Such research opens limitless vistas of inquiry into the use of artificial intelligence (AI) frameworks in advancing wildlife protection efforts by learning from past poaching activity to prescribe actionable recommendations.

Conclusion

Theory and research can inform policy, prompting interventions which aim to divert individual and community involvement in poaching. Alternative livelihoods through economic development, for example, may serve as a solution to both poaching and human–wildlife conflict in rural and peri-urban areas that rely heavily upon crop cultivation and livestock production.

Conservation International is working with governments to provide alternative livelihoods for rural communities through such community-driven approaches. For example, the Herding 4 Health programme builds capacity among farmers in high-biodiversity rural areas so that degraded rangelands can be restored, and farmers can become more resilient to climate change and natural disasters. Over the next five years, Conservation International will cover more than 1.5 million hectares (3.7 million acres) of rangeland, with the target of eventually reaching more than 25.5 million hectares (about 63 million acres) in 2025 (Price, 2020). Such community-driven approaches are crucial to preventing illegal poaching because the pandemic and climate change-related disasters have led rural communities to over-exploit resources through poaching.

DELON OMROW

Further reading

Birdwell, I. (2022). *Combatting Illegal Poaching of Wildlife*. African Union.

Duffy, R. V., & J. Humphreys. (2016). Poaching, wildlife trafficking and human security. *Whitehall Papers*, 86(1): 22–37.

Hübschle, A. (2017). The social economy of rhino poaching: Of economic freedom fighters, professional hunters and marginalized local people. *Current Sociology*, 65(3): 427–447.

Ntuli, H., A. Sundström, M. Sjöstedt, E. Muchapondwa, S. C. Jagers, & A. Linell. (2021). Understanding the drivers of subsistence poaching in the Great Limpopo Transfrontier Conservation Area: What matters for community wildlife conservation? *Ecology and Society*, 26(1): 1–22.

Stoett, P., & D. Omrow. (2021). *Spheres of Transnational Ecoviolence: Environmental Crime, Human Security, and Justice*. Palgrave Macmillan.

References

Birdwell, I. (2022). *Combatting Illegal Poaching of Wildlife*. African Union.

Carter, N. H., J. V. López-Bao, J. T. Bruskotter, M. Gore, G. Chapron, A. Johnson, Y. Epstein, M. Shrestha, J. Frank, O. Ohrens, & A. Treves. (2017). A conceptual framework for understanding illegal killing of large carnivores. *Ambio*, 46: 251–264.

Clark, C. (1990). *Mathematical Bioeconomics: The Optimal Management of Renewable Resources*. Wiley.

Duffy, R. V., & J. Humphreys. (2016). Poaching, wildlife trafficking and human security. *Whitehall Papers*, 86(1): 22–37.

Fang, F., H. Nguyen, R. Pickles, & A. Lemieux. (2017). PAWS: A deployed game-theoretic application to combat poaching. *AI Magazine*, 38(1): 23–36.

Goswami, R. (2022, May 25). *Now, an Algorithm to Save Wildlife from Poaching*. East Mojo. https://www.eastmojo.com/environment/2022/

05/25/now-an-algorithm-to-save-wildlife-from-poaching/.

Harrison, M., D. Roe, J. Baker, G. Mwedde, H. Travers, A. Plumptre, A. Rwetsiba, & E. J. Milner-Gulland. (2015). *Wildlife Crime: A Review of the Evidence on Drivers and Impacts in Uganda.* International Institute for Environment and Development.

Homans, G. C. (1958). Social behaviour as exchange. *American Journal of Sociology*, 63(6): 597–606.

Hübschle, A. (2017). The social economy of rhino poaching: Of economic freedom fighters, professional hunters and marginalized local people. *Current Sociology*, 65(3): 427–447.

Kahler, J. S., & M. L. Gore. (2012). Beyond the cooking pot and pocket book: Factors influencing noncompliance with wildlife poaching rules. *International Journal of Comparative and Applied Criminal Justice*, 36(2): 103–120.

Kahler, J. S., G. J. Roloff, & M. L. Gore. (2013). Poaching risks in community-based natural resource management. *Conservation Biology*, 27(1): 177–186.

Lau, J. (2020). Three lessons for gender equity in biodiversity conservation. *Conservation Biology*, 34(6): 1589–1591.

Mavhunga, C. (2014). *Transient Workspaces: Technologies of Everyday Innovation in Zimbabwe.* MIT Press.

Mavhunga, C. (2022, August 24). *All-Female Vegan Rangers Leading Anti-Poaching in Zimbabwe.* VOA. https://www.voanews.com/a/africa_all-female-vegan-rangers-leading-anti-poaching-zimbabwe/6209933.html.

Ntuli, H., & E. Muchapondwa. (2017). Effects of wildlife resources on community welfare in Southern Africa. *Ecological Economics*, 131: 572–583.

Ntuli, H., A. Sundström, M. Sjöstedt, E. Muchapondwa, S. C. Jagers, & A. Linell. (2021). Understanding the drivers of subsistence poaching in the Great Limpopo Transfrontier Conservation Area: What matters for community wildlife conservation? *Ecology and Society*, 26(1): 1–22.

Ostrom, E. (2007). A diagnostic approach for going beyond panaceas. *Proceedings of the National Academy of Sciences of the United States of America*, 104(39): 15181–15187.

Price, K. (2020). *Poaching, Deforestation Reportedly on the Rise Since COVID-19 Lockdowns.* Conservation International. https://www.conservation.org/blog/poaching-deforestation-reportedly-on-the-rise-since-covid-19-lockdowns.

Wyatt, T., D. van Uhm, & A. Nurse (2020). Differentiating criminal networks in the illegal wildlife trade: Organized, corporate and disorganized crime. *Trends Organized Crime*, 23: 350–366.

Xu, L., S. Gholami, S. McCarthy, & B. Dilkina. (2020). *Stay Ahead of Poachers: Illegal Wildlife Poaching Prediction and Patrol Planning Under Uncertainty with Field Test Evaluations.* International Conference on Data Engineering (ICDE).

DELON OMROW

17. Water crimes

Introduction

With few exceptions, the amount of fresh water and its resources are not rich in the thousands of years old land of Iranshahr (Iran), and the average annual rainfall does not exceed 200 millimetres. Iranians have been looking for a solution to this problem for a long time, through the use of underground springs and rivers for agriculture. The evolution of Iran's water laws has gone through many ups and downs in the contemporary period. Iran has outlined its major policies for realising social justice in Principles 44, 45, 48 and 50 of the Constitution, with the general policies related to water and vision approved in 2003 (1382) and 2025 (1404).

General policies are decided in accordance with the first paragraph of Article 110 of the Constitution of the Islamic Republic of Iran, including things such as economic security, energy, water resources, the mining sector, natural resources, and the transportation sector. In the field of environment and natural resources, especially water resources, policy criteria include stabilising the development process by relying on environmental protection and optimal use of resources; and realisation of sustainable development, based on knowledge of the social, economic, cultural and environmental fields of the country, in such a way that, while improving the quality of life, the rights of current and future generations are also preserved. Land use planning is based on the relative advantages of the regions, in such a way that every Iranian can be proud of the region in which they live with dignity and peace. Knowing the elements of Islamic and Iranian culture, art, knowledge and civilisation, as elements of national identity and taking advantage of the historical and cultural advantages of different regions of the country, is a way for the active participation of regions in sustainable development. Organising the national space, creating regional balance, and strengthening the regional role of the country by taking advantage of the social, cultural, economic and natural capacities and advantages of the land, with the aim of improving the country's international status, are all important considerations.

From the point of view of water theorists in Iran, water laws should address three areas:

1. Allocation of water resources and pollution control, which usually requires obtaining a licence for water extraction or waste disposal.
2. Water laws should be in line with broad social goals for sustainable development and environmental protection and should also be in harmony with customary and traditional rules.
3. Water laws should have the necessary structures and institutional organisations to facilitate implementation.

Also, the way of cooperation of government institutions with non-governmental water organisations and private companies should be specified.

In the international arena, some environmental experts and theorists believe that in the analysis of water-related crimes, a distinction should be made between 'crimes against water' and 'water crimes'. For example, environmental harm may be due to the commission of a crime (surface water pollution), the purpose of a crime (theft) or the means of committing a crime (intentional poisoning). In general, water crimes around the world are divided into seven categories: (1) water corruption; (2) organised water crimes; (3) water pollution; (4) water theft; (5) water fraud; (6) water terrorism; and (7) water cyber-attacks.

In order to deal with water crimes in Iran, several laws have been approved, which include criminal titles such as: Water Pollution; Unauthorised use of water; Unauthorised drilling and exploitation of water that belongs to another and aggressive seizure of water belonging to another; Wasting water; Unauthorised interference in water facilities; Destruction of water resources; Encroachment on the bed and privacy of water resources; Theft from water installations; and Buying and selling stolen property of water facilities. Harms associated with building water dams are also increasingly an issue in domestic and international arenas. If dams are built without respecting the rights of downstream countries and reasonable and fair principles and win–win diplomacy, they may cause irreparable damage and become the basis for committing crimes.

Water laws

The vast land, which has been known as 'Iranshahr' since several thousand years ago, has been looking for a solution to the water shortage problem due to its lack of abundant water. In the contemporary era, there are relevant laws at several levels of important documents and ordinary laws that have been approved by the legislative assembly. The principles of the Constitution in order to realise social justice, in the economic part, are divided into three sectors: public, cooperative and private, with a focus on public ownership and the authority of the government (Principle 44), public wealth (Principle 45), exploitation of natural resources (Principle 48) and the public duty to protect the environment and ban economic and other activities that are associated with its pollution (Principle 50).

The approval of the water law and the nationalisation of water in 1968 (1347) is considered a great development because in its Article 1, water is considered part of national wealth, and Article 2 prohibits the privatisation of all kinds of natural and human-made resources. The law of 1968 (1347) thus aimed to nationalise water in order to put an end to the undisputed rule of private rights over water resources and make it subject to public rights. The law of fair distribution was approved in 1982 (1361). This law is the most important law that was passed after the Islamic revolution in the field of water along with the previous law, namely the law of water and its nationalisation.

Since the beginning of 2020 (1399), the Ministry of Energy of Iran, using successful global experiences and taking advantage of the knowledge of experts and specialists and attracting the participation of stakeholders, put the drafting of the Water Law Bill on the agenda. After going through the preliminary stages of drafting the bill and gathering global experiences and related documents and laws, in the period from October to March, opinions were exchanged and received by 71 official institutions from the main stakeholders of the water sector. The publication of the first edition of the proposed water bill received comments from experts and activists and more than 1,600 comments were received from 76 legal and natural persons during a 40-day period. In the end, this Ministry compiled the results and summaries of the studies and consensus in the form of the proposed water law.

The most recent proposed changes are contained in this draft of Iran's comprehensive Water Law, which aims to provide a suitable legal basis for the future developments of the country's water management. The fifth chapter of this draft deals with violations, crimes, and compensation for the resulting damage, and includes the following:

1. Digging a well or an aqueduct without obtaining a permit (Article 92).
2. Intentional violation of this law (Article 93).
3. Opening the water distribution window or changing distribution or unauthorised intervention in water measuring devices in a way that causes changes in the operation of water facilities or causes damage.
4. Transferring water to one's irrigation channels or network without the right or without the permission of the competent authorities or preventing another person's right to water.
5. Deliberately wasting water belonging to another person in a way that causes damage.
6. Exploitation of wells and aqueducts or other water sources without a licence and without complying with the provisions of this law.
7. Obstructing the duties of irrigation officials or the machines of regional water companies.
8. Construction of facilities in the bed and legal boundaries of rivers, streams, canals, wetlands, seashores and lakes without the permission of the Ministry of Energy.
9. Exploitation of sand, clay, or bedrock and the boundaries of rivers, streams, and canals, and the legal boundaries of seashores and natural lakes and behind dams without complying with legal regulations.
10. Unauthorised exploitation of surface waters, rivers, streams, canals and seas and lakes without complying with regulations (numbers 3 to 10 based on Article 94 of the draft).
11. Pollution of water sources (Article 95).
12. Discharge of any polluting substances, municipal or industrial sewage, scum, garbage and any additional objects in the sanctuaries of the surface waterbed and the feeding area of the aquifers (Article 96).
13. Unauthorised destruction and encroachment on the privacy and bed of rivers,

SHARAREH ABTAHI

water streams, natural rivers, public canals, marshes, ponds, natural marshes and wetlands, natural springs, both dry and cold, mineral or non-mineral, drainage of natural gorges, natural gorges, seas and lakes, whether natural or constructed, as well as coastal and man-made lands (Article 97).

The punishments prescribed in this draft are a fine up to twice the damage caused, restitutio in integrum, compensation for the damage caused according to the opinion of the Ministry of Energy expert, in addition to the punishments prescribed in the Islamic Penal Code, imprisonment from six months to one year. In this draft, a special branch is foreseen to deal with complaints and lawsuits related to water affairs in the judiciary of each province.

This draft plan has not yet been approved by the Islamic Parliament and has not gone through the steps of becoming effective. Accordingly, the rest of this entry will discuss existing laws pertaining to water crimes in Iran, the substantive concerns of which will also be addressed in the draft plan.

There are two categories of crime across diverse Iranian laws which will be discussed in this entry.

Anthropocentric approach

This is a point of view in which the environment is viewed as a tool and its supporting purpose is to protect humans and serve their interests. In this approach, natural resources are considered exclusively as 'tools' to ensure human survival without considering the rights of or duties to other plant and animal species.

Anthrobiocentric approach

In this approach, humans and non-human animals are protected equally, and nature is cherished because it is considered to have value in itself (Kopnina & Cherniak, 2015).

In the laws of Iran, water crimes reflect each of the above categories, first through the list of criminal titles in the laws and then the legal articles as discussed below.

Water pollution

1. Water pollution

Any action that is known to be a threat to public health, such as contaminating drinking water or distributing contaminated drinking water, unsanitary disposal of human and animal excreta and waste materials, dumping poisonous substances in rivers, littering the streets and illegal killing of animals, illegal use of raw sewage or the water of sewage treatment plants, is prohibited for agricultural purposes and the perpetrators will be sentenced to imprisonment for up to one year if they are not subject to stricter sanctions according to special laws.

The meaning of environmental pollution is the spreading or mixing of foreign substances into water or air or soil or earth to the extent that its physical, chemical or biological quality is harmful to humans or other living organisms or plants or works or buildings that

(Regulations related to the implementation of Article 1 of the Law on Determining the Sanctuaries of Lakes Built Behind Dams approved in 1967 (1346); Article 12 of the Hunting and Fishing Law approved in 1967 (1346); Article 9 of the Protection and Improvement Law 1977 (1353); Article 46 of the Fair Water Distribution Law 1982 (1361); Regulations for preventing water pollution approved in 1994 (1373); the Law on the Protection and Exploitation of Water Resources of the Islamic Republic of Iran approved in 1995 (1374); Article 689 of the Islamic Penal Code 1996 (1375); Article 2 of the Waste Management Law 2004 (1383)).

Regarding the prevention of water pollution, in addition to the above-mentioned laws, there is also the approval letter of the Council of Ministers dated 2014 (1393) as well as other upstream documents that deal with these issues.

Since Iran is an oil-rich country, cases of water pollution by oil and its products are also criminalised in the laws.

- Oil pollution: the spread and mixing of one or more pollutants, including crude oil, petroleum and petrochemical products, into water, air, or soil to the extent and duration that the physical, chemical or biological quality of that contact is harmful to humans or other living organisms. Or plants or works and buildings that are harmful, change them.

This refers to a different, institutional or infrastructural type of harm and offence, related to pollution. The phrase 'change them' refers to the obligation of the polluter to modify harmful plants or works and buildings.

- Degradation: any irreversible change in the environment (Regulations for removing environmental pollution from petroleum activities, 2009 (1388)).

In Iran, the antrobiocentric approach governs water pollution prevention laws.

2. Water and unauthorised use of water

Any person without obtaining the legal distribution of water, electricity, gas and sewage network and/or who shares communication and information technology services in relation to the aforementioned services without permission, commits a crime. In Iranian laws, this unauthorised use is considered theft (Punishment law for unauthorised users of water, electricity, telephone, sewage and gas, 2017 (1396)).

In Iran, the anthropocentric approach governs theft of water.

The Fair Water Distribution Law approved in 1982 (1361) designates the crimes caused by unauthorised extraction and exploitation of water. Article 5 of the law refers to non-prohibited areas, where one is allowed to dig a well and use its water for domestic, drinking, sanitary and garden purposes up to the irrigation capacity of 25 cubic metres per day, and it is not necessary to have a drilling and exploitation licence, but the situation must be reported to the Ministry of Energy.

The use of underground water resources, with the exception of the cases mentioned in Article 5 of this law, requires that the digging of any type of wells and aqueducts and developing springs in any region of the country, must be done with the permission and approval of the Ministry of Energy, the said Ministry taking into account the hydrological features of the region (identification strata of the earth and water), and the provisions provided in this law are related to the issuance of drilling and exploitation permits.

Article 3 of the Fair Water Distribution Law views unauthorised exploitation as referring to three types of exploitation:

1. The well was drilled within the one-year period of the permit timeframe but is used without obtaining the permit, which is illegal use of underground resources.
2. Exploiting more than the permitted limit for consumption from the underground aquifer (in drinking and sanitation more than 25 cubic metres per day and in other wells more than the amount specified in the issued permit).
3. The utilisation is up to the permitted limit (even in some cases less than the permitted limit), but the type of consumption has changed (for example, irrigation, sanitation or for drinking). In this type of violation, the extracted water does not reach the desired consumption for which the permit was issued, or the permit is agreed upon, but the type of consumption is different.

One example of unauthorised exploitation of underground water sources, which plays a very important role in creating a water crisis, is the over-taking of water from wells that have an exploitation licence, that is, extracting more water than the permitted limit stated in the licence. In addition to the reduction of underground water tables, this gradually causes land subsidence and salinisation of the aquifer in the plains, and it also has harmful effects on the environment (Article 45 of the Fair Water Distribution Law approved in 1982 (1361)).

In Iran, the anthropocentric approach governs crimes caused by unauthorised extraction and exploitation of water.

3. Unauthorised drilling and exploitation of water that belongs to another and aggressive seizure of water belonging to another

Anyone who seizes another's water without legal permission and anyone intentionally taking water without the right or permission of the responsible authorities for the channels or irrigation networks (Article 45 of the Fair Water Distribution Law approved in 1982 (1361)).

4. Wasting water

Holders of consumption licences are required to avoid unreasonable consumption and avoid waste of water and to use specific channels in such a way as to ensure that consumption is reasonable and economical. Depending on the case, the Ministry of Energy or the Ministry of Agriculture will outline the situation and provide technical instructions to the consumer so that they can respond to the problem within a reasonable period of time. The said warning, which will not exceed one year, means that the consumer must follow the technical instructions and, if the above-mentioned solution does not work, the violator will be dealt with according to Article 45 of this law, which states that it is illegal for anyone to intentionally waste water in one way or another to the detriment of others (Article 25 and 45 of the Fair Water Distribution Law approved in 1982 (1361)).

5. Unauthorised interference in water facilities

The users of water from common channels and headwaters are responsible for the maintenance of common facilities, and no one has the right to construct and change the section and new water channel and branch without the permission of the Ministry of Energy, and each upstream user is responsible for the damage caused to the downstream users by their unconventional action (Article 36 of the Fair Water Distribution Law approved in 1982 (1361)).

Anyone who deliberately and without permission opens a valve or divider or changes the distribution of water or interferes with water measuring devices without authorisation or disrupts the use of water facilities in some way commits an offence (Article 45 of the Fair Water Distribution Law approved in 1982 (1361)).

6. Destruction of water resources

If as a result of the implementation of civil and industrial projects and agricultural development and construction of dams and related facilities or as a result of the use of surface and underground water resources in the area or region of canals and wells or any type of water resources exploitation facility belonging to the property, or damage is caused to it or as a result of the implementation of the mentioned plans, the water of canals, wells, rivers and springs belonging to natural or legal persons and their rights are reduced or dried up, an order will be made to compensate for the damage (Article 44 of the Fair Water Distribution Law approved in 1982 (1361)).

This law is mainly human-centred and assessment is made purely from an economic point of view.

7. Encroachment on the bed and privacy of water resources

In the law related to the bed and boundaries of rivers, streams, canals, marshes, natural ponds and water supply, irrigation and drainage networks, approved in 2000 (1379), the definitions of boundaries and bed are provided. It is worth noting that clause X of Article 1 of the regulation mentioned in the 2004 (1382) amendment provided a new and more comprehensive definition of privacy. According to this definition, the sanctuary is that part of the land around the river, channel, natural or traditional stream, marsh and natural ponds, which is necessary as an easement for their complete benefit and quantitative and qualitative protection, and according to the regulations by the Ministry of Energy or water companies. The qualitative boundary of rivers and canals for exploitation and dredging operations is determined from 1 to 20 metres, and the qualitative boundary of water of rivers, natural springs and ponds will be up to 150 metres. The quality boundary for rivers, natural reservoirs and ponds providing drinking water has also been set at 150 metres.

According to Note 3, Article 2 of the Law on Equitable Water Distribution, it is prohibited to create any kind of embankment, excavation and encroachment on the boundaries of rivers except with the permission of the Ministry of Energy. In this way, it can be said that in addition to the riverbeds, the right of privacy also belongs to the government, and therefore permission to encroach and occupy and build any buildings is subject to the approval of the Ministry of Energy.

8. Theft from water installations

Anyone who steals the means and belongings of public use that were created or installed at the expense of the government or with the capital of the government or the joint capital of the government and the non-governmental sector or by non-governmental public institutions and organisations or charitable institutions, such as water, electricity, gas exploitation facilities, etc. will be sentenced to imprisonment from one to five years, and if the perpetrator is an employee of the relevant organisations, they will be sentenced to the maximum punishment (Article 659 of the Islamic Penal Code (sanctions and deterrent punishments), 1996 (1375)).

Any soldier who steals military equipment and supplies (other than weapons, ammunition, and explosives) and funds and goods belonging to the government or what is in the possession of the armed forces will be sentenced to imprisonment from one to five years (Article 89 of the Criminal Law of the Armed Forces 2003 (1382)).

9. Buying and selling stolen property of water facilities

Anyone, who knowingly with convincing evidence that the property was obtained as a result of theft, hides it, accepts it or trades it, shall be imprisoned from six months to three years and receive up to 74 lashes. If the accused has made the trading of stolen property their profession, they will be sentenced to the maximum punishment (Article 662 of the Islamic Penal Code approved in 2013 (1392)).

According to the Law on Reduction of Punishment of 2020 (1399), the punishment for this crime is reduced by half, that is, imprisonment from three months to one and a half years or receiving up to 37 lashes.

As is clear, all the aforementioned crimes are informed by a human-centred approach.

Dams and water systems

The construction of internal and external dams will potentially cause crimes in the future and this is currently relevant to Iran's water system both domestically and internationally: in the last few decades, along with the intensification of global warming and climate change, parts of the world, especially the Middle East region, have faced a water crisis under the influence of consecutive droughts, increasing demand for water and excessive harvesting. Water for agriculture, industry and drinking is at critical levels in countries of the Middle East and Central Asia.

The increase in water demand due to agricultural development, population growth, climate change and the reduction of common water resources has led different countries to make maximum use of the water available in their lands, sometimes without considering the negative effects on the downstream countries. The indiscriminate harvesting of water resources has caused tensions between countries over the past few years. Many rivers located in the common basins between countries are under the pressure of competition for the extraction of limited water resources, which may not only aggravate the water crisis, but also create the grounds for disputes and conflicts between neighbouring countries. Iran is not exempt from this crisis, and in the last five decades, the increase in average temperature, decrease in average rainfall, reduction in the renewable water resources of the country, and excessive exploitation of water resources have led to the emergence and exacerbation of the water crisis in the country. This has made transboundary water resources a significant issue (Water, Environment and Natural Resources Foresight Group, 2018 (1397)).

The common cross-border watersheds of Iran are the Tigris–Euphrates–Arvandroud basin, Aras basin, Etrak basin, Hirmand basin, and Harirud basin. A comparison of the five shared border watersheds of Iran with the other 281 shared watersheds of the world shows that, in regard to the quantity of water resources (pertaining to agricultural water stress indices and human water stress), the environmental water stress index and the index of pollution caused by sewage, in two of the basins the conditions of danger are very high. Indeed, the Tigris–Euphrates and Aras basins are heavily affected by the indiscriminate construction of dams in their upper reaches, and therefore the risk level of these two basins on the local ecosystem is very high. Across 14 water indicators, the results show that the common border basins of Iran are in very high-risk conditions (Water, Environment and Natural Resources Foresight Group, 2018 (1397)). Each basin has its own context and crisis indicators.

(1) *The Euphrates sub-basin* is shared between five countries: Turkey (28%), Iraq (47%), Syria (22%), Jordan (0.0003%) and Saudi Arabia (3%). A total of 13 large dams have been built or are under construction on the Euphrates River by three countries: Turkey, Syria and Iraq. The Tigris watershed is shared between four countries: Iran, Iraq, Syria and Turkey. Since the 1930s, many

dams have been built or are being built in the Tigris River basin and on its tributaries. The total capacity of these dams is over 116 billion cubic metres.

In recent years, Turkey has planned to build eight dams in this area as part of the GAP project, the most important of which is the Ilisu Dam, with a capacity of more than 12 billion cubic metres. With the completion of the GAP project, Turkey will be able to control one third of the water entering the Tigris. So far, the Tigris River has not been the direct subject of multilateral negotiations between Iran, Syria, Turkey and Iraq, and the agreements reached so far have mainly been on both the Tigris and Euphrates Rivers, with more emphasis on the Euphrates (Water, Environment and Natural Resources Foresight Group, 2018 (1397)).

The most important negative effects of controlling the waters of the Tigris and Euphrates basin on Iran are intensification of micro dust centres, the threat to the ecosystem of the Persian Gulf, climate change in the region, the threat to the health of the people of the region by polluted micro dust, migration flows and social and security consequences for the country. Because the sources of the Tigris and Euphrates originate from the mountains under the sovereignty of Turkey, that country therefore uses the term border waters instead of common waters and considers the use of these waters as its sovereign right. Also, Turkey believes that the entire Tigris and Euphrates basins should be considered as one basin and that the rights of each country should be generally calculated for both basins (Water, Environment and Natural Resources Foresight Group, 2018 (1397)).

(2) The *Hirmand watershed* is a closed watershed that covers large parts of southwestern Afghanistan and small parts of southeastern Iran. This basin includes a number of rivers that originate from the highlands of Afghanistan and flow towards Hamun's lakes and fresh water wetlands and finally towards the Godzare brackish water hole in Afghanistan, which is located at the end of the Sistan basin. The government of Afghanistan has so far built and operated 13 dams and 34 diversion dams in the Hirmand watershed and upstream of the Hamun wetlands. The construction of the Kamal Khan Dam has been one of the most challenging issues between Iran and Afghanistan in recent years. It is said that by building the Kamal Khan Dam, Afghanistan intends to divert a part of Hirmand water directly to Godzare in Afghanistan before it enters Iran. The most important negative effects of the Hirmand basin water containment by Afghanistan are: (1) the drying up of Hamun's international wetlands; (2) local climate change in the region in the form of an increase in temperature and a decrease in rainfall; (3) increasing the duration and speed of the 120-day winds in Sistan; (4) desertification and movement of quicksands; (5) intensification of the occurrence of fine dust; (6) the emptying of the border and the threat to the country's security and national unity; (7) the intensification of immigration and marginalisation; (8) intensification of poverty of the people of Sistan; and (9) intensification of smuggling and waste of investments made, especially in the 46,000-hectare project (Water, Environment and Natural Resources Foresight Group, 2018 (1397)).

(3) The *Harirud watershed* is shared by the three countries of Afghanistan, Iran and Turkmenistan. Following the opening of the Dosti Dam on the Harirud River on the common border of Iran and Turkmenistan, Afghanistan announced that it plans to build several dams on the Harirud upstream of the Dosti Dam. The most important impact of the reduction of Harirud water entering the Iranian border is the impact on drinking water sources in the north-eastern part of the country, especially in the metropolis of Mashhad. Depopulation of the border and migration to other urban areas, in addition to creating social problems for the migrants and intensifying marginalisation in the host cities, will also increase the costs of securing the border (Water, Environment and Natural Resources Foresight Group, 2018 (1397)).

(4) The *Etrak watershed* is another shared border basin between Iran and Turkmenistan, located in the north-east of the country. An area of 1.79% of this 33,500 square kilometre basin is located in Iran. The most important challenges of the Etrak basin are: (1) reduction in the quality and quantity of water resources due to drought, soil erosion, pollution caused by agricultural run-off, excessive extraction of underground water resources, and industrial pollution; (2) changing the course of the river and as a result changing the official border of the two countries; and (3) the creation of numerous micro dust centres in the country of Turkmenistan, especially in the

Qara Qom desert, which has direct negative environmental effects on the plains of North Khorasan, Razavi Khorasan and Golestan (Water, Environment and Natural Resources Foresight Group, 2018 (1397)).

(5) The *Kura–Ares watershed*, with an area of 188,000 square kilometres, is located between the countries of Iran, Armenia, Azerbaijan, Georgia and Turkey. An area of 31% of this basin is located in Azerbaijan, 23% in Iran, 16% in Georgia, 16% in Armenia and 14% in Turkey. Two main rivers, the Kura and Aras, flow in this basin, which, after joining each other in Azerbaijan, finally flow into the Caspian Sea (Mazandaran Sea). Human interventions in the Kura and Aras rivers have caused the amount of water entering the Caspian Sea (Mazandaran Sea) to decrease by 40% and 27%, respectively. The pollution of the Aras River, especially caused by the industrial activities of Armenia, as well as changing the course of the river and as a result changing the official border of the country, are the most important challenges related to this basin (Water, Environment and Natural Resources Foresight Group, 2018 (1397)).

The latest joint project of the Islamic Republic of Iran and the Republic of Azerbaijan is the Giz Galasi Dam, which, according to high-ranking officials of the two countries, is a positive symbol of water diplomacy and regional stability. The Giz Galasi Dam is an embankment dam on the Aras River straddling the international border between Azerbaijan and Iran. It is located in Jabrayil District, Azerbaijan, and Khoda Afarin County, East Azerbaijan Province, Iran, 12 km (7.5 mi) downstream of the Khoda Afarin Dam. Built both to generate electricity and to irrigate the plains in the region, it is the third joint Azerbaijan–Iran project on the Aras River. The Giz Galasi Reservoir will provide 12,000 hectares (30,000 acres) of land with water. The project was developed via an agreement between the Soviet Union and Iran in October 1977. The project was completed in 1982. In 1993, the area where the dam was to be built was occupied by the Republic of Nagorno-Karabakh. Between 28 June and 2 July 1994, during the first official visit of the President of Azerbaijan, Heydar Aliyev, to Iran, a memorandum on the implementation of the project was signed. In February 2016, the governments of Azerbaijan and Iran signed an agreement on cooperation in the field of construction, operation, use of energy and water resources of the Khoda Afarin and the Giz Galasi reservoirs. On 18 October 2020, Azerbaijan returned control of its side of the dam to Iran. On 19 May 2024, President of Azerbaijan, Ilham Aliyev, and President of Iran, Ebrahim Raisi, met at the site of the Giz Galasi hydroelectric complex to inaugurate it, in addition to commissioning the Khoda Afarin hydroelectric complex.

Conclusion

This entry has provided a snapshot of current and emerging water crime issues in Iran. On the one hand, greater attention has been paid to matters of pollution within domestic law, with varying degrees of attention to human and non-human interests. On the other hand, cross-national sharing of water basins, and the construction of dams and waterways that favour specific nations, have the potential to not only harm local environments and ecological systems, but to generate conflict between countries over access to and use of water resources.

SHARAREH ABTAHI

Further reading

Constitution of the Islamic Republic of Iran.

Eberlein, C., Drillisch, H., Ayboga, E. & Wenidoppler, T. (2010). 'The Ilisu Dam in Turkey and the Role of Export Credit Agencies and NGO Networks', *Water Alternatives*, 3(2): 291–312.

Hoekstra, A. Y., Chapagain, A., Aldaya, M. & Mekonnen, M. (2011). *The Water Footprint Assessment Manual: Setting the Global Standard*. London: Earthscan Publishing.

Iraq, Government of (2002). *Position Paper Indicating Iraq's Position on the Utilisation of the Tigris River Waters*. Baghdad.

Kolars, J. & Mitchell, W. (1991). *The Euphrates River and the Southeast Anatolia Development Project*. Carbondale: Southern Illinois University Press.

Kopnina, H. & Cherniak, B. (2015). 'Cultivating a Value for Non-Human Interests through the Convergence of Animal Welfare, Animal Rights, and Deep Ecology in Environmental Education', *Education Sciences*, 5(4): 363–379.

Taheri Demeneh, M., Kazemi, M., & Safari Gharibvand, K. (2023). 'Foresight of the Water Issue in Isfahan', *Sustainable City*, 5(4): 53–71. doi:10.22034/jsc.2021.236478.1265.

United Nations Environment Programme (2006). *History of Environmental Change in the Sistan Basin: Based on Satellite Image Analysis:*

1976–2005. http://hdl.handle.net/20.500.11822/7690.

Water, Environment and Natural Resources Foresight Group, 2018 (1397). *Investigating the Effects of Water Regulation Programs of Neighboring Countries in Shared Border Basins on Iran.* Development and Foresight Research Center.

References

Legislation and regulation

Amending regulations related to the bed and boundaries of rivers, streams, canals, marshes, natural ponds and water supply, irrigation and drainage networks (2004/1382).

Constitution of the Islamic Republic of Iran (Approved in 1979, revised in 1989) (Approved in 1358, revised in 1368).

Criminal Code of the Armed Forces (2003/1382).

Fair Water Distribution Law (1982/1361).

Hunting and Fishing Law (1967/1346) with subsequent amendments.

Regulations related to the implementation of Article 1 of the Law on Determining the Sanctuaries of Lakes Built behind Dams (1967/1346).

Islamic Penal Code (2013/1392).

Law on Determining the Sanctuaries of Lakes Built Behind Dams (1967/1346).

Law on Equitable Water Distribution (1983/1361).

Law on Reducing Imprisonment (2020/1399).

Law on the Protection and Exploitation of Water Resources of the Islamic Republic of Iran (1995/1374).

Protection and Improvement Law (1974/1353).

Punishment law for unauthorised users of water, electricity, telephone, sewage and gas (2017/1396).

Regulations for preventing water pollution (1994 /1373).

Regulations for removing environmental pollution from petroleum activities (2009/1388).

The fifth book of the Islamic Penal Code (deterrent punishments) (1996/1375).

Waste Management Law (2004/1383).

Water Law Bill (2020/1399).

General references

Kopnina, H. & Cherniak, B. (2015) 'Cultivating a Value for Non-Human Interests through the Convergence of Animal Welfare, Animal Rights, and Deep Ecology in Environmental Education', *Education Sciences*, 5(4): 363–379.

Water, Environment and Natural Resources Foresight Group, 2018 (1397). *Investigating the Effects of Water Regulation Programs of Neighboring Countries in Shared Border Basins on Iran.* Development and Foresight Research Center.

18. Water theft

Introduction

Internationally, water theft has long been recognised as a global issue relevant to human security and environmental crime (Baird et al., 2021; Eman, 2023). It involves the illegal acquisition of water from natural watercourses, such as lakes, rivers and groundwater systems, and of controlled water by pumping, diversion and impoundment (Brisman et al., 2020). The aim of this entry is to provide an international overview of water theft. It begins by highlighting the definitions of water theft used in legal, socio-political and green criminological frameworks. It then moves onto a discussion of how this crime has evolved over time into a global issue, currently being embedded in the unjust practices of water privatisation, largely within developing nations. The last section illustrates the international nature and extent of the issue through discussion of contemporary and emerging forms of water theft.

Defining water theft

A focal point in green criminology is that environmental crime needs to be defined and studied in relation to harm, and not solely on the basis of legal definitions. This focus means exploring beyond the legal definitions of crime to include social and ecological notions of harm (Baird et al., 2021; White, 2021). The 'taking of water from the river' is generally not in itself criminalised or a crime in its own right. Rather, the status of this activity is defined by whether it is subject to legal restrictions and/or licensing provisions. This means that taking water is not 'theft' unless it has been expressly prohibited and/or involves breach of licence conditions (Baird et al., 2021).

However, some green criminologists argue that the privatisation of water undermines basic human rights and is thus harmful. This is because privatisation enables companies to limit and profiteer from water even though water is essential to life and therefore should be available to all regardless of capacity to pay. The privatisation of water also simultaneously forces marginalised and vulnerable populations to steal water because of supply stress and fear of water insecurity (Brisman et al., 2020; Johnson et al., 2017). Such a state of affairs might be perceived as 'institutionalised water theft' even if considered legitimate within the legal realm of global water management. In many cases, states act as a facilitator that allows water corporations to exploit the world's freshwater resources without being held accountable for the social consequences.

There are anomalies, conjectures and disputations about water theft, with some, such as Felbab-Brown (2017), questioning whether the phenomenon exists at all. The Global Initiative (2014, cited in Brisman et al., 2020: 8) refers to water theft as the illegal acquisition of water from natural watercourses, such as lakes, rivers and groundwater systems, and piped or harnessed water, both of which are designated as 'non-revenue water', meaning water that is 'lost' before reaching its intended consumer. Loss of water through theft can occur in a variety of ways, including damaging or removing water meters, physically installing a connection to water distribution pipes, and stealing aid tanks. The European Report on Water Crime defines water theft as the theft of or illegal acquisition of surface water and/or ground water from public and private properties through pumping, impoundment, diversion of natural watercourses, meter tampering and illegal tappings, without a licence or in contravention of licence conditions that causes changes to water flows and access to neighbouring farms, livestock and riparian zone management (Barclay and Bartel, 2015; European Water Crimes Project, 2019; Segato et al., 2017).

Water theft could also be defined as a 'water crime' because the illegal extraction of water can alter the hydrological structure and ecological integrity of natural watercourses, subsequently impacting water quality and availability for plants and animals, and further undermining the legitimate institutional arrangements that ensure equitable distribution for all water users. On the other hand, water theft could also be defined as a 'water-related crime' because no harm is intentionally being committed by the illegal extraction of fresh water; rather it is just seen as contravening water laws and licence conditions (European Water Crimes Project, 2019; Segato et al., 2017). One implication of the latter definition is that it may cause water thefts to be trivialised, inadequately responded to, or even overlooked as something that has harmful consequences altogether (Eman et al., 2017).

Evolution of water theft

Criminologists refer to water crime as a contemporary crisis embedded in the politics of privatisation, poverty and climate change. It is important to note the historical contexts, laws and regulations involving the theft of water as well (Brisman et al., 2018). Indeed, water theft is not only an issue of contemporary global concern, but also an ancient one that dates back thousands of years to antiquity and is closely linked to the creation of irrigation and water management practices.

Some of the first laws pertaining to water theft originated in Ancient Mesopotamia, where the Code of Hammurabi (1790 BC) restricted the theft and misuse of water wheels, a water management technology used to increase the flow of water through irrigation canals. The first water commissioner of Ancient Rome, Sextus Julius Frontinus, observed a number of obscure tappings on the Roman public aqueducts in 97 AD. Groups known as the 'water-men' would illegally install hidden pipes on the public aqueducts in order to divert fresh water for personal uses and profit. This practice was also evident in the European Middle Ages when, for example, private dwellings in outer London would extract clean water to avoid using polluted water from the River Thames (Baird and Walters, 2020). Water theft is thus not a new phenomenon and in varying forms has existed throughout the ages. It especially comes to the fore when the value of fresh water is heightened during times of drought.

Today, freshwater resources are commodified and exploited under a global system of water privatisation, tenured under individual legal ownership and delivered to consumers often at exorbitant prices. The adoption of neoliberal economic policies has allowed national governments and corporate monopolies to profit from what is essential to life and a basic human right (Brisman et al., 2018; Johnson et al., 2017). However, even ancient and medieval societies upheld water as a common good, not an exclusive private commodity. Fresh water was not seen as limitless, but as a precious resource that required preservation and sophisticated management confined to the local commons. The people of the ancient world maintained a spiritual relationship with water, which was embedded in deep respect for its qualities and necessities. They did not have the benefit of desalination, technologies of water purification and international networks of water distribution that today appear to influence contemporary views that fresh water is and can be an endless resource for commercial exploitation (Baird and Walters, 2020).

The theft of water has evolved over time, from a simple act of illegally diverting water onto a neighbouring property, to a global issue embedded within the preferential, inequitable and unjust practices of water privatisation, with devastating human and environmental consequences (Johnson et al., 2017). Within this international framework, for example, the local commons, especially disadvantaged populations within water-scarce nations, have to endure the penalties of unequal water distribution, while large corporate entities and national governments control water resources in harmful ways without legal consequence (Baird and Walters, 2020; Barlow and Clarke, 2017). By contrast, it is noteworthy that ancient societies did not penalise and sanction those who were vulnerable for unlawful use and extraction of fresh water. Instead, those who were penalised and sanctioned were the affluent classes seeking to monopolise and exploit the perceived finite resources of water. The reverse is true today.

While acknowledged as a problem, there is surprisingly little knowledge of the nature and extent of water theft or the harms it inflicts upon future generations. Research into water theft is underexplored in all disciplines and what is detailed in the literature is suggestive and speculative (Loch et al., 2020). Nonetheless, the uneven distribution of fresh water around the globe had led to a situation in which water theft is on the rise. It is estimated that 30 per cent to 50 per cent of the global supply of fresh water is illegally stolen or purchased (Brisman et al., 2020). Water theft is a common occurrence within nations and regions experiencing chronic water stress (e.g., south-eastern Europe, Kenya and Mexico), and marginalised deprived areas and disadvantaged populations (e.g., slums and refugees) are particularly vulnerable to this phenomenon (see Meehan, 2013). Corruption plays a major part in water theft and smuggling, with petty bribes given to corrupt water management operators to delay and falsify water readings and conceal illegal connections (Brisman et al., 2020; The Global Initiative, 2014). Mercenaries and organised crime syndicates also illegally transit and smuggle water across borders. For example, in 2008, rebel factions in Sudan illegally seized a UNICEF water rig that was vital for meeting the critical water needs of thousands of refugees (The Global Initiative, 2014). Moreover, there is an urgent need to critically examine the theft of water in relation to 'legal and governance frameworks that prioritise the human right to water and ecological sustainability over private interests' (Johnson et al., 2017: 160).

Responding to water theft

When water crimes are addressed, they are mostly responded to by reactive community initiatives or intelligence-orientated policing strategies, and green criminologists argue that 'different types of crime prevention models are needed to address specific water crimes' before they occur (Meško and Eman, 2020: 87). In Australia, for example, some water regulators have employed remote-sensing techniques or technologies, such as satellite imagery and drones, to detect illegal water diversions and better target compliance and enforcement efforts on the ground (Baird, 2023). There are, however, immense difficulties in trying to detect, prevent and prosecute water crimes such as water theft.

First, many natural watercourses are interconnected and flow between surface and groundwater systems and coastal estuaries, and they are geographically dispersed across local and transnational scales. Second, some water crimes are also clandestine in nature and there are limited resources and specialists available to support detection, prevention and prosecution within policing services (Brisman et al., 2020; Eman, 2016; Eman et al., 2017). These challenges make it incredibly difficult to pinpoint the origins and understand the harms of water theft, especially noting that water is a constantly flowing resource. The rights of access and ownership to water under competing regimes of public and private water management further exacerbate the ability to comprehend the victims, offenders and harms of water theft in a legal sense. This is quite problematic given there are various key stakeholders (e.g., industries such as fishing, farming and tourism) and dependencies (e.g., communities, animals, plants) in freshwater resources.

The rights of national sovereignty permit nation states to exercise their power over transboundary watercourses that flow through their jurisdiction. This could be used to provide critical water supplies to support a nation's citizens and economy but, also, for political and territorial control over other people's territories. Water has always served as a historical and territorial source of conflict (events witnessed today in the Middle East). Indeed, water crimes committed in one jurisdiction may go unforeseen and unpenalised because they may not be defined as an illegal activity by that jurisdiction's lawmakers (Frederick, 1996; Gleick and Heberger, 2012; Johnson et al., 2017). Issues pertaining to water crime, human rights and national security are complex and require further close scrutiny. Meanwhile, loopholes and inconsistencies within and between environmental legal frameworks, both within and between jurisdictions, have allowed water crimes to be reported and recorded under diverse offence categories (Brisman et al., 2020; Eman et al., 2017; Segato et al., 2017). For example, large-scale water theft may be recorded as a simple stolen property offence, overlooking the hidden transgressions of corruption and environmental harm, or it might be listed as a regulatory transgression, disregarding the broader elements of criminality and the importance of ecological justice.

Furthermore, the rewards for water theft are more commonly ingrained in the global capitalist system that enables opportunities for offending (Baird, 2023). Fresh water, commonly referred to as 'blue gold', is a lucrative commodity used for agricultural production and trading. Thus, its value or wealth is only likely to be enhanced under conditions of water scarcity and drought, becoming more of a desirable target for offenders (Barlow and Clarke, 2017; Eman, 2016). However, the penalties imposed by courts for water theft in Australia, for example, are minor and inconsequential compared to the overall profits available to companies that engage in water theft for commercial purposes. Fines and penalties may simply be calculated into the 'cost of doing business' (White, 2016: 118), which perpetuates corporate environmental harm in which fines and penalties, small or large, have little deterrent impact. Governments might also see their interests as being served by the continued profitability of corporate agricultural entities rather than risking fines that are debilitating.

Contemporary and emerging water issues

Water theft is a significant issue around the globe, especially in periods of prolonged drought, water scarcity and human conflict which can drive people to steal water for survival, domestic use and their own pecuniary benefit. For example, drought in Cape Town, South Africa, sparked social fears of water insecurity in 2018 that resulted in theft from local watercourses and fire hydrants (Baird and Walters, 2020). Refugees from war-torn Syria have forced Jordan and Lebanese residents to compete with refugees over access to fresh water, which has caused them to steal water through illegal tappings and ground water extraction (Baird and Walters, 2020). Water theft is also a daily occurrence in Mexico, where marginalised communities install illegal taps on state water supplies and develop informal water cartels to obtain access to the water that they need to survive (Meehan, 2010; 2013). These international examples suggest the issue of water theft, while common, nonetheless reflects important geopolitical and socio-economic differences within and between nation states.

Furthermore, water theft provides lucrative opportunities for organised crime groups worldwide (Eman and White, 2020). Organised crime groups in Europe, Asia and South America partake in water crimes to secure power and territory in marginalised communities and embed themselves in legal economies. Corrupt water management is estimated to be worth $1 trillion every year. This in turn jeopardises the legal management and integrity of the existing supply chain and is also commonly associated with other criminal offences such as fraud, bribery and misappropriation of funds (Eman and White, 2020). For example, in Pakistan, 'water tanker mafias' bribe police and water officials to illegally tap into the state's municipal water supply, pumping the water into private tankers and delivering it to water-scarce slums and communities at an inflated cost (Hadid and Sattar, 2018).

The theft of water has also been associated with marijuana cultivation in California, with more than 12 billion gallons of water stolen in the past decade (Felbab-Brown, 2021; Weigand-Shahani, 2018). California first legalised medicinal marijuana in 1996 under the Compassionate Use Act, which allowed medical patients to use marijuana prescribed by a physician but did not specify a limit on the amount of marijuana or number of plants they could own. Since then, the number of marijuana sharply increased with 80 per cent of the market sourced from California alone (Weigand-Shahani, 2018). Given that marijuana is a water-intensive or thirsty crop, the increase in farms came with an exponentially higher amount of water needed to support large-scale cultivation (Felbab-Brown, 2021). Farmers who wish to grow marijuana in California must apply for water rights, which is a costly and time-consuming process that takes a minimum of one year, and licence holders must comply with strict water use regulations (Weigand-Shahani, 2018). Such pressures in relation to water policy and usage have created powerful incentives for marijuana farmers to circumvent the high costs, taxes and legal risks associated with marijuana cultivation (Weigand-Shahani, 2018). This has caused farmers to siphon water from neighbouring hydrants, tanks and canals with illegal pipelines, use trucks to divert water from unprotected and ecologically threatened rivers and wetlands, and purchase illegally sold water from community wells (Felbab-Brown, 2021; Wicker, 2021). By the end of 2020, illegal cannabis cultivation extracted anything from 11 million litres up to 37 million litres of water per day. The full legalisation of marijuana is unlikely to reduce this water theft (Felbab-Brown, 2021).

One of the more egregious challenges and emerging forms of water theft involves floodplain harvesting (the diversion and impoundment of water flowing across floodplains into private on-farm storage) in Australia's Murray–Darling Basin (MDB). In 2021, the Select Committee on Floodplain Harvesting (2021: x) noted that the 'New South Wales [NSW] Government has failed to meet its obligations under the Murray–Darling Basin Agreement by allowing the unchecked growth of unregulated floodplain harvesting extraction to volumes well in excess of the 1994 Murray–Darling Basin Cap'. The capacity of private on-farm storage to hold floodplain waters in NSW has also increased by 142 per cent since 1994 (Slattery and Johnson, 2021; see also Brown et al., 2022). There is this 'kind of legal–illegal [water] theft' in the northern catchments of the MDB in which irrigators can legally extract excessive amounts of water, purposed for environmental flows, that may be otherwise illegal or harmful elsewhere (Beasley, 2021: 224–225). This unchecked growth in floodplain harvesting is, arguably, constituent of a broader culture of over-extraction, mismanagement and maleficence, predicated on decades of exploitation and harmful water policy since European settlement, which has enabled the state–corporate theft of water. Collusive arrangements between rogue irrigators and deviant state actors in northern NSW have enabled opportunities to harvest and impound unmetered and unregulated floodplain waters without a licence for three decades (Baird, 2023). This illegal take has been facilitated by water bureaucrats employing ministerial discretion and power to lift water restrictions, change water policy and prioritise floodwater events for corporate benefit in the northern MDB. For example, in February 2020, a former water minister in NSW lifted an embargo (intended to replenish downstream communities) to allow northern irrigators to freely extract and divert floodplain water without a licence. There have also been multiple attempts to legalise floodplain harvesting without a licence in the NSW State Parliament (Select Committee on Floodplain Harvesting, 2021). While floodplain harvesting became licensed, metered and regulated in March 2023 (National Resource Access Regulator, 2024), this legal–illegal take of water at the time, coupled with drought, led to a significant decline of inland flows along the lower Darling River and into the Menindee Lakes, contributing to the death of millions of native fish in 2019 (Australian Academy of Sciences, 2019). The social and ecological impacts have been considerable and devastating (Maloney et al., 2020).

Conclusion

Water theft is a social, political and economic issue that societies have wrestled with, and regulated, for millennia. Green criminologists argue that there is much to learn and adopt from the diverse history of water theft in devising criminological agendas for the future. This entry has explored some of the complexities associated with water theft, and examined how fresh water is currently being commodified, exploited and tenured under policies of water privatisation. This has posed major threats and risks regarding human rights and ecological justice and sustainability. There are also several emerging forms of water theft that are intrinsically linked to and undertaken for the purposes of organised crime, drug cultivation and enhancing national security. These, too, have real and potential harmful impacts and thus require greater academic inquiry.

ALEXANDER BAIRD

Further reading

Baird A (2024) 'Farmers as allies towards ecological justice: Lessons from water markets, colonialism and theft in Australia's Murray–Darling Basin'. In Lobo M, Mayes E and Bedford L (eds) *Planetary Justice: Stories and Studies of Action, Resilience and Solidarity*, Bristol University Press.

Barclay E and Bartel R (2015) 'Defining environmental crime: The perspective of farmers', *Journal of Rural Studies*, 39: 188–198. https://doi.org/10.1016/j.jrurstud.2015.01.007.

Brisman A, McClanahan B, South N and Walters R (2018) *Water, Crime and Security in the Twenty-First Century: Too Dirty, Too Little, Too Much*, Palgrave Macmillan.

Eman, K. (2023). The Harms and Crimes of Water Theft and Pollution. *Oxford Research Encyclopedia of Criminology*. Retrieved 9 Dec. 2024, from https://oxfordre.com/criminology/view/10.1093/acrefore/9780190264079.001.0001/acrefore-9780190264079-e-773.

Mao K and Zhao Z (2023) 'Authoritarian environmentalism and epistemological violence: A southern green criminology analysis of the 2014 Lanzhou water crisis and the Belt and Road Initiative expansion into the global water sector', *International Journal for Crime, Justice and Social Democracy*, 12(4): 27–38.

References

Australian Academy of Sciences (2019) 'Investigation of the causes of the mass fish kills in the Menindee Region NSW over the summer of 2018–2019'. AAS, 18 February.

Baird A (2023) *Drain the State: Exploring Water Theft in Australia's Murray–Darling Basin*, PhD thesis, Deakin University.

Baird A and Walters R (2020) 'Water theft through the ages: Insights for green criminology', *Critical Criminology*, 28: 371–388. https://doi.org/10.1007/s10612-020–09526–0.

Baird A, Walters R and White R (2021) 'Water theft malfeasance in Australia', *International Journal of Crime, Justice and Social Democracy*, 9(3): 83–97. doi:10.5204/ijcjsd.v10i1.1604

Barclay E and Bartel R (2015) 'Defining environmental crime: The perspective of farmers', *Journal of Rural Studies*, 39: 188–198. https://doi.org/10.1016/j.jrurstud.2015.01.007.

Barlow M and Clarke T (2017) *Blue Gold: The Battle Against Corporate Theft of the World's Water*. Routledge.

Beasley R (2021) *Dead in the Water: A Very Angry Book About Our Greatest Environmental Catastrophe... The Death of the Murray–Darling Basin*, Allen & Unwin.

Brisman A, McClanahan B, South N and Walters R (2018) *Water, Crime and Security in the Twenty-First Century: Too Dirty, Too Little, Too Much*, Palgrave Macmillan.

Brisman A, McClanahan B, South N and Walters R (2020) 'The politics of water rights: Scarcity, sovereignty and security'. In Eman K, Meško G, Segato L and Migliorini M (eds) *Water, Governance and Crime* (pp. 17–29), Springer.

Brown P, Colloff MJ, Slattery M, Johnson W and Guarino F (2022) 'An unsustainable level of take: On-farm storages and floodplain water harvesting in the northern Murray–Darling Basin, Australia', *Australasian Journal of Water Resources*, 26(1): 43–58.

Eman K (2016) 'Water crimes: A contemporary (security) issue', *CRIMEN-časopis za krivične nauke*, 1: 44–57.

Eman K (2023) 'The harms and crimes of water theft and pollution'. In Pontell HN (ed.) *Oxford Research Encyclopedia of Criminology and Criminal Justice* (pp. xx–yy), Oxford University Press.

Eman K and White R (2020) 'Water and organised crime'. In Eman K, Meško G, Segato L and Migliorini M (eds) *Water, Governance, and Crime Issues* (pp. 47–59), Springer. https://doi.org/10.1007/978-3-030-44798-4_4.

Eman K, Kuhar S and Meško G (2017) 'Water crimes and policing', *Journal of Criminal Justice and Security*, 19(2): 105–119.

European Water Crimes Project (2019) *Impel Project Water Crimes*, European Union Network for the Implementation and Enforcement of Environmental Law.

Felbab-Brown V (2017) *Water Theft and Water Smuggling: Growing Problem or Tempest in a Teapot?*, Brookings.

Felbab-Brown V (2021) *Pot, Water Theft, and Environmental Harms in the US and Mexico*, Brookings.

Frederick KD (1996) 'Water as a source of international conflict', *Resources for the Future*, 123: 9–12.

Gleick PH and Heberger M (2012) 'Water conflict chronology'. In Gleick PH *The World's Water* (pp. 175–214), Island Press.

Hadid D and Sattar A (10 September 2018) *For Karachi's Water Mafia, Stolen H20 is a Lucrative Business*, NPR.

Johnson H, South N and Walters R (2017) 'The commodification and exploitation of fresh water: Property, human rights and green criminology', *International Journal of Law, Crime and Justice*, 44: 146–162. https://doi.org/10.1016/j.ijlcj.2015.07.003

Loch A, Pérez-Blanco CD, Carmody E, Felbab-Brown V, Adamson D and Seidl C (2020) 'Grand theft water and the calculus of compliance', *Nature Sustainability*, 3(12):1012–1018.

Maloney M, Boehringer G, MacCarrick G, Satija M, Graham M and Williams R (2020) *The 2019 Inquiry into the Health of the Barka/Darling River and Menindee Lakes*, Australian Peoples' Tribunal for Community and Nature's Rights.

Meehan K (2010) *Greywater and the Grid: Explaining Informal Water Use in Tijuana*, PhD thesis, School of Geography and Development, University of Arizona.

Meehan K (2013) 'Disciplining de facto development: Water theft and hydrosocial order in Tijuana', *Environment and Planning D: Society and Space*, 21(2): 319–336. https://doi.org/10.1068/d20610

Meško G and Eman K (2020) 'Policing water crimes'. In Eman K, Meško G, Segato L and Migliorini M (eds) *Water, Governance, and Crime Issues* (pp. 75–91), Springer.

National Resource Access Regulator (2024) *Floodplain Harvesting*, NSW State Government.

Segato L, Mattioli W, Capello N and Migliorini M (2017) 'Environmental crimes in the water sector', *Water Utility Journal*, 20: 13–27.

Select Committee on Floodplain Harvesting (2021) *Floodplain Harvesting*, NSW Legislative Council.

Slattery M and Johnson B (2021) *Floodplain Water Harvesting in the Northern New South Wales Murray–Darling Basin*, Slattery & Johnson.

The Global Initiative (2014) *Water, Water Everywhere? Charting the Growth of Organised Water Theft*, The Global Initiative.

Weigand-Shahani A (2018) 'Illegal water use, marijuana, and California's environ-

ment', *Environmental Law Reporter. News & Analysis*, 48: 10625.
White R (2016) 'Reparative justice, environmental crime and penalties for the powerful', *Crime, Law and Social Change*, 67: 117–132. doi:10.1007/s10611-016-9635-5.
White R (2021) *Theorising Green Criminology: Selected Essays*, Routledge.
Wicker J (24 July 2021) 'Marijuana farmers blamed for water theft as drought grips American west', *The Guardian*.

ALEXANDER BAIRD

19. Wildlife trafficking

Introduction

Wildlife trafficking involves the transport, distribution, and sale of a wild species of plant or animal, including the whole specimen, its parts, or derived products, that contravenes laws and/or other regulatory measures. Wildlife trafficking harms public health, rural livelihoods, ecosystems, political accountability, and the individual lives of trafficked wildlife. This entry provides an overview of the theory and typologies relating to wildlife trafficking, while noting key policy and research gaps. Corruption, fraud, financial crime, social media, and online marketplaces are all notable facilitators of wildlife trafficking. Emerging issues in addressing wildlife trafficking are also identified, such as the persistence of "plant blindness", as well as the under-recognition of regions and other taxonomic groups deemed not worth prioritising. Wildlife trafficking is a constantly evolving challenge and addressing it will require continued research effort, and consideration of numerous complexities in policymaking arenas at local, national, and international levels.

Wildlife trafficking can occur on a purely domestic basis, where the chain linking the extraction of wildlife to the end consumer is all within a country's borders. Conversely, in the transnational sense, wildlife trafficking is the process by which wildlife is harvested from a country of origin and is eventually delivered to a foreign destination country in a way that contravenes international or state wildlife laws. Uses of trafficked wildlife include traditional medicines (i.e., powders, dried wildlife), processed commodities (i.e., skins, furs, timber, textiles, furniture, cosmetics, and perfume), collectors' items (i.e., rare specimens, pets, and to supply zoos, laboratories), and food (i.e., bushmeat, seafood, and to supply restaurants) (Wyatt, 2022). Though there have been numerous attempts to measure the true magnitude and value of the global illegal wildlife trade, the covert nature of wildlife trafficking means that estimates have not been robust or replicable. Notwithstanding the severity and immense impacts of other types of trafficking activities, such as the trafficking of persons, drugs, and arms, wildlife trafficking has been suggested to be one of the costliest forms of trafficking (Doody et al., 2021).

Consequences and impacts

The consequences of wildlife trafficking are far-reaching, both in terms of geography, and in the various aspects and sectors of society that are affected. The overexploitation of wild fauna and flora is known to be one of the largest contributors to global biodiversity loss (Maxwell et al., 2016). Wildlife trade can also facilitate the spread of emerging and re-emerging zoonotic diseases and pose significant threats to public health (Beirne, 2021; Chomel et al., 2007; Swift et al., 2007). The risk is especially pronounced for trafficked animals, as they do not undergo health inspections.

There are a number of threats to both individual and state security that emanate from any type of organised trafficking activity. Depending on the intensity of trafficking and degree of organised crime involvement, trafficking can:

- challenge high-quality national governance and the state foundations of responsive democratic rule;
- impede the detection and prosecution of criminal activity, as illegitimate behaviour becomes the norm;
- promote the decay of functioning domestic social structures and financial structures; and
- expose international system vulnerabilities by illuminating components that can be exploited (Mandel, 2010).

The corruption tactics used by transnational criminal networks further interfere with political legitimacy, accountability, and perceived integrity of state structures (Mandel, 2010). Simultaneously, the violence used by organised crime threatens the safety of law-abiding citizens and government officials, while undermining the government's ability to protect its citizens (Mandel, 2010).

In addition to the aforementioned anthropogenic consequences and violence against humans, it is also important to consider the harm, suffering, and injury that wildlife trafficking causes to non-human animals. Animals that are used in live wildlife trafficking processes experience stress, pain, trauma, and high mortality rates. It is important to recognise that victims of wildlife trafficking include not only humans and the state, but wild plants, animals, ecosystems, biodiversity, and the broader environment (Wyatt, 2022).

Wildlife trafficking can also threaten the survival of populations of endangered species through the unsustainable extraction of species from their habitats. This not only harms the target species but can have cascading effects throughout their ecosystems. For example, the decline of a top predator such as sharks can cause top-down impacts on their ecosystems, including behavioural changes in other species, and/or the over-abundance of prey species that have few other predators (e.g., Ferretti et al., 2010). The over-abundance of prey species can cause the subsequent over-harvesting of the next trophic level, including declines in flora abundance (Ripple and Beschta, 2012). On the other hand, the decline of a prey species for illegal trade (e.g., Lindsey et al., 2011) limits food availability for predators, which can contribute to their decline, behaviour change, and/or push them into further conflict with people (e.g., livestock farmers; Trinkel, 2013). This, in turn, can further drive pre-emptive or retaliatory illegal hunting of predators and trade in their parts. Biodiversity losses for wildlife trafficking also contribute to significant losses for communities that benefit from living near healthy ecosystems, including financial losses with reduced wildlife-based opportunities, such as tourism and legal hunting (Lindsey et al., 2011).

These environmental impacts of wildlife trafficking may be increasingly exacerbated by the effects of climate change. For example, prolonged drought periods can cause a decline in primary productivity, and therefore a decline in populations of herbivores. This can then place even more pressure on carnivore populations that are already being illegally hunted and experiencing conflict with local communities (Trinkel, 2013). Ecosystems can also be damaged through the introduction of invasive species that are released from wildlife trafficking, which can also spread novel diseases to native wildlife (Wyatt, 2022). In short, there are numerous interlinking pathways in which wildlife trafficking can negatively impact ecosystems, and perhaps even further drive wildlife trafficking.

Theory pertaining to wildlife crime

Despite a number of possible synergies, the literature from conservation studies and criminology has yet to be fully integrated (Boratto and Gibbs, 2021). Conservation biology historically explored threats to wildlife by focusing on natural sciences theory and tools such as ecology, population modelling, genetics, and resource management with little emphasis on the role of social factors and compliance (Boratto and Gibbs, 2021). Research on wildlife trafficking was initially dominated by theory from natural resource management to explore how harvesting and trading wildlife can be done sustainably (Sas-Rolfes et al., 2019). The field of economics has also played an important role in exploring property rights, the use of "the commons", and the impact of decisions on trade bans, farming, and managing stockpiles (Sas-Rolfes et al., 2019). Much of this preliminary research focused on high-value and large charismatic mammals, such as elephants, rhinoceroses, and tigers (Sas-Rolfes et al., 2019). For instance, economic research has suggested that organised poaching of elephants may be quite sensitive to the probability of interception by anti-poaching patrols yet have little relationship to the black-market price of ivory, which has important implications for proponents of "flooding the market" approaches (Lopes, 2015). While all these approaches are incredibly important contributions, the lack of collaboration between the fields of conservation and criminology in particular is limiting knowledge development (Boratto and Gibbs, 2021).

Von Essen et al. (2014) outline a variety of theories to explain wildlife crime offending and deviance from conservation rules. These theories can be separated into criminology's "instrumental perspective" and "normative perspective". The instrumental perspective includes rational choice theory, wherein the individual evaluates the costs and benefits of committing the offence and is driven by utility maximisation, whereas counter-efforts focus on fear-based deterrence and situational crime prevention (Clarke and Cornish, 2001; von Essen et al., 2014). In other words, the offender chooses to commit a crime because of their beliefs that they will get away with it, and that the benefits outweigh the costs (Moreto and Pires, 2018). Wildlife trafficking has also been explained using the routine activity approach, which situates the offender as having the opportunity to commit a crime due to shifting routine activities of everyday people (Moreto and Pires, 2018). Wildlife crime can therefore occur anytime a motivated offender finds themselves with a suitable target and a lack of capable guardians. Capable guardians are not limited to law enforcement personnel but can include the simple presence of everyday people (Moreto and Pires, 2018). Situational crime prevention refers to strategies that disrupt the immediate context and environmental factors that allow wildlife crimes to take place (Kretser et al., 2017). Examples of situational crime prevention to reduce wildlife trafficking include screening entrance points to protected areas; surveillance technologies, extending guardianship and opportunities to report wildlife trafficking; and implementing social marketing campaigns (Kretser et al., 2017; Kurland et al., 2017).

While approaches focused on the actors (individual offenders) and stages (segment of the illegal trade) can explain much of illicit activity, product-focused approaches are also useful (Moreto and Lemieux, 2015). For example, the CRAVED theft framework posits that wildlife theft is dependent on the animal's concealability, removability, availability, value, enjoyability, and disposability (von Essen et al., 2014). Since these factors change as wildlife moves along the illicit supply chain, a more suitable and comprehensive model that has been proposed is the CAPTURED framework, which focuses on the wildlife product's concealability, availability, processability, transferability, usability, removability, enjoyability, and disposability (Moreto and Lemieux, 2015).

Examples of normative theories to explain non-compliance focus on the role of morals and socialisation (Moreto and Gau, 2017). Compliance is dependent on whether the law is perceived as legitimate and consistent with internalised norms such that the law also represents "the right thing to do". The normative perspective is essential to explain the conundrum that occurs when traditional law enforcement methods and deterrence (detection and punishment) prove insufficient to deter crimes (von Essen et al., 2014). Approaches to protect wildlife from illegal activities can combine multiple models including crime prevention, traditional law enforcement deterrence, changing social norms, and sometimes approaches that are based on sustainable conservation such as hunting restrictions, licensing, and generating funds for conservation.

Protecting species from wildlife trafficking is contingent on changing human behaviour at each stage of the supply chain. Currently, the illegal consumption of wildlife is receiving increasing research attention. Much of the research on this topic has focused on understanding the motivations behind illegal hunting, with comparatively less research focused on the transit stages of wildlife trafficking. The types of actors involved in wildlife trafficking can range from opportunistic individuals to organised crime groups (UNODC, 2020). For some people, the profits from trafficking wildlife are used for basic subsistence, while others use the profits to become multimillionaires, differences which make behavioural change more difficult. Highlighting such complexity, a typology of wildmeat traffickers has been proposed by Gore et al. (2021), which includes: trading charities (who are filling a social purpose, such as cultural or medicinal); mutual societies (with disposable incomes who enjoy collecting rare species); business sideliners (who have legal businesses and venture into wildlife trafficking to supplement existing income); criminal diversifiers (who are operating other illicit supply chains and incorporate wildlife); and opportunistic irregulars (who take advantage of trafficking opportunities when they arise) (Gore et al., 2021).

Corruption and fraud

Corruption involves the abuse of entrusted power for rent-seeking and private gain (OECD, 2018). Officials can therefore play a passive role such as accepting a bribe, or a more active one, such as extortion (Interpol and UNEP, 2016). Corruption is widespread across all nodes of a wildlife trafficking network – including park rangers, conservation practitioners, police, military, and customs officers, diplomats, port authorities, entry–exit inspectors, investigators, prosecutors, magistrates, and elected officials (van Uhm and Moreto, 2018; OECD, 2018; Anagnostou and Doberstein, 2022).

To facilitate wildlife trafficking, rangers can provide information, equipment, and stolen wildlife contraband from stockpiles to supply poachers (Milliken et al., 2012;

OECD, 2018). Further along the supply chain, traffickers can be aided by officials who are willing to accept bribes for inaction. In the illegal trade in live wild animals, corrupt certified veterinarians may be involved (OECD, 2018). Customs officials can misreport the number of animals being transported and lie about the species being trafficked. Diplomats can use their immunity to transport illegal wildlife, Convention on International Trade in Endangered Species of Wild Fauna and Flora (CITES) representatives can supply fraudulent CITES permits, and members of the judiciary can destroy documents and evidence, and grant bail or give light sentences (OECD, 2018). One of the challenges to eliminating wildlife trafficking-related corruption is that when wildlife contraband is seized, authorities usually do not further investigate corruption at the early stages of the trafficking chain (OECD, 2018).

Corruption can be differentiated into petty and grand. Petty corruption may be ad hoc and involve a small bribe to a low-level official to achieve a passive or minor facilitating action among targets (Mandel, 2010), such as turning a blind eye to an illegal wildlife product being smuggled. Grand corruption, on the other hand, may involve larger sums of money to high-level officials, and is generally pre-planned to influence important and/or a large number of decisions (Mandel, 2010; OECD, 2018). Grand corruption and petty corruption often coexist. Organised crime groups view bribes to corrupt officials as simply a "cost of doing business". For example, in certain Mexican drug trafficking networks, it is common for the organised crime group to establish an informal bribery contract with border and government officials of higher standing, and the money then trickles down to customs control agents (Basu, 2014). Both parties also occasionally agree on a certain percentage of contraband shipments to be seized, which is simply considered an operational cost for the drug traffickers (Basu, 2014). This also happens in wildlife trafficking, when leaders of the network allow a "fall guy" to get caught and arrested for smuggling wildlife, then the wildlife is seized by the government and sold back to the group (Christy, 2010).

Fraudulent practices often work in tandem with corrupt practices. Fraud, or criminal deception, has been noted extensively in wildlife trafficking. Examples include falsely declaring live animals as dead; incorrect species classification; exporting unauthorised specimens among authorised specimens; exporting to individuals or places other than those indicated on the permits; falsely identifying the exporter on the permits; and/or changing the permit number or entity code (WCO, 2015).

Emerging issues

Biases in media reporting are thought to contribute to the problem of wildlife trafficking, as these may misrepresent the scale of the issue for less charismatic species, and therefore fail to garner public interest and awareness (Chawla et al., 2020). For example, scholars are increasingly calling attention to the issue of "plant blindness", which refers to the neglect of plants in research and policy arenas, and in this context, the insufficient attention placed on understanding and stopping the illegal trade in wild plant species (Margulies et al., 2019). The illegal plant trade is in fact a serious threat to hundreds of species that are exploited for timber, horticulture, and ornamental purposes. It is also worth noting that media reporting contributes to the aforementioned formation of norms surrounding wildlife use and trade.

The ill-informed de-prioritisation of certain taxonomic groups is not limited to plants. Invertebrates are also typically perceived to be of less importance than vertebrate animals and do not receive the same level of attention and resources (Losey et al., 2022). Researchers have found extensive availability of insects and arachnids on popular online commerce platforms, including many species that have legislation restricting and prohibiting their trade. Many arthropods are sold to provide services, such as biological pest control, pollination, education, and entertainment (Losey et al., 2022). Aside from large charismatic megafauna, exotic birds, reptiles, amphibians, and fish are also increasingly popular choices for pets.

Another newly observed trend is increasing domestic and international market demand for species from relatively "new locations", such as Latin America and the Caribbean, especially reptiles, amphibians, birds, and small mammals (Gluszek et al., 2021). Though these regions are experiencing immense wildlife trafficking pressure, they have not yet received the interventions and research attention that are needed to better protect the region's natural heritage.

Financial crime

Financial crimes are an essential part of the wildlife trafficking process (Viollaz et al., 2018). Tax evasion and money laundering are common to all actors in an organised wildlife trafficking network, as they must try to conceal the origin of their illegal profits (Viollaz et al., 2018). The Financial Action Task Force (FATF) is an intergovernmental organisation working to combat money laundering on an international scale. The FATF was established in 1989 by the G7 Summit, but it was not until June 2020 that they recognised wildlife trafficking as a financial threat and money laundering crime (FATF, 2020). The 2020 report highlighted that wildlife traffickers often use front companies, and layer funds through cash deposits and e-transfers. Wildlife traffickers hide their identities and avoid detection by using money mule accounts and low-value payments (FATF, 2020). To combat this, more collaboration and intelligence sharing is needed from law enforcement, customs, financial intelligence units, and compliance officers.

Technology

Wildlife trafficking is often conducted through the surface web (Lavorgna and Sajeva, 2021). The role of social media and e-commerce platforms in facilitating online wildlife trafficking has become increasingly more prominent (Stringham et al., 2021). This includes general marketplaces (e.g., eBay, Amazon, Alibaba), private messaging apps (e.g., WhatsApp), and social media platforms (e.g., Facebook, Instagram, Pinterest, Etsy) (Lavorgna and Sajeva, 2021; Wyatt et al., 2022). Wildlife trafficking that occurs online is also often intermingled with legitimate companies and merchants that are involved in the legal wildlife trade (Lavorgna, 2014). There has been little law enforcement pressure to date to cause a shift of the trade to the dark web (Lavorgna and Sajeva, 2021). As such, the private sector and civil society also have a large role to play.

One possible solution to support government agencies tasked with preventing the illegal trade of wildlife online is to shift the burden of prevention to the social media and e-commerce websites that facilitate the trade. Engaging with the private sector can be an efficient way to tackle online wildlife trafficking, especially to monitor and prevent offenders from using their sites for illegal transactions. In addition, these platforms could be held liable for illegal transactions and could be required to take steps to inhibit the illegal sale of protected species, such as through the introduction of comprehensive policy and tagging/flagging illegal transactions (Losey et al., 2022). It is important for protocols to be established to ensure long-term compliance with wildlife legislation among companies that offer online marketplaces, social media platforms and courier services (Wingard and Pascual, 2018).

Conclusion

Domestic and international wildlife trafficking are constantly evolving phenomena. Experts have noted that wildlife trafficking is becoming more transnationalised and sophisticated (Gluszek et al., 2021). When a valued wildlife species is diminished in the wild, this can lead to captive breeding for commercial purposes, or a species substitution to replace the same market. Similarly, when law enforcement efforts are intensified in one geographic or online location, wildlife traffickers will often shift their activities elsewhere, if possible. Interventions to address wildlife trafficking must consider the complexities stemming from the interactions between the taxonomic unit being trafficked, the geographic distribution of the taxa, the degree of product transformation (Roberts and Hinsley, 2020), and the degree of professionalisation of the trafficking network. All of these complexities highlight the need for ongoing research effort and increased collaborative efforts across sectors and jurisdictions to mitigate wildlife trafficking.

Michelle Anagnostou

Further reading

Esmail, Nafeesa, Bonnie C. Wintle, Michael Sas-Rolfes, Andrea Athanas, Colin M. Beale, Zara Bending, Ran Dai et al. "Emerging illegal wildlife trade issues: A global horizon scan." *Conservation Letters* 13, no. 4 (2020): e12715.

Margulies, Jared D., Leigh-Anne Bullough, Amy Hinsley, Daniel J. Ingram, Carly Cowell, Bárbara Goettsch, Bente B. Klitgård, Anita Lavorgna, Pablo Sinovas, and Jacob Phelps.

"Illegal wildlife trade and the persistence of 'plant blindness'." *Plants, People, Planet* 1, no. 3 (2019): 173–182.

Phelps, Jacob, Duan Biggs, and Edward L. Webb. "Tools and terms for understanding illegal wildlife trade." *Frontiers in Ecology and the Environment* 14, no. 9 (2016): 479–489.

Sas-Rolfes, M., D.W.S. Challender, A. Hinsley, D. Veríssimo, and E.J. Milner-Gulland. *Illegal Wildlife Trade: Scale, Processes, and Governance* (vol. 44). Annual Review of Environment and Resources. Annual Reviews Inc., 2019. https://doi.org/10.1146/annurev-environ-101718-033253.

Thomas-Walters, Laura, Amy Hinsley, Daniel Bergin, Gayle Burgess, Hunter Doughty, Sara Eppel, Douglas MacFarlane et al. "Motivations for the use and consumption of wildlife products." *Conservation Biology* 35, no. 2 (2021): 483–491.

UNODC. *World Wildlife Crime Report 2024: Trafficking in Protected Species*. United Nations, Vienna, 2024.

References

Anagnostou, Michelle, and Brent Doberstein. "Illegal wildlife trade and other organised crime: A scoping review." *Ambio* 51, no. 7 (2022): 1615–1631.

Basu, Gautam. "Concealment, corruption, and evasion: A transaction cost and case analysis of illicit supply chain activity." *Journal of Transportation Security* 7 (2014): 209–226.

Beirne, P. "Wildlife trade and COVID-19: Towards a criminology of anthropogenic pathogen spillover." *The British Journal of Criminology* 61, no. 3 (2021): 607–626.

Boratto, R., and C. Gibbs. "Advancing interdisciplinary research on illegal wildlife trade using a conservation criminology framework." *European Journal of Criminology* 18, no. 6 (2021): 777–798. https://doi.org/10.1177/1477370819887512.

Chawla, Malaika Mathew, Arjun Srivathsa, Priya Singh, Iravatee Majgaonkar, Sushma Sharma, Girish Punjabi, and Aditya Banerjee. "Do wildlife crimes against less charismatic species go unnoticed? A case study of Golden Jackal Canis aureus Linnaeus, 1758 poaching and trade in India." *Journal of Threatened Taxa* 12 (2020): 15407–15413.

Chomel, B.B., A. Belotto, and F.X. Meslin. "Wildlife, exotic pets, and emerging zoonoses." *Emerging Infectious Diseases* 13, no. 1 (2007): 6.

Christy, Bryan. "The kingpin." *National Geographic Magazine*, 2010. https://www.nationalgeographic.com/magazine/article/asia-wildlife-trade.

Clarke, R., and D. Cornish. "Rational choice," in R. Paternoster and R. Bachman, eds, *Explaining Crime and Criminals: Essays in Contemporary Criminological Theory*, 23–42. Roxbury, 2001.

Doody, J. Sean, Joan A. Reid, Klejdis Bilali, Jennifer Diaz, and Nichole Mattheus. "In the post-COVID-19 era, is the illegal wildlife trade the most serious form of trafficking?" *Crime Science* 10, no. 1 (September 13, 2021): 19. https://doi.org/10.1186/s40163-021-00154-9.

FATF. *Money Laundering and the Illegal Wildlife Trade*. Financial Action Task Force (FATF), Paris, 2020. www.fatf-gafi.org/publications/methodandtrends/documents/money-laundering-illegal-wildlife-trade.html.

Ferretti, Francesco, Boris Worm, Gregory L. Britten, Michael R. Heithaus, and Heike K. Lotze. "Patterns and ecosystem consequences of shark declines in the ocean." *Ecology Letters* 13, no. 8 (2010): 1055–1071.

Gluszek, S., D. Ariano-Sánchez, P. Cremona, A. Goyenechea, D.A. Luque Vergara, L. McLoughlin, A. Morales et al. "Emerging trends of the illegal wildlife trade in Mesoamerica." *ORYX* 55, no. 5 (2021): 708–716. https://doi.org/10.1017/S0030605319001133.

Gore, M.L., R. Mwinyihali, L. Mayet, G.D.M. Baku-Bumb, C. Plowman, and M. Wieland. "Typologies of urban wildlife traffickers and sellers." *Global Ecology and Conservation* 27 (2021). https://doi.org/10.1016/j.gecco.2021.e01557.

Interpol, and UNEP. Strategic Report: Environment, peace and security – a convergence of threats. INTERPOL and UN Environment, 2016. https://www.unep.org/resources/report/strategic-report-environment-peace-and-security-convergence-threats.

Kretser, Heidi, Emma Stokes, Serge Wich, David Foran, and Alexa Montefiore. "Technological innovations supporting wildlife crime detection, deterrence, and enforcement." *Conservation Criminology* (2017): 155–177.

Kurland, Justin, Stephen F. Pires, Sara C. McFann, and William D. Moreto. "Wildlife crime: A conceptual integration, literature review, and methodological critique." *Crime Science* 6, no. 1 (April 28, 2017): 4. https://doi.org/10.1186/s40163–017–0066–0.

Lavorgna, Anita. "Wildlife trafficking in the Internet age." *Crime Science* 3 (2014): 1–12.

Lavorgna, Anita, and Maurizio Sajeva. "Studying illegal online trades in plants: Market characteristics, organisational and behavioural aspects, and policing challenges." *European Journal on Criminal Policy and Research* 27, no. 4 (2021): 451–470.

Lindsey, P.A., S.S. Romañach, C.J. Tambling, K. Chartier, and R. Groom. "Ecological and financial impacts of illegal bushmeat trade in Zimbabwe." *Oryx* 45, no. 1 (January

2011): 96–111. https://doi.org/10.1017/S0030605310000153.
Lopes, Adrian A. "Organized crimes against nature: Elephants in southern Africa." *Natural Resource Modeling* 28, no. 1 (2015): 86–107.
Losey, J.E., C. Chen, A.E. Davis, J.F. Deitsch, J.G. Gertin, J.A. Gorneau, E.M. Hallock et al. "Insects and spiders on the web: Monitoring and mitigating online exploitation of species and services." *Global Ecology and Conservation* 36 (2022). https://doi.org/10.1016/j.gecco.2022.e02098.
Mandel, Robert. *Dark Logic: Transnational Criminal Tactics and Global Security*. Stanford University Press, 2010.
Margulies, J.D., L.-A. Bullough, A. Hinsley, D.J. Ingram, C. Cowell, B. Goettsch, B.B. Klitgård, A. Lavorgna, P. Sinovas, and J. Phelps. "Illegal wildlife trade and the persistence of 'plant blindness'." *Plants People Planet* 1, no. 3 (2019): 173–182. https://doi.org/10.1002/ppp3.10053.
Maxwell, S.L., R.A. Fuller, T.M. Brooks, and J.E. Watson. "Biodiversity: The ravages of guns, nets and bulldozers." *Nature* 536, no. 7615 (2016): 143–145.
Milliken, Tom, Jo Shaw, Richard H. Emslie, Russell D. Taylor, and Chris Turton. "The South Africa–Viet Nam Rhino Horn Trade Nexus." *Traffic* (2012): 134–136.
Moreto, William D., and Jacinta M. Gau. "Deterrence, legitimacy, and wildlife crime in protected areas." *Conservation Criminology* (2017): 45–58.
Moreto, William D., and Andrew M. Lemieux. "From CRAVED to CAPTURED: Introducing a product-based framework to examine illegal wildlife markets." *European Journal on Criminal Policy and Research* 21 (2015): 303–320.
Moreto, William D., and Stephen F. Pires. *Wildlife Crime: An Environmental Criminology and Crime Science Perspective*. Carolina Academic Press, 2018.
OECD. *Strengthening Governance and Reducing Corruption Risks to Tackle Illegal Wildlife Trade: Lessons from East and Southern Africa*. Illicit Trade. OECD, 2018. https://doi.org/10.1787/9789264306509-en.
Ripple, William J., and Robert L. Beschta. "Trophic cascades in Yellowstone: The first 15 years after wolf reintroduction." *Biological Conservation* 145, no. 1 (2012): 205–213.
Roberts, David L., and Amy Hinsley. "The seven forms of challenges in the wildlife trade." *Tropical Conservation Science* 13 (2020): 1940082920947023.
Sas-Rolfes, M., D.W.S. Challender, A. Hinsley, D. Veríssimo, and E.J. Milner-Gulland. *Illegal Wildlife Trade: Scale, Processes, and Governance* (vol. 44). Annual Review of Environment and Resources. Annual Reviews Inc., 2019. https://doi.org/10.1146/annurev-environ-101718–033253.
Stringham, Oliver C., Adam Toomes, Aurelie M. Kanishka, Lewis Mitchell, Sarah Heinrich, Joshua V. Ross, and Phillip Cassey. "A guide to using the Internet to monitor and quantify the wildlife trade." *Conservation Biology* 35, no. 4 (2021): 1130–1139.
Swift, L., P.R. Hunter, A.C. Lees, and D.J. Bell. "Wildlife trade and the emergence of infectious diseases." *EcoHealth* 4, no. 1 (2007): 25–30. https://doi.org/10.1007/s10393–006–0076-y.
Trinkel, Martina. "Climate variability, human wildlife conflict and population dynamics of lions Panthera leo." *Naturwissenschaften* 100, no. 4 (2013): 345–353.
UNODC. *World Wildlife Crime Report 2020: Trafficking in Protected Species*. 2020.
van Uhm, Daan P., and William D. Moreto. "Corruption within the illegal wildlife trade: A symbiotic and antithetical enterprise." *The British Journal of Criminology* 58, no. 4 (2018): 864–885.
Viollaz, Julie, Jessica Graham, and Leonid Lantsman. "Using script analysis to understand the financial crimes involved in wildlife trafficking." *Crime, Law and Social Change* 69, no. 5 (2018): 595–614.
Von Essen, Erica, Hans Peter Hansen, Helena Nordström Källström, M. Nils Peterson, and Tarla Rai Peterson. "Deconstructing the poaching phenomenon: A review of typologies for understanding illegal hunting." *British Journal of Criminology* 54, no. 4 (2014): 632–651.
WCO. "Illegal wildlife trade: An outline of the problems facing Peru." World Customs Organization News, 2015. https://mag.wcoomd.org/magazine/wco-news-78/illegal-wildlife-trade-an-outline-of-the-problems-facing-peru/.
Wingard, James, and Maria Pascual. "Catch me if you can: Legal challenges to illicit wildlife trafficking over the internet." 2018. https://www.legal-atlas.com/uploads/2/6/8/4/26849604/digital-dangers-catch-me-if-you-can-july-2018.pdf.
Wyatt, Tanya. *Wildlife Trafficking: A Deconstruction of the Crime, Victims and Offenders* (2nd ed.). Palgrave Macmillan, 2022. https://link.springer.com/book/10.1007/978-3-030-83753-2.
Wyatt, Tanya, Ophelia Miralles, Francis Massé, Raulff Lima, Thiago Vargas da Costa, and Dener Giovanini. "Wildlife trafficking via social media in Brazil." *Biological Conservation* 265 (2022): 109420.

PART III

CRIMES OF CONTAMINATION

20. Air pollution

Introduction

Air pollution has become recognised as one of contemporary society's major environmental harms. Yet it arguably attracts relatively little criminological attention, in part because many activities that cause air pollution are ostensibly legal (e.g., use of motor vehicles, some forms of domestic heating, commercial production processes) but also because control of air pollution and mechanisms to address pollution problems frequently fall outside the criminal law.

Air pollution basically consists of chemicals or particles in the air that have potential to harm the health of humans, animals and plants. Air pollution can also damage buildings and lead to further degradation of the environment. While air pollution may typically be thought of as smoke or exhaust emanating from factories, other commercial activities and vehicles, air pollution comes in many different forms included gases, liquid droplets and solid particles. This includes pollution caused by domestic activities. Air pollution should thus be seen as a consequence of lawful (sometimes regulated) activity. But it is also a consequence of harmful human activity that may not strictly be classed as criminal but is so harmful in its effects that it should meet the definition of being an environmental crime.

Air pollution as environmental harm

Air pollution remains a significant environmental harm issue, representing a major threat to human health and contributing to many early deaths globally each year. The American Lung Association's 2023 *State of the Air* report concluded that 'nearly 36% of Americans – 119.6 million people – still live in places with failing grades for unhealthy levels of ozone or particle pollution' (American Lung Association, 2023). The European Environment Agency in its 2022 report on the health impacts of air pollution in Europe also concluded that in 2020, air pollution led to numerous premature deaths in the 27 European Union Member States. These included exposure to concentrations of fine particulate matter above the 2021 World Health Organization guideline level that 'resulted in 238,000 premature deaths; exposure to nitrogen dioxide above the respective guideline level led to 49,000 premature deaths. Acute exposure to ozone caused 24,000 premature deaths' (European Environment Agency, 2023). Claims have been made that air pollution is linked to 40,000 early deaths a year in the UK (Roberts, 2016).

Green criminologists Mike Lynch and Paul Stretesky identify that 'the extent of air pollution victimisation incidents in the United States, indicates that green victimisation due to air pollution exposure in the United States is 33.6 billion times more likely than a violent street crime victimisation incident' (Lynch and Stretesky, 2014: 88). While it is acknowledged that this figure was based on estimates rather than comprehensive, verifiable data, the level of premature deaths indicated from official sources identifies deaths from air pollution as an issue of environmental crime. So too, are the problems of regulating and addressing air pollution as a contemporary environmental harm issue.

The causes of air pollution

Air pollution has a variety of different causes, both legal and illegal. However, at the core of air pollution, some of the most harmful components to human health are airborne particles with a diameter equal to 2.5 micrometres or less (PM2.5) which are small enough to pass through the lungs and into the body with potential to cause major health problems (Schraufnagel et al., 2019: 411).

Much air pollution is anthropocentric in nature, being caused by human activity. This is not new. As a species, humans have long interacted with and transformed their environments – for example, burning wood in fires in order to cook food. In so doing, they have simultaneously introduced contaminants into the environment (in this example, in the form of woodsmoke and cooking-related pollutants). The scale and intensity of the pollution, however, makes a significant difference, particularly in regard to its dispersal throughout the atmosphere, waterways and land masses. This shapes the capacity of the Earth to replenish and rejuvenate itself insofar as the benefits of pollution for humans (such as cooked food) can over time, and depending on the methods and types of pollution (fossil fuel pollution), destroy and diminish ecological resilience and environmental heath generally. The more pollutants there are (such as plastics and carbon dioxide emissions) and the more their concentration in particular spaces and zones (such as oceans and the upper atmosphere), the more risk and hazard they present to humans, specific environments and non-human animals and plants.

Treadmill of production theory (Schnaiberg et al., 2002) identifies that changes in production accelerate environmental degradation and thus air pollution as part of environmental harm is a consequence of production when the methods used for production negatively impact on the environment. This theory uses the terms ecological withdrawals, ecological disorganisation and ecological additions to describe the effects of pollution. Ecological additions are the pollutants emitted into the ecosystem from the legal operation of production processes. Thus, pollution is directly linked to harmful production processes and subsequent consumption.

The use of domestic appliances such as wood burning stoves and cars also causes significant air pollution even though their use is generally legal and subject to minor regulation. The level of pollution caused in this way is difficult to quantify but is recognised as being significant. For instance, preliminary research indicates that there was a decline in anthropogenic air pollution in nations responding to the COVID-19 pandemic. NASA's Earth observatory found satellite-derived concentrations of nitrogen dioxide (NO_2) in eastern and central China from early 2020 were 10–30% lower than comparable periods in 2019 (Patel and Stevens, 2020). Thus, evidence suggests that changes in human behaviour during the pandemic (e.g., fewer cars in use and lower levels of travel during lockdown periods) resulted in lower levels of air pollution. Levels of pollution are tied to specific types and frequencies of activities as well as degrees of toxicity (which refers to a particularly harsh or harmful quality of the substance, which can contribute to negative health and environmental effects).

Air pollution and public policy

Air pollution is integrated into public policy because of both international and domestic law. At an international level, the UN Declaration on the Environment sets out broad principles on the quality of the environment as follows.

> Principle 1 – Man (*sic*) has the fundamental right to freedom, equality and adequate conditions of life, in an environment of a quality that permits a life of dignity and well-being, and he (*sic*) bears a solemn responsibility to protect and improve the environment for present and future generations.
> Principle 2 – The natural resources of the Earth, including the air, water, land, flora and fauna and especially representative samples of natural ecosystems, must be safeguarded for the benefit of present and future generations through careful planning or management, as appropriate.

In addition, the Aarhus Convention adopted in 1998 had as its objective a contribution to the protection of the right of every person of present and future generations to live in an environment adequate to his or her health and well-being. Some states have explicitly enshrined the right to live in a healthy environment into their constitution (including Algeria, Argentina, Belgium, Cuba, Portugal and South Africa. The UN also identified that 120 states are parties to at least one binding regional treaty proclaiming the right to a healthy environment. In July 2022, the UN General Assembly voted to recognise the right to a clean, healthy and sustainable environment as a universal right.

Elsewhere human rights instruments have been used to suggest that state failure to deal with air pollution goes against provisions that enshrine a right to live in a healthy environment into European law. Various provisions of the European Convention on Human Rights (ECHR), for example, set out standards to be applied in respect of the right to life and the right to peaceful enjoyment of possessions. Cases have been brought before the European Court of Human Rights where failure to deal with pollution has infringed on an individual's rights (See e.g., *Lopez Ostra v. Spain* 1994 which concerned smells, noise and polluting fumes that impacted on the individual's right to respect for their private and family life).

At a domestic level, several states also have air quality legislation. For example, both the US and the UK have Clean Air Acts designed to control pollution and regulate polluting activities. The UK also has an Environmental Protection Act 1990, which forms part of the regulatory approach to dealing with pollution by designating certain forms of pollution as a public nuisance. This falls within the power of local authorities to require measures that reduce or eliminate the nuisance. Thus, public policy creates regulatory and enforcement frameworks to deal with pollution and harmful emissions, acting as social controls to address pollution. Emissions controls can, for example, create mechanisms for punishing those who drive fuel-inefficient vehicles by imposing higher road taxes on these vehicles (where applicable) or by prohibiting high polluting vehicles from being used on public roads.

Excessive pollution, particularly that consisting of harmful emissions that contribute to air pollution and/or climate change, can thus be the subject of regulatory or criminal sanctions aimed at changing both corporate and individual behaviour and ensuring compliance with environmental standards aimed at ensuring air quality. A range of environmental legislation serves this function, generally allowing for administrative, regulatory or criminal penalties to be deployed, often with discretion left to environmental regulators to decide on the appropriate mechanism to pursue in respect of the specific breach of regulations. Regulations such as the aforementioned Clean Air Act and Environmental Protection Act 1990 (amongst others) provide tools that allow regulators to require remedial action to be taken where polluting activity is at issue. However, while environmental statutes may contain both civil and criminal sanctioning powers, 'civil penalties are most typically involved as the legal remedy against environmental wrongdoers. Criminal penalties are usually invoked only when environmental statutes have been wilfully or knowingly broken' (Situ and Emmons, 2000: 38).

In the US, the Environmental Protection Agency (EPA) as the main environmental regulator has been charged with dealing with air pollution and arguably has an obligation to do so. In the landmark case of *Massachusetts v. Environmental Protection Agency*, 549 U.S. 497 (2007), the state of Massachusetts, 11 other states and several cities brought a lawsuit to force the EPA to regulate carbon dioxide emissions and several other greenhouse gases. The case hinged on an interpretation of the Clean Air Act and its definition of air pollution. The US Supreme Court concluded that greenhouse gases constituted 'air pollutants' as defined by the Clean Air Act and accordingly the EPA was required to determine whether emissions of greenhouse gases from new motor vehicles contributed to air pollution which may reasonably be anticipated to endanger public health or welfare. Thus, the EPA as regulator can consider the polluting effects of new vehicles and take action to ensure that they are appropriately controlled.

An example of this is the 'Dieselgate' case where Volkswagen AG (VW) was alleged to have intentionally equipped its diesel cars with software designed to evade emissions standards aimed at smog reduction. The EPA identified that VW installed the 'defeat device' in four-cylinder Volkswagen and Audi vehicles from model years 2009 to 2015, including the Jetta, Beetle and Golf from those model years as well as the 2014–2015 Passat. The EPA's view was that Volkswagen's actions violated the Clean Air Act under which automakers must certify to the EPA that their vehicles meet federal emissions standards for controlling air pollution. Volkswagen AG (VW) pleaded guilty to three criminal felony counts, and agreed to pay a $2.8 billion criminal penalty, as a result of the company's long-running scheme to sell approximately 590,000 diesel vehicles in the US by using a defeat device to cheat on emissions tests mandated by the EPA and the California Air Resources Board (CARB), and by lying and obstructing justice to further the scheme. In separate civil resolutions of environmental, customs and financial claims, VW agreed to pay $1.5 billion. This includes EPA's claim for civil penalties against Volkswagen for vehicle importation and sale and customs fraud. The Dieselgate affair represents a major environmental crime which also extended into regulatory action in the EU, albeit the potential penalties were lower in the UK and the nature of EU emissions regulations meant that a loophole 'made it more difficult to prove criminal intent' (Spapens, 2018: 98).

Action to address air pollution might also be taken at state level. In Europe, the Court of Justice of the European Union (CJEU) has taken action against several European states for failure to comply with European Union (EU) air quality standards. EU legislation aims to manage and improve air quality and the 2008 ambient air quality directive (2008/50/EC) sets legally binding limits for concentrations in outdoor air of major air pollutants that impact public health, such as particulate matter (PM10 and PM2.5) and nitrogen dioxide (NO_2). As well as having direct effects, these pollutants can combine in the atmosphere to form ozone, a harmful air pollutant (and potent greenhouse gas) which can be transported great distances by weather systems.

The Directive states:

> In order to protect human health and the environment as a whole, it is particularly important to combat emissions of pollutants at source and to identify and implement the most effective emission reduction measures at local, national and Community level. Therefore, emissions of harmful air pollutants should be avoided, prevented or reduced and appropriate objectives set for ambient air quality taking into account relevant World Health Organization standards, guidelines and programmes.

Yet despite these measures being in place, several EU states have been identified as not meeting air quality standards as a result of a failure to address air pollution. For example, in 2018, the European Commission took France, Germany, Hungary, Italy, Romania and the UK to the CJEU. In 2018 the European Court of Justice (ECJ) ruled that Poland had persistently breached EU air quality limits and failed to act quickly enough to improve the situation. In April 2019 the European Environment Bureau stated that only 13 of the EU's [then] 28 Member States had filed their 'National Air Pollution Control Programmes' by the required April 2019 deadline. In 2020 (*European Commission v. Romania*, C-638/18) the European Commission also concluded that Romania had systematically and persistently violated limit values for PM10 emissions in the capital city Bucharest since 2007 and at least until 2016 (except for 2013). In November 2021, the European Commission referred Portugal to the CJEU for the Member State's poor air quality resulting from nitrogen dioxide (NO_2) levels that had repeatedly breached EU standards. This is not an exhaustive list of all breaches of EU air quality legislation but demonstrates the extent to which EU states have struggled to comply with EU standards on air quality. It also exposes how some communities are disproportionately exposed to harmful air pollution, constituting both a social and an environmental injustice.

Addressing air pollution problems

Ambient air pollution remains a leading health and environmental concern. Much air pollution is the result of lawful activity albeit regulation to manage air pollution and its impacts has been created at international level to set the frameworks for controlling and monitoring pollution. As a result, countries have an obligation to deal with air pollution under international law and the required controls are often embedded in national laws and monitoring regimes that provide mechanisms for enforcing controls on pollution and requiring remediation or reduction. Yet air pollution remains a persistent problem that requires regulatory actions in respect of companies who go beyond their permitted activity, criminal enforcement respect of deliberate polluting behaviour and social action to address and change consumer behaviour that causes air pollution.

To compound matters, there is an association between climate change and specific environmental harms such as air pollution, which exacerbates existing health problems.

> An estimated 4.2 million premature deaths every year globally are linked to ambient air pollution, mainly from heart disease, stroke, chronic obstructive pulmonary disease, lung cancer, and acute respiratory infections in children. New models estimate that fossil-fuel-related greenhouse gas emissions account for about 65% of the excess mortality rate attributable to air pollution. Furthermore, climate and weather strongly affect where and when air pollution occurs. (World Meteorological Organization, 2020: 27)

As this illustrates, weather systems influence the movement of air pollutants and the actions of winds and precipitation are factors in how and where air pollutants are dispersed and who is most affected by them. Global warming makes things like the pollution crisis even worse and there is a need to consider air pollution, ozone depletion, persistent pollutants and climate change as interlinked and serious problems.

ANGUS NURSE

Further reading

Alm, J. and Shimshack, J. (2014) Environmental Enforcement and Compliance: Lessons from Pollution, Safety, and Tax Settings, *Foundations and Trends in Microeconomics*, 10(4), 209–274. http://dx.doi.org/10.1561/0700000048

Germani, A. R., Morone, P. and Testa, G. (2011) *Enforcement and Air Pollution: An Environmental Justice Case Study*. MPRA Paper No. 38656. Available at: https://mpra.ub.uni-muenchen.de/38656/1/MPRA_paper_38656.pdf (accessed 1 October 2023).

Heydon, J. (2023) Between Ordinary Harm and Deviance: Evaluating the UK's Regulatory Regime for Controlling Air Pollution from Wood Burning Stoves, *The British Journal of Criminology*, 63(6), 1504–1522. https://doi.org/10.1093/bjc/azac102

Konisky, D. M. and Woods, N. D. (2010) Exporting Air Pollution? Regulatory Enforcement and Environmental Free Riding in the United States, *Political Research Quarterly*, 63(4), 771–782. https://doi.org/10.1177/1065912909334429

Potoski, M. and Woods, N. D. (2002) Dimensions of State Environmental Policies, *Policy Studies Journal*, 30, 208–226. https://doi.org/10.1111/j.1541-0072.2002.tb02142.x

Walters, R. (2014) Toxic Atmospheres: Air Pollution, Trade and the Politics of Regulation. In R. White (Ed.), *Transnational Environmental Crime* (pp. 321–337), Abingdon: Routledge.

Weait, M. (1989) The Letter of the Law? An Enquiry into Reasoning and Formal Enforcement in the Industrial Air Pollution Inspectorate, *The British Journal of Criminology*, 29(1), 57–70. https://doi.org/10.1093/oxfordjournals.bjc.a047790

References

American Lung Association (2023) *State of the Air 2023: Key Findings*. Available at: https://www.lung.org/research/sota/key-findings (accessed 1 December 2023).

European Environment Agency (2023) *Health Impacts of Air Pollution in Europe, 2022*, Copenhagen: European Environment Agency. Available at: https://www.eea.europa.eu/publications/air-quality-in-europe-2022/health-impacts-of-air-pollution (accessed 20 December 2023).

Lynch, M. and Stretesky, P. (2014) *Exploring Green Criminology: Towards a Green Criminological Revolution*, Farnham: Ashgate.

Patel, K. and Stevens, J. (2020) Airborne Nitrogen Dioxide Plummets Over China. *Earth Observatory NASA*.

Roberts, M. (2016) UK Air Pollution 'Linked to 40,000 Early Deaths a Year', BBC News Online. Available at: http://www.bbc.co.uk/news/health-35629034 (accessed 1 October 2023).

Schnaiberg, A., Pellow, D. and Weinberg, A. (2002) The Treadmill of Production and the Environmental State. In A. P. J. Mol and F. H. Buttel (Eds.), *The Environmental State under Pressure* (pp. 15–32), London: Elsevier North-Holland.

Schraufnagel, D., Balmes, J., Cowl, C., Matteis, S., Jung, S., Mortimer, K., Perez-Padilla, R., Rice, M., Riojas-Rodriguez, H. and Sood, A. (2019) Air Pollution and Noncommunicable Diseases: A Review by the Forum of International Respiratory Societies, *Chest*, 155, 409–416.

Situ, Y. and Emmons, D. (2000) *Environmental Crime*, Thousand Oaks, CA: Sage.

Spapens, T. (2018) The 'Dieselgate' Scandal: A Criminological Perspective. In T. Spapens, R. White, D. van Uhm and W. Huisman (Eds.), *Green Crimes and Dirty Money* (pp. 91–112), London: Routledge.

World Meteorological Organization. (2020) *WMO Provisional Statement on the State of the Global Climate in 2019*. Geneva: World Meteorological Organization.

21. Fast fashion

Introduction

Mass consumption of clothing and textiles leaves a pollution footprint at each step of the clothing's life cycle. The fashion industry is not only a significant perpetrator of environmental harm, but a reinforcer of social and economic inequality. The 'fashion industry' is a conglomerate of businesses and corporate 'taste-makers' whose strategic marketing and social media influence and engineer the continuous rotation of appealing clothing and aesthetic styles. Fashion trends are created and discarded quickly; what was once 'relevant' or 'cool' is swiftly forgotten as the new hit trend emerges. In practice, this creates a perpetuating cycle of consume, discard, consume. The manufacturing of textiles, distribution of cheap clothing, and disposal of unwanted garments all create diverse types of waste and impact different groups of people. This entry will provide a brief overview of how fast fashion is hazardous to air, water, and land. The consequences of fast fashion include social harms which are transnational in impact. Analysis of these harms includes acknowledging how fast fashion functions and profits off poverty by encouraging poor workplace conditions, and cheap labour, which simultaneously disrupts and blocks the success and sustainability of local economies. Fast fashion is thus a multifaceted and complex social and environmental problem.

Fast fashion

'Fast Fashion' is a term which describes the attitude of mass production and consumption of garments associated with the fashion industry. The practical implications of producing mass-manufactured, poor-quality clothing creates an exorbitant amount of waste and environmental harm. As this entry will explore in greater detail, fast fashion is purposely structured around designing clothing which is short-loved and short-lived. Garments are created and sold in a 'trend'-driven industry, only to last one or two 'seasons' before falling apart. Being 'trend driven', this creates a perpetual desire for purchasing appealing clothing, whilst older clothes disintegrate, allowing the consumer to justify buying more clothing. As trends proliferate, clothing and textile waste continue to pile up and pass through a chain of redistribution and destruction.

Whilst some suggest 'fashion' and sustainable manufacturing practices are 'the future', changing consumer behaviour and what fashion means to them (i.e., a functional product instead of entertainment), is directly at odds with the current fast fashion mentality, which is driven by the fashion industry. Because environmental harm occurs in the fashion industry through a number of different culprits, ascribing responsibility to one company is difficult, making analysis of state–corporate crime challenging, not to mention criminal prosecutions (Simončič, 2021; Chan, Ren and Liu, 2022).

Fast fashion can be described as an act of 'democratising' clothing accessibility. The rapidly changing fashion industry has provided easily available, affordable and 'trendy' clothing to the masses quickly and effectively, allowing most people across the world to have access to clothing. Whilst clothing has become more accessible for those on a low income, their garments are still of inferior quality and are not intended for longevity. This means that consumers of cheap clothing are not benefiting from this access and will spend more money due to the continuous need to replace their rapidly disintegrating clothing. Counter-fast fashion movements such as 'upcycling' (where consumers mend, alter, or create new clothing out of discarded textiles) is increasingly hard for individuals to do, as reusing clothes for other purposes is increasingly more difficult due to the poor quality of new clothing, which results in more discarded clothing to clog landfill (Wazir, 2021).

Exportation is the wealthy nation's solution for textile waste, as importers based in poorer countries or regions purchase hundreds of bales of mixed clothing to sort and resell to small businesses and popular markets. Clothing waste from charities unable to sell garments, clothes from deceased estates, and textiles destined for landfill are bargained for and sold from wealthy countries to locations in Africa, Pakistan, and India, which contribute to the highly saturated second-hand clothing economy. The importation and distribution of second-hand clothing may provide poor nations with businesses and an income, but they damage local economies and keep people in poverty, whilst giving them the burden of disposing other countries' waste (Besser, 2021; Wazir, 2021).

The production and disposal of textiles is thus as much a human rights issue as an environmental one, as workers in both ends of the manufacturing and waste process are paid inadequate compensation for their labour and are subjected to dangerous work environments and health risks (Kozlowski, Bardecki and Searcy, 2012). The second-hand clothing industry thrives off discarded clothing and charity donations, which eventually become waste, affecting the poorest of populations. This effectively sustains global inequalities and colonial dependence between the Global North and South (Manieson and Ferrero-Regis, 2023). The importation and redistribution of recycled clothing acts as a vehicle for the textile industry to shift the environmental hazards associated with mass production onto low-income countries and vulnerable people who suffer the blame for the environmental degradation (Bick, Halsey and Ekenga, 2018). The environmental consequences of fast fashion and textile waste have an immense detrimental impact on plants and animals as well as on water, land, and air quality.

Water

Huge quantities of water are used in turning raw materials into textiles, which results in tonnes of water pollution a year. Cotton, for example, is one of the most used and versatile fibres but requires intensive farming and significant volumes of water to produce, even though the regions which produce cotton face water scarcity (Ravasio, 2012). Dyeing clothing involves using a range of chemicals that are toxic to humans, either directly or indirectly, such as chrome, copper, and zinc, which are carcinogenic. During the dyeing process, colours are fixed into the fabric using chemicals, but may not fully 'stick' to the fibres, resulting in most of the dye being washed directly off the fabric and polluting the water (Rukhaya et al., 2021). Second-hand clothing includes laundering at an industrial scale, which generates chemical-laden wastewater. Mass-scale cleaning of second-hand clothing with detergents further weakens these cheaply made textiles, making any recycling efforts almost purposeless as they disintegrate further.

Due to the emergence of plastic-based oil and synthetic fibres like rayon and polyester, the artificial fibres are micro-thin and near invisible, meaning that when they are laundered they break off and are released into waste and sewage pipes and eventually accrue within waterways, clog pipes, and wash up on beaches. Because these fibres are miniscule, they are not collected by current wastewater treatment systems, resulting in thousands of micro-plastics traveling into lakes, rivers, and oceans. Fish and other aquatic animals ingest these tiny fragments, mistaking them as food, which disrupts their digestive system, mating patterns, and kills them, greatly contributing to marine ecosystem degradation (Ruggiero, Schamber and Schroeder, 2021). Chemical-laden wastewater causes an oily scum that also prevents the penetration of sunlight, disrupting photosynthesis and depleting oxygen, which is essential for marine animal plant life to live (Kant, 2012). Even outside of waterways, when clothing ends up in landfill, any residual chemicals in the fabric seep into groundwater, further polluting local freshwater sources elsewhere (Drennan, 2015). The water pollution adversely impacts the health of humans and non-human animals as well as plant species. Although the creation, laundering, and disposal of textile pollution causes harm to aquatic life and different waterway types, the full impact and extent of textile pollution is unknown (Brooks et al., 2017).

Air

Textile treatment facilities release harmful toxins into the atmosphere. Spinning, weaving, and dyeing textiles on an industrial scale all contribute to air contamination through carbon emissions. Tanneries emit carcinogenic fumes, boilers produce nitrogen and sulphur, and formaldehyde, acids, and other volatile compounds are produced during the batch dyeing, drying, and curing of textiles for the purpose of fast fashion (Rukhaya et al., 2021).

Landfill or incineration of textile waste is the final destination for discarded clothing. Unsold materials, off-cuts, and dirty or damaged clothing are dumped in massive landfill deposits or incinerated to save space. The slums in the outskirts of New Delhi, for example, have tonnes of waste dumped daily, which are incinerated legally or through unregulated trash burning. Fires can erupt due to the build-up of methane gas that decomposing waste produces. Burning of waste damages air quality, making daily life difficult for those living in or around these burning sites. Waste-to-energy incinerators may 'solve' the problem of physical waste, but they release carbon dioxide, highly toxic ash, and carcinogens into the local atmosphere (Besser, 2021; Baloyi et al., 2024).

Whilst air quality is a concern for busy, smoggy cities, rapid deforestation for the production of textile fibres has become a global concern. Viscose, for example, is a semi-synthetic fibre made from wood pulp, which is highly sought after in the fashion industry because it imitates silk. Manufactured cellulose fabrics such as viscose, lyocell, and rayon have been created from the pulp of ancient and endangered old-growth forests. One solution to the decline of air quality (trees) is being sawn down to be twisted into clothes destined for landfill (McCullough, 2014).

Harmful toxins are pumped into the atmosphere when textiles are produced and are inadvertently inhaled by the industry's staff. When fibres are dyed and turned into rolls of fabric, workers in 'sweatshops' create garments for wealthy countries to consume across the other side of the world. After these clothes are worn, they are discarded and shipped to other countries. Each of these processes (transporting goods to markets, transporting waste for disposal) involves burning fuel for transport, sending more carbon dioxide into the air. If left to rot in landfill, their decomposition causes toxic fumes which are inhaled by local communities.

Earth

The fast fashion industry causes soil erosion, degradation of land, and deforestation. The manufacturing of clothing relies on intensive animal farming for their hides, fur, or wool. Animal agriculture itself causes immense environmental harm, but the fast fashion industry still relies on accumulating a range of 'raw materials' to create garments from plant and non-human animal sources. Land-clearing for the purpose of planting and harvesting clothing fibres contributes to the destruction of native forests and animal species. The planting and harvesting of plant fibres contributes to deforestation, as companies seek cheaper alternatives to animal-based sources. At an industry level, the textile industry is estimated to use over 15,000 different chemicals throughout the manufacturing process. This includes plantations for fabrics, which rely on pesticides (including herbicides and insecticides), which leach into the earth, decreasing biodiversity and causing soil infertility. Because fast fashion uses exhaustive resources which cause soil degradation and erosion, it requires manufacturers to move, further expand, and create new plantations on fertile soil. Meanwhile, what happens at the end of the clothing life cycle also continues to generate waste (Augustine, 2021). For example, natural degradable fibres like bamboo and viscose are still treated with harmful pesticides when manufactured into fabrics and contribute to immense deforestation as well as contaminated waste. Land-clearing, understandably, destabilises local flora and fauna as well as pushing species out of their natural habitat.

Textile waste sits alongside plastic and other waste products that take years if not centuries to decompose, creating piles of rubbish and over-filling landfill sites. Landfills and dumpsites not only severely damage the land itself and negatively affect the quality of life for human and non-human animals living nearby, but due to having no real solution for disposal, textile waste continues to build, without end. The crisis in how to manage textile and other waste products has, in turn, been lucrative for 'ecomafia' and organised criminal networks that specialise in trafficking, moving, and illegally dumping waste (Past, 2013).

Animals

Land-clearing, soil degradation, and pollution are significant outcomes stemming from breeding animals for the purposes of textile production. The process of tanning animal hides (literally, their skins) creates wastewater, which pollutes the land, whilst solid wastes, such as hair, greases, chemicals, oils, fleshing, and trimming waste, are all common outcomes of the process, which all fall under the tannery term 'sludge' (Hira et al., 2022). The processes involved in trapping, catching, plucking, and skinning is traumatising and painful for animals and some are bred, raised, and killed for this purpose alone. For example, in northern Australia, saltwater crocodiles are raised and skinned for the purpose of 'high-value leather products' for the fashion industry. Even though these practices harm the land and the animals, it is the decline in profitability that is the main public concern – as the popularity of crocodile skin in the fashion industry wanes, the livelihood of the workers is also threatened (Saalfeld et al., 2000).

The living conditions of animals bred for their skins can be immensely cruel as well, such as overcrowding birds in sheds, and housing otherwise aquatic animals such as ducks on land. The limited production of 'exotic' animal fibres that are used in the fashion industry enhances the prestige and aesthetic of garments (think here of the mink fur industry). However, trapping and hunting land animals for their skin can result in near or actual extinction of a species. The Tibetan antelope, for example, is killed for its wool to make shawls. As one shawl requires three to five antelopes, it is no surprise that they are one of the many endangered species that suffer as a consequence of fast fashion (Lakshmanan, Jose and Chakraborty, 2016). The environmental harm that fast fashion causes, either directly or consequentially and over time, changes an animal's relationship with the land or waterways in which they subsist. Whether they are farmed on land for their skins, in inhumane conditions, or if they swim freely in the textile and cotton-choked waterways and pipelines, the full extent of the harm textile pollution causes for animal life is immense even if not yet fully known.

Greenwashing

High fashion brands and those working in the fast fashion industry may, on the surface, appear to be making more sustainable choices in how they produce textiles, but this is not the reality. Corporations in the fast fashion industry might advertise that they are more 'environmentally friendly' than others, and claim that a product is 'sustainable', but these claims are largely performative rather than substantive, and to an extent rely on a lack of transparency about their supply chain (Chan, Ren and Liu, 2022).

Greenwashing refers to campaigns that provide misleading representations of environmental virtue when in fact harm continues to occur or even expand. For instance, brands may highlight their passion for the environment by using 'eco-friendly' packaging for their garments. The packaging of fashion garments itself thus may be peddled as a sign of being 'eco-friendly'. But the purpose of such packaging is, in essence, to assist in the transportation of garments and/or to emphasise a product's visibility and desirability. Both the packaging and the product are intentionally designed to go straight to landfill after use (Rukhaya et al., 2021). These kinds of 'greener' clothing packaging and designs represent a miniscule portion of a fashion brand's overall production, simply offering consumers more options in things to buy, as opposed to actively trying to minimise their environmental footprint. Fashion marketing buzzwords such as 'eco-friendly', 'sustainable fabric', or even 'ethical production' have little real clarity of meaning but can manipulate consumers into believing they are contributing to holistic change (Sinisalo, 2020).

Unless and until fast fashion companies find a solution to the disposal of their own textile waste, enhance the working conditions of those at every stage of the supply chain, and minimise their overall environmental footprint, there is no such thing as sustainable or 'environmentally friendly' fashion.

Conclusion

Fast fashion causes environmental destruction which threatens the survival of plants, humans, and non-human animals. The fashion industry knows that their practices impact the Earth and its inhabitants, both because of their detailed knowledge of production processes (and their effects on workers and local environments) and through activist and media exposure of the social and environmental harms generated by fast fashion. At every stage in the production, transportation, and eventual 'disposal' of textiles, some element of environmental harm is perpetrated. Whilst there are conscious consumer movements such as 'slow fashion' and 'upcycling', these efforts are hindered by the increasingly rapid production of poorer-grade clothing. As there is yet no real solution on how to manage textile waste; it continues to clog waterways, pollute fertile land, and poison clean air. Unless the clothing industry changes its practices, the price of fashion will continue to extend past garments and textiles, to cost the lives of humans and non-human animals and the destruction of environments.

ASH BARNES AND CHELSEA HICKMAN

ASH BARNES AND CHELSEA HICKMAN

Further reading

Baloyi, R. B., Gbadeyan, O. J., Sithole, B., & Chunilall, V. (2024). Recent advances in recycling technologies for waste textile fabrics: A review. *Textile Research Journal*, 94(3–4), 508–529.

Besser, L., (2021). *Dead White Man's Clothes.* Video: ABC.

Bick, R., Halsey, E. & Ekenga, C. C., (2018). The global environmental injustice of fast fashion. *Environmental Health*, 17, 1–4.

Chan, H. L., Ren, S. & Liu, N. (eds.), (2022). *Operations Management in the Era of Fast Fashion: Technologies and Circular Supply Chains*. Springer Nature.

Ruggiero, M., Schamber, A. & Schroeder, O., (2021). *Fast Fashion and Ocean Pollution: Exploring Problems and Potential Solutions.* White Paper, Clear Blue Sea.

Simončič, K., (2021). Fast fashion: A case of social harm and state–corporate crime. *The Howard Journal of Crime and Justice*, 60, 343–369.

References

Augustine, N., (2021). Assessing climate change's impact on agriculture. *Perspectives on Critical Issues*, 31.

Baloyi, R. B., Gbadeyan, O. J., Sithole, B., & Chunilall, V. (2024). Recent advances in recycling technologies for waste textile fabrics: A review. *Textile Research Journal*, 94(3–4), 508–529.

Besser, L., (2021). *Dead White Man's Clothes.* Video: ABC.

Bick, R., Halsey, E. & Ekenga, C. C., (2018). The global environmental injustice of fast fashion. *Environmental Health*, 17, 1–4.

Brooks, A., Fletcher, K., Francis, R. A., Rigby, E. D. & Roberts, T., (2017). Fashion, sustainability, and the Anthropocene. *Utopian Studies*, 28, 482–504.

Chan, H. L., Ren, S. & Liu, N. (eds.), (2022). *Operations Management in the Era of Fast Fashion: Technologies and Circular Supply Chains*. Springer Nature.

Drennan, K., (2015). Picking up the threads. *Alternatives Journal*, 41, 21–23.

Hira, A., Pacini, H., Attafuah-Wadee, K., Sikander, M., Oruko, R. & Dinan, A., (2022). Mitigating tannery pollution in sub-Saharan Africa and South Asia. *Journal of Developing Societies*, 0169796X221104856.

Kant, R., (2012). Textile dyeing industry an environmental hazard. *Natural Sciences*, 4, 22–26.

Kozlowski, A., Bardecki, M. & Searcy, C., (2012). Environmental impacts in the fashion industry: A life-cycle and stakeholder framework. *Journal of Corporate Citizenship*, 45, 17–36.

Lakshmanan, A., Jose, S. & Chakraborty, S., (2016). Luxury hair fibers for fashion industry. In S. S. Muthu & M. A. Gardetti (eds.), *Sustainable Fibres for Fashion Industry.* Springer, pp. 1–38.

Manieson, L. A. & Ferrero-Regis, T., (2023). Castoff from the West, pearls in Kantamanto? A critique of second-hand clothing. *Journal of Industrial Ecology*, 27(3), 811–821.

McCullough, D. G., (2014). Deforestation for fashion: Getting unsustainable fabrics out of the closet. *The Guardian.* https://www.theguardian.com/sustainable-business/zara-h-m-fashion-sustainable-forests-logging-fabric#comments [accessed 10/03/2022].

Past, E., (2013). 'Trash is gold': Documenting the ecomafia and Campania's waste crisis. *Interdisciplinary Studies in Literature and Environment*, 20, 597–621.

Ravasio, P., (2012). How can we stop water from becoming a fashion victim. *The Guardian.* https://www.theguardian.com/sustainable-business/water-scarcity-fashion-industry [accessed 15/11/2024].

Ruggiero, M., Schamber, A. & Schroeder, O., (2021). *Fast Fashion and Ocean Pollution: Exploring Problems and Potential Solutions.* White Paper, Clear Blue Sea.

Rukhaya, S., Yadav, S., Rose, N. M., Grover, A. & Bisht, D., (2021). Sustainable approach to counter the environmental impact of fast fashion. *Pharma Innovation Journal*, SP10-8, 517–523.

Saalfeld, K., Fukuda, Y., Duldig, T. & Fisher, A. (2000). Wildlife trade management plan for the saltwater crocodile (*Crocodylus porosus*) in the Northern Territory of Australia, 2016–2020. Northern Territory Department of Land Resource Management, Darwin. (This is a Wildlife Trade Management Plan prepared under the Environment Protection and Biodiversity Conservation Act.)

Simončič, K., (2021). Fast fashion: A case of social harm and state–corporate crime. *The Howard Journal of Crime and Justice*, 60, 343–369.

Sinisalo, C., (2020). Effect of greenwashing on brand image and buying behaviour in fast fashion: a consumer perspective. Bachelor's thesis, Haaga-Helia University of Applied Sciences.

Wazir, Z., (2021). How fast fashion dumps into the Global South. https://www.usnews.com/news/best-countries/articles/2021-11-11/how-dead-white-mans-clothing-is-clogging-the-global-south.

ASH BARNES AND CHELSEA HICKMAN

22. Illicit waste trafficking

Introduction

Global waste trade emerged in the 1970s when the Global North had started to impose stricter regulations on the disposal of waste. At the end of the 1980s, the Basel Convention was the first addition to the international framework to regulate waste shipments. In its wake, illicit waste trafficking emerged as a problem. Although the size of the problem is unknown, there remains a gap between amounts of waste produced and accounted for as legitimately processed or disposed of, and those illegally dealt with. Huge profits, weak enforcement systems, the complexity of rules, and the range of actors involved in the waste trade chain continue to provide incentives for non-compliance. Perpetrators range from small-scale entrepreneurs to mid-sized and large-scale corporations and organised crime groups. Cross-border law enforcement cooperation, both between waste-producing countries in the Global North and recipients in the Global South, remains difficult because of a lack of legal and practical frameworks for information exchange, and economic interests.

Dynamics of the waste trade

The transfrontier shipment of waste is a large and global business. For example, estimates are that about 15 per cent of all trade in the European Union (EU) concerns waste (IMPEL–TFS, 2006). In 2009 a similar estimate was made for all trade leaving the port of Rotterdam, which handles about half of all goods leaving the EU on seagoing vessels (UNEP, 2018; Spapens, Mehlbaum & Neve, 2019). In this respect, cross-border illicit waste trafficking (IWT) can be viewed as transnational environmental crime, involving the illegal trade, shipping, and processing of waste (White, 2011; Elliott, 2012). Illicit waste mostly originates from the Global North and is trafficked mainly to countries in the Global South, such as China, Nigeria, and Ghana, but also to other Western African and South-East Asian countries, such as Malaysia, the Philippines, Thailand, Cote d'Ivoire, and Gambia (Nellemann et al., 2016; Favarin & Aziani, 2020). The exact size of the illegal movement of waste across the globe is unknown (Rucevska et al., 2015). By comparing the amounts of waste generated and registered as treated or legitimately disposed of, Meneghini and colleagues (2017) estimated that in the EU, between 2010 and 2014, 13 per cent of non-hazardous waste and 33 per cent of hazardous waste was unaccounted for. Although there is a growing scientific interest in IWT as a transnational form of crime, a lack of empirical research remains (Favarin & Aziani, 2020).

Waste is in several respects an ambiguous term. Waste is the designation of an object or liquid when it is discarded. However, with a few exceptions such as asbestos and chemicals such as PFAS (perfluoroalkyl and polyfluroalkyl substances), most types of waste may be suitable to be wholly or partly reused after sorting or treatment. This applies for instance to plastics, paper, metals, e-waste, household waste, end-of-life vehicles and vessels, oil and chemical waste, and polluted soil. The designation of waste therefore depends on place and time. Ambiguity also applies to the distinction between hazardous and non-hazardous waste. The fact that waste is considered hazardous refers to the negative impact it has on the health of flora, fauna, ecosystems, and humans, when it is directly dumped in the environment. Hazardous waste may however be (partly) reused after treatment whilst waste that is considered to be non-hazardous, such as plastics, may have detrimental effects on the health of ecosystems when dumped. The fact that waste may be used as raw material implies that its status may revert back to that of a commodity. In the EU, for example, the principle of free movement of goods also applies to waste. In the United States, waste may also be moved freely from one state to another. As a consequence, waste is shipped to countries or states where the costs for treatment are lower.

The global waste trade emerged in the second half of the 1960s when governments in the Global North started to regulate waste disposal more strictly (Brownell, 2011). After this, disposal costs increased, whereas the price of virgin raw materials remained low. On the one hand this created little incentive for recycling and recovery, whereas, on the other hand, demand for secondary raw materials such as scrap metal and waste paper increased in upcoming economies, such as Japan and Taiwan. From the 1970s onwards, the global waste trade started to grow exponentially, promoted by the fact that transfrontier shipment of waste was almost entirely unregulated (Waugh, 2000). In addition, in the 1980s, brokers increasingly started to export toxic waste from the United States to South America, Africa, and Eastern Europe where disposal (in practice, dumping) was cheap and enforcement weak. Critics labelled these practices as 'garbage imperialism' (Brownell, 2011). Indeed, the United States exported much of its waste to countries over which it had political or economic leverage, and in a similar vein Western European countries shipped hazardous waste to their former colonies (Brownell, 2011; Favarin & Aziani, 2020). Although a regulatory framework had been introduced from the second half of the 1980s onwards, illicit waste trafficking remains a serious problem because of huge profits, weak enforcement systems, the complexity of rules, and the range of actors involved in the waste trade chain (UNEP, 2018, see also Albers, 2014).

Legal frameworks

In the 1980s international awareness about the detrimental effects of hazardous waste exports to countries in the Global South increased. In response, the Basel Convention on the Control of Transboundary Movements of Hazardous Wastes and their Disposal was opened for signature in 1989. The Convention entered into force in 1992, although up to now the United States has refused to ratify it. The basis of the Basel Convention is that waste should be shipped only between countries that have appropriate facilities to treat it or to dispose of it in an environmentally sound way. The Convention does not prohibit waste shipment but relies on procedures of 'prior informed consent', meaning that exporters must notify shipments with the competent authority in their country and seek approval based on the requirements set out in the Convention.

In 1995 the Convention was expanded with the so-called Ban Amendment. The amendment was intended to prevent export of hazardous waste to the developing world, by prohibiting shipments for final disposal from OECD to non-OECD countries and banning all shipments of hazardous wastes. However, the Ban Amendment did not enter into force until 2019 because of opposition from several developed countries, which for instance argued that a distinction should be made between waste destined for final disposal and waste for recycling or recovery purposes, as well as developing countries which feared that their economies could suffer from the loss of revenue generated by the recovery of materials from hazardous waste (Mitsilegas et al., 2022).

Another important legal instrument is the OECD Council Decision on the Control of Transfrontier Movements of Waste Destined for Recovery Operations, which was issued in 2001 and amended in 2004. The decision also covers non-hazardous waste and only allows export to OECD countries and to non-OECD countries depending on the response of the importing country.

Although these legal frameworks aim at protecting the environment, the Basel Convention in particular received criticism for essentially formalising the conditions of the trade instead of banning it, which would have promoted treatment and recovery in waste-producing countries, as well as creating incentives for producing less waste. The Convention was also criticised because of the vagueness of definitions, especially the term 'environmentally sound management' and the definition of waste itself (Brownell, 2011). Another problem is that the Basel Convention does not impose a clear obligation to make illicit waste trafficking a criminal offence. Activists argued that waste trade is fundamentally environmentally unsound, and the convention has merely established a global toxic waste trade notification system (Brownell, 2011).

Waste-trafficking actors

Illicit waste trafficking involves a range of actors and facilitators. To begin with, small-scale entrepreneurs may engage in collecting waste and shipping it abroad. Such actors are involved in shipping items such as discarded household appliances, e-waste, computers, car batteries and tyres, and end-of-life vehicles, usually under the pretext that it concerns second-hand goods to which the Basel Convention does not apply (Bisschop, 2012; Sahramäki et al., 2017). The leading actors in these cases vary from one-man companies to small family businesses which may or may not establish legal entities to facilitate illicit waste trafficking.

TOINE SPAPENS

Second, illicit waste trafficking involves mid-sized and large corporations in the waste sector who combine legitimate activities with rule violations, such as mixing recyclable and hazardous waste (Neve, 2013; Spapens, Mehlbaum & Neve, 2019). Based on a study of 13 selected cases in three EU Member States, Sahramäki and colleagues (2017) concluded that offenders usually had advanced knowledge of the waste market and of the legislation and regulations. Traders may buy specific or different types of waste from small-scale collectors or directly from waste producers (Neve et al., 2016). For instance, buyers or intermediaries from countries in the Global South operate in Western European countries to acquire recyclable waste on behalf of companies or traders in their countries of origin (Neve et al., 2016). Next, transporters play an important role in shipping waste abroad, by road, sea, train, or inland waterways. During investigation cases, transporting companies usually avoid being labelled as suspects by directing responsibility to their clients and claiming they had no knowledge about the waste shipments being potentially illegal (Neve et al., 2016). Supporting actors may provide specific services, such as import/export companies and freight forwarders who take care of organising shipments and arranging the necessary transport and customs documents. Finally, waste sampling companies may contribute to the process, for instance by wrongly assessing the toxicity of liquid waste or polluted soil.

Third, illicit waste trafficking is associated with organised crime groups. For example, several years ago Europol claimed that such groups were heavily involved in the trafficking and trade of e-waste (Europol, 2015). Indeed, if one takes as a starting point the definition, 'a structured group of three or more persons, existing for a period of time and acting in concert with the aim of committing one or more serious crimes or offences [...] in order to obtain directly or indirectly a financial or other material benefit', as included in the United Nations Convention against Transnational Organized Crime, the label applies to many cooperatives which are involved in illicit waste trafficking. It is less clear, however, whether traditional organised crime groups or syndicates have 'discovered' illicit waste trafficking as an additional market besides drug trafficking, extortion, and other criminal activities. Concrete examples are rare, one being the alleged involvement of the Camorra in dumping toxic and radioactive waste off the coast of Somalia (Interpol, 2016). In most cases, however, illicit waste trafficking can be viewed as corporate rather than traditional organised crime.

Modi operandi

The business process of transfrontier shipment of waste is complex and offers illicit operators several opportunities to evade regulations (Sahramäki et al., 2017; Spapens, Mehlbaum & Neve, 2019; Andreatta & Favarin, 2020; Morganti et al., 2020). The most important method is to avoid the regulatory system altogether by not notifying shipments. Perpetrators correctly assess the risk of getting caught as low, as this would require physical inspection of shipments. One way of avoiding notification is by declaring the goods to be second-hand instead of waste. As the Basel Convention is unclear about this distinction, countries differ in terms of rules. Germany, for example, requires that second-hand goods, such as discarded computers or vehicles, must be functional upon export. If they do not work, they are waste. The Netherlands, however, only check if the goods are carefully packed to avoid damage during transportation (Spapens, Mehlbaum & Neve, 2019). Of course, this may lead to arguments in the courtroom about whether or not the term waste applies to goods that can be repaired or refurbished.

The second main method of waste trafficking is to notify but hide the true nature of the waste. The system of classification of waste is complicated and leaves much room for diverse interpretation. Correct classification may also be problematic when different types of waste are loaded in a container. Perpetrators may deliberately classify waste in a wrong category, for example to hide that it is hazardous, but also to evade higher taxes that may apply to specific types of waste. In some cases, inspectors will see neatly packed waste representing what is mentioned on transport documents when opening a container, whereas there may be other sorts of (hazardous) wastes present in the back of the container. Mixing recyclable and hazardous waste is also common practice (Spapens, Mehlbaum & Neve, 2019). Almost all recyclable waste also contains materials that may be considered hazardous, such as agricultural plastics that may contain pesticides, and whether or not thresholds are exceeded may lead to complicated debates, for example with regard to sampling.

Third, exporters may choose to route their shipments via ports where the risk of inspection is considered lowest, a tactic of so-called 'port hopping'. Sending waste to final destinations via detours has also been observed as a modus operandi. Waste may for instance be notified as destined for a recipient in one country, and approved for this, yet sold to a recipient in another country while en route. Technically, such a change should be notified again, but in practice it is almost impossible for departure countries to keep track of waste shipments once these have left the port. Such en-route sales usually involve shell companies to avoid the risk of having to take back shipments, should these be intercepted in the country of destination. This risk may also be reduced by repackaging shipments originating from different countries at intermediary destinations, making it almost impossible to trace back their origin and hold the actors involved accountable. Consequently, intercepted containers may simply end up abandoned in, for instance, Asian ports.

Prevention and stronger enforcement

Measures to reduce the opportunities for illicit waste trafficking should combine upstream and downstream interventions. From a preventative perspective, upstream measures focus on reducing the amount of waste produced and promoting treatment and recycling in the countries where the waste is produced, instead of viewing waste primarily as a commercial good. From a repressive angle, enforcement authorities in countries of origin should be properly staffed and equipped to carry out physical inspections, as well as to investigate both criminal groups and corporate offenders involved in illicit waste trafficking. For instance, powers can be granted to allow application of covert investigation methods such as wiretapping. The justice chain should be enabled to prosecute and punish offenders, including the setting of adequate criminal penalties. Cooperation is essential, both within and across jurisdictions. Tackling illicit waste trafficking is a shared responsibility of administrative enforcement and inspection agencies, customs services, the police and the public prosecution service and a rapid proactive exchange of information between different national authorities is crucial. Effective cross-border cooperation and information sharing between countries of origin is another requirement for success. However, although there is an extensive international legal and practical framework in place for police and judicial cooperation, as well as customs cooperation, administrative authorities have few formalised legal instruments. Formal 'diagonal' cross-border cooperation between agencies with different tasks and orientations is limited, and in the EU became almost impossible after the introduction of the so-called GDPR Directive in 2018. Systems of notification such as EU-TWIX for interceptions of trafficked wildlife do not exist for waste. Despite the fact that illicit waste trafficking is inherently transnational, even in the EU most investigations stop at the national border (Mehlbaum & Spapens, 2017).

Downstream disruption focuses on the countries of destination or on the transit countries. Such countries could prevent illicit waste trafficking by imposing stricter bans on waste imports. China is an example where the government has been cracking down harder on waste trafficking since 2013 (Rucevska et al., 2015). Furthermore, in 2017 China banned import of plastic scraps completely. This caused displacement of waste to other South-East Asian countries, most notably to Thailand, Malaysia, Vietnam, and the Philippines. However, these countries have since all taken steps to restrict the import of foreign plastic waste (Uhm, 2020).

Law enforcement cooperation between EU Member States and major destination countries in Africa and Asia has proven to be difficult. Competent bodies in countries of origin are often unable to verify whether a specific company in the country of destination exists and if so, whether it can process specific types of waste without harming the environment (Mehlbaum & Spapens, 2017). In practice, it is therefore impossible to verify that waste will be treated or disposed of in an environmentally sound way. Although in Asia things have improved, finding the right person or even the competent authority in African countries is problematic, and staff often do not have official e-mail addresses, while requests almost always go unanswered (Mehlbaum & Spapens, 2017). In addition, lack of trust because of corruption in countries in the Global South also presents barriers to effective cooperation. The emphasis is therefore on building personal contacts with trustworthy Asian and African law enforcement personnel, for instance during seminars organised by cooperation networks such as IMPEL (EU Network for the Implementation and Enforcement of Environmental Law) and the World Customs Organization. Such cooperation networks have indeed worked to improve cooperation and also by experimenting with joint inspection operations such as Demeter, which started in 2009 and has been repeated several times since (Mitsilegas et al., 2022).

Conclusion

It will be interesting to see how the global waste trade and, in its wake, illicit waste trafficking will develop in the future. China, a major destination country, has increasingly restricted waste imports, including a total ban on specific types of waste that became effective in 2019. Waste trade from the Global North to the Global South depends on the availability of cheap sea transport, but disruption caused by the COVID-19 pandemic has substantially increased the costs. Finally, in Western European countries, to take another example, there is a growing incentive to use recycled raw materials, by which corporations also promote a 'green' image, and it is expected that, also because of newly developed technologies, the use of secondary materials will increase in the near future, although virgin materials for the moment remain cheaper than those that have been recycled. In the end, the best prevention of illicit waste trafficking is to reduce the amount of waste that is being produced.

TOINE SPAPENS

Further reading

Brownell, E. (2011). Negotiating the new economic order of waste. *Environmental History*, 16(2), 262–289.

Favarin, S. & Aziani, A. (2020). The global waste trafficking and its correlates. *Journal of Contemporary Criminal Justice*, 36(3), 351–383.

Rucevska, I., Nellemann, C., Isarin, N., Yang, W., Liu, N., Yu, K., Sandnæs, S., Olley, K., McCann, H., Devia, L., Bisschop, L., Soesilo, D., Schoolmeester, T., Henriksen, R. & Nilsen, R. (2015). *Waste Crime – Waste Risks: Gaps in Meeting the Global Waste Challenge.* United Nations Environment Programme & GRID-Arendal.

Sahramäki, I., Favarin, S., Mehlbaum, S., Savona, E., Spapens, T. & Kankaanranta, T. (2017). Wasting opportunities: Prevention of illicit cross-border waste trafficking. *European Journal of Policing Studies*, 5(2), 1–61.

UNEP (2018). *The State of Knowledge of Crimes that Have Serious Impacts on the Environment.*

References

Albers, J. (2014). *Responsibility and Liability in the Context of Transboundary Movements of Hazardous Wastes by Sea*. Springer.

Andreatta, D. & Favarin, S. (2020). Features of transnational illicit waste trafficking and crime prevention strategies to tackle it. *Global Crime*, 21, 130–153.

Bisschop, L. (2012). Is it all going to waste? Illegal transport of e-waste in a European trade hub. *Crime, Law and Social Change*, 58(3), 221–249.

Brownell, E. (2011). Negotiating the new economic order of waste. *Environmental History*, 16(2), 262–289.

Elliott, L. (2012). Fighting transnational environmental crime. *Journal of International Affairs*, 66(1), 87–104.

Europol (2015). *Exploring Tomorrow's Organised Crime*. European Police Office.

Favarin, S. & Aziani, A. (2020). The global waste trafficking and its correlates. *Journal of Contemporary Criminal Justice*, 36(3), 351–383.

IMPEL–TFS (2006). *IMPEL–TFS Seaport Project II: International cooperation in enforcement hitting illegal waste shipments.* Project report September 2004–May 2006, IMPEL.

Interpol (2016). *Assessing the Links between Organised Crime and Pollution Crimes*. Interpol Pollution Crimes Working Group.

Mehlbaum, S. & Spapens, T. (2017). *Enforcing the EU-WSR: Challenges of Cross-border Cooperation.* Tilburg University, Project BlockWaste.

Meneghini, C., Favarin, S., Andreatta, D. & Savona, E. (2017). *An Exploratory Estimation of the Extent of Illicit Waste Trafficking in the EU*. UCSC Transcrime, Project BlockWaste.

Mitsilegas, V., Fasoli, E., Giuffrida, F. & Fitzmaurice, M. (2022). *The Legal Regulation of Environmental Crime: The International and European Dimension*. Brill.

Morganti, M., Favarin, S., & Andreatta, D. (2020). Illicit waste trafficking and loopholes in the European and Italian legislation. *European Journal on Criminal Policy and Research*, 26(1), 105–113.

Nellemann, C., Henriksen, R., Kreilhuber, A., Stewart, D., Kotsovou, M., Raxter, P., Mrema, E. & Barrat, S. (Eds.) (2016). *The Rise of*

Environmental Crime: A Growing Threat to Natural Resources, Peace, Development and Security. United Nations Environment Programme.

Neve, R. (2013). *Geglobaliseerde afvalcriminaliteit: illegale praktijken in de afvalstromen naar Afrika en China.* Politie, Dienst Landelijke Informatieorganisatie.

Neve, R., van Doorn, M., Fortuin, B., in 't Veld, M., Mac Gillavry, D., Stokman, A. & van Zanden, N. (2016). *Dreigingsbeeld Milieucriminaliteit 2016.* Nationale politie.

Rucevska, I., Nellemann, C., Isarin, N., Yang, W., Liu, N., Yu, K., Sandnæs, S., Olley, K., McCann, H., Devia, L., Bisschop, L., Soesilo, D., Schoolmeester, T., Henriksen, R. and Nilsen, R. (2015). *Waste Crime – Waste Risks: Gaps in Meeting the Global Waste Challenge.* United Nations Environment Programme & GRID-Arendal.

Sahramäki, I., Favarin, S., Mehlbaum, S., Savona, E., Spapens, T. & Kankaanranta, T. (2017). Wasting opportunities: Prevention of illicit cross-border waste trafficking. *European Journal of Policing Studies*, 5(2), 1–61.

Spapens, T., Mehlbaum, S. & Neve, R. (2019). Preventing illicit waste: Exports from the Netherlands to China. In *Transnational Crime: European and Chinese Perspectives*, V. Mitsilegas, S. Hufnagel, A. Moiseienko, S. Yanan & L. Mingxiang (Eds.) (pp. 215–234). Routledge.

Uhm, Y. (2020). Plastic waste trade in Southeast Asia after China's import ban: Implications of the new Basel Convention amendment and recommendations for the future. *California Western Law Review*, 57(1), 1–42.

UNEP (2018). *The State of Knowledge of Crimes that Have Serious Impacts on the Environment.*

Waugh, T. (2000). Where do we go from here: Legal controls and future strategies for addressing the transportation of hazardous wastes across international borders. *Fordham Environmental Law Journal*, 11(2), 477–544.

White, R. (2011). *Transnational Environmental Crime: Toward an Eco-global Criminology.* Routledge.

TOINE SPAPENS

23. Space junk

Introduction

This entry discusses the jettisoned materials produced in the course of human exploration and commercialisation of space, in Earth orbit and beyond. Often described as space 'junk' or debris, such objects are produced in various ways and are rapidly increasing in number. The implications of such accumulation are discussed as well as proposals for mitigation and the prospects for international agreements. Speculative ventures in pursuit of the commercial realisation of space tourism and planetary colonisation are increasing and likely to lead to further orbital pollution.

'Space junk' refers to non-functioning anthropogenic material that has been abandoned off-Earth, usually in Earth orbit, but also in other extra-terrestrial locations. This often includes satellites, robots, rockets, and their associated parts. This entry provides an introduction to the topic of space junk by focusing on four key areas:

1. The creation of space debris in off-Earth locales.
2. Accidental collisions and intentional satellite destruction.
3. Mitigation strategies for addressing space junk.
4. Governance and politics.

The creation of space debris in off-Earth locales

As a scientific phenomenon, planet Earth is a magnificent spectacle. Occupying the *goldilocks zone*, it is just the right distance away from the Sun – 150 million miles – to be hospitable to life. This means the Earth is not so close that it is forced into uncontrollable, runaway climatic change, like the planet Venus, nor so far from the Sun that it becomes unable to support complex life forms (like the planet Mars). The proximity of planet Earth to its nearest star has enabled life to flourish in conditions not detected anywhere else in the known Universe. The evolution of *Homo sapiens* is, however, relatively recent. If the Earth is *c.*4.5 billion years old and this is represented as 24 hours, modern humans have been making their mark on the planet for only around three seconds, emerging approximately 300,000 years ago. In this time, humans have changed their environment, and many suggest we now live in the era of the Anthropocene, a geological epoch typified by humans' unique ability to destroy the natural world (Brisman and South, 2018).

Among the most significant markers of the 'Age of the Anthropocene' is the rapidity of the development of technologies of propulsion, measurement, calculation, and communication during and following World War II. These provided the basis for subsequent developments in space exploration and space technology as well as Cold War missile weaponry. This technological innovation and advancement has transformed modern life, in part by aiding globalisation and connectivity. For instance, satellites in Earth orbit are now fundamental to the telecommunications industry and navigation systems. They also enable weather forecasting, global communication, and serve vital governmental and military functions (Aydin, 2019).

One of the consequences of enhanced anthropogenic capability in outer space is the accumulation of space junk, otherwise referred to as *space debris* (Chobotov, 2002), *space waste* (Hobbs et al., 2019), or more broadly as *space pollution* (Brito et al., 2013). This problem was not unforeseen. In 1978, the science-fiction writer Arthur C. Clarke, credited with the first conception of the geo-synchronous satellite, wrote in his novel of the future, *The Fountains of Paradise*, 'For two hundred years, satellites of all shapes and sizes, from loose nuts and bolts to entire space villages, had been accumulating in Earth orbit. … Three-quarters of this material was abandoned junk, much of it long forgotten. Now it had to be located, and somehow disposed of' (Clarke, 1978: 37).

Human-created matter in outer space has been increasing exponentially in the Anthropocene. As of 2021, there were 27,000 pieces of space junk being tracked by NASA and other space agencies, and millions more pieces of debris exist that are too small to track (NASA, 2021).

Space junk, however, is not just limited to Earth orbit. If we accept the definition provided at the beginning of this entry, it is also clear that humans have abandoned non-functioning material in other places around the solar system including on asteroids, planets, and moons. For instance, the Apollo missions sent humans to the moon and objects were left there, including the flag of the United States of America and various items of scientific equipment. Since then, several unsuccessful missions have resulted in spacecraft crash-landing on the lunar surface, thereby contributing more 'junk' on the lunar surface (Lampkin and Wyatt, 2022).

Space junk – and particularly that existing in Earth orbit – is problematic for a multitude of reasons. First, colliding debris can cause the material to fragment, creating more individual debris components. Debris creates issues for spacecraft navigating Earth orbit, posing a health and safety risk to humans aboard such spacecraft or space stations. Furthermore, debris can adversely affect the functionality of intact satellites and equipment, causing communication problems on Earth. There is also a philosophical question regarding the morality of polluting off-Earth locales with defunct matter, and whether humans should be making the same mistakes in space that they continue to make on planet Earth (Takemura, 2019).

Accidental collisions and intentional satellite destruction

The number of satellites in Earth orbit has been increasing since the dawn of the space age when the first satellite (Sputnik-1) was launched by the Soviet Union in 1957 (Lampkin, 2020). As of April 2022, there were 8,290 satellites orbiting the Earth in various orbital ranges, of which 5,400 are still functioning (European Space Agency, 2022).

Due to the sheer size of Earth orbit, the 'Big Sky Theory' suggests that the chance of two satellites colliding has been *negligible* (Knecht, 2001 in Lampkin, 2021). Nonetheless, in 2009, such a collision did occur. As Sturza and Carretero (2021: 1) recall:

> On 10 February 2009, the 689-kg Iridium-33 satellite collided with the 900-kg COMOS-2251 satellite approximately 800-km above Siberia. Twelve years later, the consequence of that collision is 1,433 trackable debris objects with apogees up to 1,650-km, plus a likely much larger number of lethal non-trackable (LNT) debris objects.

Whilst this has been the only large-scale satellite collision in human history so far, it serves as a reminder of the very real possibility of human and scientific error which may plague Earth orbit in the future as the number of satellites continues to increase. This prospect is referred to as the *Kessler Syndrome* (Tulczyjew et al., 2021), whereby the ever-increasing amount of space debris in Earth orbit makes it difficult to successfully and safely track existing space debris, and to conduct space missions that must navigate the clustered orbital debris environment.

Whilst Kessler Syndrome is a concern for future space missions, accidentally colliding satellites are not the only risk of debris formation. In the context of international governmental and military insecurity, anti-satellite (A-SAT) weapons tests have also led to a great deal of space debris littering Earth orbit, following the use of rockets to destroy orbiting satellites, in anticipation of such a capability being used as a wartime act of aggression. Military equipment and navigation systems rely on the capability of functioning satellites which therefore become strategic targets.

A-SAT testing was commonplace in the Cold War era (particularly from the 1960s to 1980s) but is less prevalent today. However, A-SAT tests have been conducted recently by China in 2007, the United States in 2008, India in 2019, and Russia in 2021 (Lampkin, 2021). Although the intended aim of such actions is the destruction of a rocket or other device, the known and inevitable consequence is the creation of large quantities of space debris. So, while the costs of A-SAT testing and further space debris accumulation are well documented (i.e., risk to future space missions and humans in Earth orbit), state-facilitated A-SAT testing may lead to harm despite the known risks. There have been calls for an international ban on A-SAT testing (Liemer and Chyba, 2010) but so far, such testing remains merely subject to diplomatic disapproval in the political arena owing to the non-binding nature of any relevant international law. While the 1967 United Nations 'Outer Space Treaty on Principles Governing the Activities of States in the Exploration and Use of Outer Space, including the Moon and Other Celestial Bodies' makes several references to the peaceful uses of outer space, A-SAT testing is not specifically illegal according to the treaty, and it is not compulsory for states to enshrine such principles in domestic laws. The Outer Space Treaty (OST) is a set of guidelines governing the use of outer space designed in the Cold War era when reliable and consistent access to space was limited to the United States and the Soviet Union (Wortman, 2020). The power of these two nations raised concerns about space warfare, the use of nuclear substances in outer space, and attempts at national appropriation of celestial bodies. The OST was formulated to address these issues but remains only a set of international guidelines, rather than enforceable international law with criminal penalties.

Regardless of debates around the legality and future of A-SAT testing, it remains the case that Earth orbit is already littered with anthropogenic debris. Consequently, a growing body of knowledge and research exists with the aim of preventing further debris creation and enabling the removal of existing debris.

Mitigation strategies for addressing space junk

As with any form of pollution, the most effective mechanism for preventing its occurrence is to refrain from producing it in the first place, a philosophy akin to the precautionary principle in environmental law (Wolf and Stanley, 2014). As such, a ban on A-SAT testing that leads to a cessation of the practice would prevent some future debris creation. Similarly, investigating satellite collision avoidance strategies, such as mapping debris orbits and calculating collision probabilities, would then allow a state or company to attempt to remove or alter the orbital path of debris that may be likely to collide (An et al., 2022). This is an example of what is known as *space traffic management* or *space situational awareness*, where existing debris is closely monitored to try to prevent collisions and resultant debris. Current initiatives will develop the technologies required to service satellites and prolong their functional life, to enable collection of junk (Koryanov et al., 2021), and to shield debris in ways that prevent explosions (Miller et al., 2021) – another source of debris creation.

At present, the main strategy for removal of objects is based upon the influence of gravity or human interventions (for instance, using lasers, slingshots, or nets) to move them into lower orbits (Chobotov, 2002) and return them into Earth's atmosphere where most will burn up. This itself creates atmospheric harm although some (but not all) could be reclaimed on re-entry. Of course, large objects that survive re-entry may pose a highly significant health and safety risk for humans and animals on Earth's surface.

Other options for orbital debris include forcing objects into 'space storage' areas – orbits that are specifically designated for non-functioning matter. The aim of 'storage' or 'graveyard' orbits (Stakem, 2018) is to create a place that prevents debris from re-entering Earth's atmosphere, but that also does not pose a risk to existing functioning satellites or space stations. This does not fully resolve the problem as the debris still exists, but it does prevent the environmental harm that might otherwise be created through atmospheric re-entry.

Governance and politics

The 1972 UN 'Convention on International Liability for Damage Caused by Space Objects' sets out the principle that '[a] launching State shall be absolutely liable to pay compensation for damage caused by its space object on the surface of the earth or to aircraft flight' (Article II), and this also extends to bodies operating on behalf of a state. Further Articles concern the liability of launching states (and others) in cases where damage occurs to objects – or persons or property on board such objects – 'elsewhere than on the surface of the earth'. There is therefore an *in principle* basis for accountability and the application of 'polluter pays' claims. However, as Ormrod (2013: 734) notes, 'fault' is difficult to prove, and international law provides 'no incentive to protect the space environment'. Critics of the 1967 Outer Space Treaty argue that 'the treaty and its corollaries were developed for and in service of a few wealthy, powerful nations at the expense of latecomers' (Rand, 2019) but it may now be difficult to rein in the most recent 'latecomers' who have commercialised launch capabilities, relieving some states of the enormous costs involved, in pursuit of profitable ventures in orbital tourism and planetary colonisation (Seymour, 2021), with the inevitable result of further pollution of the exosphere.

Such commercialisation of outer space is a relatively new, twenty-first-century phenomenon. This is important, because much of the international law that pertains to outer space was developed and drafted in the Cold War era of the previous century. The focus of the OST, for instance, on the fair use of outer space reflects political and military concerns of the period in which the law was drafted, a time synonymous with secrecy and the protection of state intelligence and weapons (Burgess and Dubbs, 2007). Due to the decline in public interest in space exploration following the Cold War, private companies have filled the deficit of reduced state funding for space missions (Lampkin and White, 2023). Consequently, because privatisation has enabled space activities to continue, they have had almost free rein on what expansion looks like. Billionaires like Elon Musk have managed to take command of the skies, launching thousands of new satellites virtually unopposed. The state welcomes such private investment, which contributes positively to their nation's economy through the creation of jobs, research, and development. Unfortunately for the Earth and orbital environments, this free rein of new investment has (and will continue) to create an increasing amount of space junk (Lampkin and Wyatt, 2023).

Conclusion

According to Rand (2019) there is now 'a pressing need to revise international rules to reduce waste in space' and enable 'broader international participation in orbital environmental governance'. This entry has outlined the history and technologies that have brought us to this point and the parallels with the anthropocentric treatment and pollution of planet Earth should be obvious.

Space junk is, however, more than just an undesirable side effect of a new space industrial revolution; it might also be seen as emblematic of a particular view of the future which is now being shaped by 'a tiny minority of ultra-wealthy individuals and private-sector companies' whose speculative ventures are 'ultimately about dictating policy and ownership' beyond the Earth (Lam et al., 2024; Shaw, 2021).

In order to prevent state–corporate investment resulting in an ultra-contaminated orbital environment, both nation states and private companies must be held accountable for the pollution-related harms that they are producing now and into the future. Without such accountability, those who are creating the most pollution will not only escape prosecution but will undoubtedly accelerate their destructive practices.

JACK A. LAMPKIN AND NIGEL SOUTH

Further reading

Castronuovo, M.M. (2011) 'Active Space Debris Removal: A Preliminary Mission Analysis and Design,' *Acta Astronautica*, 69(9–10): 848–859.

Darwin, C. (1859) *The Origin of Species*. Hammersmith: Harper Press (published in 2011).

Eski, Y. (2023) *A Criminology of the Human Species: Setting an Unsettling Tone*. Cham: Springer Nature Switzerland.

Kessler, D.J., Johnson, N.L., Liou, J.C. and Matney, M. (2010) 'The Kessler Syndrome: Implications to Future Space Operations,' *Advances in the Astronautical Sciences*, 137(8): 1–15.

Lampkin, J.A. and White, R. (2023) *Space Criminology*. Basingstoke: Palgrave Macmillan.

Lampkin, J.A. and Wyatt, T. (2023) 'An Astro-Green Criminological Examination of Orbital Space Debris,' *Criminology & Criminal Justice*, 1–18.

References

An, J., Li, X., Zhang, Z., Zhang, G., Man, W., Hu, G. and He, J. (2022) 'Path Planning for Self-Collision Avoidance of Space Modular Self-Reconfigurable Satellites,' *Aerospace*, 9(3): 141–168.

Aydin, I. (2019) *Geopolitics of Outer Space: Global Security and Development*. Washington DC: Westphalia Press.

Brisman, A. and South, N. (2018) 'Green Criminology, Zemiology, and Comparative and Inter-Relational Justice in the Anthropocene Era.' In: Boukli, A. and Kotzé, J. (eds) *Zemiology: Reconnecting Crime and Social Harm*. Cham: Palgrave Macmillan.

Brito, T.P., Celestino, C.C. and Moraes, R.V. (2013) *A Brief Scenario About the 'Space Pollution' Around the Earth*. Journal of Physics Conference Series. Available at: https://iopscience.iop.org/article/10.1088/1742–6596/465/1/012020/pdf (accessed: 6 April 2022).

Burgess, C. and Dubbs, C. (2007) *Animals in Space: From Research Rockets to the Space Shuttle*. Chichester, UK: Praxis Publishing Ltd.

Chobotov, V.A. (2002) 'Orbital Debris Hazards Assessment and Mitigation Strategies.' In: Smirnov, N.N. (ed.) *Space Debris: Hazard Evaluation and Mitigation*. London: Taylor and Francis.

European Space Agency (2022) *Space Debris by the Numbers*. Available at: https://www.esa.int/

Safety_Security/Space_Debris/Space_debris_by_the_numbers (accessed: 8 April 2022).
Clarke, A. (1978) *The Fountains of Paradise*. London: Victor Gollancz.
Hobbs, S., Stansbery, G. and Matos de Carvalho, T. (2019) 'Space Waste.' In: Letcher, T.M. and Vallero, D.A. (eds) *Waste: A Handbook for Management* (2nd ed.). Amsterdam: Elsevier.
Knecht, W.R. (2001) 'Modeling the Big Sky Theory,' *Human Factors and Ergonomics Society Annual Meeting Proceedings*, 45(2): 87–91.
Koryanov, V., Toporkov, A. and Pozdnyakov, A. (2021) 'The Concept of a Long-Term Service Station to Increase the Life Duration of Some Satellites or to Remove Space Debris,' *Journal of Space Safety Engineering*, 8(1): 23–28.
Lam, A., South, N. and Brisman, A. (2024) 'If There Was an Observer on Mars, They Would Probably be Amazed that We Have Survived this Long': Environmental Decline, Elite Escapes and Arks in Space.' In: Eski, Y. and Lampkin, J.A. (eds) *Crime, Criminal Justice and Ethics in Outer Space: International Perspectives*. Abingdon: Routledge.
Lampkin, J.A. (2020) *Uniting Green Criminology and Earth Jurisprudence*. Abingdon: Routledge.
Lampkin, J.A. (2021) 'Mapping the Terrain of an Astro-Green Criminology: A Case for Extending the Green Criminological Lens Outside of Planet Earth,' *Astropolitics: The International Journal of Space Politics and Policy*, 18(3): 238–259.
Lampkin, J.A. and White, R. (2023) *Space Criminology*. Basingstoke: Palgrave Macmillan.
Lampkin, J.A. and Wyatt, T. (2022) 'Widening the Scope of "Earth" Jurisprudence and "Green" Criminology? Towards Preserving Extra-Terrestrial Heritage Sites on Celestial Bodies.' In: Gacek, J. and Jochelson, R. (eds) *Green Criminology and the Law*. Cham: Palgrave Macmillan.
Lampkin, J.A. and Wyatt, T. (2023) 'An Astro-Green Criminological Examination of Orbital Space Debris,' *Criminology & Criminal Justice*, 1–18.
Liemer, R. and Chyba, C.F. (2010) 'A Verifiable Limited Test Ban for Anti-Satellite Weapons,' *The Washington Quarterly*, 33(3): 149–163.
Miller, J., Davis, B., McCandless, R., Delgado, A., Henderson, D., Parado, A., Rodriguez, D. and Sandy, M. (2021) 'Project Review: Experimental Hypervelocity Impacts of Non-Spherical Projectiles on Whipple Shields,' *Orbital Debris Quarterly News*, 25(4): 1–14.
NASA (2021) *Space Debris and Human Spacecraft*. Available at: https://www.nasa.gov/mission_pages/station/news/orbital_debris.html (accessed: 6 April 2022).
Ormrod, J. (2013) 'Beyond World-Risk Society? A Critique of Ulrich Beck's World Risk Society Thesis as a Framework for Understanding Risk Associated with Human Activity in Outer Space,' *Environment and Planning D: Society and Space*, 31: 727–744.
Rand, L.R. (2019) 'The Politics of Space Junk,' *Perspectives on History*, June. Available at: https://www.historians.org/publications-and-directories/perspectives-on-history/summer-2019/politics-of-space-junk (accessed: 23 June 2022).
Seymour, R. (2021) 'Why the Billionaire Space Race Is the Colonial Fantasy Reborn,' *New Statesman*, 20 July. Available at: https://www.newstatesman.com/politics/2021/07/why-billionaire-space-race-colonial-fantasy-reborn (accessed: 23 June 2022).
Shaw, M. (2021) 'Billionaire Capitalists Are Designing Humanity's Future. Don't Let Them,' *The Guardian*, 5 February. Available at: https://www.theguardian.com/commentisfree/2021/feb/05/jeff-bezos-elon-musk-spacex-blue-origin (accessed: 23 June 2022).
Stakem, P. (2018) *Orbital Debris: The Problem and the Mitigation*. PRRB Publishing.
Sturza, M.A. and Carretero, G.S. (2021) *Consequences of LEO Satellite Collisions: The Fragments*. Available at: https://www.viasat.com/content/dam/us-site/space-and-network-operations/documents/AS-04_Sturza_Consequences%20of%20LEO%20Satellite%20Collisions%20%20The%20Fragments.pdf (accessed: 8 April 2022).
Takemura, N. (2019) 'Astro-Green Criminology: A New Perspective Against Space Capitalism,' *Toin University of Yokohama Research Bulletin*, 40: 7–16.
Tulczyjew, L., Myller, M., Kawulok, M., Kostrzewa, D. and Nalepa, J. (2021) 'Predicting Risk of Satellite Collisions Using Machine Learning,' *Journal of Space Safety Engineering*, 8(4): 339–344.
Wolf, S. and Stanley, N. (2014) *Wolf and Stanley on Environmental Law* (6th ed.). Abingdon: Routledge.
Wortman, R. (2020) 'Research Viewpoint Modernizing the Outer Space Treaty for National Appropriation,' *Astropolitics: The International Journal of Space Politics and Policy*, 18(2): 170–182.

24. Toxic legacy of the military

Introduction

This entry illustrates the destructive impact of armed conflict on human and non-human environments, providing global examples of environmental harm and an overview of the strengths and limitations of the existing international law developed to address it. The scope and scale of military pollution is vast but often goes unacknowledged or is deemed inevitable collateral damage. However, public concerns over the deliberate environmental devastation perpetuated during the Vietnam and Gulf Wars acted as turning points, focusing international attention on the need for a legal framework that protects the environment itself from wartime harm. Yet despite widespread recognition that excessive environmental damage by the military is unacceptable, there have been few examples in which perpetrators are held accountable. Effective enforcement mechanisms are seen as lacking and requiring individual state responsibility to monitor and address violations has not worked. Gaps in the framework persist. As climate change impacts worsen, researchers urgently call for effective and meaningful change.

From deforestation in Vietnam (Westing, 2013b) to desertification in Afghanistan (Saba, 2001), from resource depletion in the Democratic Republic of Congo (Renner, 2004) to biodiversity loss in Rwanda (Kanyamibwa, 1998), through to noxious air in Kuwait (Issa and Vempatti, 2018) and contaminated drinking water in the United States (Andrews et al., 2021), the soil, water and air, and flora and fauna across the globe have been impacted by the machinations of warfare. Reasons ranging from military vehicle exhaust (Watson Institute, 2019) and hazardous waste burn pits (Coughlin and Szema, 2019) to unexploded munitions and landmines (Berhe, 2007) to the depletion of uranium (Savabieasfahani et al., 2020; White, 2008), deliberate scorched-earth tactics, indiscriminate bombing (Hulme, 1997) and the development and deployment of increasingly destructive nuclear (Pilger, 2001), biological (Harris, 1995) and chemical weapons (Oatsvall, 2013) have led to devastating environmental destruction with repercussions for human and non-human life well beyond the length of a conflict.

Military pollution is transboundary by nature, impacting communities and countries outside conflict zones and even in times of peace. Military bases act as significant sources of environmental contamination (Hamilton, 2016), and weapons testing and training exercises cause widespread harm to their surroundings (Bobonis et al., 2020). There is scholarly consensus that modern warfare and the concomitant technological advances have resulted in ever more environmental destruction (Hupy, 2008; Closmann, 2009). However, with the advent of television, a global 24/7 news cycle, the internet and social media, environmental devastation is being recorded, documented, and shared as never before. Public pressure has influenced the response to the environmental devastation in both the Vietnam and Gulf Wars, providing the impetus for key changes to international environmental law. However, a review of the literature illustrates the limitations of existing legal frameworks to hold violators accountable and deter future harm, and researchers have continued to reiterate the urgency in protecting the environment upon which all life depends, as the spectre of global environmental catastrophe grows.

Toxic weapons of war

Warfare in the twentieth century was unprecedented in its scale. Competition for increasingly lethal and destructive weapons led to the development of chemical, biological, radiological, and nuclear weapons – referred to as CBRN weapons.

Chemical weapons (CWs) are characterised as weapons derived from chemical agents which have a direct toxic effect on human and non-human life. CWs were first developed and deployed by the German Army during World War I (Szinicz, 2005). The use of CWs was prohibited in the 1925 Geneva Protocol; however, they continued to be used in colonial wars throughout the 1930s and 1940s, such as Italy's extensive use against Ethiopian troops between 1935 and 1936 (Grip and Hart, 2009). The long-term toxic effects of CWs only became a focus for researchers after World War II (WWII), when the scale of dumped and abandoned CW munitions became apparent. From China (Deng and Evans, 1997: 105) to the Baltic (Glasby, 1997), the improper disposal of CWs after WWII caused harm to human and non-human life as well as broader ecosystems. The most extensive environmental damage by CWs remains the US Air Force's (USAF) use of chemical defoliants during the Vietnam War. Between 1962 and 1971 the USAF destroyed 3.1 million hectares (31,000 sq/km) of Vietnam's natural forests, grasslands, and agricultural land through the deployment of 20 million gallons (91 million litres) of chemical defoliants known as Agents Orange, White, and Blue during Operation Ranch Hand (Oatsvall, 2013). It proved to be strategically ineffective, and extremely costly in terms of loss of life and biodiverse habitats. Research on Agent Orange exposure has focused on impacts to human health; however, the impacts upon the biodiverse environments which were targeted has received much less scholarly attention, with much still unknown about the impact of USAF's operation on natural flora and fauna (Truong and Dinh, 2021).

Biological weapons (BWs) differ from CWs in that the primary antagonists are microbial organisms which multiply within a target organism to cause death and disease in humans, animals, and wider ecosystems (Leitenberg, 1971: 25). The development of BWs emerged after WWI, with the first use by the Imperial Japanese Army between 1936 and 1945. The Japanese Army murdered thousands of Chinese prisoners-of-war by exposing them to deadly pathogens such as *Pasteurella pestis* (plague) and *Bacillus anthracis* (anthrax) (Harris, 1995; Fong, 2000). In Britain, Gruinard Island off the north-west coast of Scotland was used for BW testing, leading to the island being quarantined from 1943 until 1990. British military scientists released anthrax spores into the air through controlled detonations during 1942 and 1943 (Manchee et al., 1981). This resulted in the deaths of several livestock – the deaths of other wildlife were not recorded. The island required extensive environmental remediation work after the war, including the removal and destruction of contaminated topsoil. The US military conducted BW tests at the Dugway Proving Ground in Utah between 1951 and 1969. This included the release of "Rocky Mountain spotted fever, psittacosis, Q fever, anthrax, brucellosis, plague, tularemia, and hydatid disease" (Choffnes, 2001: 60) all of which have subsequently become endemic among the native wildlife.

Radiological weapons (RWs) and *nuclear weapons* (NWs) both emit forms of ionising radiation (IR) through the breakdown of radioactive material. The advent of the Atomic Age began during World War II, when the US military detonated the first nuclear bomb at the Trinity site in New Mexico. This event reshaped global politics and introduced the threat of an anthropogenic mass extinction. The detonation of nuclear weapons for lethal (strategic military) or non-lethal (testing) purposes creates significant environmental challenges in terms of radioactive fallout and subsequent IR contamination. The bombing of the Japanese cities of Hiroshima and Nagasaki by the USAF in August 1945 remains the only offensive use of nuclear weapons during a military conflict. Studies conducted in the decades after the attacks on Hiroshima and Nagasaki demonstrated that survivors who were exposed to IR of the blasts were five times more likely to develop leukaemia or solid cancer than unexposed subjects (Preston et al., 2004). The testing of nuclear weapons provides a further avenue for exposure to deadly IR. At the site of Semipalatinsk, for example, Soviet scientists conducted 456 above- and below-ground nuclear weapons tests between 1949 and 1991 (Kassenova, 2022; Logachev et al., 2008). Studies have shown how residents of the city of Dolan, located near the Semipalatinsk test site, were subject to irradiation and long-life radionuclides contaminating their environment, and continue to demonstrate higher mortality from cancer, higher rates of stillbirth, and higher rates of birth defects, all of which are linked to exposure to IR (Chenal et al., 2006: 91). The environment around Dolon is characterised by continuing radioactive contamination from long-life radionuclides, primarily caesium and plutonium (Stegnar and Wrixon, 1998).

RWs are a broad category which range from so-called "dirty bombs" to depleted uranium (DU) munitions. The use of DU by the US military in its armour and munitions provides the most widespread examples of RWs. From the 1970s onwards, the US military sought to utilise DU, a by-product of enriching uranium, for its cheap unit cost and high-density properties. British and US forces used DU munitions extensively during the First Gulf War (1990–1991), following which a confidential report from the British Atomic Energy Authority (BAEA) outlined the toxic legacy of DU use in the conflict. The report stated that DU is a known carcinogen and predicted that it could lead to the deaths of half a million Iraqis after the conflict (Pilger, 2001). Further, a report submitted to the UN Commissioner on Human Rights in 1998 outlined that the death rate of Iraqi children under five years old increased sevenfold between 1989 and 1993 with cancers such as lymphoblastic leukaemia contributing to this alarming rise (Birchard, 1998). Despite serious concerns, British and US military forces continued to use DU munitions, including during the Second Gulf War (2003–2011). Across both Gulf Wars over 1,200 tonnes of DU munitions were used. During the same time period instances of cancer among Iraqis tripled (Fathi et al., 2013). The fragmentation of DU is particularly problematic, with Iraqi oncologist Dr Jawad Al-Ali powerfully articulating the dangers of DU in the air, when he stated, "The dust carries death" (Pilger, 2001: 9). International concern over the use of DU munitions is demonstrated by a series of votes in the European Parliament in 2001 and at the UN Human Rights Convention in 2002 to ban its use. Britain and the US have consistently resisted banning DU munitions, and evidence has emerged that the US military used DU munitions during the Syrian Civil War (Oakford, 2017).

The world's largest institutional polluter

Recent research suggests that the United States military is the world's largest institutional polluter, emitting more greenhouse gases than most medium-sized countries (Belcher et al., 2020; Crawford, 2019). Oil consumption is estimated at one million barrels per day, contributing five per cent of total global emissions (Solarin et al., 2018). Further examples of the gross excesses of the US military in relation to environmental damage include the use of chemical defoliants in Vietnam and the continued use of depleted uranium as described above. However, more recent research into environmental destruction has illustrated widespread environmental damage in Afghanistan after two decades of occupation by the US military. Burn pits, in which metal, plastic, medical materials, and human waste were incinerated, produced highly toxic air pollution (Atherton, 2021). The widespread use of landmines, and US military convoys utilising open fields as alternative routes for travel, decimated Afghanistan's agricultural industry, which shrank from 71 per cent of its GDP in 1994 to 24 per cent in 2013 (Hussona, 2019).

The US military is also one of the largest sources of domestic pollution, responsible for toxins spread across 40 million acres of US soil (Brockovich, 2021). More than two-thirds of all Superfund sites, highly contaminated areas designated by the federal government for remediation, are connected to the US military (Brockovich, 2021). Pollution from US military bases has caused widespread environmental contamination and negative health outcomes in service men and women, their families, non-human life, and wider ecosystems (Hamilton, 2016).

The US military's use of aqueous film forming foam (AFFF) as a fire-fighting foam on both domestic and international bases is an emerging environmental catastrophe. AFFF contains per- and poly-fluoroalkyl substances (PFAS), man-made chemicals utilised for their water, heat, and stain resistant properties. In 2022, the EPA proposed that two members of the PFAS class of chemicals, including those in AFFF, be designated as hazardous substances (EPA, 2022). PFAS are also known as "forever chemicals" for their persistent nature. AFFF has contaminated the water, soil, and air of bases and their surrounding communities throughout the United States (EWG, n.d.) and overseas, including in Australia (Middleton, 2009), Germany (Mori, 2020), and the United Kingdom (Salvidge, 2022). According to the Environmental Working Group, PFAS have been discharged into the environment in over 700 military sites across the United States (EWG, n.d.).

A further example of domestic pollution is Camp Lejeune Marine Corps Base in Jacksonville, North Carolina. Toxic contaminants found in the base's drinking water have been linked to infertility, birth defects, childhood leukaemia, and neurobehavioural impacts (Jung et al., 2022). The base was declared a Superfund site in 1989 after over one million people were thought to have been exposed to a cocktail of toxic chemicals in their water. In 2005, criminal investigations led by the EPA found no illegal actions in the military handling of the water contamination and the Department of Justice declined to prosecute (Magner, 2014). Camp Lejeune illustrates the difficulty of confronting environmental injustice when it is perpetuated by the US military, a trend that is continued at an international scale.

International legal frameworks

The codification of the laws and customs of war can be traced to the mid-nineteenth-century Lieber Code, which outlined the rules of conduct for Union soldiers during the US Civil War (1861–1865) (Lieber, 1863; Jensen and Teixeira, 2004). Issued in 1863, the Lieber Code does not explicitly discuss the environment; however, scholars argue that the environment is referenced through the restriction of the destruction of property that is not militarily necessary, including resources utilised by humans for survival (Jensen and Teixeira, 2004). Protection of property was reiterated and expanded upon on an international scale in the 1907 Convention Respecting the Laws of Customs and War on Land at the Hague, which made it unlawful to destroy or seize enemy property, with the exception for military necessity. It further required the occupying force to actively protect the resources and property of the occupied territory (ICRC, 1988; Jensen and Teixeira, 2004). In 1945, Article 6(1) of the Nuremberg Charter made "wanton destruction of cities, towns or villages, or devastation not justified by military necessity" a war crime.

However, it was not until 1977 that two important developments in international environmental law came into force:

(1) *Additional Protocol I (Protocol I), Relating to the Protection of Victims of Armed Conflicts, to the Geneva Conventions*

(2) *The Convention on the Prohibition of Military or Any Other Hostile Use of Environmental Modification Techniques* (ENMOD)

These two agreements are widely accepted as the first set of international laws to directly address the impact of armed conflict on the environment itself (Pilloud et al., 1987). Driven by widespread destruction during the Vietnam War by the USAF's use of chemical defoliants, participants of the United Nations Conference on the Environment in Stockholm acknowledged the necessity for regulating the harmful impacts of war on the natural environment (Daft, 2019). Out of these deliberations Article 55 of Additional Protocol I (UN, 1977a) emerged. It states:

> 1. *Care shall be taken in warfare to protect the natural environment against widespread, long-term and severe damage. This protection includes a prohibition of the use of methods or means of warfare which are intended or may be expected to cause such damage to the natural environment and thereby to prejudice the health or survival of the population.*
>
> 2. *Attacks against the natural environment by way of reprisals are prohibited.*

ENMOD was the result of bilateral discussions between the US and USSR during disarmament talks to address the prohibition of the "use of environmental or geophysical modification activity as a weapon of war" (UN, 1977b). ENMOD covers a range of ways in which states may not disrupt the "natural equilibrium permitting life" such as triggering earthquakes or manipulating the weather or climate (Pilloud et al., 1987: 420). For example, Article 1 of ENMOD states:

> States parties undertake not to engage in military or any other hostile use of environmental modification techniques having widespread, long-lasting or severe effects as the means of destruction, damage or injury to another State party. (UN, 1977b)

Scholars have discussed the key differences between these two agreements, arguing that the purpose of the Protocol is to protect the natural environment *from* damage whereas ENMOD directly addresses the prohibition of environmental modification techniques *used as a weapon* (Pilloud et al., 1987). Additionally, Protocol I applies specifically to times of war whereas ENMOD focuses on environmental modification used for any hostile purposes, thus covering incidents outside formal armed conflict. Further, ENMOD provides definitions for its three conditions, "widespread, long-lasting or severe" and requires only one of three be met, while Protocol I requires all three conditions to be met for a violation to occur.

Over a decade later, the atrocities of the Gulf War renewed concern in the international community around the destruction of the environment during armed conflict, resulting in the Rio Declaration on Environment and Development in 1993. Principle 24 states:

> Warfare is inherently destructive of sustainable development. States shall therefore respect international law providing protection for the environment in times of armed conflict and cooperate in its further development, as necessary. (UN, 1993)

However, there was no substantive change to existing international law.

It was not until the creation of an International Criminal Court and the Rome Statute that governs it in 2002 that a significant shift in international law occurred. The Rome Statute adopted the language of Protocol I in Article 8(2)(b)(iv) which classified environmental damage as a war crime (Lawrence and Heller, 2007). The Article prohibits:

> ...intentionally launching an attack in the knowledge that such attack will cause incidental loss of life or injury to civilians or damage to civilian objects or widespread, long-term and severe damage to the natural environment which would be clearly excessive in relation to the concrete and direct overall military advantage anticipated. (ICC, 2011)

The most recent update on international environmental law and armed conflict comes from the International Law Commission (ILC), which has undertaken the Protection of the Environment in Relation to Armed Conflicts (PERAC) project since 2013 to organise and clarify existing legal frameworks addressing environmental law and armed conflict (ILC, 2022). In 2022, 27 principles and a preamble were submitted by the drafting committee to the ILC with the recommendation that they be adopted by the Commission and put forward for a vote at the UN General Assembly (ILC, 2022). Some key sections include the application of the principles before, during, or after armed conflict and in situations of occupation, and the mention of protecting the environment of Indigenous peoples (ILC, 2022).

Accountability and its limitations

The prosecution of crimes against the environment dates back to the Nuremberg Military Tribunals (1946–1949) (Jensen and Teixeira 2004; Lawrence and Heller, 2007). In 1948, General Lothar Rendulic of the German Wehrmacht was convicted of violating Article 6(1) for engaging in scorched-earth policies in Finland. Nine civilian administrators were subsequently listed in the United Nations War Crimes Commission as war criminals for their extensive exploitation of Polish forests (Jensen and Teixeira 2004; Schmitt, 1997).

Despite these precedents there has been only one meaningful prosecution of environmental crime during armed conflict since the adoption of Protocol I and ENMOD prior to the Rome Statute – the burning of Kuwaiti oil fields by withdrawing Iraqi forces during the Gulf War. More than 700 oil wells were destroyed, spilling 60 million barrels of oil, 10 million of which were released into the Gulf (UN, 2022). Ten million cubic metres of soil were contaminated with oil, 50,000 cubic metres of raw sewage were discharged into Kuwait Bay, and to this day two-fifths of the country's freshwater reserve remains contaminated (Linden et al., 2004). Researchers have found negative impacts on birds, marine life, and prawn fisheries (Westing, 2013a; Evans et al., 1993; Al Bakri and Kittaneh, 1998). Iraq paid reparations of $52.4 billion to Kuwait, with the last payment in January 2022 (UN, 2022). Environmental damage cited in the legal decision include contamination of freshwater aquifers, coastal and desert areas including 26 million cubic metres of contaminants that need to be removed to landfills (UN, 2022). It is important to note that Iraq was held liable through a legal standard derived from Security Council Resolution 687 as Iraq was not a party to either ENMOD or Protocol I (UN, 2022) and despite subsequent calls for other incidents of environmental harm to be prosecuted, including NATO's repeated bombing of industrial complexes in Yugoslavia, no others have met the threshold for doing so (IEER, 1999; UN, 2000).

Herein lies one of the main criticisms of existing legal frameworks to protect the environment during armed conflict – the lack of an effective enforcement mechanism. For both ENMOD and Protocol I, state parties who have ratified the agreement are expected to comply to its terms by essentially self-policing violations and paying out reparations (Lawrence and Heller, 2007). Unsurprisingly, this has not proven is an effective enforcement mechanism and the threat of reparations an ineffective deterrent to environmental destruction during armed conflict.

Article 8(2)(b)(iv) of the Rome Statute is the first explicitly ecocentric war crime and researchers have identified several key elements that should allow for more effective enforcement of this Article than either Protocol I or ENMOD; namely, the ICC's status as an independent prosecutor, its mandatory jurisdiction over state parties, and unlike the previous agreements, the potential ability to prosecute crimes committed anywhere in the world (Lawrence and Heller, 2007). However, there has yet to be a single prosecution or investigation launched under this Article. Lawrence and Heller (2007: 71) outline the limitations of Article 8(2)(b)(iv) including the continued use of vague language from Protocol I without any clarification of the terms "widespread, long-term and severe", a test of proportionality which is weighted too heavily against finding an incident disproportionate, the subjectivity of an incident's intentionality and the fact that the Article does not apply to internal armed conflict. This final point is important as there is little research into the environmental consequences of internal conflicts despite constituting the majority of armed conflicts since World War II. During the Rwandan Civil War (1990–1994), for example, there was an increase in poaching of endangered mountain gorillas and mining in national parks to fund the conflict (Plumptre et al., 1997).

Prosecution by the ICC is further limited by the fact that the US and other major military polluters are not a party to the ICC, and the US and Russia object to its soldiers appearing before international tribunals (Jensen and Teixeira, 2004). The ICC also refers to itself as "the court of last resort" and does not seek jurisdiction before State parties have had an opportunity to do so (ICC, 2011). It lacks universal territorial jurisdiction and may only investigate and prosecute crimes committed within member states, crimes committed by nationals of member states, or crimes in situations referred to the Court by the United Nations Security Council (ILC, 2022). Further, gathering evidence of environmental damage continues to be a challenge due to lack of access to sites and funding (Biswas, 2000).

Scholars also argue that existing legal frameworks do not address the myriad ways in which armed conflicts can negatively impact the environment including the lack of explicit protections for safeguarding biodiversity and the unacknowledged connection between the uncontrolled circulation of arms and the destruction of the environment and wildlife (Durant and Brito, 2019). Funding for armed conflicts often relies on the exploitation of natural resources such as diamonds, coltan, timber, and ivory, which causes widespread environmental damage (Douglas and Alie, 2014; Christy, 2015; Smith, 2015; Brito et al., 2018; Zedany and Al-Kich, 2013). Research into the impact of war on wildlife has demonstrated proximity to armed conflict as the biggest predictor of wildlife decline (Douglas and Alie, 2014; Gaynor et al., 2016; Brashares et al., 2014).

Conclusion

The International Criminal Court, ENMOD, and Protocol I are useful in their ability to set normative customs relating to armed conflict and environmental protection but have proved to be judicially ineffective (Jensen and Teixeira, 2004). Scholars agree that a new treaty requires significant political will and must include clear definitions, enforceable protections, and prohibitive consequences. After the release of the PERAC project's principles there have been calls for a Fifth Geneva Convention dedicated to establishing better environmental protections related to any military activity, before, during, and after armed conflict (Durant and Brito, 2019). Scholars have argued that criminalising individual members of the military responsible for environmental damage is the only effective deterrent going forward, as it circumvents the limitations of achieving state responsibility (Jensen and Teixeira, 2004; Lawrence and Heller, 2007).

There is nonetheless cause for hope that wanton environmental destruction by global military forces can successfully be challenged. In the United States a landmark congressional bill was passed in 2012 after consistent pressure from members of the military personally affected by contamination at Camp Lejeune, providing medical care for health conditions and allocating $2.2 billion in compensation to those affected, and massive clean-up efforts at bases across the States are underway (Veterans Association, 2022). Coverage of the recent Russian invasion of Ukraine has included a robust and durable focus on the environment that has already documented large-scale fires at oil depots and munitions dumps (Mathiesen et al., 2022), and chemical spills at power stations, chemical warehouses, and power plants (Weir, 2022; Surma, 2022, Mathiesen et al., 2022, Marsi, 2022). Researchers hope that, as was the case with the Vietnam and Gulf Wars, public sentiment will be a driving force to progress legal changes that further protect the environment upon which all life depends.

LILY RUBINO

Further reading

Austin, J.E. and Bruch, C.E. (eds.), 2000. *The Environmental Consequences of War: Legal, Economic, and Scientific Perspectives*. Cambridge University Press.

Biswas, A.K., 2000. Scientific assessment of the long-term environmental consequences of war. In J.E. Austin and C.E. Bruch, (eds.), *The Environmental Consequences of War: Legal, Economic, and Scientific Perspectives*, pp. 303–315. https://thirdworldcentre.org/wp-content/uploads/2020/07/RPP-Jan-3-00-Scientific-Assessment-of-the-Long-Term-Environmental-Consequences-of-War.pdf

Burton, D. and Lin, H.C., 2022. *Military and Conflict-Related Emissions: Kyoto to Glasgow and Beyond*. https://militaryemissions.org/wp-content/uploads/2022/06/military-emissions_final.pdf

Butko, A., 2018. Ukraine's Donbas bears the brunt of toxic armed conflict. *UNEP*. https://www.unep.org/news-and-stories/story/ukraines-donbas-bears-brunt-toxic-armed-conflict.

International Criminal Court (ICC), 2011. *Rome Statute of the International Criminal Court*. https://www.icc-cpi.int/sites/default/files/RS-Eng.pdf

Khan, M., 2022. *The Environmental Impacts of War and Conflict*. K4D Helpdesk Report. Institute of Development Studies. doi:10.19088/K4D.2022.060

Lawrence, J.C. and Heller, K.J., 2007. The first ecocentric environmental war crime: The limits of Article 8 (2)(b)(iv) of the Rome Statute. *Georgetown Environmental Law Review*, *20*, 61–96.

Lieber, F., 1863. *Instructions for the Government of Armies of the United States in the Field*. https://avalon.law.yale.edu/19th_century/lieber.asp

Mauri, D., 2022. The use of CBRN weapons in armed conflict. In A. de Guttry, M. Frulli, F. Casolari, and L., Poli, (eds.), *International Law and Chemical, Biological, Radio-Nuclear (CBRN) Events*, pp. 358–379. Brill Nijhoff.

United Nations (UN), 1977a. *Protocol Additional to The Geneva Conventions of 12 August 1949, and Relating to The Protection of Victims of International Armed Conflicts (Protocol I), of 8 June 1977*. https://www.un.org/en/genocideprevention/documents/atrocity-crimes/Doc.34_AP-I-EN.pdf

United Nations (UN), 1977b. *Convention on the Prohibition of Military or Any Other Hostile Use of Environmental Modification Technique*. https://www.un.org/disarmament/enmod/

United Nations, 1993. *Report of the United Nations Conference on Environment and Development*. https://daccess-ods.un.org/tmp/4102273.58341217.html.

References

Al Bakri, D. and Kittaneh, W., 1998. Physicochemical characteristics and pollution indicators in the intertidal zone of Kuwait: Implications for benthic ecology. *Environmental Management*, *22*(3), 415–424.

Andrews, D.Q., Hayes, J., Stoiber, T., Brewer, B., Campbell, C. and Naidenko, O.V., 2021. Identification of point source dischargers of per- and polyfluoroalkyl substances in the United States. *AWWA Water Science*, *3*(5), e1252.

Atherton, K.D., 2021. U.S. forces are leaving a toxic environmental legacy in Afghanistan. *Scientific American*. https://www.scientificamerican.com/article/u-s-forces-are-leaving-a-toxic-environmental-legacy-in-afghanistan/

Belcher, O., Bigger, P., Neimark, B. and Kennelly, C., 2020. Hidden carbon costs of the "everywhere war": Logistics, geopolitical ecology, and the carbon boot-print of the US military. *Transactions of the Institute of British Geographers*, *45*(1), 65–80.

Berhe, A.A., 2007. The contribution of landmines to land degradation. *Land Degradation & Development*, *18*(1), 1–15.

Birchard, K., 1998. Does Iraq's depleted uranium pose a health risk? *The Lancet*, *351*(9103), 657.

Biswas, A.K., 2000. Scientific assessment of the long-term environmental consequences of war. In *The Environmental Consequences of War: Legal, Economic, and Scientific Perspectives*, pp. 303–315. https://thirdworldcentre.org/wp-content/uploads/2020/07/RPP-Jan-3-00-Scientific-Assessment-of-the-Long-Term-Environmental-Consequences-of-War.pdf

Bobonis, G.J., Stabile, M. and Tovar, L., 2020. Military training exercises, pollution, and their consequences for health. *Journal of Health Economics*, *73*, 102345.

Brashares, J.S., Abrahms, B., Fiorella, K.J., Golden, C.D., Hojnowski, C.E., Marsh, R.A., McCauley, D.J., Nuñez, T.A., Seto, K. and

Withey, L., 2014. Wildlife decline and social conflict. *Science, 345*(6195), 376–378.
Brito, J.C., Durant, S.M., Pettorelli, N., Newby, J., Canney, S., Algadafi, W., Rabeil, T., Crochet, P.A., Pleguezuelos, J.M., Wacher, T. and de Smet, K., 2018. Armed conflicts and wildlife decline: Challenges and recommendations for effective conservation policy in the Sahara-Sahel. *Conservation Letters, 11*(5), p.e12446.
Brockovich, E., 2021. *Superman's Not Coming: Our National Water Crisis and What We the People Can Do About It*. Vintage.
Chenal, C., Legue, F. and Nourgalieva, K., 2006. Delayed effects of low-level acute irradiation and chronic environmental radioactive contamination on DNA lymphocytes of people living in Dolon, a settlement located in the vicinity of the Semipalatinsk nuclear test site (Kazakhstan). *Science of the Total Environment, 369*(1–3), 91–98.
Choffnes, E., 2001. Germs on the loose. *Bulletin of the Atomic Scientists, 57*(2), 57–61.
Christy, B. 2015. How killing elephants finances terror in Africa. *National Geographic* (August) https://www.nationalgeographic.com/tracking-ivory/article.html
Closmann, C.E. ed., 2009. *War and the Environment: Military Destruction in the Modern Age*. Texas A&M University Press.
Coughlin, S.S. and Szema, A., 2019. Burn pits exposure and chronic respiratory illnesses among Iraq and Afghanistan veterans. *Journal of Environment and Health Sciences, 5*(1), 13–14.
Crawford, N.C., 2019. *Pentagon Fuel Use, Climate Change, and the Costs of War*. Watson Institute, Brown University.
Daft, S., 2019. Environmental destruction is a war crime, but it's almost impossible to fall foul of the laws. *The Conversation*. https://theconversation. com/environmental-destruction-is-a-war-crime-but-its-almost-impossible-to-fall-foul-of-the-laws-121180.
Deng, H. and Evans, P.O.M., 1997. Social and environmental aspects of abandoned chemical weapons in China. *The Nonproliferation Review, 4*(3), 101–108.
Douglas, L.R. and Alie, K., 2014. High-value natural resources: Linking wildlife conservation to international conflict, insecurity, and development concerns. *Biological Conservation, 171*, 270–277.
Durant, S.M. and Brito, J.C., 2019. Protect environment from armed conflicts. *Nature, 571*(7766), 478.
Environmental Protection Agency (EPA), 2022. *Proposed Designation of Perfluorooctanoic Acid (PFOA) and Perfluorooctanesulfonic Acid (PFOS) as CERCLA Hazardous Substances*. www.epa.gov/superfund/proposed-designation-perfluorooctanoic-acid-pfoa-and-perfluorooctanesulfonic-acid-pfos
Environmental Working Group (EWG), n.d. *708 Military Sites With Known or Suspected Discharges of PFAS*. https://www.ewg.org/interactive-maps/2020-military-pfas-sites/map/
Evans, M.I., Symens, P. and Pilcher, C.W.T., 1993. Short-term damage to coastal bird populations in Saudi Arabia and Kuwait following the 1991 Gulf War marine pollution. *Marine Pollution Bulletin, 27*, 157–161.
Fathi, R.A., Matti, L.Y., Al-Salih, H.S. and Godbold, D., 2013. Environmental pollution by depleted uranium in Iraq with special reference to Mosul and possible effects on cancer and birth defect rates. *Medicine, Conflict and Survival, 29*(1), 7–25.
Fong, P., 2000. Inter arma enim silent leges: The impunity of Japan's secret biological warfare unit. *New England Journal of International & Comparative Law, 6*, 1–15.
Gaynor, K.M., Fiorella, K.J., Gregory, G.H., Kurz, D.J., Seto, K.L., Withey, L.S. and Brashares, J.S., 2016. War and wildlife: Linking armed conflict to conservation. *Frontiers in Ecology and the Environment, 14*(10), 533–542.
Glasby, G.P., 1997. Disposal of chemical weapons in the Baltic Sea. *Science of the Total Environment, 206*(2–3), 267–273.
Grip, L. and Hart, J., 2009. The use of chemical weapons in the 1935–36 Italo-Ethiopian War. *SIPRI Arms Control and Non-proliferation Programmme*, 1–8.
Hamilton, J.W., 2016. Contamination at US military bases: Profiles and responses. *Stanford Environmental Law Journal, 35*, 223–249.
Harris, S.H., 1995. *Factories of Death: Japanese Biological Warfare, 1932–45, and the American Cover-up*. Routledge.
Hulme, K., 1997. Armed conflict, wanton ecological devastation and scorched earth policies: How the 1990–91 Gulf Conflict revealed the inadequacies of the current laws to ensure effective protection and preservation of the natural environment. *Journal of Armed Conflict Law, 2*(1), 45–81.
Hupy, J., 2008. The environmental footprint of war. *Environment and History, 14*(3), 405–421.
Hussona, J. 2019. The reverberating effects of explosive violence on agriculture in Afghanistan. *Action on Armed Violence (AOAV)*. https://aoav.org.uk/2019/the-reverberating-effects-of-explosive-violence-on-agriculture-in-afghanistan
Institute for Energy and Environmental Research (IEER), 1999. *NATO Bombing in Balkans Could Result in Widespread Ecological Disaster*. https://ieer.org/resource/press-releases/nato-bombing-in-balkans-could-result-in-widespread-ecological-disaster/.
International Committee of the Red Cross (ICRC), 1988. *Treaties, States Parties and*

Commentaries. https://ihl-databases.icrc.org/ihl/INTRO/195
International Criminal Court (ICC), 2011. *Rome Statute of the International Criminal Court*. https://www.icc-cpi.int/sites/default/files/RS-Eng.pdf
International Law Commission (ILC), 2022. *Analytical Guide to the Work of the International Law Commission*. https://legal.un.org/ilc/guide/8_7.shtml
Issa, N. and Vempatti, S., 2018. Oil spills in the Arabian Gulf: A case study and environmental review. *Environment and Natural Resources Research*, *8*(1), 144–153.
Jensen, E.T. and Teixeira Jr, J.J., 2004. Prosecuting Members of the US military for wartime environmental crimes. *Georgetown International Environmental Law Review*, *17*, 651.
Jung, K., Khan, A., Mocharnuk, R., Olivo-Marston, S. and McDaniel, J.T., 2022. Clinical encounter with three cancer patients affected by groundwater contamination at Camp Lejeune: A case series and review of the literature. *Journal of Medical Case Reports*, *16*(1), 1–12.
Kanyamibwa, S., 1998. Impact of war on conservation: Rwandan environment and wildlife in agony. *Biodiversity & Conservation*, *7*(11), 1399–1406.
Kassenova, T., 2022. *Atomic Steppe: How Kazakhstan Gave Up the Bomb*. Stanford University Press.
Lawrence, J.C. and Heller, K.J., 2007. The first ecocentric environmental war crime: The limits of Article 8(2)(b)(iv) of the Rome Statute. *Georgetown Environmental Law Review*, *20*, 61–96.
Leitenberg, M., 1971. The problem of chemical and biological warfare: A study of the historical, technical, military, legal and political aspects of CBW, and possible disarmament measures. *SIPRI Vol. 1: The Rise of CB Weapons*.
Lieber, F., 1863. *Instructions for the Government of Armies of the United States in the Field*. https://avalon.law.yale.edu/19th_century/lieber.asp
Linden, O., Jerneloev, A. and Egerup, J., 2004. *The Environmental Impacts of the Gulf War 1991*. International Institute for Applied Systems Analysis (IIASA). http://pure.iiasa.ac.at/7427/
Logachev, V.A., Savkin, M.N. and Logacheva, L.A., 2008. Nuclear tests in the USSR and their influence on the health of the population of the Russian Federation.
Magner, M., 2014. *A Trust Betrayed: The Untold Story of Camp Lejeune and the Poisoning of Generations of Marines and Their Families*. Da Capo Press.
Manchee, R.J., Broster, M.G., Melling, J., Henstridge, R.M. and Stagg, A.J., 1981. Bacillus anthracis on Gruinard Island. *Nature*, *294*(5838), 254–255.
Marsi, F., 2022. Can Ukraine hold Russia accountable for environmental crimes? www.aljazeera.com/amp/features/2022/5/16/can-ukraine-hold-russia-accountable-for-environmental-crimes
Mathiesen, K., Guillot, L. and Zimmermann, A., 2022. Ukraine's nuclear nightmare is only part of the war's environmental horrors. www.politico.eu/article/ukraine-war-russia-nuclear-power-plant-map-zaporizhzhia-nightmare-environment/
Middleton, H., 2009. The campaign against US military bases in Australia. In L. Blanchard and L. Chan, (eds.), *Ending War, Building Peace*, pp. 121–135. Sydney University Press.
Mori, K., 2020. Domestic environmental policy and Status of Forces Agreement: US military presence and new water pollution risk in Germany. In S. Kawana and M. Takahashi, (eds.), *Exploring Base Politics*, pp. 77–92. Routledge.
Oakford, S., 2017. The United States used depleted uranium in Syria. *Foreign Policy*. https://foreignpolicy.com/2017/02/14/the-united-states-used-depleted-uranium-in-syria/
Oatsvall, N.S., 2013. Trees versus lives: Reckoning military success and the ecological effects of chemical defoliation during the Vietnam War. *Environment and History*, *19*(4), 427–458.
Pilger, J., 2001. Iraq: The great cover-up. *New Statesman*, *130*(4521), 8–9.
Pilloud, C., Sandoz, Y., Swinarski, C. and Zimmermann, B. (eds.), 1987. *Commentary on the Additional Protocols of 8 June 1977 to the Geneva Conventions of 12 August 1949*. Martinus Nijhoff Publishers.
Plumptre, A.J., Bizumuremyi, J.B., Uwimana, F. and Ndaruhebeye, J.D., 1997. The effects of the Rwandan civil war on poaching of ungulates in the Parc National des Volcans. *Oryx*, *31*(4), 265–273.
Preston, D.L., Pierce, D.A., Shimizu, Y., Cullings, H.M., Fujita, S., Funamoto, S. and Kodama, K., 2004. Effect of recent changes in atomic bomb survivor dosimetry on cancer mortality risk estimates. *Radiation Research*, *162*(4), 377–389.
Renner, M., 2004. Pillage and plunder: The vast natural resources of the Congo are once again fuelling war, exploitation and poverty – and Western consumers are profiting. *Alternatives Journal*, *30*(4), 22–26.
Saba, D.S., 2001. Afghanistan: Environmental degradation in a fragile ecological setting. *International Journal of Sustainable Development and World Ecology*, *8*, 279–289. https://www.tandfonline.com/doi/abs/10.1080/13504500109470086
Salvidge, R., 2022. High levels of toxic chemicals found in Cambridgeshire water supply. www.theguardian.com/environment/2022/feb/

08/high-levels-of-toxic-chemicals-found-in-cambridgeshire-drinking-water
Savabieasfahani, M., Ahamadani, F.B. and Damghani, A.M., 2020. Living near an active US military base in Iraq is associated with significantly higher hair thorium and increased likelihood of congenital anomalies in infants and children. *Environmental Pollution, 256*, 113070.
Schmitt, M.N., 1997. Green war: An assessment of the environmental law of international armed conflict. *Yale Journal of International Law, 1*, 36–50.
Smith, J.H., 2015. "May it never end": Price wars, networks, and temporality in the "3 Ts" mining trade of the Eastern DR Congo. *HAU: Journal of Ethnographic Theory*, *5*(1), 1–34.
Solarin, S.A., Al-Mulali, U. and Ozturk, I., 2018. Determinants of pollution and the role of the military sector: Evidence from a maximum likelihood approach with two structural breaks in the USA. *Environmental Science and Pollution Research*, *25*(31), 30949–30961.
Stegnar, P. and Wrixon, T., 1998. Semipalatinsk revisited. *International Atomic Energy Agency, Bulletin*, *40*(4), 12–14.
Surma, K., 2022. *Activists Deplore the Human Toll and Environmental Devastation from Russia's Unprovoked War of Aggression in Ukraine*. insideclimatenews.org/news/04032022/activists-deplore-the-human-toll-and-environmental-devastation-from-russias-unprovoked-war-of-aggression-in-ukraine/.
Szinicz, L., 2005. History of chemical and biological warfare agents. *Toxicology*, *214*(3), 167–181.
Truong, K.N. and Dinh, K.V., 2021. Agent Orange: Halt-century effects on the Vietnamese wildlife have been ignored. *Environmental Science & Technology*, *55*(22), 15007–15009.
United Nations (UN), 1977a. *Protocol Additional to the Geneva Conventions of 12 August 1949, and Relating to the Protection of Victims of International Armed Conflicts (Protocol I), of 8 June 1977*. https://www.un.org/en/genocideprevention/documents/atrocity-crimes/Doc.34_AP-I-EN.pdf.
United Nations (UN), 1977b. *Convention on the Prohibition of Military or Any Other Hostile Use of Environmental Modification Technique*. https://www.un.org/disarmament/enmod/
United Nations, 2000. *Final Report to the Prosecutor by the Committee Established to Review the NATO Bombing Campaign Against the Federal Republic of Yugoslavia*. https://www.icty.org/en/press/final-report-prosecutor-committee-established-review-nato-bombing-campaign-against-federal
United Nations (UN), 2022. *Iraq Makes Final Reparation Payment to Kuwait for 1990 Invasion*. https://news.un.org/en/story/2022/02/1111632
Veterans Association, 2022. *Camp Lejeune Water Contamination Health Issues*. https://www.va.gov/disability/eligibility/hazardous-materials-exposure/camp-lejeune-water-contamination/
Watson Institute, 2019. *Costs of War: Environmental Costs*. https://watson.brown.edu/costsofwar/costs/social/environment
Weir, D., 2022. Environmental trends in the Ukraine conflict 10 days in. *CEOBS*. https://ceobs.org/environmental-trends-in-the-ukraine-conflict-10-days-in/
Westing, A.H., 2013a. The Gulf War of 1991: Its environmental impact. In Arthur H. Westing, *Arthur H. Westing: Pioneer on the Environmental Impact of War*, pp. 51–75. Springer.
Westing, A.H., 2013b. The second Indochina war of 1961–1975: Its environmental impact. In Arthur H. Westing, *Arthur H. Westing: Pioneer on the Environmental Impact of War*, pp. 35–49. Springer.
White, R. 2008. Depleted uranium, state crime and the politics of knowing. *Theoretical Criminology*, *12*(1), 31–54.
Zedany, A. and Al-Kich, A., 2013. Libyan gazelles risk being "poached to extinction". *France 24*, 1 February.

PART IV

CRIMES OF USE AND MODIFICATION

25. Animal abuse in wildlife crime and conservation

Introduction

A common trend concerning wildlife conservation is that freeborn animals are referred to in mass terms, as 'wildlife', and with reference to their species, rather than as sentient individuals with interests. This entails that individual protection and welfare are subordinate to conservation and protection at species level. This entry argues that this policy therefore fails to acknowledge the intrinsic value of freeborn animals, leaving them unprotected from harm and that this ultimately also results in lack of protection at species level. This is transparent in the enforcement of two conventions dedicated to prevent wildlife from going extinct: CITES (The Convention on International Trade in Endangered Species of Wild Fauna and Flora); and the Bern Convention (The Bern Convention on the Conservation of European Wildlife and Natural Habitats). This issue is exemplified through the practice and policy of the enforcement of these two conventions in Norway.

Trends and concepts

This entry is about human-caused legal and illegal animal harm and animal deaths that continue despite international conventions established in order to protect freeborn animals. The world is facing a human-caused extinction crisis. The Intergovernmental Science-Policy Platform on Biodiversity and Ecosystem Services (IPBES) is an independent intergovernmental body established by states to strengthen the science–policy interface for biodiversity and ecosystem services for the conservation and sustainable use of biodiversity, long-term human well-being and sustainable development. It was established in Panama City, on 21 April 2012 by 94 governments. According to IPBES (2019), one million species are threatened with extinction. In 2022, the second IPBES report showed that humankind relies on 50,000 species, whether for food, medicine or for other purposes (IPBES, 2022). From an anthropocentric point of view, there are ample reasons for protecting nature and wildlife.

This entry, however, adopts a non-anthropocentric approach in that it rejects the notion that wildlife exists to serve humans and that it is a resource that humans are free to exploit. I respect that animals are sentient with intrinsic value and interests (Regan, 2004) and adopt a species justice approach (White, 2013). A species justice approach acknowledges that animals have rights not to be subjected to harm and/or be killed by humans.

Before I outline ways in which animals suffer from harm despite conservation efforts, some defining of central concepts is in order. By 'animals', I refer to all sentient animals other than the human animal. The concept of 'theriocide' refers to the intentional killing of an animal, whether lawful or as breach of law (Beirne, 2014). Theriocides are also a consequence of neglect or destruction of habitat. 'Speciesism' refers to humans' discrimination and oppression of other animal species based on them belonging to a non-human species. 'Freeborn animal' refers to an animal who is born outside human control or who, despite being bred in human captivity, has preserved natural behaviour. The term 'wildlife' refers to more than one freeborn animal, who live under their natural conditions, and finally, with 'wildlife abductions' and theriocides, I refer to freeborn animals who have been abducted from their natural habitats against their will or interests, or who have been killed by humans therein, whether legally or illegally.

International conventions

Many conventions exist in order to protect nature from destruction and loss. They have been developed alongside an increasing loss of nature and biological/ecological collapses. For example, an international Convention to Protect the Oceans and Ecosystems of the Seas was established in 2002, not least to address illegal, unreported and unregulated (IUU) fishing. CITES was implemented in 1975 and the Bern Convention later the same decade. In addition to these, there is the Convention on Biodiversity, amongst others. These conventions were implemented as efforts to achieve broad and international agreement for the protection of nature, and to halt the losses caused by unsustainable exploitation, not at individual animal level but for the protection of natural habitats and species.

Conventions are formulated in ways that give room for discretion and different interpretations allow states with different interests to join the agreements. There are thus differences in political decisions about wildlife management and their outcomes; nation states differ in how they comply with the goals of wildlife conservation set out in CITES and the Bern Convention (Sollund, 2021a, p. 11). Differences in practices concerning the integration of individual and species protection and justice are integrated into states' conservation efforts. While the member states sign the same conventions, the implementation and the enforcement of these conventions vary because of their very different domestic law-making processes and the different interpretations of what the legal implications of the treaties entail (Wyatt, 2021a; Trouwborst et al., 2017; Goyes, 2024). This is not only manifest at national state levels, but also in federations (countries comprised of provinces or states that have their own jurisdictional powers) where conventions and legislation are differently prioritised and practised at the regional government level, as in Germany (Stefes, 2024).

The suffering of animals is grossly under-reported and neglected, not the least in the seas where, for example, thousands of individuals are caught in trawls – harming both individual fish and destroying the ecosystems causing more direct and indirect harm. The focus in the United Nations Convention on the Law of the Sea (UNCLOS) is nonetheless not on the harms and deaths inflicted on fish (and other marine animals), but on them as resources that are depleted through IUU. According to the FAO (United Nations Food and Agriculture Organization), IUU fishing represents up to 26 million tons of fish caught annually. As the fish are estimated in tons, no worries are raised about the individual suffering of each fish, whether dragged out of the sea by a hook cutting into the flesh of the mouth, or when packed together in nets as they slowly suffocate. The ways in which fish are abused and killed goes on seemingly without any regard to research that clearly documents the ability of fish to suffer as well as their cognitive and social skills (Pouca and Brown, 2017).

Fish, sea mammals and other animals of the seas are also covered by CITES, which is meant to protect listed species from trade if they are endangered, and the Bern Convention, which also protects their habitats. Catch and release of fish, which is permitted in places such as Norway, goes on without attention to the suffering of wild, freeborn salmon, who are also red listed as near threatened in that country. The wild salmon is also threatened by contamination from farmed salmon, with lice and other diseases spreading from the salmon industry (Thorstad et al., 2021).

Another important international agreement is the International Whaling Commission (IWC). It decided in 1982 to introduce a moratorium on commercial hunting of all whale species (Rueness et al., 2019). The minke whale was as a consequence listed in Appendix I of CITES. Norway objected to the moratorium and has since conducted commercial hunting of the species. Norway along with Iceland and Japan are the only countries in the world that disrespected the moratorium, and Japan withdrew from the IWC in 2019 (IWC, n.d.). Norway is exporting whale products from the quota of 1,278 minke whales per year. However, Norway can only export to non-CITES members, since whales are listed in Appendix I, and must produce an assessment report, a non-detriment finding, which is a risk assessment, where the species vulnerability is considered in relation to how well it is managed (Rueness et al., 2019). One report produced in 2019 underlines several uncertainties that makes it impossible to give certain assessment. They included: 'I) Uncertainties inherent in survey and monitoring methods; II) uncertainties stemming from fundamental data gaps in the population biology of minke whales; and III) uncertainties stemming from environmental changes' (Rueness et al., 2019, p. 7). Despite such uncertainties, Norway continues the whale hunts.

Norway will be used as a case study to demonstrate the paradoxical implementation and enforcement of the CITES and Bern conventions and to demonstrate the legal and illegal harms committed at state level (Goyes and Sollund, 2016; Sollund, 2021a). One reason to focus on Norway is that this country can become an example for other countries that are bound by the same conventions, insofar as the impact of international nature conventions is gradually withering away. The issue of rewilding of large predators such as wolves, for instance, creates debate not only in Norway, but also in countries like Italy and

Spain, which have much larger wolf populations than Norway (Fajardo del Castillo, 2021). These debates put the public spotlight on the dynamics and effectiveness of nature protection conventions.

CITES and Norway

CITES was established in 1973 and came into effect in 1975. CITES is an international trade convention with 183 parties. Its goal is to prevent species from going extinct because of unsustainable trade, though a certificate system whereby sale/import/export/re-export permits can be obtained depending on the degree of endangerment of the individual animal (and plant) species. This functions through an appendix system, where species are listed in the Appendix I, II, or III, depending on their endangerment status. The Appendix I species are threatened with extinction and therefore generally banned from trade, whereas Appendix II species can be traded contingent on an export permit from the CITES authority in the country from where the animal (or plant or product) is taken, after which the CITES authority in the import country will issue an import permit. Appendix III species are those for which a country where these species live have asked about monitoring of the species and trade. Through the conferences of the parties that take place every two to three years, decisions are made regarding up-listing or down-listing species.

The general trend is that the number of species that are listed is increasing; there are currently 6,610 animal species and 34,310 plant species listed. It is, however, problematic that many species never reach any list, and therefore go silently extinct. It is also a problem that species that become listed thereby also become more interesting for collectors who want the rarest species in their collections. CITES is therefore accused of failing at protecting endangered species from extinction and for being an anthropocentric trade convention promoting and prolonging wildlife trade and thus contributing to species extinction (Goyes and Sollund, 2016; Sollund, 2019, 2023). A general problem with CITES is that the tracking system of trade in CITES-listed species is unsatisfactory and there is under-reporting because many parties to the convention fail to deliver the biannual reports; there are even countries that have never filed a trade report (Wyatt, 2021a).

Norway joined CITES in 1976. The management authority of CITES in Norway is the Norwegian Environment Agency. Since Norway joined CITES, the regulation under which it is implemented has been revised several times, and the laws through which CITES has been implemented have varied as a consequence, from CITES being implemented under Customs legislation, then the Wildlife Act and currently, under the Nature Diversity Act. The potential punishment varies under these different acts, and this means that punishment for breaches of CITES has varied from nothing to administrative sanctions in the form of minor fines, to four years in prison (in 1998), the harshest sentence ever imposed in Norway for wildlife trafficking (Sollund, 2019). There has also been variation in how this legislation should be interpreted (Sollund, 2019). This in turn has led to very lenient sentences being imposed for serious and repeated wildlife trafficking crimes, which is a general problem worldwide (Wyatt, 2021b).

A prominent feature of the enforcement of CITES in Norway has been the practice of killing the animals who are seized by the Norwegian authorities (Sollund, 2019; Sollund, 2021b). This has led to the death of hundreds, perhaps thousands of reptiles. Exotic reptiles were banned in Norway from 1976 to 15 August 2017, after which the ban was partly lifted and a positive list introduced (Sollund, 2021b). In this period, reptiles who were seized by the police during house searches or by customs were killed (Sollund, 2019; Sollund, forthcoming).

Animals who have been killed after they have been confiscated by customs include parrots, and also other species such as a Bengal cat, a Serval and raccoons (Sollund, 2019). Norway has therefore been accused of enforcing CITES in a paradoxical way, killing the animals the convention aims to protect (Sollund, 2019). Such critiques may have contributed to changes in the CITES regulation in Norway from May 2021, where in the revision of § 29 it is stated that the authorities must aim to rehome or return animals of CITES Appendix I species. This is an improvement on previous practice; however, the wording does not preclude that animals included Appendix I may still be killed, since the wording in the paragraph is only that 'the Environment Agency shall consider the possibility' of rehoming or returning the animal. To 'consider a possibility' is weakly formulated and therefore provides little certainty with respect to animal lives and animal rights. Moreover, this paragraph includes only CITES Appendix I species, which will likely entail that non-CITES listed or Appendix II or III species will continue to be killed in practice, as before. The formulation is therefore speciesist, in that only species affiliation is valued, not the intrinsic value of each animal, as established in the Animal Welfare Act in Norway.

An example of how this killing policy evolved is an incident from Oslo airport, which took place in the autumn of 2019. This involved three African grey parrot chicks (*Psittacus erithacus*) who were listed on Appendix I of CITES, after being up-listed in 2017. Their arrival followed an incident a bit earlier, when a man arrived with three parrots (*Eclectus roratus*) listed in Appendix II. The veterinarians at the airport, on orders from the Norwegian Environment Agency (NEA), killed them. Then the three African grey chicks arrived. They were so small they needed to be hand fed. They stayed in the facilities of the border veterinarians a few weeks before the NEA decided they too should be killed. The veterinarian who had to execute the order was very upset about the decision and about having to do this since, as she said:

> I have euthanized many animals, but I cried when I euthanized these birds. Because I thought it was hell euthanizing them. They understood. It is completely different with a dog, they don't understand anything. But these, they understood, as my colleague and I entered, that this was big shit. (quoted in Sollund, 2021b, p. 13)

This type of killing is often referred to as euthanasia, implying there is some kind of mercy involved in the act. The word is for example used when one must kill a dog because of old age. As this story reveals, however, although the veterinarian felt mercy and compassion, these feelings were not allowed to prevent her from killing them, she had to, since this was her job. She also said that she did not *want* to be the executioner of the NEA. Through these theriocides, the birds each had a potential lifespan of 60 years stolen from them, and according to the veterinarian, they wanted to live.

To kill an animal is not a breach of animal welfare legislation. It depends on the manner in which the animal is killed, and whether it is 'necessary' harm. It is believed that animals can be 'humanely' killed. The concept 'humane' is another anthropocentric term implying that humans more than other species possess the ability to act with kindness. This is wrong. There is ample evidence of empathy in non-human species (Decety et al., 2016; De Waal and Preston, 2017).

Euthanasia is also used in regard to humans when a person suffering from disease, paralysis or old age can travel to countries where euthanasia is permitted for people who themselves want assistance to die. As pointed out by Francione (2008), however, to kill an animal is counter to animal welfare, because an animal who is killed can never *fare well.* To kill someone, when this is not consensual, is the utter and most serious form of violence. It is animal murder, whether homicide or theriocide (Beirne, 2014). The fact that the killing is done as routine, as the case is for confiscated wildlife in Norway, or in large industrial systems in the meat industry, does not change this fact. The killed parrots suffered because they knew what was happening to them, and they were deprived of potential future well-being. They were potentially also prevented from future suffering, but this does not outweigh the harm that was done to them and is an invalid argument. For example, in homicide trials it is not regarded as a mitigating circumstance that an offender has prevented his victim from future potential suffering in life, unless, of course, the case concerns euthanasia. Whether euthanasia can be accepted (and also as a term for needless killing), would depend on an individual's potential for a happy life. If an individual who is well and with life prospects is killed, this is not euthanasia, but murder/theriocide. Referring to such killing as euthanasia is a euphemism disguising the true character of the act and serving as its legitimation.

Norway and the Bern Convention

Norway has implemented the Bern Convention through the Nature Diversity Act. Norway has through the affiliation to Bern a special responsibility for large carnivores: the brown bear, wolf, lynx and wolverine. These species are endangered in Norway, wolves critically, while brown bears, wolverine and lynx are all very endangered [*sterkt truet*]. The population of these species were, in 2022 in Norway, according to WWF Norway (n.d.), 125–129 wolves, 160 brown bears, 395 lynx and 386 wolverines. Despite the status of endangerment and counter to its obligations to the Bern Convention and the Nature Diversity Act, Norway is both licensing hunts and authorising regular quota hunts in relation to these species (Sollund, 2017). Norway is implementing the Bern Convention through a geographical zone system, through which these large carnivores are allowed to live in five per cent of Norwegian territory. It is stated by the Supreme Court in Norway that wolves living within a wolf zone shall enjoy particular protection, while wolves wandering outside wolf territory may be shot more or less regularly.

Despite this zone system, which is also disputed (Trouwborst et al., 2017), Norway has in the recent years started killing wolves within wolf zones too. It has been established in two court cases, in *Oslo Tingrett* (District Court) and in *Borgarting lagmannsrett* (Court of Appeal, 6 June 2022), that Norway killed the Letjenna pack illegally in the winter of 2019–2020, a breach of the Nature Diversity Act, and consequently also failed to fulfil its obligations to the Bern Convention. These acts of killing thus merit the term *organized state theriocide* (Sollund, 2017; Sollund and Goyes, 2021). Despite the appeal case of the Letjenna family group pending in the court system, the Norwegian government continued to kill an increasing number of wolves within wolf zones. In 2021–2022 it was decided that 28 wolves within wolf zones should be killed, of whom 20 were shot, in addition to the 26 wolves outside wolf zones. This killing is not sustainable at species level, since the Norwegian wolves suffer heavily from inbreeding (Liberg et al., 2005).

The manner in which these wolf hunts take place is also extremely abusive and in itself in breach of the Norwegian Wildlife Law and the Animal Welfare Act: wolves are hunted down with dogs, and by the use of helicopters from which hunters use automatic shotguns. The hunts take place every winter and can go on for days, as the family members of the packs are killed one by one, with the panic and suffering this implies. The Bern Convention Appendix IV states that the use of aircraft is not allowed, which represents another breach of the convention.

Suffering in the legal and illegal wildlife trade

Animals who are victims of wildlife trade suffer regardless of whether they are abducted or killed legally or illegally. The measures through which animals are captured, encaged and transported often entails physical injuries, such as broken legs or wings, suffocation, starvation or dehydration (Sollund, 2011, 2013; Wyatt, 2014; Wyatt et al., 2022). Estimates from a Brazilian study showed that only one in ten of the individuals who are trafficked are still alive when reaching the destination (RENCTAS, 2014). A report about the parrot trade in Mexico revealed that 65,000 to 78,500 Mexican parrots are captured each year and that the mortality rate for captured parrots exceeds 75–90 per cent before they reach the buyer (Guzmán et al., 2007). In the parrot trade, birds are systematically broken down to 'accommodate' them to the owners' interests, through medication, the use of a cloth covering the cage, to put them in darkness and through deprivation of their usual diet (Roldán-Clarà et al., 2017). Animals who are destined for the 'pet trade' suffer in captivity through social media as well, when they are exposed in manners and positions intended to generate 'likes' (Lavorgna, 2014; Nekaris et al., 2013, Wyatt et al., 2022), such as when slow loris are 'tickled' or primates are dressed up in clothes.

In addition to the physical injuries, freeborn animals suffer psychological trauma from being captured and/or killed, whether their deaths were intended or not, and from being kept in a cage. Examples of legal wildlife trade, which are extremely abusive, include the export of freeborn parrots from South America to Singapore (Sinovas et al., 2017), a process in which parrots are abducted from their homes, partner and flock, forcefully transported across the globe as cargo in airplanes, for them to then live and end their lives in a cage in Singapore.

Other examples of extremely abusive, yet legal wildlife trade include the breeding and abduction and caging of moon bears, who have a hole drilled into their stomach through which bile is regularly extracted, for use in traditional Asian medicine (Feng et al., 2009). Tigers are also farmed and kept for the use of their different body parts for medicinal purposes (Tobias and Morrison, 2014). Lions are bred and kept in cages until they are released in an enclosure where trophy hunters can kill them. Reptiles, such as crocodiles, are bred under bad conditions, for the use of their skin. Exports of reptile skins like these are important for the Colombian state budget, which also perpetuates the practice (Sollund, 2019).

As each fish that is dragged out of the sea suffers, so too do the far larger minke whales are harpooned by Norwegian hunters. The mammalian order Cetacea includes over 80 known species of whales, dolphins and porpoises and they are documented to be highly intelligent, complex, social beings (Simmonds, 2006). Undoubtedly, this contributes to their suffering when they are targeted by hunters. A study of hunting of minke whales in West Greenland in 2002 showed that none died immediately; the average time it took to die was 16 minutes while five took 300 minutes to die (n = 131) (Simmonds, 2006, p. 114).

Species justice and animal rights

As shown in relation to the Norwegian wolf hunts, the methods that are used when the state orchestrates the hunt are worse than the illegal practices in ordinary hunting. The suffering in legal hunting still cannot be underestimated. In Norway in 2021–2022, 29,276 elks, 52,806 deer, 21,720 foxes, 33,660 forest doves, and 14,730 hares were killed by hunters, to mention some of the species targeted. Foxes are hunted in the summer, just as they are raising their cubs.

From this it can be deduced that freeborn animals do not have rights. On 15 October 1987, the Universal Declaration for Animal Rights was proclaimed at the headquarters of UNESCO (United Nations Educational, Scientific and Cultural Organization). It is stated in Article 2 that all animals are entitled to respect, and in Article 4, concerning freeborn animals: 'All wild animals have the right to liberty in their natural environment, whether land, air or water, and should be allowed to procreate.' The international conventions that should secure the lives of freeborn animals largely fail to offer them genuine protection; one reason is that they are regarded as 'mass' 'wildlife' who are given value only insofar as their species is in danger. As shown, even this meagre protection is easily withdrawn if this is of anthropocentric interest. Yet, in the UNESCO declaration it is also stated in Article 3 that: 'All animals have the right to the attention, care and protection of man.'

Animal rights and species justice may refer to two different things. Animal rights should imply individual rights to life and freedom, free from human-inflicted harm. Species justice, understood narrowly as a species capacity for survival, is what seems to guide 'nature conservation' and 'predator management'. Thereby, animals can be 'harvested' as long as this 'harvesting' is not detrimental to the species. As long as the species survive, authorities say that they fulfil nature conservation goals. As long as individuals of a species are deliberately killed, however, this is not species justice. Nature conservation language does not include species justice.

Conclusion

Whether humans target animals legally or illegally, their suffering remains the same. The UNESCO Declaration on Animals Rights points in the direction of the Declaration of Human Rights, which distributes certain rights to all humans at an individual level. Similarly, animal rights should be acknowledged for all sentient beings, whether a human or non-human animal. To counter the nature crisis, it is urgent to adopt a view of nature that incorporates individual animal rights to *not* be have harm inflicted, in addition to the protection they should enjoy at the species level.

RAGNHILD SOLLUND

Further reading

Beirne, P. (2014). Theriocide: Naming animal killing. *International Journal for Crime, Justice and Social Democracy*, *3*(2), 49–66.

Beirne, P. (2018). *Murdering animals: Writings on theriocide, homicide and nonspeciesist criminology*. Springer.

Goyes, D., & Sollund, R. (2016). Contesting and contextualising CITES: Wildlife trafficking in Colombia and Brazil. *International Journal for Crime, Justice and Social Democracy*, *5*(4), 87–102.

Maher, J., Pierpoint, H., & Beirne, P. (Eds.). (2017). *The Palgrave international handbook of animal abuse studies*. Palgrave Macmillan.

Nurse, A., & Wyatt, T. (2020). *Wildlife criminology*. Bristol University Press.

Sollund, R. (2017). Perceptions and law enforcement of illegal and legal wolf killing in Norway:

Organized crime or folk crime? *Palgrave Communications*, *3*(1), 1–9.
Sollund, R. (2019). *The crimes of wildlife trafficking: Issues of justice, legality and morality*. Routledge.
Sollund, R., & Goyes, D. R. (2021). State-organized crime and the killing of wolves in Norway. *Trends in Organized Crime*, 1–18.
White, R. (2013). *Environmental harm: An eco-justice perspective*. Policy Press.
White, R. (2017). Animal abuse resulting from wildlife habitat destruction. In J. Maher, H. Pierpoint and P. Beirne, (eds.), *The Palgrave international handbook of animal abuse studies* (pp. 249–268). Palgrave Macmillan.
White, R. (2018). Green victimology and non-human victims. *International Review of Victimology*, *24*(2), 239–255.
Wyatt, T., Maher, J., Allen, D., Clarke, N., & Rook, D. (2022). The welfare of wildlife: An interdisciplinary analysis of harm in the legal and illegal wildlife trades and possible ways forward. *Crime, Law and Social Change*, *77*(1), 69–89.

References

Beirne, P. (2014). Theriocide: Naming animal killing. *International Journal for Crime, Justice and Social Democracy*, *3*(2), 49–66.
Cohen, S. (2013). *States of denial: Knowing about atrocities and suffering*. John Wiley & Sons.
De Waal, F. B., & Preston, S. D. (2017). Mammalian empathy: Behavioural manifestations and neural basis. *Nature Reviews Neuroscience*, *18*(8), 498–509.
Decety, J., Bartal, I. B. A., Uzefovsky, F., & Knafo-Noam, A. (2016). Empathy as a driver of prosocial behaviour: Highly conserved neurobehavioural mechanisms across species. *Philosophical Transactions of the Royal Society B: Biological Sciences*, *371*(1686), 20150077.
Fajardo del Castillo, T. (2021). Wolf (dis)protection in Spain: Exceptions to the rules in the Bern Convention and in the Habitats Directive as a conservation and management tool. *Revista Catalana de Dret Ambiental*, *12*(1), 1–47.
Feng, Y., Siu, K., Wang, N., Ng, K. M., Tsao, S. W., Nagamatsu, T., & Tong, Y. (2009). Bear bile: Dilemma of traditional medicinal use and animal protection. *Journal of Ethnobiology and Ethnomedicine*, *5*(1), 1–9.
Francione, G. L. (2008). *Animals as persons: Essays on the abolition of animal exploitation*. Columbia University Press.
Goyes, D. R. (2024). National legislative adoption of international wildlife law after treaty ratification. *Crime, Law and Social Change*, *81*(2), 143–162.
Goyes, D., & Sollund, R. (2016). Contesting and contextualising CITES: Wildlife trafficking in Colombia and Brazil. *International Journal for Crime, Justice and Social Democracy*, *5*(4), 87–102.
Guzmán, J. C. C., Saldaña, M. E. S., Teyeliz, A. C., Grosselet, M., & Gamez, J. S. (2007). The illegal parrot trade in Mexico: Defenders of wildlife. www.defenders.org/mexicanparrot (accessed 25 June 2012).
International Whaling Commission (IWC) (n.d.). iwc.int.
IPBES (2019). Global assessment report on biodiversity and ecosystem services of the Intergovernmental Science-Policy Platform on Biodiversity and Ecosystem Services. E. S. Brondizio, J. Settele, S. Díaz, & H. T. Ngo (Eds.). IPBES Secretariat, Bonn, Germany.
IPBES (2022). https://doi.org/10.5281/zenodo.3831673
Lavorgna, A. (2014). Wildlife trafficking in the Internet age. *Crime Science*, *3*(1), 1–12.
Liberg, O., Andrén, H., Pedersen, H. C., Sand, H., Sejberg, D., Wabakken, P., ... & Bensch, S. (2005). Severe inbreeding depression in a wild wolf *Canis lupus* population. *Biology Letters*, *1*(1), 17–20.
Nekaris, K. A. I., Campbell, N., Coggins, T. G., Rode, E. J., & Nijman, V. (2013). Tickled to death: Analysing public perceptions of 'cute' videos of threatened species (slow lorises – *Nycticebus* spp.) on Web 2.0 Sites. *PLoS One*, *8*(7), e69215.
Pouca, C. V., & Brown, C. (2017). Contemporary topics in fish cognition and behaviour. *Current Opinion in Behavioral Sciences*, *16*, 46–52.
Rede Nacional de Combate ao Trafico de Animais Silvestres (RENCTAS) (2014). 1st National Report on the Traffic of Wild Animals. https://www.renctas.org.br/wp-content/uploads/2014/02/RELATORIO-INGLES_final.pdf (accessed 5 September 2021).
Regan, T. (2004). *The case for animal rights*. University of California Press.
Roldán-Clarà, B., Toledo, V. M., & Espejel, I. (2017). The use of birds as pets in Mexico. *Journal of Ethnobiology and Ethnomedicine*, 13(1), 1–18.
Rueness, E. K., Asmyhr, M. G., Kausrud, K., Nilsen, E. B., Øien, N., de Boer, H., Eldegard, K., Hindar, K., Hole, L. R., Järnegren, J., Kirkendall, L., Måren, I. E., Nielsen, A., Thorstad, E. B., & Velle, G. (2019). *A CITES risk assessment for the common minke whale (Balaneoptera acutorostrata): Opinion of the Panel on Alien Organisms and Trade in Endangered Species (CITES) of the Norwegian Scientific Committee for Food and Environment* (VKM report 2019: 10). Norwegian Scientific

Committee for Food and Environment (VKM), Oslo, Norway.
Simmonds, M. P. (2006). Into the brains of whales. *Applied Animal Behaviour Science*, *100*(1–2), 103–116.
Sinovas, P., Price, B., King, E., Hinsley, A., & Pavitt, A. (2017). Wildlife trade in the Amazon countries: An analysis of trade in CITES listed species. UN Environment – World Conservation Monitoring Centre.
Sollund, R. (2011). Expressions of speciesism: The effects of keeping companion animals on animal abuse, animal trafficking and species decline. *Crime, Law and Social Change*, *55*, 437–451.
Sollund, R. (2013). Animal trafficking and trade: Abuse and species injustice. In R. Walters, D.S. Westerhuis and T. Wyatt, (eds.), *Emerging issues in green criminology* (pp. 72–92). Palgrave Macmillan.
Sollund, R. (2017). Perceptions and law enforcement of illegal and legal wolf killing in Norway: Organized crime or folk crime? *Palgrave Communications*, *3*(1), 1–9.
Sollund, R. (2019). *The crimes of wildlife trafficking: Issues of justice, legality and morality*. Routledge.
Sollund, R. (2021a). Introduction to Special Issue of CRIMEANTHROP: Criminal Justice, Wildlife Conservation and Animal Rights in the Anthropocene. *Revista Catalana de Dret Ambiental*, *12*(1).
Sollund, R. (2021b). The development of the enforcement of CITES in Norway: Discretionary omissions and theriocides. *Revista Catalana de Dret Ambiental*, *12*(1).
Sollund, R. (2023). The dark side of nature conventions: A call to end anthropogenic wildlife destruction. *Criminology & Criminal Justice*, 17488958231181309.
Sollund, R. (forthcoming). *Wildlife trade: Parallel harms and crimes*. Routledge.
Sollund, R., & Goyes, D. R. (2021). State-organized crime and the killing of wolves in Norway. *Trends in Organized Crime*, 1–18.
Stefes, C. (2024). Paper tigers and local perseverance: Wildlife protection in Germany. In Sollund, R., & Lie, M. S. B. (Eds.), *Criminal justice, wildlife conservation and animal rights in the Anthropocene* (pp. 125–150). Bristol University Press.
Thorstad, E. B., Forseth, T., & Fiske, P. (2021). *Status for norske laksebestander i 2021*. Norsk institutt for naturforskning. https://hdl.handle.net/11250/2830680
Tobias, M. C., & Morrison, J. G. (2014). Animal rights in China. In M.C. Tobias and J.G. Morrison, (eds.), *Why life matters* (pp. 245–255). Springer.
Trouwborst, A., Boitani, L., & Linnell, J. D. (2017). Interpreting 'favourable conservation status' for large carnivores in Europe: How many are needed and how many are wanted? *Biodiversity and Conservation*, *26*(1), 37–61.
White, R. (2013). *Environmental harm: An eco-justice perspective*. Policy Press.
WWF Norway (n.d.). http://www.wwf.no (accessed 19 July 2022).
Wyatt, T. (2014). Non-human animal abuse and wildlife trade: Harm in the fur and falcon trades. *Society & Animals*, *22*(2), 194–210.
Wyatt, T. (2021a). *Is CITES protecting wildlife? Assessing implementation and compliance*. Routledge.
Wyatt, T. (2021b). *Wildlife trafficking: A deconstruction of the crime, victims and offenders*. Springer Nature.
Wyatt, T., Maher, J., Allen, D., Clarke, N., & Rook, D. (2022). The welfare of wildlife: An interdisciplinary analysis of harm in the legal and illegal wildlife trades and possible ways forward. *Crime, Law and Social Change*, *77*(1), 69–89.

RAGNHILD SOLLUND

26. Climate change and environmental crimes

Introduction

This entry examines the relationship between climate change and crimes that affect the environment. Global warming is radically altering the basis of life on Earth as we know it. The entry examines climate-related harms and risks, specific climate-related crimes, and the perpetrators of climate crimes. The impetus for work in the area of climate change criminology stems from the transformative changes besetting human societies and global ecosystems due to global warming. From a criminological point of view, these changes also feature a variety of significant environmental crimes, old and new. Rapid changes to the climate are linked to various harmful activities, some of which are key contributors to global heating, and others reflect its impacts and consequences.

Climate-related harms and risks

One result of climate change is widespread climate disruption. This refers to how increases in global average temperature trigger sharp changes in weather and disrupt longer-term weather and climate patterns. This takes the form of prolonged droughts, super storms, increased intensity of cyclones and hurricanes, and unusual precipitation events involving snow and rain. Climate disruption produces harms and risks that add further contexts and specific limits and pressures on crime and criminality.

The effects of global heating also increase other kinds of risks that affect human communities, non-human animals and plants, and ecosystems, and it is vulnerable communities globally who have historically contributed the least to current climate change that are disproportionately affected. Key risks identified by the Intergovernmental Panel on Climate Change (IPCC) (2014) include a distributional shift and reduced fisheries catch potential at low latitudes; compounded stress on water resources; increased mass coral bleaching and mortality; reduced crop productivity and livelihood and food security; and the loss of livelihoods, settlements, infrastructure, ecosystem services and economic stability. Other risks include the spread of vector-borne diseases – the coronavirus pandemic illustrating just how quickly future risks can translate into present harms. Climate change has also caused local species losses, increases in disease, and mass mortality events of plants and animals, resulting in the first climate-driven extinctions, ecosystem restructuring, increases in areas burned by wildfire, and declines in key ecosystem services (IPCC, 2022a).

Global warming is accelerating, and in-built biophysical feedback loops (such as melting ice sheets), mean that it is likely to happen even faster than it already is today as time goes by. The current trends as regards global warming are unequivocal. The planet is heating up at an unprecedented rate. Greenhouse gas emissions continue to rise, despite scientific warnings and UN-oriented political commitments, and the main cause continues to be fossil fuel emissions from energy use and industry (IPCC, 2022a, 2022b; World Meteorological Organization, 2020a, 2020b).

The impact of disasters, while affecting everyone around the world, is nonetheless unequal in consequence. This is due to a combination of geographical location and socio-economic circumstance. It has been pointed out that:

> Approximately 3.3–3.6 billion people live in contexts that are highly vulnerable to climate change. Human and ecosystem vulnerability are interdependent. Regions and people with considerable development constraints have high vulnerability to climate hazards. Increasing weather and climate extreme events have exposed millions of people to acute food insecurity and reduced water security, with the largest adverse impacts observed in many locations and/or communities in Africa, Asia, Central and South America, LDCs, Small Islands and the Arctic, and globally for Indigenous Peoples, small-scale food producers and low-income households. Between 2010 and 2020, human mortality from floods, droughts and storms was 15 times higher in highly vulnerable regions, compared to regions with very low vulnerability. (IPCC, 2023: 5)

Such trends are also driving displacement from the most affected areas, thereby generating potential flow-on conflicts as people are forced to move due to catastrophe. Climate disruption on this scale and complexity constitutes harm landscapes that are unprecedented in human history.

Climate-related crimes

At a global level, climate impacts are manifest in a series of developments. For instance, the divides between the global North and South, geographically and metaphorically, are deepening as crises related to food production and distribution, energy sources and pollution, and changing climates re-order the international political environment (IPCC, 2014, 2018, 2022a, 2022b, 2023; Oxfam, 2018; Clark et al., 2020). Social inequality and environmental injustice will be the drivers of conflicts for many years to come, as the most dispossessed and marginalised of the world's population suffer the brunt of food shortages, undrinkable water, climate-induced migration, and general hardship in their day-to-day lives. The necessities of life – food, water, shelter, security, healthy environments – are under pressure. Scarcity of natural resources, such as fresh water, affect the quality, quantity and access to goods that are essential to life itself.

Pressures to survive in increasingly arduous conditions create all manner of opportunities for crime and violence, from human trafficking and illegal border crossings to gang stand-over tactics in the acquisition of food and water. Predicted rises in the number and intensity of natural disasters due to climate change are correlated with increases in violence against women in those regions experiencing extreme weather events (Wachholz, 2007). At the same time, men are disproportionately involved in group, domestic, interpersonal and self-violence when income and food security is no longer possible (White, 2023). Insecurities of place and position are exacerbated in the context of failing states and countries that simply do not have the resources to put into human services and social infrastructure (Crank & Jacoby, 2015). A form of 'climate apartheid' may well become entrenched as the world's wealthy move into secure residential enclaves; in essence, walled sanctuaries to isolate them from the majority population (Brisman, South & Walters, 2018).

A wide range of crimes and harms are associated with climate change, including contributing to it (White, 2018). Specific criminal and environmental offences linked to climate change include offences that contribute to climate change (e.g., unlicensed pollution, destruction of habitat and forests), those arising from its consequences (e.g., water theft, wildlife poaching), civil unrest and criminal activities (e.g., food riots, people smuggling), and offences pertaining to regulation and law enforcement associated with mitigation and adaptation strategies (e.g., carbon trading fraud, corruption). There is an intrinsic connection between crimes affecting the environment and climate change, and vice versa. Climate-related crimes can be summarised according to three types of crime category (Tables 26.1a–c). As indicated, crime and criminality are linked to climate change in a variety of respects and there is a two-way influence between crime and climate change. Examples of these kinds of crimes are further described below.

Crimes that affect the environment contributing to climate change

The illegal exploitation of natural resources is contributing in many ways to global warming and climate-related issues (Nellemann et al., 2018; United Nations Office on Drugs and Crime (UNODC), 2022; UNODC & World Wildlife Fund, 2023). An exemplar of this is illegal logging and land clearing, each of which contributes to deforestation which, in turn, contributes to carbon emissions. Moreover, the damage resulting from crimes that affect the environment also lowers ecosystem resilience to the effects of climate change. From illegal felling of trees to illegal clearing of native vegetation, the ecological and climate impacts of crimes affecting the environment are enormous. Acknowledgement of the consequences of widescale destruction of the environment has generated increasing interest in the notion of 'ecocide' as a criminal offence. A recent formulation views ecocide as 'unlawful or wanton acts committed with knowledge that there is a substantial likelihood of severe and either widespread or long-term damage to the environment being caused by those acts' (Stop Ecocide International, 2021). This proposed crime is under review in the European Union and several countries and regions have begun incorporating ecocide-type laws into their list of criminal offences.

Climate change affecting existing categories of crime

Climate change is already having an impact on existing categories of crime in that rising temperatures have been linked to increased levels of aggression and social conflict, scarcity of

ROB WHITE

Table 26.1a Crimes affecting the environment contributing to climate change

Type of Crime	Examples of Harm
Deforestation	Diminishing of carbon sinks; adding to carbon emissions
Illegal mining	Air pollution; polluting freshwater systems
Wildlife trafficking	Undermines the functioning of ecosystems affecting mitigation of climate change impacts
Land grabs and changing land uses	Lost carbon stock and sequestration, adding to carbon emissions

Source: White (2024).

Table 26.1b Climate change affecting existing categories of crime

Type of Crime	Examples of Harm
Water crimes	Resource scarcity and water theft
Clandestine migration	Climate refugees
Illegal mining	Rare earth minerals for new renewable energy systems
Social conflict	Aggression and violence over scarce resources, social strains arising from biophysical changes, changes in routine activities depending on weather

Source: White (2024).

essential natural resources such as water, and the loss of infrastructure due to disaster and slow-onset crises such as rising sea levels (Europol, 2022; Interpol Innovation Centre, 2022; White, 2018). There is concern that climate change is associated with changes in rates and types of crimes as people move from place to place and interact with new communities. An exemplar of how climate change is affecting existing categories of crime is illegal mining. The switch to renewable energy has been accompanied by the scramble to exploit deposits of lithium and other minerals which have the special properties needed for technologies such as batteries. Criminal gangs and networks have moved into this space in recent years (Nellemann et al., 2018). Other existing categories of crime affected by climate change include water theft, clandestine migration and increasing levels of aggression and violence over scarce resources (Agnew, 2011; Ranson, 2014). Existing categories of crime such as piracy (i.e., stealing and robbing ships at sea) likewise warrant further attention insofar as the demise of fishing grounds in some places means that people desperate for their livelihood may turn to crimes on the open seas (UNODC, 2011).

Cross-over crimes associated with climate change

Cross-over crimes refer to crimes that intersect, for example, human trafficking, drug trafficking and fisheries crime and which therefore simultaneously result in severe threats to human rights, environmental sustainability, and global security (UNODC, 2011). Such crimes may be interconnected across different jurisdictions, which compounds their impact and exacerbates their harmful consequences. Conflicts over resources provide an indication of emergent crimes related to climate change. These include protest actions and aspects of eco-terrorism directed at environmental policy change through to food riots and climate-induced migrations of people. An exemplar of cross-over crime is fraud associated with insurance scams after disasters such as wildfire or flood have taken place. These kinds of crime are made more likely and easy to accomplish when criminals utilise cyber-skills to create false identities and launder money via crypto-currency and the like (White, 2024). Other crimes pertain to corruption, state–corporate crime, illegal solar panel and battery waste trafficking and negligent homicide (e.g., failure to curtail excessive carbon emissions).

Table 26.1c *Cross-over crimes associated with crimes affecting the environment and climate change*

Type of Crime	Examples of Harm
Homicide	Killing of park rangers, environmental activists, local residents
Organised crime groups and networks	Fraudulent green investments, low-price food on-sales
Corruption	Direct (criminal such as document fraud) and moral (unethical policies and practices that foster carbon emission pollution)
Disaster-related fraud	Building practices, insurance claims, victim scams and identity theft

Source: White (2024).

Perpetrators of climate-related crimes

Offenders and perpetrators of climate-related crimes can be identified from the point of view of the particular social forces involved (White, 2018: 46):

- Crimes by the less powerful – basic survival (for example, loss of land, lack of rain, changes in temperatures), through to illegal migration, foraging for food in reserves, water theft and street riots;
- Crimes by the powerful – protection of privilege and defence of profit motive, through to enclosures of land, hoarding of food and other basics, and the establishment of private armies/security;
- Crimes by organised criminals – new criminal opportunities, such as carbon emission fraud, illegal trafficking of people and substances, dumping of waste, and illegal trade in food and water;
- Crimes by the state – collusion with powerful interests, denial of human/ecological rights, failures of intervention or to regulate, and buying of land for food production/consumption somewhere else.

New crimes may also be stimulated by and arise because of government policy. For example, the trading of carbon credits on the open market (which allows polluters to buy 'offsets' instead of reducing their pollution directly) opens the door to carbon fraud (Martin & Walters, 2013; Walters & Martin, 2013). Moreover, the sequestration of land in places such as Latin America and Africa can result in the eviction of local people from their traditional lands, itself another negative consequence of climate change policy as well as reflecting the imposition of specific forms of 'conservation' (Bulkeley & Newell, 2010; Duffy, 2010, 2022). The effects of the commodification of carbon thus put pressure on communities located well away from the originating industries.

Climate change has been associated with the advent of varying types of natural disaster which are projected to increase in intensity and frequency in the foreseeable future. These include such phenomena as floods, cyclones, extreme heat spells and so on. Study of disasters (both human-created and natural) has revealed substantial instances of criminality (Green, 2005; Thornton & Voigt, 2007; Sergi, 2017). These include crimes pre-disaster (e.g., poor construction standards such as omission of steel reinforcing in concrete), during the disaster (e.g., looting, rape) and post-disaster (e.g., insurance fraud, misappropriation of aid funds, embezzlement by local authorities). The kinds of crimes associated with disasters include crimes against the person as well as corporate, white-collar and state crimes. Moreover, the scale of recent disasters indicate that other forms of criminality may be associated with these events, including the collapse of public order, enforced climate-induced migration and the increase or further entrenchment of local gang cultures.

The sheer scale of the problems created by the consequences of climate change have also generated retrospective consideration of the main culprits behind the causes of climate change. At a formal level, governments worldwide agreed in the 1990s that climate change is caused by humans, and that measures needed to be taken then to prevent the catastrophic consequences emerging today. To a large degree, climate contrarianism has postponed needed action around climate change mitigation, through campaigns of mis- and disinformation. For some, this is deemed to be a crime of 'postericide' (McKinnon, 2021).

Conclusion

Criminology as a field has been somewhat slow in responding to the challenges of climate change, although this is changing (see for example, Agnew, 2011; Crank & Jacoby, 2015; Kramer, 2020; Holley, Phelan & Shearing, 2021; Holley & Shearing, 2017; White, 2018).

There are many different crimes that contribute to and/or are exacerbated by climate change. The destruction of environments and pumping of pollutants into the atmosphere are interconnected reasons why global warming is continuing apace. In many instances, such environmental harms are perfectly legal, regardless of how serious the damage is or whether they are contributing to the present existential crisis for humanity. How best to respond to climate change, and the crimes associated with climate change, are the biggest issues of the current era.

ROB WHITE

Further reading

Agnew, R. (2011) 'Dire forecast: A theoretical model of the impact of climate change on crime', *Theoretical Criminology*, 16(1): 21–46.

Crank, J. & Jacoby, L. (2015) *Crime, Violence, and Global Warming*. Abingdon: Routledge.

Farrell, S., Ahmed, T. & French, D. (eds) (2012) *Criminological and Legal Consequences of Climate Change*. Oxford: Hart Publishing.

Holley, C. & Shearing, C. (eds) (2017) *Criminology and the Anthropocene*. Abingdon: Routledge.

Kramer, R. (2020) *Carbon Criminals, Climate Crimes*. New Brunswick, NJ: Rutgers University Press.

White, R. (2018) *Climate Change Criminology*. Bristol: Policy Press.

References

Agnew, R. (2011) 'Dire forecast: A theoretical model of the impact of climate change on crime', *Theoretical Criminology*, 16(1): 21–46.

Brisman, A., South, N. & Walters, R. (2018) 'Climate apartheid and environmental refugees', in K. Carrington, R. Hogg, J. Scott & M. Sozzo (eds) *The Palgrave Handbook of Criminology and the Global South*. Basingstoke: Palgrave Macmillan, pp. 301–321.

Bulkeley, H. & Newell, P. (2010) *Governing Climate Change*. London: Routledge.

Clark, H. et al. (2020) 'A future for the world's children? A WHO-UNICEF-Lancet Commission', *The Lancet*, 395: 605–658.

Crank, J. & Jacoby, L. (2015) *Crime, Violence, and Global Warming*. Abingdon: Routledge.

Duffy, R. (2010) *Nature Crime: How We're Getting Conservation Wrong*. New Haven, CT: Yale University Press.

Duffy, R. (2022). *Security and Conservation: The Politics of the Illegal Wildlife Trade*. Princeton: Yale University Press.

Europol (2022) *Environmental Crime in an Age of Climate Change: Threat Assessment 2022*. Europol.

Green, P. (2005) 'Disaster by design: Corruption, construction and catastrophe', *British Journal of Criminology*, 45(4): 528–546.

Holley, C. & Shearing, C. (eds) (2017) *Criminology and the Anthropocene*. Abingdon: Routledge.

Holley, C., Phelan, L. & Shearing, C. (2021) *Criminology and Climate: Insurance, Finance and the Regulation of Harmscapes*. Abingdon: Routledge.

Interpol Innovation Centre (2022) *Crime, Law Enforcement and Climate Change*. Background Paper. Lyon: Interpol.

IPCC. (2014) *Climate Change 2014 Synthesis Report, Approved Summary for Policymakers*. Geneva: IPCC.

IPCC. (2018). *Special Report: Global Warming of 1.5°C: Summary for Policymakers*. Geneva: IPCC.

IPCC (2022a) *Climate Change 2021: The Physical Basis*. Cambridge: Cambridge University Press.

IPCC (2022b) *Climate Change 2022: Impacts, Adaptation and Vulnerability. Summary for Policymakers*. Geneva: IPCC.

IPCC (2023) *Synthesis Report of the IPCC Sixth Assessment Report (AR6), Summary for Policymakers*. Geneva: IPCC.

Kramer, R. (2020) *Carbon Criminals, Climate Crimes*. New Brunswick, NJ: Rutgers University Press.

Martin, P. & Walters, R. (2013) 'Fraud risk and the visibility of carbon', *International Journal for Crime, Justice and Social Democracy*, 2(2): 27–42.

McKinnon, C. (2021) 'Postericide and intergenerational ethics', in S. M. Gardiner (ed.) *The Oxford Handbook of Intergenerational Ethics* (online edn). https://doi.org/10.1093/oxfordhb/9780190881931.013.44

Nellemann, C., Henriksen, R., Pravettoni, R., Stewart, D., Kotsovou, M., Schlingemann, M., Shaw, M. & Reitano, T. (eds) (2018) *World Atlas of Illicit Flows*. A RHIPTO-Interpol-GI Assessment. RHIPTO-Norwegian Center for Global Analyses, Interpol and the Global

Initiative Against Transnational Organized Crime. www.rhipto.or www.interpol.int.
Oxfam (2018) *Reward Work, Not Wealth*. Nairobi: Oxfam.
Ranson, M. (2014) 'Crime, weather and climate change', *Journal of Environmental Economics and Management*, 67: 274–302.
Sergi, A. (2017) 'Building sites: Criminal groups exploit natural disasters', *IHS Jane's Intelligence Review*, February: 42–45.
Stop Ecocide International (2021) *Independent Expert Panel for the Legal Definition of Ecocide, Commentary and Core Text*, June 2021. https://static1.squarespace.com/static/5ca2608ab914493c64ef1f6d/t/60d7479cf8e7e5461534dd07/1624721314430/SE+Foundation+Commentary+and+core+text+revised+%281%29.pdf
Thornton, W. & Voigt, L. (2007) 'Disaster rape: Vulnerability of women to sexual assaults during Hurricane Katrina', *Journal of Public Management and Social Policy*, 13(2): 23–49.
UNODC (2011) *Transnational Organized Crime in the Fishing Industry: Focus on: Trafficking in Persons, Smuggling of Migrants, Illegal Drugs Trafficking*. Vienna: United Nations.
UNODC (2022) *Illegal Wildlife Trade and Climate Change: Joining the Dots*. Vienna: UNODC.
UNODC & World Wildlife Fund (2023) *Crimes that Affect the Environment and Climate Change*. Vienna: UNODC & WWF.
Wachholz, S. (2007). '"At risk": Climate change and its bearing on women's vulnerability to male violence', in P. Beirne & N. South (eds) *Issues in Green Criminology: Confronting Harms Against Environments, Humanity and Other Animals*. London: Routledge, pp. 161–185.
Walters, R. & Martin, P. (2013) 'Crime and the commodification of carbon', in R. Walters, D. Westerhuis & T. Wyatt (eds) *Emerging Issues in Green Criminology*. Basingstoke: Palgrave Macmillan.
White, R. (2018) *Climate Change Criminology*. Bristol: Policy Press.
White, R. (2023) 'David and Goliath: The male burdens of patriarchal capitalism', in E. Milne, P. Davies, J. Heydon, K. Peggs & T. Wyatt (eds) *Gendering Green Criminology*. Bristol: Bristol University Press.
White, R. (2024) *Global Law Enforcement in the Harm Landscapes of Climate Change*. Vienna: United Nations Office on Drugs and Crime.
World Meteorological Organization (2020a). *WMO Provisional Statement on the State of the Global Climate in 2019*. Geneva: WMO.
World Meteorological Organization (2020b). *State of the Global Climate 2020*. Geneva: WMO.

ROB WHITE

27. Food crime

Introduction

Food crime is a rapidly growing research area in criminology that blurs the boundary between criminal practices and harmful but legal activities, as well as challenging the limitations of the usual constructions of victimhood. Some perspectives on food crime are rooted in traditional understandings of crime and also consider food crime through the lenses of corporate and state–corporate crimes. The growing importance of green criminology in food crime studies is also visible. Scholars adopting a green criminological perspective have sought to develop new understandings of food crime by exploring the impact of socially normalised practices and systemic harms that are rooted in the normal functioning of the capitalist food system. These food-related harms include harms against non-human animals, the environment, and communities living in that environment as well as food workers.

Even though both isolated deviancy and systemic harm are woven into the fabric of food production systems, criminological study of the intersections of food, crime and harm has not been prolific (Gladkova, 2021). Rizzuti (2020) argues that it is only within the last two decades that criminology has considered specific harmful acts under the label of 'food crime'.

Defining food crime

While it is not certain when the term 'food crime' was first used (Tourangeau and Fitzgerald, 2020), Croall's (2007) chapter on food crime in the edited book *Issues in Green Criminology: Confronting Harms Against Environments, Humanity and Other Animals* is often considered a starting point. Since then, the definition of food crime has evolved and spanned a broad spectrum of licit and illicit activities. Cheng (2012), considering food crime in China, describes food crime broadly as a set of practices that violate laws, regulations and customs that should be respected by members of the food industry. Croall's conceptualisation is expansive enough to cover the 'crimes that directly involve the processing, production, and sale of food, as well as those that are more indirectly involved in local and global food trades (such as tax evasion)' (Croall, 2013: 167). Gray and Hinch (2015) argue that food crime should be analysed criminologically by investigating the criminogenic factors and complexities of the contemporary food production system. For them, food crimes include a range of illicit behaviours, ranging from economic and physical harms to both the humans and non-human animals involved in the food industry, to food adulteration and the misrepresentation of food quality.

All the above authors also recognise the importance of exploring food-related issues where no laws are being broken but environmental, social, and physical harms still occur. For instance, in the *Handbook of Food Crime*, Gray (2018) argues for the necessity of a food crime perspective that questions the concepts of crime and harm in relation to food issues and includes a broad variety of illegal, criminal, harmful, unjust, unethical, or immoral food-related practices. Likewise, Croall (2013: 173) suggests study should focus on individual and cultural factors determining food production and consumption in light of a wider capitalist and corporate 'culture of callousness' and organisational dynamics that lead to crime and harm.

Food crime research

Much research into food crime also addresses harms across the licit–illicit spectrum. Croall (2013) lists eight different types of food crimes – food fraud, food poisoning, food mislabelling, illicit trade practices, food pricing, crimes of exploitation in food production, crimes against non-human animals, and financial crimes. Several of these areas have garnered widespread attention.

For example, food fraud, by far one of the most prolific research fields, considers different fraudulent activities committed inside the food sector. Food fraud is a phenomenon that encompasses 'the deliberate and intentional substitution, addition, tampering or misrepresentation of food, food ingredients or food packaging; or false or misleading statements made about a product for economic gain' (Spink and Moyer, 2011: 158). Criminological research into food fraud has focused on the organisational aspects of fraudulent activities. Lord et al. (2017a; 2017b) explore the situated nature of food fraud and the role of legitimate, occupational actors in creating criminogenic dynamics. Ruth et al. (2018) investigate the factors determining fraud vulnerability in various supply chains, while Flores Elizondo et al. (2019) focus on the prosecution of food fraud through the lens of the (in)effectiveness of the UK's Fraud Act 2006. International research into food fraud draws particular attention to the Chinese milk industry (Liu, 2009; Yang et al., 2020).

Food mislabelling (Lawrence, 2008; Croall, 2013) is another key research area. It is associated with analysis of the complex nature and regulation of ingredients and processing, which often lead to giving false impressions to customers. For instance, food manufacturers may be breaking guidelines when using labels such as 'traditional', 'homemade', etc. if the production process does not reflect the meaning of these terms (Croall, 2007). Anti-competitive trade practices, which are illegal in some jurisdictions (Gluck, 2008), reveal the uneven power dynamics in the food supply chains, whereby major supermarkets put excessive pressure on producers, which often leads to frauds and cheaper substitutes. Food pricing associated with fraud (Blythman, 2011) is also done at the expense of customers, with 'bargain deals' and changes in pricing during a season (higher at the start and reduced towards the end) as examples.

Intersections with other perspectives

While some researchers specifically refer to their work as involving studies of food crime, there is also growing acknowledgement of food crime in criminological perspectives examining the intersections between state–corporate, corporate, and environmental harms (Gray and Hinch, 2015). Croall (2013) observes that much food crime can be described as state–corporate crime and a variety of financial crimes have implicated food in their commission, from food subsidies fraud in the EU to the growth of wine investment fraud. For instance, Lawrence's research (2008) documented the journey of a soya cargo from a South American Cargill terminal to Liverpool. The research found that the soya actually travelled directly from South America to the United Kingdom. Yet, on paper, it also went to the Turks and Caicos Islands tax haven before heading to Liverpool, which altered the details of the transaction process. This kind of falsification of paperwork hides the size of a cargo, its sale price and, most importantly, the taxable profit, and the use of tax havens deprives countries of legitimate tax returns (Croall, 2013).

Food poisoning is another example of activities that have come to criminological attention (Pennington, 2003; Williams, 2007). Food poisoning results from neglect of or disregard for regulations involving the handling of food, thus it stems from the breaking of laws (Croall, 2013). Additionally, food poisoning research intersects with state–corporate crime research. In investigating mass salmonella poisoning by the Peanut Corporation of America, Leighton (2016) demonstrates that this corporate crime was facilitated by substantial weaknesses in regulation and accordingly labels it a state-facilitated corporate crime. Tombs and Whyte (2010) develop this line of thinking further by discussing food poisoning as corporate harms (rather than crimes). They highlight the corporate responsibility for large numbers of food-related illnesses and deaths, most of which result from criminal breaches of food hygiene and food safety legislation. Yet, prosecutions of food-related breaches are rare. Additionally, there is little official information on food poisoning-related deaths, even though between 100 and 200 people in the UK die directly as a result of salmonella and campylobacter every year. Tombs and Whyte (2010) state that this does not present the full extent of food poisoning-related deaths. Adopting the harm perspective also reveals that food poisoning cases have lasting and complex effects on health and increase the average person's chances of dying from any other disease or condition (Tombs and Whyte, 2010).

Criminological research into harmful labour practices (Davies, 2018; 2020) and crimes against food producers (Tourangeau and Fitzgerald, 2020) also show how food crime scholarship benefits from adopting multidisciplinary perspectives. The situation of migrant workers in agriculture, fishing, and food processing has been described as 'new slavery' (Lawrence, 2008: 111), and there remain a number of controversial practices that may still be legal, but which are seen as 'ethically' or 'morally' problematic (Davies and Ollus, 2019). Many exploitative labour practices are not classed as crimes even if they are reported since they are instead considered as simply regulatory violations or civil breaches, or even possibly legal supply chain practices (Tombs and Whyte, 2007). Brisman et al. (2016) document the human rights consequences of forced labour in the case of rural workers, also demonstrating how exploitation is embedded into the fabric of the globalised industrial food system. Similarly, Fitzgerald (2015) discusses the normalised yet problematic conditions in slaughterhouses across the globe, also highlighting inadequate enforcement of safety regulations. Del Prado-Lu (2018) also demonstrates the adverse effects on food producers by discussing the health risks from pesticides and the lack of social and health protection for farmers, particularly in the Global South. Hinch (2018) reveals how exploitation and harm are perpetuated in his analysis of forced labour in the cocoa industry; governments are often complicit in exploitation in the name of protecting commercial interests.

Green criminological perspectives have also been applied to the analysis of harms involving food producers. Biopiracy of genetic resources is one such example. Walters (2004, 2006, 2010) pioneered the research into corporate exploitation of food production by examining the social, economic and ecological risks of genetically modified (GM) foods. He explained how corporations sought to 'manipulate and monopolize world trade in the food industry' (Walters, 2004: 162) through trying to impose GMO products into new global markets. Goyes and South (2016) and Goyes (2020) further advanced this body of knowledge, describing how corporate actors profit from marketing agricultural and pharmaceutical products derived from Indigenous knowledge, further disadvantaging local communities, and fuelling injustice and inequality.

Food crime and green criminology

The cross-pollination of food crime studies with green criminology research has been increasing. An important aspect of this is the focus on crimes and harms against non-human animals. Croall (2013) had already singled out crimes and harms against non-human animals in her list of food crimes, drawing upon a green criminological non-speciesist lens (Agnew, 1998; Beirne, 2007; White, 2018). Criminal actions include regulatory non-compliance and inhumane and illegal actions against animals designated as food sources (Tourangeau and Fitzgerald, 2020).

Illegal, unreported and unregulated fishing – exceeding commercial quotas, fishing without a licence, exploitation of endangered species (White, 2008) – provides an example of regulatory non-compliance that results in grave harm to marine species and ecosystems. Moreover, illegal fishing often has transnational criminal dimensions (Petrossian and Clarke, 2019; Belhabib and Le Billon, 2020), including enforcement evasion, misreporting, document forging, money laundering, labour abuses, tax evasion, piracy and trafficking. The scale of threat to the marine ecosystems is so extensive that García Ruiz et al. (2022) are calling for a new Blue Criminology to examine such harms and crimes.

Illegal actions against animals treated as 'livestock' include inhumane treatment and living conditions, inhumane transportation, and inhumane slaughter (Tourangeau and Fitzgerald, 2020). Tourangeau and Fitzgerald (2020) describe Canadian Maple Leaf Farms being fined for inhumane treatment of chickens during transportation, and regular breaches of EU laws in the transportation of animals in Europe. In the United Kingdom, veterinarians and meat hygiene inspectors working for the Food Standards Agency (FSA) inside abattoirs reported a total of 9, 511 animal welfare breaches between July 2014 and June 2016 (Wasley and Robbins, 2016). Animal Equality – an international animal protection organisation – continues to document woeful breaches of animal welfare regulation in the UK and beyond.

Yet, it is also evident that much of the harm against animals in food production (particularly at industrial scale) is legal, normalised and sometimes actively promoted. In response, green criminology has been particularly helpful in examining this type of harm and advocating non-speciesist criminology (Beirne, 2007) amongst other measures. Industrial meat production is an example of such harm. It is an 'ordinary act' characterised by conformity with existing capitalist norms of meat production, rather than an act of deviance (Brisman and South, 2018). Beirne (2014: 55) coined the term 'theriocide' to summarise the diverse ways human actions cause the deaths of animals. The activities that the term covers include intensive rearing regimes.

Speciesism is a label that attempts to encompass the magnitude of this kind of animal abuse (South, 2007; Sollund, 2012).

It refers to 'a set of widely shared beliefs that result from, and support, oppressive social arrangements' with respect to the treatment of non-human animals by humans (Sollund, 2012: 194). Regarding intensive farming, Sollund documents how prejudice against animals was transformed into a harmful, exploitative practice because of ideological legitimations promulgated by the meat industry and state authorities. Wyatt (2014) further expands the research on the human–animal relationship in food production by investigating animal abuse that takes place on English and Welsh pig farms. She applies the environmental justice perspective to recognise the harm and suffering of non-human animals in addition to exploring environmental degradation and human health concerns resulting from the industrialisation of pig farming. Concluding that industrialisation should not be the way forward, she suggests boosting financial incentives for high welfare farms and helping larger farms transition to a smaller scale. One of the more recent criminological forays into industrial farming through a socio-legal lens is Schally's (2017) investigation of the discursive construction of harm and the presentation of animal harms as 'business as usual' by US agribusiness. She undertook a case study of Tyson Foods in the US to investigate the techniques of legitimation of harm-doing, concluding that researchers and activists need to focus future endeavours on developing discourses of resistance to these harms.

Legal and normalised harms in food production are also committed against the environment itself and humans inhabiting that environment. Once again, green criminological research into industrial farming provides a useful case study for these issues. Sollund (2015) says that industrial farming should be of interest for green criminological exploration as it opens multiple avenues for studies of harm construction, denial, and neutralisation. Larsen (2012: 44) concurs, suggesting that agricultural production can also be viewed as 'structural violence or structural damage' and its damage-wreaking consequences should be considered criminal in both a judicial and a moral sense.

Ritchie (2004: 179) shows that the legal practice of industrial farming, that 'impoverishes rural communities, pollutes our rivers, depletes our soils, destroys our wilderness, extinguishes wildlife species, mistreats animals, and sickens and kills people' should be interrogated rather than taken for granted. Passas (2005) also stresses that factory farming results in social and environmental grievances and harms, creating concerns for environmental justice (Gladkova, 2020). Overall, industrial farming operations lead to deforestation resulting from growing animal feed crops, are water- and energy-intensive, generate greenhouse gas emissions and result in water supply contamination (Weis, 2013).

In addition to harms from industrial farming, there are other food harms embedded in the capitalist food system that result in environmental degradation. Boekhout van Solinge (2010) investigates deforestation in Brazil linked to agricultural production, discussing global consumption patterns and their hidden harms and debating the conundrum of responsibility for harm in the context of globalisation. Gray and Hinch (2015), while considering transformations of the food industry by corporatisation, touch upon agribusinesses' negative effects on traditional farming. White and Yeates (2018) demonstrate the intersections between the dominant food production practices and climate change. Additionally, Long and Lynch (2018) consider the problem of food waste and its regulation, emphasising the grave risks to both the environment and society.

Food harm and sustainability

Intersections of food and emerging technologies have also become the focus of criminology scholars. For example, Walters (2018) continues research into genetic technologies in food by applying the lens of political economy to food production, distribution and consumption and analysing the role of knowledge politics in constructing public and political discourses around food. Laestadius et al. (2018) develop a discussion around carnist technologies – technologies designed to meet human demand for animal-based foods – and their facilitation of food crimes and harms. They argue that technologies that increase efficiency in animal rearing, second-generation technologies for cellular agriculture, and plant-based analogues of animal products, do not challenge the carnist ideology and that the neoliberal ethos behind such technologies perpetuates systemic food harms.

EKATERINA GLADKOVA

Despite pessimistic prognoses, food crime scholars in criminology also focus their research on hopeful futures for food production and discuss alternatives for more sustainable and socially just food systems. Brisman (2009) argues that pursuing food justice is important not only for public health reasons but also to prevent and reduce crime. Booth et al. (2018) focus on food democracy and citizens' activities of opposition to the current food system resulting in the emergence of new food systems. Such initiatives – such as farmers' markets and community gardens – are underpinned by democratic processes and constitute a participatory movement whereby citizens can exert some modicum of control over their food system.

Conclusion

Food crime research in criminology is growing, which mirrors the growing concern about the unsustainable nature of our global food system. The food crime literature currently covers a spectrum of illegal and legal behaviours, and various types of crimes and harms. Issues of power, interests, speciesism and environmentalism are intertwined with how we produce and consume food now and into the future.

Ekaterina Gladkova

Further reading

Cheng, H. (2012). Cheap Capitalism: A Sociological Study of Food Crime in China. *The British Journal of Criminology*, 52, 254–273.

Croall, H. (2007). Food Crime, in Beirne, P., and South, N. (eds), *Issues in Green Criminology: Confronting Harms Against Environments, Humanity and Other Animals*. Cullompton: Willan.

Croall, H. (2013). Food Crime: A Green Criminology Perspective, in South, N., and Brisman, A. (eds), *Routledge International Handbook of Green Criminology*. Abingdon: Routledge, pp. 167–183.

Fitzgerald, A. (2015). *Animals as Food: (Re)connecting Production, Processing, Consumption, and Impacts*. East Lansing, MI: Michigan State University Press.

García Ruiz, A., South, N., and Brisman, A. (2022). Eco-Crimes and Ecocide at Sea: Toward a New Blue Criminology. *International Journal of Offender Therapy and Comparative Criminology*, 66(4), 407–429. https://doi.org/10.1177/0306624X20967950

Goyes, D., and South, N. (2016). Land-Grabs, Biopiracy and the Inversion of Justice in Colombia. *The British Journal of Criminology*, 56(3), 558–577. https://doi.org/10.1093/bjc/azv082

Gray, A. (2018). A Food Crime Perspective, in Hinch, R., and Gray, A. (eds), *A Handbook of Food Crime: Immoral and Illegal Practices in the Food Industry and What to Do About Them*. Bristol: Policy Press, pp. 11–26.

Passas, N. (2005). Lawful but Awful: Legal Corporate Crimes. *The Journal of Socio-Economics*, 34, 771–786.

Ritchie, M. (2004). The High Price of Cheap Food, in Passas, N., and Goodwin, N. (eds), *It's Legal but It Ain't Right: Harmful Social Consequences of Legal Industries*. Ann Arbor, MI: University of Michigan Press, pp. 77–92.

Walters, R. (2006). Crime, Bio-Agriculture and the Exploitation of Hunger. *The British Journal of Criminology*, 46(1), 26–45.

White, R., and Yeates, J. (2018). Farming and Climate Change, in Gray, A., and Hinch, R. (eds), *A Handbook of Food Crime: Immoral and Illegal Practices in the Food Industry and What to Do About Them*. Bristol: Policy Press, pp. 341–362.

References

Agnew, R. (1998). The Causes of Animal Abuse: A Social-Psychological Analysis. *Theoretical Criminology*, 2, 177–209.

Beirne, P. (2007). Animal Rights, Animal Abuse and Green Criminology, in Beirne, P., and South, N. (eds), *Issues in Green Criminology: Confronting Harms Against Environments, Humanity and Other Animals*. Cullompton: Willan, pp. 55–83.

Beirne, P. (2014). Theriocide: Naming Animal Killing. *International Journal for Crime, Justice and Social Democracy*, 3(2), 49–66.

Belhabib, D., and Le Billon, P. (2020). Editorial: Illegal Fishing as a Trans-National Crime. *Frontiers in Marine Science*, 7, 162. doi:10.3389/fmars.2020.00162

Blythman, J. (2011). The Food Chain Is Almost Broken: Who Will Reforge the Links of Trust? *The Observer*, 5 June. www.joannablythmanwriting.com

Boekhout van Solinge, T. (2010). Deforestation Crimes and Conflicts in the Amazon. *Critical Criminology*, 18(4), 263–277.

Booth, S., Coveney, J., and Paturel, D. (2018). Counter Crimes and Food Democracy: Suspects and Citizens Remaking the Food System, in Gray, A., and Hinch, R. (eds), *A Handbook of Food Crime: Immoral and Illegal Practices in the Food Industry and*

What to Do About Them. Bristol: Policy Press, pp. 367–383.
Brisman, A. (2009). Food Justice as Crime Prevention. *Journal of Food Law & Policy*, 5(1). https://scholarworks.uark.edu/jflp/vol5/iss1/3.
Brisman, A., and South, N. (2018). Green Criminology and Environmental Crimes and Harms. *Sociology Compass*, 13, 1–12.
Brisman, A., McClanahan, B., and South, N. (2016). Fractured Earth, Forced Labour: A Green Criminological Analysis of Rights and the Exploitation of Landscapes and Workers in Rural Contexts, in Donnermeyer, J. F. (ed.), *The Routledge International Handbook of Rural Criminology*. Abingdon: Routledge.
Cheng, H. (2012). Cheap Capitalism: A Sociological Study of Food Crime in China. *The British Journal of Criminology*, 52, 254–273.
Croall, H. (2007). Food Crime, in Beirne, P., and South, N. (eds), *Issues in Green Criminology: Confronting Harms Against Environments, Humanity and Other Animals*. Cullompton: Willan, pp. 206–229.
Croall, H. (2013). Food Crime: A Green Criminology Perspective. In South, N., and Brisman, A. (eds), *Routledge International Handbook of Green Criminology*. Abingdon: Routledge, pp. 167–83.
Davies, J. (2018). From Severe to Routine Labour Exploitation: The Case of Migrant Workers in the UK Food Industry. *Criminology & Criminal Justice*, 1–17.
Davies, J. (2020). Corporate Harm and Embedded Labour Exploitation in Agri-food Supply Networks. *European Journal of Criminology*, 17(1), 70–85. doi:10.1177/1477370819874416
Davies, J., and Ollus, N. (2019) Labour Exploitation as Corporate Crime and Harm: Outsourcing Responsibility in Food Production and Cleaning Services Supply Chains. *Crime, Law and Social Change*, 72(1), 87–106.
Del Prado-Lu, J. (2018). Impact of Hazardous Substances and Pesticides on Farmers and Farming Communities, in Hinch, R., and Gray, A. (eds), *A Handbook of Food Crime: Immoral and Illegal Practices in the Food Industry and What to Do About Them*. Bristol: Policy Press.
Fitzgerald, A. (2015). *Animals as Food: (Re)connecting Production, Processing, Consumption, and Impacts*. East Lansing, MI: Michigan State University Press.
Flores Elizondo, C., Lord, N., and Spencer, J. (2019). Food Fraud and the Fraud Act 2006: Complementarity and Limitations, in Monaghan, C., and Monaghan, N. (eds), *Financial Crime and Corporate Misconduct: A Critical Evaluation of Fraud Legislation*. Abingdon: Routledge, pp. 48–62.
García Ruiz, A., South, N., and Brisman, A. (2022). Eco-Crimes and Ecocide at Sea: Toward a New Blue Criminology. *International Journal of Offender Therapy and Comparative Criminology*, 66(4), 407–429. https://doi.org/10.1177/0306624X20967950
Gladkova, E. (2020). Farming Intensification and Environmental Justice in Northern Ireland. *Critical Criminology*, 28, 445–461. https://doi.org/10.1007/s10612-020-09488-3
Gladkova, E. (2021). Food Production Harms in the European Context: The EU as an Enabler or a Solution?, in Lord, N., Inzelt, É., Huisman, W., and Faria, R. (eds), *European White-Collar Crime: Exploring the Nature of European Realities*. Bristol: Bristol University Press, pp. 125–142.
Gluck, M. (2008). *The Great Wine Swindle: The Secrets behind the Wines You Love*. London: Gibson Square.
Goyes, D. R. (2020). Monopolising Seeds, Monopolising Society: A Guide to Contemporary Criminological Research of Biopiracy, in South, N., and Brisman, A. (eds), *Routledge International Handbook of Green Criminology* (2nd ed.). Abingdon: Routledge.
Goyes, D., and South, N. (2016). Land-grabs, Biopiracy and the Inversion of Justice in Colombia. *The British Journal of Criminology*, 56(3), 558–577. https://doi.org/10.1093/bjc/azv082
Gray, A. (2018). A Food Crime Perspective, in Hinch, R., and Gray, A. (eds), *A Handbook of Food Crime: Immoral and Illegal Practices in the Food Industry and What to Do About Them*. Bristol: Policy Press, pp. 11–26.
Gray, A., and Hinch, R. (2015). Agribusiness, Governments and Food Crime: A Critical Perspective, in Sollund, R. (ed.), *Green Harms and Crimes: Critical Criminology in a Changing World*. Basingstoke: Palgrave Macmillan, pp. 97–116.
Hinch, R. (2018). Chocolate, Slavery, Forced Labour, Child Labour and the State, in Hinch, R., and Gray, A. (eds), *A Handbook of Food Crime: Immoral and Illegal Practices in the Food Industry and What to Do About Them*. Bristol: Policy Press. ISBN 978-1-4473-3601-3.
Laestadius, L., Deckers, J., and Baran, S. (2018). Food Crimes, Harms and Carnist Technologies, in Hinch, R., and Gray, A. (eds), *A Handbook of Food Crime: Immoral and Illegal Practices in the Food Industry and What to Do About Them*. Bristol: Policy Press, pp. 295–311.
Larsen, G. (2012). The Most Serious Crime: Eco-Genocide Concepts and Perspectives in Eco-Global Criminology, in Ellefsen, R., Sollund, R., and Larsen, G. (eds), *Eco-Global Crimes*. Farnham and Burlington, VT: Ashgate Publishing Limited, pp. 33–56.
Lawrence, F. (2008). *Eat Your Heart Out: Why the Food Business Is Bad for the Planet and Your Health*. London: Penguin Books.
Leighton, P. S. (2016). Mass Salmonella Poisoning by the Peanut Corporation of America: State–

Corporate Crime Involving Food Safety. *Critical Criminology*, 24, 75–91.
Liu, C. (2009). Profits above the Law: China's Melamine Tainted Milk Incident. *Mississippi Law Journal*, 79, 371–417.
Long, M., and Lynch, M. (2018). Food Waste (Non)Regulation, in Hinch, R., and Gray, A. (eds), *A Handbook of Food Crime: Immoral and Illegal Practices in the Food Industry and What to Do about Them*. Bristol: Policy Press, pp. 331–346.
Lord, N., Flores Elizondo, C., and Spencer, J. (2017a). The Dynamics of Food Fraud: The Interactions Between Criminal Opportunity and Market (Dys)Functionality in Legitimate Business. *Criminology and Criminal Justice*, 17(5), 605–623.
Lord, N., Spencer, J., Albanese, J., and Flores Elizondo, C. (2017b). In Pursuit of Food System Integrity: The Situational Prevention of Food Fraud Enterprise. *European Journal on Criminal Policy and Research*, 23, 483–501.
Passas, N. (2005). Lawful but Awful: Legal Corporate Crimes. *The Journal of Socio-Economics*, 34, 771–786.
Pennington, T. (2003). *When Food Kills: BSE, E. coli, and Disaster Science*. Oxford: Oxford University Press.
Petrossian, G., and Clarke, R. (2019). Illegal Commercial Fishing, in Natarajan, M. (ed.), *International and Transnational Crime and Justice*. Cambridge: Cambridge University Press, pp. 132–137. doi:10.1017/9781108597296.022
Ritchie, M. (2004). The High Price of Cheap Food, in Passas, N., and Goodwin, N. (eds), *It's Legal but It Ain't Right: Harmful Social Consequences of Legal Industries*. Ann Arbor, MI: University of Michigan Press, pp. 178–193.
Rizzuti, A. (2020). Food Crime: A Review of the UK Institutional Perception of Illicit Practices in the Food Sector. *Social Sciences*, 9(7), 112. https://doi.org/10.3390/socsci9070112
Ruth, S. M., Luning, P. A., Silvis, I. C. J., Yang, Y., and Huisman, W. (2018). Differences in Fraud Vulnerability in Various Food Supply Chains and Their Tiers. *Food Control*, 84, 375–381.
Schally, J. (2017). *Legitimizing Corporate Harm: The Discourse of Contemporary Agribusiness*. Basingstoke: Palgrave Macmillan.
Sollund, R. (2012). Speciesism as Doxic Practice Versus Valuing Difference and Plurality, in Ellefsen, R., Sollund, R., and Larsen, G. (eds), *Eco-global Crimes*. Farnham and Burlington, VT: Ashgate, pp. 181–199.
Sollund, R. (2015). *Green Harms and Crimes: Critical Criminological Perspectives* Basingstoke: Palgrave Macmillan.
South, N. (2007). The Corporate Colonization of Nature: Bio-Prospecting, Bio-Piracy and the Development of Green Criminology, in Beirne, P., and South, N. (eds), *Transnational Environmental Crime*. Cullompton: Willan, pp. 76–89.
Spink, J., and Moyer, D. (2011). Defining the Public Health Threat of Food Fraud. *Journal of Food Science*, 76, R157–R163.
Tombs, S., and Whyte, D. (2007). *Safety Crime*. Cullompton: Willan Publishing.
Tombs, S., and Whyte, D. (2010). Crime, Harm and Corporate Power, in Muncie, J., Talbot, D., and Walters, R. (eds), *Crime: Local and Global*. Cullompton: Willan Publishing, pp. 137–172.
Tourangeau, W., and Fitzgerald, A. (2020). Food Crime and Green Criminology, in South, N., and Brisman, A. (eds), *Routledge International Handbook of Green Criminology* (2nd ed.). Abingdon: Routledge, pp. 205–221.
Walters, R. (2004). Criminology and Genetically Modified Food. *The British Journal of Criminology*, 44, 151–167.
Walters, R. (2006). Crime, Bio-Agriculture and the Exploitation of Hunger. *The British Journal of Criminology*, 46(1), 26–45.
Walters, R. (2010). *Crime, Political Economy and Genetically Modified Food*. Abingdon and New York: Routledge.
Walters, R. (2018). Food, Genetics and Knowledge Politics, in Gray, A., and Hinch, R. (eds), *A Handbook of Food Crime: Immoral and Illegal Practices in the Food Industry and What to Do About Them*. Bristol: Policy Press.
Wasley, A., and Robbins, J. (2016). FSA: 4,000 Major Breaches of Animal Welfare Laws at UK Abattoirs in Two Years. *The Guardian*, 28 August. https://www.theguardian.com/environment/2016/aug/28/fsa-4000-breaches-animal-welfare-laws-uk-abattoirs-two-years
Weis, T. (2013). *The Ecological Hoofprint: The Global Burden of Industrial Livestock*. London and New York: Zed Books.
White, R. (2008). Environmental Harm and Crime Prevention. *Trends and Issues in Crime and Criminal Justice*, no. 360. Canberra: Australian Institute of Criminology. https://www.aic.gov.au/publications/tandi/tandi360
White, R. (2018). Green Victimology and Non-Human Victims. *International Review of Victimology*, 24(2), 239–255. https://doi.org/10.1177/0269758017745615
White, R., and Yeates, J. (2018). Farming and Climate Change, in Gray, A., and Hinch, R. (eds), *A Handbook of Food Crime: Immoral and Illegal Practices in the Food Industry and What to Do About Them*. Bristol: Policy Press, pp. 341–362.
Williams, R. (2007). Cadbury Fined £1m for Salmonella Offences. *The Guardian*, 17 July.

www.guardian.co.uk/commentisfree/2007/jul/17/uk.business
Wyatt, T. (2014). A Criminological Exploration of the Industrialisation of Pig Farming. *Internet Journal of Criminology*, 12–28.
Yang, Y., Huisman, W., Hettinga, K. A., Zhang, L., and van Ruth, S. M. (2020). The Chinese Milk Supply Chain: A Fraud Perspective. *Food Control*, 113, 1–10. https://doi.org/10.1016/j.foodcont.2020.107211

EKATERINA GLADKOVA

28. Genetically modified organisms

Introduction

In this entry, the issue of genetically modified organisms (GMOs) will be approached from the theoretical perspective of *green criminology* – a "conceptual umbrella" within whose analytical frame the bio-physical and socio-economic consequences of the various sources of environmental crime and harm can be examined. These include pollution, deterioration of resources, loss of biodiversity, and climate change (South, 1998; Lynch and Stretesky, 2003; White, 2008; South, Brisman and Beirne, 2013). It is within this theoretical framework that criminologist Walters (2004; 2011) underlines how we are currently witnessing the dramatic emergence of a "food crisis", that, with its related theme of "food safety" – regarding production, sale and distribution of food – is certainly an issue of planetary importance.

One of the main objectives of this entry is to examine GMOs in the light of notions of crime that go beyond conventional definitions. Clearly, this kind of approach opens huge epistemological questions, which we do not presume to resolve quickly. Without going into detail, it is clear that criminology has to redefine the "lenses" through which it observes the worlds of crime to include global environmental risks and harms. It also has to take an active part in the social and political spheres that inevitably cross these theoretical areas. In brief: emerging environmental harms and injustices require "a new academic way of looking at the world but also a new global politics" (South, 2010: 242). This is, in fact, the "double nature" that animates green criminology.

Genetically modified food and green criminology

The World Food Programme reports that there are 795 million people worldwide who are undernourished (UNWFP, 2017). The fact that ten per cent of the world's population lives in a daily state of starvation and food insecurity is an international crisis that criminology can no longer ignore. The global food crisis, in fact, has also reinvigorated debates about agricultural development and genetically modified (GM) food, as well as posing deeply divided debates about poverty, debt and security. In this context, a peculiar scenario is that of genetically modified food and of the production and technological processes involved that, in their turn, imply multiple dimensions as regards power, economy, environmental risks, and harm (see also Latour, 1999; Natali, 2013).

The GMO debate often takes on ideological aspects and raises dilemmas that, because they are oriented according to very specific ethical and political alignments, end up becoming insoluble. For example, consider the following question, often asked during public and scientific debates: who benefits from GMOs? The answer is first, the multinationals, who gain new profits in monopoly markets (through the management of patents, for example). But so too do the environmental associations and militant anti-GMO groups looking for a common enemy to fight, a scapegoat (almost a "super-villain") on whom to unload their collective anxieties, perhaps even in order to generate some form of "moral panic".

GM proponents argue that current technology promises increased agricultural productivity, lower costs, and improved environmental outcomes. It is argued that GM is a breakthrough technology that promises to feed the world's hungry (Hindmarsh, 2008) as well as contributing to global food security (Tait and Barker, 2011).

Critics of this new agrigenetics technology raise a number of issues including:

- the risk and uncertainty regarding the development of GM crops, particularly when regulated by a narrow scientific cohort (Hindmarsh, 2008);
- economic harm created through GM contamination via gene-flow (of non-GM conventional to organic produce) and inadequate storage and transportation loss;
- environmental harm including the breeding of wild weed species (Knispel et al., 2008), and the demise of beneficial insects (Zhao et al., 2011);
- toxin persistence and unintended effects on soil biota (Vadakattu and Watson, 2004);
- safety of long-term ingestion of GM foods (Carmen, 2004);
- consumer choice and the "right to know";

- concentration of capital and privatisation of genetic information and its influence on the control of agricultural production (Pechlaner and Otero, 2010); and
- the deviant and illegal activities of corporate actors in controlling and monopolising the production, distribution and regulation of GM technologies, seeds and plants (Walters, 2011).

On closer inspection, these opposing sides reflect, more or less directly, the ambiguous nature of GMOs, which can be in its turn associated with the idea of *phàrmakon* (Resta, 2008): a *remedy*/panacea/cure-all for the hunger of the world, for food crisis and insecurity, for environmental deterioration and for climate change; and, at the same time, a *poison* capable of producing, even in small cumulative doses, dangerous and sinister alterations to the balance of the ecosystem.

The ambivalence ingrained in the concept of *phàrmakon* – being remedy and poison at the same time – links technological innovations to law. If the code of technology is "we can do everything we can do", turning this statement into a question "*can* we do everything we *can* do?" – and therefore questioning ourselves about the consequences to be avoided with legal tools – means highlighting the limits deriving from simplified and excessively linear approaches to technology. To posit that every innovation is beneficial or, on the contrary, intrinsically harmful, would mean reducing economic, ethical and political evaluation to the expression of expert opinion on the danger (Testart, 2013). However, the global debates about food insecurity and injustice necessitate adopting a pluralistic analytical lens capable of transcending disciplinary boundaries to understand the complexities of food production, trade and consumption. To fulfil this task, it is necessary to take a sensitive look at the issue and to pick up even the most ambiguous and difficult-to-catch signals, such as those gravitating around the GMOs – new "objects" that challenge the traditional dichotomies between nature and culture, nature and politics, between the "natural" and what is, or would be, "against nature" (Latour, 1991).

GMOs and knowledge production

In 2002, Zambia expressed its refusal to accept genetically modified corn. The then president of Zambia defined the corn stored in the local depots of the World Food Programme as "poisoned food", since it was genetically modified, thus justifying his refusal of food aid. Naturally, he was heavily criticised for taking this position, particularly considering the conditions of malnutrition that were devastating the population of Zambia – along with the populations of many other developing countries. During his empirical investigation of this issue, Walters (2011) highlighted how, in similar cases, it is crucial to take into account the (inter)cultural dimension of these phenomena. For example, a society like that of Zambia sees corn as the source of life, and the introduction of an extraneous and "unnatural" element, such as genetically modified corn, is seen as a real "contamination". Moreover, the case of Zambia's resistance towards food aid containing genetically modified corn is interesting in that it demonstrates the ways by which countries and multinational companies from the West exercise their political and economic power and also how actors possessing minor power can sometimes resist the dominant ones. In such contexts, one can also ask: are the Zambians victims of a food crisis or victims of the power wielded by the multinationals or both?

Accordingly, a green criminology perspective needs to go beyond the limits of mono-dimensional approaches by on the one hand recognising the role that the global political economy has in the dynamics concerning GMOs, and, on the other, recognising and highlighting the different concepts of nature upheld by some countries compared to others. In this sense, a perspective sensitive to the dimensions of power and, at the same time, to the (inter)cultural dimensions in the environmental field is able to help sensitise scientific and cultural reflection towards new perspectives through which humans can relate to the environment, to nature and to its modification. To this end, the experiences and traditions of distinctive cultures are extremely useful to study. For instance, investigation highlights how the Zambian government's refusal of GMOs not only expresses a precautionary approach required in the face of scientific uncertainty but is also rooted in the will to protect the landscape and the national territory from the (unpredictable) impact of unfamiliar and difficult to control agricultural practices.

Continuing along the criminological itinerary suggested here, the GMO issue can also be fruitfully explored in a further sense, seeing this exploration as an encounter between green and cultural criminology. The latter is an approach that seeks to incorporate a concern with the cultural significance of the environment, environmental crime, and environmental harm into the green criminological enterprise (Brisman and South, 2014). In the context of food production, it is evident that food has now assumed an iconic dimension and value: the food industries no longer sell just food, but also the lifestyle, the social image, and the desires it represents. Contemporary capitalism is seen as an "essentially cultural enterprise", whose economic productivity and political vitality are intrinsically linked to its cultural representations. Capitalism produces and launches on the market material products but also, simultaneously, the images and meanings related to them. The consumers "make their choices" within this seductive imagery created by the market and by the advertising industry.

Thus, to be for or against GMOs means adopting a specific social identity, more or less *green*, and more or less aware of the ecological consequences. We know very well that our knowledge and perception of environmental issues derive to a great extent from the media, which tend to provide simplified representations of the good–evil dichotomy. This is why it is important to evaluate the cultural dimensions that contribute significantly to the contours of the public debate on such issues. An example is the media representation of GMO, of the protests by *NO GMO*, and of the dynamics of representation of the socio-environmental conflict. More importantly, modern consumption presents a multiplicity of manifestations that cannot be reduced to a single interpretative perspective. To try and understand this consumption in all its complexity, one must take into account the fact that the markets are also necessarily part of political and cultural matrices that give to the acts of consumption a specific meaning and resonance (Brewer and Trentmann, 2006). This is why a cultural perspective represents a useful key to the understanding of these processes.

The successful establishment of GM "friendly" national regulatory institutions has been critically examined in previous work in Australia (Hindmarsh and Parkinson, 2012) and the UK (Walters, 2011). Such works concluded that the direct application of economic power, astute policy alliances and ownership and privileging of certain knowledge has contributed to the dominance of the GM lobby. More broadly, biotech companies have sought political influence through substantial public relation campaigns, focused lobby groups, and through sponsorship and advertising in influential scientific journals (Walters, 2011: 23–26) as well as through public exhibitions (Hindmarsh, 2008) and public inquiries as forms of knowledge/power (Hindmarsh and Parkinson, 2012). In this sense, it is crucial to critically analyse the way this knowledge production is increasingly privatised, controlled and selectively deployed by corporate and state interests and how this is transformed into economic and political power. Given the money to be made from world hunger, and the monopolisation of the biotech industry, it is not surprising that the Monsantos of the world are entering the next phase of the GM food technology era firmly focused on public relations in re-branding and messaging their genetic products. The shift has now moved from farmers, politicians, supermarkets, and scientists to the global consuming public in an attempt to capture the hearts, minds, stomachs, and pockets of future generations.

Green cultural criminology

Science and technology per se have significantly and positively impacted on global food production, distribution and consumption. The advent of food genetics and biotechnology, however, has provided deeply divided and politicised dimensions to discourses, policies and practices about food security. Within such global debates, scientific knowledge resources have been selectively produced and deployed to counter the politicisation of GM crops and to encourage the rapid adoption of this technology. In highly contested social and environmental issues, what is researched – and what is not – and how that knowledge is authorised and deployed, have significant power effects that pose serious social, economic and environmental consequences.

Some relevant points in the GMO debate deserve to be considered in more depth from a green and cultural criminological perspective. First, it seems essential to take into account that the context is much wider than the human world alone, that it is continuously transforming, is neither predictable nor transparent, and that the separation between the social and natural worlds is, not uncommonly, a "visual effect" derived from the cognitive, dichotomous and mechanistic devices elaborated so far. In other words, we need to bring nature and the non-human into the human equation. Nature has never been truly "pure" and a "safe, good and just" natural order does not exist except in the abstract. However, this recognition does not stop us from developing and fostering notions of *respect* towards nature that include those progressive, silent, cumulative and diffused processes capable, in the long run, of influencing the circular relationship between human beings and environment (Adam, 2000).

Second, the introduction of new technology and innovations in agriculture has always been accompanied by discourses on the benefits of the particular technology. The development of GM crops is a prime example of an environmental regulatory issue featuring a proliferation of contested knowledge – from detailed agronomic and ecological research data to scientific reviews, technology assessments, public inquiries, economic and risk analyses, media reportage, and policy documents. Notwithstanding all this, little clarity or social agreement exists on the productive capacity, ecological or social consequences of GM crop regimes, or confidence in GM commercialisation. Such knowledge contestations reflect conflicts between expert scientific knowledge and local knowledge and understandings (Liberatore and Funtowicz, 2003). In the specific environmental scenario, the active participation of citizens represents a vital ingredient when focusing on and defining public policies.

In this context, the precautionary principle allows one to problematise the distribution of risks and their social acceptability in cases where insufficient knowledge is apparent. This problematisation, necessary for a democratic reappropriation of the socio-environmental issues, requires the expansion of expert knowledge and multiple understanding of environment and environmental issues. To achieve this, it is necessary, on the one hand, to introduce all the relevant knowledge, produced by the scientific community *and* by the people and, on the other, particularly, as regards the GMO question, to "take care" of the delicate link between communication and science. As White (2008: 78) suggests, science can and must represent the main tool to use in the deliberations concerning the intervention and the impact of humans on the environment, but science is still *only one kind* of knowledge in the complex web that links politics, democracy and technology. Who develops and "owns" knowledge, what knowledge is seen to be authoritative in these contexts, and how it is extended to decision makers, are important questions.

Third, it is clear that the production and dissemination of GM food knowledge remains deeply politicised and polarised. The GM crops debate intersects a number of highly controversial "science, technology, environment and society" debates characterised by considerable complexity and uncertainty, high risk, susceptibility to politicisation by interested parties, and a divisive polarisation of viewpoints. In these issues, "authoritative" knowledge is a valuable commodity and those in the position to control knowledge production and communication exert significant political and economic power (see also Stehr, 2005). Importantly, the introduction of GM technologies reduces reliance on local knowledge through restrictions on farmer experimentation and evaluation, and with the decline in independent sources of knowledge, farmers are more reliant on private knowledge sources that are also the main beneficiaries of the technology. These "structural" changes to the knowledge networks of farmers, intensified by patent-protected GM resources and knowledge exclusivity, thus influence what and how decisions are made about GM crop adoption.

Conclusion

If we imagine the "social" and the "natural" as the two banks of a turbulent river, we can say that criminology is located on those banks, attempting to connect them. This is an effective image to describe the highly complex context in which green criminology moves, introducing into the *mainstream* of the criminological field perturbing elements, of which the phenomenon of GMOs constitutes a clear example. It is also along these lines that (green) criminology is trying to redefine its role and its language, enhancing its constitutive and original interdisciplinary nature, that goes beyond the hyper-specialisation of experts and technicians.

Following this path, criminology will be able to contribute to the building of a theoretical perspective capable of keeping together the many dimensions – political, economic, social, ecological and cultural – that constitute the "reality" of GMOs. In doing this, it will contribute to defining the notions of social and environmental risk, harm and justice linked to GMOs, and force us to ask ourselves if technology can effectively do all that we want it to. This is a reflexive exercise useful in creating a vision of who we *can* be and who we want to become, projecting ourselves into an idea of a really sustainable future. Following this trail, in order to protect nature effectively, it is necessary to bring back into the "dialogue" – as Latour (1991; 1999) has demonstrated – the multiplicity of natures that have been "silenced" for too long by a rigid and myopic anthropocentrism. This is possible only by recognising that humans are "capable", in the etymological sense of the word, that is, able to deal with a multiplicity of experiential and knowledge levels, among them the "unexpected", the "unheard of", and the "emerging". This last capacity is essential to the very idea of justice and essential in responding to ever new forms of social and environmental injustice.

LORENZO NATALI AND REECE WALTERS

Further reading

Adam, B. (2000), The temporal gaze: The challenge for social theory in the context of GM food, *The British Journal of Sociology*, 51: 125–142.

Carmen, J. (2004), Is GM food safe to eat?, in R. Hindmarsh and R. Lawrence (eds) *Recoding Nature: Critical Perspectives on Genetic Engineering*, Sydney: UNSW Press, pp. 82–93.

Walters, R. (2004), Criminology and genetically modified food, *British Journal of Criminology*, 44(2): 151–167.

Walters, R. (2007), Food crime, regulation and the biotech harvest, *European Journal of Criminology*, 4(2): 217–235.

Walters, R. (2018), Food, genetics and knowledge politics, in A. Gray and R. Hinch (eds) *A Handbook of Food Crime: Immoral and Illegal Practices in the Food Industry and What to Do About Them*, Bristol: Policy Press, pp. 265–280.

References

Adam, B. (2000), The temporal gaze: The challenge for social theory in the context of GM food, *The British Journal of Sociology*, 51: 125–142.

Brewer, J. and Trentmann, F. (2006), *Consuming Cultures, Global Perspectives: Historical Trajectories, Transnational Exchanges*, London: Bloomsbury Publishing.

Brisman, A. and South, N. (2014), *Green Cultural Criminology. Constructions of Environmental Harm, Consumerism and Resistance to Ecocide*, London and New York: Routledge.

Carmen, J. (2004), Is GM food safe to eat?, in R. Hindmarsh and R. Lawrence (eds) *Recoding Nature: Critical Perspectives on Genetic Engineering*, Sydney: UNSW Press, pp. 82–93.

Hindmarsh, R. (2008), Food and environmental security in the Indian Ocean region: Questioning the GM doubly green revolution, in T. Doyle and M. Risely (eds) *Crucible for Survival: Environmental Security in the Indian Ocean Region*, New Brunswick, NJ: Rutgers University Press, pp. 182–214.

Hindmarsh, R. and Parkinson, A. (2012), The public inquiry as a contested political technology: GM crop moratoria review in Australia, *Environmental Politics*, 23(2): 293–311.

Knispel, A., McLachlan, S., van Acker, R. and Friesen, L. (2008), Gene flow and multiple herbicide resistance in escaped canola populations, *Weed Science*, 56(1): 72–80.

Latour, B. (1991), *We Have Never Been Modern*, Cambridge, MA: Harvard University Press.

Latour, B. (1999), *Politics of Nature: How to Bring the Sciences into Democracy*, Cambridge, MA: Harvard University Press.

Liberatore, A. and Funtowicz, S. (2003), Democratising expertise: "Expertising" democracy. What does it mean and why bother?, *Science and Public Policy*, 30(3): 146–150.

Lynch, M. and Stretesky, P. (2003), The meaning of green: Contrasting criminological perspectives, *Theoretical Criminology*, 7(2): 217–238.

Natali, L. (2013), The contemporary horizon of green criminology, in N. South and A. Brisman (eds) *Routledge International Handbook of Green Criminology*, London and New York: Routledge, 73–84.

Pechlaner, G. and Otero, G. (2010), Neoliberalism and food vulnerability: The stakes for the South, in G. Lawrence, K. Lyons and T. Wallington (eds) *Food Security, Nutrition and Sustainability*, London: Earthscan, pp. 79–86.

Resta, E. (2008), *Diritto vivente*, Roma-Bari: Laterza.

South, N. (1998), A green field for criminology? A proposal for a perspective, *Theoretical Criminology*, 2(2): 211–234.

South, N. (2010), The ecocidal tendencies of late modernity: Transnational crime, social exclusion, victims and rights, in R. White (ed.) *Global Environmental Harm: Criminological Perspectives*, Cullompton: Willan, pp. 228–247.

South, N., Brisman, A. and Beirne, P. (2013), A guide to a green criminology, in N. South and A. Brisman (eds) *Routledge International*

Handbook of Green Criminology, London and New York: Routledge, pp. 27–42.
Stehr, N. (2005), *Knowledge Politics: Governing the Consequences of Science and Technology*, Boulder, CO: Paradigm Publishers.
Tait, J. and Barker, G. (2011), Global food security and the governance of modern biotechnologies, *Science and Society*, 12(8): 763–788.
Testart, J. (2013), *A chi convengono gli OGM?*, Turin: Lindau.
United Nations World Food Programme (UNWFP) (2017), Available at https://publications.wfp.org/en/annual-report/2017/?_ga=2.12119165.876615723.1728657542-2038003815.1728657541 (last accessed 11 October 2024).
Vadakattu, G. and Watson, S. (2004), Ecological impacts of GM cotton on soil biodiversity. CSIRO. http://www.environment.gov.au/system/files/pages/ca807cf6–8ad9–478f-9d7d-f3894704642d/files/bt-cotton.pdf
Walters, R. (2004), Criminology and genetically modified food, *British Journal of Criminology*, 44(2): 151–167.
Walters, R. (2011), *Eco Crime and Genetically Modified Food*, London and New York: Routledge.
White, R. (2008), *Crimes Against Nature: Environmental Criminology and Ecological Justice*, Cullompton: Willan.
Zhao, Y. Y., Liu, F., Yang, G. and You, M. S. (2011), PsOr1, a potential target for RNA interference-based pest management, *Insect Molecular Biology*, 20(1): 97–104.

LORENZO NATALI AND REECE WALTERS

29. Online environmental crimes

Introduction

Online environmental crimes refers to the digitalisation of illegal activities which directly harm both humans and the environment. Tech-savvy criminals in an interconnected, digital age have extended their reach through the Internet to engage in various environmental crimes such as the sale of ozone-depleting substances; the illicit trade in hazardous waste and pollution; illegal, unregulated and unreported fishing; and illegal logging and associated trade in stolen timber. The most common type of online environmental crime, however, is the illegal wildlife trade. The digitalisation of criminal commerce and the velocity of illicit transactions via social platforms have created an expansive hub between sellers and buyers via email, discussion groups, telephony and other modes of communication, facilitating the dissemination of wildlife trade information. In contrast to the regulation of traditional "bricks-and-mortar" marketplaces, auction websites and chat rooms on thematic websites facilitate transactions with increased anonymity, making it easy to buy and sell endangered products across borders and to evade domestic legislation.

The Internet has grown exponentially since its advent, establishing a global communication network and eliminating conventional notions of space and distance. It has also changed the nature of interpersonal communications, the distribution and accessibility of information and, finally, legitimate economical activities (O'Neill, 2000; Pastor-Satorras and Vespignani, 2007). Demeau et al. (2019) assert that the digitalisation of wildlife trafficking parallels online drug trafficking insofar as criminals use the Internet to promote "products" and favour alternative means of communication in order to finalise exchanges and transactions. Whereas wildlife traffickers will exploit loopholes online, dealers will also find ways to exploit online platforms to illegally sell narcotics due to the lack of consistent international legislation regulating online pharmacies and synthetic substances (Lavorgna, 2014).

In a technology-driven world, the illegal wildlife trade has increased at all levels: locally, nationally and internationally. The combination of techniques for machine learning and social media analysis by the Global Initiative Against Transnational Organized Crime (GITOC) reveals that the most expansive markets for online environmental crimes may be totally off the radar, often attached to personal phone numbers and in clear violation of many platforms' policies. With mounting pressure being placed on online companies to regulate this illegal trade on the "surface web" – that is, the small portion of the Internet accessible with standard web search engines, criminal groups have moved on to anonymous networks such as the "dark web" or "darknet" to illegally traffic animals. These clandestine websites are easily created, removed, or altered by simple modifications to web addresses, and criminal networks do not provide identifying information such as their location or source (Sullivan, 2016). A 2018 report by GITOC also surmises that illicit wildlife markets will expand on the "dark web", growing in scope and scale alongside other criminal activities like illegal drugs and arms sales.

Regulation

Research suggests that the turnover of online marketplaces is extremely high – in fact, the majority of auction websites are shut down a year after they are launched (Lavorgna, 2016). The International Fund for Animal Welfare (IFAW) conducted its first review of online environmental crimes in 2005, focusing specifically on the wildlife market on the Internet. The organisation uncovered approximately 9,000 ads for animals and animal-derived products in one week. With eBay auction sites being the most prominent platform for online environmental crimes, the "dark web" has garnered the attention of law enforcement personnel who track emerging markets, the geographic locations that they serve, and the range of products being offered online. One of the preferred methods of governing online markets is "scraping". With many online marketplaces using off-the-shelf auction software, "scraping" tools monitor trends in consumer behaviour and identify highly coveted items. Ironically, the untraceability of the "dark web" makes online marketplaces relatively easy to "scrape" in their entirety, enabling authorities to gather data on consumer demand for illegally traded goods without accessing closed social-media groups or forums (Wright, 2019).

Consider, for example, the FloraGuard project in the United Kingdom, which uses AI search algorithms in tandem with human analysis, drawing upon subject matter experts in the fields of conservation science, criminology, law enforcement, and information and communications technology (ICT) (Whitehead et al., 2021). The project is an example of a socio-technical workflow involving multidisciplinary approaches to the investigation of Internet-facilitated illegal wildlife trade. While Step 1 involves the identification of species of interest with the help of conservation scientists and law enforcement officers, Step 2 involves other actors such as ICT scientists, criminologists and other diverse participants in the creation of a lexicon for website searches. Cross-disciplinary exchanges of information occur and key inputs and outputs are produced to achieve interdisciplinary participation.

TRAFFIC, a non-governmental organisation, works across the globe to combat the illegal wildlife trade and document endangered species products being sold on the Internet. In 2010, the organisation began routinely monitoring online markets, recording the number of advertisements selling illegal wildlife. This data was then disseminated to enforcement agencies through workshops held with China's Management Authority for CITES (Convention on International Trade in Endangered Species of Wild Fauna and Flora). Not long thereafter, TRAFFIC decided to conduct more thorough and comprehensive analyses of online monitoring in China, working alongside website and platform managers and with enforcement agencies such as the National Forest Police Bureau to train e-commerce professionals on a range of relevant issues: the latest code words used to conceal illegal transactions, changes in legislation, and species identification (Yu and Jia, 2015). Today, TRAFFIC monitors the monthly total number of illegal wildlife product advertisements (TWPA) and the number of new wildlife product advertisements (NWPA). It searches code words pertaining to items such as ivory, rhino horn, tiger bone, hawksbill shells, pangolin scales, leopard bones, saiga horn, hornbill casques and much more. With each code word searched individually on various websites, web links and descriptions of each seller and trader are recorded and then sent to website/platform owners so that they can delete the posts.

TRAFFIC also regulates methods of payment among buyers and sellers, detecting sales of illegal wildlife products through "guaranteed transactions". Once a transaction takes place, the buyer pays money to a "guaranteed" intermediary who alerts the seller. The seller then sends the product to the buyer and, upon careful inspection for authenticity, the buyer instructs the intermediary to release the money to the seller. TRAFFIC tracks these financial flows with the hope of intercepting these transactions by identifying courier companies used to deliver illegal wildlife products to buyers. Established partnerships with many courier companies allow TRAFFIC to build capacity and develop procedures to ensure said companies do not work as unwitting conduits for illegal wildlife transactions via online markets.

Perhaps one of the most notorious online markets, "Silk Road" 1.0 and 2.0, served as an online hub for selling drugs, weapons and illegal services. The "Silk Road" was an eBay-style marketplace for drugs and other illicit goods that, at its peak in 2012, was processing an estimated $15 million in transactions annually. In 2013, the FBI shut down "Silk Road" 1.0 and arrested Ross Ulbricht, the founder of the website. Not long thereafter, "Silk Road" 2.0 was launched, and authorities acted swiftly to infiltrate the online market, resulting in the arrest of its administrator, Blake Benthall. In November 2014, Operation Onymous was launched by law enforcement units and prosecutors in Europe and the United States of America. The campaign set out to tackle illegal markets by identifying vendors and administrators across various regions of the world. Most of the transactions were carried out by Bitcoin, a decentralised cryptocurrency which is processed and validated by a peer-to-peer network. While Bitcoin promises increased levels of anonymity, all its transactions are stored in a public ledger and information on Bitcoin users can be obtained from exchanges – for example, institutions converting Bitcoin into other currencies or vice versa. Operation Onymous was coordinated by Europol's European Cybercrime Centre (EC3), Eurojust, the FBI, the US Immigration and Customs Enforcement's (ICE) Homeland Security Investigations (HSI) and the operation led to the arrest of 17 individuals and the seizure of

Bitcoins amounting to US$1 million as well as drugs, gold and silver.

Theoretical frameworks

Several criminological theories have been used to explain different types of cybercrimes. Said theories include routine activities (Bossler and Holt, 2009; Reyns, 2013) social learning theory (Hawdon et al., 2019; Holt et al., 2010), situational crime prevention (Mayhew et al., 1976; Felson and Clarke, 1998) and general strain theory (Patchin and Hinduja, 2011). Situational crime prevention offers an opportunity to think about a crime in sequential phases. The concept of "crime scripts" (Cornish, 1994) is helpful here, describing the essential stages of criminal activity. These "scripts" lay bare the modus operandi of offenders involved in different types of criminal activities. Hancock and Laycock (2010) employ "crime scripts" to investigate human trafficking, distinguishing functions, categories, and actions, as well as by stressing the pinch-points for interventions. Lavorgna (2014) applies Hancock and Laycock's (2010) model of "crime scripts" to online wildlife trafficking, identifying key players operating on websites and other social media platforms. The use of "script" categories helps identify the crime, the criminal's lifestyle and their online network.

The crux of strain theory, on the other hand, suggests that crime is the result of the differential access to legitimate, institutionally defined means to achieve culturally defined goals – notably, the "American Dream" or, simply put, monetary success (Merton, 1938). Social structures and institutionally determined means do not always provide equal opportunities for all members of society, leading to deviant adaptations and, inevitably, criminal behaviour. Structural strain theory outlines five responses to such strain: ritualism; conformity; innovation; retreatism; and rebellion. Revised versions of strain theory have led to multiple vistas of cybercrime inquiry. Drawing upon Durkheim's (1897/1987) discussion of anomie and Merton's (1938) strain theory, Messner and Rosenfeld's institutional anomie theory (IAT) (2013) explores online crimes as a means of achieving the "American Dream" based on four values: achievement at any cost; intensive individualism; universalism (everyone should succeed); and the fetishism of money.

Dearden et al. (2021) apply Messner and Rosenfeld's (2013) institutional anomie theory (IAT) to a variety of cybercrimes, some of which include online environmental crimes and the illegal wildlife trade. The authors argue that the economic goals associated with the digitalisation of wildlife trafficking lead to higher rates of cybercriminal behaviour. Moreover, the authors discovered that IAT correlates with self-reported online offending behaviour, serving as a significant predictor of online environmental crimes. Consistent with the original notions of strain theory and anomie, criminals engage in online environmental crimes because they prioritise financial and market success at all costs. Noteworthy predictors of online environmental crimes include gender, race, age, and "dark web" use.

Addressing online environmental crimes

There are many challenges with regulating online environmental crimes – chief among these is under-resourcing of law enforcement, which leads to weak regulation of the cyber sphere. This is especially dire for developing countries that are the source of these illegal wildlife items. The international community, however, is slowly addressing the low prioritisation of online environmental crimes – for example, the European Multidisciplinary Platform Against Criminal Threats (EMPACT) is a security initiative driven by European Union Member States and has made the decision to include environmental crime as one of its ten priorities. Relatedly, the Coalition to End Wildlife Trafficking Online is a partnership with tech companies to tackle various cybercrimes.

Anonymity seems to be an insurmountable problem, too. "Tor", short for The Onion Router, is one example of an anonymous network which facilitates anonymous communication over a wide area network and conceals the names of the parties that are communicating as well as the data through layers of encryption. Tor is a free, open-source software for enabling anonymous communication and directing Internet traffic through overlay networks. It conceals users' location and information from anyone performing network surveillance or traffic analysis. The UK Parliamentary Office of Science and Technology has declared that banning anonymity systems such as Tor is not a policy option in the UK and that it is completely legal. As such, this encourages semi-anonymous trading and selling of wildlife online. Some conservationists reveal that the illegal wildlife trade has fully migrated to the "dark web", as is evidenced in "fishing trips" – that is, where motivated sellers place want adverts for certain items, hoping to lure potential buyers. Other partnerships like the EU Wildlife Cybercrime Project and EnviCrimeNet have started to build capacity for cyber investigations among law enforcement, adding cyber and financial investigations to environmental crime investigations, an approach used by the Basel Institute.

Harrison et al. (2016) assert that the majority of illegal products sold on the "dark web" are "by-catch" products, which refers to items sold for other reasons, but that contain illegal wildlife products. For example, on Alphabay market, sellers promoted hallucinogenic cacti to the drug market, and counterfeit Chanel bags produced from reptile skin, both of which contained "by-catch" products (Wright, 2019). Alphabay has also been notorious for the illegal trade of rhino horn and elephant ivory, in conjunction with illicit narcotics and illegally mined diamonds.

Wright (2019) explores the economic geography of seller and buyer locations on the "dark web", arguing that sellers are usually located geographically close to buyers in consumer countries. This means that the flow of sales on the "dark web" is typically in-country, or in-continent, rather than international. "Dark web" markets were also predominantly a European and North American phenomenon, with illegal dealers and sellers expanding the range of code words to make it difficult to detect online environmental crimes. Yu and Jia (2015) reveal that code words used to describe products evolve to evade online regulation. For example, in 2012, the only code words for ivory on Chinese websites were "象牙, XY, xiangya". However, by 2014, there were 22 code words for ivory, including terms for ivory such as "African materials, yellow materials, white plastic, and jelly". In March 2014, TRAFFIC turned its attention to social media's code words for online environmental crimes. In complete contrast to posted advertisements on regular websites, social media platforms such as Facebook and Instagram allow sellers to reach out to potential customers. Consider, for example, the use of "agents" by social media sellers. "Agents" receive a financial incentive for reposting information about illegal wildlife products onto their own social media platforms, protecting the anonymity of the seller and extending what is referred to as a discreet Internet circle comprised of sellers, "agents" and buyers. In fact, in 2015, Facebook and Instagram accounted for almost 80 per cent of the online wildlife trafficking (Krishnasamy and Stoner, 2016). Unequivocally, social media has empowered sellers to manage their followers regularly and block those who never buy products, post updates or those suspected of being law enforcement personnel.

Yet another challenge associated with online environmental crimes is the distinction between fake and genuine wildlife products. TRAFFIC personnel examine written product descriptions and images posted online, especially those advertising items such as ivory, rhino horn, hawksbill shell, and pangolin scale. Oftentimes, it is difficult to distinguish "knockoff" from genuine products, so personnel have to rely exclusively on the seller's detailed description for informed judgement. In many cases, the seller may use images which might not represent the products advertised online, deceiving both consumers and law enforcement personnel. Such false advertisements end up being included within the statistics as representing illegal wildlife products, skewing the data. For example, many of the terms associated with online wildlife trafficking are polysemic – in other words, the data may lead to false positives when monitoring websites: ivory can refer wildlife products, but has also been a code word for drugs and pornography (Harrison et al., 2016).

Emerging topics and issues

One of the emerging topics and issues related to online environmental crimes is the use of industry-led approaches for detection and prevention. Since 2018, more than 11.6 million advertisements for illegal wildlife goods have been removed or blocked from online platforms, as a direct result of the partnership between the International Fund for Animals Welfare (IFAW), World Wide Fund for Nature (WWF) and TRAFFIC and the Coalition to End Wildlife Trafficking Online. As of today, the coalition is comprised of 47 companies including Facebook, Google, Etsy,

Microsoft, Poshmark, eBay, and even TikTok (Looby, 2021).

Despite such efforts, online environmental crimes show no sign of abating: IFAW's recent report illustrates that 20 per cent of the advertisements online are for live exotic pets, while other species such as pangolins are trafficked online for their scales in traditional medicine, or leather goods, like purses, belts and boots (IFAW, 2022). With government agencies lacking the capacity or the resources to monitor all online transactions and physical shipments of wildlife, the trade continues. One industry-led approach is the use of wildlife experts, who serve as "cyber spotters" to help identify the correct species online and what that animal's protection status is. "Cyber spotters" scour the Internet, using keywords to detect the illegal trade in wildlife. This information is then shared with coalition members and the keywords are fed into algorithms so they can be identified again. Education and awareness campaigns are also used by industry: companies utilise pop-up ads to deter purchases. If a potential buyer of ivory searches for a keyword that might lead to authentic ivory products, that person will see a pop-up ad which lists protections and prohibitions in place for elephants. More automated methods are being explored to detect illegal wildlife posts, leading to new algorithms with new keywords. IFAW and Baidu, China's biggest search engine, have taken proactive measures, creating an artificial intelligence tool that identifies wildlife products online.

Another industry-led practice is leveraging national legislation to combat online environmental crimes. The United States is an instructive example here: through the Lacey Act, American law enforcement personnel and lawyers can prosecute online sellers based on violations of foreign laws when there is a connection to the US. In December 2020, the Department of Justice extradited a Chinese citizen from Malaysia to the US for financing a turtle-trafficking ring that smuggled 1,500 protected turtles out of the US (Looby, 2021). The aim is to arrest not only traffickers, but also the leaders of the syndicates.

Conclusion

The role of the Internet in facilitating the sale of illegally sourced wildlife products is a major techno-social development. The online trade in illegally sourced wildlife represents a hybrid of online and offline activities and it poses extremely complex problems for prevention and prosecution. Responding to this phenomenon requires a range of skill sets and innovative strategies. For example, research and enforcement teams have increasingly turned to exploring the potential use of artificial intelligence (AI), including the use of algorithms, to search for online content that contains information about the illegal wildlife trade.

Most importantly, however, wildlife conservation should not be politicised insofar as select countries are stigmatised for cultural and traditional use of wildlife products. China has borne the brunt of international campaigns – some of which have led to rising rates of anti-Asian racism. Education and awareness, again, are key here because online wildlife trafficking takes place in other countries like the US and Japan but does not get as much media attention. Online environmental crimes are truly international in nature and a global problem.

Delon Omrow

Further reading

Demeau, E., Vargas, M. and Jeffrey, K. (2019). Wildlife trafficking on the Internet: A virtual market similar to drug trafficking? *Revista Criminalidad*, *61*(2), 101–112.

Harrison, J.R., Roberts, D.L. and Hernandez-Castro, J. (2016). Assessing the extent and nature of wildlife trade on the dark web. *Conservation Biology*, *30*(4), 900–904.

IFAW. (2022). *Annual Report, July 2021–June 2022*. IFAW.

Stoett, P. and Omrow, D. (2021). *Spheres of Transnational Ecoviolence: Environmental Crime, Human Security, and Justice*. Palgrave Macmillan.

Wright, J. (2019). *Darknet Usage in the Illegal Wildlife Trade: Tools and Guidance*. Oxford University Press.

References

Bossler, A. and Holt, T. (2009). On-line activities, guardianship, and malware infection: An examination of routine activities theory. *International Journal of Cyber Criminology*, *3*(1), 400–420.

Cornish, D.B. (1994). The procedural analysis of offending and its relevance for situational prevention. In R.V. Clarke (ed.), *Crime Prevention Studies* (pp. 151–196). Criminal Justice Press.

Dearden, T., Parti, K. and Hawdon, J. (2021). Institutional anomie theory and cybercrime:

Cybercrime and the American Dream. *Journal of Contemporary Criminal Justice*, *1*, 1–22.
Demeau, E., Vargas, M. and Jeffrey, K. (2019). Wildlife trafficking on the Internet: A virtual market similar to drug trafficking? *Revista Criminalidad*, *61*(2), 101–112.
Durkheim, E. (1987). *Suicide: A Study in Sociology* (J.A. Spaulding and G. Simpson, Trans.). Routledge and Kegan Paul (original work published 1897).
Felson, M. and Clarke, R.V. (1998). *Opportunity Makes the Thief: Practical Theory for Crime Prevention*. Police Research Series, Paper 98. Home Office.
Hancock, G. and Laycock, G. (2010). Organised crime and crime scripts: Prospects for disruption. In K. Bullock, R.V. Clarke and N. Tilley (eds), *Situational Prevention of Organised Crimes* (pp. 172–193). Willan Publishing.
Harrison, J.R., Roberts, D.L. and Hernandez-Castro, J. (2016). Assessing the extent and nature of wildlife trade on the dark web. *Conservation Biology*, *30*(4), 900–904.
Hawdon, J., Bernatzky, C. and Costello, M. (2019). Cyber-routines, political attitudes, and exposure to violence-advocating online extremism. *Social Forces*, *98*(1), 329–354.
Holt, T.J., Burrus, G.W. and Bossler, A.M. (2010). Social learning and cyber-deviance: Examining the importance of a full social learning model in the virtual world. *Journal of Crime and Justice*, *33*(2), 31–61.
IFAW. (2022). *Annual Report, July 2021–June 2022*. IFAW.
Krishnasamy, K. and Stoner, S. (2016). *TRADING FACES: A Rapid Assessment on the Use of Facebook to Trade Wildlife in Peninsular Malaysia*. http://www.traf cj.org/publication/16_Trading_Faces.pdf
Lavorgna, A. (2014). Internet-mediated drug trafficking: Towards a better understanding of new criminal dynamics. *Trends in Organized Crime*, *17*(4), 250–270.
Lavorgna, A. (2016). How the use of the internet is affecting drug trafficking practices. In European Monitoring Centre for Drugs and Drug Addiction (ed.), *The Internet and Drug Markets*. Publications Office of the European Union.
Looby, C. (2021, December 9). In wildlife traffickers, the internet finds a cancel target everyone agrees on. Mongabay. https://news.mongabay.com/2021/12/in-wildlife-traffickers-the-internet-finds-a-cancel-target-everyone-agrees-on/.
Mayhew, P., Clarke, R.V., Sturman, A. and Hough, M. (1976). *Crime as Opportunity*. Home Office Research Study no. 34. Her Majesty's Stationery Office.
Merton, R.K. (1938). Social structure and anomie. *American Sociological Review*, *3*, 672–682.
Messner, S.F. and Rosenfeld, R. (2013). *Crime and the American Dream* (5th ed.). Wadsworth (original work published 1994).
O'Neill, M.E. (2000). Old crimes in new bottles: Sanctioning cybercrime. *George Masson Law Review*, *9*(2), 237–288.
Pastor-Satorras, R. and Vespignani, A. (2007). *Evolution and Structure of the Internet: A Statistical Physics Approach*. Cambridge University Press.
Patchin, J.W. and Hinduja, S. (2011). Traditional and non-traditional bullying among youth: A test of general strain theory. *Youth & Society*, *43*(2), 727–751.
Reyns, B.W. (2013). Online routines and identity theft victimization: Further expanding routine activity theory beyond direct-contact offenses. *Journal of Research in Crime and Delinquency*, *50*(2), 216–238.
Sullivan, B. (2016). *Illegal Wildlife Traders Aren't Welcome on the Dark Web*. http://motherboard.vice.com/read/illegal-wildlife-traders-arent-welcome-on-the-dark-web.
Whitehead, D., Cowell, C., Lavorgna, A. and Middleton, S. (2021). Countering plant crime online: Cross-disciplinary collaboration in the FloraGuard study. *Forensic Science International: Animals and Environments*, *1*. doi: https://doi.org/10.1016/j.fsiae.2021.100007.
Wright, J. (2019). *Darknet Usage in the Illegal Wildlife Trade: Tools and Guidance*. Oxford University Press.
Yu, X. and Jia, W. (2015). *Moving Targets: Tracking Online Sales of Illegal Wildlife Products in China*. http://static1.1.sqspcdn.com/static/f/157301/26245505/1432122394320/China-monitoring-report.pdf?token=Q8AuzEmc9lBrlrqSNkYIn6E%2FseI%3D.

DELON OMROW

PART V

ENVIRONMENTAL INJUSTICE AND VICTIMISATION

30. Conservation colonisation

Introduction

Conservation colonisation refers to the process(es) in which Indigenous peoples are displaced from their lands or places of cultural importance for the sake of conservation. This experience is not limited to just the immediate act of removal but can include the broader social and systemic dimensions that contributed to that removal, along with the aftermath of dispossession. To these ends, conservation colonisation expands on the definition of colonisation – the action or process of settling among and establishing control over the Indigenous people of the area – and situates it within a conservation context. Conservation colonisation can serve as the umbrella for conservation actions such as fortress conservation, militarised conservation, or conservation-related displacement. When we contextualise this within the broader space of human–environment relationships, we can begin to see a dimension of conservation which continues to exploit and disvalue Indigenous peoples, knowledge, and lands. Scholarship on the linkages between conservation and colonisation is well established by Indigenous authors. However, further research on the generational, both social and ecological, impacts of conservation-related colonisation is needed.

The practice of conservation colonisation

Conservation colonisation is a practice that mirrors that of the settler colonial tendency of the Euro-Western powers of North America, Canada, and Western Europe. This shared history of conservation and colonialism encompasses the land dispossession of Indigenous peoples (e.g., Wilson, 2021; Shahabuddin & Bhamidipati, 2014); government-sanctioned removal of Indigenous rights to natural resources and territories (e.g., Lima et al., 2020; Johnstone, 2011); Othering of Indigenous peoples (e.g., Weldemichel, 2020; van Holstein & Head, 2018); and the murder of Indigenous environmental defenders (e.g., Zeng et al., 2022; Scheidel et al., 2020), among others. Conservation colonisation has allowed for social inequities that marginalise Indigenous people to be strengthened and reinforced (Abraham, 2019), despite notions of good intentions (Eichler & Baumeister, 2021).

For present purposes, this entry emphasises the role that conservation has had in enabling settler colonialism. Settler colonialism reflects an ongoing power system that normalises the oppression of Indigenous peoples and the exploitation of lands and resources (Cox, 2017). Settler colonialism is encompassed by interlocking dimensions of oppression that uniquely affect Indigenous peoples (Cox, 2017). This entry delves into these dimensions of conservation colonisation and how and why it has manifested to become a prominent issue for both biodiversity and Indigenous peoples.

Conservation colonisation has culminated in the protection of Indigenous territories for non-Indigenous and/or non-local people. This has resulted in the extraction of Indigenous knowledge, resources, and lives so as to appease the ideals of non-Indigenous Euro-Western conservation practitioners, often at the expense of Indigenous communities (Lee, 2021). As such, the legacies of non-Indigenous Western conservation are often intertwined with the legacies of colonialism, ultimately deepening local inequality and reinforcing global injustices (Collins et al., 2021). When we contextualise further, we can see that the ostensibly systematic integration of colonialism within conservation spaces has allowed for the systemic erasure and exploitation of Indigenous peoples.

Presently, conservation has transcended beyond being simply an alleviation of biodiversity loss and a form of natural resource preservation. Conservation has the opportunity to support the lives and livelihoods of Indigenous and local peoples (Hoffman et al., 2021; Nikolakis & Hotte, 2022), while simultaneously furthering biodiversity protection efforts (Ens et al., 2016; Dawson et al., 2021) Modern conservation practices that continue to perpetuate these neocolonial ideals pose a human rights (Gavin et al., 2015; Larsen et al., 2020); development (Jackson, 1993; Mukoni, 2013); sustainability (Niesenbaum, 2019; Jones, 2021); environmental (Eichler & Baumeister, 2018); gendered (Walker, 2001; James et al., 2021); and racialised (Rudd et al., 2021; Kepe, 2009) issue. Recognition of these issues reflects a need for restructuring modes of conservation that are extractive, to more adequately account for the socio-ecological, socio-political, and socio-ecological impacts of conservation on local and Indigenous people.

Deploying the existing conservation literature within a framework of decoloniality is not possible within an inherently colonial system. What is meant by this is that *non-Indigneous Western conservation is a derivative of colonialism*. The establishment of conservation was for the continuation of natural resource extraction by and for white, usually wealthy, non-Indigenous people (Duffy, 2022; Taylor, 2016). This means that conservation initiatives are generally going to have an underlying goal that directly *benefits* non-Indigenous communities while simultaneously directly *harming* Indigenous ones. This bifurcated colonial conservation is thus based on ingrained and nurtured systems of racialisation, prejudice, and sexism which dictate who can benefit from natural resource use and who is harmed by the other's consumption. In sum, due to the injustice that is foundational to the colonial framework of conservation, decolonisation is not possible unless we start to dismantle these systems of harm.

Types of conservationism

Two approaches to conservation are particularly important to consider in understanding the dynamics of conservation colonisation: neoliberal conservation and green violence.

Neoliberal conservation

Neoliberal conservation arose as a means of addressing poverty and economic development within conservation projects (Fletcher, 2020). Neoliberal conservation (1) often consists of distinct power dimensions that are aligned with both conservation and neoliberal-economic values, (2) often has a strong reliance on extravagance to produce a product for the market system, often to the social detriment of local communities, and (3) establishes an unequal distribution of social impacts which leverages pre-existing social inequities (Holmes & Cavanagh, 2016).

In theory, neoliberal conservation sits at the intersection of neoliberalism (with its stress on markets, profitability, and market-based incentives) and community-based conservation (with an emphasis on values pertaining to land and species preservation and conservation) to address shared socio-political and socio-economic dynamics (McCarthy, 2005). Neoliberal conservation thus introduces a 'win–win' scenario for conservation which can fulfil the interests of big international non-governmental organisations, conservationists, and donors (land and species protection and restricted uses) while also appearing to address the needs of local communities (social developmental concerns) (Büscher & Dressler, 2012).

Assessments of neoliberal conservation projects, however, indicate that the practice is rarely successful in implementing intended outcomes (Fletcher, 2020). In essence, under the guise of neoliberal conservation, local communities, by conserving wildlife, are conserving the ideals and practices of external, largely non-Indigenous and Western, communities. For example, protected areas or national parks may protect species, which only benefits tourists, and often substantially limits or prohibits local people from using the park territories (e.g., Dahlberg et al., 2010) or from being able to engage in subsistence hunting (e.g., LaRocco, 2020; Lynch & Genco, 2022). This discrepancy in who can reap the benefits of conservation, as well as who is negatively impacted by conservation, has appeared as an unintended outcome of neoliberal conservation, which disproportionately negatively impacts local and Indigenous communities. This relates to the practices of conservation which concurrently dehumanise Indigenous people and advance the conservation and political interests of the state and investors (Loperena, 2016).

Neoliberal conservation has routinely negatively impacted Indigenous peoples, with the sole intent of uplifting the ideals, material interests, and aspirations of Western individuals, communities, and organisations (Musavengane & Leonard, 2019). This can extend to the neocolonial motive of land and resource control which fundamentally is structured to exploit Indigenous people, territories, and resources (Domínguez & Luoma, 2022; Crowe & Shryer, 1995). Singh and van Houtum (2002) further suggest that these territorial dimensions of conversation illuminate a greater issue regarding land control and land access which are complicated because of neoliberal practices. For example, Wieckardt et al. (2022) describe the case of ecotourism ventures' ability to legitimise the activities and strengthen the power of nature conservation organisations to secure protected areas with regard to the Green Life Project in Sumatra, Indonesia. This is further illustrated through the use of conservation easements in the United States, which are undergirded by stark racial supremacy projects but safeguarded by nature preservation claims (see Van Sant et al., 2020). Seen in tandem with the capitalist and imperialist motivations of Western colonial powers, neoliberal conservation has the potential to exacerbate social inequities in areas of conservation interest (e.g., Segi, 2014). The goals of Western conservation have often continued to perpetuate neoliberal fortress conservation which results in the displacement and exclusion of Indigenous peoples.

However, for as long as there has been colonialism, there has been resistance against colonial powers. Indigenous peoples have been resistant to colonial powers in relation to conservation matters as well (see Asiyanbi et al., 2019; Njau, 2014; Beinart & Hughes, 2007). For instance, in framing illegal hunting and fishing as resisting neocolonialism, Nils Peterson et al. (2017) argue that the introduction of neoliberal conservation has actually increased the frequency of wildlife crime activities insofar as residents' traditional subsistence and recreational activities are socially reconstructed as crimes, and yet they continue their traditional practices nonetheless. This resistance to neoliberal conservation has allowed for many conservation projects to not only not meet their preservation goals, but also exacerbate social conflicts.

Green violence

Green violence, or the deployment of violence for the sake of environmental and biodiversity protection, can broadly be considered a delayed effect of settler colonialism (Bersaglio, 2018). However, green violence can also ultimately be used as a tool to establish control over areas of conservation interest and the communities within those areas (Woods, 2019). For instance, the specific targeting of green violence engaged in by Indigenous peoples (e.g., 'environmental defenders') can result in greater incarceration rates (Paudel et al., 2020); increased disenfranchisement (Marler, 2013); land grabbing (Holmes, 2014; Benjaminsen & Bryceson, 2012); as well as international justification for violence towards people who commit, or are suspected of committing conservation-related offences (Witter & Satterfield, 2019; Bocarejo & Ojeda, 2016). In short, institutional responses to this form of green violence have essentially authorised the destruction of the lives and livelihoods of individuals who share spaces with the species or areas of conservation interest (Mushonga & Matose, 2020).

On the other hand, one of the most systemic forms of elite violence, and arguably the most debilitating, is the Othering of Indigenous and non-white people *for the sake of* conservation. Othering is upheld in conservation spaces using 'white-authorized green violence' (Marijnen & Verweijen, 2016). This type of violence is essentially justified by equating Indigenous people as a threat to conservation interests (see Büscher & Ramutsindela, 2016). This process of Othering has unethical and deadly consequences, including the authorisation of and legitimacy given to green militarisation (Massé, Lunstrum, & Holterman, 2018; Annecke & Masubelele, 2016); violent anti-poaching policies (Mogomotsi & Madigele, 2017; de Jong & Butt, 2023); displacement (Murdock, 2021; Milgroom & Claeys, 2024); and the systematic criminalisation of Indigenous people and their practices (Snook et al., 2020; Rodríguez et al., 2023). Conservation-related violence of this sort often 'alienates people within and around protected areas and turn[s] them against wildlife conservation' (Massé, 2020). This shift in othering has made the Western conservation priorities incompatible with the priorities of Indigenous peoples. Indeed, human rights atrocities are no stranger to many leading conservation organisations (see Ramutsindela et al., 2022) and thus building relationships that are grounded in militarised security will be no small feat.

The perpetuation of elite-driven violence globally has also garnered feelings of distrust and contempt towards conservation practice and conservation practitioners (e.g., Duan et al., 2022). This violence leaves lasting effects. As such, one of the prominent questions about green violence is the degree to which violence connected to conservation ought to be considered as 'green violence' at all (Verweijen, 2020). For example, Lunstrum (2017) studied the types of violence that Facebook users advocated against rhino poachers, and found that an overwhelming number of users, predominantly non-African users, advocated the killing of suspected poachers. Acts of violence that occur in the digital world (Hammond et al., 2022; Büscher, 2016) or that result in direct legitimisation for violence to occur against those perceived as threats to conservation (Trogisch & Fletcher, 2022; Howson, 2018) warrant further critical investigation. Green violence within the conservation sector is linked to a concept of conservation which is acting to incite fear in relation to communities who threaten the Western ideal of pristine wilderness (e.g., Vinyeta, 2022; Chatterjee, 2019). Further, green violence legitimises acts of violence against those who threaten these ideals of what a natural space or what conservation is 'supposed' to look like.

Conclusion

When we consider the global experience of conservation colonisation, we see hotspots of colonial practices occurring in the non-Western world, such as the use of Nepalese military forces to enact land securitisation in areas of conservation interest (Dongol & Neumann, 2021); the displacement of Indigenous communities for the establishment of protected areas in Southern Africa post-World War II (Munro, 2021); and the selective eviction of Indigenous communities in Nicaragua in areas of conservation interest (Sylvander, 2021). Colonial conservation practices also continue to occur in the Western nations, with some historical examples including the banning of the subsistence lifestyle of the Inuit of Nunavik by state policies (Gombay, 2014), and the extermination of bison in order to inflict violence against American Indigenous peoples in the North American prairies (Mamers, 2019).

Globally, therefore, there is still a need to prioritise Indigenous voices within the conservation sector worldwide (see Reyes-García & Benyei, 2019). The majority of studies demonstrating positive outcomes for both conservation and well-being come from cases where Indigenous peoples and local communities have a central role in the project (Dawson et al., 2021). The emphasis on centring Indigenous peoples and local communities in conservation projects allows for a deeper conversation on how to undo colonial harm in conservation spaces. Conservation decolonisation necessitates a break from the Western conception of wildlife conservation in favour of centring local, formerly colonised community realities and experiences.

Conservation colonisation has essentially allowed non-Indigenous and Western power elites to harm local and Indigenous communities and uphold the prerogatives of settler-colonialists (van Holstein & Head, 2018). Western conservation is likewise frequently dependent on the upholding of colonial structures in order to operate, with terrible social and ecological ramifications. Instituting a decolonial agenda to conservation which encompasses both conservation policy and practice is necessary if we are to rectify the harm that has resulted from conservation colonisation. Further research is therefore needed on the socio-ecological effects of conservation colonisation; strategies for conservation decolonisation which are grounded in the needs, experiences, and voices of local and Indigenous peoples; and how conservation science can be utilised as a tool to establish anti-colonial, intersectional, and consensual partnerships with local and Indigenous peoples.

Aalayna R. Green

Further reading

Adams, W. B., & Mulligan, M. (2012). *Decolonizing Nature: Strategies for Conservation in a Post-Colonial Era*. Routledge.

Apostolopoulou, E., Chatzimentor, A., Maestre-Andrés, S., Requena-i-Mora, M., Pizarro, A., & Bormpoudakis, D. (2021). Reviewing 15 years of research on neoliberal conservation: Towards a decolonial, interdisciplinary, intersectional and community-engaged research agenda. *Geoforum*, *124*, 236–256.

Brittain, S., Ibbett, H., de Lange, E., Dorward, L., Hoyte, S., Marino, A., Milner-Gulland, E. J., Newth, J., Rakotonarivo, S., Veríssimo, D., & Lewis, J. (2020). Ethical considerations when conservation research involves people. *Conservation Biology*, *34*(4), 925–933. https://doi.org/10.1111/cobi.13464.

Collins, Y. A., Macguire-Rajpaul, V., Krauss, J. E., Asiyanbi, A., Jiminez, A., Mabele, M. B., & Alexander-Owen, M. (2021). Plotting the coloniality of conservation. *Journal of Political Ecology*, *28*(1), 968–989.

Domínguez, L., & Luoma, C. (2020). Decolonising conservation policy: How colonial land and conservation ideologies persist and perpetuate Indigenous injustices at the expense of the environment. *Land*, *9*(3), 65. https://doi.org/10.3390/land9030065.

Eichler, L., & Baumeister, D. (2021). Settler colonialism and the US conservation movement:

Contesting histories, indigenizing futures. *Ethics, Policy & Environment*, *24*(3), 209–234.
Fletcher, M. S., Hamilton, R., Dressler, W., & Palmer, L. (2021). Indigenous knowledge and the shackles of wilderness. *Proceedings of the National Academy of Sciences*, *118*(40), e2022218118.
Garnett, S. T., Burgess, N. D., Fa, J. E., Fernández-Llamazares, Á, Molnár, Z., Robinson, C. J. … & Leiper, I. (2018). A spatial overview of the global importance of Indigenous lands for conservation. *Nature Sustainability*, *1*(7), 369–374.
Gavin, M. C., McCarter, J., Mead, A., Berkes, F., Stepp, J. R., Peterson, D., & Tang, R. (2015). Defining biocultural approaches to conservation. *Trends in Ecology & Evolution*, *30*(3), 140–145.
Jackson, C. (1993). Environmentalisms and gender interests in the Third World. *Development and Change*, *24*, 649–677.
Kashwan, P. V., Duffy, R., Massé, F., Asiyanbi, A. P., & Marijnen, E. (2021). From racialized neoliberal global conservation to an inclusive and regenerative conservation. *Environment: Science and Policy for Sustainable Development*, *63*(4), 4–19.
Larsen, P. B., Le Billon, P., Menton, M., Aylwin, J., Balsiger, J., Boyd, D., First, M., Lambrick, F., Santos, C., Storey, H., & Wilding, S. (2020). Understanding and responding to the environmental human rights defenders crisis: The case for conservation action. *Conservation Letters*, *14*, e12777.
Marijnen, E., & Verweijen, J. (2016). Selling green militarization: The discursive (re)production of militarized conservation in the Virunga National Park, Democratic Republic of the Congo. *Geoforum*, *75*, 274–285.
Mollett, S., & Kepe, T. (Eds.). (2018). *Land Rights, Biodiversity Conservation and Justice: Rethinking Parks and People* (1st ed.). Routledge. https://doi.org/10.4324/9781315439488.
Mukoni, M. (2013). Traditional gender roles of men and women in natural resource conservation among the Vhavenda People in Zimbabwe: Implications for sustainable development. *International Journal of Humanities and Social Science*, *5*(4), 1.
Mullenbach, L. E., Breyer, B., Cutts, B. B., Rivers L., III, & Larson, L. R. (2022). An antiracist, anticolonial agenda for urban greening and conservation. *Conservation Letters*, e12889.
Ramutsindela, M., Matose, F., & Mushonga, T. (Eds.). (2022). In M. Ramutsindela, F. Matose and
T. Mushonga, (eds.), *The Violence of Conservation in Africa: State Militarization and Alternatives*. Edward Elgar Publishing.
Rudd, L. F., Allred, S., Bright Ross, J. G., Hare, D., Nkomo, M. N., Shanker, K., & Dávalos, A. (2021). Overcoming racism in the twin spheres of conservation science and practice. *Proceedings of the Royal Society B*, *288*(1962), 20211871.
Trisos, C. H., Auerbach, J., & Katti, M. (2021). Decoloniality and anti-oppressive practices for a more ethical ecology. *Nature Ecology & Evolution*, *5*(9), 1205–1212.

References

Abraham, T. (2019). Shooting a tiger: Big-game hunting and conservation in colonial India. *Conservation and Society*, *17*(3), 314–315.
Annecke, W., & Masubelele, M. (2016). A review of the impact of militarisation: The case of rhino poaching in Kruger National Park, South Africa. *Conservation and Society*, *14*(3), 195–204.
Asiyanbi, A. P., Ogar, E., & Akintoye, O. A. (2019). Complexities and surprises in local resistance to neoliberal conservation: Multiple environmentalities, technologies of the self and the poststructural geography of local engagement with REDD+. *Political Geography*, *69*, 128–138.
Beinart, W., & Hughes, L. (2007). Resistance to colonial conservation and resource management. In W. Beinart & L. Hughes, (eds.), *Environment and Empire* (pp. 269–288). Oxford University Press.
Benjaminsen, T. A., & Bryceson, I. (2012). Conservation, green/blue grabbing and accumulation by dispossession in Tanzania. *The Journal of Peasant Studies*, *39*(2), 335–355.
Bersaglio, B. (2018). Green violence: Market-driven conservation and the reforeignization of space in Laikipia, Kenya. In S. Mollett and T. Kepe, (eds.), *Land Rights, Biodiversity Conservation and Justice* (pp. 71–88). Routledge.
Bocarejo, D., & Ojeda, D. (2016). Violence and conservation: Beyond unintended consequences and unfortunate coincidences. *Geoforum*, *69*, 176–183.
Büscher, B. (2016). ‘Rhino poaching is out of control!’: Violence, race and the politics of hysteria in online conservation. *Environment and Planning A*, *48*(5), 979–998.
Büscher, B., & Dressler, W. (2012). Commodity conservation: The restructuring of community conservation in South Africa and the Philippines. *Geoforum*, *43*(3), 367–376.
Büscher, B., & Ramutsindela, M. (2016). Green violence: Rhino poaching and the war to save Southern Africa’s peace parks. *African Affairs*, *115*(458), 1–22.
Chatterjee, E. (2019). Green and white nationalism. *The London Review of Books*, 6 September.
Collins, Y. A., Macguire-Rajpaul, V., Krauss, J. E., Asiyanbi, A., Jiminez, A., Mabele, M. B., & Alexander-Owen, M. (2021). Plotting the

coloniality of conservation. *Journal of Political Ecology*, *28*(1), 968–989.
Cox, A. (2017). Settler colonialism. *Literary and Critical Theory*, doi:10.1093/OBO/9780190221911-0029.
Crowe, D. M., & Shryer, J. (1995). Eco-colonialism. *Wildlife Society Bulletin*, 26–30.
Dahlberg, A., Rohde, R., & Sandell, K. (2010). Comparing access rights and ideological legacies in three countries. *Conservation and Society*, *8*(3), 209–224.
Dawson, N., Coolsaet, B., Sterling, E., Loveridge, R., Nicole, D., Wongbusarakum, S., … & Rosado-May, F. (2021). The role of Indigenous peoples and local communities in effective and equitable conservation. *Ecology and Society*, *26*(3), 19. https://doi.org/10.5751/ES-12625-260319.
de Jong, M., & Butt, B. (2023). Conservation violence: Paradoxes of 'making live' and 'letting die' in anti-poaching practices. *Environment and Planning E: Nature and Space*, *6*(4), 2400–2423.
Domínguez, L., & Luoma, C. (2020). Decolonising conservation policy: How colonial land and conservation ideologies persist and perpetuate indigenous injustices at the expense of the environment. *Land*, *9*(3), 65.
Dongol, Y., & Neumann, R. P. (2021). State making through conservation: The case of post-conflict Nepal. *Political Geography*, *85*, 102327.
Duan, W., Su, N., Jiang, Y., & Shen, J. (2022). Impacts of social trust on rural households' attitudes towards ecological conservation: Example of the Giant Panda Nature Reserves in China. *Forests*, *13*(1), 53. https://doi.org/10.3390/f13010053.
Duffy, R. (2022). *Security and Conservation: The Politics of the Illegal Wildlife Trade*. Yale University Press.
Eichler, L., & Baumeister, D. (2021). Settler colonialism and the US conservation movement: Contesting histories, Indigenizing futures. *Ethics, Policy & Environment*, *24*(3), 209–234. https://doi.org/10.1080/21550085.2021.2002623.
Ens, E., Scott, M. L., Rangers, Y. M., Mortiz, C., & Pirzl, R. (2016). Putting Indigenous conservation policy into practice delivers biodiversity and cultural benefits. *Biodiversity and Conservation*, *25*, 2889–2906.
Fletcher, R. (2020). Neoliberal Conservation. *Oxford Research Encyclopedia of Anthropology*. Retrieved 9 Dec. 2024, from https://oxfordre.com/anthropology/view/10.1093/acrefore/9780190854584.001.0001/acrefore-9780190854584-e-300.
Gavin, M. C., McCarter, J., Mead, A., Berkes, F., Stepp, J. R., Peterson, D., & Tang, R. (2015). Defining biocultural approaches to conservation. *Trends in Ecology & Evolution*, *30*(3), 140–145.
Gombay, N. (2014). 'Poaching': What's in a name? Debates about law, property, and protection in the context of settler colonialism. *Geoforum*, *55*, 1–12.
Hammond, N. L., Dickman, A., & Biggs, D. (2022). Examining attention given to threats to elephant conservation on social media. *Conservation Science and Practice*, *4*(10), e12785.
Hoffman, K. M., Dabis, E. L., Wickham, S. B., Schang, K., Johnson, A., Larking, T., Lauriault, P. N., Quynh Le, N., Swerdfager, E., & Trant, A. J. (2021). Conservation of Earth's biodiversity is embedded in Indigenous fire stewardship. *Proceedings of the National Academy of Sciences*, *118*(32), e2105073118.
Holmes, G. (2014). What is a land grab? Exploring green grabs, conservation, and private protected areas in Southern Chile. *The Journal of Peasant Studies*, *41*(4), 547–567.
Holmes, G., & Cavanagh, C. J. (2016). A review of the social impacts of neoliberal conservation: Formations, inequalities, contestations. *Geoforum*, *75*, 199–209.
Howson, P. (2018). Slippery violence in the REDD+ forests of Central Kalimantan, Indonesia. *Conservation and Society*, *16*(2), 136–146.
Jackson, C. (1993). Environmentalisms and gender interests in the Third World. *Development and Change*, *24*, 649–677.
James, R., Gibbs, B., Whitford, L., Leisher, C., Konia, R., & Butt, N. (2021). Conservation and natural resource management: Where are all the women? *Oryx*, 1–8.
Johnstone, N. (2011). Commercialism and conservationism: Law in the forests of Indonesia – from colonization to climate change. *Asia Pacific Journal of Environmental Law*, *14*(1/2), 21–42.
Jones, E. (2021). Capital and control: Neocolonialism through the militarization of African wildlife conservation. *Flux: International Relations Review*, *11*(2), 28–37.
Kepe, T. (2009). Shaped by race: Why 'race' still matters in the challenges facing biodiversity conservation in Africa. *Local Environment*, *14*(9), 871–878.
LaRocco, A. A. (2020). Botswana's hunting ban and the transformation of game-meat cultures, economies and ecologies. *Journal of Southern African Studies*, *46*(4), 723–741.
Larsen, P. B., Le Billon, P., Menton, M., Aylwin, J., Balsiger, J., Boyd, D., First, M., Lambrick, F., Santos, C., Storey, H., & Wilding, S. (2020). Understanding and responding to the environmental human rights defenders crisis: The case

for conservation action. *Conservation Letters*, *14*, e12777.
Lee, E. (2021). Indigenous peoples shift conservation through best practices. *Nature Human Behavior*, *5*, 666–667.
Lima, M., do Vale, J. C. E., de Medeiros Costa, G., dos Santos, R. C., Correia Filho, W. L. F., Gois, G., de Oliveira-Junior, J. F., Teodoro, P. E., Rossi, F. S., & da Silva Junior, C. A. (2020). The forests in the Indigenous lands in Brazil in peril. *Land Use Policy*, *90*, 104258.
Loperena, C. A. (2016). Conservation by racialized dispossession: The making of an eco-destination on Honduras's North Coast. *Geoforum*, *69*, 184–193.
Lunstrum, E. (2017). Feed them to the lions: Conservation violence goes online. *Geoforum*, *79*, 134–143.
Lynch, M., & Genco, L. (2022). Hunting as a crime? A cautionary note concerning how ecological biodiversity and anti-hunting arguments contribute to harms against indigenous people and the rural poor. *Criminological Encounters*, *5*(1), 183–194.
Mamers, D. T. (2019). Human–bison relations as sites of settler colonial violence and decolonial resurgence. *Humanimalia*, *10*(2), 10–41.
Marijnen, E., & Verweijen, J. (2016). Selling green militarization: The discursive (re)production of militarized conservation in the Virunga National Park, Democratic Republic of the Congo. *Geoforum*, *75*, 274–285.
Marler, T. E. (2013). The intersection of a military culture and Indigenous peoples in conservation issues. *Communicative & Integrative Biology*, *6*(6), e26665.
Massé, F. (2020). Conservation law enforcement: Policing protected areas. *Annals of the American Association of Geographers*, *110*(3), 758–773.
Massé, F., Lunstrum, E., & Holterman, D. (2018). Linking green militarization and critical military studies. *Critical Military Studies*, *4*(2), 201–221.
McCarthy, J. (2005). Devolution in the woods: Community forestry as hybrid neoliberalism. *Environment and Planning A*, *37*(6), 995–1014.
Milgroom, J., & Claeys, P. (2024). Participation is not the answer: Epistemic violence and authoritarian practices in conservation-forced displacement. *The Journal of Peasant Studies*, 1–27.
Mogomotsi, G. E., & Madigele, P. K. (2017). Live by the gun, die by the gun: Botswana's 'shoot-to-kill' policy as an anti-poaching strategy. *South African Crime Quarterly*, *60*, 51–59.
Mukoni, M. (2013). Traditional gender roles of men and women in natural resource conservation among the Vhavenda People in Zimbabwe: Implications for sustainable development. *International Journal of Humanities and Social Science*, *5*(4), 1.
Munro, P. (2021). Colonial Wildlife Conservation and National Parks in Sub-Saharan Africa. *Oxford Research Encyclopedia of African History*. Retrieved 9 Dec. 2024, from https://oxfordre.com/africanhistory/view/10.1093/acrefore/9780190277734.001.0001/acrefore-9780190277734-e-195.
Murdock, E. G. (2021). Conserving dispossession? A genealogical account of the colonial roots of western conservation. *Ethics, Policy & Environment*, *24*(3), 235–249.
Musavengane, R., & Leonard, L. (2019). When race and social equity matters in nature conservation in post-apartheid South Africa. *Conservation and Society*, *17*(2), 135–146.
Mushonga, T., & Matose, F. (2020). Dimensions and corollaries of violence in Zimbabwe's protected forests. *Geoforum*, *117*, 216–224.
Niesenbaum, R. A. (2019). The integration of conservation, biodiversity, and sustainability. *Sustainability*, *11*(17), 4676.
Nikolakis, W., & Hotte, N. (2022). Implementing 'ethical space': An exploratory study of Indigenous–conservation partnerships. *Conservation Science and Practice*, *4*(1), e580.
Nils Peterson, M., von Essen, E., Hansen, H. P., & Peterson, T. R. (2017). Illegal fishing and hunting as resistance to neoliberal colonialism. *Crime, Law and Social Change*, *67*, 401–413.
Njau, M. N. (2014). Colonialism and marginalization of African Indigenous knowledge on land and soil conservation in Kenya, a case of the Kikuyu Community. *Asian Journal of Humanities and Social Studies*, *2*(4), 596–603.
Paudel, K., Potter, G. R., & Phelps, J. (2020). Conservation enforcement: Insights from people incarcerated for wildlife crimes in Nepal. *Conservation Science and Practice*, *2*(2), e137.
Ramutsindela, M., Matose, F., & Mushonga, T. (2022). Conservation and violence in Africa. In *The Violence of Conservation in Africa* (pp. 2–21). Edward Elgar Publishing.
Reyes-García, V., & Benyei, P. (2019). Indigenous knowledge for conservation. *Nature Sustainability*, *2*(8), 657–658.
Rodríguez, I., Inturias, M., Masay, E., & Peña, A. (2023). Decolonizing wildfire risk management: Indigenous responses to fire criminalization policies and increasingly flammable forest landscapes in Lomerío, Bolivia. *Environmental Science & Policy*, *147*, 103–115.
Rudd, L. F., Allred, S., Bright Ross, J. G., Hare, D., Nkomo, M. N., Shanker, K., Allen, T., Biggs, D., Dickman, A., Dunaway, M., Ghosh, R., González, N. T., Kepe, T., Mbizah, M. M., Middleton, S. L., Oommen, M. A., Paudel, K., Sillero-Zubiri, C., & Dávalos, A. (2021). Overcoming racism in the twin spheres of conservation science and practice. *Proceedings of the Royal Society B*, *288*(1962), 20211871.
Scheidel, A., Del Bene, D., Liu, J., Navas, G., Mingorría. S., Demaria, F., Avila, S., Roy, B., Ertör, I., Temper, L., & Martínez-Alier, J. (2020). Environmental conflicts and defend-

ers: A global overview. *Global Environmental Change*, *63*, 102104.
Segi, S. (2014). Protecting or pilfering? Neoliberal conservationist marine protected areas in the experience of coastal Granada, the Philippines. *Human Ecology*, *42*, 565–575.
Shahabuddin, G., & Bhamidipati, P. L. (2014). Conservation-induced displacement: Recent perspectives from India. *Environmental Justice*, *7*(5), 122–129.
Singh, J., & Van Houtum, H. (2002). Post-colonial nature conservation in Southern Africa: Same emperors, new clothes? *GeoJournal*, *58*, 253–263.
Snook, J., Cunsolo, A., Borish, D., Furgal, C., Ford, J. D., Shiwak, I. Flowers, C. T. R., & Harper, S. L. (2020). 'We're made criminals just to eat off the land': Colonial wildlife management and repercussions on Inuit well-being. *Sustainability*, *12*(19), 8177.
Sylvander, N. (2021). 'Territorial cleansing' for whom? Indigenous rights, conservation, and state territorialization in the Bosawas Biosphere Reserve, Nicaragua. *Geoforum*, *121*, 23–32.
Taylor, D. E. (2016). *The Rise of the American Conservation Movement: Power, Privilege, and Environmental Protection*. Duke University Press.
Trogisch, L., & Fletcher, R. (2022). Fortress tourism: Exploring dynamics of tourism, security and peace around the Virunga transboundary conservation area. *Journal of Sustainable Tourism*, *30*(2–3), 352–371.
van Holstein, E., & Head, L. (2018). Shifting settler-colonial discourses of environmentalism: Representations of indigeneity and migration in Australian conservation. *Geoforum*, *94*, 41–52.
Van Sant, L., Hardy, D., & Nuse, B. (2020). Conserving what? Conservation easements and environmental justice in the coastal US South. *Human Geography*, *14*(1), 31–44.
Verweijen, J. (2020). A microdynamics approach to geographies of violence: Mapping the kill chain in militarized conservation areas. *Political Geography*, *79*, 102153.
Vinyeta, K. (2022). Under the guise of science: How the US Forest Service deployed settler colonial and racist logics to advance an unsubstantiated fire suppression agenda. *Environmental Sociology*, *8*(2), 134–148.
Walker, B. L. E. (2001). Sisterhood and seine-nets: Engendering development and conservation in Ghana's marine fishery. *Professional Geographer*, *53*(2), 160–177.
Weldemichel, T. G. (2020). Othering pastoralists, state violence, and the remaking of boundaries of Tanzania's militarized wildlife conservation sector. *Antipode*, *52*(5), 1496–1518.
Wieckardt, C. E., Koot, S., & Karimasari, N. (2022). Environmentality, green grabbing, and neoliberal conservation: The ambiguous role of ecotourism in the Green Life privatised nature reserve, Sumatra, Indonesia. *Journal of Sustainable Tourism*, *30*(11), 2614–2630.
Wilson, D. (2021). European colonisation, law, and Indigenous marine dispossession: Historical perspectives on the construction and entrenchment of unequal marine governance. *Maritime Studies*, *20*, 387–407.
Witter, R., & Satterfield, T. (2019). Rhino poaching and the 'slow violence' of conservation-related resettlement in Mozambique's Limpopo National Park. *Geoforum*, *101*, 275–284.
Woods, K. M. (2019). Green territoriality: Conservation as state territorialization in a resource frontier. *Human Ecology*, *47*, 217–232.
Zeng, Y., Twang, F., & Carrasco, L. R. (2022). Threats to land and environmental defenders in nature's last strongholds. *Ambio*, *51*, 269–279.

31. Environmental justice

Introduction

Low-income, communities of colour and indigenous communities face disproportionate burdens of harm from environmental pollution throughout the world. This environmental injustice spawned a movement that acknowledges this unequal burden from environmental harms and seeks to reduce or remove communities from harm. This entry plots an overview of the evolution of the academic study of environmental justice, the grassroots movement that evolved to attract attention and change policy, and the governmental response. It concludes with a discussion of future directions for government action to remedy environmental injustice

In the 1980s in the United States, the academic study and grassroots movement to define, study, and push for policy changes about the unequal burdens of environmental harm borne by low-income, minority, and indigenous communities moved forward in earnest. Today, it continues to push for governmental change to unburden these communities (Ozymy and Jarrell, 2021a). Living near toxic waste dumps, petroleum refineries, chemical plants, and other sources of toxic pollution creates a significant health burden for these communities. These burdens are often the result of governmental policies and the actions by polluters may often be criminal actions with serious health consequences. All these issues remain underappreciated (Pulido, 2017; McDonald and Jones, 2018; Ozymy and Jarrell, 2020). For example, civil and administrative remedies for fenceline communities near industrial sites are often inadequate and fail to remove the chronic harms these communities face from industrial pollution (Stretesky and Lynch, 1999; Pulido, 2015). It is important therefore to explore the possibilities of community and government action to end environmental injustice and reduce or remove harms caused by toxic pollution in these communities.

In our backyard

An estimated 40 per cent of human deaths around the world are attributed to environmental factors, particularly toxic pollution (Bullard et al., 2009). The unfortunate reality in the developed and developing world is that industrialisation has brought about significant environmental harms from pollution. Moreover, the facilities that spew toxic pollution into the air and water and generate toxic waste are disproportionately located in low-income communities of colour and indigenous communities (Mohai and Bryant, 1992; Balazs et al., 2012). From the 1960s onwards it was becoming increasingly apparent just how devastating the world's industrial pollution problem was for so many communities located next to ongoing and legacy sources of industrial pollution.

One of the first cases to draw worldwide media attention to the problem of industrial pollution 'in our backyard' occurred near Niagara Falls, New York. For years the Hooker Chemical Company had used an abandoned canal as a chemical dump and sold the property to the city of Niagara Falls for one dollar, indemnifying themselves from legal liability in the process (Beck, 1979). By the 1950s, the expansion of middle-class housing in the area meant the construction of over 100 homes and a school on the site. By the 1970s, community groups, led by activist Lois Gibbs, brought national attention to the chemical leaching occurring in their basements, parks, and nearby spaces that, in turn, was causing significant birth defects and other health problems. By 1978, a state of emergency was declared, many of the residents were relocated, and the US Congress passed the Comprehensive Environmental Response, Compensation, and Liability Act (CERCLA), also known as the Superfund, to begin identifying and prioritising toxic waste sites across the country for remediation. The Love Canal tragedy brought attention to the health problems caused by living near toxic pollution, although in this instance the community itself was predominately white, particularly amongst homeowners in the area. The broader problem of who was being most affected by these toxic sites subsequently became of great interest to both academics and grassroots social movements by the beginning of the 1980s.

The academic study of environmental justice

Working on a lawsuit with his wife in Houston, Texas, a young sociologist, Robert

Bullard, unearthed a terrible corollary to Love Canal. His research found that 75 per cent of all private landfills and 100 per cent of landfills owned by the City of Houston, as well as roughly 75 per cent of the incinerations, were located in African American neighbourhoods (Dicum, 2006). Not only were toxic sites disproportionately located in minority communities, Bullard found that they were intentionally sited there per governmental policy (Bullard, 2000). Bullard went on to articulate a broader theory of *environmental racism*, where political leaders make intentional choices to burden non-white communities with these environmental harms. He also developed the academic study of environmental justice that focuses on how low-income, communities of colour and indigenous communities face disproportionate environmental harms as a result of structurally racist policies (Bullard, 1990; Pulido, 2017). For his community and academic work history will likely remember Bullard as the 'father' of the environmental justice movement, given that his academic work fused well with his activism and the role he played in the broader social justice movement.

The academic study of environmental justice was further solidified in 1990, when Bunyan Bryant and Paul Mohai organised a conference at the University of Michigan on Race and the Incidence of Environmental Hazards (U.S. EPA, 2024b). The publication of a book from the conference, *Race and the Incidence of Environmental Hazards*, brought significant academic attention to the study of environmental justice and in 1992, the university was the first in the United States to create undergraduate and graduate degrees focusing on environmental justice (University of Michigan, 2024). In 1992, environmental justice as a legitimate field of academic study was further enhanced when the Deep South Center of Environmental Justice was founded at Xavier University by Beverly Wright and a number of community groups (Deep South Center, 2024). In 1994, the Environmental Justice Resource Center (EJRC) was founded at Clark Atlanta University.

By the end of the 1990s, the academic study of environmental justice provided sufficient evidence that environmental injustice existed across the United States and abroad. Settling that question opened up additional room to move research towards related questions of the effects of living near industrial pollution and to study the government's past and ongoing response to injustices. Some of this research takes novel, theoretical approaches to examining structural racism in capitalism that undergirds and thwarts efforts to ameliorate injustices (Pulido, 2015, 2017).

Studies of population health have also taken novel approaches towards examining cancer risks and health inequalities as these pertain to environmental justice (Alvarez and Rosenfeld Evans, 2021). Other studies have shown racial disparities in air pollution exposures (Perlin et al., 1999; Li et al., 2019), water pollution (Balazs et al., 2012), and drinking water violations (McDonald and Jones, 2018). Studies also demonstrate the effect of hydrocarbon exposure (e.g., lead poisoning) on communities vulnerable to environmental injustice (Sansom et al., 2018). Research has begun to extend the field of inquiry towards other, more contemporary environmental harms that may disproportionately affect minority and low-income communities, such as fracking (Zwickl, 2019). And still other scholars have examined the changing nature of social movements and environmental groups, focusing analysis on energy justice issues and how the energy transition (e.g., shift from coal-fired power to solar power) will affect various low-income groups (Mullen and Marsden, 2016; Carley et al., 2021; Memmott et al., 2021), while others are studying residential contamination in environmental justice communities after severe weather events (Horney et al., 2018).

Studies focusing on government responses to environmental justice, with a lens towards improving outcomes, have focused on issues like zoning and land use policies pertaining to hazardous waste storage and elimination (Wilson, 2017). Others have constructed distributive justice schemes for environmental justice communities or legal options for more comprehensive remedies for these communities (such as recognising and compensating them in prosecutions as victims of environmental crime) (Schlosberg, 2013; Youngblood, 2019; Ozymy and Jarrell, 2020). Studies on environmental enforcement show important findings, like disproportionately fewer enforcement actions in Hispanic communities (Konisky and Reenock, 2018), air pollution inequality and state-level policy that ignores less-well-off neighbourhoods (Bullock et al., 2018), or regulatory compliance bias in regard to pollution controls (Konisky and Reenock, 2013).

Studies outside the US include air quality offsets and environmental injustice in South Africa (Langerman, 2019) and the social harms caused by the coal industry in India (Oskarsson and Bedi, 2018). Other studies have examined possible solutions to urban air pollution problems plaguing communities in Belgium (Loopmans et al., 2022). Research into many topics in these areas is fruitful and ongoing, but more is needed, and there is much to learn from how frameworks of environmental justice in the Global South can be applied in the Global North, and vice versa (Natarajan, 2021). The struggles against water privatisation in South Africa and Colombia, and community responses to disasters such as the Bhopal chemical plant disaster in India, also highlight the global–local nature of environmental injustices and responses to these.

The grassroots movement for environmental justice

If Bullard's legal and academic work may be cited as the genesis for the academic study of environmental justice in the United States, the social movement to ameliorate environmental justice can be traced to Warren County, North Carolina. The spark that set off a larger, worldwide movement was a protest held over the siting of a landfill for toxic polychlorinated biphenyls (PCBs). The protest was organised by the group, the Warren County Citizens Concerned (WCCC) (United Church of Christ, 2024). Community reaction had been building for years and by 1978, Dollie Burwell and Ken and Debra Ferruccio instigated community meetings to organise against the landfill (Burwell and Cole, 2007). Some have argued that for her role here and over the decades, Dollie Burwell should be properly acknowledged as the 'mother' of the US environmental justice movement (Berndt, 2017).

In 1983, the US General Accounting Office (GAO) provided empirical support for activist claims, finding that among the hazardous waste sites studied, three out of four were in low-income African American communities (U.S. EPA, 2024b). In 1987, the United Church of Christ Commission on Racial Justice issued a report on toxic waste and race that brought international attention to the environmental justice issue (United Church of Christ, 1987). By 1990, another important step in the organisation of the environmental justice movement was the founding of the Indigenous Environmental Network (IEN) to extend the social movement to the organisation of indigenous communities facing environmental harms (U.S. EPA, 2024a). In 1991, the First National People of Color Environmental Leadership Summit, attended by some 1,100 delegates from all 50 US States as well as Mexico, Puerto Rico, Chile, and the Marshall Islands, adopted a declaration of 17 principles of environmental justice that helped to articulate a broader vision for the movement (Berndt, 2021). The movement continued to build through the 1990s, with broader organisations, such as the National Black Environmental Justice Network, founded in 1999, developing larger strategies and organisation to address health disparities borne by African American communities throughout the United States (National Black Environmental Justice Network, 2024).

In the United States, the social movement for environmental justice became animated in the 1980s, and their political action prompted a series of government responses by the 1990s, including when the US EPA held the first environmental equity workshop, followed by the creation of an Environmental Equity Working group two years later. In 1992, the EPA opened the Office of Environmental Equity; in 1993, the National Environmental Justice Advisory Council (NEJAC) was created; and by 1994, President Bill Clinton signed Executive Order 12898, directing the US EPA to address issues of environmental injustice. A small grants programme was created in 1994 to help environmental justice groups build collaborative partnerships (U.S. EPA, 2024b). In 2010, the EPA established environmental justice as a priority for the agency, Plan EJ 2014, that set up a roadmap to integrate environmental justice issues into EPA decision making, and EJSCREEN in 2015 to help with screening and mapping needs, and finally it chartered a course for the agency's broader programme for environmental justice with EJ 2020 Action Agenda (U.S. EPA, 2024c; 2024d; 2024e). Programmes are now centralised in the EPA's Office of Environmental Justice (U.S. EPA, 2024f).

Conclusion

The US government focused primarily in the 1990s on acknowledging environmental justice as a policy problem and integrating activists into the planning process. However, their strategy for reducing the disparities of health effects caused by pollution has failed on many fronts (Konisky, 2016; Ozymy and Jarrell, 2021a). Nonetheless, there are a few pathways that present themselves for advancing environmental justice.

One path is to improve the regulatory response to environmental justice issues. For example, during his first term of office President Biden made commitments to move beyond simply integrating stakeholder participation at the EPA to prioritising it within the US Department of Justice. This would represent the further evolution of integrating environmental justice within agencies over the last three decades and a logical extension to prioritise environmental justice communities for regulatory enforcement. However, it is unlikely that Republicans share this commitment and long-term funding for the US EPA and the Department of Justice have been declining in real terms for decades (Ozymy et al., 2021; Ozymy, 2022). Reimagining the government's commitment to environmental justice would mean shifting focus to prioritise known areas of injustice and would require the additional use of criminal enforcement tools against large corporations, which has been historically rare across air, water, hazardous waste, and other environmental media (Ozymy and Jarrell, 2021b; Ozymy and Jarrell, 2021c; Ozymy and Jarrell Ozymy, 2021).

A second path forward is to improve the status of environmental justice communities within the legal system. Environmental crimes are slow to manifest, difficult to prove guilt or liability under the law, and many of these crimes affect environmental justice communities (Adler and Lord, 2010; Jarrell and Ozymy, 2014). The place of crime victims' rights has become more prominent in the United States through an alignment between conservative needs to punish crime and liberal needs to expand civil rights and the movement, which began in the 1980s, has gained significant strength in the last few decades (Cassell, 2005; Beloof, 2007; Cassell and Joffe, 2011). There have been a series of important legal cases integrating the idea of crime victims' rights at the federal level as well, including compensation for harm, and environmental justice communities have been recognised as victims of environmental crimes in US federal court, but have yet to receive restitution (Jarrell and Ozymy, 2014; Ozymy and Jarrell, 2020). Prosecutors could expand this precedent and seek greater integration of environmental justice communities in their criminal case selection, but also in their broader prosecutorial strategy against industrial polluters on behalf of victims. This strategy would go hand in hand with a stronger regulatory response.

The final path ahead may simply be the joining up of a US movement that began with the needs of African Americans and then extended to other low-income, indigenous, and minority groups, with a larger global movement tied to decarbonisation and energy transition needs. Research has already pointed to energy justice groups and energy activism linking broader energy transition to the problems faced by groups disproportionally affected by industrial pollution (Carley et al., 2021; Memmott et al., 2021). Such alliances, while not unproblematic (Konisky, 2016; Russo and Martin, 2020), also prefigure the need for fundamental social change and transformations in the global political economy.

MELISSA JARRELL OZYMY AND JOSHUA OZYMY

Further reading

Bullard, Robert D. (1996). Solid Waste Sites and the Houston Black Community. 53 *Social Inquiry*, 273–288.

Bullard, Robert D., Johnson, Glenn S., and Torres, Angel O. (2009). Addressing Global Poverty, Pollution, and Human Rights. In Robert D. Bullard (ed.), *The Quest for Environmental Justice: Human Rights and the Politics of Pollution* (San Francisco: Sierra Club Books) 279–298.

Burwell, Dollie and Cole, Luke W. (2007). Environmental Justice Comes Full Circle: Warren County Before and After. 1 *Golden Gate Environmental Law Journal*, 9–40.

Jarrell, Melissa L. (2009). Environmental Crime and Injustice: Media Coverage of a Landmark Environmental Crime Case. 6 *Southwest Journal of Criminal Justice*, 25–44.

Konisky, David M. (2016). Environmental Justice Delayed: Failed Promises, but Some Hope for the Future. 58 *Environment: Science and Policy for Sustainable Development*, 4–15.

Natarajan, Usha. (2021). Environmental Justice and the Global South. In Sumada A. Atapattu,

Carmen G. Gonzalez, and Sara L. Seck (eds), *Environmental Justice and Sustainable Development* (Cambridge: Cambridge University Press) 39–57.

Ozymy, Joshua and Jarrell, Melissa L. (2021a). Seizing the Political Moment: How the Environmental Protection Agency Can Reimagine Itself and Its Commitment to Environmental Justice. 14 *Environmental Justice*, 372–382.

United Church of Christ. (1987). *Toxic Wastes and Race: A National Report on the Racial and Socio-Economic Characteristics of Communities with Hazardous Waste Sites* (New York: United Church of Christ).

U.S. EPA. 2024a. Learn About Environmental Justice. Available from: https://www.epa.gov/environmentaljustice/learn-about-environmental-justice

References

Adler, Robert and Lord, Charles. (2010). Environmental Crimes: Raising the Stakes. 59 *The George Washington Law Review*, 781–861.

Alvarez, Camila H. and Rosenfeld Evans, Clare. (2021). Intersectional Environmental Justice and Population Health Inequalities: A Novel Approach. 269 *Social Science & Medicine*, 1.

Balazs, Carolina L., Morello-Frosch, Rachel, Hubbard, Alan E., and Ray, Isha. (2012). Environmental Justice Implications of Arsenic Contamination in California's San Joaquin Valley: A Cross-Sectional, Cluster-Design, Examining Exposure and Compliance in Community Drinking Water Systems. 11 *Environmental Health*, 84–85.

Beck, Eckhart C. (1979). The Love Canal Tragedy. Available from: https://archive.epa.gov/epa/aboutepa/love-canal-tragedy.html

Beloof, Douglas E. (2007). Weighing Crime Victims' Interests in Judicially Crafted Criminal Procedure. 56 *Catholic University Law Review*, 1135.

Berndt, Brooks. (2017). A Case for the Mother of the Environmental Justice Movement: Dollie Burwell. Available from: https://www.ucc.org/pollinator_a_case_for_the_mother_of_the_environmental_justice_movement/

Berndt, Brooks. (2021). 30th Anniversary: The First National People of Color Environmental Leadership Summit. Available from: https://www.ucc.org/30th-anniversary-the-first-national-people-of-color-environmental-leadership-summit/

Bullard, Robert D. (1990). *Dumping in Dixie: Race, Class, and Environmental Quality* (Boulder, CO: Westview Press).

Bullard, Robert D. (2000). *Dumping in Dixie: Race, Class, and Environmental Quality* (London: Routledge).

Bullard, Robert D., Johnson, Glenn S., and Torres, Angel O. (2009). Addressing Global Poverty, Pollution, and Human Rights. In Robert D. Bullard (ed.), *The Quest for Environmental Justice: Human Rights and the Politics of Pollution* (San Francisco: Sierra Club Books), 279–298.

Bullock, Clair, Ard, Kerry, and Saalman, Grace. (2018). Measuring the Relationship between State Environmental Justice Action and Air Pollution Inequality, 1990–2009. 35 *Review of Policy Research*, 466–490.

Burwell, Dollie and Cole, Luke W. (2007). Environmental Justice Comes Full Circle: Warren County Before and After. 1 *Golden Gate Environmental Law Journal*, 9–40.

Carley, Sanya, Engle, Caroline, and Konisky, David. (2021). An Analysis of Energy Justice Programs Across the United States. 152 *Energy Policy*, 1–25.

Cassell, Paul G. (2005). Recognizing Victims in the Federal Rules of Criminal Procedure: Amendments in Light of the Crime Victims' Rights Act. 835 *Brigham Young University Law Review*, 835–925.

Cassell, Paul G. and Joffe, Steven. (2011). The Crime Victims' Expanding Role in a System of Public Prosecution: A Response to the Critics of the Crime Victims' Rights Act. 105 *Northwestern University Law Review*, 164–183.

Deep South Center of Environmental Justice. (2024). Our Story. Available from: https://www.dscej.org/our-story

Dicum, Gregory. (2006). Meet Robert Bullard, the Father of Environmental Justice. Available from: https://grist.org/article/dicum/

Horney, Jennifer A., Casillas, Gaston A., Baker, Erin, Stone, Kahler W., Kirsch, Katie R., Camargo, Krisa, Wade, Terry L., and McDonald, Thomas J. (2018). Comparing Residential Contamination in a Houston Environmental Justice Neighborhood Before and After Hurricane Harvey, 8 *PLoS One*.

Jarrell, Melissa L. and Ozymy, Joshua. (2014). Few and Far Between: Understanding the Role of the Victim in Federal Environmental Crime Cases. *Crime, Law, and Social Change* 61: 563–584.

Konisky, David M. (2016). Environmental Justice Delayed: Failed Promises, but Some Hope for

the Future. 58 *Environment: Science and Policy for Sustainable Development*, 4–15.
Konisky, David M. and Reenock, Christopher. (2013). Compliance Bias and Environmental (In)Justice. 75 *The Journal of Politics*, 506–519.
Konisky, David M. and Reenock, Christopher. (2018). Regulatory Enforcement, Riskscapes, and Environmental Justice. 46 *Policy Studies Journal*, 7–36.
Langerman, Kristy E. (2019). An Environmental Justice Perspective on Air Quality Offsets. 29 *Clean Air Journal*, 88–101.
Li, Zhengyan, Konisky, David M., and Zirogiannis, Nickolaos. (2019). Racial, Ethnic, and Income Disparities in Air Pollution: A Study of Excess Emissions in Texas. 14 *PLoS ONE*.
Loopmans, Maarten, Smits, Linde, and Kenis, Anneleen. (2022). Rethinking Environmental Justice: Capability Building, Public Knowledge, and the Struggle Against Traffic-Related Air Pollution. 40 *Environment and Planning C: Politics and Space*, 705–723.
McDonald, Yolanda J. and Jones, Nicole E. (2018). Drinking Water Violations and Environmental Justice in the United States, 2011–2015. 108 *American Journal of Public Health*, 1401–1407.
Memmott, Trevor, Carley, Sanya, and Konisky, David M. (2021). Who Participates in Energy Activism? Profiling Political Engagement in the United States. 77 *Energy Research & Social Science*, 102095.
Mohai, Paul and Bryant, Bunyan. (1992). Environmental Racism: Reviewing the Evidence. In Bunyan Bryant and Paul Mohai (eds), *Race and the Incidence of Environmental Hazards: A Time for Discourse* (Boulder, CO: Westview Press) 163–176.
Mullen, Caroline and Marsden, Greg. (2016). Mobility Justice in Low Carbon Energy Transitions. 18 *Energy Research & Social Science*, 109–117.
Natarajan, Usha. (2021). Environmental Justice and the Global South. In Sumada A. Atapattu, Carmen Gonzalez, Sara L. Seck (eds), *Environmental Justice and Sustainable Development* (Cambridge: Cambridge University Press) 39–57.
National Black Environmental Justice Network. (2024). Our History. Available from: https://www.nbejn.com/our-history
Oskarsson, Patrik and Bedi, Heather P. (2018). Extracting Environmental Justice: Countering Technical Renditions of Pollution in India's Coal Industry. 5 *The Extractive Industries and Society*, 340–347.
Ozymy, Joshua. (2022). The Persistence of Vision. *The Environmental Forum* May/June, 27–33.
Ozymy, Joshua and Jarrell, Melissa L. (2020). Of Sex Crimes and Fencelines: How Recognition of Environmental Justice Communities as Crime Victims under State and Federal Law Can Help Secure Environmental Justice. 38 *Pace Environmental Law Review*, 109–146.
Ozymy, Joshua and Jarrell, Melissa L. (2021a). Seizing the Political Moment: How the Environmental Protection Agency Can Reimagine Itself and Its Commitment to Environmental Justice. 14 *Environmental Justice*, 372–382.
Ozymy, Joshua and Jarrell, Melissa L. (2021b). Does the Criminal Enforcement of Federal Environmental Law Reduce Crime? The Case of the Resource Conservation and Recovery Act. 11 *Environmental and Earth Law Journal*, 65–88.
Ozymy, Joshua and Jarrell, Melissa L. (2021c). Illegal Discharge: Exploring the History of the Criminal Enforcement of the U.S. Clean Water Act. 32 *Fordham Environmental Law Review*, 195–230.
Ozymy, Joshua and Jarrell Ozymy, Melissa L. (2021). Exploring Charging and Sentencing Patterns in U.S. Clean Air Act Criminal Prosecutions. 61 *Natural Resources Journal*, 225–248.
Ozymy, Joshua, Menard, Bryan, and Jarrell, Melissa L. (2021). Persistence or Partisanship: Exploring the Relationship between Presidential Administrations and Criminal Enforcement by the U.S. Environmental Protection Agency, 1983–2019. 81 *Public Administration Review*, 49–63.
Perlin, Susan A., Sexton, Ken, and Wong, David W.S. (1999). An Examination of Race and Poverty for Populations Living Near Industrial Sources of Air Pollution. 9 *Journal of Exposure Analysis & Environmental Epidemiology*, 29–32.
Pulido, Lauren. (2015). Geographies of Race and Ethnicity I: White Supremacy vs. White Privilege in Environmental Racism Research. 39 *Progress in Human Geography*, 809–817.
Pulido, Lauren. (2017). Geographies of Race and Ethnicity II: Environmental Racism, Racial Capitalism, and State-Sanctioned Violence. 41 *Progress in Human Geography*, 524–533.
Russo, Thomas N. and Martin, Ethan. (2020). Environmental Justice and the Energy Transition: How the Energy Industry Can Do Better. 37 *Climate and Energy*, 17–28.
Sansom, Garrett T., Kirsch, Katie R., Stone, Kahler W., McDonald, Thomas J., and Horney, Jennifer. (2018). Domestic Exposures to Polycyclic Aromatic Hydrocarbons in a Houston, Texas

Environmental Justice Neighborhood. 11 *Environmental Justice*, 183–191.

Schlosberg, David. (2013). Theorising Environmental Justice: The Expanded Sphere of a Discourse. 22 *Environmental Politics*, 37–55.

Stretesky, Paul B. and Lynch, Michael J. (1999). Corporate Environmental Violence and Racism. 30 *Crime, Law and Social Change*, 163–180.

United Church of Christ. (1987). *Toxic Wastes and Race: A National Report on the Racial and Socio-Economic Characteristics of Communities with Hazardous Waste Sites* (New York: United Church of Christ).

United Church of Christ. (2024). A Movement is Born: Environmental Justice and the UCC. Available from: https://www.ucc.org/a_movement_is_born_environmental_justice_and_the_ucc

University of Michigan, School of Environment and Sustainability. (2024). History of Environmental Justice Education at SEAS. Available from: https://seas.umich.edu/academics/master-science/environmental-justice/history-environmental-justice

U.S. EPA. (2024a). Learn About Environmental Justice. Available from: https://www.epa.gov/environmentaljustice/learn-about-environmental-justice

U.S. EPA. (2024v). Environmental Justice Timeline. Available from: https://www.epa.gov/environmentaljustice/environmental-justice-timeline

U.S. EPA. (2024c), Plan EJ 2014. Available from: https://www.epa.gov/environmentaljustice/plan-ej-2014

U.S. EPA. (2024d). EJSCREEN: Environmental Justice Screening and Mapping Tool. Available from: https://www.epa.gov/ejscreen

U.S. EPA. (2024e). EJ 2020 Action Agenda: EPA's Environmental Justice Strategy. Available from: https://www.epa.gov/environmentaljustice/ej-2020-action-agenda-epas-environmental-justice-strategy

U.S. EPA. (2024f). Environmental Justice. Available from: https://www.epa.gov/environmentaljustice

Wilson, Benjamin F. (2017). It's Not 'Just' Zoning: Environmental Justice and Land Use. 49 *Urban Lawyer*, 717–726.

Youngblood, Candice Y. (2019). Put Your Money Where Their Mouth Is: Actualizing Environmental Justice by Amplifying Community Voices. 46 *Ecology Law Quarterly*, 455–484.

Zwickl, Klara. (2019). The Demographics of Fracking: A Spatial Analysis of Four U.S. States. 161 *Ecological Economics*, 202–215.

MELISSA JARRELL OZYMY AND JOSHUA OZYMY

32. Environmental racism

Introduction

This entry provides an overview of the field of environmental racism, from its roots elucidating the relationship between race and hazardous waste sites to its expansion into an explanatory concept that underpins the workings of social, economic, and political institutions including the conservation and wider environmental movements. Global examples illustrate how Black, Indigenous and People of Color (BIPOC) communities are disproportionately burdened with environmental harms largely perpetrated by powerful interests, grounded and entrenched in the ideologies and logics of Whiteness. Corporate, state, and environmental decision-making, bound up in systemic racism, have prompted BIPOC communities to call for greater accountability, remediation, and protection of the environment. BIPOC communities remain at the forefront of activism demanding a more equal Earth for all.

As a concept and field of research, environmental racism centres race as a principal variable in deciphering the unequal distribution of environmental hazards and harms throughout the world. While early works in this field built the evidence base for environmental racism, later contributions offered more explanatory frameworks for environmental racism's production and reproduction, including the entrenched ideologies that result in the disproportionate perpetuation of environmental harms against BIPOC communities. These works have included an exploration of how environmental racism manifests slowly as the accumulation of environmental hazards, how harms are exacerbated by existing inequalities and how these realities can be utilised to obfuscate causation, allowing perpetrators to escape responsibility and avoid remediation. Further research has demonstrated the deleterious environmental and social impacts on BIPOC communities enacted by powerful transnational corporations, often with state complicity. These communities have also been disenfranchised in the global movement to safeguard the environment despite their long history leading environmental and climate justice causes. Centring BIPOC voices in both academia and the environmental justice movement is seen as a starting point to addressing the inequities that the field of environmental racism evinces.

Environmental racism: rooted in activism

The term 'environmental racism' emerged during the 1980s, following activism among the predominantly Black communities of Warren County, North Carolina in the United States. The state government planned to transport thousands of tons of PCB (polychlorinated biphenyls) contaminated soil into the county through the creation of an industrial landfill (McGurty, 2009). PCBs are highly toxic compounds known to pose serious health risks, leading to dementia, cardiovascular disease, cancer, reduced fertility, and birth defects (Montano et al., 2022). The PCBs had been released into the soil through the illegal dumping of toxic manufacturing waste by the Ward Transformer Company during the late 1970s. Whilst the Black communities of Warren County were ultimately unsuccessful in their attempt to stop the construction of the toxic landfill, four years of activism and resistance raised awareness of the need for an environmental justice movement within the United States and beyond. In 1987, the United Church of Christ's (UCC) Commission for Racial Justice produced a report entitled *Toxic Wastes and Race in the United States* which articulated in the literature, for the first time in the USA, the connection between race and environmental inequality. As the primary conclusion of the report states: 'Race proved to be the most significant among variables tested in association with the location of commercial hazardous waste facilities. This represented a consistent national pattern' (UCC, 1987: xiii).

The findings of the UCC report inspired more research into the nexus of race and environmental hazards, providing further evidence in support of the UCC's thesis on environmental racism (Anderton et al., 1994; Mohai & Bryant, 1992). Robert Bullard's *Dumping in Dixie: Race, Class, and Environmental Quality* published in 1990 remains a key text revealing the relationship between the placement of hazardous waste facilities, ethnic minority communities, and the suffering that results from exposure to toxic environments (Bullard, 1990). However, direct causation between pollution and negative health impacts is difficult to prove through technocratic forms of knowledge such as epidemiological studies – studies that institutions, environmental policies, and the legislative systems legitimise. This is especially so when environmental hazards are compounded with existing systemic and structural issues. In Ingrid Waldron's book, *There's Something in the Water: Environmental Racism in Indigenous and Black Communities* (2021), she argues that disproportionate exposure to environmental harms in Black and Indigenous communities in Canada are often worsened by existing 'structural determinants of health' (2021: 66) such as low educational attainment and unemployment. These communities are both more vulnerable to the impacts of hazardous contaminants and pollution and less likely to have the resources to effectively fight back when perpetrators of harm use the lack of conclusive scientific evidence of harm from pollution to avoid accountability.

On a global scale, environmental racism is generally attributed to the disproportionate impact of environmental damage on communities whose race or ethnicity is different from those creating and perpetuating the harm. Overwhelmingly, these harmful activities are legally protected and committed by predominantly White affluent nations and corporate actors on non-White communities (P. Davies et al., 2019; Potter, 2010). Hugh Marbury (1995) argues that developed nations' exportation of hazardous waste to countries in the Global South constitutes environmental racism at the international level. Researchers have continued to argue this point, most recently focusing on electronic waste, with studies highlighting toxic dumping across countries in the Gulf of Guinea (Okafor-Yarwood & Adewumi, 2020), Ghana (Akese & Little, 2018) and India (Mundada et al., 2004). China's increasingly outsized role in the importation of electronic waste from the West has exposed communities near the country's recycling sites to lead poisoning from contaminated drinking water (Grossman, 2007; Shi et al., 2016). International agreements such as the Basel Convention (signed in 1989) were established in response to calls for increased regulation of hazardous waste with advocacy movements largely emerging on the African continent (Nagy, 1998), where researchers and advocates have long proposed holistic strategies for mitigating environmental racism in the global e-waste trade (Daum et al., 2017). While works focusing on the unequal distribution of environmental hazards build the evidence base for environmental racism, other works in the field seek to offer more explanatory frameworks for the production and reproduction of environmental racism.

Explanatory frameworks in environmental racism

Over the past 30 years, scholars such as Laura Pulido have sought to understand the social, political, and economic dynamics which have enabled and reproduced geographies of racialised inequality. Research had previously focused on the ways in which decision-makers were explicitly influenced by racist ideologies, and how this impacted upon the injurious distribution of environmental hazards (Hamilton, 1995). However, in her study of environmental hazards within Latino communities in Los Angeles, Pulido argues that rather than situating the problem with individual decision-makers, there is much more explanatory potential in the concept of Whiteness (drawing on Lipsitz, 1998), and particularly in White privilege. Pulido did not seek to diminish the ways in which racist ideologies influence the development of racialised environmental injustice but rather that environmental racism is a far more pervasive, historically contingent, and structural issue (Pulido, 2017b). By moving beyond a focus on evidence of individual racism for particular incidents and acts, Pulido and other scholars highlight how forms of racism are entrenched within institutions and policies, broadening the field's scope of inquiry.

The neoliberal world order

An area which was initially overlooked within analysis of environmental racism was the coevalness or connectedness of the neoliberal state and corporate interests in the production of racialised geographies of environmental hazards. Pulido (2017a) argues that environmental racism is entwined with racial capitalism, whereby industry profits at the expense of non-White communities. Thus, there is little incentive, within industry, to develop policies and regulations that disrupt the status quo. Other scholars have presented environmental racism perpetuated by corporate entities as a form of state-sanctioned violence against communities deemed 'expendable'

(Grisafi, 2020; Pellow, 2016). According to Charles Mills (2001), this disposability is the result of a perception of non-White lives as 'trash'. Similarly, John D. Márquez (2014) contends that this 'racial expendability' is codified through the state and its legal frameworks and reinforced through over-policing, incarceration, urban development, and economic segregation (Dillon, 2012; McKittrick, 2011; Wilson, 2019). Thom Davies (2022) applies Rob Nixon's (2011) concept of 'slow violence' to characterise the environmental harm experienced by the predominantly Black communities of 'Cancer Alley' in Louisiana at the hands of corporate industry. 'Cancer Alley' is an unprecedented 85-mile cluster of 136 petrochemical plants and seven oil refineries, so named because of the purported high incidences of cancer in the population. Davies attests that the toxic accumulation of pollution in residents' bodies and the surrounding environment amounts to a form of institutional violence perpetuated over time. A violence against Black bodies that is enabled by the state and its entanglement with the logics of racial capitalism which deems the harms against marginalised communities for the sake of progress and profit an acceptable trade-off.

Global state–corporate harms

The global power dynamics that enable state–corporate environmental harms against marginalised groups, including those exacerbating the climate crisis, are felt acutely throughout the Global South where resource exploitation by Western economies is pervasive. The US parent company of a chemical plant in Bhopal, India, ignored fervent community protests calling for safer, more responsible conditions in observation of the company's own policies (Gupta & Gupta, 2008). In 1984, the mismanagement of this facility led to a toxic chemical leak that killed 8,000 people. Hundreds of thousands more suffered from associated neurological disorders, tuberculosis, and lung fibrosis (Gupta & Gupta, 2008). Further, corporate environmental pollution from activities like mining and oil drilling by multinational energy companies on local communities of color have posed serious health risks, from Mexico to Australia (Lloyd-Smith & Bell, 2003; Tetreault, 2020). Extractive industries have been associated with other forms of environmental racism as well, including energy poverty (Fakier, 2018; Gamu et al., 2015) and food injustice (Heydon, 2020; Kurz et al., 2021). During South African Apartheid, weak governmental regulations allowed largely White-owned mining corporations to operate with impunity, inflicting further suffering on the country's predominantly Black communities (Llewellyn, 2018).

Indigenous groups have been identified as especially susceptible to global environmental harms perpetrated by corporate entities and state complicity given their marginality from decision-making processes and deep ties to the local environments (Carrington et al., 2016). Global issues of significance include: land grabs and land use criminalisation by the state in favour of extractive industry (Regan, 1998) or environmental preservation (Laudati, 2010; Muehlmann, 2013); violent conflicts over resources and territories (Pérez-Rincón et al., 2019; van Solinge, 2010); the specific vulnerability of Indigenous people to environmental pollution, particularly in countries with loose regulations (San Sebastián et al., 2001); and human rights abuses, including the state-sanctioned killing of Indigenous activists (Lynch et al., 2018; Turner, 1997).

Hegemony and military power

States often operate as perpetrators of environmental racism within and through the entrenchment in the hegemonic logics that underlie their institutions. For example, through political, economic, and military imperialism, the United States has produced and maintained conditions for the disposability of non-White lives across the globe. The primary organ of US imperialism, state influence overseas, and the hammer through which neoliberal capitalist logics have been imposed upon the world is the US military. The US military has been routinely operationalised against non-White communities both domestically and overseas. This has been initiated through the deployment of direct violence, material support for brutal authoritarian regimes and/or the imposition of extreme environmental hazards.

During the Vietnam War (1954–1975), the US military deployed chemical, ballistic, and explosive ordnance against populations in Cambodia, Laos, and Vietnam at levels heretofore unrivalled. What remained following US withdrawal in 1975, is what Davorn

Sisavath (2019) has described as a 'wasteland'. Situating his work in Ban Naphia, Laos, Sisavath illustrates how communities have adapted to the environmental hazards resulting from the saturation of military waste which continue to interrupt their daily lives. Sisavath reads this waste as a material 'archive' which narrates an alternative history of US militarism in Laos as the convergence of US state power, capitalism, and environmental destruction. The US military has also, allegedly, illegally dumped toxic waste from its operations into a Zimbabwean mine during the 1980s (Mpanya, 2019), and in Afghanistan, burn pits incinerating a myriad of toxic waste polluted the land, water, and air for both service members and local communities (Coughlin & Szema, 2019).

Racism in the environmental movement

The environmental movement has often sought policy solutions from the state as a method for eradicating environmental hazards (Bullard, 2002; Lowman et al., 2013; Norton et al., 2007), which frequently gives primacy to the environmental aspect of the problem rather than the social, political, or economic drivers (Wright, 2021). Willie Jamaal Wright (2021) and others (Pulido et al., 2016; Van Sant et al., 2021) argue that this situation continues to elide the ways in which the state is a primary driver of environmental racism and broader geographies of inequality. The unequal burden placed on developing countries to combat ecological degradation caused by the world's economic superpowers is underscored in the limitations of international treaties. The advanced economies of the United States and Europe, for example, demand global action on climate change while regularly falling short of their commitments to the Paris Climate Accords. The failure of these economic superpowers to implement or enforce domestic regulations positions them as top greenhouse gas emitters, a status that undermines international calls for rural people in the Global South to change their behaviours to preserve the world's remaining 'pristine environments' (Rudd et al., 2021). This is reflective of the preservationist ideals that founded the modern conservation movement, guided by racist ideologies, dispossessing Indigenous communities, and disavowing local knowledge.

This colonial legacy can be found in the leadership structures of many international conservation efforts today (Kashwan et al., 2021). Centuries of land dispossession and the forced migration of local and Indigenous people have endured under the auspices of 'environmental protection'. 'Fortress conservation' received its name by displacing local communities and forest-dwelling people whose ancestral ranges overlap with key biodiversity areas. Sometimes referred to as 'conservation refugees' (Dowie, 2011), these communities lose access to their lands and traditional livelihoods through the processes of eviction (Brockington & Igoe, 2006) and resource use criminalisation (Laudati, 2010) associated with the establishment of protected areas and national parks (Brockington & Igoe, 2006; Laudati, 2010). Despite the apparent consensus among researchers that 'externally controlled conservation' has been associated with ineffective conservation and negative social outcomes for communities, they continue (Dawson et al., 2021).

Climate change mitigation strategies have also dispossessed and disadvantaged already marginalised groups (Paulose, 2021). As Lohmann (2016) points out, the United Nations programme REDD+ (Reducing Emissions from Deforestation and Forest Degradation) incentivises companies from developed economies to cheaply purchase (read dispossess) Indigenous land for 'forest protection' to offset centuries of non-Indigenous carbon emissions. Other examples include bioenergy monocultures for reforestation (Bose, 2016) as well as green energy projects, which are frequently backed by third party funders such as the World Bank. The impacts of hydropower, generally regarded as a critical source of renewable energy, have proven damaging for local environments and human populations. The construction and operation of hydroelectric dams has been associated with ecosystem destruction, racialised decision-making by governments and international financial institutions, and human rights violations against Indigenous people (Paulose, 2021).

Ways forward

A lack of representation for non-White voices, and particularly those of BIPOC women, persists in environmental decision-making in the state, corporate, and NGO sectors (Taylor, 2015). Lohmann (2016) argues that the same structures of systemic racism driving the disproportionate exposure of BIPOC communities to environmental hazards are also responsible for the harmful stereotypes that fail to recognise minority communities as champions of environmental causes. Such racist axioms belie a long history of environmental and climate justice movements led by BIPOC communities (Bullard & Wright, 1990; Ritchie, 2021; Turner, 1997). Though they collectively represent just six per cent of the global human population, Indigenous groups have gained worldwide attention for their increasingly organised resistance movements for environmental justice across North America (Cortés Calderón, 2018; Heydon, 2020), South America (Rodriguez-Garavito & Arenas, 2005), Europe (Lawrence & Raitio, 2006), Asia (Paulose, 2021), Africa (Turner, 1997), and Australia (Scambary, 2013). However, marginalised BIPOC communities will continue to be under-served if policymakers, corporate actors, and conservation leaders fail to elevate and work with these critical perspectives.

Systemic racism is as pervasive in conservation science as it is in conservation practice, limiting opportunities for BIPOC researchers and practitioners (Rudd et al., 2021). The discipline is dominated by White scholars who are able to afford the costs associated with higher education and the low-paying career opportunities that follow, reinforcing a system known as 'academic imperialism' (Bratman & DeLince, 2022; Chilisa, 2011). Challenging these structures requires inclusive pedagogic strategies that elevate BIPOC perspectives and epistemologies (Bratman & DeLince, 2022; Pulido & De Lara, 2018). These might include reforms to degree programmes, course syllabi, institutional support, and advancement opportunities (Rudd et al., 2021). Encouragingly, efforts to confront the problem of exclusionary environmentalism and colonial conservation have gained momentum in recent years (Goyes, 2019; 2023; Kashwan et al., 2021; Murdock, 2019; White, 2023).

Conclusion

Since the term 'environmental racism' first emerged, scholars across academic disciplines have challenged the bounds of its definition. What began as a movement against the unequal distribution of environmental hazards in communities of Colour, has expanded to include other racialised decisions about the environment and their associated impacts on the health and well-being of BIPOC communities. This has most often referred to the actions of governments and corporations, but it can also be seen in the environmental movement itself, which has historically pursued its agenda regardless of racialised harm. On a global scale, environmental problems are often exported to the Global South by the advanced economies which bear responsibility for them. These include the harmful but legal practices of hazardous waste dumping and resource extractivism; but they also include 'environmentally friendly' activities like carbon offsets and conservation initiatives. Research connecting the entrenched ideologies of Whiteness and White privilege as an explanatory concept for environmental racism have shown the need for challenging the social, economic, and political logics that underpin societal, state, and environmental institutions. Creating the conditions for BIPOC participation and leadership on these issues across academia, public and private sectors, and environmental activism are a critical first step in addressing the myriad inequities elucidated by the field of environmental racism.

Lily Rubino and Alexandra Lebron

Further reading

Akese, G. A., & Little, P. C. (2018). Electronic waste and the environmental justice challenge in Agbogbloshie. *Environmental Justice*, *11*(2), 77–83.

Bullard, R. D. (1990). *Dumping in Dixie: Race, Class, and Environmental Quality*. Routledge.

Kashwan, P. V., Duffy, R., Massé, F., Asiyanbi, A. P., & Marijnen, E. (2021). From racialized neocolonial global conservation to an inclusive and regenerative conservation. *Environment: Science and Policy for Sustainable Development*, *63*(4), 4–19.

Lipsitz, G. (1998). *The Possessive Investment in Whiteness*. Temple University Press.

Pulido, L., & De Lara, J. (2018). Reimagining 'justice' in environmental justice: Radical ecologies, decolonial thought, and the Black Radical Tradition. *Environment and Planning E: Nature and Space*, *1*(1–2), 76–98.

Ritchie, J. (2021). Movement from the margins to global recognition: Climate change activism by young people and in particular Indigenous

youth. *International Studies in Sociology of Education, 30*(1–2), 53–72.
Rudd, L. F., Allred, S., Bright Ross, J. G., Hare, D., Nkomo, M. N., Shanker, K., Allen, T., Biggs, D., Dickman, A., Dunaway, M., Ghosh, R., & Dávalos, A. (2021). Overcoming racism in the twin spheres of conservation science and practice. *Proceedings of the Royal Society B, 288*(1962), 20211871.
Shi, J., Zheng, G. J. S., Wong, M. H., Liang, H., Li, Y., Wu, Y., Li, P., & Liu, W. (2016). Health risks of polycyclic aromatic hydrocarbons via fish consumption in Haimen Bay (China), downstream of an e-waste recycling site (Guiyu). *Environmental Research, 147*, 233–240.
Sollund, R. A., & Runhovde, S. R. (2020). Responses to wildlife crime in post-colonial times. Who fares best? *The British Journal of Criminology, 60*(4), 1014–1033.
Tetreault, D. (2020). The new extractivism in Mexico: Rent redistribution and resistance to mining and petroleum activities. *World Development, 126*, 104714.
United Church of Christ. Commission for Racial Justice. (1987). *Toxic Wastes and Race in The United States: A National Report on the Racial and Socio-Economic Characteristics of Communities with Hazardous Waste Sites.* Public Data Access.

References

Akese, G. A., & Little, P. C. (2018). Electronic waste and the environmental justice challenge in Agbogbloshie. *Environmental Justice, 11*(2), 77–83.
Anderton, D. L., Anderson, A. B., Oakes, J. M., & Fraser, M. R. (1994). Environmental equity: The demographics of dumping. *Demography, 31*(2), 229–248.
Bose, P. S. (2016). Vulnerabilities and displacements: Adaptation and mitigation to climate change as a new development mantra. *Area, 48*(2), 168–175.
Bratman, E. Z., & DeLince, W. P. (2022). Dismantling white supremacy in environmental studies and sciences: An argument for anti-racist and decolonizing pedagogies. *Journal of Environmental Studies and Sciences, 12*(2), 193–203.
Brockington, D., & Igoe, J. (2006). Eviction for conservation: A global overview. *Conservation and Society, 4*(3), 424–470.
Bullard, R. D. (1990). *Dumping in Dixie: Race, Class, and Environmental Quality*. Routledge.
Bullard, R. (2002). Environmental justice challenges at home and abroad. In N. Low, (ed.), *Global Ethics and Environment* (pp. 47–60). Routledge.
Bullard, R. D., & Wright, B. H. (1990). The quest for environmental equity: Mobilizing the black community for social change. *Race, Poverty & the Environment, 1*(2), 3–17.
Carrington, K., Hogg, R., & Sozzo, M. (2016). Southern criminology. *The British Journal of Criminology, 56*(1), 1–20.
Chilisa, B. (2011). *Indigenous Research Methodologies*. Sage Publications.
Cortés Calderón, S. V. (2018). Security, justice, and forest protection! An indigenous community's fight against illegal deforestation and organised crime in Cheran, Mexico. In I. Arroyo-Quiroz and T. Wyatt, (eds.), *Green Crime in Mexico* (pp. 63–73). Palgrave Macmillan.
Coughlin, S. S., & Szema, A. (2019). Burn pits exposure and chronic respiratory illnesses among Iraq and Afghanistan veterans. *Journal of Environment and Health Sciences, 5*(1), 13–14.
Daum, K., Stoler, J., & Grant, R. J. (2017). Toward a more sustainable trajectory for e-waste policy: A review of a decade of e-waste research in Accra, Ghana. *International Journal of Environmental Research and Public Health, 14*(2), 135.
Davies, P., Hernandez, M. P., & Wyatt, T. (2019). Economy versus environment: How corporate actors harm both. *Critical Criminology, 27*(1), 85–99.
Davies, T. (2022). Slow violence and toxic geographies: 'Out of sight' to whom? *Environment and Planning C: Politics and Space, 40*(2), 409–427.
Dawson, N., Coolsaet, B., Sterling, E., Loveridge, R., Gross-Camp, N., Wongbusarakum, S., … & Rosado-May, F. J. (2021). The role of indigenous peoples and local communities in effective and equitable conservation. *Ecology and Society, 26*(3), 19.
Dillon, S. (2012). Possessed by death: The neoliberal-carceral state, Black feminism, and the afterlife of slavery. *Radical History Review, 2012*(112), 113–125.
Dowie, M. (2011). *Conservation Refugees: The Hundred-Year Conflict Between Global Conservation and Native Peoples*. MIT Press.
Fakier, K. (2018). Women and renewable energy in a South African community: Exploring energy poverty and environmental racism. *Journal of International Women's Studies, 19*(5), 165–176.
Gamu, J., Le Billon, P., & Spiegel, S. (2015). Extractive industries and poverty: A review of recent findings and linkage mechanisms.

The Extractive Industries and Society, *2*(1), 162–176.
Goyes, D. (2019). *Southern Green Criminology: A Science to End Ecological Discrimination*. Emerald.
Goyes, D. (ed.). (2023). *Green Crime in the Global South: Essays on Southern Green Criminology*. Palgrave Macmillan.
Grisafi, L. (2020). Prosecuting international environmental crime committed against indigenous peoples in Brazil. *HRLR Online*, *5*, 26.
Grossman, E. (2007). *High Tech Trash: Digital Devices, Hidden Toxics, and Human Health*. Island Press.
Gupta, A. D., & Gupta, A. D. (2008). Corporate social responsibility in India: Towards a sane society? *Social Responsibility Journal*, *4*(1–2), 209–216.
Hamilton, J. T. (1995). Testing for environmental racism: Prejudice, profits, political power? *Journal of Policy Analysis and Management*, *14*(1), 107–132.
Heydon, J., 2020. Indigenous environmental victimisation in the Canadian oil sands. In N. South & A. Brisman (eds), *Routledge International Handbook of Green Criminology* (pp. 333–347). Routledge.
Kashwan, P. V., Duffy, R., Massé, F., Asiyanbi, A. P., & Marijnen, E. (2021). From racialized neocolonial global conservation to an inclusive and regenerative conservation. *Environment: Science and Policy for Sustainable Development*, *63*(4), 4–19.
Kurz, D. J., Saikim, F. H., Justine, V. T., Bloem, J., Libassi, M., Luskin, M. S., Withey, L. S., Goossens, B., Brashares, J. S., & Potts, M. D. (2021). Transformation and endurance of Indigenous hunting: Kadazandusun-Murut bearded pig hunting practices amidst oil palm expansion and urbanization in Sabah, Malaysia. *People and Nature*, *3*(5), 1078–1092.
Laudati, A. A. (2010). The encroaching forest: Struggles over land and resources on the boundary of Bwindi Impenetrable National Park, Uganda. *Society and Natural Resources*, *23*(8), 776–789.
Lawrence, R. and Raitio, K., 2006. Forestry conflicts in Finnish Sapmi: Local, national and global links. *Indigenous Affairs*, *4*, 36–43.
Lipsitz, G. (1998). *The Possessive Investment in Whiteness*. Temple University Press.
Llewellyn, L. (2018). Mining corporations, democratic meddling, and environmental justice in South Africa. *Social Sciences*, *7*(12), 259.
Lloyd-Smith, M., & Bell, L. (2003). Toxic disputes and the rise of environmental justice in Australia. *International Journal of Occupational and Environmental Health*, *9*(1), 14–23.
Lohmann, L. (2016). Expanding the concept of environmental racism. *Chain Reaction*, (127), 35–36.
Lowman, A., McDonald, M. A., Wing, S., & Muhammad, N. (2013). Land application of treated sewage sludge: Community health and environmental justice. *Environmental Health Perspectives*, *121*(5), 537–542.
Lynch, M. J., Stretesky, P. B., & Long, M. A. (2018). Green criminology and native peoples: The treadmill of production and the killing of Indigenous environmental activists. *Theoretical Criminology*, *22*(3), 318–341.
Marbury, H. J. (1995). Hazardous waste exportation: The global manifestation of environmental racism. *Vanderbilt Journal of Transnational Law*, *28*, 251.
Márquez, J. D. (2014). *Black-Brown Solidarity: Racial Politics in the New Gulf South*. University of Texas Press.
McGurty, E. (2009). *Transforming Environmentalism: Warren County, PCBs, and the Origins of Environmental Justice*. Rutgers University Press.
McKittrick, K. (2011). On plantations, prisons, and a black sense of place. *Social & Cultural Geography*, *12*(8), 947–963.
Mills, C. W. (2001). Black trash. In L. Westra and B.E. Lawson, (eds.), *Faces of Environmental Racism* (pp. 73–91). Rowman & Littlefield.
Mohai, P., & Bryant, B. (1992). Race, poverty, and the environment. *EPA Journal*, *18*, 6.
Montano, L., Pironti, C., Pinto, G., Ricciardi, M., Buono, A., Brogna, C., ... & Motta, O. (2022). Polychlorinated biphenyls (PCBs) in the environment: Occupational and exposure events, effects on human health and fertility. *Toxics*, *10*(7), 365.
Mpanya, M. (2019). The dumping of toxic waste in African countries: A case of poverty and racism. In B. Bryant and P. Mohai, (eds.), *Race and the Incidence of Environmental Hazards* (pp. 204–214). Routledge.
Muehlmann, S. (2013). *Where the River Ends: Contested Indigeneity in the Mexican Colorado Delta*. Duke University Press.
Mundada, M. N., Kumar, S., & Shekdar, A. V. (2004). E-waste: A new challenge for waste management in India. *International Journal of Environmental Studies*, *61*(3), 265–279.
Murdock, E. G. (2019). Nature where you're not: Rethinking environmental spaces and racism. In S.M. Meagher, S. Noll and J.S. Biehl, (eds.), *The Routledge Handbook of Philosophy of the City* (pp. 301–313). Routledge.
Nagy, I. V. (1998). The transboundary shipments of hazardous wastes. In D.K. Asante-Duah

and I.V. Nagy, (eds.), *International Trade in Hazardous Wastes* (pp. 81–99). Routledge.
Nixon, R. (2011). *Slow Violence and the Environmentalism of the Poor*. Harvard University Press.
Norton, J. M., Wing, S., Lipscomb, H. J., Kaufman, J. S., Marshall, S. W., & Cravey, A. J. (2007). Race, wealth, and solid waste facilities in North Carolina. *Environmental Health Perspectives, 115*(9), 1344–1350.
Okafor-Yarwood, I., & Adewumi, I. J. (2020). Toxic waste dumping in the Global South as a form of environmental racism: Evidence from the Gulf of Guinea. *African Studies, 79*(3), 285–304.
Paulose, R. M. (2021). Crouching tiger, hidden dragon: Hydropower and crimes against humanity. In R. M. Paulose, (ed.), *Green Crimes and International Criminal Law* (pp. 257–294). Vernon Press.
Pellow, D. N. (2016). Toward a critical environmental justice studies: Black Lives Matter as an environmental justice challenge. *Du Bois Review: Social Science Research on Race, 13*(2), 221–236.
Pérez-Rincón, M., Vargas-Morales, J., & Martinez-Alier, J. (2019). Mapping and analyzing ecological distribution conflicts in Andean countries. *Ecological Economics, 157*, 80–91.
Potter, G. (2010). What is green criminology. *Sociology Review, 20*(2), 8–12.
Pulido, L. (2017a). Geographies of race and ethnicity II: Environmental racism, racial capitalism and state-sanctioned violence. *Progress in Human Geography, 41*(4), 524–533.
Pulido, L. (2017b). Rethinking environmental racism: White privilege and urban development in Southern California. *Annals of the Association of American Geographers, 90*(1), 12–40.
Pulido, L., & De Lara, J. (2018). Reimagining 'justice' in environmental justice: Radical ecologies, decolonial thought, and the Black Radical Tradition. *Environment and Planning E: Nature and Space, 1*(1–2), 76–98.
Pulido, L., Kohl, E., & Cotton, N. M. (2016). State regulation and environmental justice: The need for strategy reassessment. *Capitalism Nature Socialism, 27*(2), 12–31.
Regan, A. J. (1998). Causes and course of the Bougainville conflict. *The Journal of Pacific History, 33*(3), 269–285.
Ritchie, J. (2021). Movement from the margins to global recognition: Climate change activism by young people and in particular Indigenous youth. *International Studies in Sociology of Education, 30*(1–2), 53–72.
Rodriguez-Garavito, C. A., & Arenas, L. C. (2005). Indigenous rights, transnational activism, and legal mobilization: The struggle of the U'wa people in Colombia. In B. de Sousa Santos & C. A. Rodriguez-Garavito (eds), *Law and Globalization from Below* (pp. 241–266). Cambridge University Press.
Rudd, L. F., Allred, S., Bright Ross, J. G., Hare, D., Nkomo, M. N., Shanker, K., Allen, T., Biggs, D., Dickman, A., Dunaway, M., Ghosh, R., & Dávalos, A. (2021). Overcoming racism in the twin spheres of conservation science and practice. *Proceedings of the Royal Society B, 288*(1962), 20211871.
San Sebastián, M., Armstrong, B., Córdoba, J. A., & Stephens, C. (2001). Exposures and cancer incidence near oil fields in the Amazon basin of Ecuador. *Occupational and Environmental Medicine, 58*(8), 517–522.
Scambary, B. (2013). *My Country, Mine Country: Indigenous People, Mining and Development Contestation in Remote Australia*. ANU Press.
Shi, J., Zheng, G. J. S., Wong, M. H., Liang, H., Li, Y., Wu, Y., Li, P., & Liu, W. (2016). Health risks of polycyclic aromatic hydrocarbons via fish consumption in Haimen Bay (China), downstream of an e-waste recycling site (Guiyu). *Environmental Research, 147*, 233–240.
Sisavath, D. (2019). The US Secret War in Laos: Constructing an archive from military waste. *Radical History Review, 2019*(133), 103–116.
Taylor, D. E. (2015). Gender and racial diversity in environmental organizations: Uneven accomplishments and cause for concern. *Environmental Justice, 8*(5), 165–180.
Tetreault, D. (2020). The new extractivism in Mexico: Rent redistribution and resistance to mining and petroleum activities. *World Development, 126*, 104714.
Turner, T. E. (1997). Oil workers and oil communities in Africa: Nigerian women and grassroots environmentalism. *Labour, Capital and Society/ Travail, capital et société, 30*(1), 66–89.
UCC. Commission for Racial Justice. (1987). *Toxic Wastes and Race in The United States: A National Report on the Racial and Socio-Economic Characteristics ofCommunities with Hazardous Waste Sites*. United Church of Christ. Commission for Racial Justice. Public Data Access.
Van Sant, L., Milligan, R., & Mollett, S. (2021). Political ecologies of race: Settler colonialism and environmental racism in the United States and Canada. *Antipode, 53*(3), 629–642.
van Solinge, T. B. (2010). Deforestation crimes and conflicts in the Amazon. *Critical Criminology, 18*(4), 263–277.
Waldron, I. R. (2021). *There's Something in the Water: Environmental Racism in Indigenous & Black Communities*. Fernwood Publishing.
White, R. (2023). Colonialism, knowledge, and the White Man's Burden. In D. Goyes (ed.), *Green Crime in the Global South: Essays on Southern*

Green Criminology (pp. 285–313). Palgrave Macmillan.
Wilson, B. M. (2019). *America's Johannesburg: Industrialization and Racial Transformation in Birmingham*. University of Georgia Press.
Wright, W. J. (2021). As above, so below: Anti-Black violence as environmental racism. *Antipode*, *53*(3), 791–809.

33. Non-human animal victimology

Introduction

Non-human criminology is a proposed area of non-speciesist scholarship that focuses on non-human animals as victims of harm. This entry provides an overview that demonstrates the types of activity that victimologists would undertake to reveal more about these neglected victims. The development of non-human animal victimology is briefly contextualised in the context of existing scholarship on non-speciesist criminology, after which the non-human animal as victim is considered. A brief introduction to victimology is provided, and the status of non-human animals as 'ideal victims' is considered. Theories and philosophies relating to non-humans as victims, both legally and conceptually, are outlined and the benefits and challenges of pursuing a non-human animal victimology agenda are discussed.

Conceptual orientation

Non-human animal victimology is an emerging area of concern that builds on work from green criminology, critical animal studies, and animal abuse studies. It proposes that non-human animals be granted 'victim' status and sets out an agenda for research and advocacy along the lines of victimological study relating to humans. As such, non-human animal victimology would consider (1) the nature, extent and patterns in victimisation of non-human animals; (2) the consequences and impacts of victimisation for non-human animals; (3) interactions between non-human animal victims and the criminal justice system (and other organisations), as well as victim–offender relationships; and (4) philosophy and theories of non-human animal victimisation (Flynn, 2024).

There is much debate in the literature on the appropriate terminology when referring to animals that are not human. All proposed examples seem to result in the reduction of the vast range of life that constitutes non-human animals into one category of 'other' (Beirne, 2007), thus the quest for non-speciesist terminology continues. Here, consistent with Flynn and Hall's (2017) proposal and Flynn's work that follows, the term non-human animal victimology is used. Whilst this may not be entirely satisfactory, the distinction from the dominant *human* victimology is important.

Non-human animal victimology is a recently proposed sub-discipline, with a long history of related scholarship behind it. As a specific body of work, it was first proposed by Flynn and Hall (2017), in their paper 'The case for a victimology of nonhuman animal harms'. However, research and writing on non-human animals as sufferers of harm has a much longer, albeit marginalised, past. Within criminology, such considerations became more recently associated with green criminology, which was interested in harms against environments, humanity and *other animals* (Beirne and South, 2007). There are also numerous examples of scholars focusing their work on harms against non-human animals and constructing them as 'victims' or adopting a species justice perspective (White, 2013), the most notable of whom is Beirne (1999; 2018). In terms of applying the language of victimisation to non-human animals, notable examples are Sollund (2011; e.g., referring to abduction rather than poaching of animals) and Beirne's (2014) proposed use of the term 'theriocide' to describe the killing of non-human animals whether legal or illegal.

Non-human animal victimology, then, can be seen as closely related to animal abuse studies (see, for example, Maher et al. (2017)), critical animal studies (e.g., Taylor and Twine, 2014), animal law (e.g., Favre, 2019) and philosophy (e.g., Browning and Birch, 2022), including the vast body of literature on animal rights. It is also aligned with the concept of species justice (Beirne, 1999; Sollund, 2021; White, 2013), whilst some elements may overlap with vegan academic movements, such as vegan studies (Wright, 2021), vegan sociology (Wrenn, 2022), and vegan criminology (Flynn, 2022).

Non-human animals as victims

With some limited exceptions, usually involving 'higher-order' mammals, such as apes (Fox, 2012) and cetaceans (Doornbos and Whitehead, 2024), in most jurisdictions, non-human animals cannot be legally recognised as *victims* of a crime. Similarly, non-human animals are not treated as offenders, though here there are historical exceptions (see Girgen, 2003). Despite this, non-human animals unarguably suffer abuse, maltreatment, and harm. Which of these harms might be considered acceptable varies (across countries and cultures, as well as individuals), but at least some of these are legally proscribed. Yet even if that is a crime related to animal welfare or cruelty, the non-human animal who has suffered the harm is not considered a victim. This raises the question of whether such offences should be really be considered *victimless* crimes.

Flynn and Hall (2017), among others, have provided examples of the range and extent of harms inflicted upon non-human animals, from direct illegal harm (such as causing unnecessary suffering of a domestic animal), to indirect illegal harm (such as pollution of waterways), to legal regulated harm that may be considered culturally unacceptable (for example, fur farming), to legal regulated harm that is generally culturally acceptable (such as farming and medical vivisection). Taken in their entirety, every year hundreds of billions of non-human animals experience pain, injury, suffering, and death caused by human actions, including illegal activity. They contend that these harms can no longer be ignored by victimologists.

Introducing victimology

In simple terms, victimology is the study of victims. It considers the extent and patterns of victimisation, the consequences and impacts of victimisation, the relationship and experiences of victims and various organisations, but most notably the criminal justice system, as well as the victim–offender relationship. Victimology also deals with theories and philosophies of victimisation. An intersectional approach is taken, which recognises differential experiences impacted by the unique confluence of victim characteristics, circumstances and oppressions (Daigle, 2021; Hall, 2009; Walklate, 2018). Victimology has also championed 'victim rights' and challenged myths and misconceptions. Thus, there is also a recognised overlap between academic victimology and victim advocacy and activism (van Dijk, 1988).

Victimology may be crudely considered to have followed two paths. A positivist stance, which seeks to objectively capture 'facts' of victimisation, and a critical stance, which aims to paint a more accurate picture and challenge orthodox assumptions about victims and victimisation (Mawby and Walklate, 1994). Both approaches have a part to play in considering non-human animal victims, but it is within a more critical, radical (green) victimology where Flynn and Hall (2017) have argued non-human animal victimology is likely to flourish. They note that non-human animals can be recognised as a form of 'real, complex, contradictory and often politically inconvenient victims' (Kearon and Godey, 2007: 31), which have been excluded by political and economic considerations heavily influenced by power inequalities (Ruggerio and South, 2010). Critical radical victimology has already shown a willingness to consider 'problematic' victims, such as those of corporate and white-collar crime, and the families of homicide victims, whilst victims of environmental harm (Hall, 2013; 2014) are of growing interest.

Non-human animals as forgotten victims

One may ask the question, then, where are the non-human animals in victimology? Flynn and Hall (2017) and Flynn (2024) consider why non-human animals are the forgotten victims of both procedural and academic endeavours. In doing this, they consider the victimological concept of the ideal victim, and the anthropocentrism of victimology and the criminal justice system.

Christie (1986) proposed the concept of the ideal victim as that innocent, deserving individual, who is most readily afforded victim status by society, law enforcement, and the courts. The features of the ideal victim can be summarised as (1) weak; (2) carrying out an innocent (or 'respectable') project; (3) being blameless within the context of the offence; (4) co-operating with authorities; and (5) being victimised by a 'big bad' offender who is (6) a stranger. Beyond the scope of this entry, we might variously argue about different species of non-human animal, and different types of harm, such that there are clearly situations where a non-human animal would appear to meet these criteria and those where they do not, but they may still be constructed as 'ideal' (for example, a companion animal subjected to abuse by her 'owner'). We might also argue whether the inability to 'co-operate with authorities' and make their victimisation known are achievable for non-human animals, but where they are not, this is clearly not through wanton obstruction, but the very lack of voice that makes non-human animals so vulnerable.

We can certainly point to numerous examples where the public and media response to animal cruelty, abuse, and neglect suggests that non-human animals are 'ideal victims'. This may be less the case when we consider the criminal justice response, however. In contrast, there are also various normalised harms experienced by uncountable non-human animals that receive no such attention from the public, who may in fact be participants in such cruelty, for example, by consuming the products of (intensive) farming. Most of these harms are also likely to be legal.

This led Flynn and Hall (2017) to declare that criminology and victimology are themselves speciesist. Such is the anthropocentric focus of these fields of study, and of legal and criminal justice systems, that a final condition of the ideal victim should be added to the list: (7) the victim is human. Further, within this speciesist perspective, there is also clear evidence of hierarchical speciesism (Flynn and Hall, 2017), also referred to as the 'Bambi effect' (Ferreday, 2011) or the 'scala naturae' (Nussbaum, 2017). Companion animals such as dogs and cats, for example, rate more highly than mice, rats or snakes. Herein, not only are certain types of non-human animals afforded lesser (legal) protections than others seen to be higher in the hierarchy, but the consequences of their commodification are entirely normalised, regardless of the substantial harm, or victimisation, that this causes.

Justifications for non-human animal victimology

Various legal and philosophical perspectives have been used to argue whether non-human animals (should) have rights, liberties and/or legal protections (see, for example, Nussbaum, 2017), including utilitarianism (Singer, 1975), interest theories of legal rights (Feinberg, 1974; Kramer, 2015), and the subjects-of-a-life position (Regan, 1986). Contrastingly, one may draw on various feminist (e.g., Adams, 2015) and eco-feminist (Sollund, 2013; 2020) perspectives that reject rights-based discourse, instead critiquing the patriarchal hegemony and drawing parallels between the oppression of human (often women and people of colour) and non-human animals. Banwell (2023) expands this to further consider shared sources of oppression using the framework of war crimes and crimes against humanity, to argue non-human animals should be granted legal personhood and the status of 'protected persons' during the ongoing war against non-human animals.

Flynn and Hall (2017), explicitly focusing on the justification for perceiving non-human animals as 'victims', argued that this could not be based on a 'rights' argument alone. Instead, they draw on the work of Boutellier (2000) and the concept of the victimalisation of morality. Put simply, this argues that the twin processes of globalisation and secularisation have resulted in a decline in common standards of morality, which have instead been replaced by a common appreciation of the impacts of harm and a shared sympathy for those who have suffered. They extended this to non-human animals as sufferers of harm, adopting a social harm or zemiological (Hillyard, 2006), as opposed to legal, perspective. This public concern is apparent in many cases, including illegal acts of cruelty and in response to legal activities (most notably, in the UK, the recent outcry relating to trophy hunting). However, this theory may not extend to all non-human animals due to hierarchical speciesism.

Returning to the concept of the non-human animal as victim, Nurse (2016) considers whether non-human animals have welfare rights as a result of existing legislation (referring specifically to the UK's Animal Welfare Act 2006), an idea that is also explored by Stucki (2020), who considers whether non-human animals should have *fundamental* legal rights in the future. Similarly, Levitt et al. (2024) have compiled a collection of essays relating to *Animals as Crime Victims*, many of which adopt legal perspectives. Indeed, it is regularly lamented that non-human animals are considered property in most legal jurisdictions, whilst non-natural entities, such as companies, have legal personhood with attendant rights and duties. The most well-known efforts to recognise legal non-human animal rights are the work of the Nonhuman Rights Project (NhRP) and the Great Ape Project. It must also be acknowledged that various jurisdictions have, recently, undertaken processes of de-objectification of non-human animals and environmental entities in their legal or constitutional doctrines (see, for example, Echeverria and Leroux, 2019; Pranshu, 2020), yet, as Gacek and Jochelson (2020) explore, there remains substantial scope for interdisciplinary developments between green criminology and law, to advance a less anthropocentric perspective.

Non-human animal victimology has, to this point, side-stepped the legal rights issue, arguing that, from a victimological perspective, non-human animals can be conceptualised as 'victims' because of the legal and illegal harms to which they are subjected, regardless of their status in law (Flynn, 2024; Flynn and Hall, 2017). Similarly, it has been argued that representation of non-human animal 'victims', such as in court cases, whilst benefitting from legal recognition of victim status, is not dependent on it. Take for example the limited instances of courtroom animal advocates (previously in the Canton of Zurich, Switzerland and currently in Connecticut, USA), where an attorney is permitted to represent the interests of non-human animals victimised under existing criminal legislation (e.g., animal cruelty laws). The Animal Legal Defense Fund (ALDF)'s Courtroom Animal Advocate Program (CAAP) provides model legislation that can be used for this purpose (ALDF, 2019), but this does not create legal victim status (although the ALDF does use this language). Similarly, there have been successful efforts to introduce species victim impacts into court deliberations through either 'victim' impact statements or the use of expert witnesses (see, e.g., MacBeath and Whitfort, 2024, discussing Hong Kong SAR, South Africa, and Zambia). Following the existing legislation argument set out above, Lynch (2023: 21) also argues that welfare and protection laws may already (in principle) 'allow certain animals standing in the courts as valid petitioners'. Alternatively, Kymlicka (2017) suggests a third way to conceptualise animals in law that avoids the person/property dilemma, instead constructing non-human animals as 'workers' or 'family members' (as the recent, but as yet untested, Pet Abduction Act 2024 appears to do in England, Wales and Northern Ireland).

The benefits of a non-human animal victimology

The benefits of introducing non-human animal victimology may relate to both non-human animal interests as well as human interests. Non-human animals are an under-represented, 'hidden', and heavily victimised group (Flynn and Hall, 2017). This should sit comfortably within critical victimology's expanded notion of victimhood. Their inclusion should also be seen as a further push to decolonise criminology. As Flynn and Hall (2017) point out, a Global South perspective of victimisation, or one based on indigenous thought (Fraundorfer, 2018), may look vastly different, even from a more legalistic perspective. For example, Ecuador's constitutional court has recognised the constitutional rights of nature (and afforded these equal status as human rights). Whilst in 2022, it held that non-human animals are subjects of rights, calling for new legislation to protect these.

Flynn (2024) has also argued that victimological enquiry is important because it focuses on the victim and consequences of victimisation, not just the crime and the offender. The findings of victimology research could also be used to inform policy and support advocacy and activism. It is further claimed that, from a critical perspective, which victims should be considered worthy of study, and whose voices should be heard, should not be determined by the anthropocentric and institutionally speciesist practices of government or formal systems of justice.

Regarding benefits to victimology and others' interests, there is a well-established body of literature on the intersection of victims, as well as research demonstrating an overlap between human and non-human animal victimisation. Flynn (2024) summarises this in relation to the co-occurrence of non-human animal and familial abuse (for example, Ascione and Arkow, 1999; Turgoose and McKie, 2019), criminal careers research demonstrating versatility of offending (for example, Farrington, 2003; Piquero et al., 2003) and links to other forms of concomitant criminality (Levitt et al., 2016), as well as the graduation hypothesis (see Walters, 2014). Continued research into non-human animal victimisation can only further illuminate these links, revealing more about their impact and the effectiveness of responses to them. Non-human animal harm may also have predictive value for human victimisation, and vice versa. Ignoring this area of research thus minimises the importance of non-human animal harm and impacts negatively on responses to victimisation as a whole (Flynn, 2024).

Challenges for non-human animal victimology

This entry has considered the arguments proposed to support an expansion of victimology to include non-human animals. However, this does not come without challenges. These relate to the boundaries of study, difficulties of research involving non-human animals and the collection of relevant data, and criticisms relating to competing rights.

The first potential challenge relates to deciding what should be included within a non-human animal victimology. Flynn (2024) has set out a framework of study encompassing the key foci of human victimology as they pertain to non-human animals. It is argued there is scope for black letter positivist exploration of the nature, extent, and patterns within non-human animal 'victimisation' (following the welfare law perspective of acquired rights or victimhood), to more critical research and advocacy adopting a social harms definition of victimisation. Flynn (2022) has also explored the idea of a vegan victimology that would construct all species of non-human animal as (potential) victims of human violence. The challenge, then, is whether these different perspectives can sit comfortably alongside one another, or whether legal vs social harm vs vegan 'factions' may result in fragmentation and division among victimologists. Relatedly, this raises concerns about hierarchical speciesism being further advanced, through focus on research and the pursuit of victim rights for those animals 'most like us'.

Scholars have also acknowledged a range of potential difficulties undertaking studies of non-human animals as victims. First, these relate to conceptual challenges, such as how to avoid unhelpful anthropomorphism and how to capture and give voice to non-human animals when filtered through human experience, perceptions, and constructs (such as rights themselves) (Flynn, 2024). Second, these relate to more pragmatic concerns, such as where and how to access relevant data and funding, the ability to publish, and the need for collaboration with stakeholders from other disciplines (for example, veterinarians) (Flynn, 2024; Lynch and Genco, 2023; Maher, 2021). In many jurisdictions, reliable, routine data are not collected even on criminalised non-human animal harms. In the USA, the FBI incorporated animal cruelty offences into their National Incident-Based Reporting System in 2016. However, Beirne and Lynch (2023) point out that these data are themselves substantially skewed by the speciesist concerns and practices of state law enforcement, thus questioning the validity of any patterns found in such data.

Finally, there are challenges relating to competing rights (Lynch, 2023). It is important to consider how to respond when the interests of non-human animal victims, human victims, and environmental entities (for example, watercourses) do not align. This challenge is exacerbated by concerns about protecting economic activity (Rice, 2013). More formal recognition of victimhood and animal interests (or rights) has the potential to greatly expand the scope of criminal law, drawing more people into the organs of state control. This 'net-widening' (Hall and Farrall, 2013) may be of particular concern should it impact unequally on marginalised groups who already suffer as a result of structural inequalities. Flynn and Hall (2017) do not see these as insurmountable challenges, but rather as ones that victimology must already grapple with when considering competing *human* rights. Addressing this, White (2018) applies an eco-justice perspective, highlighting the importance of social and ecological context when weighing up competing interests and harms. It is clear that such issues will need to be further considered as green victimologies expand, as will concerns that inclusion of non-human animals may somehow be seen as minimising the experiences of human victimisations, rather than adding to our understanding of them.

Conclusion

Recent publications demonstrate examples of research pertinent to non-human animal victimology. This includes work on the portrayal of animal cruelty in news media reports (Morton et al., 2022), on the use of images of polar bears as ideal non-human victims in climate change reporting (Lam and Tegelberg, 2020), using evidence of poaching (here, of turtle nests) as a form of 'victim reporting' (Pheasey et al., 2021: 10), debating the extent and use of animal abuse registries (Lynch and Genco, 2018), and using wildlife (species) impact statements in prosecutions in Scotland and Hong Kong (Whitfort, 2019). Stephens Griffin and Griffin (2021) have also called for violence against non-human animals to be taken seriously as a form of social harm, whilst Tschakert et al. (2021), discussing climate justice, propose an alternative 'multi-species' justice. The volume, focus, and use of the language of victimisation across these works is promising. A more coherent body of scholarship would support the collation of current knowledge and the identification of the undoubtedly numerous research gaps in our understanding of the nature, extent, experiences of, and responses to non-human animal victimisation. This would also allow us to chart examples of hierarchical speciesism in the limited research that already exists. A non-human animal victimology would also help to systematise scholarly activity in this field and produce findings to support informed advocacy.

MELANIE FLYNN

Further reading

Beirne, P. (1999). For a nonspeciesist criminology: Animal abuse as an object of study. *Criminology*, *37*(1): 117–148. https://doi.org/10.1111/j.1745-9125.1999.tb00481.x

Flynn, M. and Hall, M. (2017). The case for a victimology of nonhuman animal harms. *Contemporary Justice Review*, *20*(3): 299–318. https://doi.org/10.1080/10282580.2017.1348898

Corte Constitucional del Ecuador, Sentencia No. 253-20-JH/22. http://esacc.corteconstitucional.gob.ec/storage/api/v1/10_DWL_FL/e2NhcnBldGE6J3RyYW1pdGUnLCB1dWlkOic3ZmMxMjVmMi1iMzZkLTRkZDQtYTM2NC1kOGNiMWIwYWViMWMucGRmJ30= (A press release in English, relating to the case, can be found at https://animal.law.harvard.edu/news-article/landmark-ruling/.)

Gacek, J. and Jochelson, R. (2020). Animals as something more than mere property: Interweaving green criminology and law. *Social Sciences*, *9*(7): 122. https://doi.org/10.3390/socsci9070122

Hall, M. (2014). Environmental harm and environmental victims: Scoping out a 'green victimology'. *International Review of Victimology*, *20*(1): 129–143. https://doi.org/10.1177/0269758013508682

Lynch, M.J. (2023). Writs of habeas corpus for nonhuman primates in the United States and the Nonhuman Rights Project: Legal processes and arguments used to secure nonhuman animal rights. *International Journal for Crime, Justice and Social Democracy*, *12*(3): 15–26. https://doi.org/10.5204/ijcjsd.2598

Milburn, J. (2021). The analytical philosophers: Peter Singer's *Animal Liberation* and Tom Regan's *The Case for Animal Rights*. In L. Wright (Ed.). *The Routledge Handbook of Vegan Studies* (pp. 39–49). Routledge.

Sollund, R. (2021). Nonspeciesist criminology, wildlife trade, and animal victimization. *Oxford Research Encyclopedias, Criminology and Crime Justice*. https://doi.org/10.1093/acrefore/9780190264079.013.608

White, R. (2018). Green victimology and non-human victims. *International Review of Victimology*, *24*(2): 239–255. https://doi.org/10.1177/0269758017745615

References

Adams, C. (2015). *The Sexual Politics of Meat: A Feminist-Vegetarian Critical Theory*. Bloomsbury Publishing.

Animal Legal Defense Fund (ALDF) (2019). *Animal Legal Defense Fund Model Legislation: Courtroom Animal Advocate Program (CAAP) Law*. https://aldf.org/wp-content/uploads/2019/08/ALDF-Model-CAAP-Law-2019.pdf

Ascione, F.R. and Arkow, P. (Eds.). (1999). *Child Abuse, Domestic Violence, and Animal Abuse: Linking the Circles of Compassion for Prevention and Intervention*. Purdue University Press.

Banwell, S. (2023). *The War Against Nonhuman Animals: A Non-Speciesist Understanding of Gendered Reproductive Violence*. Palgrave Macmillan.

Beirne, P. (1999). For a nonspeciesist criminology: Animal abuse as an object of study. *Criminology*, *37*(1): 117–148. https://doi.org/10.1111/j.1745-9125.1999.tb00481.x

Beirne, P. (2007). Animal rights, animal abuse and green criminology. In P. Beirne and N. South (Eds.). *Issues in Green Criminology: Confronting Harms Against Environments, Humanity and Other Animals* (pp. 55–86). Willan.

Beirne, P. (2014). Theriocide: Naming animal killing. *International Journal for Crime, Justice and Social Democracy*, *3*(2): 49–66. https://doi.org/10.5204/ijcjsd.v3i2.174

Beirne, P. (2018). *Murdering Animals: Writings on Theriocide, Homicide and Nonspeciesist Criminology*. Palgrave Macmillan.

Beirne, P. and Lynch, M.J. (2023). On the geometry of speciesist policing: The Federal Bureau of Investigation's Animal Cruelty Data. *International Journal for Crime, Justice and Social Democracy*, *12*(2). https://doi.org/10.5204/ijcjsd.2631

Beirne, P. and South, N. (Eds.). (2007). *Issues in Green Criminology: Confronting Harms*

Against Environments, Humanity and Other Animals. Willan.

Boutellier, H. (2000). *Crime and Morality: The Significance of Criminal Justice in Post-Modern Culture*. Kluwer.

Browning, H. and Birch, J. (2022). Animal sentience. *Philosophy Compass*, *17*(5): e12822. https://doi.org/10.1111/phc3.12822

Christie, N. (1986). The ideal victim. In E.A. Fattah (Ed.). *From Crime Policy to Victim Policy* (pp. 17–30). Palgrave Macmillan. https://doi.org/10.1007/978-1-349-08305-3_2

Daigle, L.E. (2021). *Victimology: The Essentials* (3rd ed.). Sage.

Doornbos, E. and Whitehead, J. (2024). Whales and dolphins now have legal personhood in the Pacific – but one treaty won't be enough to protect them. *The Conversation*. https://theconversation.com/whales-and-dolphins-now-have-legal-personhood-in-the-pacific-but-one-treaty-wont-be-enough-to-protect-them-227615#:~:text=Whales%20and%20dolphins%20have%20been,(New%20Zealand)%20and%20Tonga.

Echeverria, H. and Leroux, F.J.B.R. (2019). The rights of nature in Ecuador: An overview of the new environmental paradigm. In C. La Follette and C. Maser (Eds.). *Sustainability and the Rights of Nature in Practice* (pp. 279–293). CRC Press. https://doi.org/10.1201/9780429505959

Farrington, D.P. (2003). Key results from the first forty years of the Cambridge study in delinquent development. In T.P. Thornberry, and M.D. Krohn (Eds.). *Taking Stock of Delinquency: An Overview of Findings from Contemporary Longitudinal Studies* (pp. 137–184). Kluwer/Springer.

Favre, D.S. (2019). *Animal Law: Welfare, Interests, and Rights* (3rd ed.). Aspen Publishing.

Feinberg, J. (1974). The rights of animals and unborn generations. In W.T. Blackstone (Ed.). *Philosophy and Environmental Crisis* (pp. 43–68). University of Georgia Press.

Ferreday, D. (2011). Becoming deer: Nonhuman drag and online utopias. *Feminist Theory*, *12*(2): 219–225. https://doi.org/10.1177/1464700111404288

Flynn, M. (2022, September 6). Nonhuman animals as victims: Advancing a vegan victimology. Invited keynote presentation to the Vegan Society Research Day, Manchester, UK. https://www.youtube.com/watch?v=pdyEljA7WMw&list=PLwq-YHBuff5f76XgglJCZE-dRfBCUDqnk&t=12s

Flynn, M. (2024). Proposing a nonhuman animal victimology. In L. Levitt, D.B. Rosengard and J. Rubin (Eds.). *Animals as Crime Victims* (pp. 113–130). Edward Elgar Publishing.

Flynn, M. and Hall, M. (2017). The case for a victimology of nonhuman animal harms. *Contemporary Justice Review*, *20*(3): 299–318. https://doi.org/10.1080/10282580.2017.1348898

Fox, J. (2012). Great ape personhood. *Law School Student Scholarship*, *102*. https://scholarship.shu.edu/student_scholarship/102/?utm_source=scholarship.shu.edu%2Fstudent_scholarship%2F102&utm_medium=PDF&utm_campaign=PDFCoverPages

Fraundorfer, M. (2018). The rediscovery of indigenous thought in the modern legal system: The case of the great apes. *Global Policy*, *8*(1): 17–25. https://doi.org/10.1111/1758-5899.12517

Gacek, J. and Jochelson, R. (2020). Animals as something more than mere property: Interweaving green criminology and law. *Social Sciences*, *9*(7): 122. https://doi.org/10.3390/socsci9070122

Girgen, J. (2003). The historical and contemporary prosecution and punishment of animals. *Animal Law*, *9*(97): 97–133. https://www.animallaw.info/sites/default/files/lralvol9_p97.pdf

Hall, M. (2009). *Victims of Crime: Policy and Practice in Criminal Justice*. Willan.

Hall, M. (2013). *Victims of Environmental Harm: Rights, Recognition and Redress under National and International Law*. Routledge.

Hall, M. (2014). Environmental harm and environmental victims: Scoping out a 'green victimology'. *International Review of Victimology*, *20*(1): 129–143. https://doi.org/10.1177/0269758013508682

Hall, M. and Farrall, S. (2013). The criminogenic consequences of climate change: Blurring the boundaries between offenders and victims. In N. South and A. Brisman (Eds.). *International Handbook of Green Criminology* (pp. 120–133). Routledge.

Hillyard, P. (2006). Crime obsessions: Crime isn't the only harm. *Criminal Justice Matters*, *62*: 26–46. http://dx.doi.org/10.1080/09627250508553097

Kearon, T. and Godey, B. (2007). Setting the scene: A question of history. In S. Walklate (Ed.). *Handbook of Victims and Victimology* (pp. 17–36). Willan Publishing.

Kramer, M.H. (2015). Do animals and dead people have legal rights? *Canadian Journal of Law and Jurisprudence*, *14*(1): 29–54. https://doi.org/10.1017/S0841820900002368

Kymlicka, W. (2017). Social membership: Animal law beyond the property/personhood impasse. *Dalhousie Law Journal*, *40*(1): 123–155.

Lam, A. and Tegelberg, M. (2020). #Sickbear: Photographing polar bears as ideal nonhuman animal victims. In A. Lam and M. Tegelberg, (eds.), *Criminal Anthropocenes: Media and Crime in the Vanishing Arctic* (pp. 107–143). Palgrave Macmillan. https://doi.org/10.1007/978-3-030-46004-4_4

Levitt, L., Hoffer, T.A. and Loper, A.B. (2016). Criminal histories of a subsample of animal cruelty offenders. *Aggression and Violent*

Behavior, *30*: 48–58. https://doi.org/10.1016/j.avb.2016.05.002

Levitt, L., Rosengard, D.B. and Rubin, J. (Eds.). (2024). *Animals as Crime Victims*. Edward Elgar Publishing.

Lynch, M.J. (2023). Writs of habeas corpus for nonhuman primates in the United States and the Nonhuman Rights Project: Legal processes and arguments used to secure nonhuman animal rights. *International Journal for Crime, Justice and Social Democracy*, *12*(3): 15–26. https://doi.org/10.5204/ijcjsd.2598

Lynch, M.J. and Genco, L. (2018). Animal abuse registries: Expanded interest in animal protection mimics other criminal justice policies, but should green criminologists hop on the band-wagon? *Contemporary Justice Review*, *21*(4): 351–370. https://doi.org/10.1080/10282580.2018.1531713

Lynch, M.J. and Genco, L.J. (2023). Deer slayers: Examining the scope of and arguments for and against legal deer theriocide in the US. *Sustainability*, *15*(7): 5987. https://doi.org/10.3390/su15075987

MacBeath, A. and Whitfort, A. (2024). *Species Victim Impact Statements: Giving a Voice to the Unheard Victims of Environmental Crime*. Global Initiative Against Transnational Organised Crime. https://globalinitiative.net/analysis/species-victim-impact-statements-envitonmental-crime/

Maher, J. (2021). Documenting harm to the voiceless: Researching animal abuse. In P. Davies, P. Leighton and T. Wyatt (Eds.). *The Palgrave Handbook of Social Harm* (pp. 167–195). Palgrave Macmillan.

Maher, J., Pierpoint, H. and Beirne, P. (Eds.). (2017). *The Palgrave International Handbook of Animal Abuse Studies*. Palgrave Macmillan.

Mawby, R. and Walklate, S. (1994). *Critical Victimology: International Perspectives*. Sage.

Morton, R., Hebart, M.L., Ankeny, R.A. and Whittaker, A.L. (2022). Portraying animal cruelty: A thematic analysis of Australian news media reports on penalties for animal cruelty. *Animals*, *12*(21): 2918. https://doi.org/10.3390/ani12212918

Nurse, A. (2016). Beyond the property debate: Animal welfare as a public good. *Contemporary Justice Review*, *19*(2): 174–187. https://doi.org/10.1080/10282580.2016.1169699

Nussbaum, M.C. (2017). Working with and for animals: Getting the theoretical framework right. *Denver Law Review*, *94*(4): 609–625. https://digitalcommons.du.edu/dlr/vol94/iss4/5/

Pheasey, H., Glen, G., Allison, N.L., Fonseca, L.G., Chacón, D., Restrepo, J. and Valverde, R.A. (2021). Quantifying illegal extraction of sea turtles in Costa Rica. *Frontiers in Conservation Science*, *2*. https://doi.org/10.3389/fcosc.2021.705556

Piquero, A. R., Farrington, D. P., and Blumstein, A. (2003). The criminal career paradigm. *Crime and Justice*, *30*: 359–506. https://doi.org/10.1086/652234

Pranshu, P. (2020). A study of animals as legal persons. *Indraprastha Law Review*, *I*(I): 1–10. https://indraprasthalawreview.in/wp-content/uploads/2020/10/ggsipu_uslls_ILR_2020_V1-I1-09-pranjal_pranshu.pdf

Regan, T. (1986). A case for animal rights. In M.W. Fox & L.D. Mickley (Eds.). *Advances in Animal Welfare Science 1986/87* (pp. 179–189). The Humane Society of the United States.

Rice, T. (2013). Letting the apes run the zoo: Using tort law to provide animals with a legal voice. *Pepperdine Law Review*, *40*(4): 6. https://digitalcommons.pepperdine.edu/plr/vol40/iss4/6

Ruggiero, V. and South, N. (2010). Critical criminology and crimes against the environment. *Critical Criminology*, *18*: 245–250. https://doi.org/10.1007/s10612-010-9121-9

Singer, P. (1975). *Animal Liberation: A New Ethics for Our Treatment of Animals*. HarperCollins.

Sollund, R. (2011). Expressions of speciesism: The effects of keeping companion animals on animal abuse, animal trafficking and species decline. *Crime, Law and Social Change*, *55*(5): 437–451. https://doi.org/10.1007/s10611-011-9296-3

Sollund, R. (2013). The victimization of women, children and nonhuman species through trafficking and trade: Crimes understood through an ecofeminist perspective. In N. South and A. Brisman (Eds.). *Routledge International Handbook of Green Criminology* (pp. 317–330). Routledge.

Sollund, R. (2020). Wildlife crime: A crime of hegemonic masculinity. *Social Sciences*, *9*(6): 93. https://doi.org/10.3390/socsci9060093

Sollund, R. (2021). Nonspeciesist criminology, wildlife trade, and animal victimization. *Oxford Research Encyclopedias, Criminology and Crime Justice*. https://doi.org/10.1093/acrefore/9780190264079.013.608

Stephens Griffin, N. and Griffin, N. (2021). Beyond meat? Taking violence against non-human animals seriously as a form of social harm. In P. Davies, P. Leighton and T. Wyatt (Eds.). *The Palgrave Handbook of Social Harm* (pp. 281–310). Palgrave Macmillan. https://doi.org/10.1007/978-3-030-72408-5_12

Stucki, S. (2020). Towards a theory of legal animal rights: Simple and fundamental rights. *Oxford*

Journal of Legal Studies, *40*(3): 533–560. https://doi.org/10.1093/ojls/gqaa007

Taylor, N. and Twine, R. (Eds.). (2014). *The Rise of Critical Animal Studies: From the Margins to the Centre*. Routledge.

Tschakert, P., Schlosberg, D., Celermajer, D., Rickards, L., Winter, C., Thaler, M., Stewart-Harawira, M. and Verlie, B. (2021). Multispecies justice: Climate-just futures with, for and beyond humans. *WIREs Climate Change*, *12*(2): e699. https://doi.org/10.1002/wcc.699

Turgoose, D. and McKie, R. (2019, July 5). Domestic violence and abuse (DVA), companion animals and independent agency: Why as criminologists we need to converse beyond speciesism, towards an intersectional approach. Presentation to the British Society of Criminology Conference on Public Criminologies Invisible Victims Panel, University of Lincoln, UK.

van Dijk, J. (1988). Introduction: The rediscovery of the crime victim. In M. Maguire and J. Pointing (Eds.). *Victims of Crime: A New Deal?* (pp. 1–13). Open University Press.

Walklate, S. (Ed.). (2018). *Handbook of Victims and Victimology* (2nd ed.). Routledge.

Walters, G.D. (2014). Testing the direct, indirect, and moderated effects of childhood animal cruelty on future aggressive and non-aggressive offending. *Aggressive Behavior, 40*(3): 238–249. https://doi.org/10.1002/ab.21514

White, R. (2013). *Environmental Harm: An Eco-Justice Perspective.* Policy Press. https://doi.org/10.56687/9781447300427-005

White, R. (2018). Green victimology and non-human victims. *International Review of Victimology*, *24*(2), 239–255. https://doi.org/10.1177/0269758017745615

Whitfort, A. (2019). Wildlife crime and animal victims: Improving access to environmental justice in Hong Kong. *Journal of International Wildlife Law and Policy*, *22*(3): 203–230. https://doi.org/10.1080/13880292.2019.1677055

Wrenn, C.L. (2022). What is vegan sociology? On the Pulse Seminar Series. The Vegan Society, 26 April. https://www.youtube.com/watch?v=PCMB51aZp_8&list=PLwq-YHBuff5eDSvpT0jYU9ekFVGZ-guWX

Wright, L. (Ed.). (2021). *The Routledge Handbook of Vegan Studies*. Routledge.

34. Environmental victimisation

Introduction

This entry examines the processes of environmental victimisation from the wide and plural perspective of green criminology. In doing this, it suggests some theoretical frameworks for an interdisciplinary understanding of environmental issues in the criminological field, highlighting the importance of epistemologically comprehending the impact of colonialism, anthropocentrism and androcentrism on environmental victimisation and, methodologically, conducting empirical research on social perceptions pertaining to environmental crime and harm.

Processes of environmental victimisation

In the criminological field, the processes of environmental victimisation have, until recently, received little empirical attention and environmental victims often remain hidden in the shadows of mainstream criminology (Hall, 2013; White, 2011; Davies et al., 2014; Williams, 1996). Overall, environmental victimisation poses a series of new questions that criminal justice systems have generally been unprepared to face (Hall, 2013, pp. 219–220). These questions touch on several interrelated issues.

First, environmental harms can affect an extended group, a community of victims, sometimes representing rival interests, and/or even with transnational consequences. Second, the perpetrators are often corporations or states, which are structurally immunised by the criminal justice system (due to their ability to formulate self-serving laws, hire expensive legal counsel, bribe officials, and so on) and, in many cases, they are not even based in the same territory where the environmental harm was suffered, as is the case with transnational corporations, for example (White, 2011, 2013; Barak, 2015; Böhm, 2019; Whyte, 2020). Here we see the importance of developing a notion of 'crime' that encompasses 'lawful, but awful' acts and omissions (Hillyard et al., 2004; Passas, 2005). Third, the causality nexus is extremely complex to reconstruct insofar as, for example, pollution may originate from many sources and take a long period of time to demonstrate harm (e.g., plastics in the ocean). Finally, to overcome anthropocentrism the concept of environmental victims must also embrace animals other-than-humans and the ecosystems affected by human harmful activities (Wyatt, 2022; White, 2008). However, this also raises another issue, that is, how to understand the harms caused to other-than-human animals and to ecosystems. How can we measure or comprehend the harms perpetrated to beings that can't speak? (Wyatt, 2022; Pali and Aertsen, 2021).

Another important issue is the divide between humans and other-than-humans, since there are cultural differences to consider in these relationships. Epistemologically, this divide does not make sense to Indigenous communities which preserve their identities as peoples-nature, in the sense that they are not simply humans living in harmony with nature; they *are* nature (Krenak, 2020). Harms caused to these peoples intrinsically have the consequence of causing harm to the environment; harms perpetrated against their environment tend to harm the peoples. From this perspective we can develop the interconnected relationship between ecocide and genocide, and between genocide and ecocide.

The idea of a connection between ecocide and genocide was first developed with the case of Agent Orange in the Vietnam War. It was considered to define, for the first time, the concept of ecocide, as articulated by Richard Falk (Lynch et al., 2021). The idea that the opposite process can also be truth – that genocide can also cause ecocide – derives from the connection with epistemicide of cultures of groups who are the guardians of the forests (Budó, in press; Goyes et al., 2021).

The relevant scientific literature clearly shows that systematic denial of harm and responsibility further frustrate efforts to create causal connections between offenders and victims (Williams, 1996). The strategies and techniques of neutralisation on the part of corporations or the state in cases where they are causing environmental harms include literally denying the problem (Cohen, 2001; Budó, 2021); justifying the harms in the name of economic development (with so-called 'sustainable development' being one of the main greenwashing strategies); putting out the perspective that what is seen as damaging is normal and in the national interest; and reproaching, blaming, dividing, and confusing the victims (Williams, 1996). It is important, therefore, to explore the process of victimisation as an active social process, which implies relationships of power, control, and resistance (White, 2011).

The impacts of environmental victimisation are diverse and far-reaching. The complexity of the concept of environmental harm, including the definition of victim, is also related to the epistemological problem of the coloniality of knowledge (Quijano, 2000). The experiences of environmental harm and victimisation can be construed as a framework of disputes that have concrete consequences. In this regard, it is important to comprehend how colonialism and racism are responsible for hierarchising peoples, animals, and territories and thereby to differentially legitimise environmental destruction (Rodríguez, 2022). Not everyone is treated the same conceptually, socially, and materially, and there are major differences in who is considered a bona fide environmental victim and who or what is not. Concerning this approach, the epistemologies of the South are integral to the construction of a Southern Green Criminology (Connell et al., 2018; Goyes, 2019). They reveal that the people seen as *others* and as *objects* by modern rationality are the most affected by environmental harms even though they are less responsible for them: they include women, non-white people, and those mainly based in the Global South (WHO, 2010; Pulido, 1996; Goyes, 2019).

When talking about cisheteropatriarchy, it is also important to highlight how women, and especially racialised and gender dissidents, have been inferiorised and treated as the other to be invaded and dominated, and whose work is not considered valuable, in a process which has the same epistemic basis and economic interests as the colonial domination over nature (Sollund, 2012; Milne et al., 2023; Ferdinand, 2022; Mies and Shiva, 2014). That is why research on victims of environmental crimes should always consider the intersection between systems of oppression, such as gender, race, sexuality, and class. At a global level, this is expressed, for example, by the migration of harms from the Global North to the Global South, the double patterns of safety and regulation used by transnational companies (Böhm, 2019), and the disputes over territory within which these companies sometimes engage (Whyte, 2020).

Doing empirical research on environmental victimisation

Social and cultural perspectives are the basis for an empirical clarification of what constitutes environmental victimisation (Hall, 2013, pp. 225–226). In many cases, to understand the different narratives orbiting around a broadly understood case of environmental crime, it is necessary to comprehend the perceptions of that harm *from the inside*, that is, starting from the symbolic and cultural perspectives expressed by the social actors affected, to study harm *from their perspective*.

This approach to harm raises the following kinds of questions. How do people live and make sense of their experiences in polluted places? From the inhabitants' perspective, what is the relationship between their knowledge of the risks living and working in a contaminated environment, their lived experiences of environmental suffering and injustice, and their responses to these threats and experienced harms? What can they want or expect from the justice system if anything? (Bisschop and Vande Walle, 2013; White, 2013).

Empirical research on the inhabitants of highly polluted places, for example, has revealed that there are multiple interpretations guiding their decision to act – or to abstain from acting – in response to their environmental victimisation (Natali, 2010). Moreover, social and cultural perspectives on environmental victimisation processes show that experiences of environmental suffering are not simply individual; they are actively and collectively created starting from the position that the residents as a group occupy in the wider social macro-cosmos (Auyero and Swistun, 2009, p. 159). In order to include this form of knowledge it is necessary to rethink the hierarchy of knowledge (Quijano, 2000), created by modernity and colonialism, to analyse critically the supposed clear division between knowledge and non-knowledge – between what can be recognised as 'scientific', and thus 'real', and what instead remains at the margins even though it, too, is 'real'.

When undertaking these empirical investigations, it is essential to question simplistic concepts about the relationship between victims and environmental harms, noting that victims often disagree on the definition and interpretation of that reality. Contrary to what is identified in the predominant scientific literature, social experiences of environmental suffering are full of doubts, disagreements, suspicion, fears, and hopes (Auyero and Swistun, 2009). The mechanism of denial, in particular, helps us to understand the silences, the apathy and a wide range of other possible responses by those who witness daily the destruction of their environment (Williams, 1996; White and Heckenberg, 2014; Cohen, 2001).

At the same time, collective and political reactions to environmental harm can also be deadly for environmental victims. For example, in 2021, Global Witness (2021) reported that 220 people around the world were killed while defending their territories. This number is the highest in the series, but it is nevertheless still way under-reported. Institutional violence, such as police shootings and arrests of activists are also a reality for those who are not passive in the face of environmental destruction.

Methodologically, empirical research of this import requires a peculiar sensitivity to the situation on the part of the researcher. Respect for local knowledge and culture and acknowledgement of the dimensions of political and economic power that may be present in the contexts studied are crucial factors for relevant and ethical research. With respect to this, collaborative methods of collection and construction of data help in approaching the 'truths' in the narratives of research participants (Natali et al., 2023).

It is crucial to highlight the importance of developing qualitative methods that explore the reality of environmental harm, starting from the knowledge of those social actors who are direct victims of its consequences (Natali, 2010, 2016). This sensitivity to the symbolic perspectives of the social actors surveyed is necessary to get the researcher closer to the 'truths' disclosed in their narratives. Remaining alert to such nuances – including ambiguities, contradictions, and disagreements – is a fundamental challenge when attention is focused on the narratives that people construct about their complex experiences of environmental contamination. These theoretical and methodological sensibilities may be enhanced thanks to what Brisman and South (2014) conceptualise as a 'green cultural criminology', a criminological perspective that tries to imagine new modes of critically analysing the intersection of culture, crime, justice, and environment.

When considering the results of such qualitative research on environmental victimisation, the first issue concerns the multiple, confused, and contradictory viewpoints of people affected by environmental harm (Auyero and Swistun, 2009). This 'haziness' affects their perceptions of the impact of pollution on health and the natural world and is related to: (1) the constitutive uncertainty around the toxicity of some substances present in the environment; (2) the discursive universes dominated by those social actors – businesses, the state, mass media, local daily papers, local authorities – empowered to enact an efficient 'work of confusion' regarding the issue of pollution; and (3) the relational and physical basis of risk perception (Auyero and Swistun, 2009). Thus, confusion and doubt result from a process of social construction in a non-neutral social space. It concerns, in fact, both social and natural worlds that are also structured according to power, in which some social actors, the most powerful, have more influence than others.

Qualitative and collaborative research methods may contribute to facilitating various steps towards social and political recognition of victims, and the visualisation of environmental harm connected to human activity (Natali and de Nardin Budó, 2018). This process can be assisted by shedding light on that 'twilight state' where environmental harms arise as happenings that do not yet exist in the social and discursive sphere (Szasz, 1994, p. 31) – where the voices of victims have not yet been heard. This aspect may well be linked with a green criminological perspective that goes beyond a binary and modernist approach to crime, harm, and criminal justice. Such an approach, offering the victims a chance to *narrate* – both to themselves and to others – their personal and collective experience of environmental suffering and victimisation, is paramount to the development of more efficient and satisfying answers than those offered by legislation alone (Hall, 2017).

Environmental engagement and discourses

Environmental activism by environmental victims and social movements has been the main way to provide awareness to the public about the processes of environmental destruction throughout the world. From the Bhopal disaster to the dam collapses in Brazil, we can see how the victims and environmental organisations are struggling for accountability for perpetrators, recognition and reparation for past harms, and prevention of future harms.

Citizens' active participation is vital for the processes of reparation, even though environmental issues are mostly left to 'experts' (Natali, 2010; Natali et al., 2023). Science can and must be the main tool in deliberations concerning the interventions to repair the impact of humans on the environment. However, science offers only one kind of knowledge (White, 2008, p. 78). An important step in creating the conditions for knowledge, recognition, and possible reparation in the aftermath of environmental crime is to give value to the reflexive and narrative dimensions of knowledge and include the voices of victims in contexts also open to other actors (institutions, experts, civil society).

Questions concerning environmental harm and victimisation also present complex practical challenges as they involve intrinsically multidisciplinary fields that are highly politicised and global in their reach (White, 2011). Including in criminological discourses the most advanced theorising about nature should help to progressively sensitise decision-makers to the necessity of changing traditional visions that inform policy options and laws relating to the environment. Many authors have noted how the prevailing image of nature seriously limits the conception of juridical constructions and criminal justice policies to effectively meet environmental victims' needs and repair harms (Cullinan, 2011). Given this, it is necessary to ask how one can translate the conceptual openness inaugurated by green criminology into policies capable of operating concretely (see White, 2023).

To address environmentally destructive activities by listening to environmental victims and respecting the complexity of environmental harm, we could draw inspiration from criminologists' considerable interest in restorative justice mechanisms (Pali et al., 2022; Pali and Aertsen, 2021; Natali and Hall, 2022; Budó and Pali, 2023). Of course, restorative justice cannot be expected to be effective in all, or even many, cases of environmental crimes. Nonetheless, it can contribute to repairing the resulting harms of environmental victimisation. That is why, in the environmental field, it seems necessary to imagine a different system of justice, orienting towards possible futures, utilising languages and models of justice other than the traditional ones. Restorative justice – based on the idea of spontaneous participation and aimed at constructing, together and actively, a work of reparation on an act's destructive effects – represents a possible horizon that is increasingly feasible (see also White, 2017).

In any event, to deal with the reality of environmental crimes and harms, it is also important to understand the colonial and racial dimensions of the knowledge produced by the powerful if we are to address ecological destruction (Rodríguez, 2022), and the power imbalance between stakeholders in most cases of environmental harm (Aertsen, 2018). A change in the relationship between humans and nature, to overcome anthropocentrism and the conception that nature is just a resource for capitalist development, is also a related project to decolonisation. Such a change is not only vital for reparation of past harms, but for the survival of all human life on the planet (Stretesky et al., 2013; Whyte, 2020).

Conclusion

A progressive social and environmental policy should focus on ameliorating situations characterised by harms and socio-environmental injustice (both at the individual and collective level), and on protecting the well-being of the most exposed and vulnerable groups in society. Among its aims would be social and environmental justice (distributive equity), social and environmental security (protection against serious environmental risks), peaceful management of socio-environmental conflicts, and the strengthening of public participation in environmental policymaking. For human environmental victims, such an approach is essential. It also provides an important platform for developing measures to better recognise and protect the rights and status of non-human animals, plants, and specific ecosystems.

LORENZO NATALI AND MARÍLIA DE NARDIN BUDÓ

Further reading

Hall, M. (2013). *Victims of Environmental Harm: Rights, Recognition and Redress under National and International Law*. Abingdon: Routledge.

Milne, E., Davies, P., Heydon, J., Peggs, K., and Wyatt, T. (eds.) (2023). *Gendering Green Criminology*. Bristol: Bristol University Press. https://doi.org/10.51952/9781529229646.ch001

Natali, L. (2016). *A Visual Approach for Green Criminology: Exploring the Social Perception of Environmental Harm*. Basingstoke: Palgrave Macmillan.

Natali, L. (2024). The social perception of environmental victimization: A visual and sensory methodological proposal. *Crime, Law and Social Change* 81: 561–580.

Spapens, T., White, R., and Kluin, M. (2014). *Environmental Crime and Its Victims: Perspectives within Green Criminology*. Abingdon: Routledge.

White, R. (2015). Environmental victimology and ecological justice. In Wilson, D., and Ross, S. (eds.) *Crime, Victims and Policy*. Basingstoke: Palgrave Macmillan, 33–52.

Wyatt, T. (2022). *Wildlife Trafficking: A Deconstruction of the Crime, Victims and Offenders* (2nd ed.). Basingstoke: Palgrave Macmillan.

References

Aertsen, I. (2018). Restorative justice for victims of corporate violence. In Forti, G., Mazzucato, C., Visconti, A., and Giavazzi, S. (eds.) *Victims and Corporations: Legal Challenges and Empirical Findings* (pp. 235–258). Milan: Wolters Kluwer.

Auyero, J., and Swistun, D. A. (2009). *Flammable: Environmental Suffering in an Argentine Shantytown*. Oxford: Oxford University Press.

Barak, G. (2015). The crimes of the powerful and the globalization of crime. *Revista Brasileira de Direito* 11(2): 104–114.

Bisschop, L., and Vande Walle, G. (2013). Environmental victimisation and conflict resolution: A case study of e-Waste. In Walters, R., Westerhuis, D., and Wyatt, T. (eds.) *Emerging Issues in Green Criminology: Exploring Power, Justice and Harm* (pp. 34–56). Basingstoke: Palgrave Macmillan.

Böhm, M. L. (2019). *The Crime of Maldevelopment*. New York: Routledge.

Brisman, A., and South, N. (2014). *Green Cultural Criminology: Constructions of Environmental Harm, Consumerism and Resistance to Ecocide*. Abingdon: Routledge.

Budó, M. N. (2021). Corporate crime and the use of science in the case of asbestos: Producing harm through discursive shields. *Journal of White Collar and Corporate Crime* 2(2): 81–96. https://doi.org/10.1177/2631309X20978718

Budó, M. N. (in press). Os limites coloniais da criminalização do ecocídio perante o Tribunal Penal Internacional. *Sortuz: Oñati Journal of Emergent Socio-Legal Studies*.

Budó, M. N., and Pali, B. (2023). Restorative responses to harms caused by asbestos companies. *Journal of Victimology* 15: 171–204.

Cohen, S. (2001). *States of Denial: Knowing About Atrocities and Suffering*. Cambridge: Polity Press.

Connell, R., Pearse, R., Collyer, F., Maia, J., and Morrell, R. (2018). Re-making the global economy of knowledge: Do new fields of research change the structure of North–South relations? *British Journal of Sociology* (69): 738–757. doi.org/10.1111/1468-4446.12294.

Cullinan, C. (2011). *Wild Law: A Manifesto for Earth Justice*. Vermont: Chelsea Green Publishing.

Davies, P., Francis, P., and Wyatt, T. (eds.) (2014). *Invisible Crimes and Social Harms*. Basingstoke: Palgrave Macmillan.

Ferdinand, M. (2022). *Uma ecologia decolonial: pensar a partir do mundo caribenho*. São Paulo: Ubu.

Global Witness (2021). *The Industries Causing the Climate Crisis and Attacks Against Land and Environmental Defenders*. https://www.globalwitness.org/documents/20190/Last_line_of_defence_-_low_res_-_September_2021.pdf

Goyes, D. R. (2019). *Southern Green Criminology: A Science to End Ecological Discrimination*. Bingley, UK: Emerald.

Goyes, D. R., South, N., Abaibira, M. A., Baicué, P., Cuchimba, A., and Ñeñetofe, D. T. R. (2021). Genocide and ecocide in four Colombian Indigenous communities: The erosion of a way of life and memory. *The British Journal of Criminology* 61(4): 965–984. https://doi.org/10.1093/bjc/azaa109

Hall, M. (2013). *Victims of Environmental Harm: Rights, Recognition and Redress under National and International Law*. Abingdon: Routledge.

Hall, M. (2017). Exploring the cultural dimensions of environmental victimization. *Palgrave Communication* 3: 17076.

Hillyard, P., Pantazis, C., Tombs, S., and Gordon, D. (eds.) (2004). *Beyond Criminology: Taking Harm Seriously*. London: Pluto Press.

Krenak, A. (2020). *Ideas to Postpone the End of the World*. Toronto: House of Anansi Press.

Lynch, M., Fegadel, A., and Long, M. (2021). Green criminology and state–corporate crime: The ecocide–genocide nexus with examples from Nigeria. *Journal of Genocide Research* 23(2): 236–256.

Mies, M., and Shiva, V. (2014). *Ecofeminism*. London: Zed Books.

Milne, E., Davies, P., Heydon, J., Peggs, K., and Wyatt, T. (eds.) (2023). *Gendering Green*

Criminology. Bristol: Bristol University Press. https://doi.org/10.51952/9781529229646.ch001
Natali, L. (2010). The big grey elephants in the backyard of Huelva, Spain. In White, R. (ed.) *Global Environmental Harm: Criminological Perspectives* (pp. 193–209). Cullompton: Willan Publishing.
Natali, L. (2016). *A Visual Approach for Green Criminology: Exploring the Social Perception of Environmental Harm*. Basingstoke: Palgrave Macmillan.
Natali, L., and de Nardin Budó, M. (2018). A sensory and visual approach for comprehending environmental victimization by asbestos industry in Casale Monferrato. *European Journal of Criminology* 16(6): 708–726.
Natali, L., and Hall, M. (2022). A green criminological approach to environmental victimisation and restorative justice. In Burgess, J. P., Centemeri, L., and Topçu, S. (eds.) *Rethinking Environments: A Critical Perspective on Recovery After Disaster*. Abingdon: Routledge, 165–184.
Natali, L., Suman, A., and De Nardin Budó, M. (2023). What about environmental 'victims'? Methodological reflections for an activist criminology. In Canning, V., Martin, G., and Tombs, S. (eds.) *International Handbook of Activist Criminology* (pp. 215–231). Bingley, UK: Emerald.
Pali, B., and Aertsen, I. (2021). Inhabiting a vulnerable and wounded Earth: Restoring response-ability. *International Journal of Restorative Justice* 4(1): 3–16.
Pali, B., Tepper, F., and Forsyth, M. (eds.) (2022). *The Palgrave Handbook of Environmental Restorative Justice*. Basingstoke: Palgrave Macmillan.
Passas, N. (2005). Lawful but awful: 'Legal corporate crimes'. *The Journal of Socio-Economics* 34(6): 771–786.
Pulido, L. A. (1996). Critical review of the methodology of environmental racism research. *Antipode* 28(2):142–159.
Quijano, A. (2000). Coloniality of power and Eurocentrism in Latin America. *International Sociology* 15(2): 215–232.
Rodríguez, I. (2022). Restor(y)ing the past to envision an 'other' future: A decolonial environmental restorative justice perspective. In Pali, B., Tepper, F., and Forsyth, M. (eds.) *The Palgrave Handbook of Environmental Restorative Justice* (pp. 531–561). Basingstoke: Palgrave Macmillan.
Sollund, R. (2012). The victimization of women, children and non-human species through tracking and trade: Crimes understood through an ecofeminist perspective. In South, N., and Brisman, A. (eds.) *Routledge International Handbook of Green Criminology* (pp. 512–528). Abingdon: Routledge.
Stretesky, P., Long, M., and Lynch, M. (2013). *The Treadmill of Crime: Political Economy and Green Criminology*. Abingdon: Routledge.
Szasz, A. (1994). *Ecopopulism: Toxic Waste and the Movement for Environmental Justice*. Minneapolis: University of Minnesota Press.
White, R. (2008). *Crimes Against Nature: Environmental Criminology and Ecological Justice*. Cullompton: Willan Publishing.
White, R. (2011). *Transnational Environmental Crime: Towards an Eco-Global Criminology*. Abingdon: Routledge.
White, R. (2013). Resource extraction leaves something behind: Environmental justice and mining. *International Journal for Crime and Justice* 2(1): 50–64.
White, R. (2017). Reparative justice, environmental crime and penalties for the powerful. *Crime, Law and Social Change: An Interdisciplinary Journal* 67(2): 117–132.
White, R. (2023). *Advanced Introduction to Applied Green Criminology*. Cheltenham, UK and Northampton, MA, USA: Edward Elgar Publishing.
White, R., and Heckenberg, D. (2014). *Green Criminology: An Introduction to the Study of Environmental Harm*. Abingdon: Routledge.
Whyte, D. (2020). *Ecocide: Kill the Corporation before It Kills Us*. Manchester: Manchester University Press.
WHO (2010). *Environment and Health Risks: A Review of the Influence and Effects of Social Inequalities*. Copenhagen: World Health Organization.
Williams, C. (1996). An environmental victimology. *Social Science* 23(1): 16–40. Reprinted in White, R. (ed.) (2009). *Environmental Crime: A Reader*. Cullompton: Willan Publishing, pp. 200–222.
Wyatt, T. (2022). *Wildlife Trafficking: A Deconstruction of the Crime, Victims and Offenders* (2nd ed.). Basingstoke: Palgrave Macmillan.

35. Indigenous people and environmental crime

Introduction

Global populations with deep historic ties to their lands and natural resources are collectively known as 'Indigenous'. The interconnectedness these communities share with the natural world makes them especially susceptible to the social and ecological pressures caused by environmental crimes and harms. The traditional ecological knowledge of Indigenous people is also of significant value to criminals looking to exploit the environment for profit as well as conservationists who seek to protect it. Previously uncontacted groups now balance geopolitical and socio-economic considerations with their traditional belief systems. The range of outside influences that have been experienced in these historically marginalised communities has led to diverse interactions with environmental crime. This entry primarily explores Indigenous people as occupying the roles of victim, offender, and defender and the considerable overlap that often exists between them. The implications of these different orientations for criminal justice, conservation, and human rights are also discussed.

Overlapping roles in environmental crime

Environmental crime has become one of the most serious threats to human security, economic development, biodiversity protection, and public health in recent decades, the impacts of which are acutely felt by the world's Indigenous people. Increasing at a higher rate than the global GDP, these illicit activities include illegal logging; illegal, unregulated, and unreported (IUU) fishing; illegal wildlife trade (IWT); illicit mining; and hazardous waste crimes. According to the Financial Action Task Force (FATF), environmental crime recently surpassed human trafficking to become the world's third most lucrative transnational crime, only trailing trafficking in drugs and firearms (FATF, 2021). The violent social conflict that frequently accompanies these crimes has been associated with piracy, civil war, forced child labour, and terrorism (Brashares et al., 2014; Nellemann et al., 2016).

Indigenous people, many of whom share their ancestral ranges with ecologically significant species of flora and fauna, include roughly 476 million people worldwide (World Bank, 2022). While it would be inadvisable to discuss these geographically and culturally diverse populations as a monolith, Indigenous environmental ontologies across the Americas, Oceania, Africa, Asia, and Europe tend to centre around two main themes. These are: (1) the interconnected well-being of humanity and nature and (2) an inherent spiritual and cultural significance for all elements of nature (Goyes et al., 2021). Given their inextricable relationship with the natural environment, Indigenous people's knowledge has been targeted by criminals looking to profit from the illegal trade in natural resources and other products (van Uhm & Grigore, 2021) as well as in conservation efforts aimed at protecting the environment (Chaudhuri, 2013; Ohlson et al., 2008). The historical exploitation of Indigenous populations by outside interests often positions them in such binary terms, as victim or resister. In the case of crimes against the environment, however, the situation is more complex.

Although the scale of environmental destruction from Indigenous 'criminal' offences is generally understood to be far less than those committed by state and corporate actors, their underlying motivations can have important implications. Socio-economic conditions like poverty and loss of traditional livelihoods have been identified as precursors to Indigenous people's participation in the illegal wildlife trade (Bartholomew et al., 2021; Leberatto, 2016; van Uhm & Grigore, 2021). Absent any external influence, however, involvement in knowingly illegal resource use for subsistence or tradition demonstrates a certain autonomy in Indigenous decision-making (Eichler & Baumeister, 2018; Tanalgo, 2017). Alternatively, a victim–offender overlap may exist, in which these processes are co-occurring. Many governments have effectively criminalised traditional activities on land designated for environmental protection (Duffy, 2010), extractive industry like mining (Heydon, 2020) or industrial agriculture (Mol, 2017; van Solinge, 2010).

The roles Indigenous people occupy at the different stages of environmental crime have overlapped in other ways as well. Researchers have described the trajectory of environmental offenders to defenders and influencers in their communities (Goyes et al., 2021; Whittington-Jones et al., 2020). While hard-to-reach populations like Indigenous groups remain underexplored, researchers have observed diverse interactions with environmental crimes and harms among these communities. While they only constitute an estimated six per cent of the world's population, such findings have important implications for humanity and the environment.

Victimisation and environment-related transgressions

To understand Indigenous people's interactions with the natural world, specifically to the extent that a crime is alleged, researchers must appreciate how environmental transgressions and value associations are socially and culturally constructed across distinct human populations. Green criminology has been identified as well positioned to address the borderless and transnational nature of environmental crime (Goyes et al., 2021). While dominant Western perspectives on the environment tend to be anthropocentric, non-spiritual, and sceptical, green criminological approaches reflect many Indigenous philosophies by acknowledging the intrinsic value of non-human animal and plant life and their impact on global ecosystems (van Uhm, 2018).

It is critical that researchers also consider how words like 'crime' can have different meanings across languages depending on the translation (Wyatt & Arroyo-Quiroz, 2018). This, in addition to distinct legal and cultural understandings of crime, can be of great consequence in understanding the processes of criminal offending and victimisation across global societies. Southern criminology, which elevates the perspectives and experiences of the Global South in the production of criminological knowledge, is also key to studying how crimes of the state are frequently discordant with Indigenous livelihoods and systems of justice (Carrington et al., 2016).

Victims of environmental crime

It is often useful to think about environmental crimes and harms through a historical lens in which certain activities that were once permitted are now considered illegal. The failure of the United States government to regulate bison hunting in the late 1800s, for example, resulted in the species' unabated slaughter over a 25-year period, a crucial resource and cultural loss for Native Americans. Moloney and Chambliss (2014) refer to this governmental inaction as the 'state crime of omission'. The authors argue that this is underscored by the fact that the US government was engaged in open conflict with Native American groups at the time and had already provided legislative protections to other big game species. The state-sanctioned decimation of the American bison by non-Indigenous hunters directly threatened the traditional hunting activities and livelihoods of the native population. Although today's governments and powerful corporations are held to higher standards than their predecessors, they still manage to avoid accountability in cases of Indigenous victimisation from environmental crimes.

State–corporate environmental crime

It is often easier to identify the victims of green crimes than the perpetrators. Indigenous inhabitants depend on elements of the immediate natural environment for survival, including for food, water, and medicine. The destruction of these resources undermines their own self-interests. The far more pervasive destroyers of the environment include private transnational companies, typically based in the West, whose activities are often enabled by governmental corruption (Wolf, 2011). Despite many countries having granted legal protections for their Indigenous populations, a lack of enforcement means these groups are frequently the victims of large-scale environmentally destructive activities like logging, mining, and even green energy projects. While the official policy in Brazil, for example, is to protect its Indigenous population, the Bolsonaro government (which ruled from 2019 to 2023) was accused of state–corporate environmental crime by neglecting these citizens to develop the country's forested areas for economic growth (Grisafi, 2020).

Forest conversion for industrial agriculture is the main source of illegal deforestation in the tropics, driven by Western demand for export products like beef, soy, palm oil, and leather. Violent territorial conflicts have long existed between Indigenous forest inhabitants and loggers or landowners seeking agricultural expansion. Indigenous people have been the victims of intentional forest fires; violent acts of racism and discrimination, including murder, torture, kidnapping, and rape; and a high suicide rate among Indigenous youth who see a grim future without the forest and natural resources they depend on (Mol, 2017; van Solinge, 2010). Previously uncontacted populations are also at serious risk of contracting unfamiliar diseases, compounded by their reduced access to important medicinal plants long used in the treatment of illness and disease (van Solinge, 2010).

Justice and environmental crimes

Grisafi (2020) alleges that acts of genocide are being committed against Indigenous people in the Amazon through state–corporate environmental destruction designed to target these communities based on ethnic identity. Citing forcible transfer, extermination, and the persecution of Indigenous people, she argues that crimes against humanity have been committed and discusses the need for such cases to be adjudicated by the International Criminal Court (ICC). Other scholars have echoed calls to establish a precedent for investigating and prosecuting intertwined international and green crimes (Paulose, 2021).

Environmental courts have been advocated in the administration of restorative justice for environmental crimes and harms against both people and place (Hall, 2017). This is especially relevant for Indigenous victims and defendants whose belief systems are compatible with the restorative justice principles of forgiveness, harmonious relations, and holistic perspectives. The New Zealand Environmental Court set a precedent for applying this type of justice in cases of pollution, land development, and deforestation. The restorative measures applied have ranged from defendant apology to financial compensation to reforesting (White, 2014). It is unclear how successful these accountability measures would be in cases of non-Indigenous offenders, such as corporate polluters. However, White (2017) considers how 'reparative' justice administered by specialist environmental courts through sanctions may be used to repair harm and deter future corporate offending.

Victim–offender nexus

Legal and illegal environmental degradation has led to drastically reduced opportunities for traditional hunting, trapping, and fishing (Heydon, 2020; Lawrence & Raitio, 2006; van Solinge, 2010). 'Tertiary green crimes' have been identified as those committed as the result of such environmental victimisation (Potter, 2016). Ironically, environmental regulations restricting access to natural resources have also pushed many Indigenous people towards 'criminality'. Through the process of net-widening, the legal definitions of criminal behaviour are broadened to include activities not previously proscribed by the law (McMahon, 1990). With their traditional livelihoods criminalised and stigmatised, Indigenous communities have faced persistent accusations of illegal resource use and trespassing on newly private or protected lands. Consideration of the complex 'victim–offender overlap' (Hall, 2013) in these cases allows for a more nuanced understanding of Indigenous experiences with environmental crime.

Offenders of environmental crime

Hunting and gathering

Overwhelmingly, Indigenous offences against the environment pertain to the illegal removal or consumption of protected flora and fauna. While Indigenous and non-Indigenous hunting for sustenance is legally protected in many countries, with some basic restrictions for protected species (Tanalgo, 2017), regulations are often poorly enforced, and over-hunting has become a significant problem in places like Peru (Leberatto, 2016). In other countries, including neighbouring Colombia, wildlife hunting and plant foraging for subsistence and/or medicine constitutes a crime. Breaches of expected behaviour in these cases are sometimes adjudicated in Indigenous systems of justice, but the most extreme are handled by the state (Goyes et al., 2021).

Unsurprisingly, participation in Indigenous hunting is often gendered. Men and boys typically participate in hunts while women and girls process game meat for consumption or sale (Lyana, 2014) or hold no discernible role at all (Tanalgo, 2017). The most common Indigenous hunting techniques include traditional methods like snaring, spears, scavenging, and the use of hunting dogs. There has also been some evidence of non-traditional air guns or explosive baits (Kanagavel et al., 2016; Tanalgo, 2017). Wild game meat has been targeted for both sustenance and trade (Lyana, 2014) and has been used by some communities for purposes other than consumption, including in medicines, musical instruments, and cremation (Kanagavel et al., 2016).

In countries such as Tanzania and the Philippines, Indigenous hunters have been observed targeting larger mammals for their meat and high protein content (Lyana, 2014; Tanalgo, 2017). In other areas, including Peninsular Malaysia and the Western Ghats region of India, large mammals appear to be too much work for traditional hunting efforts. Smaller animals, such as the critically endangered Sunda pangolin, are more frequently targeted for their higher value in the illegal market (Bartholomew et al., 2021; Kanagavel et al., 2016). Despite this diversity in hunting preferences and a trade that is largely opportunistic and informal (Leberatto, 2016; Paudel et al., 2020), local law enforcement has mostly focused its efforts on the larger, charismatic species (Kanagavel et al., 2016). They have also been accused of inequitable and biased treatment of suspected Indigenous offenders (Paudel et al., 2020).

Global environmental impacts

Though tempting, researchers have cautioned against idealising Indigenous–environment relationships as a utopian panacea (Goyes et al., 2021). For example, during the annual Mayan festival in the Yucatán known as *kots kaal pato*, piñatas are filled with captured iguanas and endangered opossums who are subsequently beaten to death by the community (Borges and Martín, 2015). Despite such cases of Indigenous groups targeting vulnerable species, there is little evidence to suggest that traditional hunting has led to species population decline or extinction (Bartholomew et al., 2021; van Solinge, 2010).

Researchers have found that Indigenous hunters often engage in self-regulation and local management (Roldán-Clarà, 2018; Tanalgo, 2017). When a resource becomes scarce in the environment, many communities with taboos against commercial hunting adjust their subsistence hunting practices to avoid upsetting the ecological balance (Aisher, 2016; Kurz et al., 2021). By contrast, the activities that serve to limit traditional hunting can actually serve as greater threats to local wildlife populations. These include agricultural expansion (Kanagavel et al., 2016; Roldán-Clarà, 2018) and major road construction (Pattiselanno & Krockenberger, 2021), which are known to facilitate wildlife trade.

Nevertheless, the integration of skilled Indigenous hunters in the global wildlife trade should be of concern to conservation practitioners. The opportunity for additional income has been cited by former and current Indigenous hunters as a significant motivation for poaching (Bartholomew et al., 2021; Leberatto, 2016; van Uhm & Grigore, 2021). A lack of formal education in Indigenous communities has resulted in high illiteracy rates and a deficiency of marketable skills for legal employment. Such conditions, combined with the loss of traditional livelihood, have incentivised criminal participation (Bartholomew et al., 2021; Roldán-Clarà, 2018; van Uhm & Grigore, 2021). Many convicted offenders have expressed remorse about the socio-economic conditions that led to their involvement in the illicit trade and about forest degradation in general (Leberatto, 2016; Paudel et al., 2020; Tanalgo, 2017), reflecting the inherent conflict between Indigenous ecocentric value systems and the economic incentives in environmental destruction.

Studies have also revealed that convicted Indigenous offenders had underestimated the risks and possessed a limited understanding of the potential sanctions associated with their environmental crimes (Paudel et al., 2020). The outsized proportion of offenders apprehended by law enforcement who are poor and/or Indigenous is also concerning and points to a broader trend in IWT where low-level poachers face greater risks and experience lesser rewards than professional dealers and kingpins. As the resource use of Indigenous people has been criminalised in many places, bias training for enforcement officers could be beneficial in addressing the apparent targeting of these individuals in IWT arrests. In their crime script analysis, Viollaz et al. (2021) identified important variations in the laying, monitoring, and use of snares for poaching in Vietnam. Such distinctions in the snaring decision-making process may inform targeted law enforcement approaches to professional poaching versus local subsistence hunters.

Indigenous knowledge and expert use of the natural environment are of high value to organised crime groups operating in borderlands, in particular. The lack of economic opportunities for Indigenous people has made them prime targets for serving as guides or informants for trafficking in drugs, timber, and/or wildlife (van Uhm & Grigore, 2021). Simultaneously helping and harming their own future survival, these individuals fill the role of both victim and offender in the environmental crimes they facilitate. Given the environmental stewardship historically practised by Indigenous people, conservation interests should empower the traditional beliefs upheld in these communities and incorporate them in efforts to protect the environment (Tanalgo, 2017).

Defenders against environmental crime

The role of local and Indigenous communities as guardians of the environment has been emphasised in community-based wildlife crime prevention by conservationists and criminologists alike. Locally controlled conservation initiatives have generally achieved more long-term success in improving conservation and social outcomes than externally controlled efforts that seek to change local behaviours (Dawson et al., 2021). Early examples of 'cooperative' strategies had been established somewhat paternalistically in response to local and Indigenous overhunting and overfishing of endangered species. Critics at the time argued that greater clarity and an improved sense of ownership over environmental protection efforts was needed among Indigenous communities for these efforts to be sustainable (Horowitz, 1998).

Subsequent conservation efforts have moved beyond cooperation to focus on leadership opportunities for Indigenous and local people. 'Co-management' strategies were developed to preserve Indigenous self-determination in environmental protection efforts and provide a more balanced power-sharing structure. Through these schemes, Indigenous communities are able to retain their traditional and legal rights to hunt, fish, gather, and farm but with added regulations applied to their traditional management system. The exclusion of Indigenous voices from decision-making processes, however, has compromised these efforts (Ohlson et al., 2008).

The vocal approval and participation of Indigenous leadership has been critical in garnering local support for certain controversial conservation projects. In response to sharp declines in African leopard populations, a partnership between the Barotse Royal Establishment (BRE) of the Lozi People of Western Zambia and the NGO Panthera introduced synthetic furs as viable alternatives to leopard skins for ceremonial attire. While many members of the Lozi tribe continue to prefer the authentic skins to the synthetic ones, most are accepting of the initiative primarily because of their reluctance to go against leadership directives (Whittington-Jones et al., 2020).

Reflecting the shift away from militarised conservation strategies and towards a greater role for Indigenous people, a participatory approach known as 'social fencing' was implemented at the Periyar Tiger Reserve (PTR) in Southern India. The participation of former forest-dwelling communities, and particularly Indigenous women, in the voluntary surveillance of forest boundaries appears to have had a positive effect on both conservation and Indigenous livelihoods (Chaudhuri, 2013). The project has received criticism, however, for the decision-making power that rests with Park authorities as well as its emphasis on 'marketable' skills to reduce forest dependency. Detractors argue that the development and modernisation of Indigenous communities and their disenfranchisement from conservation policy undermine their right to self-determination.

The intersectionality of gender and indigeneity in such programmes can have important implications for forest protection, however. In their comparative analysis of two Indigenous populations in the Philippines, Gabriel et al. (2020) found that the more gender-restrictive community, where there was no obvious role for women in environmental protection activities, experienced greater degradation of their natural environment. While the two communities occupy a similar range, the more gender-inclusive community demonstrated greater resilience to environmentally destructive events. Prevention efforts, including rock barriers to mitigate soil erosion, are led by the tribe's women, who also install warning signs to deter specific forms of local hunting in areas deemed sacred and vital to the community's well-being. Interestingly, these women were also accepted by their tribe as hunters of non-endangered wild animals.

Resistance movements

The world's Indigenous populations have mobilised their opposition to the destruction of their natural environment through both violent and non-violent resistance movements. Peaceful public protests and social movement strategies have featured far more frequently than violent responses. However, the threat of Indigenous resistance movements to the existing state and corporate power structures have precipitated a robust counter-resistance that has tended towards violence in recent decades. Though the official number is unknown, it is estimated that hundreds of Indigenous activists have been murdered or disappeared since the turn of the century (Boele et al., 2001; Lynch et al., 2018; Mol, 2017). Global Witness (Hines, 2023) further reports that Indigenous women face gender-specific threats such as sexual violence.

While global environmental and Indigenous rights movements have not always been aligned, the two interest groups have been able to wage successful campaigns against state–corporate power. The Ogoni people of Nigeria provided one of the earliest examples in their international campaign against Shell Oil and the Nigerian government in the early 1990s. After violent and deadly military retaliations against Ogoni activists, Shell eventually withdrew its operations (Boele et al., 2001). Similar efforts have come from the U'Wa people of Colombia and the Sámi of Finland, Europe's last remaining Indigenous population. Both have achieved relative success in collaborating with environmental interests to challenge their governments and the oil and logging industries, respectively (Lawrence & Raitio, 2006; Rodríguez-Garavito & Arenas, 2005). While NGOs have access to substantial resources and international contacts, Indigenous advocacy groups wield political influence with the larger movement to assert their collective rights.

Other communities have similarly channelled their environmental victimisation from capitalist extractivism into unlikely success stories of organised resistance and even self-governance. The North American Free Trade Agreement (NAFTA), a reinforcement of neoliberal economic policies that disadvantage vulnerable communities, enabled rampant legal and illegal resource extraction and hazardous waste dumping throughout Mexico (Mohai et al., 2009). In the state of Michoacán, the government-sanctioned convergence of illicit timber and drug trafficking has been dominated by the cartels through paramilitarised deforestation. In response, the Indigenous Cherán community organised their own security strategies to defend against the violent extractivism. This led to a community rebellion in 2011 that forcefully ejected members of the cartel as well as the colluding mayor and other local officials. What began as a defence movement ultimately developed into a broader struggle for Indigenous political, social, and environmental rights, appropriately encapsulated by their slogan: 'security, justice and forest protection' (Cortés Calderón, 2018).

Conclusion

It is important to recognise that Indigenous people are a non-monolithic group and that individual global populations operate in different ways and according to distinct needs and priorities. However, the philosophies, ontologies, and epistemologies that have been observed in these communities generally assign great significance to the natural environment, both in terms of its inherent value as well as its relationship with humanity. While some traditional customs and activities exploit and harm highly valued species (Borges & Martín, 2015), hunting is largely intended for subsistence and done with a degree of self-regulation.

Indigenous resource use has been criminalised by many governments around the world who have displaced forest-dwelling people in favour of environmental protection or extractive industry. The far more profound threat to species and ecosystems, however, is legal and illegal corporate pollution and extractivism, which also inflict considerable suffering on local and Indigenous populations. As a global movement, these communities have transformed and modernised their resistance to environmental victimisation through strategies that include social networking, public protests, and legal action. These individual groups are becoming increasingly organised through international collaborative partner-

ALEXANDRA LEBRON

ships, including with the global environmental movement, to assert their collective rights and shared interests (Rodríguez-Garavito & Arenas, 2005).

Scholars have emphasised the importance of confronting *academic imperialism* (Bratman & DeLince, 2022; Chilisa, 2011) as well as the specific advantages that researchers of Indigenous heritage offer in studying these issues (Goyes et al., 2021; van Uhm & Grigore, 2021). A poor understanding of the complex victim–offender overlap can obfuscate the nuanced roles Indigenous people fill at the different stages of environmental crime. To address the underrepresentation of Indigenous contributions to the discipline, critical criminologists have advocated moving beyond the traditional urban paradigm in research towards more inclusive approaches (Goyes & South, 2021). Green criminology, specifically, serves as an important decolonial tool for investigating environmental harms in addition to crimes (Wolf, 2011).

Alexandra Lebron

Further reading

Brashares, J. S., Abrahms, B., Fiorella, K. J., Golden, C. D., Hojnowski, C. E., Marsh, R. A., … & Withey, L. (2014). Wildlife decline and social conflict. *Science*, *345*(6195), 376–378.

Dawson, N., Coolsaet, B., Sterling, E., Loveridge, R., Nicole, D., Wongbusarakum, S., … & Rosado-May, F. (2021). The role of Indigenous peoples and local communities in effective and equitable conservation. *Ecology and Society*, *26*(3), 19.

Eichler, L., & Baumeister, D. (2018). Hunting for justice: An indigenous critique of the North American model of wildlife conservation. *Environment and Society*, *9*(1), 75–90.

Goyes, D. R., & South, N. (2021). Indigenous worlds and criminological exclusion: A call to reorientate the criminological compass. *International Journal for Crime, Justice and Social Democracy*, *10*(3), 115–128.

Goyes, D. R., Abaibira, M. A., Baicué, P., Cuchimba, A., Ñeñetofe, D. T. R., Sollund, R., … & Wyatt, T. (2021). Southern green cultural criminology and environmental crime prevention: Representations of nature within four Colombian Indigenous communities. *Critical Criminology*, *29*(3), 469–485.

Lynch, M. J., Stretesky, P. B., & Long, M. A. (2018). Green criminology and native peoples: The treadmill of production and the killing of Indigenous environmental activists. *Theoretical Criminology*, *22*(3), 318–341.

van Uhm, D. P., & Grigore, A. G. (2021). Indigenous people, organized crime and natural resources: Borders, incentives and relations. *Critical Criminology*, *29*(3), 487–503.

White, R. (2014). Indigenous communities, environmental protection and restorative justice. *Australian Indigenous Law Review*, *18*(2), 43–54.

Wolf, B. (2011). 'Green-collar crime': Environmental crime and justice in the sociological perspective. *Sociology Compass*, *5*(7), 499–511.

References

Aisher, A. (2016). Scarcity, alterity and value: Decline of the pangolin, the world's most trafficked mammal. *Conservation and Society*, *14*(4), 317–329.

Bartholomew, C. V., Zainir, M. I., Zalipah, M. N., Husin, M. H., & Abdullah, M. T. (2021). Wildlife hunting practices by the Indigenous people of Terengganu, Peninsular Malaysia. In M. T. Abdullah, C. V. Bartholomew, and A. Mohammad *Resource Use and Sustainability of Orang Asli: Indigenous Communities in Peninsular Malaysia*. Springer, pp. 137–151.

Boele, R., Fabig, H., & Wheeler, D. (2001). Shell, Nigeria and the Ogoni. A study in unsustainable development: I. The story of Shell, Nigeria and the Ogoni people–environment, economy, relationships: conflict and prospects for resolution 1. *Sustainable Development*, *9*(2), 74–86.

Borges, H., & Martín, T. (2015, May 19). The Mexican town that bashes piñatas full of live animals. *VICE*. https://www.vice.com/en_uk/article/kwzjea/yucatan-animal-sacrifice-tradition-876.

Brashares, J. S., Abrahms, B., Fiorella, K. J., Golden, C. D., Hojnowski, C. E., Marsh, R. A., … & Withey, L. (2014). Wildlife decline and social conflict. *Science*, *345*(6195), 376–378.

Bratman, E. Z., & DeLince, W. P. (2022). Dismantling white supremacy in environmental studies and sciences: An argument for anti-racist and decolonizing pedagogies. *Journal of Environmental Studies and Sciences*, *12*(2), 193–203.

Carrington, K., Hogg, R., & Sozzo, M. (2016). Southern criminology. *The British Journal of Criminology*, *56*(1), 1–20.

Chaudhuri, T. (2013). From policing to 'social fencing': Shifting moral economies of biodiversity conservation in a South Indian Tiger Reserve. *Journal of Political Ecology*, *20*(1), 376–394.

Chilisa, B. (2011). *Indigenous Research Methodologies*. Sage Publications.

Cortés Calderón, S. V. (2018). Security, justice, and forest protection! An indigenous community's fight against illegal deforestation and organised crime in Cheran, Mexico. In I. Arroyo-Quiroz and T. Wyatt, (eds.), *Green Crime in Mexico*. Palgrave Macmillan, pp. 63–73.

Dawson, N., Coolsaet, B., Sterling, E., Loveridge, R., Nicole, D., Wongbusarakum, S., … & Rosado-May, F. (2021). The role of Indigenous peoples and local communities in effective and equitable conservation. *Ecology and Society*, *26*(3), 19.

Duffy, R. (2010). *Nature Crime: How We're Getting Conservation Wrong*. Yale University Press.

Eichler, L., & Baumeister, D. (2018). Hunting for justice: An indigenous critique of the North American model of wildlife conservation. *Environment and Society*, *9*(1), 75–90.

FATF. (2021). *Money Laundering from Environmental Crimes*. Financial Action Task Force.

Gabriel, A. G., De Vera, M., & B. Antonio, M. A. (2020). Roles of Indigenous women in forest conservation: A comparative analysis of two indigenous communities in the Philippines. *Cogent Social Sciences*, *6*(1), 1720564.

Goyes, D. R., & South, N. (2021). Indigenous worlds and criminological exclusion: A call to reorientate the criminological compass. *International Journal for Crime, Justice and Social Democracy*, *10*(3), 115–128.

Goyes, D. R., Abaibira, M. A., Baicué, P., Cuchimba, A., Ñeñetofe, D. T. R., Sollund, R., … & Wyatt, T. (2021). Southern green cultural criminology and environmental crime prevention: Representations of nature within four Colombian Indigenous communities. *Critical Criminology*, *29*(3), 469–485.

Grisafi, L. (2020). Prosecuting international environmental crime committed against Indigenous peoples in Brazil. *Columbia Human Rights Law Review*, *5*, 26–59.

Hall, M. (2013). *Victims of Environmental Harm: Rights, Recognition and Redress under National and International law*. Routledge.

Hall, M. (2017). *Exploring Green Crime: Introducing the Legal, Social and Criminological Contexts of Environmental Harm*. Bloomsbury Publishing.

Heydon, J. (2020). Indigenous environmental victimisation in the Canadian oil sands. In A. Brisman and N. South, (eds.), *The International Handbook of Green Criminology* (2nd edn). Routledge, pp. 333–347.

Hines, A. (2023, May 10). Decade of defiance. *Global Witness*. https://www.globalwitness.org/en/campaigns/environmental-activists/decade-defiance/.

Horowitz, L. S. (1998). Integrating indigenous resource management with wildlife conservation: A case study of Batang Ai National Park, Sarawak, Malaysia. *Human Ecology*, *26*(3), 371–403.

Kanagavel, A., Parvathy, S., Nameer, P. O., & Raghavan, R. (2016). Conservation implications of wildlife utilization by Indigenous communities in the southern Western Ghats of India. *Journal of Asia-Pacific Biodiversity*, *9*(3), 271–279.

Kurz, D. J., Saikim, F. H., Justine, V. T., Bloem, J., Libassi, M., Luskin, M. S., … & Potts, M. D. (2021). Transformation and endurance of Indigenous hunting: Kadazandusun-Murut bearded pig hunting practices amidst oil palm expansion and urbanization in Sabah, Malaysia. *People and Nature*, *3*(5), 1078–1092.

Lawrence, R., & Raitio, K. (2006). Forestry conflicts in Finnish Sapmi: Local, national and global links. *Indigenous Affairs*, *4*, 36–43.

Leberatto, A. C. (2016). Understanding the illegal trade of live wildlife species in Peru. *Trends in Organized Crime*, *19*(1), 42–66.

Lyana, A. Z. (2014). Perceptions of African Indigenous hunting communities in Tanzania on use of game meat resources. *Journal of Human Ecology*, *48*(1), 43–52.

Lynch, M. J., Stretesky, P. B., & Long, M. A. (2018). Green criminology and native peoples: The treadmill of production and the killing of Indigenous environmental activists. *Theoretical Criminology*, *22*(3), 318–341.

McMahon, M. (1990). 'Net-widening' vagaries in the use of a concept. *The British Journal of Criminology*, *30*(2), 121–149.

Mohai, P., Pellow, D., & Roberts, J. T. (2009). Environmental justice. *Annual Review of Environment and Resources*, *34*, 405–430.

Mol, H. (2017). Agro-industry expansion through 'strategic alliances': The shifting dynamics of palm oil-related dispossession. In D. R. Goyes, H. Mol, A. Brisman, and N. South, (eds.), *Environmental Crime in Latin America*. Palgrave Macmillan, pp. 163–186.

Moloney, C. J., & Chambliss, W. J. (2014). Slaughtering the Bison, controlling Native Americans: A state crime and green criminology synthesis. *Critical Criminology*, *22*(3), 319–338.

Nellemann, C., Henriksen, R., Kreilhuber, A., Stewart, D., Kotsovou, M., Raxter, P., … & Barrat, S. (2016). *The Rise of Environmental Crime: A Growing Threat to Natural Resources, Peace, Development and Security*. United Nations Environment Programme (UNEP).

Ohlson, D., Cushing, K., Trulio, L., & Leventhal, A. (2008). Advancing Indigenous self-determination through endangered species protection: Idaho gray wolf recovery. *Environmental Science & Policy*, *11*(5), 430–440.

Pattiselanno, F., & Krockenberger, A. (2021). Road development and Indigenous hunting in Tanah Papua: Connecting the facts for future wildlife conservation agendas. *Forest and Society*, *5*(1), 181–189.

Paudel, K., Potter, G. R., & Phelps, J. (2020). Conservation enforcement: Insights from people incarcerated for wildlife crimes in Nepal. *Conservation Science and Practice*, *2*(2), e137.

Paulose, R. M. (2021). Crouching tiger, hidden dragon: Hydropower and crimes against humanity. In R.M. Paulose, (eds.), *Green Crimes and International Criminal Law*. Vernon Press, pp. 257–294.

Potter, G. (2016). The criminogenic effects of environmental harm: Bringing a 'green' perspective to mainstream criminology. In T. Spapens, R. White, and M. Kluin, (eds.), *Environmental Crime and its Victims*. Routledge, pp. 25–40.

Rodríguez-Garavito, C. A., & Arenas, L. C. (2005). Indigenous rights, transnational activism, and legal mobilization: The struggle of the U'wa people in Colombia. In B. de Sousa Santos and C. A. Rodríguez-Garavito, (eds.), *Law and Globalization from Below: Towards a Cosmopolitan Legality*. Cambridge University Press, pp. 241–266.

Roldán-Clarà, B. (2018). Traditional bird trader families: Towards a new approach. In I. Arroyo-Quiroz and T. Wyatt, (eds.), *Green Crime in Mexico*. Palgrave Macmillan, pp. 137–148.

Tanalgo, K. C. (2017). Wildlife hunting by Indigenous people in a Philippine protected area: A perspective from Mt. Apo National Park, Mindanao Island. *Journal of Threatened Taxa*, *9*, 10307–10313.

van Solinge, T. B. (2010). Deforestation crimes and conflicts in the Amazon. *Critical Criminology*, *18*(4), 263–277.

van Uhm, D. P. (2018). The social construction of the value of wildlife: A green cultural criminological perspective. *Theoretical Criminology*, *22*(3), 384–401.

van Uhm, D. P., & Grigore, A. G. (2021). Indigenous people, organized crime and natural resources: Borders, incentives and relations. *Critical Criminology*, *29*(3), 487–503.

Viollaz, J., Long, B., Trung, C. T., Kempinski, J., Rawson, B. M., Quang, H. X., … & Gore, M. L. (2021). Using crime script analysis to understand wildlife poaching in Vietnam. *Ambio*, *50*(7), 1378–1393.

White, R. (2014). Indigenous communities, environmental protection and restorative justice. *Australian Indigenous Law Review*, *18*(2), 43–54.

White, R. (2017). Reparative justice, environmental crime and penalties for the powerful. *Crime, Law and Social Change*, *67*, 117–132.

Whittington-Jones, G., Yeta, I., Naude, V., Lishandu, M., Chibeya, D., Dickerson, T., & Dunnink, J. (2020). Product-based crime script of targeted leopard poaching for skin use in ceremonial attire by the Lozi People of Western Zambia. In A. M. Lemieux, (ed.), *The Poaching Diaries: Crime Scripting for Wilderness Problems*. Center for Problem-Oriented Policing, pp. 8–16.

Wolf, B. (2011). 'Green-collar crime': Environmental crime and justice in the sociological perspective. *Sociology Compass*, *5*(7), 499–511.

World Bank. (2022, April 14). *Indigenous Peoples*. https://www.worldbank.org/en/topic/indigenouspeoples.

Wyatt, T., & Arroyo-Quiroz, I. (2018). Green harms and crimes in Mexico. In In I. Arroyo-Quiroz and T. Wyatt, (eds.), *Green Crime in Mexico*. Palgrave Macmillan, pp. 1–22.

PART VI

OFFENDERS AND PERPETRATORS

36. Agriculture

Introduction

Whilst farming practices (as opposed to hunting and gathering) have existed for eons, by the twentieth century these had evolved in many parts of the world into large-scale commercial enterprises. Contemporary practices incorporate crop and animal specialisation, uniform monocultures, mechanisation of labour, consolidation of farms and market concentration, the application of chemical inputs, and the use of genetically modified crops. Evolving cultural values and political sensibilities mean that modern agriculture is fraught with conflict, with animal welfare and climate change being most prominent. Agriculture broadly and farmers individually can be pre-eminent in environmental harm and crime. Farmers are also victims of the effects of climate change and in some instances are at the forefront of conservation efforts.

Agricultural practices

The agricultural cultivation of food and goods through the practice of farming dates back to 13,000 years ago, with the practice being widespread and established in human populations for approximately 7,000 years (Bulliet et al., 2008). The transition from hunting and gathering to more intensive farming of crops and animals has been recognised as a primary catalyst behind the rapid growth in human populations insofar as a greater abundance of food supplies supported larger and denser populations. This shift has had widespread and dramatic changes beyond mere food supply, as it changed the way humans have lived and interacted. Some of its consequences have included increased leisure time compared to the hunting and gathering era, the pursuit and development of sophisticated cultural pursuits, and new forms of social division and conflict related to competition over land and natural resources and the emergent social hierarchies. The social surplus afforded by agricultural production paved the way for new divisions of labour, both technical (e.g., artisans and tradespeople who worked outside agricultural production) and social (e.g., the formation of a power elite comprised of non-productive layers such as priests and members of the ruling classes). Land ownership and control over agricultural production have been vital components in the dynamics of social life over many centuries.

Contemporary agricultural practices are a far cry from early agricultural practices, which were much smaller in scale and intended to support smaller and more localised populations (JH Bloomberg School of Public Health, 2016). In a United States context, for example, by the early 1900s, whilst most Americans were farmers or at least lived rurally, the production of crops was varied, and the farming of animals was diversified, often occurring outdoors with food being produced primarily by humans and working animals (Ikerd, 1996) rather than relying on mechanical devices such as tractors and automated milking machines. Since then, innovations in agricultural practices have allowed food production to keep pace with and even exceed population growth.

Today, much of the world's food production takes place on 'industrial' farms where large-scale operations collectively produce massive crop outputs and millions of animals and animal by-products for consumption. Whilst subsistence farming and small-scale agricultural businesses still exist the world over, crop and animal specialisation, uniform monocultures, mechanisation of labour, the consolidation of farms and market concentration, the introduction and widespread application of chemical inputs and reliance on genetically modified crops dominate food and fibre production and create an array of environmental impacts (JH Bloomberg School of Public Health, 2016).

Conflicts over agriculture and the environment

The environment considered broadly includes flora, fauna, land, air and water (the 'natural environment'), as well as the built and cultural environment (the human 'social environment'). Agriculture can impact on each, resulting in philosophical and ideological conflicts over 'right' and 'wrong'. Indeed, evolving cultural values and political sensibilities mean that modern agriculture is fraught with conflict – in effect, these are ground zero for various issues which dominate social discourse and the political psyche in the twenty-first century. Conflicts surrounding animal welfare, climate change, and oil and gas extraction are the most prominent.

Some view agricultural farming as immoral on animal welfare grounds. The catalysts for such views vary but tend to focus on concerns around the ethics of industrial farming and the cruel treatment farm animals may experience, as well as associated notions of animal intelligence and sentience (see Harari, 2015). Examples of animal welfare issues include mulesing and tail-docking of sheep, use of sow stalls for pigs and feed lots for cattle, battery farming and debeaking of poultry, live animal exports, and abattoir practices generally (White, 2013).

With regard to climate change, the focus is on the harm to the environment caused by agricultural farming operations, including land clearing, the methane emissions from cows (in particular), and the deleterious use of chemicals and pesticides. The production of food is responsible for 30 per cent of greenhouse gas emissions. Of this, 31 per cent comes from livestock and fishers, 27 per cent from crop production, 24 per cent from land use including the removal of carbons sinks such as forests, while the supply chain accounts for 18 per cent (Ritchie & Roser, 2020).

Farmers both large and small advance a 'right to farm' which views agricultural land and products, including animals, as business products and theirs to farm (see Becker & Condon, 2019). While these debates are nuanced and those involved subscribe to varied perspectives that are not easily captured by binary comparisons, the desire of farmers and/or their belief in different philosophies of land and environmental management may conflict with evolving environmental sensibilities and policies (Mulrooney et al., forthcoming). Regardless of ideological perspective, agriculture is severely impacted by climate change, contributes to it and, as such, farmers can be seen as both victims and offenders of environmental harm and crime.

Agricultural offenders

Whilst farmers are casualties of climate change, they may also be environmental offenders. In agriculture and the production of food more broadly, some harm is tolerated and the consequences are understood as the by-product of such activities. Farming activities can inadvertently damage the environment (in the sense of not being intentionally harmful), including the over-extraction of water and depletion of groundwater, run-off from intensive livestock operations, use of chemicals which can pollute soil or waterways, soil erosion or degradation, and the destruction of habitat and biodiversity. For example, Blackwell et al. (2024) argue that a drastic shift towards plant-based diets may have unintended consequences which are a product of the conversion of grasslands into arable production, including potentially adverse impacts on yield stability, biodiversity, soil fertility and beyond. Social and cultural heritage can also be affected by the actions of farmers, such was the case in Victoria, Australia, where a farmer damaged a 1,500-year-old Aboriginal cultural site (see de Kruijff, 2024).

More deliberate acts of environmental crime and harm have also been perpetrated by farmers and the agricultural sector. For example, notwithstanding international pressure and belated attempts to arrest the trend by the Brazilian government, farmers and loggers deforest (both illegally and lawfully) large tracts of the Amazon (Lopes, 2019). The effects of such actions are global: the Amazon serves as the Earth's lungs releasing oxygen and storing carbon dioxide.

Agricultural offending against the environment may be perpetrated by an individual farmer whilst other such examples venture into the arena of white-collar or corporate crime undertaken by industry and corporations, often in the name of profit maximisation. Farmers, for instance, may undertake land management practices which harm biodiversity in direct contravention of existing laws and regulations. This can include the illegal clearing of native vegetation or the use of chemical sprays and inputs that are illegal in order to increase production (see Anaduaka et al., 2023).

Political conflicts are at the core of many of these issues and environmental crime or harm may have human consequences at a local or farm level. For example, illegal native vegetation clearing refers to acts that harm native vegetation without permission. In an Australian context, up until the late 1980s, the removal of native vegetation was a legally condoned practice. This has created ambiguity for farmers who are often responsible for these offences (see Davies, 2019). There is an ongoing debate over the right to clear farmland, particularly the right to clear woody weeds which impede productivity and undermine environmental ends, the restriction of which has angered many farmers.

In 2014, battles over illegal land clearing came to a head when a farmer shot and killed a New South Wales (NSW) environment officer during a departmental visit. The farmer had a long history of non-compliance with the NSW Native Vegetation Act 2003 and, subsequently, had been prosecuted on several occasions by the NSW Land and Environment Court. The core of this case revolved around a farmer motivated by retaliation and revenge owing to perceptions of persecution. Notably, while this case was progressing through the courts, the then NSW Government repealed the Act and introduced new and less onerous legislation with lighter penalties for non-compliance. As such, considering themes of property rights and a 'right to farm', discourse surrounding this murder by some political leaders and media outlets framed the crime as the product of bad legislation and government encroachment more generally (see Holden, 2021).

Larger-scale and industrial farms engaging in illegal or non-compliant farming practices and behaviours cause considerable harm. Useful to consider is White's (2013) outline of eco-justice, including three interrelated components – environmental justice (humans), ecological justice (specific environments) and species justice (non-human animals, and plants) (White, 2022). These categories are not mutually exclusive, and harms caused may simultaneously impact humans, animals and the environment alike.

Regarding anthropocentric concerns, the issue of environmental degradation and its implications on farmer well-being when it comes to yields and crop destruction (such as floods and drought) ought to be considered. There is also the human implication of certain behaviours and actions which may harm animals and/or the environment while also exacting a human cost. For instance, in Queensland, Australia, concerns were expressed that a Macadamia plantation using agrichemicals was causing not only deformities in the fish at a nearby hatchery but was also possibly linked to a cancer cluster amongst residents whose homes back on to a creek shared with the plantation (see Brisbane Times, 2010).

The bulk of the attention – and associated concerns – surrounding industrial farming have been those of a biocentric nature, with harm caused to ecosystems through land clearing and/or the use of pesticides and other chemicals. Similarly, the scale of industrial farming and its associated harm to animals have brought animal cruelty to another level. Harari (2015) argues that the treatment of domesticated animals in industrial farms amounts to the worst crime in history. Another example is the farming of Atlantic salmon on the coastline of Tasmania, Australia. The intensity of these fish farms is credited with causing disease, reduction in oxygen levels and environmental stress adjacent to a World Heritage Area. It has also brought about political attention around issues with environmental regulation and transparency (see Coulter, 2022).

With respect to ecocentric concerns, the theft of coveted elements such as water, particularly in times of drought, is pertinent. This includes the pumping, impoundment or diversion of water from irrigation channels, river systems, dams or groundwater bores without a licence or in contravention of licence conditions that cause changes to flow and reduce water access to neighbouring farms. A useful example is missing water in the Murray–Darling Basin in Australia where more than two trillion litres of water vanished during a time of severe drought (Slezak et al., 2021).

Irrigators in the Barwon–Darling catchment – in the Northern Basin where figures indicate there has been significantly more water missing – have been charged with tampering with water meters. In other cases, floodplains in the protected wetlands of the Macquarie Marshes have been harvested or altered by irrigators and graziers, not only contributing to the missing flow of water but also harming the ecosystems of semi-permanent wetlands. Impacts can also be acutely felt by communities further along the river, such as those around the mouth of the Murray River in South Australia.

Farmers as victims of environmental harm

Farmers are significantly impacted by environmental catastrophes such as floods and droughts as well as global trends pertaining to climate change, and farming as an industry faces major hurdles. For example, increases in extreme weather events, such as drought, flooding, extreme heat and associated bushfires, and temperature variability, have placed serious pressure on the agricultural sector and farmers. In terms of livestock, extreme heat and limited access to water reduces productivity and can lead to significant animal welfare issues and increased mortality rates. For instance, during a recent drought in Australia, between 2017–2019, suggested to be the worst in 800 years, a number of farmers were charged with animal cruelty offences as feed ran short and water ran dry.

Biosecurity is another concern as both livestock and crops may be impacted by changes in the distribution and occurrence of disease or pests brought about by changing conditions, leading to animal welfare threats and wider social and economic implications. Consequential increased costs will be borne by the public as food security is placed at risk, with costs inequitably felt by those in the lowest socio-economic quintile (see Khalil et al., 2018).

Disagreements between advocates of the right and need to farm and those who view such practices as immoral and/or environmentally destructive and unsustainable can lead to actual physical confrontation and conflict between such activists and farmers (Katz & McPherson, 2020; Monaghan, 2013). Examples include farms being trespassed upon, whether physically or technologically (such as with use of drones), by activists seeking to expose harmful practices and/or make a political point towards the reduction or eradication of certain types of farming.

In certain cases, this invasion of private property has also been accompanied by vandalism, sabotage, harassment and threats (Ceccato et al., 2022). In one example from Australia, an animal rights group created a website (Aussie Farms) detailing the location and contact details of numerous farms, raising concerns around privacy, trespass and biosecurity threats (Barnes & White, 2020). Such conflicts and experiences can have a significant negative impact on farmers and their families. For example, Ceccato et al. (2022) found that fear of animal rights activism among farmers has a negative impact on their children's well-being, their economic productivity, and their own quality of life. They note that such fear has led to reduced trust in strangers more broadly.

In a study on farmers' perspectives of environmental crime, Barclay and Bartel (2015) found almost half of the 1926 respondents to a nation-wide survey of Australian farmers had experienced some type of environmental crime over the previous two years. Trespassing was the most frequently experienced incidence. However, other harms often associated with agriculture include chemical spray drift, bushfires owing to inadequate land management, weed infestations from neighbouring farms, the altering of water courses upstream causing flooding and/or increased salinity on the farm, and water theft. Farmers also experienced other forms of victimisation related to environmental harm perpetrated by others. For example, resource extraction (such as coal seam gas extraction; fracking) may impinge upon property rights, and cause damage to the land and environment (see Smee, 2022), while the outward growth of urban city centres and encroachment onto farmland may see the imposition of power grids and conflicts over odours associated with farming (Caffyn, 2021).

Farmers as environmentalists and custodians of the land

Not all farmers see the environment as a commodity to be exploited. Indeed, some recognise the symbiotic relationship between environmental protection and increased productivity. For example, Peter Andrews, a grazier from New South Wales, Australia, began converting severely degraded, salinated land though 'natural sequence farming'. This involves re-establishing how a natural system worked prior to intervention, thus addressing soil degradation and water loss and restoring biodiversity (Andrews, 2006).

Another farmer from Victoria, the late John Fenton, adopted these principles in the 1960s and 'sacrificed' a quarter of his property for replanting of vegetation and creation of wetlands. This led to enhanced water conservation, natural cycling of water and nutrients back into the soil making the land more resilient, restoration of biodiversity, and provision of shelter for livestock. Whilst his actions were disparaged, naysayers may well feel rebuffed given that Fenton's vision has resulted in much greater yields from his livestock (Courtney, 2022).

Motivated by witnessing the harm caused by extreme weather on her family farmland and business, Anike Molesworth (2021) sought to advance and advocate the role of farmers in protecting their land, food and future, through sustainable farming and environmental conservation. Other practices include Indigenous 'firestick farming' – a reversion to millennia-old practices of cool burning to minimise the release of carbon emissions, suppress weeds and promote rejuvenation of native flora species. Ultimately, many farmers, as well as those involved in the development of agricultural technology, put conservation efforts and the climate at the forefront of their practices.

Conclusion

Agriculture has developed into a sophisticated, expansive sector that has a significant influence on both the environment and society. Food production has advanced significantly because of modern agricultural methods, yet these practices may also present enormous ethical and environmental challenges. The disputes in society about production and conservation are reflected in the issues around land usage, climate change, animal welfare and the concept of eco-justice more broadly. Farmers face dangers from climate change and sociopolitical conflicts, and they are both perpetrators of and victims of environmental degradation. Farmers also serve as important land stewards by promoting environmental preservation and employing sustainable farming practices, techniques, and tools. The future of agriculture depends on understanding these sometimes-conflicting interests, encouraging innovation, and supporting methods that support both food security and environmental sustainability.

KYLE MULROONEY, ALISTAIR HARKNESS AND MATTHEW BOX

Further reading

Barnes, A., & White, R. (2020). Mapping emotions: Exploring the impact of the Aussie Farms map. *Journal of Contemporary Criminal Justice*, 36(3), 303–326. https://doi.org/10.1177/1043986220910306

Ceccato, V., Lundqvist, P., Abraham, J., Göransson, E., & Svennefelt, C. A. (2022). Farmers, victimization, and animal rights activism in Sweden. *The Professional Geographer*, 74, 1–14.

Monaghan, R. (2013). Not quite terrorism: Animal rights extremism in the United Kingdom. *Studies in Conflict and Terrorism*, 36(11), 933–951.

Mulrooney, K. J. D. (2021). *The NSW Farm Crime Survey*. The Centre for Rural Criminology, University of New England. https://spark.adobe.com/page/zsV05pknxXl7N/

White, R. (2013). *Environmental harm: An eco-justice perspective* (1st ed.). Policy Press. https://doi.org/10.2307/j.ctt9qgsq7

References

Anaduaka, E. G., Uchendu, N. O., Asomadu, R. O., Ezugwu, A. L., Okeke, E. S., & Ezeorba, T. P. C. (2023). Widespread use of toxic agrochemicals and pesticides for agricultural products storage in Africa and developing countries: Possible panacea for ecotoxicology and health implications. *Heliyon*, 9(4), e15173. https://doi.org/10.1016/j.heliyon.2023.e15173

Andrews, P. (2006). *Back from the brink: How Australia's landscape can be saved*. ABC Books.

Barclay, E., & Bartel, R. (2015). Defining environmental crime: The perspective of farmers. *Journal of Rural Studies*, 39, 188–198.

Barnes, A., & White, R. (2020). Mapping emotions: Exploring the impact of the Aussie Farms map. *Journal of Contemporary Criminal Justice*, 36(3), 303–326. https://doi.org/10.1177/1043986220910306

Becker, J., & Condon, M. (2019, August 20). NSW government introduces new 'right to farm' laws to protect farmers from activists. ABC News. https://www.abc.net.au/news/rural/2019–08–20/new-nsw-right-to-farm-laws/11431934

Blackwell, M. S. A., Takahashi, T., Cardenas, L. M., et al. (2024). Potential unintended consequences of agricultural land use change driven by dietary transitions. *NPJ Sustainable Agriculture*, 2(1), Article 1. https://doi.org/10.1038/s44264–023–00008–8

Brisbane Times (2010, April 21). Lawsuit blames farm chemicals for two-headed fish. *Brisbane Times*. https://www.brisbanetimes.com.au/national/queensland/lawsuit-blames-farm-chemicals-for-twoheaded-fish-20100421-sune.html.

Bulliet, R. W., Crossley, P. K., Headrick, D. R., Johnson, L. L., & Hirsch, S. W. (2008). *The Earth and its peoples: A global history* (vol. I). Houghton Mifflin.

Caffyn, A. (2021). Contesting countryside smells: The power of intensive livestock odours. *Journal of Rural Studies*, 86, 554–565.

Ceccato, V., Lundqvist, P., Abraham, J., Göransson, E., & Svennefelt, C. A. (2022). Farmers, victimization, and animal rights activism in Sweden. *The Professional Geographer*, 74, 1–14.

Coulter, E. (2022, May 24). Tasmania's salmon industry must reform and be transparent, parliamentary inquiry says. ABC News. https://www.abc.net.au/news/2022-05-24/tas-salmon

-industry-reform-parliamentary-inquiry-transparency/101094476
Courtney, P. (2022, September 3). Farmer John Fenton's obsession with planting trees was ridiculed but he created a legacy. ABC News. https://www.abc.net.au/news/2022–09–03/john-fenton-leaves-an-environmental-tree-legacy-at-lanark/101402066
Davies, A. (2019, August 1). NSW farmers granted amnesty for illegal land clearing. *The Guardian*. https://www.theguardian.com/australia-news/2019/aug/01/nsw-farmers-granted-amnesty-for-illegal-land-clearing
de Kruijff, P. (2024, April 9). Farmer charged with harming Aboriginal heritage over change to Lake Bolac stone arrangement. ABC News. https://www.abc.net.au/news/2024–04–09/farmer-charged-lake-bolac-aboriginal-stone-arrangement-damage/103683214
Harari, Y. N. (2015, September 25). Industrial farming is one of the worst crimes in history. *The Guardian*. https://www.theguardian.com/books/2015/sep/25/industrial-farming-one-worst-crimes-history-ethical-question
Holden, K. (2021, May 3). An environmental worker was shot dead, so why do locals say the murderer was the real victim? *The Sydney Morning Herald*. https://www.smh.com.au/national/an-environmental-worker-was-shot-dead-so-why-do-locals-say-the-murderer-was-the-real-victim-20210503-p57odp.html.
Ikerd, J. E. (1996). Maintaining the profitability of agriculture. In Proceedings of the AAEA Preconference on Sustainable Agriculture, Sponsored by the AAEA Extension Committee San Antonio, Texas July 27, 1996 (ed.), *Economist's role in the agricultural sustainability paradigm* (27–37). University of Missouri.
JH Bloomberg School of Public Health. (2016, August 10). Food system primer. Johns Hopkins Bloomberg School of Public Health. https://www.foodsystemprimer.org/.
Katz, C., & McPherson, T. (2020). Veganism as a food ethic. In H. L. Meiselman (ed.), *Handbook of eating and drinking: Interdisciplinary perspectives* (pp. 1137–1155). Springer.
Khalil, A. T., Iqrar, I., Bashir, S., Ali, M., Khalil, A. H., & Shinwari, Z. K. (2018). Preemptive and proactive strategies for food control and biosecurity. In A. M. Grumezescu and A. M. Holban, (eds.), *Food safety and preservation* (pp. 39–58). Elsevier.
Lopes, M. (2019, September 8). Why Brazilian farmers are burning the rainforest – and why it's so hard for Bolsonaro to stop them. *Washington Post*. https://www.washingtonpost.com/world/the_americas/why-brazilian-farmers-are-burning-the-rainforest--and-why-its-difficult-for-bolsonaro-to-stop-them/2019/09/05/3be5fb92-ca72–11e9–9615–8f1a32962e04_story.html
Molesworth, A. (2021). *Our sunburnt country*. Pan Macmillan Australia.
Monaghan, R. (2013). Not quite terrorism: Animal rights extremism in the United Kingdom. *Studies in Conflict and Terrorism*, 36(11), 933–951.
Mulrooney, K. J. D., Camilleri, M., Donnermeyer, J. F., & Harkness, A. (forthcoming). Considerations of access to justice in the context of disaster. In M. Statz, & D. Newman (eds), *Whose rural? Global reflections on positionality and place in rural access to justice scholarship*. Hart Publishing.
Ritchie, H., & Roser, M. (2020, January 15). Environmental impacts of food production. Our World in Data. https://ourworldindata.org/environmental-impacts-of-food
Slezak, M., Doman, M., Shatoba, K., Timms, P., & Palmer, A. (2021, April 8). Billions of litres of water vanishes from Australia's most vital river network. ABC News. https://www.abc.net.au/news/2020–09–03/the-mystery-of-the-murray-darlings-vanishing-flows/12612166
Smee, B. (2022, March 13). In Queensland's food bowl, farmers fear the gas bores from next door. *The Guardian*. https://www.theguardian.com/australia-news/2022/mar/13/in-queenslands-food-bowl-farmers-fear-the-gas-bores-from-next-door
White, R. (2013). *Environmental harm: An eco-justice perspective* (1st ed.). Policy Press. https://doi.org/10.2307/j.ctt9qgsq7
White, R. (2022). Green criminology, environmental harms and eco-justice. In D. Nelken & C. Hamilton (eds), *Research handbook of comparative criminal justice* (pp. 315–331). Edward Elgar Publishing.

37. Biopiracy and bioprospecting

Introduction

Biological and genetic resources are essential for human and non-human existence. From the seeds that nourish humanity to the chemicals that heal, all components fundamental for life repose in nature. For millennia, nature and native inhabitants co-created biodiversity – rich in biological and genetic resources. More recently, applying their technologies to extract and isolate, corporations moved to transform natural compounds into commodities to commercialise and sell. Yet, who can fairly claim ownership over biological and genetic resources and the derived products, especially those which local communities have been using for centuries? Nonetheless, since the dawn of the twentieth century, intellectual property rights have enabled corporations to exclude others from making, using, or selling their biological and genetic resource-based 'inventions'. In doing so, corporations have successfully monopolised natural compounds. The term 'biopiracy' has emerged as part of a critique of the monopolisation of nature and of unfair practices that only benefit one among the many actors involved in the creation of bio-products. According to this critical view, claiming property rights over the elements that allow humans to survive equals the monopolisation of the sources of life and therefore of life itself.

Biopiracy, bioprospecting, and biotechnology

'Biopiracy' is a term applied to the appropriation, monopolisation, and patenting of biological and genetic resources in ways that are unfair, unjust, and sometimes – but not always – illegal. Examples can be diverse, and the science and law involved can be complex but, in general, biopiracy is accompanied by impacts that are epistemologically, sociologically, and symbolically detrimental to the original owners or cultivators as well as damaging to the ecosystems disturbed. Proponents of the term 'biopiracy' argue that powerful transnational companies, mainly in the agrochemical and pharmaceutical sectors, have misused the differential legal and political power of their host nations to skew law systems and unfairly assert ownership and rights to commercial development of these resources through use of novel biotechnologies (Goyes and South, 2016; South, 2007; Goyes, 2020).

'Bioprospecting' is a term that refers to the exploitation and appropriation of biological and genetic resources as a legitimate enterprise. Its proponents use this term to designate the virtues of the scientific endeavour to identify and subsequently exploit materials and properties found in biodiverse environments or sites, for use in new commercial and beneficial applications that are sold as products protected by intellectual property regimes. As a process, bioprospecting therefore usually involves: (1) the systematic study of biological and genetic resources; (2) the transformation of a specific natural resource into a commodity; (3) the commodification and marketing of the resulting product; and, alongside this, (4) the process of applying the law to protect rights and profits (Goyes, 2020).

The same event can be labelled as 'biopiracy' or as 'bioprospecting' depending on the interests, values, and stance of the person conducting the evaluation. While 'bioprospecting' is a term that seeks to forefront the contributions of biotechnology corporations to human well-being, 'biopiracy' seeks to denounce the unfair practices ingrained in the production of commodities and in the distribution of benefits. The presentation of bioprospecting as benign is challenged by its critical designation as biopiracy: what for 'bioprospecting' is progress, for 'biopiracy' is theft.

Not every use of biological or genetic resources to produce products beneficial to humanity needs to be problematic and labelled as biopiracy, and various efforts have been made to reconcile the advantages of biotechnology with issues of social and environmental justice. The 1992 Rio de Janeiro Convention on Biological Diversity and the 2010 Nagoya Protocol list a number of principles seeking to inform bioprospecting processes with principles of fairness. However, in practice, bioprospecting frequently results in outcomes that favour elite interests; they therefore fit the description of biopiracy.

'Biotechnology' is central to the dynamics contested by 'biopiracy' and 'bioprospecting' proponents. The 1992 Rio de Janeiro Convention on Biological Diversity defines biotechnology as 'any technological application that incorporates biological systems, living organisms, or derivatives thereof, to produce or to refine products or processes for specific use' (p. 3).

Biotechnology and the law

Biotechnologies have changed the world in various ways, co-evolving with changes to social institutions and processes of globalisation (Juma, 2005). According to Zelder (2005), markets targeted by biotechnology can be thought of as red, green, and white: *red* bioprospecting and biotechnology processes are aimed at medical products; *green* bioprospecting and biotechnology processes are applied to agriculture (e.g., development of genetically modified crops and herbicides); and *white* bioprospecting and biotechnology processes are employed in industrial chemistry. The result has been an 'unexpected variety of products that include chemicals, genes, metabolic pathways, structures, materials and behaviours' (Beattie et al., 2011: 341).

Diverse forms of biotechnology exist. *Biogenetics* uses recombinant DNA technologies to develop products from living beings (Soberón Mainero, 2003). '*Bio-mimicry* designs and builds biotechnologies based on models of biological mechanisms and structures found in nature (Lurie-Luke, 2014). Bio-mimicry is a term that acknowledges that the origin of ideas and designs might lie within complex local ecosystems without association with the criticism put forward by writers on 'biopiracy'. Regardless of the type of biotechnology, its insertion in the capitalist market means that the purpose is to create profit for corporations by monetising the 'discoveries' of useful natural components.

While criticism has been noted, it is nevertheless argued by powerful state and corporate actors that a 'variety of treaties and national laws have been enacted worldwide to control the use of intellectual property and to establish equitable benefit sharing' (Beattie et al., 2011: 342). For example, the 1992 Rio de Janeiro Convention on Biological Diversity, the 2001 Plant Genetic Resources Treaty of the Food and Agriculture Programme of the United Nations, the 2002 Bonn Guidelines, and the 2010 Nagoya Protocol have been important. Critics argue, however, that such agreements have also been weakened by compromises and lobbying related to trade-related intellectual property (Braithwaite, 2000: 179–181) which can in some cases lead to them acquiring the status of being 'placeless, universal and global' (Robinson, 2010: 42) – and thus, in essence, inapplicable and useless. These international treaties, moreover, seem to further disenfranchise already marginalised rural communities. The Rio Convention, for instance, assigns sovereignty in the area of genetic resources to the state and not to the Indigenous communities (Kim, 2010).

Origins and historical background

As a term and concept, 'biopiracy' seems to date back to the early 1990s and originate with the work of Mooney (1993; 2000), an activist working with the Canadian NGO Rural Advancement Foundation International (RAFI, now ETC; Robinson, 2010). Mooney (1993: 5) devised the term 'bio-piracy' as a synonym of 'klepto-monopoly', with both concepts describing a corporate 'drive to establish exclusive monopolies over life' (Mooney, 1993: 6). These are based on generating high profits from the sale of agricultural and pharmaceutical products derived from Indigenous knowledge and 'resources' in an unequal and unjust transaction with 'source' communities that did not benefit in terms of returned financial or living standards improvements. The term has subsequently been widely used by activists and academics. For example, Shiva (1997; 2001: 49) says, 'Biopiracy refers to the use of intellectual property systems to legitimize the exclusive ownership and control over biological resources and biological products and processes that have been used over centuries in non-industrialized cultures' (see also Mgbeoji, 2006).

The term 'biopiracy' was created amidst discussions of what later became the 'ecologically unequal exchange' theory. This theory posits that the global flows of commodities operate in a highly unfair, asymmetric, manner. The products originating in countries rich in biological and genetic resources are sold at prices much lower than the human and land labour embodied in them; by contrast, the processed commodities of biotechnologically advanced nations are sold for significantly higher prices than the labour invested in them (Honborg, 1998). Consequently, the term 'biopiracy' seeks to convey that biotech corporations can only develop their commodities thanks to the human labour of Indigenous peoples in source countries, who in interaction with ecosystems, co-created vast biological and genetic diversity. While these basic resources are the most valuable element of biotechnology commodities, corporations do not acknowledge the intellectual, and labour, investment of Indigenous communities, during processes of distribution of profits and benefits. Moreover, rural communities in source countries often guide corporations in understanding the potential applications of biological resources. This unremunerated use of biological resources and related knowledge amounts to theft – or biopiracy.

The key question of the biopiracy versus bioprospecting debate hinges on ownership: are biotechnology resources fairly and legitimately obtained or unfairly acquired and illegitimately stolen? Is it fair to claim ownership and profit individually from products that depend on a historical collective effort? In one sense, of course, these are not new questions. The age of colonial expansions and expropriation was driven by exploration in search of new forms of wealth derived from nature (flora and fauna) and the land (Crosby, 1993). From the nineteenth century onwards, developments in legal arrangements originating in the global North benefited the growth of corporate enterprises that operated transnationally. Through the use of trademarks and patent law based upon recognition of an individual or corporate actor as an innovator, and upon the taking of original or novel steps to add efficacy and value to something, definitions of intellectual property rights (IPR) have become accepted in ways that benefit such enterprises. Supporters maintain that IPR has successfully pushed forward innovation while also adopting conservation protocols and providing returns to communities and ecosystems of origin. Since the late twentieth century this has become a more controversial subject, recognising past injustice and with related debates influencing the drafting of conventions, treaties, and protocols at national and international levels.

Critiques underlying the 'biopiracy' concept

One obvious criticism of the use of legal systems to claim ownership over products derived from biological diversity is that it seems to perpetuate colonialism. The pattern is familiar: the accrual of wealth and power by some, usually in the global North, based on a strategy of 'discovery' and 'monopoly' that usually excludes and disadvantages those who have been traditional cultivators for generations in the global South. Processes of 'propertisation and monopolisation' (Chandra, 2015) remove from free access and the 'common interest' what should be more freely available. The knowledge and contributions of long-standing guardians of the local ecological conditions that have supported biodiversity may receive limited or no recognition.

The dynamics of colonial 'discovery', denial of value and knowledge outside the Western canon, and the extraction and commercialisation of biological products, all create harms in five realms: distributive; ecological; sociological; symbolic; and epistemological (Goyes, 2020).

- *Distributive harms* are derived from monopolisation of products. When a corporation claims exclusive ownership of a product, local communities – that have contributed to its existence – need to start paying fees for a product that was previously theirs (Conforto, 2004).
- *Ecological harms* happen when the market has an interest in the increased use of their products and not of other alternatives found in nature. Interest in promoting corporate products leads to monoculture, which results in loss of biodiversity (Zedan, 2005).
- *Sociological harms* happen when biotechnology transforms the composition of societies by centralising processes of product exchanges, for example, replacing bartering with dealing exclusively with corporations (Shiva, 1997).
- *Symbolic harms* pertain to the fact that in biopiracy 'life forms are treated as if they are mere machines' (Shiva, 1997: 23) and thus bioprospecting suggests that everything in the world needs to be efficient and useful; everything should be a means towards the end of 'progress'.
- *Epistemological harms* are produced by biopiracy by sending the message that biotechnology corporations are the ultimate knowledge creators that shall lead humanity to progress and that other more 'backward' communities lack the knowledge to fruitfully exploit the natural resources that

they were lucky to be bestowed by nature (Goyes, 2020).

Green criminology's first discussion of biopiracy was South's (2007) description of the processes by which the transnational mobility of corporations facilitates the transfer of knowledge and rights from their Indigenous origins to legally protected, private and profit-oriented monopolisers of intellectual property. White (2008) examined biopiracy in the context of threats to biodiversity, the corporate control and use of genetically modified organisms, and the exploitation of natural resources in the developing countries. Goyes and South (2017) further augmented criminological knowledge of biopiracy by analysing the monopolisation of seeds. They argue that biopiracy has evolved from appropriating via patents, to using the entire legal framework – not only that related to intellectual property rights – to gain ownership of multiple biological and genetic resources simultaneously. Wyatt and Brisman (2016) studied biopiracy related to plant hybridisation and commercialisation, while Goyes (2020) has explored biopiracy in the field of agribusiness.

Discussion and negotiation continue at the level of international treaties and the work of the World Intellectual Property Organization (Javed et al., 2022) to find ways to make bioprospecting processes fair – but the key debates endure. Those arguing that bioprospecting has led to life-saving discoveries in bio-medicines also reject claims that traditional communities have been unfairly treated or denied access to traditional lands and local ecosystems. There is also a future-facing argument that the horizons of the bio-sciences are now set beyond the locations of the past and advances in manipulation of genetic materials mean a preoccupation with 'species' and 'specimens' is out of date in a world where 'next-generation' micro-biological techniques are being developed.

It is undeniable that global health and medicine have benefited from scientific developments based on discoveries unlocking the power of nature. Whether such benefits have been equitably distributed is one question that follows, and the answer is generally agreed to be in the negative. However, while the biopiracy critique remains necessary, it may also need refining. For example, a narrow focus on IPR and patents tends to produce debate and analysis that are limited and circular, limiting consideration of future developments. The 'ever increasing spiral of biopiracy' that disproportionately impacts upon rural communities, afro-descendants, Indigenous groups, and peasants (Goyes and South, 2016) cannot be attributed solely to what IP drives or permits but is related to contemporary processes of constant economic demand as well as the legacy of historical justifications for colonialism.

Conclusion

As Robinson (2010: 52) argues, the critique offered by the concept of 'biopiracy' is not simply a 'rhetorical tool for developing countries to seek "benefits" from the spoils of genetic resource exploitation'. Biopiracy aims its deepest criticism at the colonial matrix of power that presents modernity as 'salvation, progress, development' (Mignolo, 2018: 107) – within which bioprospecting is a valuable tool – while neglecting and even denying the shadow side of such 'progress': the social and environmental harms on which Western high living standards depend. So, at its deepest, the term 'biopiracy' seeks to denounce the Western theft, distortion, and destruction of Indigenous knowledges about the use of nature (Grosfoguel, 2013), the erasure of the history of creation of biological riches, and the Northern appropriation of the profits that are partly based on the efforts of many communities in the global South. Bioprospecting thus advances the disappearance of alternative cosmovisions, that, as Robinson (2010: 52) notes, are often 'rooted in complex cultural and spiritual connections to plants and animals'. Such varied 'corporeal engagements with animate and vegetative worlds' require 'alternate ways of "seeing, knowing and doing"' and a wider lens is therefore needed.

DAVID R. GOYES AND NIGEL SOUTH

Further reading

Goyes, D. R. (2020). Monopolising seeds, monopolising society: A guide to contemporary criminological research on biopiracy. In A. Brisman and N. South (Eds.), *Routledge International*

Handbook of Criminology (pp. 222–238). Routledge.

Mooney, P. (1993). Bio-pirates patent indigenous knowledge … and indigenous people too. *Echoes*, *4*, 4–6.

Shiva, V. (1997). *Biopiracy, the Plunder of Nature and Knowledge*. South End Press.

South, N. (2007). The 'Corporate Colonisation of Nature': Bio-prospecting, bio-piracy and the development of green criminology. In P. Beirne and N. South (Eds.), *Issues in Green Criminology: Confronting Harms against Environments, Humanity and other Animals* (pp. 230–247). Willan.

References

Beattie, A. J., Hay, M., Magnusson, B., de Nys, R., Smeathers, J. and Vincent, J. F. (2011). Ecology and bioprospecting. *Australian Ecology*, *36*(3), 341–356.

Braithwaite, J. (2000). *Global Business Regulation*. Cambridge University Press.

Chandra R. (2015). *The Cunning of Rights: Law, Life, Biocultural*. Oxford University Press.

Conforto, D. (2004). Traditional and modern-day biopiracy: Redefining the biopiracy debate. *Environmental Law and Litigation*, *19*(2), 357–396.

Crosby, A. (1993). *Ecological Imperialism: The Biological Expansion of Europe, 900–1900*. Cambridge University Press.

Goyes, D. R. (2020). Monopolising seeds, monopolising society: A guide to contemporary criminological research on biopiracy. In A. Brisman and N. South (Eds.), *Routledge International Handbook of Criminology* (pp. 222–238). Routledge.

Goyes, D. R. and South, N. (2016). Land-grabs, bio-piracy and the inversion of justice in Colombia. *British Journal of Criminology*, *56*(3), 558–577.

Grosfoguel, R. (2013). The structure of knowledge in Westernized universities: Epistemic racism/sexism and the four genocides/epistemicides of the long 16th century. *Human Architecture: Journal of the Sociology of Self-Knowledge*, *11*(1), 73–90.

Honborg, A. (1998). Towards an ecological theory of unequal exchange: Articulating world system theory and ecological economics. *Ecological Economics*, *25*(1), 127–136.

Javed, G., Priya, R. and Deepa, V (2022). Protection of traditional health knowledge: International negotiations, national priorities and knowledge commons. *Society and Culture in South Asia*, *6*(1), 98–120.

Juma, C. (2005). Biotechnology in a globalizing world: The coevolution of technology and social institutions. *BioScience*, *55*(3), 265–272. https://doi.org/10.1641/0006-3568(2005)055[0265:BIAGWT]2.0.CO;2

Kim, T. J. (2010). Expanding the arsenal against biopiracy: Application of the Concession Agreement Framework to prevent misappropriation of biodiversity. *SMU Science and Technology Law Review*, *14*(1), 69–126.

Lurie-Luke, E. (2014). Product and technology innovation: What can biomimicry inspire? *Biotechnology Advances*, *32*(8), 1494–1505.

Mgbeoji, I. (2006). *Global Biopiracy: Patents, Plants, and Indigenous Knowledge*. Cornell University Press.

Mignolo, W. (2018). *On Decoloniality*. Duke University Press.

Mooney, P. (1993). Bio-pirates patent indigenous knowledge … and indigenous people too. *Echoes*, *4*, 4–6.

Mooney, P. (2000). Why we call it biopiracy. In H. Svarstad and S. S. Dhillion (Eds.), *Responding to Bioprospecting* (pp. 37–44). Spartacus Forlag.

Robinson, D. (2010). Locating biopiracy: Geographically and culturally situated knowledges. *Environment and Planning A: Economy and Space*, *42*(1), 38–56.

Shiva, V. (1997). *Biopiracy, the Plunder of Nature and Knowledge*. South End Press.

Shiva, V. (2001). *Protect or Plunder? Understanding Intellectual Property Rights*. Zed Books.

Soberón Mainero, F. X. (2003). *La ingeniería genética, la nueva biotecnología y la era genómica* [*Genetic Engineering, New Biotechnology and the Genomic Era*] (3rd ed.). Fondo de Cultura Económica.

South, N. (2007). The 'Corporate Colonisation of Nature': Bio-prospecting, bio-piracy and the development of green criminology. In P. Beirne and N. South (Eds.), *Issues in Green Criminology: Confronting Harms against Environments, Humanity and other Animals* (pp. 230–247). Willan.

White, R. (2008). *Crimes Against Nature: Environmental Criminology and Ecological Justice*. Willan.

Wyatt, T. and Brisman, A. (2017). The role of denial in the 'theft of nature': comparing biopiracy and climate change. *Critical Criminology*, *25*, 325–341.

Zedan, H. (2005). Patents and biopiracy: The search for appropriate policy and legal

responses. *The Brown Journal of World Affairs*, *12*(1), 189–205.
Zelder, O. (2005). White biotechnology: Science, fiction and reality. *Journal of Biotechnology*, *118*(1), 1.

DAVID R. GOYES AND NIGEL SOUTH

38. Corporate environmental crime

Introduction

Despite the existence of environmental protection legislation, corporate environmental crime remains widespread, and the transnational corporation is at the forefront of contemporary environmental harm. Corporations are responsible for various harms to the natural environment including 'illegal emissions to air, water and land; hazardous waste dumping; and illegal manufacturing practices' (Tombs and Whyte, 2015: 47). Corporate environmental crimes have both simple and complex explanations. In simple terms, corporate environmental crimes take place when corporations choose to break the law to maximise profits; taking direct and deliberate action to bypass or ignore environmental laws. Corporate environmental crimes can also occur when corporations are negligent in respect of their obligations under environmental protection legislation. But there is also a more complex explanation that can apply when the very nature of corporate activity and drive for profits places undue pressure on staff who have no choice but to break the law.

The nature of corporate environmental crimes

The demands of modern consumerism and the operation of markets result in production practices that inevitably cause environmental harms. For example, 'industrial pollution of the air, water and land, toxic waste sites, deforestation, species extinction, excessive pesticide use and pollution, climate change, the excessive use of fossil fuels, acid rain, a growing reliance on coal and oil, the environmental effects of drilling for oil or mining coal ... are the problems of the modern world', many of which are linked to corporate activity (Lynch and Stretesky, 2014: 11). Several of these harms are the result of legal corporate activity, although the legal and the illegal often go side by side where corporations may, for example, go beyond permitted levels of pollution. Green criminology recognises that 'eco-global crimes are often transnationally organised, with damage being caused by legal transnational corporations, such as British Petroleum in the Gulf of Mexico, and the destruction of the soil and forest in the Ecuadorian Amazon caused by Chevron and Texaco' (Sollund, 2012: 3). This reflects the reality that the global operations of transnational corporations can have significant negative consequences for the communities in which they operate and the wider environment, yet their actions are often legal given the relative lack of regulation for corporate practice in relation to environmental harm. For example, lawful activities such as oil extraction and the operation of polluting factories may result in harmful consequences for ecosystems but may fall outside the strict legalistic definition of crimes where these are unintended or accidental consequences of a lawful activity. But activities such as corruption and the bribing of officials and deliberate harm caused to communities by ignoring environmental regulations, polluting water sources and ignoring the effects of oil spills and pollution can amount to corporate crime.

In principle, many environmental offences committed by corporations are not crimes according to a strict socio-legal definition which defines crimes according to the criminal law. Instead, they are arguably 'quasi-criminal' regulatory offences, committed when corporations are found to be in breach of permit regulations or acting in a way that falls outside expected standards of operation and corporate norms. As a result, corporate environmental crime can include a range of activities, both deliberate and accidental and can also include accidents and 'upset' incidents (e.g., equipment breakdowns causing pollution) that may not be deliberate actions on the part of a corporation but that nonetheless cause environmental harm, whilst falling short of being a crime.

The strict definition of environmental crimes holds that 'an environmental crime is an unauthorised act or omission that violates the law and is therefore subject to criminal prosecution and criminal sanctions. This offence harms or endangers people's physical safety or health as well as the environment itself' (Situ and Emmons, 2000: 3). For corporations, a vested interest in committing environmental crimes may stem from an anthropocentric viewpoint on the environment as a natural resource to be exploited and also be influenced by the drive to maximise profits and minimise costs. Accordingly, where the costs of environmental compliance become too expensive, corporations arguably have an incentive to commit environmental crime.

Contemporary ideas on corporate environmental crime have also expanded the concept to include greenwashing (discussed later in this entry) and planned obsolescence in product manufacture. In this latter idea, corporations are alleged to have deliberately designed products to limit their lifespan, ensuring that consumers will need to buy replacements. This raises questions about the sustainability of products, particularly in respect of electronic products where consumers are potentially being defrauded into buying a product that they will have to replace sooner than might be necessary (Bisschop et al., 2022).

Causes of corporate environmental crimes

Research suggests that the causes of corporate environmental crime lie in the operation of neoliberal markets and the drive for profits that lie at the heart of the modern corporation. It has been said that the systematic causal chains that underpin much environmental harm are located at the level of the global political economy – within which the transnational corporation stands as the central social force (White, 2011). Globalisation is a factor because international systems of production, distribution and consumption encourage corporations to see environmental harms as something that can either be considered as an 'externality', something that their system of production does not need to consider, while in fact the nature of production processes continues to generate environmental harms (Lynch et al., 2020).

The first responsibility of many corporate actors is to the company's shareholders; this means first ensuring the profitability and ongoing sustainability of the corporation. Second, managers and directors have a responsibility to provide for sustainable growth and profits that will increase shareholder dividends and increase the company's market share. Adam Smith's concept of 'the invisible hand' holds that markets operate by self-regulation where a healthy market is one in which there is a steady supply of buyers and sellers, and the market regulates itself. But the market is concerned only with the sale and purchase of products and less so with 'hidden' or external costs such as environmental harm. So, the market considers that unprofitable corporations cannot survive and that self-regulation weeds out weak corporations. But the market does not always charge the 'real' cost of goods, for example the costs of deforestation or the cost to corporations to reduce the pollution caused by production. The corporation may consider some of these costs and seek to reduce them and make choices about the extent to which they are prepared to comply with environmental laws. In this sense, corporate environmental crime is 'a product of motivation and opportunity conditioned by the quality of law enforcement' (Situ and Emmons, 2000: 67) and there is an inherent conflict between drivers to make money and the costs of regulatory compliance.

This conflict has been recognised by UK and US governments who employ the principles of risk-based regulation (discussed later in this entry), which seeks a regulatory approach to enforcing corporate activity rather than the traditional criminal justice-based retributive punishment approach. However, the regulatory approach is in part based on the idea that there is a distinction between 'productive corporate innovation' and 'unproductive activities such as organized crime' (Baumol, 1990: 893). But corporate compliance with environmental regulations operates along a continuum where environmental non-compliance can be a form of business innovation that allows corporations to be creative in when and how they comply with the law.

Corporate crime and corporate environmental responsibility

Corporations can also engage in 'greenwashing' which is defined as 'the act of misleading consumers regarding the environmental practices of a company (firm-level greenwashing) or the environmental benefits of a product or service (product-level greenwashing)' (Delmas and Burbano, 2011: 66). This can occur when 'corporations creatively manage their reputations with the public, financial community, and regulators so as to hide deviance, deflect attributions of fault, obscure the nature of the problem of allegation, reattribute blame, ensure an entity's reputation, and finally, appear to be in a leadership position' (Laufer, 2003: 255). This definition illustrates how greenwashing can be a deliberate tactic to hide wrongdoing, deflect claims of environmental harm and allow corporations to deliberately spread misinformation about environmental performance that presents a misleading picture of environmental compliance. Contemporary debates also consider the extent to which corporations act responsibly towards the environment and embed this within their operating practices. The concepts of corporate social responsibility (CSR) and corporate environmental responsibility (CER) are used to promote mechanisms through which corporations can demonstrate accountability and transparency and potentially be held accountable for the environmental harm they cause. CER has been defined as 'the commitment of business to take the environment into account in decision-making processes and involves environmental commitment and awareness, transparent reporting, measuring and auditing and means going beyond regulatory compliance' (Bisschop, 2010: 350).

But many corporations which have CSR or CER policies in place also commit environmental crimes. McBarnet (2006) identifies creative compliance as a tool through which corporations circumvent and undermine legal regulation by essentially engaging in symbolic compliance whilst continuing with harmful and sometimes illegal business practices. Corporations may also engage in constructive compliance, using their sustainability reporting as a tool to appear compliant with regulation whilst at the same time making it all but impossible for staff to comply with the law and meet their objectives. Where this happens the 'rogue employee' argument can be used, so that in the event of enforcement action, the company is able to protect itself by pointing to its CSR/CER policies and the employee's failure to comply with these.

Corporate environmental crime enforcement

Where corporate crime arguably distinguishes itself from mainstream crime is in the enforcement response. Corporate environmental crime is often not the responsibility of mainstream policing agencies but instead often falls within the remit of environmental regulators like the Environmental Protection Agency in the US and the Environment Agency in the UK. Specialist regulators like Ofwat, the water services regulator (UK) also enforce specific sectors.

This regulatory response to corporate environmental crimes remains outside mainstream policing action because corporations are considered to be different from the 'traditional' street criminal who is the subject of much policing activity. First, corporations are legal actors, generally seen to act responsibly and so not considered by the state to be inherently criminal. This perception reflects corporate activity in providing jobs, contributing to the economy by providing goods and services and paying taxes. Accordingly, governments rely on corporations to contribute to society and lawful corporations are seen as beneficial through philanthropic corporate activity allied to their contribution to the economy. In a globalised world, corporations also provide for poorer societies through providing jobs and services that some Global South states may struggle to provide. Corporations are thus not generally subject to the same criminal regime as individual offenders and indeed, there are sometimes challenges in prosecuting corporations. One difficulty is in establishing that the offending *actus reus* was committed on behalf of the company rather than by an individual, another is to establish the corporate *mens rea*, that the decision and 'guilty mind' were at the level of the corporation rather than that of an individual employee.

Economic instruments, informational devices, voluntary agreements and command and control regulation are some of the techniques modern states use to protect the environment and deal with corporate environmental crimes. The principle of enforcement in corporate environmental crime is that corporate norms and the natural drive of corporations to behave ethically will automatically provide for self-regulation. As a result, corporate environmental crime is dealt with via regulatory mechanisms that view corporate offending as an aberration rather than the norm. With this perspective in place, fines and administrative sanctions are thought more effective than prosecution, with the aim of impacting on corporate profits whilst allowing the corporation to continue business.

In addition, the principle of 'risk-based regulation' is adopted by Global North governments, with the aim of reducing the regulatory burden on business in line with the principle that corporations should not have to allocate excessive resources to complying with legislation and should be allowed to concentrate on their core business of innovation and providing products. The risk-based regulation concept holds that inspections and other regulatory activity should only take place when necessary, so that enforcement action should not be overly burdensome on business. The enforcement approach is designed to work alongside corporate activity so that a regulatory approach is taken where settlements and allowing corporations to amend their behaviour are favoured approaches with criminal prosecution considered to be a last resort. The idea is that sanctions imposed on business should be proportionate, meaningful and not overly punitive, with the purpose of sanctions being to change behaviour (Stretesky et al., 2013: 236).

This approach to enforcement differs from the retributive justice approach of mainstream criminal enforcement where prison is arguably the main sanction for serious offending. There are debates concerning the 'benefits' of sending corporate managers to prison. In one sense this would signal to corporations that their behaviour is considered serious, unacceptable and will be punished, invoking deterrence principles. However, given the lawful activity carried out by corporations, a punishment visited on individual managers is potentially ineffective as that manager can simply be replaced and the 'rogue employee' argument can be deployed, where the corporation simply argues that the individual staff member was at fault, not the corporate entity. Individualised punishment in the form of prison sentences also fails to address the environmental harm caused, whilst many transnational corporations can simply absorb fines as being the cost of doing business.

Addressing corporate environmental crime

In responding to corporate environmental crime, contemporary green criminology and environmental law debates have raised questions about the adequacy of the criminal law as the appropriate enforcement tool. First, much corporate environmental harm falls outside the remit of the criminal law and would be caught by other justice systems (civil, administrative and regulatory). As a result, application of criminal penalties is limited, and the use of criminal penalties is sometimes at the discretion of environmental regulators who are significant players in environmental enforcement. In addition, the adequacy of the criminal law to deal with environmental problems is questionable. The criminal law generally punishes and applies retributive justice whereas green criminological perspectives on corporate environmental crime contend that the focus should be on repairing the harm caused by corporate wrongdoing.

The reality is that the individualistic nature of criminal prosecution potentially lacks any real deterrent effect, particularly in the case of the transnational corporation. In addition, major corporations often have the resources to frustrate prosecution activity and indeed can withstand multiple prosecutions, either factoring in the cost of fines as the cost of doing business or having the resources to settle cases.

ANGUS NURSE

Further reading

Doyon, J. (2014) Corporate environmental crime in the electronic waste industry: The case of Executive Recycling, Inc. In A. Nurse, *Critical Perspectives on Green Criminology. Internet Journal of Criminology*. Nottingham: New University Press/Flashmouse Publishing Ltd, pp. 68–88.

Gibbs, C. (2012) Corporate citizenship and corporate environmental performance. *Crime Law and Social Change*, 57, 345–372. https://doi.org/10.1007/s10611-012-9365-2

Gibbs, C. and Simpson, S. S. (2009) Measuring corporate environmental crime rates: Progress and problems. *Crime Law and Social Change*, 51, 87–107. https://doi.org/10.1007/s10611-008-9145-1

Greife, M., Stretesky, P. B., O'Connor Shelley, T. and Pogrebin, M. (2017) Corporate environmental crime and environmental justice. *Criminal Justice Policy Review*, 28(4), 327–346. doi:10.1177/0887403415576742.

Johnson, E., Schwartz, J. and Inlow, A. (2020) The criminalization of environmental harm: A study of the most serious environmental offenses prosecuted by the U.S. federal government, 1985–2010. *Environmental Sociology*, 6(3), 307–321. doi:10.1080/23251042.2020.1748269

Lynch, M., Stretesky, P. and Long, M. (2020) The treadmill of production and the treadmill of law: Propositions for analyzing law, ecological disorganization and crime. *Capitalism Nature Socialism*, 31(1), 107–122. doi:10.1080/10455752.2018.1545241

Nurse, A. (2015) Creative compliance, constructive compliance: Corporate environmental crime and the criminal entrepreneur. In *Exploring Criminal and Illegal Enterprise: New Perspectives on Research, Policy and Practice*. Bingley, UK:

Emerald Publishing, pp. 97–119. https://doi.org/10.1108/S2040-724620150000005012
Ozymy, J. and Jarrell, M. (2015) Corporate environmental crime and environmental victimization: Exploring new legal precedents for securing recognition and restitution for environmental justice communities. *Environmental Justice*, 8(2), 47–50. https://doi.org/10.1089/env.2014.0036
Rorie, M. (2015) An integrated theory of corporate environmental compliance and overcompliance. *Crime, Law and Social Change*, 64(2), 65–101. https://doi.org/10.1007/s10611–015–9571–9
Simpson, S., Gibbs, C., Rorie, M., Slocum, L., Cohen, M. and Vandenbergh, M. (2013) An empirical assessment of corporate environmental crime-control strategies. *The Journal of Criminal Law and Criminology*, 103(1), 231–278. http://www.jstor.org/stable/24615613.
Walker, K. and Wan, F. (2012) The harm of symbolic actions and green-washing: Corporate actions and communications on environmental performance and their financial implications. *Journal of Business Ethics*, 109, 227–242. https://doi.org/10.1007/s10551-011-1122-4
White, R. (2017) Reparative justice, environmental crime and penalties for the powerful. *Crime Law and Social Change*, 67(2), 117–132. https://doi.org/10.1007/s10611-016-9635-5
Zou, H. L., Zeng, R. C., Zeng, S. X. and Shi, J. J. (2015) How do environmental violation events harm corporate reputation? *Business Strategy and the Environment*, 24, 836–854. doi:10.1002/bse.1849.

References

Baumol, J. (1990) Entrepreneurship: productive, unproductive and destructive. *Journal of Political Economy*, 98(5), 893–921.
Bisschop, L. (2010) Corporate environmental responsibility and criminology. *Crime, Law and Social Change*, 53(4), 349–364. https://doi.org/10.1007/s10611-009-9227-8
Bisschop, L., Hendlin, Y. and Jaspers, J. (2022) Designed to break: Planned obsolescence as corporate environmental crime. *Crime, Law and Social Change*, 78, 271–293. https://doi.org/10.1007/s10611-022-10023-4
Laufer, W. S. (2003) Social accountability and corporate greenwashing, *Journal of Business Ethics*, 43, 253–261.
Delmas M. A. and Burbano V. C. (2011) The drivers of greenwashing. *California Management Review*, 54, 64–87.
Lynch, M. and Stretesky, P. (2014) *Exploring Green Criminology*. Farnham: Ashgate.
Lynch, M., Stretesky, P. and Long, M. (2020) The treadmill of production and the treadmill of law: Propositions for analyzing law, ecological disorganization and crime. *Capitalism Nature Socialism*, 31(1), 107–122. doi:10.1080/10455752.2018.1545241
McBarnet, D. (2006) After Enron will 'Whiter than White Collar Crime' still wash? *The British Journal of Criminology*, 46(6), 1091–1109. https://doi.org/10.1093/bjc/azl068
Situ, Y. and Emmons, D. (2000) *Environmental Crime*. Thousand Oaks, CA: Sage.
Sollund, R. (2012) Introduction. In R. Ellefsen, R. Sollund and G. Larsen (eds), *Eco-Global Crimes: Contemporary Problems and Future Challenges*. Farnham: Ashgate, pp. 3–14.
Stretesky, P., Long, M. and Lynch, M. (2013) Does environmental enforcement slow the treadmill of production? The relationship between large monetary penalties, ecological disorganization and toxic releases within offending corporations. *Journal of Crime and Justice*, 36(2), 233–247. doi:10.1080/0735648X.2012.752254
Tombs, S. and Whyte, D. (2015) *The Corporate Criminal*. Abingdon: Routledge.
White, R. (2011) *Transnational Environmental Crime: Towards an Eco-Global Criminology*. London: Routledge.

39. Organised environmental crime

Introduction

In the twenty-first century, environmental crime has become a significant new form of organised criminal activity, with disastrous impacts on the environment and costs for future generations (OECD 2016; van Uhm 2023; Walters 2014; White 2011). The rising global scarcity of natural resources increasingly attracts organised crime groups across the world. Traditionally, organised crime groups are linked to international smuggling activities, such as drugs, arms and human trafficking (Gambetta 1993; Thoumi 1995; Zhang and Chin 2002; Siegel et al. 2003; Varese 2011), but the extraction and trafficking of natural resources have increasingly become connected to the criminal portfolios of modern organised crime (Boekhout van Solinge 2014; van Uhm and Wong 2021). Criminal networks have become involved in a range of illegal environmental markets, including timber, wildlife, waste and minerals and metals (UNODC 2012; Miklaucic and Brewer 2013; Interpol 2016).

A lucrative enterprise

In recent years, environmental crime has become one of the largest black markets following in the footsteps of drugs and weapons with estimates of between 91 and 276 billion USD annually (Table 39.1) (UNEP/Interpol 2016; GFI 2017; World Bank 2019). This value would make environmental crime the fourth largest crime in the world after drug trafficking (344 billion USD), counterfeit crimes (288 billion USD) and human trafficking (157 billion USD) (UNEP/Interpol 2016).

Illegal logging and trade in forest products is the most lucrative form of environmental trade and generates revenues between 50.7 and 157 billion USD annually (UNEP/Interpol 2016: 20; World Bank 2019: 18). Illegal mining and trade in minerals and metals is the next most lucrative category with revenues estimated between 12 and 48 billion. Illegal fishing is estimated between 11 and 36 billion USD (UNEP/Interpol 2016: 20; World Bank 2019: 18), the global illegal wildlife trade has been estimated between 7 and 23 billion USD (van Uhm 2016), and the illegal trade and dumping of hazardous waste is estimated between 10 and 12 billion. The environmental black market is one of the fastest-growing forms of crime: these environmental offences increase by 5–7 per cent per year, or two to three times the pace of the global economy, which reflects the urgency to prevent and react to crimes against the environment (UNEP/Interpol 2016).

Diversification and crime convergence

Recent decades have seen an international diversity of organised crime groups involved in environmental crimes influenced by socio-economic, cultural, political and ecological conditions of society (van Uhm and Siegel 2021). Environmental black markets attracted both traditional organised crime and crime groups that are considered much more fluid, complex networks of legal and illegal actors. Organised crime groups rapidly shift from 'traditional' organised crime activities, such as drug or human trafficking, to the illegal trade in natural resources (Elliott 2009; Nellemann et al. 2016; van Uhm 2023). Therefore, the classic image of hierarchical well-structured organised crime specialising in one kind of criminal activity appears to be too narrow (see Paoli 2002). Organised crime syndicates diversify into the lucrative business of tropical timber, endangered species, and natural minerals and metals alongside their traditional activities (Interpol 2016; Miklaucic and Brewer 2013; UNODC 2012). The developing interconnectedness between environmental crime and other serious crimes shows that traditional lines of separation are no longer appropriate for understanding and dealing with the increasing complexities of organised environmental crime (Interpol 2015; Shelley 2017; van Uhm et al. 2021).

In order to understand the evolution of organised crime into environmental crime, Figure 39.1 presents the environmental crime continuum (van Uhm 2018). Five points are situated on the environmental crime continuum. Each single point displays a form of convergence between organised crime (situated on the far left) and environmental crime (situated on the far right). The level of diversification of organised crime into environmental crime gradually increases during the stages: from minor diversification of organised crime groups, expanding their

Table 39.1 The monetary value of environmental crime

Environmental crime	Value (USD)	Source
Illegal logging and trade	51–157 billion	UNEP 2016; GFI 2017; World Bank 2019
Illegal extraction and trade in minerals/ mining	12–48 billion	GITOC 2016; UNEP 2016; GFI 2017
Illegal fisheries	11–36 billion	UNODC 2011; UNEP 2016; World Bank 2019
Illegal trade and poaching of wildlife	7–23 billion	Haken 2011; van Uhm 2016; UNEP 2016
Illegal trade and dumping of hazardous waste	10–12 billion	UNEP 2015; UNEP 2016
Total	**91–276 billion**	

illegal activities with environmental crimes to a limited extent based on alliances with environmental crime groups (1) to overall domination over environmental crimes (5). The model of various relationships between organised crime and environmental crime may assist our theoretical understanding of the convergence between environmental crime and other serious crimes (van Uhm and Nijman 2022).

First, *alliances* between organised crime groups and environmental crime groups may be established for expert knowledge or operational services akin to social relationships within legitimate business settings (Gounev and Ruggiero 2012; Makarenko 2004). The nature of alliances may vary: it can include one-off, short-term relationships or long-term relationships (Morselli 2009; Paoli 2003). Alliances are established to share information such as communication technologies and counter-surveillance techniques, or to provide access to smuggling routes. For instance, alliances arrange for minerals and metals to be smuggled along routes established for other types of illicit commodities (Europol 2011; Nellemann et al. 2014; van Uhm et al. 2022). Therefore, the first stage reflects minor diversification of crime groups, extending their illegal activities into environmental crimes to a limited degree, based on alliances with environmental crime organisations.

Second, *crime mutualism* between organised crime groups and environmental crime groups may be established in a long-term way for sharing natural resources, stopping mutual adversaries, and spreading crime (Felson 2006: 185; Moreto et al. 2019). This may involve symbiotic relationships that include both illegitimate and legitimate activities for conscious mutual benefits (Passas 2005). Crime mutualism embodies barter trade such as wildlife being exchanged for drugs and stolen cars, or camouflage, when a legitimate company is used to shield illegal trafficking (Austrac 2010; Chiszar et al. 2002; van Uhm et al. 2021). Crime-related camouflage methods allow criminals to hide illegal activities in plain sight (Felson 2006: 283). This second stage involves a higher degree of diversification, as the organised crime groups become increasingly involved in environmental crime through crime mutualism.

Third, environmental crime organisations and other criminal organisations could *converge* into a single entity that displays characteristics of both groups simultaneously (Miklaucic and Brewer 2013: xiv). In this scenario, the crime groups might eventually converge completely and become one and the same in the middle of the continuum (Makarenko 2001: 22–24). This represents the confluence of different forms of illegal activities as well as the ability to diversify (Shelley and Kinnard 2018: 117). An example would be a criminal enterprise involved in both human trafficking and fisheries, or a timber trader involved in the supply of weapons utilising multiple trade lines (Lichtenwald et al. 2009; UNODC 2011; van Uhm et al. 2022). Stage three displays hybrid and multifaceted crime groups with the capability to diversify into environmental crime and retain their traditional crime characteristics.

Fourth, criminal groups may *transform* into entrepreneurial organisations in order to adapt to changing circumstances (Dishman 2001; Williams 1998). In this metamorphosis, the

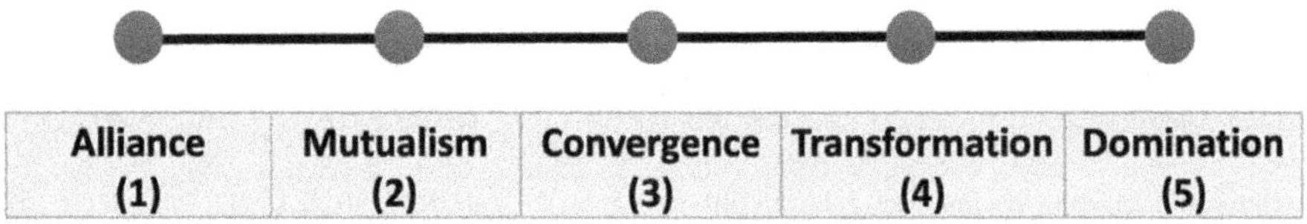

Figure 39.1 *The environmental crime continuum*

organised crime groups decide to depart from their traditional activities and reshape their features in order to infiltrate a new criminal market (Bovenkerk and Chakra 2004: 5), in this case the environmental crime market. This career shift changes the way that the criminal groups perform their operations because they become fixated so keenly on one criminal activity that they drop the other altogether. An example is the infiltration of criminal organisations into the illegal trade in minerals for the expanding computer and cell-phone markets (Sutherland 2011). In stage four, the ultimate aims and motivations of the crime group have actually changed in order to diversify into the illegal trade in natural resources.

Fifth, criminal organisations may start to *dominate* a specific area or trade line (Cressey 1969: 28). By monopolising elements of trade lines or by controlling the entire supply chain through the use of violence, intimidation, or extortion, criminal groups may effectively achieve control, reputation, and authority (Albanese 1985; Varese 2011). In contrast to the symbiotic relationships between crime groups in the earlier stages (1, 2, and 3), the latter two stages (4 and 5) display antithetical relations in which there is competition between criminal groups vying for market shares (Passas 2005; van Uhm and Moreto 2018). The caviar trade serves as an example as it has reportedly been controlled by the Russian mafia competing with local fishers (van Uhm and Siegel 2016). In this final stage, the organised crime groups dominate (parts of) an environmental crime market completely.

Black markets in gold, wildlife and timber

The three examples below delve into the role of diversification and crime convergence in three organised environmental crime hotspots: the Darién Gap, the Golden Triangle and the eastern edge of the Congo basin.

The Gulf Clan cartel and the gold business in Darién

The Darién jungle on the border of Colombia and Panama has a reputation for being a dangerous, violent, and lawless wilderness. By its highly strategic location and the entangled network of rivers in the middle of the jungle, the Darién Gap has suffered disproportionately from endemic conflict over natural resources and has become a haven for organised crime groups vying for social and territorial control. Even though the Gulf Clan cartel is notorious for the cocaine business, they transformed their features in order to diversify into the gold business in Darién. By raising 'extortion taxes' to be paid by local miners, and by importing miners from abroad, the Gulf Clan increasingly dominates the gold mines by means of violence and intimidation. This illustrates how the criminal infrastructure and know-how developed by the Gulf Clan cartel to exert control and power within the context of drug trafficking can be used to diversify into the gold industry through criminal mutualistic relations with under- and upper-world actors.

The Gulf Clan cartel has gained local support by providing security services and social controls, while generating alternative incomes for local communities where mining offers a way to make a living in the political economy of Darién. Simultaneously, the lives and cultures of Indigenous and Afro-descendant communities are diminished through displacement, land grabbing, and ecocidal harms, including large-scale deforestation and pollution. Influenced by this dual reality, diversifying organised crime groups into gold mining colours the socio-economic and geopolitical landscape, but not least, threatens the survival of one of the greatest biodiverse areas of our planet, the jungles of Darién (van Uhm 2020, 2023).

Chinese organised crime and wildlife trafficking in the Golden Triangle

The Golden Triangle, the area where the borders of Laos, Myanmar, and Thailand meet, has become notorious as a major opium-cultivation area, but it has also been identified as one of the world's most critical hubs for illegal wildlife trade. Due to reduced governance of the transboundary frontiers where geopolitical boundaries and biodiversity hotspots overlap, alliances between crime groups, militias, and corrupt officials complicate the situation. Improved trading conditions and infrastructures as well as mutualistic relations between Chinese criminal entrepreneurs provided opportunities for Chinese organised crime to diversify into illegal wildlife trade and facilitated cross-border trafficking of contraband. Nowadays a new Chinese organised crime generation has emerged – some coming from Triad members – but they consider themselves no longer members.

Chinese organised crime groups invest in casinos in the Golden Triangle borderlands, which facilitated lucrative illegal wildlife trade deals alongside drug trafficking and prostitution. Highly professional Chinese smuggling gangs added wildlife trafficking to their criminal portfolios and used their drug-smuggling infrastructure to diversify, influenced by repressive drug policies and the rising value of wildlife. Some Chinese organised crime networks use their drug trafficking profits to invest in the illegal trade in wildlife, such as tiger bones and rhino horn. Other Chinese crime groups pay local poachers in both money and equipment and outsource the smuggling part of the wildlife trade to local smuggling entrepreneurs. However, the lives of human and non-human communities are also affected through poaching, displacement, and violence; in the past decennia several endangered species, including the rhino and tiger, disappeared from the biodiverse jungles of the Golden Triangle (van Uhm & Wong 2021; van Uhm 2023).

Militias and deforestation in the eastern edge of the Congo basin

Located on the eastern edge of the Congo basin, the border area between the Democratic Republic of Congo, Rwanda, and Uganda is home to a tremendous range of endangered species living in a variety of natural environments and climates. However, violence, wars, and conflicts in the border area between the Democratic Republic of Congo, Rwanda, and Uganda resulted in institutional collapse, lawlessness, and unbridled exploitation of natural resources. In order to finance their arms and munitions, militia groups focus their operations on deforestation for tropical timber and charcoal alongside mineral and metal extraction, drugs, and the ivory trade, facilitated by a complex web of power dynamics and mutualistic relationships. For example, armed groups control secure systems of extortion and patronage within the charcoal and timber trades, increasing their status and power. Militia groups such as the FDLR, M23, ADF, and Mai-Mai groups are socio-economically and politically embedded in the local communities, providing access to natural resources, generating economic income, and offering protection and social prestige among the inhabitants.

Due to the presence of armed groups, interfering with or blocking the trades triggers conflicts, disputes, and clashes, illustrated by the prevalence of intense violence and dozens of killings each year. Moreover, the rapid deforestation of one of the world's last remaining biodiversity hotspots ensures that both human and non-human inhabitants are suffering directly from deforestation and habitat loss, while the reduction of ecosystem functions may affect living conditions for all of us. While several species are on the brink of extinction, suffering from great habitat loss, animals flee to the last silos of natural habitats, which are targeted directly by organised environmental crime involved in the extraction of resources (van Uhm et al. 2022; van Uhm 2023).

Green criminology and organised crime

Organised crime groups across the world have been linked to environmental crimes in recent decades. Alliances between organised crime and environmental crime groups are established for expert knowledge or operational services, including access to smuggling routes. For instance, the Colombian Gulf Clan cartel controls large parts of the Darién jungle, and therefore timber smuggling rings in and around Katíos National Park operate under the control of the Gulf Clan cartel and pay extortion taxes to transport the timber through the Gulf of Urabá for export abroad. Crime mutualism is reflected by clear appointments between wildlife poachers and organised crime groups, illustrated by Chinese crime groups that outsource not only the tasks of poaching of wildlife, but also product promotion, or product smuggling to localised crime groups.

Some organised crime groups and environmental crime groups converge and form a single entity that displays characteristics of both groups simultaneously, illustrated by several militia groups in Eastern Congo that control diverse illegal trades, including minerals, metals, timber, arms and ivory. Some of these groups consist of different substructures that control different illegal submarkets and collaborate with each other, while in other situations the substructures are involved in the illegal activities simultaneously. In order to adapt to changing socio-economic, political, or ecological circumstances, organised crime groups also transform their organisations, reflected by Chinese organised crime groups specialised in opium and methamphetamine, along the Laos and Myanmar borders, that adopted the smuggling of tiger bones in their criminal portfolios; they gradually transformed their organisations in order to specialise in illegal wildlife trade. Finally, organised crime groups may dominate a specific area or trade line, mirrored by the Gulf Clan cartel that started to control mining activities in Darién, but also the territories controlled by militia groups in Eastern Congo reflect the role of domination over natural wealth, resulting in high-level collaboration with officials, and also violence in the respective areas.

The diversification of organised crime into the illegal trade in natural resources can also result in tragic ecological consequences and costs for future generations. A green criminological perspective, that encompasses adverse effects on human and non-human entities, including ecosystem, animals and plants, may serve to understand this organised crime–nature dynamic. The three examples of organised environmental crime in the Darién Gap, the Golden Triangle and the eastern edge of the Congo basin all occur in what are considered to be among the most biodiverse rainforests in the world. The illegal mining with mercury in the Darién Gap contaminates the ground and water, which are essential to the Darién ecosystem as well as the Indigenous and Afro-communities' lives and cultures. And illegal deforestation in the Congo basin, the second largest rainforest in the world, affects not only its human and non-human inhabitants; these forests generate water supplies, enhance biodiversity and mitigate climate change through their natural binding of carbon dioxide, which is important for the entire planet.

These organised environmental crime activities not only destroy their natural environment, but they may directly affect the sentient, pain-feeling of non-human animals that are subject to criminal and harmful behaviour; during poaching and trafficking the individual animals are killed or suffer significantly during transportation or at the final destination when they are kept in captivity. Moreover, the poaching and wildlife trade pushes many endangered species to the brink of extinction. The animal species in such biodiverse landscapes, such as macaws in the Darien jungles, big cats in the Golden Triangle region, and the mountain gorillas of the Virungas, face large-scale habitat loss due to the disappearance and pollution of the tropical forests. From an ecocentric perspective, macaws, tigers and mountain gorillas are considered to be crucial keystone species that have a disproportionally large effect on the composition of the ecosystem and its ecosystem functions. With several species close to extinction, suffering from great habitat loss, animals flee to the last silos of natural habitats, which are targeted directly by organised crime groups. There, the victimisation of human and non-human inhabitants continues, which illustrates how environmental and social harms are intrinsically intertwined. Therefore, the effects on the ecosystems of the world's last remaining biodiversity hotspots of organised environmental crime groups can have serious local and global consequences.

Conclusion

This entry has shed light on how organised crime groups are involved in environmental black markets alongside their traditional activities and how environmental crime converges with other serious crimes. Even though the rising global scarcity of natural resources increasingly attracts organised crime, there is a lack of understanding of criminal diversification in general, and the involvement of organised crime in environmental crimes specifically. The problems of illegal mining, wildlife trade and deforestation are most damaging in politically unstable, economically depressed regions with a high level of biodiversity, where organised crime groups contribute to environmentally unsustainable practices. The victimisation of human and non-human inhabitants continues, and environmental and social harms are intrinsically intertwined in the last biodiversity hotspots on Earth. As organised crime diversifies into environmental crimes, the costs are unfathomable.

Note

Parts of this entry have been published in van Uhm DP and Nijman RC (2022) The convergence of environmental crime with other serious crimes: Subtypes within the environmental crime continuum. *European Journal of Criminology* 19(4): 542–561.

DAAN VAN UHM

Further reading

Boekhout van Solinge T (2014) The illegal exploitation of natural resources. In Paoli L (ed.) *The Oxford Handbook of Organized Crime*. Oxford University Press.

Elliott L (2012) Fighting transnational environmental crime. *Journal of International Affairs* 66(1): 87–104.

van Uhm DP (2023) *Organized Environmental Crime: Black Markets in Gold, Wildlife, and Timber*. Bloomsbury.

Walters R (2013) Eco mafia and environmental crime. In K. Carrington, M. Ball, E. O'Brien and J. M. Tauri, (eds.), *Crime, Justice and Social Democracy: International Perspectives* (pp. 281–294). Palgrave Macmillan.

White R (2011) *Transnational Environmental Crime: Toward an Eco-Global Criminology*. Routledge.

References

Albanese JS (1985) *Organized Crime: From the Mob to Transnational Organized Crime*. Anderson Publishing.

Austrac (2010) *Typologies and Case Studies Report 2010*. Australian Transaction Reports and Analysis Centre.

Boekhout van Solinge T (2014) The illegal exploitation of natural resources. In Paoli L (ed.) *The Oxford Handbook of Organized Crime*. Oxford University Press.

Bovenkerk F and Chakra BA (2004) Terrorism and organized crime. *Forum on Crime and Society* 4(1–2): 3–15.

Chiszar D, Smith HM and Costain WD (2002) *Reptiles in Association with Illicit Drugs*. University of Colorado.

Cressey D (1969). *Theft of the Nation: The Structure and Operations of Organized Crime in America*. Harper & Row.

Dishman C (2001) Terrorism, crime, and transformation. *Studies in Conflict and Terrorism* 24(1): 43–58.

Elliott L (2009) Combating transnational environmental crime: 'Joined up' thinking about transnational networks. In Kangaspunta K and Marshall IH (eds) *Eco-Crime and Justice: Essays on Environmental Crime* (pp. 55–77). UNICRI.

Europol (2011) *Organised Crime Threat Assessment (OCTA)*. Europol.

Felson M (2006) *Crime and Nature*. Sage Publications.

Gambetta D (1993) *The Sicilian Mafia: The Business of Private Protection*. Harvard University Press.

GFI. (2017) *Transnational Crime and the Developing World*. Global Financial Integrity.

GITOC. (2016) *Organized Crime and Illegally Mined Gold in Latin America*. Global Initiative against Transnational Organized Crime.

Gounev P and Ruggiero V (eds) (2012) *Corruption and Organized Crime in Europe: Illegal Partnerships*. Routledge.

Haken, J. (2011). *Transnational Crime in the Developing World*. GITOC.

Interpol (2015) *Environmental Crime and Its Convergence with Other Serious Crimes*. Interpol.

Interpol (2016) *Environment, Peace and Security: A Convergence of Threats*. Interpol.

Lichtenwald TG, Perri FS and MacKenzie P (2009) Smuggling multi-consignment contraband. *Inside Homeland Security* 7(2): 17–31.

Makarenko T (2001) Transnational crime and its evolving links to terrorism and instability. *Jane's Intelligence Review*, November: 22–24.

Makarenko T (2004). The crime–terror continuum: Tracing the interplay between transnational organised crime and terrorism. *Global Crime* *6*(1): 129–145.

Miklaucic M and Brewer J (2013) *Convergence: Illicit Networks and National Security in the Age of Globalization*. Government Printing Office.

Moreto WD, Charlton RW, DeWitt SE and Burton CM (2019) The convergence of CAPTURED fish and people: Examining the symbiotic nature of labor trafficking and illegal, unreported and unregulated fishing. *Deviant Behavior*.

Published online 24 March. https://doi.org/10.1080/01639625.2019.1594587.
Morselli C (2009) *Inside Criminal Networks*. Springer.
Nellemann C, Henriksen R, Raxter P, Ash N and Mrema E (2014) *The Environmental Crime Crisis: Threats to Sustainable Development from Illegal Exploitation and Trade in Wildlife and Forest Resources*. United Nations Environment Programme and Interpol.
Nellemann C, Henriksen R, Kreilhuber A, Stewart D, Kotsovou M, Raxter P, Mrema E and Barrat S (eds) (2016) *The Rise of Environmental Crime: A Growing Threat to Natural Resources, Peace, Development and Security*. United Nations Environment Programme.
OECD (Organisation for Economic Co-operation and Development) (2016) *Illicit Trade: Converging Criminal Networks*. OECD Reviews of Risk Management Policies. OECD Publishing.
Paoli L (2002) The paradoxes of organized crime. *Crime, Law and Social Change* 37(1): 51 97.
Paoli L (2003) *Mafia Brotherhoods: Organized Crime, Italian Style*. Oxford University Press.
Passas N (2005) Lawful but awful: 'Legal corporate crimes'. *Journal of Socio-economics* 34(6): 771–786.
Shelley L (2017) The Convergence among Diverse Forms of Crime. Working Paper. George Mason University, Virginia.
Shelley L and Kinnard K (2018) Convergence of rhino horn and ivory trade with other criminality. In Moreto WD (ed.) *Wildlife Crime* (pp. 109–134). Temple University Press.
Siegel D, Van de Bunt H and Zaitch D (eds) (2003) *Global Organized Crime: Trends and Developments*. Kluwer Academic Publishers.
Sutherland E (2011). Coltan, the Congo and your cell phone. The connection between your mobile phone and human rights abuses in Africa. University of the Witwatersrand.
Thoumi FE (1995) *Political Economy and Illegal Drugs in Colombia*. Lynne Rienner Publishers.
UNEP (2015) Waste crime – waste risks: Gaps in meeting the global waste challenge. In Nellemann C, Rucevska I et al. (eds) *A Rapid Response Assessment*. United Nations Environment Programme and GRID-Arendal.
United Nations Environment Programme. (2016) *The Rise of Environmental Crime: A Growing Threat to Natural Resources Peace, Development and Security*. United Nations Environment Programme.
UNEP/Interpol (2016) *The Rise of Environmental Crime*. Interpol.
UNODC (2011) *Transnational Organized Crime in the Fishing Industry. Focus on Trafficking in Persons Smuggling of Migrants Illicit Drugs Trafficking*. United Nations Office on Drugs and Crime.
UNODC (2012) *Digest of Organized Crime Cases. A Compilation of Cases with Commentaries and Lessons Learned*. United Nations Office on Drugs and Crime.
van Uhm DP (2016) *The Illegal Wildlife Trade: Inside the World of Poachers, Smugglers and Traders*. Springer.
van Uhm DP (2018) The diversification of organized crime into the illegal trade in natural resources. Utrecht University.
van Uhm DP (2020). The diversification of organized crime into gold mining: domination, crime convergence, and ecocide in Darién, Colombia. In Zabyelina Y and van Uhm DP (eds) *Illegal Mining: Organized Crime, Corruption, and Ecocide in a Resource-Scarce World* (pp. 105–146). Palgrave.
van Uhm DP (2023) *Organized Environmental Crime: Black Markets in Gold, Wildlife, and Timber*. Bloomsbury.
van Uhm DP and Moreto WD (2018) Corruption within the illegal wildlife trade: A symbiotic and antithetical enterprise. *British Journal of Criminology* 58(4): 864–885.
van Uhm DP and Nijman RC (2022) The convergence of environmental crime with other serious crimes: Subtypes within the environmental crime continuum. *European Journal of Criminology* 19(4): 542–561.
van Uhm DP and Siegel D (2016) The illegal trade in black caviar. *Trends in Organized Crime* 19(1): 67–87.
van Uhm DP and Siegel D (2021) Organised crime and animals. *Trends in Organized Crime*, 24: 419–424.
van Uhm DP and Wong RY (2021) Chinese organized crime and the illegal wildlife trade: Diversification and outsourcing. *Trends in Organized Crime* 24(4): 486–505.
van Uhm DP, South N and Wyatt T (2021) Connections between trades and trafficking in wildlife and drugs. *Trends in Organized Crime* 24(4): 425–446.
van Uhm DP, Tjoonk M and Bakole E (2022) Organized forest crimes: Charcoal and timber trade in Eastern DRC. In Zabyelina Y and Thachuk K (eds) *The Private Sector and Organized Crime* (pp. 149–162). Routledge.
Varese F (2011) *Mafias on the Move: How Organized Crime Conquers New Territories*. Princeton University Press.
Walters R (2014) Organized crime and the environment. In Bruinsma G and Weisburd D (eds) *Encyclopedia of Criminology and Criminal Justice* (pp. 3368–3375). Springer.
White R (2011) *Transnational Environmental Crime: Toward an Eco-Global Criminology*. Routledge.
Williams P (1998) Terrorism and organised crime: Convergence, nexus or transformation? In Jervas G (ed.) *Report on Terrorism* (pp. 69–92).

DAAN VAN UHM

Swedish Defence Research Establishment (FOA).
World Bank (2019) *Illegal Logging, Fishing, and Wildlife Trade: The Costs and How to Combat It*. World Bank.
Zhang S and Chin KL (2002) Enter the dragon: Inside Chinese human smuggling organizations. *Criminology* 40(4): 737–768.

40. Organised crime groups and networks

Introduction

Many regions around the world have experienced an increase in organised crime activities in recent years. The consequences of organised crime are immense, as it can threaten good governance, economic growth, public security, and the natural environment. Organised crime groups and networks are difficult to define, and they can differ greatly in size, structure, and function across jurisdictions and markets. Yet all organised crime groups tend to have some degree of governance, organisation, and continuity. Violence, cybercrimes, corruption, and financial crimes are common tools used by organised crime groups and networks to facilitate their activities. This entry provides an overview of organised crime group tactics, structures, networking, resiliency, and drivers. In order to reduce organised crime in the long term, there is a clear need for more collaborative approaches, as well as upstream approaches that address the systemic drivers.

Defining organised crime

Organised crime is recognised as a constantly evolving global threat and remains one of the biggest challenges to global justice (Dugato and Aziani, 2020). Economic stagnation, human rights violations, forced migration, natural resource theft, and the spread of corruption are among the consequences of organised crime. Numerous definitions have been put forth in the literature, and academics have been unable to agree on a single correct definition for exactly what constitutes "organised crime" or an "organised crime group" (Kirby and Snow, 2016). In fact, at least 200 definitions of organised crime have been proposed to date (von Lampe, 2016).

Organised crime is interpreted and conceptualised differently across jurisdictions (Lavorgna, 2020). The most globally applicable definition of an organised crime group is presented in the text of the United Nations Convention against Transnational Organized Crime, also known as the Palermo Convention, which defined the term as "a structured group of three or more persons, existing for a period of time and acting in concert with the aim of committing one or more serious crimes or offences established in accordance with this Convention, in order to obtain, directly or indirectly, a financial or other material benefit" (UNGA, 2000). Organised crime groups can generally be considered as having a governance structure of some sort, a level of sophistication and continuity to their activities, a steady supply of an illegal good or service, stable and structured links between offenders with a collective identity (i.e., some degree of organisation), alliances with political and business elites, and violence and/or corruption at the root of their activities (Papachristos and Zhao, 2015; Lavorgna, 2020).

Organised crime is not distributed evenly across geographic space (Hall, 2010). Africa and Latin America experience the highest amounts of organised crime activity and corruption globally. To a slightly lesser extent, organised crime is also prominent in Asia, and Southern and Eastern Europe (van Dijk et al., 2021). While there is reportedly less "general crime" occurring in many high-income countries, organised crime activities remain on the rise (Kirby and Snow, 2016). Global trends are pointing to an overall global increase in organised crime, including in North America, Australia, and Latin America (van Dijk et al., 2021). Advances in technology in recent decades (e.g., internet, the dark web, cryptocurrencies) have "freed" organised crime groups from many of the legal and geographic limitations that previously restricted them (Lambrechts and Hector, 2016).

The drivers of organised crimes are thought to be different from the drivers of common crimes. For example, poverty, wealth, and urbanisation are factors that are linked to common crime occurrence, although these may not be important determinants of organised crime (van Dijk et al., 2021). Inequality, poor governance, and corruption, however, are highly related to organised crime, although the interrelationships between these factors remain poorly understood (van Dijk et al., 2021).

As organised crime is a clandestine phenomenon, it is challenging methodologically to research (Kirby and Snow, 2016). Relatively little is known about how organised crime groups operate in various countries around the world. There is no question that organised crime has cascading impacts throughout all levels of society. However, the difficulties in defining organised crime contribute to difficulties in measuring organised crime and its consequences to society (Dugato and Aziani, 2020). One of the greatest efforts to fill in this knowledge gap was carried out by the Global Initiative Against Transnational Organized Crime, with the creation of the Global Organized Crime Index. Despite the limitations of using composite indicators to measure complex phenomena (Dugato and Aziani, 2020), the creation of organised crime indices is a valuable way to summarise and present information, identify trends, and to make comparisons across regions. There are multiple direct dimensions which can be used to characterise the organised crime situations in various contexts. These have been proposed broadly as (1) the organised crime groups (e.g., size, structure, relationships, modus operandi, etc.) and (2) activities (e.g., trafficking, money laundering, extortion). In addition, there are a few indirect contextual dimensions: (3) state response (e.g., law enforcement, criminal justice); (4) enablers (e.g., corruption, inequalities, low governance); and (5) civil society (e.g., non-governmental organisations, media) (Dugato and Aziani, 2020).

Once organised crime groups have significant control at the local level, they may gain enough power to participate in transnational criminal activities, including obtaining weapons and access to new markets and money-laundering opportunities. When an organised crime group establishes connections to expand their illegal businesses to other countries, they can be considered a transnational organised crime group, or a transnational criminal organisation. Many environmental crimes are indeed transnational, such as the illegal cross-border trade in waste, wildlife, timber, water, mined goods, and fish. However, organised environmental crimes can also exist wholly within the borders of one state, such as encroachment on a protected area, illegal dumping of hazardous and non-hazardous waste within state borders, and the domestic illegal trade in wildlife, timber, charcoal, mined goods, and fish. Many crimes may also be difficult to define geographically, for example, if the crime occurred in one state, but the consequences are felt in multiple states (e.g., air, land, and water pollution).

Tactics and operational features

Modus operandi is a commonly used term in criminology and related fields, which characterises the human actions, traits, and behaviours which collectively comprise the methods of operation used by organised crime (Smith, 2009). The use of violence is a staple in the modus operandi of organised crime groups and networks. Poor governance, underdevelopment, high levels of inequality, and high homicide rates are all related to organised crime at the country level (van Dijk et al., 2021). Globally, there are an estimated 65,000 homicides linked to organised crime groups and gangs each year (UNODC, 2019). Threatening and engaging in violence is often used to manage competition between organised crime groups. Violence is also used to reinforce loyalty within the group. Information on the actors involved in violence can be a potential source of compromising information, and thus, potential defectors are actively managed and discouraged within organised crime groups (Campana and Varese, 2013). Research has also found that multiple organised crime groups can benefit by jointly contributing to an act of violence as it fosters cooperation and compliance. Even discussing and sharing information about violence may in fact be a better predictor of cooperation than kinship in organised crime (Campana and Varese, 2013).

Studies of organised crime group violence have found that someone who has been subject to violent victimisation is more likely to be victimised again. Moreover, a former victim of harassment is more likely to escalate their retaliation into violence against the harasser; and that violence tends to be reciprocated by the former harasser. There is strong internal violence within organised crime groups, as previous co-offending increases the likelihood of being the victim of a violent act perpetuated by the co-offender (Niezink and Campana, 2022). Researchers have also found that gunshot victimisation of criminal offenders increases with exposure to violence within the victim's social network, and also increases the closer one is to a member of a co-offending criminal network (Papachristos et al., 2015). In other words, violence begets violence.

Cyberspace is thought to be a strong enabler of organised criminal activities, although there is limited research to date on how sophisticated organised crime groups and networks actually make use of cyberspace (Lavorgna, 2020). Cybercrimes can be beneficial for criminal networking, conducting illicit transactions, trafficking goods, and laundering money. It is important to maintain a distinction between types of cybercriminals. One type includes organised crime groups who are active offline but use cyberspace mainly to facilitate their operations. The other type includes organised cybercriminals, who specifically carry out "cybercrimes" as defined by the law (e.g., the Budapest Convention on Cybercrime, such as phishing and malware attacks, hacking, copyright infringements, etc.) (Lavorgna, 2020). Despite an increasing number of media and research reports claiming that organised crime groups are shifting their activities online, there is limited evidence to support these claims. The ability of traditional transnational organised crime groups to change their modus operandi to exploit online opportunities is under-researched, and the majority of criminal networks in cyberspace may not accurately fall into the category of organised crime (Lavorgna, 2020).

Organised crime groups

Attempts have been made to develop a typology of crime groups, including the United Nations Office on Drugs and Crime (UNODC)'s (2002) seminal analysis which produced five types of criminal networks.

- First, there are groups with a rigid hierarchy with a single leader, strong internal systems of discipline and reporting, often controlling a defined territory, and have strong social ties.
- Second, there are groups that have a "devolved hierarchy" with regional structures and leadership with their own autonomy, but still with central leadership and line of command.
- Third are groups that are associated with each other through a single governing arrangement (which can be flexible and loose), and each cluster may have its own identity and degree of autonomy.
- Fourth are core groups with a limited number of core individuals who are cohesively and horizontally organised.
- Fifth are groups that are defined by the activities of key individuals, who tend to keep a low public profile, and whose membership is based on the skills and capital that they bring to the network, rather than social or ethnic identity.

The majority of these groups carry out illicit activities in three or more countries (UNODC, 2002). The results on inter-group collaborations from this study were unclear, though external cooperation is likely for the purposes of obtaining illicit commodities to smuggle across borders into the market where the group is most active.

Organised crime networking

Modus vivendi refers to the relational quality of actors in an organised crime network, including the formation of symbiotic relationships. This allows organised crime network members to build contacts and develop social capital (Smith, 2009). Organised crimes can involve a variety of actors with varying degrees of legitimacy. A network approach has been a useful tool and conceptual framework for researchers to understand organised crime (Bouchard, 2020). Network approaches allow researchers to map social relations, criminal relations, and locations of actors in networks, and also to capture the inherent fluidity and changing dynamics of networks (Bouchard, 2020). The use of the word "networks" may make some think of loose, disorganised collaborations, as opposed to more rigid hierarchical organisations. However, "networks" encompasses criminal groupings of any kind, regardless of hierarchies and the qualitative nature of partnerships (Bouchard, 2020).

There is a growing body of research which has sought to understand the individual characteristics that explain involvement in organised crime, yet more limited is the body of research on network- or group-level characteristics of organised crime groups (Li and Liu, 2017). For example, research on the trafficking of cultural objects has generally focused on the people who loot archaeological sites, and people at the opposite end of the supply chain who purchase the stolen artefacts (Mackenzie and Davis, 2014). Similarly, wildlife trafficking research has focused on the people who illegally harvest wildlife, and the people who consume wildlife contraband. Though there are notable exceptions, and more research is needed, numerous studies on the organisational structure of drug trafficking groups point to a general lack of a formal structure and minimal hierarchy, and a network composition which is typically a series of loosely tied nodes with unstable/short-term partnerships (Li and Liu, 2017). Importantly, organised crime groups that have overlapping markets may not necessarily be in competition with one another. Collaboration across organised crime groups even with market overlap can occur when groups share similar subcultures, which may allow them to trust each other more easily. In addition, the internal organisation of organised crime groups can facilitate the establishment of norms of cooperation and coordinated responses to encounters with other groups. Furthermore, the recognition of law enforcement interventions as a common threat to both groups, and therefore a mutual enemy, can encourage collaboration (Coutinho et al., 2020).

Intermediaries and brokers in transnational trafficking networks may be chosen through prison contacts, or people who grew up in the same village as the leader/organiser (Luong, 2020). Ethnic affiliation has previously been suggested to increase the opportunities for prospective offenders to participate in organised crime when a certain ethnic group has a monopoly on a sector of the illegal market. However, this is thought to be becoming less prominent as a factor in organised crime, as new market conditions increasingly allow alliances among members from different ethnic backgrounds (Bouchard, 2020). Recent years have seen more cross-regional and cross-ethnic criminal ties. This also facilitates involvement in and access to multi-commodity networks and markets (Li and Liu, 2017; Anagnostou, 2021; van Uhm, 2023).

There is high heterogeneity in the structure, size, organisation, and operations of organised crime groups and networks across regions and crime types. One study found that a notable commonality across drug trafficking networks of various sizes in Vietnam was that leaders and organisers rarely make appearances in any actual transactions, thereby shielding, or buffering, themselves from law enforcement (Luong, 2020). These actors try to limit direct involvement and will try to control the network activities from a distance through trusted confederates, and by remaining overseas. Gender can also play a role in the organisational structure of organised crime groups. For example, drug trafficking groups in China that are composed of predominantly women members are more likely to have a decentralised structure, and less likely to have a vertical hierarchy (Li and Liu, 2017).

Opportunities and weak links

A commonality across organised crime networks is that successful trafficking operations require legitimate "covers": legal businesses and import–export trade which hide the movement of illegal goods and help to launder dirty money. Maritime ports see billions of metric tons of cargo each year, creating opportunities for organised crime activities to conceal contraband, to use fraudulent documentation, and to corrupt the officers tasked with stopping trafficking (Pourakbar and Zuidwijk, 2018). Customs address these challenges by physically inspecting cargo shipments, possibly at both the point of origin and destination, as well as reviewing the information on the shipment manifest, carrier, and shipper. Efforts to counter maritime trafficking are developed around situational crime prevention at ports, such as using surveillance cameras, barriers, smart cards, and other restrictions (Sergi, 2021). Additional measures may include conducting an X-ray or a gamma-ray scan of containers to confirm that the items match with the manifest. However, given the volume of trade, not all containers are selected for such scrutiny. These inspections can be time-consuming and costly, and may lead to delays in shipping time. Training customs officers to identify high-risk containers and investing in inspection equipment will help to improve detection efficiency (Pourakbar and Zuidwijk, 2018). Both private firms and public agencies play essential roles in securing supply chains, and partnerships between these two stakeholders are likely to benefit risk management and business firms (Pourakbar and Zuidwijk, 2018).

Some criminal organisations choose to operate in weak states in order to exploit their vulnerabilities, such as the lack of capacity to combat their activities (both operational and systemic; Lee, 2010). Weak states can be more easily criminalised through corruption, the gateway crime to undermining good governance, and facilitating organised crime (Neumann, 2013). Once a state becomes criminalised, its senior leadership is aware of and involved to some extent with transnational organised crime (Farah, 2013). "Criminal penetration" occurs at the initial stages of a criminalised state, when a criminal network manages to place a member of their network within the state structure (Miklaucic and Naím, 2013). "Criminal infiltration" occurs when the corruption becomes widespread throughout the state apparatus (Miklaucic and Naím, 2013). Criminal networks aim to corrupt rather than overthrow the government so that its officials will do as they command (Neumann, 2013). Criminal networks require corrupted, but still functioning governance structures including the infrastructures of transportation, communications, and finance (Neumann, 2013; Keefe, 2013). As all non-state groups thrive in contexts of political instability, the connections between various groups will be more common in developing countries and those recovering from conflict, though still highly context dependent (Mandel, 2010; Picarelli, 2012).

Resilience of organised crime

Criminal networks must be able to defend themselves against shocks and challenges, such as disruptions from law enforcement, policies, or other criminal groups (Munro, 2011). The ability of a criminal network to be fluid, adaptable, and to overcome external resistance is generally aided by having a loose and decentralised structure. Whether a criminal group or network succeeds or fails depends on a few factors: their vulnerability, elasticity, and adaptive capacity (Bouchard, 2007; Munro, 2011). Vulnerability considers the likelihood that an organised crime group will be exposed to attacks, and its capacity to protect itself and maintain stability (Bouchard, 2007). If the external shock/disruption is too great for the network to continue operating with the same stability, it must be elastic enough to recover from the shock and return to its original state, or a new state which maintains its operational abilities to engage in crime. Another alternative to returning to the previous structure following a shock is when an organised crime group with high capacity adapts and modifies its structures to make it less vulnerable in the future (Bouchard, 2007). Any combination of these features will enhance the resilience of organised crime groups and illegal markets. A greater focus on cooperation and intelligence-led policing is likely to weaken the resilience of transnational organised crime (Munro, 2011).

Resilience against organised crime

Resilience, in this context, can be considered as the "ability to withstand and disrupt organized criminal activities as a whole, rather than individual markets, through political, economic, legal and social measures" (Global Initiative, 2021). A country's resilience to organised crime can be measured using a number of key indicators:

(1) leadership and governance: political leadership and governance, transparency and accountability, international cooperation, national policies and laws;
(2) criminal justice and security: judicial system and detention, law enforcement, territorial integrity;
(3) economic and financial: anti-money laundering, economic regulatory capacity; and
(4) civil society and social protection: victim and witness support, prevention, and non-state actors (Global Initiative, 2021).

The type of regime is related to the resilience of a country to criminality, with full democracies having the highest resilience, and authoritarian states having the least (Global Initiative, 2021). The presence of state-embedded criminal actors is also closely correlated to poor resilience, as criminality within state institutions undermines the capacity to address organised crime (Global Initiative, 2021).

One of the challenges in combatting the trafficking of illegal goods is that when law enforcement focuses on one district or type of legality, the other branches of transnational organised crime groups are able to shift the focus of their activities elsewhere, resulting in the amount of illegal goods in circulation remaining the same (Luong, 2020). A top priority in undermining transnational organised crime is to interdict the illegal proceeds, as these proceeds would otherwise have been used to pay for supply, bribes, and infrastructure for another cycle of trafficking (Shen et al., 2021).

Conclusion

As countries increasingly feel the effects of organised crime, channels for global cooperation across law enforcement agencies must be strengthened to facilitate communication, capacity building, and information sharing. Researchers, investigators, civil society, policymakers, and private sector leaders must increasingly work together. Importantly, as many of the drivers of organised crime stem from deep-seated social and economic challenges, such as inequality and a lack of opportunities for legitimate work, decision-makers must work to address the systemic failures that cultivate crime, and shift from a reactionary-based approach to an upstream and strategic approach to reducing organised crime in the long term.

Michelle Anagnostou

Further reading

Albanese, Jay, and Philip Reichel, eds. *Transnational Organized Crime: An Overview from Six Continents*. Sage Publications, 2013.

GITOC. *Global Organized Crime Index 2023*. Global Initiative Against Transnational Organized Crime, 2023.

Kleemans, Edward R. "Theoretical perspectives on organized crime." In L. Paoli, (ed.), *The Oxford Handbook of Organized Crime*. Oxford University Press, 2014, pp. 32–52.

Paoli, Letizia. "The paradoxes of organized crime." *Crime Law and Social Change* 37 (2002): 51–97.

Van Dijk, Jan, Paul Nieuwbeerta, and Jacqueline Joudo Larsen. "Global crime patterns: An analysis of survey data from 166 countries around the world, 2006–2019." *Journal of Quantitative Criminology* (2021): 1–36.

Varese, Federico. "What is organised crime." In S. Carnevale, S. Forlati and O. Giolo, (eds.), *Redefining Organised Crime: A Challenge for the European Union*. Hart Publishing, 2017, pp. 27–56.

References

Anagnostou, Michelle. "Synthesizing knowledge on crime convergence and the illegal wildlife trade." *Environmental Challenges* 5 (2021): 100222.

Bouchard, Martin. "On the resilience of illegal drug markets." *Global Crime* 8, no. 4 (2007): 325–344.

Bouchard, Martin. "Collaboration and boundaries in organized crime: A network perspective." *Crime and Justice* 49 (July 2020): 425–469. https://doi.org/10.1086/708435.

Campana, Paolo, and Federico Varese. "Cooperation in criminal organizations: Kinship and violence as credible commitments." *Rationality and Society* 25, no. 3 (2013): 263–289.

Coutinho, James A., Tomáš Diviák, David Bright, and Johan Koskinen. "Multilevel determinants of collaboration between organised criminal groups." *Social Networks* 63 (October 1, 2020): 56–69. https://doi.org/10.1016/j.socnet.2020.04.002.

Dugato, M., and A. Aziani. "Measuring (transnational) organized crime as an indicator of global justice." *Fudan Journal of the Humanities and Social Sciences* 13, no. 2 (2020): 211–231. https://doi.org/10.1007/s40647–020–00279–2.

Farah, Douglas. "Fixers, super fixers and shadow facilitators: How networks connect." In M. Miklaucic and J. Brewer, (eds.), *Convergence: Illicit Networks and National Security in the Age of Globalization*. Military Bookshop, 2013, pp. 75–95.

Global Initiative Against Transnational Organized Crime. *Global Organised Crime Index 2021*. Global Initiative Against Transnational Organized Crime, 2021. https://globalinitiative.net/wp-content/uploads/2021/09/GITOC-Global-Organized-Crime-Index-2021.pdf.

Hall, Tim. "Economic geography and organized crime: A critical review." *Geoforum* 41, no. 6 (2010): 841–845.

Keefe, Patrick Radden. "The geography of badness: Mapping the hubs of the illicit global economy." In M. Miklaucic and J. Brewer, (eds.), *Convergence: Illicit Networks and National Security in the Age of Globalization*. Military Bookshop, 2013, pp. 97–110.

Kirby, Stuart, and Nicki Snow. "Praxis and the disruption of organized crime groups." *Trends in Organized Crime* 19 (2016): 111–124.

Lambrechts, Derica, and Michael Hector. "Environmental organised crime: The dirty business of hazardous waste disposal and limited state capacity in Africa." *Politikon* 43, no. 2 (2016): 251–268.

Lavorgna, Anita. "Organized crime and cybercrime." In T. J. Holt and A. M. Bossler, (eds.), *The Palgrave Handbook of International Cybercrime and Cyberdeviance*. Palgrave Macmillan, 2020, pp. 117–134. https://doi.org/10.1007/978-3-319-78440-3_14.

Lee, Maggy. *Trafficking and Global Crime Control*. Sage Publications, 2010, pp. 1–192.

Li, Spencer D., and Jianhong Liu. "Network characteristics and organizational structure of Chinese drug trafficking groups." *Asian Journal of Criminology* 12, no. 1 (March 1, 2017): 63–79. https://doi.org/10.1007/s11417–016–9241–6.

Luong, Hai Thanh. "The organisational structure of transnational narcotics trafficking groups in Southeast Asia: A case study of Vietnam's border with Laos." *Trends in Organized Crime*

23, no. 4 (December 1, 2020): 385–411. https://doi.org/10.1007/s12117–020–09384-w.

Mackenzie, Simon, and Tess Davis. "Temple looting in Cambodia: Anatomy of a statue trafficking network." *British Journal of Criminology* 54, no. 5 (2014): 722–740.

Mandel, Robert. *Dark Logic: Transnational Criminal Tactics and Global Security*. Stanford University Press, 2010.

Munro, P. "People smuggling and the resilience of criminal networks in Indonesia." *Journal of Policing, Intelligence and Counter Terrorism* 6, no. 1 (2011): 40–50. https://doi.org/10.1080/18335330.2011.553180.

Miklaucic, Michael, and Moisés Naím. "The criminal state." In M. Miklaucic and J. Brewer, (eds.), *Convergence: Illicit Networks and National Security in the Age of Globalization*. Military Bookshop, 2013, pp. 149–170.

Neumann, Vanessa. "Grievance to greed: the global convergence of the crime–terror threat." *Orbis* 57, no. 2 (2013): 251–267.

Niezink, Nynke M. D., and Paolo Campana. "When things turn sour: A network event study of organized crime violence." *Journal of Quantitative Criminology*, April 12, 2022. https://doi.org/10.1007/s10940–022–09540–1.

Papachristos, Andrew V., Anthony A. Braga, Eric Piza, and Leigh S. Grossman. "The company you keep? The spillover effects of gang membership on individual gunshot victimization in a co-offending network." *Criminology* 53, no. 4 (2015): 624–649.

Papachristos, Andrew V., and Sandy Y. Zhao. "Crime: Organized." In James D. Wright (ed.), *International Encyclopedia of the Social and Behavioral Sciences* (2nd ed.). Elsevier, 2015, pp. 170–175. https://doi.org/10.1016/B978–0-08–097086–8.45015–4.

Picarelli, John T. "Osama bin Corleone? Vito the Jackal? Framing threat convergence through an examination of transnational organized crime and international terrorism." *Terrorism and Political Violence* 24, no. 2 (2012): 180–198.

Pourakbar, M., and R. A. Zuidwijk. "The role of customs in securing containerized global supply chains." *European Journal of Operational Research* 271, no. 1 (November 2018): 331–340. https://doi.org/10.1016/j.ejor.2018.05.012.

Sergi, Anna. "Policing the port, watching the city. Manifestations of organised crime in the port of Genoa." *Policing and Society* 31, no. 6 (2021): 639–655.

Shen, Yeming, Thomas C. Sharkey, Boleslaw K. Szymanski, and William (Al) Wallace. "Interdicting interdependent contraband smuggling, money and money laundering networks." *Socio-Economic Planning Sciences* 78 (December 1, 2021): 101068. https://doi.org/10.1016/j.seps.2021.101068.

Smith, Robert. "Understanding entrepreneurial behaviour in organized criminals." *Journal of Enterprising Communities: People and Places in the Global Economy* 3, no. 3 (January 1, 2009): 256–268. https://doi.org/10.1108/17506200910982019.

UNGA. *United Nations Convention against Transnational Organized Crime and the Protocols Thereto*. United Nations, 2000.

UNODC. *Global Study on Homicides*. United Nations, 2019.

UNODC. *Results of a Pilot Survey of Forty Selected Organized Criminal Groups in Sixteen Countries*. United Nations, 2002.

van Dijk, Jan, Paul Nieuwbeerta, and Jacqueline Joudo Larsen. "Global crime patterns: An analysis of survey data from 166 countries around the world, 2006–2019." *Journal of Quantitative Criminology* (2021): 1–36. https://doi.org/10.1007/s10940-021-09501-0.

van Uhm, Daan. *Organized Environmental Crime: Black Markets in Gold, Wildlife, and Timber*. Bloomsbury Academic, 2023.

von Lampe, Klaus. "Definitions of organized crime." Organized Crime Research, 2016. http://www.organized-crime.de/organizedcrimed.efinitions.htm.

Michelle Anagnostou

41. State–corporate crime and the environment

Introduction

State–corporate crime refers to the serious social harms that result from the interaction of political and economic organisations and are mutually beneficial for the economic, social and political elite. This entry discusses the origins of state–corporate crime and the theoretical explanations for it. It then focuses on several case studies of state–corporate crime, ending with a discussion of several challenges for the future. The particular focus lies with those state–corporate crimes that harm the environment.

As a subtype of white-collar crime, analysis of state–corporate crime draws attention to the intersection of governmental and corporate interests in the emergence of harmful behaviours. The actions or omissions by these elites result in various (environmental) harms and victims, whose existence is often rationalised or denied by these same elites (Cohen 2001; Hall 2013). An obvious example is that of a representative of an oil and gas company that later becomes the environmental regulator or other types of so-called revolving doors between state and corporate institutions. More often, however, environmental harms occur because of much more subtle interdependencies. State–corporate crime challenges us to study organisational outcomes not as discreet acts but rather as a product of the relationships between different social institutions. Crimes and harms occur exactly because government interests are not separated from corporate ones, but instead because governments play a role in facilitating and encouraging economic prosperity (Whyte 2014). State–corporate crime theory provides a more nuanced understanding of the processes leading to deviant organisational outcomes than approaches that treat either businesses or governments as independently functioning systems.

Many state–corporate crimes concern human rights violations such as rights to food, shelter, education, and cultural life and political process. This entry focuses on those state–corporate crimes that harm the environment, which are also human rights violations, now that the United Nations General Assembly has declared that everyone on the planet has a right to a healthy environment. However, the harm to the environment extends far beyond those harms that directly impact humans to also include harms to non-human animals, plants and ecosystems.

State–corporate crime theory

Kramer and Michalowski (1990: 4) define state–corporate crimes as: 'illegal or socially injurious actions that occur when one or more institutions or political governance pursue a goal in direct cooperation with one or more institutions of economic production and distribution'. The integrated theory of state–corporate crime as developed by Kramer, Michalowski and Kauzlarich (2002) has its origins in a long critical criminological and sociological tradition of studying crimes of the powerful and of problematising their under-criminalisation (Simpson 2013). In 1916, Willem Bonger advocated the expansion of criminological and legal study to include 'crimes in the [business] suites'. Sutherland (1949: 2) gave white-collar crime international prominence by drawing attention to deviance by people and organisations of respectability and high social status, committed in the course of their occupation. He drew attention to the behaviour of large companies (petrochemistry, pharmaceuticals, weapons, banks, tobacco) which got away with their harmful behaviour because of their power to influence the imposition of more strict regulation. Continuing in this critical criminological tradition (see also Pearce & Tombs 2006), the crime referred to as state–corporate crime today is not limited to the law; it includes issues of injustice and power imbalances that generally receive less attention than criminal (or even administrative) law violations by organisations but are equally and frequently even more harmful.

Integrated theory of state–corporate crime

Kramer, Michalowski and Kauzlarich (2002) developed a theory of state–corporate crime integrating three general causes for crime and three levels of explanation. The causes of these crimes stem from the pressure for goal attainment (e.g., a culture of competition), the (perceived) opportunity of illegitimate ways to reach those goals (e.g., availability of illegal means), and the lack of effective social control (e.g., media scrutiny). Each of these domains can also be analysed at the interactional (e.g., social meaning and defining situations), organisational (e.g., corporate culture and codes of conduct) and institutional levels (e.g., economic pressure and legal sanctions). State–corporate crime reflects the specific power relations and sectoral interests of economic and political elites, which also makes it difficult to study, expose and respond to.

Within this matrix of explanations various factors are identified as contributing to the occurrence of state–corporate crime, ranging from managerial pressure and reward structures that prioritise profits within a company through to concerted ignorance of both regulators and society at large. Moreover, various actors, individuals and organisations, companies, governments and civil society actors play a role. This explanatory model makes clear that there is not one single explanation for crimes committed by political and economic elites but rather a combination of factors and actors that influence the behaviour of business and governmental organisations and their employees (for an overview see Rothe 2020). Moreover, these factors also influence each other in the emergence of the crime.

Over the years, various subtypes of state–corporate crime have been identified. The first two subtypes were identified in the original theory (Kramer, Michalowski & Kauzlarich 2002) and others were added later by other authors (Lasslett 2014; Tombs & Whyte 2020).

(1) State-facilitated corporate crime is when illegal or socially harmful business activities occur because government institutions fail to regulate them. This happens either because stricter regulation would lead to a failure to reach shared goals of business and government or because there is collusion. It emphasises that state–corporate crime can also occur as a result of inaction by not taking adequate measures to regulate the behaviour of businesses.

(2) State-initiated corporate crime is when illegal or socially harmful business activities take place at the direction or with the tacit approval of governmental actors.

(3) Corporate-initiated state crime occurs when corporations use their economic power to coerce states into illegal or socially harmful actions.

(4) Corporate-facilitated state crime refers to deviant behaviour by states for which corporations supply the means or which corporations fail to report to the respective authorities.

(5) State–corporate crime that includes crimes of globalization, which refers to the crimes committed at supranational level by transnational corporates, countries and intergovernmental institutions, and which disproportionally harm countries in the Global South.

Various scholars have contributed to the conceptual and empirical development of crimes of the powerful scholarship. For example, Green and Ward (2000) argued the importance of demonstrating that state–corporate crime occurred both objectively (because a human rights violation has occurred) and subjectively (because the public has labelled the actions or omissions as deviant). Tombs argued the importance of going beyond a focus on particular aspects of state–corporate collusion to developing a thorough analysis of the longer-term, multifaceted symbiosis between corporate and governmental interests and actors (Tombs 2012: 176).

Case studies of state–corporate environmental crime

A variety of case studies have fine-tuned state–corporate crime theory. This entry selects those that involve environmental crimes. We present them chronologically and these are by no means exhaustive in these kinds of state–corporate crimes.

- Paducah gaseous diffusion plant (Bruce & Becker 2007)
- Democratic Republic of Congo and gold and diamond industries (Mullins & Rothe 2008)
- Canadian–Alberta tar sands (Smandych & Kueneman 2013)
- Natural disaster relief (Faust & Carlson 2011): failed responses of the powerful can inflict secondary victimisation on populations beyond the harms caused by the natural disaster itself.

LIESELOT BISSCHOP, KARIN VAN WINGERDE, ABBY MURICHO ONENCAN AND SAMMIE VERBEEK

- Lynch, Burns and Stretesky (2010) studied the policy of G. W. Bush in respect of climate change as a state–corporate crime, identifying exactly that symbiosis between interests of private companies and actions of the Bush administration.
- Kramer and Michalowski (2012) have also studied climate change as a type of state–corporate crime. They concluded that the interaction between states and corporations resulted in the social and environmental harms of climate change, for instance by denying the link between climate change and human activities.
- 2010 Gulf of Mexico spill (Bradshaw 2015)
- Community resistance to a landfill (McDowell 2013)
- Standing (2015a, 2015b) studied the neoliberal political-economic system in which states and corporations are interdependent, which implies that deviant behaviour of one actor is tolerated or even facilitated by the other, and applied that to the case of illegal, unreported and unregulated fishing (IUU) in Senegal. This case study also provides insights for the crimes of globalisation subtype because it elaborates on the role of multinationals from 'home countries' in the corruption and extortion in 'host countries' via bilateral negotiations in which fishing rights are traded for development aid.
- Gold mining in Colombia (Zaitch & Gutiérrez Gómez 2015)
- Gas flaring in Nigeria (Izarali 2016)
- Land grabbing, transitional justice and economic–state crime in Afghanistan (Saeed & Parmentier 2017)
- Agrarian crisis in India, that is, the company BT Cotton (Stańczak 2017)
- Coastal land loss (Bisschop, Strobl & Viollaz 2018)
- Oil industry in Nigeria (Ai Weswasi 2019)
- Climate regulation (Michalowski & Kramer 2020)
- Coal and uranium mining on the Navajo and Hopi Islands (Robyn 2020)
- The (fast) fashion industry (Williamson & Lutz 2020; Simoncic 2021)
- The US Appalachian coal industry (Perdue 2021)
- The fossil fuel industry in Spain (Pons-Hernandez 2022)

As this list demonstrates, state–corporate crime affecting the environment is global in nature, traversing many countries in the North and the South, and comprising pollution crimes, fraud, regulatory failure, and contributing to the carbon emissions heating up the planet.

Challenges for the future

Research into environmental harms and the victims of state–corporate crime requires that we combine the insights from various disciplines. Interpreting the extent and severity of harm requires toxicological, biochemical, medical and pharmaceutical knowledge. Research into environmental crime has a long tradition of this, but this will likely have to be intensified in the future. Moreover, state–corporate crime scholarship could also benefit from integrating insights from regulation and governance studies on prevention, self-regulation and social control as potential approaches (van Erp & Almond 2020; Rodrigues de Oliviera 2019).

Research into state–corporate crime and the environment typically embraces the critical green criminological or zemiological tradition of looking at a wide variety of harms and victims (Brisman & South, 2015). A focus on harm, however, implies that it is more challenging to identify and define what can be labelled as state–corporate crimes and what cannot. For example, to what extent do we consider data manipulation by Big Tech companies to be a crime and how do we look at its harmfulness in relation to various potential victims, including the planet? And what about a theme like fake news and the power that Big Tech companies have in influencing public opinion, including opinions that deny the existence of climate change? That too is damage resulting from the undertakings at the intersection of economic and political elites.

In the literature on state–corporate crime, it has long been noted that it is precisely where economic and political interests come together that makes it much more complicated to characterise the behaviour of companies as criminal. But state–corporate crime also has more 'mundane' manifestations in our everyday consumption of technology and clothes that are connected to human rights abuses and environmental harms (Rothe & Medley 2019). A focus on harm and victimisation can break through this complexity (Dodge 2020).

Indeed, such harmful behaviour might not have been a crime in the legal sense. In many cases, governments are aware of what is going on in polluting industries, and in some cases, they even facilitate these activities by allowing them in the interest of the economy or of innovation. They therefore apply more flexible regulatory standards regarding emissions or safety margins or do not regulate at all and leave it to the industry to self-regulate. As such, many corporate crimes were 'allowed' by the state.

Prosecuting companies in criminal court has proven challenging and only a few cases lead to criminal convictions. Legal follow-through has been possible when the focus has been on civil torts and damages. This strategy might allow for a greater focus on how to force corporations to repair the physical, emotional and economic damage associated with their activities. Perhaps there is something to be said for restorative justice in this context, provided, of course, that both companies and governments are willing to enter into an open and honest dialogue about what went wrong historically (Pali, Forsyth & Tepper 2022). This requires that companies do not deny legal responsibility nor shift it to other supply chain partners or corporate entities that no longer exist. Moreover, it also requires the public authorities to be prepared to enter into dialogue even about those situations in which they may be responsible for insufficient (critical) regulation or monitoring of harmful business activities.

State–corporate crime research has a tradition of looking at the broader social context in which a crime has occurred. This contextual analysis also needs to be positioned in its economic, company and regulatory history. For example, in recent years more and more public information has become available about the harmful behaviour of companies. Several lawsuits in the United States led to the release of company documents dating back decades, for example on internal studies in the chemical, oil and gas industry, and in the pharmaceutical industry. This provides better insight into the (awareness of) historical damage caused by business activities.

Take the example of the so-called 'forever chemicals', the suite of over 4,700 per- and polyfluoroalkyl substances (PFAS) used in our non-stick cookware, hard-shell jackets, firefighting foam, plastic food wrappings or cosmetics. Once PFAS chemistry was discovered in the 1930s, PFAS have persisted and accumulated in the environment, in non-human animals and in humans. What is becoming increasingly clear thanks to historical documents is that the harmful effects of some PFAS were known by the chemical industry decades ago and yet still the phasing out of their production and use followed much later (Richter, Cordner & Brown 2018). PFAS pollution was thus perpetuated and regulated via permits by government agencies. However, the important challenge remains to label that behaviour as deviant within criminology research and within the wider society. After all, it is not just about how progressive scientific insight has made it clear that lead, glyphosate, PFAS, and other substances are harmful to people and the environment. More importantly, it is now clear that the industry was aware of that harmfulness for a long time, and that it kept it quiet or even actively tried to counteract it through rhetoric about safety margins and risks or innovation, thereby diverting attention, shifting blame and/or silencing whistleblowers.

Although case studies remain a relevant method for understanding state–corporate crimes, one important limitation is that these tend to focus on a temporary 'moment of rupture' within the relationship between the state and the corporation (Whyte 2014). This prevents a deeper, structural understanding of the causes (Davies 2022; Pons-Hernandez 2022; Bernat & Whyte 2017; Whyte 2014). Therefore, a more recent trend in literature on state–corporate crime is a shift from case studies that focus on these temporary 'moments of rupture', to a call for longitudinal and historical research that places state–corporate crime in a political, social and historical context (Davies 2022; Pons-Hernandez 2022; Perdue 2021; Michalowski & Kramer 2020; Bisschop, Strobl & Viollaz 2018; Bernat & Whyte 2017; Stańczak 2017; Bradshaw 2015; Whyte 2014).

Finally, studies that focus on causes of environmental crime tend to more or less artificially separate the characteristics of criminality at the individual, organisational or societal level. If we only consider one of the explanation levels – or a limited number of explanatory factors within each of those levels – then we ignore the way in which other levels of explanation may illuminate crime causation and consequences. A focus on the individual CEO or politician alone, for example, leads to attention being diverted from more structural and institutional causes. The search for a scapegoat on whom the blame can be laid is, however, a tried and tested (communication) strategy for companies that are involved in (lawsuits about) environmental crime. Referring to the lack of governmental oversight as the cause of the environmental crime may ignore characteristics of the company itself or of the manager at the helm. One possible response would be to punish severely and introduce codes of conduct to clarify what moral behaviour is, but we may miss some of the causes in the wider context of the company, sector, regulation or society. If we miss part of the explanation, this also has consequences for the policy that is being developed to try, punish and prevent environmental crime. After all, the most effective response is the one that is best tailored to the nature of the company, the sector and the social and regulatory environment in which it functions.

Conclusion

Environmental crime requires a comprehensive explanation, which means a combination of factors at the individual, organisational and societal level, as was initially developed in the integrated theory of state–corporate crime. Moreover, these levels also mutually influence each other. A competitive culture in a sector or even in a country creates pressure for companies to set (too) ambitious goals. Subsequently, achieving these objectives gives employees in these organisations a reason to rationalise their own norm-violating behaviour. Moreover, the behaviour of a manager can influence the culture within a company and thus encourage harmful behaviour. The challenges for tackling environmental crime therefore lie in developing robust models of the possible causes and the interactions between these different factors and between both state and corporate actors. The relational character of state–corporate crime requires us to consider the vertical relationships between different levels of organisational action: the individual; the institutional; and the political-economic. There is much work for scholars in embracing that complexity by empirically studying environmental harms.

LIESELOT BISSCHOP, KARIN VAN WINGERDE, ABBY MURICHO ONENCAN AND SAMMIE VERBEEK

Further reading

Bernat, I. & Whyte, D. (2017). State–corporate crime and the process of capital accumulation: Mapping a global regime permission from Galicia to Morecambe Bay. *Critical Criminology*, 25(1), 71–86.
Kramer, R., Michalowski, R. & Kauzlarich, D. (2002). The origins and development of the concept and theory of state–corporate crime, *Crime & Delinquency*, 48(2), 263–282.
Rothe, D.L. (2020). Moving beyond abstract typologies? Overview of state and state–corporate crime. *Journal of White-Collar and Corporate Crime*, 1(1), 7–15.
Rothe, D. & Kauzlarich, D. (2017). We are all complicit: Victimization and crimes of the powerful. In S. Walklate (ed.), *The Handbook of Victims and Victimology*. Routledge, pp. 358–363.
Tombs, S. & Whyte, D. (2020). The shifting imaginaries of corporate crime. *Journal of White Collar and Corporate Crime*, 1(1), 16–23.
Whyte, D. (2014). Regimes of permission and state–corporate crime. *State Crime Journal*, 3(2), 237–246. https://www.jstor.org/stable/10.13169/statecrime.3.2.0237

References

Ai Weswasi, E. (2019). Spending blood for oil in Nigeria: A frame analysis of Shell's neutralization of acts that led to corporate-initiated state crime. *Nordisk Tidsskrift for Kriminalvidenskab*, 106(3), 280–296.
Bernat, I. & Whyte, D. (2017). State–corporate crime and the process of capital accumulation: Mapping a global regime permission from Galicia to Morecambe Bay. *Critical Criminology*, 25(1), 71–86.
Bisschop, L.C.J., Strobl, S. & Viollaz, J.S. (2018). Getting into deep water: Coastal land loss and state–corporate crime in the Louisiana bayou. *The British Journal of Criminology*, 58(4), 886–905.
Bonger, W. (1916). *Criminality and Economic Conditions*. Little, Brown and Company.
Bradshaw, E. (2015). 'Obviously, We're All Oil Industry': The criminogenic structure of the offshore oil industry. *Theoretical Criminology*, 19(3), 376–395.
Brisman, A. & South, N. (2015). State–corporate environmental harms and paradoxical interventions: Thoughts in honour of Stanley Cohen.

In R. Sollund (ed.), *Green Harms and Crimes*. Palgrave Macmillan, pp. 27–42.
Bruce, A.S. & Becker, P.J. (2007). State–corporate crime and the Paducah gaseous diffusion plant. *Western Criminology Review*, 8, 29.
Cohen, S. (2001). *States of Denial: Knowing about Atrocities and Suffering*. Polity Press.
Davies, J. (2022). Criminogenic dynamics of the construction industry: a state–corporate crime perspective. *Journal of White Collar and Corporate Crime*, 3(2), 90–99.
Dodge, M. (2020). A black box warning: The marginalization of white-collar crime victimization. *Journal of White Collar and Corporate Crime*, 1(1), 24–33.
Faust, K. & Carlson, S. (2011). Devastation in the aftermath of Hurricane Katrina as a state crime: Social audience reactions. *Crime, Law and Social Change*, 55(1), 33–51.
Green, P. & Ward, T. (2000). State crime, human rights, and the limits of criminology. *Social Justice*, 27, 101–115.
Hall, M. (2013). *Victims of Environmental Harm: Rights, Recognition and Redress under National and International Law*. Routledge.
Izarali, M. (2016). Human rights and state–corporate crimes in the practice of gas flaring in the Niger Delta, Nigeria. *Critical Criminology*, 24(3), 391–412.
Kramer, R. & Michalowski, R. (1990). *Toward an Integrated Theory of State–Corporate Crime*. Presented at the American Society of Criminology, Baltimore, MD.
Kramer, R.C. & Michalowski, R.J. (2012). Is global warming a state–corporate crime? In R. White (ed.), *Climate Change from a Criminological Perspective*. Springer, pp. 71–88.
Kramer, R., Michalowski, R. & Kauzlarich, D. (2002). The origins and development of the concept and theory of state–corporate crime. *Crime & Delinquency*, 48(2), 263–282.
Lasslett, K. (2014). *State Crime on the Margins of Empire: Rio Tinto, the War on Bougainville and Resistance to Mining*. Pluto Press.
Lynch, M.J., Burns, R.G. & Stretesky, P.B. (2010). Global warming and state–corporate crime: The politicalization of global warming under the Bush administration. *Crime, Law and Social Change*, 54(3), 213–239.
McDowell, M. (2013). Becoming a waste land where nothing can survive: Resisting state–corporate environmental crime in a 'forgotten' place. *Contemporary Justice Review*, 16(4), 394–411.
Michalowski, R. & Kramer, R.C. (2020). Rolling back climate regulation: Trump's assault on the planet. *Journal of White-Collar and Corporate Crime*, 1(2), 123–130.
Mullins, C. & Rothe, D.L. (2008). International state–corporate crime in the Democratic Republic of Congo. *Contemporary Justice Review*, 11(2), 81–99.
Pali, B., Forsyth, M. & Tepper, F. (eds.) (2022). *The Palgrave Handbook of Environmental Restorative Justice*. Palgrave Macmillan.
Pearce, F. & Tombs, S. (2006). Hegemony, risk and governance: 'Social regulation' and the American chemical industry. *Economy and Society*, 25(3), 428–454.
Perdue, R.T. (2021). Corporate violence in the Central Appalachian coal industry: From roots to repercussions. *Critical Criminology*, 29(4), 897–913.
Pons-Hernandez, M.A. (2022). Power(ful) connections: Exploring the revolving doors phenomenon as a form of state–corporate crime. *Critical Criminology*, 30(2), 305–320.
Richter, L., Cordner, A. & Brown, P. (2018). Non-stick science: Sixty years of research and (in)action on fluorinated compounds. *Social Studies of Science*, 48(5), 691–714.
Robyn, L.M. (2020). Environmental injustices and state–corporate crime on Navajo and Hopi lands. In K. Jarratt-Snider & M.O. Nielsen (eds.), *Indigenous Environmental Justice*. The University of Arizona Press (pp. 59–91). https://doi.org/10.2307/j.ctv10qqwrm.8.
Rodrigues de Oliviera, C. (2019). Corporate crimes: The specter of genocide haunts the world. *Revista de Administração de Empresas*, 59(6), 435–441.
Rothe, D.L. (2020). Moving beyond abstract typologies? Overview of state and state–corporate crime. *Journal of White-Collar and Corporate Crime*, 1(1), 7–15. doi:10.1177/2631309X19872438
Rothe, D. & Medley, C. (2019). Beyond state and state–corporate crime typologies: The symbiotic nature, harm, and victimization of crimes of the powerful and their continuation. In M. Rorie (ed.), *The Handbook of White-Collar Crime*. Routledge, pp. 81–94.
Saeed, H. & Parmentier, S. (2017). When rabbits are in charge of carrots: Land grabbing, transitional justice and economic-state crime in Afghanistan. *State Crime Journal*, 6(1), 13–36.
Simoncic, K. (2021). Fast fashion: A case of social harm and state–corporate crime. *The Howard Journal of Crime and Justice*, 60(3), 343–369.
Simpson, S.S. (2013). White-collar crime: A review of recent developments and promising directions for future research. *Annual Review of Sociology*, 39(1), 309–331.
Smandych, R. & Kueneman, R. (2013). The Canadian-Alberta tar sands: A case study of state–corporate environmental crime. In R.

LIESELOT BISSCHOP, KARIN VAN WINGERDE, ABBY MURICHO ONENCAN AND SAMMIE VERBEEK

White (ed.), *Global Environmental Harm*. Willan, pp. 105–127.
Standing, A. (2015a). Mirage of pirates: State–corporate crime in West Africa's fisheries. *State Crime Journal*, 4(2), 175–197.
Standing, A. (2015b). Corruption and state–corporate crime in fisheries. *Anti-Corruption Resource Center*. https://www.u4.no/publications/corruption-and-state-corporate-crimein-fisheries/pdf.
Stańczak, D. (2017). State–corporate crime and the case of BT Cotton: On the production of social harm and dialectical process. *State Crime Journal*, 6(2), 214–240.
Sutherland, E.H. (1949). *White Collar Crime*. Dryden Press.
Tombs, S. (2012). State–corporate symbiosis in the production of crime and harm. *State Crime Journal*, 1(2), 170–195.
Tombs, S. & Whyte, D. (2020). The shifting imaginaries of corporate crime. *Journal of White Collar and Corporate Crime*, 1(1), 16–23.
van Erp, J. & Almond, P. (2020). Regulation and governance versus criminology: Disciplinary divides, intersections, and opportunities. *Regulation & Governance*, 14(2), 167–183.
Whyte, D. (2014). Regimes of permission and state–corporate crime. *State Crime Journal*, 3(2), 237–246. https://www.jstor.org/stable/10.13169/statecrime.3.2.0237
Williamson, S.H. & Lutz, J. (2020). Sewing responsibility: Media discourse, corporate deviance, and the Rana Plaza collapse. *Sociological Inquiry*, 90(1), 76–100.
Zaitch, D. & Gutiérrez Gómez, L. (2015). Mining as a state–corporate crime: The case of AngloGold Ashanti in Colombia. In D. Zaitch & L. Gutiérrez Gómez (eds.), *The Routledge International Handbook of the Crimes of the Powerful*. Routledge, pp. 386–397. https://doi.org/10.4324/9781315815350

PART VII

COMBATTING ENVIRONMENTAL CRIME

42. Community responses to illegal wildlife trade

Introduction

This entry critically examines the evolution and effectiveness of community interventions in reducing wildlife crime, with a focus on the inclusion of Indigenous Peoples and Local Communities (IPLCs). It discusses the transition from traditional 'fortress conservation' methods, which often excluded local populations, to more inclusive strategies that engage IPLCs as autonomous leaders, partners or stakeholders (Dawson et al. 2024). Highlighting both historical and contemporary perspectives, this entry explores the multifaceted challenges and successes associated with these approaches. By engaging with concepts such as contested illegality and the socio-economic drivers behind wildlife crime, this entry underscores the complex interplay between local traditions, legal frameworks and global conservation practices. Theoretical frameworks and case studies are utilised to provide a comprehensive understanding of how community-centric responses not only contribute to wildlife conservation but also enhance the social and ecological well-being of IPLCs. This entry aims to offer insights into the significance of community involvement in contemporary conservation practices and to propose directions for future research and policy development.

The importance of Indigenous Peoples and Local Communities

Wildlife crime poses a grave threat not only to endangered wildlife species but also to global biodiversity and socio-ecological sustainability. The concept captures the illegal hunting, harvesting, capturing of wildlife and subsequent trafficking, trade and consumption of live or dead wildlife, body parts or derivatives. Despite international regulations and concerted conservation enforcement efforts, the persistence, proliferation and evolution of wildlife crime necessitate preventative and whole-of-society measures. Such approaches increasingly recognise Indigenous Peoples and Local Communities (IPLCs) as pivotal actors in fighting wildlife crime.

Focusing on sustainable livelihoods – one of the four pillars discussed at the intergovernmental conferences on reducing the illegal wildlife trade (IWT) in Kasane, Hanoi and London – this approach complements traditional state-centred responses such as law enforcement, legal frameworks and demand reduction. IPLCs, historically marginalised and often mischaracterised as perpetrators or beneficiaries of wildlife crime, are now valued for their knowledge of local ecosystems and their potential as 'protectors' of wildlife (Cooney et al. 2017), 'fulcrum institutions' and 'change agents' (Hübschle and Shearing 2018) and the 'first line of defence' (Cooney et al. 2018).

A community is defined as a group of individuals connected by geographical proximity and social relations at a specific point in time (Kepe 1999). Communities are diverse and not homogeneous; they consist of individuals with varied backgrounds, loyalties and aspirations. Historically, the concept of 'community' has been used to group people of colour and those from different social strata, castes or religions as collective entities, as opposed to individual agency granted to colonialists and their descendants, and other elite formations. Today, the notion of community and community participation is widely recognised and embraced by government authorities, civil society and NGOs (Hübschle and Shearing 2025). It is increasingly acknowledged that community cohesion and strategic mobilisation have been crucial in driving significant social and political changes, including the dismantling of colonial systems (Williams 2006: 197). However, communities still embody a complex tapestry of influences, alliances and interests.

This entry explores the historical evolution, varieties, strengths and challenges of community responses to wildlife crime. It is loosely based on the International Union for Conservation of Nature (IUCN) First Line of Defence pathways that outline how incentives shape community attitudes and behaviours in relation to wildlife crime (IUCN 2017) and Hübschle's module developed for the United Nations Office on Drugs and Crime (UNODC) on 'Sustainable Livelihoods and Community Engagement' (Hübschle 2022). By exploring the concept of contested illegality, this entry highlights how legal frameworks sometimes clash with Indigenous and local practices and beliefs, emphasising the need for a culturally sensitive approach to conservation enforcement. It aims to provide a comprehensive understanding of how localised actions can contribute to global conservation efforts, reflecting the emergence of a conservation paradigm where community well-being and biodiversity conservation are intractably linked and mutually reinforcing objectives.

Historical context and contested illegality

Since the 1980s, community-based interventions have increasingly become a focus in conservation, prompted by a recognition that effective natural resource management must involve those who have historically lived in and around these resources. IPLCs have maintained various forms of conservation and consumption relationships with natural resources for generations. This shift in approach coincides with broader macro-political and economic developments in the Global South and the emergence of post-colonial studies advocating the principle of 'nothing about us without us' (Botha and Murphree 2022).

Historically, conservation strategies were characterised by 'fortress conservation', a model that sought to create pristine wilderness and protected areas by separating humans and wildlife, often resulting in the relocation and marginalisation of resident human populations (Brockington 2002). This exclusion began in earnest during the colonial period from the early sixteenth century to the twentieth century, where IPLCs were often forcibly evicted from their territories to make space for new settler economies and conservation areas designated for wildlife protection or elite hunting. This was not just a matter of physical displacement but also involved stripping these communities of their natural resource user rights, including hunting rights, and severing their deep cultural and ancestral connections to these territories. This model has been criticised for serving the interests of international tourism and elite subsets of society rather than supporting sustainable ecological practices. Despite its proponents claiming effectiveness, studies such as those by the Intergovernmental Science-Policy Platform on Biodiversity and Ecosystem Services (2019) indicate that biodiversity declines at a slower rate in areas managed by IPLCs.

Conservation in many parts of the world has a checkered history intricately linked to colonial oppression, systemic exclusion and eviction of IPLCs (Hübschle and Shearing 2025; Duffy 2022; Dlamini 2020). During the colonial era and continuing into the present, protected areas were frequently established at the expense of local communities, who were deprived of their land, natural resource rights and cultural heritage. Conservation laws implemented during these times were often designed to benefit colonial powers and post-colonial elites while criminalising traditional practices of IPLCs, thus turning sustainable users of natural resources into 'poachers'.

The dissonance between local customs and formal legal frameworks imposed by state or colonial powers in the present and past forms the crux of the notion of contested illegality (Hübschle 2017a, 2017b; Dore et al. 2022). Traditional practices like hunting or gathering, integral to local cultures and survival, were criminalised under new conservation laws without due consultation or respect for Indigenous Rights. This criminalisation not only alienated IPLCs but often spurred conflicts that undermined conservation goals. IPLCs did not recognise the legitimacy of anti-poaching and conservation laws, viewing them as continuations of colonial impositions that fail to acknowledge their sovereign rights and traditional knowledge. This contention highlights a critical aspect of wildlife law enforcement: the need to reconcile international and national regulations with local conservation contexts and environmental justice. The evolving legal landscape now increasingly recognises the rights and roles of IPLCs in stewardship of biodiversity, a significant shift from earlier exclusionary policies.

As we reflect on this history, it is evident that the exclusionary practices of the past continue to influence contemporary conservation efforts. Community-based conservation now seeks to rectify these injustices by involving IPLCs not only as stakeholders but as leaders in the stewardship of biodiversity. This approach challenges the traditional narratives that have long depicted local communities as antagonists rather than as essential partners, autonomous leaders or stakeholders in conservation (Dawson et al. 2024).

ANNETTE HÜBSCHLE

The cost of conservation

While traditional hunting practices remain legally contested, community engagement in wildlife trade is often shaped by a range of economic, social, and cultural factors. This section examines the multifaceted incentives that drive community participation, acknowledging that economic, social and cultural factors play significant roles in shaping these interactions with wildlife crime.

Living near or within protected areas poses substantial challenges and risks for IPLCs. These so-called human–wildlife conflicts can arise when wildlife threatens human livelihoods, property or safety. Conflicts can take several forms, including wildlife damaging crops, livestock and property, or directly endangering human lives through attacks. The presence of wildlife can necessitate costly safety measures for IPLCs, limiting their freedom of movement, especially at night, and creating an atmosphere of fear and tension. Cultural norms and beliefs significantly influence perceptions of wildlife. For instance, snakes, which generally avoid humans, are often killed out of fear when encountered. In some regions, wildlife like the aye-aye lemur in Madagascar is killed due to local beliefs that associate them with bad omens. The concept of human–wildlife conflict is also intertwined with human–human conflicts, particularly between local communities and conservation authorities or NGOs. These conflicts often stem from conservation practices that fail to align with the needs or rights of local communities. Promoting coexistence involves shifts in terminology from ‘conflict’ to ‘coexistence’ to foster a more harmonious relationship between humans and wildlife, focusing on mutual survival rather than adversarial conflict. The approach of Conservation Conflict Transformation seeks to address the underlying social conflicts that fuel conservation issues, advocating a social carrying capacity that accommodates both human and wildlife needs.

Communities living adjacent to protected areas often face economic hardships due to restricted access to natural resources, which historically constituted their livelihoods. The lack of viable economic alternatives can make illegal activities such as poaching, logging and unregulated fishing attractive. These activities often provide immediate financial relief and are perceived as opportunities to reclaim control over natural resources. The high profit margins associated with illegal wildlife products, such as ivory, rhino horn and exotic pets, further incentivise engagement in IWT. For many, the economic benefits of IWT overshadow the potential gains from participating in legal conservation efforts, which are often insufficient and delayed.

IWT can also emerge as a form of resistance or social rebellion against wildlife that pose threats to human life and property. Communities suffering from crop raiding, livestock predation and other forms of human–wildlife conflict may engage in poaching as a retaliatory measure. Moreover, the depletion of resources due to conservation policies can lead to intensified competition between humans and wildlife for the remaining resources, pushing communities towards IWT as a survival strategy.

In some cultures, hunting and trading in wildlife are traditional practices that hold cultural significance and are vital for social cohesion and identity. These activities are often part of communal rituals, traditional medicine and local economies. Legal restrictions that overlook these traditions can drive these practices underground, contributing to the persistence of IWT. The social structure within communities can also play a role, where influential community members engage in or facilitate IWT, setting a precedent for others (Hübschle 2017a, 2017b).

The absence of robust and accessible legal frameworks for sustainable wildlife management can leave communities with few alternatives but to turn to IWT. This situation is exacerbated by weak enforcement of existing wildlife protection laws, corruption and a lack of trust in authorities. When communities perceive conservation laws as unjust or see them being flouted by those with more power, they are more likely to disregard these laws themselves.

In some cases IWT provides not only financial gains but also a sense of empowerment and control over community resources. This aspect of IWT can be particularly appealing in contexts where communities feel marginalised from mainstream economic and political processes. Engaging in IWT can be seen as a way to assert control over local biodiversity that is otherwise managed by external actors, such as governments and international conservation organisations.

This complex interplay of economic, social and cultural factors underscores the need for conservation strategies to be holistic and inclusive in light of the diverse motivations and pressures that drive communities towards involvement in IWT. By addressing these underlying factors, conservation efforts can be more effective in curbing illegal activities while fostering positive community engagement in wildlife management.

IPLCs as wildlife crime fighters

The prevailing approach to fighting IWT relies on traditional crime-fighting tactics led by public law enforcement and, increasingly, private military and security companies. These entities often operate in remote areas away from robust state control and civil society oversight, which complicates enforcement efforts. The methodologies used, including command-and-control, green militarisation and hotspot policing, are largely reactive. They typically respond to incidents of poaching after they occur, with intelligence-driven policing, anti-poaching patrols, and emerging technologies like artificial intelligence-based surveillance systems attempting to pre-empt such activities. Command-and-control approaches involve strict governance and regulation of natural resources, aimed at reducing variability and unpredictability in ecosystems to make them more manageable for human benefit. However, such a centralised method often leads to exclusion of IPLCs from protected areas, sometimes even involving forced evictions in the name of anti-poaching strategies. Despite the integration of AI and advanced technologies in some landscapes, these approaches continue to operate within a framework that may marginalise local communities and overlook their valuable role in conservation. In contrast to the command-and-control model, some countries have implemented more community-inclusive strategies. Namibia, for example, employs community game guards and rhino monitors within its community conservancies. These guards are locals trained to monitor and protect wildlife, integrating traditional knowledge with modern conservation practices. This approach not only provides jobs but also helps ensure that conservation efforts are more acceptable to and actively supported by local communities.

The involvement of communities in enforcement can sometimes lead to conflicts, particularly when local norms and conservation laws are at odds. Additionally, reliance on local enforcement without adequate support and recognition can place community members at risk from well-armed poaching syndicates. Furthermore, enforcement approaches that focus excessively on surveillance and punishment without addressing underlying socio-economic drivers may lead to resistance rather than cooperation.

Community-centred conservation

The focus on community-centred conservation strategies emphasises the importance of involving IPLCs not just as partners in conservation enforcement efforts against wildlife crime, but as direct beneficiaries and managers of conservation projects. This approach is based on the principle of increasing the tangible benefits that communities derive from conservation, which in turn motivates them to protect and sustain their natural resources.

A significant portion of conservation policies and initiatives has historically been aimed at rehabilitating communities that were displaced or adversely affected by previous conservation efforts, including former poachers. Many current projects seek to provide alternative, sustainable livelihoods, compensations, and in some rare cases, actual ownership or rights over land and resources. However, these measures often need to be more aligned with the organic needs, desires and historical practices of the communities they intend to support. They also frequently serve as a form of damage control for past wrongs, highlighting the complex and sometimes contentious relationship between conservation efforts and community rights, particularly in regions like the Global South where issues of environmental and social justice are prevalent.

For example, the Namibia community conservancy model is one of the few global examples where land ownership and management rights are effectively transferred to local communities (Jones 1999). This model has shown success in fostering conservation while benefiting the local population but is not universally applicable, underscoring the challenge of replicating specific conservation models across different contexts. Well-known methods like eco-tourism and trophy hunting have traditionally been used to directly incentivise conservation by making wildlife valuable to communities through self-generated revenue from sustainable use. However, these approaches depend heavily on external markets and are vulnerable to disruptions such as diseases, political unrest, changing consumer preferences or international travel restrictions, which can undermine their effectiveness and sustainability.

In Zimbabwe, the CAMPFIRE programme is another example of a community-based conservation initiative designed to redistribute benefits from wildlife tourism and hunting back to the communities themselves (Murombedzi 1999). This programme was initially set up to empower rural district councils to manage and benefit financially from local wildlife, with the expectation that a significant portion of the revenue would be passed on to the communities. While CAMPFIRE has been successful in generating income and conserving wildlife, challenges such as underpayments, delays and the unequal distribution of benefits have highlighted the limitations and potential pitfalls of such programmes. Both the CAMPFIRE and Namibian conservancy models illustrate the potential for community-based conservation initiatives to support both biodiversity and local livelihoods. However, they also demonstrate the complexities and challenges involved in ensuring that these programmes are equitable, sustainable and adaptable to the specific cultural, social and environmental contexts of the communities they aim to serve.

An emerging tool in conservation finance is the use of social impact bonds (SIBs). These bonds are designed to attract private capital to fund projects that have clear, measurable social outcomes. In the context of conservation, SIBs can be used to fund initiatives that directly benefit both biodiversity and community welfare. These bonds typically function on a pay-for-success model, where investors are reimbursed and rewarded based on the project's outcomes. This model incentivises the achievement of specific conservation goals, such as reducing poaching activities or increasing wildlife populations, while also aiming to improve local livelihoods through employment in conservation activities.

Buffer zones are areas designated around protected regions that help mitigate the impact of human activities on core conservation areas. By integrating sustainable land use practices within buffer zones, communities can participate in activities that are compatible with conservation goals. These zones not only protect the biodiversity of the core areas but also allow for the sustainable use of natural resources by local communities, thus serving as a compromise between unrestricted access and total exclusion. Implementing buffer zones effectively requires active community involvement and can lead to enhanced stewardship of the environment by local residents.

Rights-based approaches grant local communities legal rights to manage and use the natural resources within their traditional territories. This approach recognises the intrinsic connection between Indigenous Peoples and their environments, empowering them through legal frameworks that acknowledge their rights to land and resources. Such initiatives often lead to more sustainable conservation outcomes as communities directly benefit from maintaining the ecological health of their environments.

Looking forward, the integration of community responses into conservation strategies should focus on adaptive management practices that allow for the flexible implementation of projects based on ongoing feedback and evolving community needs. By fostering an inclusive approach that values the input and expertise of local communities, conservation initiatives can create more resilient and sustainable outcomes that benefit both biodiversity and the people who depend on these natural resources. By expanding on these strategies and continually adapting to the challenges and lessons learned from community-centred conservation, it is possible to create a more inclusive and effective model for wildlife protection that directly engages and benefits those most affected by conservation policies.

Models that incentivise conservation

Alternative livelihood projects are essential in reducing environmentally harmful activities by offering less damaging or beneficial alternatives, often not involving the direct exploitation of biodiversity. These projects aim to replace harmful subsistence activities with sustainable ones, providing equivalent or greater benefits. For example, introducing alternative protein sources and income opportunities can significantly reduce the reliance on and trade in bushmeat. Despite their potential, the effectiveness of alternative livelihood projects in conservation remains under-documented and its impact questionable (Roe et al. 2015). Studies, including those by Wicander and Coad (2018), have criticised these projects for insufficient outcome monitoring, dependence on small short-term grants administered by international and local non-governmental organisations and lack of rigorous impact monitoring and evaluation. This suggests a gap between project implementation and conservation effectiveness, highlighting a critical need for better integration of conservation objectives into these livelihood alternatives and the restructuring of funding models. Prominent examples include carbon credits (e.g., REDD+), paying for ecosystem services (PES) and microcredits.

The concept of carbon credits allows companies to offset their emissions by investing in environmental conservation projects, such as forest conservation under the REDD+ framework. However, the effectiveness and ethical implications of these programmes are widely debated. Critics argue that REDD+ can lead to the alienation of land and exacerbate the marginalisation of forest-dependent communities. The complex dynamics of carbon trading and its impact on local communities necessitate a careful and inclusive approach to conservation financing. PES programmes compensate landowners for managing their land in ways that provide ecological services, such as carbon sequestration or watershed protection. While successful in some regions, the application of PES often involves restricting traditional land use, which can lead to conflicts and unintended conservation outcomes. Ensuring that these schemes are beneficial for all stakeholders, particularly Indigenous Peoples and Local Communities, is crucial for their success. Microcredit schemes provide small loans to individuals in low-income regions, empowering them to engage in sustainable livelihoods. These programmes have shown promise in conservation efforts, such as reducing fuel wood use in Pakistan. However, the effectiveness of microcredits can vary, and programmes must be designed to address the specific needs and contexts of their target communities.

However, emerging trends such as the financialisaton of nature, including new forms of conservation finance like green bonds and payments for ecosystem services, are redefining how conservation funding is structured. These mechanisms need to be critically examined to ensure they lead to equitable outcomes for IPLCs and do not perpetuate historical injustices.

Incentivising conservation through alternative livelihoods offers a pathway to sustainable development that aligns economic and environmental goals. However, the success of these models depends on their adaptability to local contexts, the involvement of local communities in their design and implementation, and ongoing monitoring and evaluation to ensure they meet both conservation and social objectives.

Failures and weaknesses of incentivisation mechanisms

Despite the promise of community-based conservation, several inherent challenges and systemic issues can undermine its efficacy. Criticisms focus primarily on governance deficits, distribution of benefits, the persistence of unequal power relationships, and issues such as elite capture and the marginalisation of vulnerable groups like women and youth. Corruption poses a significant risk, deeply intertwined with the governance of natural resources. It can distort conservation goals and hinder the equitable distribution of benefits, thereby reducing community trust and participation in conservation initiatives. Donor reliance often leads to a dependency that can stifle local initiative and sustainability. Conservation efforts financed externally must ensure that they build local capacity rather than create perpetual reliance on foreign funds. External influence from international conservation bodies and individuals can sometimes overshadow local needs and knowledge, imposing solutions that may not be culturally or contextually appropriate. Elite capture refers to the diversion of benefits meant for the entire community to a small group of powerful individuals, undermining equity and the effectiveness of conservation efforts. Marginalisation of women and youth continues to be a significant issue as these vulnerable groups are often excluded from decision-making processes, yet they are crucial for the holistic development of community resilience and sustainability. These challenges underscore the need for more nuanced and inclusive approaches that genuinely engage community stakeholders at all levels and recognise their traditional rights, access and knowledge.

Conclusion

As community-based conservation continues to address the challenges of wildlife crime, the evolution of community responses is paramount. The shift from traditional enforcement methods to approaches that integrate the needs and knowledge of IPLCs marks significant progress in how we tackle these crimes. However, the journey towards fully effective community-driven conservation strategies is ongoing and requires both reflective evaluation and forward-thinking innovation. Affected communities, scholars and practitioners are working on design principles and strategies on community-centred responses (Hübschle and Shearing 2018; 2025; Büscher and Fletcher 2019; Roe and Booker 2019). Moving forward, it will be crucial to refine these strategies to ensure they are aligned with both conservation goals and the needs of local communities, thereby fostering environments where human and wildlife coexistence is beneficial to all. This ongoing evolution of community-based conservation holds the promise of transforming the landscape of global conservation practices, making them more inclusive and effective in the face of environmental challenges. Moreover, there is a growing need to explore how climate change, which alters habitats and animal behaviour, will affect the dynamics of wildlife crime and the effectiveness of community responses. As such, integrating climate adaptation strategies into community conservation plans will be crucial.

ANNETTE HÜBSCHLE

Further reading

Cooney, Rosie, Dilys Roe, Holly Dublin, Jacob Phelps, David Wilkie, Aidan Keane, Henry Travers, Diane Skinner, Daniel W. S. Challender, James R. Allan, and Duan Biggs. 2017. From poachers to protectors: Engaging local communities in solutions to illegal wildlife trade. *Conservation Letters* 10(3): 367–374. doi:10.1111/conl.12294.

Dressler, Wolfram, Bram Büscher, Michael Schoon, Dan Brockington, Tanya Hayes, Christian A. Kull, James McCarthy, and Krishna Shrestha. 2010. From hope to crisis and back again? A critical history of the global CBNRM narrative. *Environmental Conservation* 37(1): 5–15. doi:10.1017/S0376892910000044.

Gandiwa, Edson, Ignas M. A. Heitkönig, Anne M. Lokhorst, Herbert H. T. Prins, and Cees Leeuwis. 2013. CAMPFIRE and human–wildlife conflicts in local communities bordering Northern Gonarezhou National Park, Zimbabwe. *Ecology and Society* 18(4): 7.

Hübschle, Annette and Jared Margulies. 2024. The need for a socioecological harm reduction approach to reduce illegal wildlife trade. *Conservation Biology* 38(5): e14335. doi: 10.1111/cobi.14335.

Hulme, David, and Marshall Murphree. 1999. Communities, wildlife and the 'new conservation' in Africa. *Journal of International Development* 11: 277–285.

Roe, Dilys, and Francesca Booker. 2019. Engaging local communities in tackling illegal wildlife trade: A synthesis of approaches and lessons for best practice. *Conservation Science and Practice* 1(5): e26. doi:10.1111/csp2.26.

References

Botha, Lindie, and Michael Murphree. 2022. The geopolitics of animal welfare. *Environment: Science and Policy for Sustainable Development* 64(94): 4–11. doi:10.1080/00139157.2022.2089526.

Brockington, Dan. 2002. *Fortress Conservation: The Preservation of Mkomazi Game Reserve, Tanzania.* Bloomington: Indiana University Press.

Büscher, Bram, and Robert Fletcher. 2019. Towards convivial conservation. *Conservation and Society* 17(3): 283–296. doi:10.4103/cs.cs_19_75.

Cooney, Rosie, Dilys Roe, Holly Dublin, Jacob Phelps, David Wilkie, Aidan Keane, Henry Travers, Diane Skinner, Daniel W. S. Challender, James R. Allan, and Duan Biggs. 2017. From poachers to protectors: Engaging local communities in solutions to illegal wildlife trade. *Conservation Letters* 10(3): 367–374. doi:10.1111/conl.12294.

Cooney, Rosie, Dilys Roe, Holly Dublin, and Francesca Booker. 2018. *Wild Life, Wild Livelihoods: Involving Communities on Sustainable Wildlife Management and Combating Illegal Wildlife Trade*. Nairobi, Kenya: United Nations Environment Programme.

Dawson, Neil M., Brendan Coolsaet, Aditi Bhardwaj, Francesca Booker, David Brown, Bosco Lliso, Jacqueline Loos, Adrian Martin, Malena Oliva, Unai Pascual, Pasang Sherpa, and Thomas Worsdell. 2024. Is it just conservation? A typology of Indigenous Peoples' and Local Communities' roles in conserving

biodiversity. *Environmental Conservation* 7(6): 1007–1021. doi:10.1016/j.envcon.2024.06.007.
Dlamini, Jacob S. T. 2020. *Safari Nation: A Social History of the Kruger National Park.* Athens, OH: Ohio University Press.
Dore, Ashleigh, Annette Hübschle, and Mike Batley. 2022. Towards environmental restorative justice in South Africa: How to understand and address wildlife offences. In *The Palgrave Handbook of Environmental Restorative Justice* (Eds. Brunilda Pali, Miranda Forsyth, and Felicity Tepper). Basingstoke: Palgrave Macmillan: 333–359.
Duffy, Rosaleen. 2022. *Security and Conservation: The Politics of the Illegal Wildlife Trade.* New Haven, CT: Yale University Press.
Hübschle, Annette. 2017a. Contested illegality: Processing the trade prohibition of rhino horn. In *The Architecture of Illegal Markets* (Eds. Beckert, Jens and Matías Dewey). Oxford: Oxford University Press: 177–197.
Hübschle, Annette. 2017b. The social economy of rhino poaching: Of economic freedom fighters, professional hunters and marginalized local people. *Current Sociology* 65(3): 427–447. doi:10.1177/0011392116673210.
Hübschle, Annette. 2022. *Sustainable Livelihoods and Community Engagement.* Vienna: UNODC. https://www.unodc.org/e4j/en/wildlife-crime/module-5/index.html.
Hübschle, Annette, and Clifford Shearing. 2018. *Ending Wildlife Trafficking: Local Communities as Change Agents*. Geneva: Global Initiative against Transnational Organised Crime. https://www.researchgate.net/publication/326839026_Ending_wildlife_trafficking_Local_communities_as_change_agents.
Hübschle, Annette, and Clifford Shearing. 2025. *Governing Wildlife Security: Towards Pragmatic Conservation.* Abingdon: Routledge.
Intergovernmental Science-Policy Platform on Biodversity and Ecosystems Services (IPBES). 2019. *Global Assessment Report on Biodiversity and Ecosystem Services of the Intergovernmental Science-Policy Platform on Biodiversity and Ecosystem Services*. Bonn, Germany: IPBES Secretariat.
IUCN. 2017. *Local Communities: First Line of Defence in Combatting Illegal Wildlife Trade*. Geneva: CITES.
Jones, Brian T. B. 1999. Community management of natural resources in Namibia. In IIED (ed.), *IIED Drylands Programme*. London: IIED: 1–23.
Kepe, Thembela. 1999. The problem of defining 'community': Challenges for the land reform programme in rural South Africa. *Development Southern Africa* 16(3): 415–433. doi:10.1080/03768359908440089.
Murombedzi, James C. 1999. Devolution and stewardship in Zimbabwe's CAMPFIRE Programme. *Journal of International Devlopment* 11(2): 287–293.
Roe, Dilys, and Francesca Booker. 2019. Engaging local communities in tackling illegal wildlife trade: A synthesis of approaches and lessons for best practice. *Conservation Science and Practice* 1(5): e26. doi:10.1111/csp2.26.
Roe, Dilys, Francesca Booker, Maryanne Day, Robert T. Huberman, Holly Dublin, Andrew A. Fisher, David W. Macfarlane, and Jim Hancock. 2015. Are alternative livelihood projects effective at reducing local threats to specified elements of biodiversity and/or improving or maintaining the conservation status of those elements? *Environmental Evidence* 4(22). doi:10.1186/s13750-015-0048-1.
Wicander, Sylvia, and Lauren Coad. 2018. Can the provision of alternative livelihoods reduce the impact of wild meat hunting in West and Central Africa? *Conservation and Society* 16(4): 441–458.
Williams, John J. 2006. Community participation. *Policy Studies* 27(3): 197–217. doi:10.1080/01442870600885982.

ANNETTE HÜBSCHLE

43. Disrupting environmental crime

Introduction

Crime disruption is an intervention approach which sets out to bring down the whole criminal operation as its primary objective. It aims to accomplish this by marshalling a range of prosecutorial, investigatory, regulatory and community agencies and actors in a coordinated manner. It seeks to identify wrongdoing at all levels, both civil and criminal, with a central theme being to protect the agencies concerned and to fundamentally end criminality. It does this by investigating compliance and adherence to regulatory authorities at all levels, quite different to conventional investigative methodology, and in so doing unearthing non-compliance which when pursued has a collective and often dramatic disruptive capability to the organised criminal group's ability to function. This is made possible because organised criminal groups seldom adhere to regulations, thereby creating intervention opportunities which when pursued cumulatively can become severely disruptive to their operability (Hancock and Laycock 2012; Bullock et al. 2012).

Crime disruption in theory

Crime disruption, as described here, refers to an *outcome* (i.e., disabling the capacity to commit crime), a *process* (i.e., intervention strategy involving relevant stakeholders), and a *mission* (i.e., to prevent crime and ensure communal health and safety, and to provide assurance and confidence to citizens and communities). It involves not just the police and other government authorities, but action from private citizens as well. As an enforcement practice, disrupting crime has the objective of maximising good environmental outcomes (not just enforcing the law as such). For this, interventions include multi-pronged tactics and sanctions, and networking and collaboration take place at the local level, with specific leadership provided by state officials such as the police (Barrett and White 2017; White, 2023). Individuals working together for criminal purposes are called an organised crime group. Organised criminal groups (OCGs) often include many operatives, each of which is responsible for performing different functions. However, these individuals are rarely indispensable. For example, the dishonest accountant may be responsible for false accounting, which if pursued criminally may remove that individual actor, but adopting this strategy rarely undermines the operability of the group collectively as members are replaceable. In other words, the removal of criminal actors, on its own, does little to affect the overall criminality of the group (Duijn et al. 2014). The investigative strategy, therefore, has to shift its focus from identifying individual criminal acts and actors to the collective criminality of the group and how the group's activities may be brought to an end (Sparrow et al. 1992; Kirby and Nailer 2013).

Adopting a crime disruption approach requires a different investigative mindset, one which questions the functionality of the group, collectively (Barrett and White 2017). There are three key interrelated elements to environmental crime disruption.

Scoping of activities and study of anomalies

This consists of different measures and diverse points of information collection depending on the crime and organised criminal group. For example, it may involve the testing of waste water (e.g., to ascertain the nature and extent of drug use in institutions, towns, regions), review of water and energy use (e.g., houses and residences as possible drug production centres), scrutiny of land and vehicle ownership records (e.g., land use permits, transport licences), and so on. The main orientation is towards identifying potential data sources and types of analyses that pertain to specific crimes, locations and criminal formations.

Multi-agency strategic collaboration

A core feature of crime disruption as a strategic measure is collaboration across diverse agencies. These include government agencies such as licensing bodies, utilities, insurance companies, and the police, as well as community partners such as local businesses, residents, commuters and others with an interest (material and moral) in dealing with the crime in question. This element requires formally constituting an investigation group and ensuring that the content and frequency of meetings remain relevant to its central purposes.

Multiple and continuous interventions

An important element of crime disruption is that it can involve multiple sites of intervention (e.g., the OCG's place of business, their delivery routes, accounts offices), multiple stakeholders (e.g., residential neighbours, insurance companies, utilities officers), and a range of potential intervention tactics (e.g., cutting off power for failure to pay energy bill, arrest where criminal offences can be proved). Persistence is a virtue of this model and this, in turn, requires coordination of intervention, and acknowledgement that, over time, this will lead to benefits and mutually reinforcing processes and outcomes.

Disruption is a unique multi-agency supplement to conventional prosecutorial investigations, identifying infringements within infrastructural requirements, thereby presenting intervention opportunities to interrupt and disrupt the operability of criminal organisations as a whole. Adopting multi-agency disruption of criminal infrastructure, as opposed to solely targeting individual actors within groups, makes daily operations less profitable and more complicated for the OCGs. The key is to make criminal benefits more difficult by increasing the efforts, reducing criminal profitability and increasing risk using multi-agency powers and collaboration (Cornish and Clarke 1986; Clarke 1980).

Crime disruption as practice

This approach focuses upon reducing the opportunity, limiting the method, and eliminating the motive by undertaking a detailed analysis of the group's activities. Adopting this methodology in a collective manner, by bringing together agencies affected by the criminal activity, has the effect of greatly increasing the intelligence picture and opportunities for interruption.

In the specific area of environmental crime, a crime disruption approach is useful across crime categories. It can be applied to wildlife markets, for instance. Analysis of wildlife trafficking demonstrates the importance of studying harvesting networks and the resilience of these networks to environmental law enforcement efforts (Schneider 2012; Ayling 2013). The relationship between specific networks of actors – from the local through to inter-city through to regional and transnational levels – and specific markets and marketplaces (including eBay and other Internet mechanisms) allows identification of weak points in the supply chains, as well as diverse participant motivations. A market reduction approach, as applied to the illicit endangered species trade, seeks to identify the routine patterns of those involved – those who hunt, transform, transport and buy the wildlife (the likely offenders, such as hunters, poachers, handlers, consumers); the precise wildlife being hunted, transformed, transported, and purchased (the suitable targets, such as non-human animals and plants); and those whose remit is to actually conserve and protect those species (such as conservators, police, customs and wildlife officers). By understanding the social dynamics pertaining to the specific crime, it becomes apparent who the perpetrators are and how they are linked to other stakeholders (Schneider 2012).

A similar approach can be adopted in dealing with pollution issues. To protect environments and preserve ecological integrity, it is possible to use various tactics to impede the ability of offenders to function. For example, 'environmental enforcement sweeps' are now being applied in some US cities where a specific community faces multiple environmental burdens, such as polluting industries. Such sweeps involve the use of administrative, civil and criminal enforcement tools in tandem to address the problems in a comprehensive fashion. Factory pollution, for example, might be responded to by examination of the permit compliance history of companies, investigation of violations of various environmental laws, and involvement of multiple agencies alongside community input (Dighe and Pettus 2011).

Illegal waste dumping and stockpiling

Another concrete example of crime disruption pertains to illegal waste dumping and stockpiling (see Barrett and White 2017). In this instance, the organised criminal group was mainly locally based, and involved several family members among others. The commission of the crimes occurred locally, and the harms were therefore felt most acutely at the local level. The crimes were intentional and organised and involved collection of waste skips and the storage of waste. The OCG formed a local skip hire company as a legitimate business operating across Durham and Darlington situated within the North East of England. As a permitted company, their business involved the hire of a variety of skips, approximately 100 in total covering a large area of North East England and North Yorkshire. Their business was usually with private individuals but always on a cash basis. This provided the first opportunity for manipulation with the average skip costing approximately £100 per day.

Once the full skips were collected, they would be returned to one of three industrial-sized compounds where anything of any intrinsic value would be separated and sold for recycling whilst the remainder was stockpiled. The stockpiling of the waste was supposed to be sieved down to its most basic form and landfilled at the lowest tax rate, approximately £5 per tonne (by contrast, raw waste costs approximately £120 per tonne in landfill tax). This provided the second area of manipulation. As the sites began to fill it became abundantly clear that the processing and removal of the waste was not being completed as agreed within the permits.

The starting point in disrupting this OCG was to scope their activity in full, examining all their activities to identify any wrongdoing that would assist in undermining their ability to function. Time was also spent identifying any 'quick wins'. This formed the basis of the strategy subsequently adopted. By scoping the activity of the OCG, a number of anomalies were identified. The anomalies concerned different agencies – such as local council planning breaches, utility companies, and insurance providers. These constituted the key agencies that were brought together to form a group to undermine the OCG. As per the theoretical model, the disruption of illegal waste disposal involved scoping and anomalies, multi-agency collaboration, and multiple and continuous interventions.

Scoping

The scoping element in this instance was informed by the question, 'what is it they need to function?' The answer was insightful and led to thinking about various disruption tactics. Examples include:

Vehicle insurance for the skip trucks

The penalties are severe for operating without vehicle insurance and so stopping this insurance meant liaising with insurance companies. The OCG manipulated the situation to their advantage, however. The usual knock-on effect usually manifests with the withdrawal of cover (due to the intervention of the investigation group), then the OCG reinsures with a different company, and fails to disclose information such as 'Have you ever had insurance withdrawn or revoked' and off we go again. This once again highlights the importance of continuous engagement and follow-up.

Water consumption

At the stage this OCG was scoped they owed the water supplier tens of thousands of pounds. They manipulated the goodwill of the water supplier by presenting as a well-intentioned company that was experiencing financial difficulties. The water supplier did not really want to engage in a lengthy legal process and so offered a payment plan to catch up the debt but all the while the OCG were buying time before winding up their limited company and declaring themselves bankrupt. Cutting off water supply therefore became imperative.

Environmental prosecution

The objective of the waste company was to collect waste as quickly as possible by undercutting their competitors and storing the waste. The Environment Agency (EA) are the governing agency concerning waste management. Again, the OCG engaged with the EA and manipulated their initial engagement which was to seek compliance rather than enforcement. This essentially buys time whilst the waste keeps rolling in. They manipulated the EA to hold off prosecutions while paying lip service to the special measures that had been put in place until it was too late. Communication across agencies is therefore crucial.

Planning and land use

The OCG built huge storage facilities without requisite planning authority approval in the knowledge that the legal process to remove the structures was so lengthy that they would be gone before the authorities granted a demolition notice. The timing of intervention is thus vital to disruption and preventing future harms.

The common denominator here is *manipulation of the authorities to the advantage of the OCG* which is reliant upon the prosecutorial agencies acting independently and not being interconnected. The silos of regulatory and service provision agencies meant that crucial information was not being shared, and potential actions forestalled (such as cutting off the water and power supply).

Strategic collaboration

Once scoping was completed by the police then all the affected agencies were brought together and, once a form of non-disclosure agreement was set up, then disclosure as to who they were dealing with was made. This obviously altered the complexion of everything each agency may have previously agreed with the OCG.

Some simple ground rules were then set. For example:

Agencies always work together and never do anything singularly

This is designed to intimidate the OCG such that they feel the pressure from every angle and it also prevents them from manipulating situations, for example, by saying that the Environment Agency said this, or the water supplier said that, to mask their criminal activity.

Agencies to pursue all anomalies irrespective of size to their end

This was part of the agreement between all the affected agencies at the commencement of disruption. This is to prevent one agency showing leniency while others within the cohort continue to tackle other and/or the bigger issues.

Agencies would meet regularly to discuss the disruption and map out next steps

This particular action brought together a wide range of stakeholders, with representatives from the Driver and Vehicle Standards Agency to Northern Electric to the Durham and Darlington Fire Service. Under the leadership of the Durham Constabulary, the group met on a regular basis to share information and receive updates. This also helped to secure 'buy-in' from the linked-in groups.

A vital aspect of this process is *collaborative partnership*, which involved all parties putting something in and receiving something back – specifically, regarding information sharing and the development of 'next step' manoeuvres designed to outflank the OCG. It was strategic in the sense that there was an agreed-upon mission, which meant that process was directly linked to specific outcome.

Multiple and continuous interventions

The single objective of the OCG is to manipulate any known situation to their ultimate advantage and they rely on none of the prosecutorial agencies working collectively to help achieve their goal. Undermining this activity by working collaboratively and openly provides an opportunity for the governing agencies and agencies within the private sector to make informed choices as to their activities with the OCG. Local agencies and actors can then work together to address the problem in their midst by involving driver licence-issuing agencies, power and water authorities, insurance companies, fire services, passport offices, and local health and safety authorities.

Meaningful participation can take several forms

Action can include reporting events to police through to cutting off power and water due to unpaid bills. These latter measures incapacitate the organised criminal group by making it difficult for them to carry out their activities, a classic case of crime disruption supported by, but not involving, direct police intervention.

Action includes a wide variety and number of actors

There are many stakeholders and participants associated with the crimes, from truck drivers to property managers. The obligations of landholders regarding site management and health and safety issues also provide important departure points for neighbours, employees, associates and service providers to put pressure on organised criminal groups to desist from criminal activities.

Action is continuous and multi-pronged

The idea is to apply continuous intervention, ranging from constant intrusions by regulatory inspectors through to prosecution for criminal offences. The pressure also included measures that affected the physical infrastructure of the OCG, for example, regarding water, electricity and transportation.

ROB WHITE AND STOYAN BARRETT

The key message here is that *everyone has a role* to play in crime disruption. Each tactic that is adopted cascades into an overall waterfall of blockage and denial. It becomes risky and cost-ineffective for the OCG to continue in this line of work.

Conclusion

The practice of crime disruption is characterised by close analysis and scoping of the harmful activities and the study of any anomalies associated with these activities. For example, testing of waste water in a locality may reveal substances that indicate the wrongful disposal of toxic liquid wastes. Multi-agency collaboration is vital, and this might include a wide range of government agencies, local businesses, and community partners. Another important dimension of crime disruption is that it works best when involving multiple and continuous interventions. Where there are multiple sites of intervention and multiple stakeholders intervening, this makes criminal activity that much harder to engage in and benefit from.

The key question for environmental law enforcement is 'What is it that they do, and how can we undermine it?' The emphasis is on multi-agency disruption of criminal infrastructure as opposed to only targeting individual actors within groups.

ROB WHITE AND STOYAN BARRETT

Further reading

Barrett, S. and White, R., (2017). Disrupting environmental crime at the local level: An operational perspective. *Palgrave Communications*, 3: article 2. doi:10.1057/s41599-017-0006-3.
Bjelland, H. and Vestby, A., (2017). 'It's about using the full sanction catalogue': On boundary negotiations in a multi-agency organised crime investigation. *Policing and Society*, 27(6): 655–670.
Bullock, K., Clarke, R. and Tilley, N., (2012). *Situational Prevention of Organised Crimes*. London: Routledge.
Dighe, K. and Pettus, L., (2011). Environmental justice in the context of environmental crime. *United States Attorneys' Bulletin*, 59(4): 3–14.
Hancock, G. and Laycock, G., (2012). Organised crime and crime scripts: Prospects for disruption. In K. Bullock, R. Clarke and N. Tilley, eds, *Situational Prevention of Organised Crimes*. London: Routledge.
Innes, M. and Sheptycki, J., (2004). From detection to disruption. *International Criminal Justice Review*, 14(1): 1–24.
Leong, A., (2007). *The Disruption of International Organised Crime*. Farnham, UK: Ashgate.

References

Ayling, J., (2013). What sustains wildlife crime? Rhino horn trading and the resilience of criminal networks. *Journal of International Wildlife Law & Policy*, 16(1): 57–80.
Barrett, S. and White, R., (2017). Disrupting environmental crime at the local level: An operational perspective. *Palgrave Communications*, 3: article 2. doi:10.1057/s41599-017-0006-3.
Bullock, K., Clarke, R. and Tilley, N., (2012). *Situational Prevention of Organised Crimes*. London: Routledge.
Clarke, R., (1980). 'Situational' crime prevention: Theory and practice. *The British Journal of Criminology*, 20(2): 136–147.
Cornish, D. and Clarke, R., (1986). *The Reasoning Criminal: Rational Choice Perspectives on Offending*. New York: Springer-Verlag.
Dighe, K. and Pettus, L., (2011). Environmental justice in the context of environmental crime. *United States Attorneys' Bulletin*, 59(4): 3–14.
Duijn, P., Kashirin, V. and Sloot, P., (2014). The relative ineffectiveness of criminal network disruption. *Scientific Reports*, 4: article 4238.
Hancock, G. and Laycock, G., (2012). Organised crime and crime scripts: Prospects for disruption. In K. Bullock, R. Clarke and N. Tilley, eds, *Situational Prevention of Organised Crimes*. London: Routledge.
Kirby, S. and Nailer, L., (2013). Reducing the offending of a UK organized crime group using an opportunity-reducing framework: A three-year case study. *Trends in Organized Crime*, 16(4): 397–412.
Schneider, J., (2012). *Sold into Extinction: The Global Trade in Endangered Species*. New York: Praeger.
Sparrow, M., Moore, M. and Kennedy, D., (1992). *Beyond 911*. New York: Basic Books.
White, R., (2023). *Advanced Introduction to Applied Green Criminology*. Cheltenham, UK and Northampton, MA, USA: Edward Elgar Publishing.

44. Environmental activism

Introduction

Environmental activism encompasses the collective efforts of individuals, groups and organisations to protect, preserve and restore the natural environment from the damage caused by human activities. It involves advocating policies, practices and behaviours that promote the conservation and sustainable use of natural resources and the prevention and reparation of anthropogenic (or human-caused) environmental harm. Environmental activists are driven by a deep concern for the planet's well-being and believe in the importance of collective action to combat environmental challenges. Environmental activism takes many forms, covering a variety of activities ranging from political engagement, litigation and education through civil disobedience, direct action and – at its most extreme – violent resistance, directed at individuals, institutions and systems deemed most responsible for causing environmental harm. With historical roots dating back at least to the 19th century, environmental activism has become more widespread, more visible and more controversial as environmental problems themselves have become more pressing across the late 20th and early 21st centuries.

A brief history of environmental activism

The roots of contemporary environmental activism can be traced back to the 19th century when concerns about industrialisation and its impact on the environment began to emerge (Peterson del Mar, 2012). Notable figures like Henry David Thoreau and John Muir in the US, John Ruskin in the UK, and Prussian Alexander von Humboldt were early environmental advocates, emphasising the importance of nature and wilderness and the interconnections between the human and natural worlds. Early milestones included the establishment of national parks and endangered species listings, and other conservation efforts. These early activists were driven by a desire to protect pristine wilderness areas and wildlife alongside parallel concerns around the treatment of animals (Peterson del Mar, 2006).

The modern environmental movement, leading to the widespread environmental activism we see today, emerged in the 1960s and 1970s. Events like the publication of Rachel Carson's *Silent Spring* in 1962, which exposed the detrimental effects of pesticides on ecosystems, the first Earth Day in 1970 (earthday.org/history), a pivotal moment that mobilised millions of people globally to demand environmental protection, and Arne Naess' celebrated 1972 lecture on 'Deep Ecology' (Naess, 2005), were credited with cementing a philosophical and theoretical framework for contemporary environmentalism (Belshaw, 2001). Environmentalists of this era campaigned for legislative developments such as Clean Air and Clean Water Acts, and the creation of Environmental Protection Agencies in various countries. This period also saw the formation of many international environmental campaigning groups, such as Greenpeace, Friends of the Earth and WWF (World Wide Fund for Nature), that mark the growth of widespread organised public activism (Peterson del Mar, 2012).

As well as further growth in the activities, membership and number of 'mainstream' international environmentalism groups, and the proliferation of local and single-issue campaigns around the world, the 1980s and 1990s saw the emergence and spread of the 'radical' environmental movement (Peterson del Mar, 2012). Driven by an increased sense of urgency, groups such as Earth First!, the Environmental Liberation Front (ELF), the Animal Liberation Front (ALF) and Sea Shepherd were noteworthy for developing a more confrontational approach to environmental campaigning, prioritising direct action tactics (including criminal acts), and adopting non-hierarchical, cellular organisational structures (Scarce, 2007).

The 21st century has seen a continuation in the growth of both mainstream and radical environmental activism. Numerous new organisations and campaigns have appeared, with some rapidly growing into global movements attracting widespread media and political attention, including groups such as Extinction Rebellion and Just Stop Oil. An important trend has been the continued proliferation of direct action, increasingly employed by mainstream organisations as well as radical groups. These recent trends are underpinned by the increased perception of impending environmental crisis and are particularly fuelled by young people (whose futures are most threatened), although environmental activism movements involve a wide range of participants drawn from all ages and socio-economic groups (Di Ronco, 2023). In turn, these developments have attracted increased criticism from the media, business interests and some parts of the wider public – and the increased criminalisation of environmental activism by governments around the world (Canineu, 2024; Selmini and Di Ronco, 2023).

Variation in environmental activism

'Environmental activism' (along with alternative and related terms such as environmentalism, the environmental movement or the ecology movement) is a useful umbrella term that points to a common ethos of care for nature, and activism as an effort to effect change. However, environmental activism is far from homogeneous, incorporating a vast diversity of aims, organisations and approaches that do not always align with each other beyond an agreement that current patterns of human exploitation of nature need to change. Key dimensions of variation include issues targeted and outcomes sought, size and organisational structure of activist groups, underpinning philosophies and tactics employed (White, 2023).

As large-scale international organisations and movements have continued to grow in terms of both membership and activity, so too has smaller-scale, locally focused activism proliferated. Local groups are more frequently engaged in single-issue campaigns, responding to recent and current harms and future threats to local people, environments and natural resources (such as local water quality, air pollution, or development impinging on natural environments). Some single-issue campaigns operate on an international level (such as Just Stop Oil), while many local, grassroots activist movements are also concerned with a full range of environmental issues (such as campaigns to elect local green politicians or for local or national governments to adopt green policies). While single-issue groups tend to be focused on prevention or reparation of a particular harm, multi-issue activism tends to demand broader social, economic and political change (White, 2023).

Organisationally, smaller, local and single-issue movements have tended to grow from grass-roots activism led by victims of environmental harms that have already occurred (high-profile examples here include victim-movement responses to the Bhopal disaster in India and the indigenous Ogoni people's campaign against Shell Oil in Nigeria; Williams, 1996), or community groups concerned about future threats (such as the ongoing battle to prevent future mining activity in El Salvador; Mackey, 2024), or the recent local campaign to save urban trees in Sheffield, UK; Shackle, 2023). Larger-scale national and global organisations also draw membership from those who have been victims of specific environmental harms but are predominantly supported by those seeking to prevent future damage or express sympathy for those who are already direct victims of environmental harms. As such, we can see an increasing mix of reactive, proactive and sympathetic environmental activism – from those who are already environmental victims, those who anticipate future environmental victimisation, and those who seek to support or prevent the environmental victimisation of others. Organisational structures of larger, international activist groups show marked bifurcation across 'mainstream' and 'radical' campaigns with the former (including groups like Greenpeace, WWF and Friends of the Earth) being characterised by hierarchical leadership and formal membership and the latter (including the ELF, the ALF and Earth First!) operating more as loosely connected independent cells without central leadership and with largely anonymous participants (i.e., no central membership lists) (Scarce, 2007).

An important dimension of variation within environmental activism is that of underpinning eco-philosophical approaches (Halsey and White, 1998). While all environmental activism is united in seeking change, there are significant differences in the degrees of change being sought. We can recognise three broad categories here, distinguished by how activists see human/nature relations and what would constitute 'justice' moving forwards.

For some activists, the demand is for *environmental justice*. This reflects an anthropocentric philosophical position, where humans are seen as the most important species with nature subservient to human needs. Pursuant to this, the primary reason for protecting nature is for human benefit; to sustain the needs of individuals and society. Environmental justice means ensuring equal access to natural resources for all, regardless of wealth, class, ethnicity (etc.), and including future generations. As such, activism here focuses on preventing environmental harms that undermine human health and well-being, and on disproportionate exposure to environmental harms for some socio-economic or demographic groups compared to others (of which *environmental racism* – the disproportionate environmental victimisation experienced by non-white groups – is a particular egregious example; Bullard, 1994; Pinderhughes, 1996; Henderson and Wells, 2021) (Hall, 2011; Brisman et al., 2020).

Other activists are driven by a biocentric philosophy and corresponding demands for *species justice*. Here, humans are not given special moral worth or consideration compared to other species and campaigns include those aimed at protecting animals (and plants) *from* humans, not (just) protecting them *for* humans (Celermajer et al., 2020). An illustrative example here is the difference between animal welfare activists, who seek to minimise harm to animals but ultimately recognise humanity's right to own and exploit animals for human benefit, and animal rights or animal liberation activists, who seek to protect animals from all human interference (Bekoff, 2009). A further point here is that Animal Welfare activists are often primarily concerned with the treatment of animals in captivity (including farmed animals and pets) and, as such, are not necessarily environmental activists in the usual sense of the word 'environmental'.

A third, more nuanced position is *ecocentrism*, where humans are not seen as more important or more worthy than other species but are recognised as having a unique role in understanding and ability to act and, as such, have a particular duty to preserve the overall balance of nature. The preferred outcome here is one of *ecological justice*, and the need to protect entire ecosystems from human interference (Schlosberg, 2014). One difference between an ecological justice and an environmental justice position, for example, would be in campaigning to protect wilderness for human benefits, such as eco-tourism or sustainable logging, and campaigning to protect wildernesses from all human activity (beyond, perhaps, that of indigenous communities or scientific research).

Approaches and tactics

A key dimension of variation across environmental activism is in the range and types of tactics different activists engage with in pursuit of their different goals, and within their different organisational structures and ideological positions. This variety of activist approaches can be seen, broadly, as a spectrum from 'soft' activism operating within existing legal and political frameworks, to violent resistance aimed at overthrowing existing political structures (Scarce, 2007; Williams, 1996).

At the softest end of this spectrum, individual activism includes signing petitions, writing letters to the press or to political representatives, supporting political movements or activist groups through donations and membership fees, or participating in boycotts of products, corporations or other entities implicated in particular environmental harms (consumer activism). Such methods are increasingly easy to engage with in the Internet and social media era – and are often disparagingly referred to as 'slacktivism' by other, more involved, activists. At the group level, activist organisations engage in more concerted lobbying of political parties or environment-damaging businesses, producing reports and guidance documents, and consultation with industry and political leaders. Some group activism of this type can be particularly influential (or, at least, feed in to policymaking at a high level). For example, organised 'citizen science' (such as wildlife counts or collated reports of local environmental harms) helps provide an evidential basis for many campaigns, and some larger environmental NGOs contribute not just to national policy formulation but are parties to international policy forums such as CITES (the Convention on International Trade in Endangered Species of Wild Fauna and Flora) and COP (Climate Change Conference of the Parties) (White, 2023).

Another growth area for activism operating within existing political frameworks is litigation, with activists (especially local victims groups and established NGOs, but also individual litigants) taking environmental offenders to court for cease and desist, compensation and reparation orders, supporting (or, in some cases, leading) criminal prosecutions, or suing governments for failures to maintain or enforce environmental regulations (Phelps et al., 2021; White, 2023). A recent and potentially significant example of community-led litigation from Switzerland goes further, with failure to prevent environmental harm found to be a breach of international human rights legislation (Niranjan, 2024).

Escalating from soft activism, direct action approaches have become a staple of environmental activism (Seel et al., 2000; Scarce, 2007). These involve more physical and visible activity, and include organised protests, marches and sit-ins, often incorporating visual and performative activism (Di Ronco, 2023). Such approaches can take place entirely within the law, but often involve civil disobedience such as trespass or breaching of orders against congregating in certain areas, or refusals to disperse when instructed by the police. More radical environmental activists have been increasingly willing to engage in more protracted civil disobedience and overt criminal acts, such as extended occupations (including in tree-houses or tunnels to prevent tree-felling or construction work), property damage ('ecotage') ranging from damage to machinery (such as diggers or chainsaws) to arson (such as the burning down of animal testing laboratories or housing or leisure developments on previously pristine wilderness areas), and even threatened or actual violence to individuals implicated in causing environmental harm (Loadenthal, 2017). Extreme, but very rare, examples include bombing attacks, such as those carried out by the Mexican group 'Individualidades Tendiendo a lo Salvaje' ('Individuals tending to the Wild') (ITS).

Many activism groups employ a wide range of approaches across this spectrum. For example, Greenpeace encourages consumer activism and political engagement amongst its members, employs direct action tactics targeting particular industries or sites (such as coal-fuelled power stations, whaling ships or deep-sea drilling rigs), provides consultation to industry and governments, and is an active party to international policy forums such as CITES (White, 2023).

A key component of all approaches, but particularly the more transgressive, is to obtain media coverage. Environmental activists often recognise that victory in individual campaigns may be unlikely and/or of limited overall benefit. Instead, the ultimate goal is to increase public awareness and public pressure on politicians and corporate groups to enact wider and longer-lasting legal and economic change (Di Ronco, 2023; Scarce, 2007).

Responses to environmental activism

Environmental activists have achieved numerous victories. Examples of individual successes in preventing future or redressing past environmental harms can be found in countries all over the world, and environmental activism has undoubtedly had a central role in raising awareness of issues, in developing positive legislative developments and international agreements, and in keeping environmental issues on political agendas locally, nationally and globally. However, they have also led to a range of negative responses from governments, corporate interests and the public at large – part of what has been called 'the green backlash' (Rowell, 1996).

For example, some high-profile direct action campaigns, such as blocking streets or interrupting sporting or cultural events, have led to public backlash, with members of the public critical of tactics that impinge on their day-to-day economic and social activities (Feinberg et al., 2020; Di Ronco, 2023). While concerns and criticisms raised by the public are usually levelled at the tactics employed by campaigners rather than the issues they are campaigning against, coverage of public backlash has often been linked to anti-environmental political discourse such as climate-change denial, especially in right-wing media – which is itself often controlled by individuals or corporations with interests in environmentally harmful activities such as mining or fossil fuels (Anderson, 1997; Beder, 2004).

As environmentally harmful activities are largely related to economic activity, individual corporations, industrial and economic sectors, and the systems and structures of capitalism are often the primary target of activism. In turn, environmental activism – and activists' demands for changes to industrial and economic activities and structures – are seen as a threat to corporate profit-making and overall economic growth. As such, both corporate interests and governments have been seen to respond, often aggressively, by bringing their economic and political power to bear on activists (Rowell, 1996; Di Ronco, 2023).

Corporate responses to environmental activism range from counter-campaigns of (mis) information and supporting anti-environmental voices in the media and academia, and 'greenwashing' (highlighting often-minimal steps taken to reduce environmental harm in some areas of activity, whilst underplaying ongoing environmentally harmful practices), through to lobbying governments to influence (i.e., weaken) legislative initiatives to protect the environment, and litigation action against campaigners (such as the 1997 'McLibel' case where McDonald's sued two English environmental activists for libel; Vidal, 1997, and Shell suing Greenpeace for damages after activists occupied an oil platform; Ambrose, 2023). In some cases, powerful elites have responded to environmental activism by encouraging, supporting or instigating violence against the activists (May, 2019).

Governmental responses to activism, influenced by the perceived threat to economic activity (and the lobbying activities of vested corporate interests) – although often couched in terms of the threat to the safety and freedoms of the general public – include reductions in the rights to protest and increased criminalisation of activists. These pernicious trends are increasingly prevalent around the world, with the increased repression of activism in general, and eco-justice activism in particular, seen in liberal democracies as well as authoritarian regimes (Canineu, 2024; Ruggiero, 2021; Selmini and Di Ronco, 2023). Many countries, including the UK, Australia and Italy, have seen reductions in rights to protest with restrictions placed on where, when and how protests can be lawfully conducted and increasingly onerous demands on protest organisers to provide information (e.g., on march routes and protester numbers) to, and receive permission from, the police in advance. Protests are often banned from locations where they would be most visible (such as city centres), or from key sites and events where they would be most relevant (such as near venues hosting industry expos or intergovernmental discussions on environmental issues). Previously legal forms of protest (such as 'lock-ons') are now subject to legal restrictions, and protest tactics (such as trespass or obstruction of highways) previously subject only to civil law regulation have become criminal offences. Policing has also become more visible (e.g., with increased numbers of uniformed police present), more physical (e.g., with greater uses of barriers, kettling and forceful removal of protesters), and more militarised (e.g., with greater use of riot gear and crowd-dispersal equipment such as water cannons, tear gas and rubber bullets) (Di Ronco, 2023).

Away from protests themselves, governments and police are using stronger rhetoric against activist groups, labelling them as threats, criminals or eco-terrorists in media coverage before and after protests (Jämte and Ellefsen, 2020). While some extreme examples of environmental activism may rightly be seen as terrorism (e.g., ITS, mentioned above) (Liddick, 2000), such labels are often applied inappropriately – with critics arguing that such labelling both exaggerates the realities of the threat posed by radical environmentalists as well as diluting the utility of the term 'terrorism' when applied more appropriately (Nurse, 2017; Loadenthal, 2017). However, application of these labels helps undermine public support for activist groups and justify escalation of policing tactics and can enable the use – or threat of use – of greater law enforcement resources and tougher sentences under anti-terrorism legislation, in turn acting as a deterrent against other environmental activists. The framing of radical – and even mainstream – environmental activists as serious threats to public order has also seen an increase in police surveillance of activists and the infiltration of environmentalist groups by undercover police officers who have, in turn, been found to act unlawfully against members of such groups, including examples of undercover officers engaging in long-term romantic relations with activists and acting as agents provocateurs (Hattenstone, 2011; ucpi.org.uk).

At the most extreme, and particularly in Global South countries where civil liberties are often less well protected, powerful interests that see environmental activists – or their demands – as threats to economic activity are increasingly implicated in violent responses towards activists, local and indigenous populations, and agents of environmental law enforcement (e.g., officials tasked with policing or protecting natural resources, such as park rangers seeking to prevent poaching). This includes intimidation, harassment and 'disappearing' tactics against environmental defenders by government agencies or their sympathisers (such as reported against anti-mining campaigners in El Salvador; Mackey, 2024) and the murder of activists, indigenous leaders, game wardens and environmentalists (Ruggiero, 2021). For example, NGO Global Witness reports that 1,910 'environmental defenders' were murdered between 2012 and 2022 (globalwitness.org).

Future considerations

There are tensions within and between different environmental activist groups that may be a threat to the cohesion and success of the environmental movement as a whole. Mainstream groups preferring political engagement and 'soft-action' approaches criticise radical environmentalists and those engaged in direct action for undermining the legitimacy of, public support for, and politicians' willingness to engage with the aims and demands of environmentalists and, thus, jeopardising chances for legal and political change on the scale needed for a more environmentally sound future. Counter-arguments from radical environmentalists are that the cumulative threats to the natural world – and, in turn, to humanity – are increasingly urgent, that soft-action approaches have repeatedly failed, and that engagement within existing political and economic systems perpetuates and legitimises the very systems that are responsible for the environmental challenges facing the world. Instead, they argue, the need now is for dramatic and fundamental change to global economic and political structures and the overthrow and replacement of capitalism (a similar division exists between animal welfare and animal rights campaigners, with the latter arguing that the former's approach of reforming existing animal protection laws, while well intended, perpetuates the idea that animals are primarily to be seen as property to be exploited for human interests) (Liddick, 2000; Scarce, 2007).

Despite the green backlash – and the concerted efforts of powerful vested interests to protect the status quo – environmental activism seems likely not just to continue, but to escalate as climate change and other widespread environmental harms become more visible and more and more people are directly affected by them. And despite increased governmental repression of activism and criminalisation of activists, radical activism and direct action seem likely to continue to be an important part of the activist landscape. Moreover, given that activists have been increasingly willing to commit crimes as part of their campaigning tactics, criminalisation of protest seems unlikely to be an effective deterrent against the more radical environmentalists.

Commentators have pointed to historic social justice campaigns such as the fight for women's suffrage in the UK, the civil rights movement in the US and the anti-apartheid movement in South Africa as similar examples of social movements that increasingly adopted direct action tactics, including violence, while also facing increasingly repressive responses from powerful vested interests and state institutions, but that were eventually successful in achieving demanded change – and that have come to be seen as just causes all along. But key differences here are that environmental activism is occurring globally, is seeking fundamental change to established power structures, and sees its battle as against an existential threat to humanity as whole. With such high stakes on both sides, comparisons to historical political and social justice campaigns may be of limited value.

Conclusion

Environmental activism has been a significant force driving positive change in the face of unprecedented environmental challenges. Rooted in a history of concern for the natural world, contemporary environmental activism embodies diverse principles and strategies. As we confront the urgent need for environmental stewardship, the role of environmental activists remains pivotal in shaping a sustainable and harmonious future for the planet and its inhabitants. Through the efforts of environmental activists, significant policy changes have been achieved, public awareness has increased, and corporate practices have evolved to become more environmentally responsible. At the same time, environmental activism faces significant challenges including public backlash, corporate greenwashing, and criminalisation and governmental repression. But as the world faces increasingly complex environmental challenges, environmental activism remains a critical force for positive change. By supporting and engaging in environmental activism, we can all contribute to building a healthier, greener future.

GARY R. POTTER

GARY R. POTTER

Further reading

Canineu, M.L. (2024) Environment defenders face new wave of oppression. *Newsweek*, 29 April. https://www.newsweek.com/environment-defenders-face-new-wave-oppression-opinion-1894433

Celermajer, D., Schlosberg, D., Rickards, L., Stewart-Harawira, M., Thaler, M., Tschakert, P., Verlie, B. and Winter, C. (2020) Multispecies justice: Theories, challenges, and a research agenda for environmental politics. *Environmental Politics 30*(1–2): 119–140. https://doi.org/10.1080/09644016.2020.1827608

Di Ronco, A. (2023) *Policing Environmental Protest: Power and Resistance in Pandemic Times*. Bristol: Bristol University Press.

Feinberg, M., Willer, R. and Kovacheff, C. (2020) The activist's dilemma: Extreme protest actions reduce popular support for social movements. *Journal of Personality and Social Psychology 119*(5): 1086–1111. https://doi.org/10.1037/pspi0000230

Peterson del Mar, D. (2012) *Environmentalism* (2nd ed.). London: Routledge.

Scarce, R. (2007) *Eco-Warriors: Understanding the Radical Environmental Movement* (updated ed.). London: Routledge.

References

Ambrose, J. (2023) Shell sues Greenpeace for $2.1m in damages over fossil fuel protest in North Sea, *The Guardian*, 9 November.

Anderson, A. (1997) *Media, Culture and the Environment*. London: Routledge.

Beder, S. (2004) Moulding and manipulating the news. In R. White (ed.) *Controversies in Environmental Sociology*. Cambridge: Cambridge University Press: 204–220.

Bekoff, M. (2009) *Encyclopedia of Animal Rights and Animal Welfare* (volumes 1 and 2, 2nd ed.). Westport, CT: Greenwood Publishing.

Belshaw, C. (2001) *Environmental Philosophy: Reason, Nature and Human Concern*. Montreal: McGill-Queen's University Press.

Brisman, A., South, R. and Walters, R. (2020) Global environmental divides and dislocations: Climate apartheid, atmospheric justice and the blighting of the planet. In A. Brisman and N. South (eds.) *Routledge International Handbook of Green Criminology*. London: Routledge: 187–204.

Bullard, R. (1994) *Unequal Protection: Environmental Justice and Communities of Color*. San Francisco: Sierra Club Books.

Canineu, M.L. (2024) Environment defenders face new wave of oppression. *Newsweek*, 29 April. https://www.newsweek.com/environment-defenders-face-new-wave-oppression-opinion-1894433

Carson, R. (1962) *Silent Spring*. Boston: Houghton Mifflin.

Celermajer, D., Schlosberg, D., Rickards, L., Stewart-Harawira, M., Thaler, M., Tschakert, P., Verlie, B. and Winter, C. (2020) Multispecies justice: Theories, challenges, and a research agenda for environmental politics. *Environmental Politics 30*(1–2): 119–140. https://doi.org/10.1080/09644016.2020.1827608

Di Ronco, A. (2023) *Policing Environmental Protest: Power and Resistance in Pandemic Times*. Bristol: Bristol University Press.

Feinberg, M., Willer, R. and Kovacheff, C. (2020) The activist's dilemma: Extreme protest actions reduce popular support for social movements. *Journal of Personality and Social Psychology 119*(5): 1086–1111. https://doi.org/10.1037/pspi0000230

Hall, M. (2011) Environmental victims: Challenges for criminology and victimology in the 21st century. *Varstvoslovje: Journal of Criminal Justice & Security 13*(4): 371–391.

Halsey, M. and White, R. (1998) Crime, ecophilosophy and environmental harm. *Theoretical Criminology 2*: 345–371.

Hattenstone, S. (2011) Mark Kennedy: Confessions of an undercover cop. *The Guardian*, 26 March.

Henderson, S. and Wells, R. (2021) Environmental racism and the contamination of Black lives: A literature review. *Journal of African American Studies 25*: 134–151.

Jämte, J. and Ellefsen, R. (2020) The consequences of soft repression. *Mobilization: An International Quarterly 25*(3): 383–404.

Liddick, D.R. (2000) *Eco-Terrorism: Radical Environmental and Animal Liberation Movements*. London: Bloomsbury.

Loadenthal, M. (2017) 'Eco-terrorism': An incident-driven history of attack (1973–2010). *Journal for the Study of Radicalism 11*(4): 1–34.

Mackey, D. (2024) The true cost of El Salvador's new gold rush. *The Guardian*, 4 April. https://www.theguardian.com/environment/2024/apr/04/el-salvador-gold-rush-environmental-activists-metal-mining-ban-nayib-bukele

May, R.H. (2019) Land grabbing and violence against environmentalists. In R. Rozzi, R.H. May, F.S. Chapin et al. (eds.) *From Biocultural Homogenization to Biocultural Conservation: Ecology and Ethics* (vol. 3). Cham: Springer: 109–124.

Naess, A. (2005) The shallow and the deep, long-range ecology movement: A summary. In

GARY R. POTTER

A. Drengson (ed.) *The Selected Works of Arne Naess*. Dordrecht: Springer: 2263–2269.
Niranjan, A. (2024) Human rights violated by Swiss inaction on climate, ECHR rules in landmark case. *The Guardian*, 9 April.
Nurse, A. (2017) Pirates or protectors? A critical perspective on extreme environmental activism. In M. Hall, J. Maher, A. Nurse, G. Potter, N. South and T. Wyatt (eds.) *Greening Criminology in the 21st Century: Contemporary Debates and Future Directions in the Study of Environmental Harm*. Farnham, UK: Ashgate: 120–132.
Peterson del Mar, D. (2006) *Environmentalism (Short Histories of Big Ideas)*. London: Routledge.
Peterson del Mar, D. (2012) *Environmentalism* (2nd ed.). London: Routledge.
Phelps, J., Aravind, S., Cheyne, S., Dabrowski Pedrini, I., Fajrini, R., Jones, C.A., Lees, A.C., Mance, A., Nagara, G., Nugraha, T.P., Pendergrass, J., Purnamasari, U., Rodriguez, M., Saputra, R., Sharp, S.P., Sokolowki, A. and Webb, E.L. (2021) Environmental liability litigation could remedy biodiversity loss. *Conservation Letters 14*: e12821.
Pinderhughes, R. (1996) The impact of race on environmental quality: An empirical and theoretical discussion. *Sociological Perspectives 39*(2): 231–248.
Rowell, A. (1996) *The Green Backlash*. London: Routledge.
Ruggiero, V. (2021) *Critical Criminology Today: Counter-Hegemonic Essays*. Abingdon: Routledge.
Scarce, R. (2007) *Eco-Warriors: Understanding the Radical Environmental Movement* (updated ed.). London: Routledge.
Schlosberg, D. (2014) Ecological justice for the Anthropocene. In M. Wissenburg and D. Schlosberg (eds.) *Political Animals and Animal Politics*. Basingstoke: Palgrave Macmillan: 75–89.
Seel, B., Paterson, M. and Doherty, B. (2000) *Direct Action in British Environmentalism*. London: Routledge.
Selmini, R. and Di Ronco, A. (2023) The criminalization of dissent and protest. *Crime and Justice 52*: 197–231. https://doi.org/10.1086/727553
Shackle, S. (2023) Chainsaws, disguises and toxic tea: The battle for Sheffield's trees. *The Guardian*, 24 October. https://www.theguardian.com/environment/2023/oct/24/chainsaws-disguises-and-toxic-tea-the-battle-for-sheffield-trees?utm_term=653ccd9728f86f293c6b76fe8279e926&utm_campaign=TheLongRead&utm_source=esp&utm_medium=Email&CMP=longread_email
Vidal, J. (1997) *McLibel: Burger Culture on Trial*. London: The New Press.
White, R. (2023) *Advanced Introduction to Applied Green Criminology*. Cheltenham, UK and Northampton, MA, USA: Edward Elgar Publishing.
Williams, C. (1996) An environmental victimology. *Social Justice 23*: 16–40.

45. Environmental courts

Introduction

In a world of increasing environmental concerns, specialised environmental courts are playing an increasingly important role in environmental disputation. While taking different forms, there are many environmental courts. The Land and Environment Court of New South Wales ('NSWLEC'), Australia, is touted as a world-class example of an environmental court. Providing both administrative and judicial functions, this court is paving the way with alternative dispute resolution, exploration of environmental principles such as ecologically sustainable development, the facilitation of public interest litigation, and application of an ecocentric approach to decision-making, just to mention a few examples. There are many benefits of having environmental courts in a world of growing environmental concern and thereby disputation.

No country is free from environmental concerns. Such concerns will sometimes manifest in environmental disputation. Some countries have developed specialised environmental courts to deal with such disputation. This entry is concerned with these environmental courts and will explore:

- *defining* environmental courts
- the *Land and Environment Court of New South Wales*, Australia: a case study
- the *benefits* of environmental courts.

A key finding is the importance of specialist expertise in adjudicating matters pertaining to environmental harm.

Defining environmental courts: function over title

As the United Nations Environment Programme (2022: 42) highlights, there is no one best model for an environmental court, 'no "one-size-fits-all" design. Every environmental court … reflects its national character, culture and legal system'. Indeed, five different types of environmental courts have been identified (United Nations Environment Programme 2022: 43):

A. 'Operationally independent courts (separate, fully or largely independent environmental courts)'; an example is the NSWLEC, which will be considered in more depth shortly. Other examples are the New Zealand Environment Court and the Court of Environment and Agrarian Issues of Amazona, Brazil (United Nations Environment Programme 2022: 43–44);
B. 'Decisionally independent environmental courts (within a general court, but separate and free to make their own rules, procedures and decisions)'; examples include the Planning and Environment Court in Queensland, Australia, and the Environmental Division of the Vermont Superior Court in the United States of America (United Nations Environment Programme 2022: 43; 45);
C. 'Mix of law-trained and science-trained judges (may be either model A or B above, with the two types of judges sharing decision making)'; an example is the Land and Environment Court in Sweden (a 'decisionally independent environmental court with a multidisciplinary judicial approach') (United Nations Environment Programme 2022: 43; 46);
D. 'General court judges assigned environmental cases (assigned environmental cases in addition to their regular docket, sometime without necessary interest, expertise or training)'; examples include the green bench of the High Court of Bhutan, and the Malaysian High Court, Magistrates Courts and Sessions Courts (United Nations Environment Programme 2022: 43; 50);
E. 'General court judges trained in environmental law (who may therefore be assigned to environmental law cases from time to time)'; examples include Indonesia and Mexico (United Nations Environment Programme 2022: 43; 52).

While differences exist between jurisdictions, cross-national sharing of ideas and information is also common.

The New South Wales Land and Environment Court: a case study

The NSWLEC is a statutory court established by legislation (Land and Environment Court Act 1979 (NSW) ('LEC Act')), and 'continues to be recognized as one of the most visionary and successful based on its innovations, good practices and advice for other environmental courts around the world' (United Nations Environment Programme 2022: 44). It is one of three environmental courts in Australia, the other two being the Planning and Environment Court of Queensland and the Environment, Resources and Development Court of South Australia. The Court has both administrative and judicial roles and is organised into eight classes. Class 1 hears merit appeals relating to environmental planning and protection (LEC Act, s 17); local government and miscellaneous appeals and applications (including disputes over trees and hedges) are heard in Class 2 (LEC Act, s 18); Class 3 hears land tenure, valuation, rating and compensation matters (LEC Act, s 19); environmental planning and protection, development contract and strata renewal plan civil enforcement (including judicial review and civil enforcement proceedings) are heard in Class 4 (LEC Act, s 20); Class 5 hosts the NSWLEC criminal jurisdiction, pertaining to environmental planning and protection summary enforcement (LEC Act, s 21); appeals from conviction relating to environmental offences, generally from the Local Court, are heard in Class 6 (LEC Act, s 21A); Class 7 hears other appeals relating to environmental offences (LEC Act, s 21B); Class 8 is confined to mining matters (LEC Act, s 21C).

As a rule of thumb, commissioners (both full-time and acting) hear merit appeals (exercising an administrative function) and judges hear all other matters, generally those where the exercise of power is judicial rather than administrative. However, there have been occasions where judges will determine merit appeals, either alone or with the assistance of a commissioner. Likewise, commissioners will sometimes assist a judge by sitting in on a judicial matter where the special expertise of the commissioner is needed. Qualified persons may be appointed as commissioners of the NSWLEC. Those qualifications (both formal or through experience) relate to the administration of local government or town planning, country planning or environmental planning, environmental science or matters relating to the protection of the environment and environmental assessment, law and practice of land valuation, architecture, engineering, surveying or building construction, management of natural resources or the administration and management of Crown lands, land rights for Aborigines and determining disputes involving Aborigines, or urban design or heritage (LEC Act, s 12). The biographies of each of the commissioners is available on the NSWLEC website.

The NSWLEC is an important information hub in that it makes available information such as in practice notes (which 'explain the practice and procedure and the process to be followed for different types of cases from their commencement, through to the preliminary stages and preparation, to their resolution'), annual reviews (which 'includes an overview of court performance for that year, reforms and development, involvement in education and community, and consultation with court users. Individual parts of the annual review outline the court profile, caseflow management, reforms and development, court performance and, education and community involvement' (Hamilton 2020)), judicial speeches and papers (of which there are currently over 240, contributed by both past and present judges and commissioners; Justice Preston, Chief Judge of the NSWLEC, has contributed over 100 speeches and papers. Three 'hot topics' include climate change, the role of environmental courts and tribunals including the NSWLEC, and ecologically sustainable development (Hamilton 2022)), planning principles (being 'a statement of a desirable outcome from a chain of reasoning aimed at reaching, or a list of appropriate matters to be considered in making, a planning decision' (NSWLEC; for an overview see Roseth 2005a; Roseth 2005b). There are currently 37 planning principles and three tree planning principles, and they are reviewed and updated as necessary. Information on planning principles is available elsewhere (Gerathy and Smith 2013; Nash 2013; Hewitt 2014; Hewitt and Knapman 2014; Webster and Camenzuli 2015; Poisel 2015; Hewitt 2017; Epstein and Hewitt 2017; Hamilton 2018a; Hamilton 2018b)), judicial newsletters (which are 'published every four months and provides useful summaries of recent developments in legislation, regulations, planning policies and case law both in the Land and Environment Court and in appeal courts'); and, policies (currently there are 17 policies, which 'explain particular aspects of practice and procedure, such as case management or site inspections, which are not restricted to particular types of cases (these are dealt with by the Practice Notes) or that address other matters concerning the Court, its officers and its work').

The benefits of environmental courts

Justice Preston, Chief Judge of the NSWLEC, has outlined the 'desirable dozen' being 12 benefits His Honour sees in having environmental courts. These are rationalisation, specialisation, multi-court courthouse, superior court of record, independence from government, responsiveness to environmental problems, facilitates access to justice, development of environmental jurisprudence, better court administration, unifying ethos and mission, decision-making is value adding, and flexible and innovative (Preston 2012; see also Preston 2008a). It is not the purpose of this entry to repeat in summary those benefits. Rather, a smaller list of benefits is highlighted, some of which have synergy with those of Justice Preston.

Achievement of the United Nations Sustainable Development Goals

One of the benefits of having environmental courts is global. That is, environmental courts can contribute to Global Goals, such as the United Nations Sustainable Development Goals, particularly Goal 16 'Peace, Justice and Strong Institutions', namely:

i. promote environmental rule of law at the national and international levels and ensure access to justice (Sustainable Development Goal Target 16.3);
ii. develop more effective, accountable and transparent institutions at all levels (Sustainable Development Goal Target 16.6);
iii. ensure responsive, inclusive, participatory and representative decision-making at all levels (Sustainable Development Goal Target 16.7);
iv. ensure public access to information and protect fundamental freedoms, in accordance with national legislation and international agreements (Sustainable Development Goal Target 16.10); and
v. promote and enforce non-discriminatory laws and policies for sustainable development (Sustainable Development Goal Target 16.10.b) (United Nations Environment Programme 2022: 2; United Nations Department of Economics and Social Affairs n.d.).

Not only are environmental courts well placed to contribute to Global Goals, such as the United Nations Sustainable Development Goals, they are best placed to interpret and apply environmental concepts.

Best placed to interpret and apply environmental concepts

Given the specialist knowledge of the decision-makers within an environmental court, it could be argued that such courts are best placed to interpret and apply environmental concepts. Indeed, Justice Preston of the NSWLEC gives but one example when he explains that '[i]ncreasingly, it is being recognized that a court with special expertise in environmental matters is best placed to play this role in the achievement of ecologically sustainable development' (Preston 2012: 398). Indeed, one of the seminal interpretations of the requirements of ecologically sustainable development came from the NSWLEC decision of Justice Preston (sitting with Commissioner Brown) in the Class 1 merit appeal of *Telstra Corporation Limited v Hornsby Shire Council* [2006] NSWLEC 133; (2006) 146 LGERA 10 ('*Telstra Corporation*') (an earlier exploration of ecologically sustainable development was undertaken by McLellan CJ, in *BGP Properties Pty Limited v Lake Macquarie City Council* [2004] NSWLEC 399). In the judgment His Honour considers in some depth the concept of ecologically sustainable development and lays down six principles which although they 'do not exhaustively describe the full ambit of the concept of ecologically sustainable development … do afford guidance in most situations' (*Telstra Corporation*, [120]). The gravity of the principles, and hence the articulation and dissemination of those principles, cannot be understated: 'These principles, if adequately implemented, may ultimately realise a paradigm shift from a world in which the development of the environment takes place without regard to environmental consequences, to one where a culture of sustainability extends to institutions, private development interests, communities and individuals' (*Telstra Corporation*, [120]). This guidance provided by an environmental court with specialised knowledge is invaluable as ecologically sustainable development 'is the central pivot around which all governmental decision-making is increasingly being required to revolve' (Bates 2019: 171).

Alternate dispute resolution under one roof

Justice Preston conceives this idea in terms of a 'multi-door courthouse', being 'a dispute resolution center offering intake services together with an array of dispute resolution processes under one roof' (Preston 2012: 411; see also, Preston 2008b; 2008c). The NSWLEC, as an example, offers an array of alternate dispute resolution: conciliation conferences in Classes 1–3 (LEC Act, s 34); mandatory conciliation and arbitration for certain appeals within Class 1 (LEC Act, s 34AA) and Class 8 (LEC Act, s 41A) proceedings; and, mediation, neutral evaluation and reference to a referee available for all proceedings in Classes 1, 2, 3, 4 and 8. The rationale for alternate dispute resolution 'is the saving in time it takes to dispose of matters brought before the courts, reducing the workload of the court, and the saving in costs for litigants' (Preston 2011: 2); such alternatives lead to the 'just, quick and cheap resolution' of disputes (Civil Procedure Act 2005 (NSW), s 56(1)). Conciliation conferences are the most widely used of the alternate dispute resolution processes in the NSWLEC, with such conferences involving 'a conciliator whose role is to facilitate negotiation between the parties in an attempt to resolve the issues in dispute ... If an agreement is reached by the parties ... the Commissioner [who conciliated the dispute] must then dispose of the proceedings in accordance with the agreement in the decision and set out the terms of the decision in writing' (Camenzuli, Yeung and Matthews 2019: 116).

Facilitation of public interest litigation

Public interest litigation involves 'proceedings in a court or tribunal undertaken by a private individual or community group where the dominant purpose is not to protect or vindicate a private right or interest but to protect the environment. In essence: it is litigation by a private individual to protect the environment' (McGrath 2008: 327). Arguably, environmental courts with governing Acts, Rules, and expertise are best placed to hear this important form of litigation. Public interest litigation acts as an important check on environmental decision-making. There are two primary impediments to conducting public interest litigation: standing and costs, but neither impediment is insurmountable.

Standing to bring public interest litigation before the NSWLEC is facilitated by the open standing ('any person') stance pertaining to both planning matters (Environmental Planning and Assessment Act 1979 (NSW), s 9.45 which specifies that '[a]ny person may bring proceedings in the Court [NSWLEC] for an order to remedy or restrain a breach of this Act, whether or not any right of that person has been or may be infringed by or as a consequence of that breach') and environmental matters (Protection of the Environment Operations Act 1997 (NSW), s 252 which specifies that '[a]ny person may bring proceedings in the Land and Environment Court for an order to remedy or restrain a breach of this Act or the regulations ... whether or not any right of that person has been or may be infringed by or as a consequence of that breach'). Costs rules in the NSWLEC have also been amended to facilitate public interest litigation. The default position in relation to civil proceedings brought before the NSWLEC is that costs follow the event (that is, the unsuccessful party pays the costs of the successful party) (Uniform Civil Procedure Rules 2005 (NSW), r 42.1). However, in proceedings brought in the public interest (which include civil enforcement and judicial review proceedings) the NSWLEC 'may decide not to make an order for the payment of costs against an unsuccessful applicant' (Land and Environment Court Rules 2007 (NSW), r 4.2). Justice Preston has outlined what the court needs to consider before exercising its discretion to not make an order of costs against an unsuccessful party who has brought proceedings in the public interest. Namely:

- Can the litigation be characterised as being brought in the public interest? (*Caroona Coal Action Inc v Coal Mines Australia Pty Ltd (No. 3)* [2010] NSWLEC 59; (2010) 173 LGERA 280 ('*Caroona Coal Action Inc*'), [15]).
- Are there circumstances in addition to the mere characterisation of public interest? (*Caroona Coal Action Inc*, [47]).
- Are there any countervailing considerations? (*Caroona Coal Action Inc*, [61]).

Ecocentric approach to decision-making

Expertise residing in environmental courts, along with governing legislation, practice and procedure, facilitates an ecocentric approach to decision-making. 'Ecocentrism refers to an approach to law and crime that is environment-centred rather than solely human-centred. Put simply, ecocentrism views the environment as having value for its own sake apart from any instrumental or utilitarian value to humans' (White 2022a: 62; see also, White 2017a; 2017b). The approach of the NSWLEC 'to criminal cases involving environmental offences provides a valuable illustration of how ecocentric principles can be incorporated into judicial decision-making' (White 2022b: 214). White considers the following to be central to an ecocentric approach to judicial decision-making:

- Specialised expertise, with specialised environmental courts providing 'an ideal forum for the development and deployment of such expertise' (White 2022a: 80).
- '[D]evelopment of detailed frameworks within which specific types of environmental harm can be categorised' (White 2022a: 81).
- '[I]ntersection of legislative frameworks supportive of ecological sustainability, the employment of assessment methods that categorise harm and facilitate determination of its seriousness according to ecological criteria, and the developing ecological expertise of the judiciary that is in part fostered by regular exposure to relevant experts (such as botanists, arborists, and ecologists) in the course of Court proceedings' (White 2022a: 81).
- A 'statutory context that provides for substantial penalties for environmental offences, and that provides a broad spectrum of sanctions that can be drawn upon in sentencing offenders', including the requirement that an offender '*do* something', accomplish something (White 2022a: 81).

In a world of increasing environmental concern and disputation, environmental courts light the way through their expertise, statutory framework, practice and procedure.

Conclusion

Given the environmental issues facing the world today, the most notable being climate change, coupled with the benefits of environmental courts outlined above, it is not surprising that there has been an increase in the number of such courts around the world. These courts are necessary as the world grapples with increasingly urgent and complex environmental issues. While the establishment and operation of these courts is essential, what should not be overlooked is 'judicial training and networking' to spur on judicial 'environmental law capabilities', enhance 'the quality of environmental law jurisprudence at both national and transnational levels' and to increase 'public trust and participation in environmental justice' (United Nations Environment Programme 2022: 62).

MARK HAMILTON

Further reading

Fisher, E., & Preston, B. (eds). (2022). *An Environment Court in Action: Function, Doctrine and Process*. London: Hart.

Hamman, E., Walters, R., & Maguire, R. (2015). Environmental Crime and Specialist Courts: The Case for a 'One-Stop (Judicial) Shop' in Queensland. *Current Issues in Criminal Justice 27*(1), 59–77.

Pearce, C. (2018). Does the 'One-Stop Shop' Need Refurbishing? Evaluating the Review Jurisdiction of the NSW Land and Environment Court. *Environmental and Planning Law Journal 35*(3), 235–246.

Preston, Hon Justice B. J. (2008a). Operating an Environment Court: The Experience of the Land and Environment Court of New South Wales. *Environmental and Planning Law Journal 25*(6), 385–409.

Preston, Hon Justice B. J. (2008b). The Land and Environment Court of New South Wales: Moving Towards a Multi-Door Courthouse – Part I. *Australasian Dispute Resolution Journal 19*(2), 72–82.

Preston, Hon Justice B. J. (2008c). The Land and Environment Court of New South Wales: Moving Towards a Multi-Door Courthouse – Part II. *Australasian Dispute Resolution Journal 19*(3), 144–155.

Walters, R., & Solomon Westerhuis, D. (2013). Green Crime and the Role of Environmental

Courts. *Crime, Law and Social Change 59*(3), 279–290.

Additional resources

The Planning and Environment Court of Queensland Web Page is https://www.courts.qld.gov.au/courts/planning-and-environment-court.

The Environment, Resources and Development Court of South Australia Web Page is https://www.courts.sa.gov.au/going-to-court/court-locations/environment-resources-and-development-court/.

The Land and Environment Court of New South Wales Web Page is https://lec.nsw.gov.au/. Commissioner biographies can be found at https://www.lec.nsw.gov.au/about-us/judicial-officers-and-decision-makers.html.

Practice notes can be found on the Land and Environment Court of New South Wales Web Page, at https://lec.nsw.gov.au/practice-and-procedure/practice-notes.html.

Planning principles can be found on the Land and Environment Court of New South Wales Web Page, at https://lec.nsw.gov.au/practice-and-procedure/principles/planning-principals.html.

Judicial newsletters can be found on the Land and Environment Court of New South Wales Web Page, at https://lec.nsw.gov.au/publications-and-resources/judicial-newsletters.html.

Policies can be found on the Land and Environment Court of New South Wales Web Page, at https://lec.nsw.gov.au/practice-and-procedure/policies.html.

References

Bates, B. (2019). *Environmental Law in Australia* (10th ed.). Australia: LexisNexis.

BGP Properties Pty Limited v Lake Macquarie City Council [2004] NSWLEC 399.

Camenzuli, L., Yeung, S., & Matthews, J. (2019). The Use of ADR in Resolving Planning Disputes in NSW. *Local Government Reporter 18*(7), 116–119.

Caroona Coal Action Inc v Coal Mines Australia Pty Ltd (No. 3) [2010] NSWLEC 59; (2010) 173 LGERA 280.

Civil Procedure Act 2005 (NSW).

Environment, Resources and Development Court of South Australia. https://www.courts.sa.gov.au/going-to-court/court-locations/environment-resources-and-development-court/. Accessed 23 June 2023.

Environmental Planning and Assessment Act 1979 (NSW).

Epstein, A., & Hewitt, J. (2017). Revised Planning Principle for Sex Services Premises: Yao v Liverpool City Council. *Local Government Reporter 16*(9), 154–155.

Gerathy, K., & Smith, L. (2013). View Loss in the Harbour City: Planning Principle Protects Public Domain Views – Rose Bay Marina Pty Ltd v Woollahra Municipal Council. *Local Government Reporter 11*(8), 122–124.

Hamilton, M. (2018a). Tree Dispute Principle: Demonstrating Cause of Structural Damage. *Local Government Reporter 16*(10), 179–181.

Hamilton, M. (2018b). NSWLEC Planning Principles and Tree Planning Principles Update. *Local Government Reporter 17*(9&10), 122–124.

Hamilton, M. (2020). The Website of the Land and Environment Court of New South Wales: An Important Information Hub. *Local Government Reporter 19*(6), 94–96.

Hewitt, J. (2014). Replacement of Court Planning Principles: 'Whether a New Development'. *Local Government Reporter 13*(1), 3–4.

Hewitt, J. (2017). Review of Isolation of Site Planning Principles: 193 Liverpool Road Pty Ltd v Inner West Council. *Local Government Reporter 16*(3), 45–46.

Hewitt, J., & Knapman, R. (2014). Desired Future Character Planning Principle Reviewed and Re-endorsed: Revelop Projects Pty Ltd v Parramatta City Council. *Local Government Reporter 13*(9), 152–154.

Land and Environment Court Act 1979 (NSW).

Land and Environment Court of New South Wales. https://lec.nsw.gov.au/. Accessed 23 June 2023.

Land and Environment Court Rules 2007 (NSW).

McGrath, C. (2008). Flying Foxes, Dams and Whales: Using Federal Environmental Laws in the Public Interest. *Environmental and Planning Law Journal 25*(5), 324–359.

Nash, S. (2013). New Planning Principle for Assessing Impacts on Neighbouring Properties. *Local Government Reporter 12*(1), 2–3.

Planning and Environment Court of Queensland. https://www.courts.qld.gov.au/courts/planning-and-environment-court. Accessed 23 June 2023.

Poisel, T. (2015). Seniors Living Principle: Is the First Planning Principle of Continuing Relevance? *Local Government Reporter 14*(5), 85–88.

Preston, Hon Justice B. J. (2008a). Operating an Environment Court: The Experience of the Land and Environment Court of New South Wales. *Environmental and Planning Law Journal 25*(6), 385–409.

Preston, Hon Justice B. J. (2008b). The Land and Environment Court of New South Wales: Moving Towards a Multi-Door Courthouse – Part I. *Australasian Dispute Resolution Journal 19*(2), 72–82.

Preston, Hon Justice B. J. (2008c). The Land and Environment Court of New South Wales: Moving Towards a Multi-Door Courthouse – Part II. *Australasian Dispute Resolution Journal 19*(3), 144–155.

Preston, Hon Justice B. J. (2011). The Use of Alternative Dispute Resolution in Administrative Disputes. *Symposium on the Right to Access*

to the Administrative Jurisdiction, Bangkok, Thailand.
Preston, Hon Justice B. J. (2012). Benefits of Judicial Specialization in Environmental Law: The Land and Environment Court of New South Wales as a Case Study. *Pace Environmental Law Review 29*(2), 396–440.
Protection of the Environment Operations Act 1997 (NSW).
Roseth, Snr Commissioner J. (2005a). Planning Principles and Consistency of Decisions (paper given at the Law Society's Local Government and Planning Law Seminar, 15 February).
Roseth, Snr Commissioner J. (2005b). Developing Planning Principles (paper given at the NEERG Seminar on Planning Principles, 27 July).
Telstra Corporation Limited v Hornsby Shire Council [2006] NSWLEC 133; (2006) 146 LGERA 10.
Uniform Civil Procedure Rules 2005 (NSW).
United Nations Department of Economics and Social Affairs. (n.d.). *Sustainable Development, The 17 Goals* (https://sdgs.un.org/goals). Accessed 27 June 2023.
United Nations Environment Programme. (2022). *Environmental Courts and Tribunals – 2021: A Guide for Policymakers*. Law Division; Kenya: United Nations.
Webster, D., & Camenzuli, L. (2015). Revision of the NSW Land and Environment Court's Planning Principle on Plans of Management. *Local Government Reporter 14*(3), 42–44.
White, R. (2017a). *The Sentencing of Environmental Offences Involving Non-Human Environmental Entities in the NSW Land and Environment Court*. Master of Laws (LLM) Thesis, University of Tasmania.
White, R. (2017b). Reparative Justice, Environmental Crime and Penalties for the Powerful. *Crime, Law and Social Change 67*(2), 117–132.
White, R. (2022a). Environmental Crime, Ecological Expertise and Specialist Environment Courts. In J. Gacek & R. Jochelson (eds), *Green Criminology and the Law* (pp. 61–84). Cham: Palgrave Macmillan.
White, R. (2022b). Ecocentrism and Criminal Proceedings for Offences against Environmental Laws. In E. Fisher & B. Preston (eds), *An Environment Court in Action: Function, Doctrine and Process* (pp. 213–231). London: Hart.

MARK HAMILTON

46. Environmental forensics

Introduction

This entry provides a commentary on the use of forensic sciences and methods in the investigation and understanding of environmental crimes and harms. The term "forensic" refers to the intersection of science and law. In popular discourse it usually refers to the gathering of information and evidence from crime scenes. It also involves forensic medicine, forensic psychology and forensic social work and assessments of and responses to the mental capacity and mental health of offenders. For present purposes, the focus is on forensic processes as applied to environmental issues.

Contemporary environmental crises, environmental forensics and green criminology

Scientific and technological developments have introduced into our late modern societies a new type of vulnerability, which translates into serious risks and harms for humans and natural environments. As with other disciplines, contemporary environmental crises – at the same time huge, fast and overwhelming – pose unique challenges for forensic science. One of the main reasons for this is that, being distributed over space and time, these crises present "aesthetic and technological challenges to their representation while complicating normative standards of harm, intention and causality" (Ahmed, 2017: 139). In fact, when environmental problems prove to be progressive and accretive rather than being immediately catastrophic, our ability to perceive, understand, interpret and analyse them fails (Natali, 2017). This is so for several reasons.

First, and more specifically, the harmful consequences do not materialise immediately, but only over extended periods of time. For example, environmental pollution is the result of processes that occur over varying periods of time and is often the outcome of several polluting behaviours repeated through time that may be illegal but may also be legal, so long as they remain within the authorised limits, and yet still be harmful to the environment. Moreover, in the majority of these cases, even if the polluting behaviours were to be immediately stopped, their harmful effects would still continue to be produced, because of the long periods of latency of the harms and illnesses with which they can be linked.

Second, causation can be extremely difficult to prove, both because of the temporal distance between the behaviour and the production of its harmful consequences (see also Hall, 2014: 100) and because of the complexity of the social and ecological context. As it is well known in forensic medicine, the longer the so-called chain of the damage – the pathway coming from the initial rule violation down to the final effective harm – the more difficult the technical investigation about judicial causes and judicial effects. The consequences may be visible today, but their origin goes back to a remote or near past that is very difficult to appreciate in its reality. Instead of an "origin", we should speak of a *process* which has unfolded itself over time, generating complex reactions and counter-reactions within the concerned environment – also due to nature's capacity to absorb the harm and reveal the most destructive and visible consequences only after an extended period of time. Furthermore, even when the harm is already visible and evident, attributing a cause can be extremely complex. The link between exposure to chemical agents and the illnesses of workers and/or inhabitants of the contaminated areas is a clear example. Complicated biological and natural processes are always hard to manage in judicial trials – which best perform when there are single and immediate crime causes. This is especially the case in criminal trials.

Third, environmental crimes are often described as "victimless crimes" because the victims are not easily identifiable and sometimes cannot speak for themselves (as is the case with forests and non-human animals). Moreover, in corporate crimes the space–time distance between the action (the polluting behaviours) and its harmful consequences can be great, entailing significant implications in terms of awareness and of proof of victimisation.

Investigation of environmental crimes requires environmental forensics knowledge to appreciate these complex issues and to provide accurate scientific evidence. Environmental forensic science is an expanding field and engages with environmental crimes, such as pollution, illegal trade of wildlife (wildlife forensics), waste dumping, toxicity and ecocide. It does this through methods such as tracing the fingerprints of the contamination source (Ahmed, 2017: 140, 143; see also Pires and Olah, 2022): "In terms of the study of toxicity, environmental forensic science investigations typically deal with identifying the source and age of the contaminating substances and determine the extent of environmental damage over space and time (Mudge 2007)" (Ahmed, 2017: 143).

Generally speaking, environmental forensics is the technical culture daily needed by the criminal justice system to do its work, with such work being basically about environmental rights to be protected and environmental duties to be respected. If environmental forensics is asked to give technical answers about the sources and the shapes of environmental harms, to be a scientific answer, the technical answer must first of all be an evidence-based one. And working for real evidence-based justice, the forensic science usually tries to show *what* has happened, *when* it happened and to explain *how* it has happened. In the immediate context, available scientific laws and methods do cover singular events and environmental forensics always looks for the scientific data best fitting the individual case. A key element of this is how "evidence" itself is socially constructed within legal and scientific discourses, and how different players within the criminal justice system conceptualise the nature of criminal investigation, criminal procedure, criminal evidence, and courtroom practices (see also White, 2012, 2017).

In a wider perspective, environmental forensics aims at assisting the justice system and policymakers. A good technical culture is needed by both judges (hopefully helped by accountable expert witnesses) and politicians (hopefully guided and supported by relevant criminological research) so as to achieve the double result of positive effects from the existing rules and of continuous developments of the rules themselves. In this regard, a fruitful dialogue with green criminology can make a significant theoretical and applied contribution with respect to environmental harms and crimes. For example, green criminology can use the technical evidence coming from environmental forensics to lead the way towards more effective environmental laws (the way to prevention) and also more effective victim identifications (the way to compensation). It can therefore work as an intermediate partner between environmental forensics and environmental justice.

Strategically, with regard to the distinctive features of environmental crimes, green criminologists have suggested that it is crucial to consider:

(1) who is the victim: humans, non-human animals, an entire ecosystem;
(2) where the harm takes place: at a local level, globally, or somewhere in between;
(3) what is the context in which the harm manifests itself: the natural or the built environment – urban or rural; and
(4) what is the temporal frame within which the consequences of the harm can be analysed: immediate, delayed, or intergenerational (Heckenberg and White, 2013; White and Heckenberg, 2014).

More theoretically, green criminology examines the bio-physical and socio-economic consequences of the diverse sources of environmental harm, such as pollution, the deterioration of natural resources, the loss of biodiversity, climate change and ecocide (see South et al., 2013: 28–29; Lynch and Stretesky, 2014; Natali, 2013; White, 2011, 2022) and connect issues of crucial importance for today's world: namely, environmental crimes, harm, and various forms of (in) justice relating to the environment, animal and plant species, and the planet. Three different approaches to justice exist that further define what an environmental victim might include: humans; non-human animals; and ecosystems (White, 2013). The approach focused on humans is the most traditional and anthropocentric and features prominently in mainstream environmental forensics; however, ecocentric environmental forensics approaches are also drawn upon, particularly in cases involving vulnerable and threatened animal and plant species, and illegal land clearance.

Traditionally, environmental forensics has mainly served forms of anthropocentric justice. In its typical forensic declination, environment-related justice pertains to both the criminal law and tort law: both routinely deal with environmental issues, the former aiming at punishing environmental crimes and the latter at compensating for environmental damage occurring to people. Simply speaking, criminal law is crime-centred while tort law is victim-centred. In either case, the judicial interest towards the environment can be alternatively event-focused or risk-focused according to the negative effect of the original environmental violation on humans (Casali et al., 2022). In the beginning, judicial interest stems from a rule violation. For example, judicial events are here represented by deaths and physical injuries to humans, with the environmental violation producing the legally acknowledged harmful outcomes. Risks exist when the environmental violation has harmed the environment in ways that increase the chance of negative clinical outcomes for some human groups but are not producing such outcomes yet. In other words, the judicial risk is an intermediate step along a factual line possibly getting to the judicial event. The environmental hazard is typically about human groups and individuals.

The interest of anthropocentric justice is focused on the harmful consequences occurring to humans. From a wider ecocentric perspective the environmental harm can itself be an autonomous judicial issue, regardless of the risks and the events to humans (Berry, 1999; Preston, 2011: 136–145). This extends the remit of forensic investigation to include harms to non-human entities such as rivers, trees, birds and bees. After judicial interest arises in these kinds of environmental violations, forensic science can be asked to analyse the harm, the risk and the event. Forensic ecology, with all its distinct branches, must be efficiently mobilised to properly address all the possible environmental issues. Risk as well as the harmful event must be evaluated carefully and comprehensively (White, 2022).

The progression from the rule violation to the harmful event can be usefully described through a triangular shape, where the progression from the base to the apex of the triangle is that from many rule violations to very few but serious subsequent harmful events. This is quite a typical picture in any kind of risk management, where the height of the triangle is the dimension of the preventable risk: the higher the height, the more manageable the risk.

Reorienting environmental forensics

The peculiar features of environmental crimes and environmental crises demand a new kind of forensics, one at the same time able to cooperate with many new scientific and social partners and applicable to environmental risk management (Casali et al., 2022). More traditional forensics mainly deals with crimes where the victims are typically humans, who are positioned at the end of compressed chains of the damage.

The new environmental forensics serves an ecocentric justice that aims to develop new judicial solutions. Reparative/restorative forms of ecojustice are perhaps the most promising approaches on the horizon (White, 2015, 2016; Nurse, 2016). The task for environmental forensics can here be extended to the technical estimations of the right reparation and/or restoration required in a given situation.

In this framework, naturalistic branches such as veterinary medicine and botany turn out to be as important as human medicine, thus contributing to an effective and up-to-date environmental justice response. Environmental science is a rapidly growing area indeed (Murphy and Morrison, 2007) and many different scientists work nowadays in the field of environmental forensics. Geology, climatology, glaciology and etology represent many new chapters of the forensic sciences, each featuring their own technical and sophisticated methods to better describe the environment and its pathologies (White, 2012; Ahmed, 2017: 143). One of the most promising of these techniques is remote sensing analysis, performed with data acquired by Earth observation satellites and hopefully able to compare *before versus after*, thus creating the basis for judicial evidence about environmental harms (Ahmed, 2017: 143–144). Data from remote sensing must be always filtered through the expert witness (Ahmed, 2017: 145).

The basic analytical methodology is the same for both the traditional and the new environmental forensics. The environmental forensics investigation is mainly about causal links between human actions and their judicial consequences. Causal demonstration is at the core of any forensic investigation: the level for such a causal demonstration is strictly individualistic (that event in that place at that time producing those effects). The epidemiological laws (analysis of quantitative data in order to gauge causes and distributions), that are the very first step for every technical investigation, must therefore invariably be filtered through human, plant and animal pathophysiology. Climate and Earth pathophysiologies are likewise developing as part of an up-to-date ecocentric science. In reference back to ancient philosophy (the Mileto School), nature and climate might be better described as gigantic living animals, thus having a proper dynamic physiology and a possible traumatic pathology, where the trauma can have the shape of environmental human misbehaviour. Such a perspective could perhaps offer a common methodological way for both the traditional forensics (focusing only on humans) and the new environmental forensics (focusing on all living beings as well as non-living entities such as rivers and mountains).

Both justice and forensics are always about singular cases and only scientific analysis of the pathophysiology can tailor the epidemiological evidence down to the singular cases. Inside the singular case, the criminal law asks for absolute demonstrations of causal proof (100% sure or beyond a reasonable doubt) while for tort law it is probable cause (> 50% of chance or on the balance of probabilities). For judicial risks the sufficient causal reasoning is about possible effects. The practical tools utilised for environmental forensics include things such as environmental inspections, chemical and medical tests, DNA samples, lab tests on both living and non-living samples, and cumulative historical trends. All these tools and more can be drawn upon for forensic investigations, environmental risk management and environmental research.

New tasks for environmental forensics

If criminology has had difficulties in viewing itself as a "prospective" discipline (Brisman and South, 2013: 412), normally limiting itself to the best-known crimes that do not require a radical rethinking of the horizons of space and time through which we approach crime and its consequences, this temporal myopia has also characterised environmental forensics. In this regard, it seems useful that environmental forensics can also be applied to environmental risk management and to environmental research. Talking about risks is pivotal for prevention of further harmful consequences: where there is a pure risk, there is the space for the effective prevention of some related events too. This is the prize available for putting together environmental forensics and environmental risk management. In fact, as a dynamic part of environmental science, environmental forensics must also be committed to environmental risk management (Munns et al., 2017): the knowledge coming from the series of singular cases can be used to manage the previous risks through the continuous development of rules and laws. Inside environmental risk management, environmental forensics can provide a technical contribution to maximise ecological welfare.

Much environmental research, especially around pollution issues, is oriented to forensic medicine. Beside the environmental detection of levels and values of various substances in humans, there is the need for precise estimations of such levels and values in non-human animal and plant samples. Subclinical pollution is largely unknown across species. Asbestos is one of the most famous topics of both environmental science and environmental justice. Much of the medical literature deals with the environmental pollution caused by asbestos fibres, but the few autoptic works involving the lung asbestos burden in healthy urban people (who died due to trauma injury) have shown the real harms of inner human pollution created by asbestos (Casali et al., 2015). The cumulative results of this kind of scientific research will provide wider knowledge, clearer explanations, up-to-date pollution rules, stronger prevention and a better life for many.

Conclusion

If it is true that it is extremely difficult to go from the "the mute physical fact of damage" that constitutes environmental harm to its social, political, and juridical salience (Szasz, 1994: 30–40), it becomes crucial to facilitate the social and political recognition of environmental harms and risks by shedding light on that "twilight zone" where environmental harms emerge and come to life as facts not yet in existence in the social and institutional sphere. Environmental science as a whole can give justice and society the technical means and culture so that we can protect our planet: environmental forensics is a central player in such a preventive effort.

Faced with the great complexity that characterises human–environment interactions, criminologists, lawyers, sociologists and forensic scientists often employ diverging languages and models of interpretation. However, an interdisciplinary approach will be particularly useful in exploring specific environmental scenarios of criminological relevance (Hall, 2014). Interdisciplinary dialogue, particularly between environmental forensic science and green criminology, will be crucial in protecting the planet from grave harm (see also Oosthuizen et al., 2022). With expertise in the methodologies for detection of contaminants and a sensibility to new and emerging techniques and technologies, environmental forensic science is essential to analysis of the nature, dynamics and thresholds of environmental harm (Ahmed, 2017: 145).

MICHELANGELO CASALI AND LORENZO NATALI

Further reading

Ahmed, N., 2017, Proof of ecocide: Towards a forensic practice for the proposed international crime against the environment, *Forensic Archaeology, Anthropology and Ecology*, 1(2): 139–147. https://doi.org/10.1558/aefs.36378.

Casali, M., Travaini, G.V., Di Francesco, C.V., & Genovese, U.R., 2022, Environment, environmental crimes, environmental forensic medicine, environmental risk management and environmental criminology, *Healthcare*, 10: 263.

Murphy, B., & Morrison, R., eds., 2007, *Introduction to Environmental Forensics*, Amsterdam: Elsevier.

Oosthuizen, T., Howes, L.M., & White, R., 2022, Forensic science and environmental offences: Litter, DNA analysis and surveillance, *Forensic Science International: Animals and Environments*, 2: 100042. https://doi.org/10.1016/j.fsiae.2022.100042

White, R., 2012, Environmental forensic studies and toxic towns, *Current Issues in Criminal Justice*, 24(1): 105–119. doi:10.1080/10345329.2012.12035947

References

Ahmed, N., 2017, Proof of ecocide: Towards a forensic practice for the proposed international crime against the environment, *Forensic Archaeology, Anthropology and Ecology*, 1(2): 139–147. https://doi.org/10.1558/aefs.36378.

Berry, T., 1999, *The Great Work: Our Way into the Future*, New York: Harmony/Bell Tower.

Brisman, A., & South, N., 2013, Conclusion: The planned obsolescence of planet Earth? How green criminology can help us learn from experience and contribute to our future, in N. South & A. Brisman (eds.), *Routledge International Handbook of Green Criminology*, London and New York: Routledge: 409–417.

Casali, M., Carugno, M., Cattaneo, A., ... & Pesatori, A.C., 2015, Asbestos lung burden in necroscopic samples from the general population of Milan, Italy, *Annals of Occupational Hygiene*, 59: 909–921.

Casali, M., Travaini, G.V., Di Francesco, C.V., & Genovese, U.R., 2022, Environment, environmental crimes, environmental forensic medicine, environmental risk management and environmental criminology, *Healthcare*, 10: 263.

Hall, M., 2014, The roles and use of law in green criminology, *International Journal for Crime, Justice and Social Democracy*, 3(2): 96–109.

Heckenberg, D., & White, R., 2013, Innovative approaches to researching environmental crime, in N. South & A. Brisman (eds.), *Routledge International Handbook of Green Criminology*, London and New York: Routledge: 110–131.

Lynch, M.J., & Stretesky, P.B., 2014, *Exploring Green Criminology. Toward a Green Criminological Revolution*, Farnham, UK and Burlington, VT: Ashgate.

Munns, W.R. Jr, Poulsen, V., Gala, W.R., ... & von Stackelberg, K., 2017, Ecosystem services in risk assessment and management, *Integrated Environmental Assessment and Management*, 13(1): 62–73.

Murphy, B., & Morrison, R., eds., 2007, *Introduction to Environmental Forensics*, Amsterdam: Elsevier.

Natali, L., 2013, The contemporary horizon of green criminology, in N. South & A. Brisman (eds.), *Routledge International Handbook of Green Criminology*, London and New York: Routledge: 73–84.

Natali, L., 2017, The contribution of green criminology to the analysis of historical pollution, in F. Centonze & S. Manacorda (eds.), *Historical Pollution: Comparative Legal Responses to Environmental Crimes*, Cham: Springer: 21–55.

Nurse, A., 2016, *An Introduction to Green Criminology and Environmental Justice*, London: Sage.

Oosthuizen, T., Howes, L.M., & White, R., 2022, Forensic science and environmental offences: Litter, DNA analysis and surveillance, *Forensic Science International: Animals and Environments*, 2: 100042. https://doi.org/10.1016/j.fsiae.2022.100042

Pires, S.F., & Olah, G., 2022, Wildlife crime: Issues and promising solutions, *Animals*, 12(14): 1736. https://doi.org/10.3390/ani12141736

Preston, B., 2011, The use of restorative justice for environmental crime, *Criminal Law Journal*, 35: 136–145.

South, N., Brisman, A., & Beirne, P., 2013, A guide to a green criminology, in N. South & A. Brisman (eds.), *Routledge International*

Handbook of Green Criminology, London and New York: Routledge: 27–42.
Szasz, A., 1994, *Ecopopulism: Toxic Waste and the Movement for Environmental Justice*, Minneapolis: University of Minnesota Press.
White, R., 2011, *Transnational Environmental Crime: Toward an Eco-global Criminology*, London and New York: Routledge.
White, R., 2012, Environmental forensic studies and toxic towns, *Current Issues in Criminal Justice*, 24(1): 105–119. doi:10.1080/10345329.2012.12035947
White, R., 2013, *Environmental Harm: An Eco-Justice Perspective*, Bristol: Policy Press.
White, R., 2015, Indigenous communities, environmental protection and restorative justice, *Australian Indigenous Law Review*, 18(2): 43–54.
White, R., 2016, Reparative justice, environmental crime and penalties for the powerful, *Crime, Law and Social Change*, 67(2): 117–132.
White, R., 2017, Experts and expertise in the Land and Environment Court, *Australian Journal of Forensic Sciences*, 49(4): 392–402. doi:10.1080/00450618.2016.1218544
White, R., 2022, *Theorising Green Criminology: Selected Essays*, Abingdon: Routledge.
White, R., & Heckenberg, D., 2014, *Green Criminology: An Introduction to the Study of Environmental Harm*, London and New York: Routledge.

Michelangelo Casali and Lorenzo Natali

47. Environmental law and transgression

Introduction

The substance of environmental law in a country is undergirded by the quality of its enforcement apparatus. Violations of environmental law, unlike street crime, are typically treated as a regulatory problem, rather than an issue to be solved via the criminal justice system. The majority of violations of environmental law are thus treated as civil or administrative violations, where the focus is on bringing the violator into compliance with the law. For violations involving significant harm and/or culpable conduct, however, criminal prosecution may be warranted to both punish the offender and deter future offences. This entry provides an overview of the various administrative, civil, and criminal tools that are used to punish environmental transgressions, drawing from the experience of multiple jurisdictions.

Remedies for transgressing environmental laws flow through two channels with distinct supporting philosophies that inform each approach. In the first, the state attempts to bring offenders into compliance with the law via civil or administrative remedies (U.S. EPA, 2021). In the case of more serious violations, the state may apply criminal enforcement tools to punish violators and deter future offences (Devaney, 1994; Uhlmann, 2014; 2019). Historically, countries have viewed environmental law violations as a compliance issue and most offences are managed through administrative fines and other punishments (Lynch et al., 2016; Ozymy and Jarrell Ozymy, 2022). Recognising that many transgressions had serious consequences for humans, non-human animals, and the natural environment, many countries began in earnest in the 1980s to develop criminal provisions in environmental law, as well as environmental law enforcement agencies to police and prosecute serious and chronic offences (Barton, 1991; Pendleton, 1997).

Environmental problems spur environmental laws

As much of the world began to industrialise in earnest in the 19th century, the use of fossil fuels and later the development of the modern petrochemical industry created a variety of emerging environmental challenges that began to focus public attention on the relationship between environmental hazards and health risks to humans, non-human animals, and the natural environment. In Europe and the United Kingdom, laws governing air and water pollution were passed during industrialisation, such as the German Industrial Code and British Waterworks Clauses Acts, passed in 1845, and the Spanish Water Act of 1878 (Vercher, 1990). Early examples of environmental laws from the United States at the turn of the 20th century include the Rivers and Harbors Act of 1899 and the Lacey Act of 1900, where the federal government protected the navigable waterways of the country from unpermitted alteration or obstruction and banned the unpermitted inter-state trade in wildlife (U.S. Department of Justice, 2015).

Later in the 20th century, environmental focusing events made international headlines, such as the Great Smog of London in 1952 that killed some 4,000 people and injured 100,000 more, the Santa Barbara Oil Spill off the California Coast in 1969, and a series of fires on the Cuyahoga River, which caught fire 13 times between 1868 and 1969 and which thereby brought public attention to the growing need to regulate air and water pollution. Rachel Carson's book, *Silent Spring*, published in 1962, centred the public's attention on the negative effects humans were having on the natural world, particularly the widespread use of synthetic pesticides developed after World War II, such as DDT, that were decimating wildlife and posing health risks to humans.

The 1970s witnessed a flourishing of both a new environmental movement, and laws meant to protect human health and the environment across a range of environmental media (Ozymy and Jarrell, 2021a). Laws empowering the state to regulate air and water pollution, toxic waste, and chemical substances became more commonplace or were strengthened, as were endangered species Acts. The developed world, in particular, saw significant shifts in environmental law towards better managing the risks of industrialisation alongside the needs for more robust habitat and species conservation. Decades later, these concerns have morphed into the need to decarbonise the industrial world in order to combat the damaging effects of anthropogenic climate change.

Remedies for civil violations

By the end of the 1970s it became more and more apparent to policymakers, environmental interest groups, and the public that agencies tasked with enforcing environmental laws needed a greater range of tools to enforce the law (Ozymy and Jarrell, 2021b). Policymakers historically treated violations as regulatory matters or misdemeanour violations of law, but now it was becoming evident that serious and chronic violations of environmental law resulted in significant consequences and required stiffer penalties to deter violators and in other cases, regulators needed a broader range of options to bring violators back into compliance with the law (Brickey, 2001; Ozymy and Jarrell, 2021b).

There are substantive differences between infractions that merit civil or administrative remedies, and those requiring the application of criminal enforcement tools. A first distinction is between civil and criminal liability for transgressing environmental laws. Broadly speaking, civil liability involves basic violations of law (wrongful acts), whereas criminal violations also involve intent (guilty mind) (U.S. EPA, 2024a). In the United States, environmental civil liability is 'strict liability' in that it focuses on whether a defendant violated the law and gives no consideration to whether they knew that they violated the law or intended to violate it. The burden of proof for being found guilty of a civil violation is a preponderance of the evidence standard, meaning it is truer than not that a defendant violated the law (U.S. EPA, 2024a). This is sometimes referred to as a 'balance of probabilities' standard of proof.

When companies or individuals violate environmental laws, they may do so accidentally or without intent, yet still incur civil liability for the transgression. In this instance, the state is applying principles of administrative compliance, where the goal is to bring the transgressor back into compliance with the law (Ozymy and Jarrell Ozymy, 2022). In such cases, which constitute the majority of violations, regulators may choose to focus on applying civil administrative actions or civil judicial actions (Ozymy and Jarrell, 2021b). Civil administrative actions include actions such as issuing notices of violation, administrative orders for corrective actions needed to come into compliance with the law, and the issuance of fines. The state may pursue civil judicial actions when a violator does not comply with administrative orders or come into compliance with the law. In other words, the violator must present to court for adjudication of the matter. If the state chooses to pursue a civil lawsuit against a violator, the responsible party may be found liable for the violation and consequently subject to sanctions relevant to the specific transgression (U.S. EPA, 2024a). The parties may also choose to reach a negotiated settlement. These settlements may include a consent decree, where the defendant is required to meet a set of obligations to return to compliance but need not admit guilt.

Civil remedies can take a variety of forms and administrators can be somewhat flexible when dealing with non-compliance issues. If a defendant is found liable in court or agrees to a settlement, typical options for civil penalties include fines and other monetary penalties, injunctive relief to institute corrective actions to come into compliance, or actions taken by the responsible parties to improve the environment. Administrative fines are a common remedy for transgressing the law and parameters (e.g., the size of the fine) may be set by statute (U.S. EPA, 2024b). The broad goal of such fines is to incentivise compliance and offset the economic benefit received by non-compliance (U.S. EPA, 2024a). Injunctive relief may be sought as a remedy in a civil lawsuit. This requires the transgressor to stop engaging in a specific action or series of actions that cause environmental damage or harm; and may be a temporary injunction to stop an action or a permanent injunction (U.S. EPA, 2021). Examples include seeking a temporary injunction to halt a company from discharging toxic chemicals into a river or emitting air toxins affecting a neighbouring community until the issue is legally resolved, or a permanent injunction barring certain polluting activities at a large industrial plant or petroleum refinery.

If non-compliance with environmental laws has caused harm to a neighbouring community, regulators can push for environmental mitigation and/or monitoring plans as a form of injunctive relief that require the transgressor to engage in actions to offset or mitigate past or ongoing harms (U.S. EPA, 2021). This might take the form of administrative orders on consent, which is an agreement between a regulator and an individual or business entity to agree to pay for damage

Melissa Jarrell Ozymy and Joshua Ozymy

caused by their actions and/or agree to cease certain activities, usually applied in cases where a guilty party needs to pay the cost of cleaning up pollution (U.S. EPA, 2024a). An example might be a chemical company, where an equipment failure resulted in the discharge of tens of thousands of gallons of toxic substances into a nearby river, being required to pay for the cost of clean-up.

Mitigation actions are sought as injunctive relief when the state feels that the goal is to restore the status quo in the regulatory environment (U.S EPA, 2024c). A supplemental environmental project (SEP) may be included as part of a negotiated settlement. An SEP is a voluntary agreement by the violator that provides public or environmental health benefits above and beyond what is required under the law to return to compliance (U.S. EPA, 2024d). SEPs are different to mitigation actions, as they are voluntary agreements reached through negotiation and may result in improved environmental actions beyond compliance as well as in the offseting of other penalties (U.S. EPA, 2024c). A stipulated remedy may also be included as part of a settlement, one that requires a future action and/or project in the event that the terms of a settlement are violated.

When parties reach a settlement in a civil action, they may agree to any combination of these terms as part of that negotiated settlement. Because civil actions focus on restoring the violator to compliance with the law, in the case of companies in particular, the overall prerogative of the state is always to ensure current and future operations comply with the law, and that often means injunctive relief in the form of changes to operations or physical improvements to facilities that will halt unpermitted emissions or other discharges into the environment (U.S. EPA, 2024a). A defendant may propose to remedy a violation by undertaking a set of actions that provides a concrete benefit to the public or environmental health in direct relation to the violation in question. This may be an action, like an SEP, that improves the environment beyond what is required for compliance (U.S. EPA, 2024c). Furthermore, settlements may require violators, particularly companies, to engage in other actions that go beyond basic compliance to enhance transparency with regulators and improve their image with the public, such as providing greater public access to data, engaging in electronic reporting of required regulatory data, opening themselves up to third-party compliance audits, or adopting advanced methods of environmental monitoring (U.S. EPA, 2024a).

In recent years, a number of countries have adopted environmental courts and other environmental administrative bodies to resolve environmental violations, and there is a growing literature on this topic (Fisher and Preston, 2022; Hamilton, 2021; Voigt and Makuch, 2018; Wright, 2022). The need for specialist expertise is a common theme as is the influence of ecocentrism on adjudication processes. There is also close scrutiny of how decisions are made and of substantive outcomes, particularly as these relate to environmental restorative justice (Pali, Forsyth and Tepper, 2022).

Remedies for criminal violations

While civil remedies focus on returning violators to compliance with the law, in cases that involve significant harm to the public or environment and/or culpable conduct, criminal enforcement tools are applied (Ringquist and Emmert, 1999; Ozymy and Jarrell, 2022). Unlike civil remedies, remedies for criminal conduct centre on the need to both punish the transgressor for the crime and to deter future offences (Devaney, 1994). Thus, criminal enforcement is informed by a philosophy based on deterrence of crime, rather than administrative compliance (Griefe et al., 2017; Lynch, 2017). While civil liability is strict, criminal liability is based to some degree on intent. Criminal enforcement is applied when a defendant knowingly (or neglectfully) violates an environmental law or at least knew the facts at hand when they violated the law (U.S. EPA, 2024a). A civil violation may be the result of an accident, or the liable party did not knowingly intend to break the law.

Transgression is deemed to be a 'felony' offence (or, in jurisdictions such as Australia, an 'indictable' offence) when it is serious. Because criminal violations involve actions resulting in significant harm, and culpable conduct (where the defendant has intent), criminal provisions of environmental statutes contain felony penalties that correspond to these more serious violations (Ozymy and Jarrell, 2022). Due to the seriousness of the transgression and possible penalties, unlike civil liability, criminal guilt has a higher standard of proof, being 'beyond a reasonable doubt' that a defendant is guilty of the crime with which they are charged (Brickey, 2008; U.S. EPA, 2024a). In this, criminal guilt is a very serious matter and if a defendant pleads guilty or is convicted of a crime, they have legally committed the crime, whereas with civil liability they may be found liable for damages in court or negotiate a consent decree with prosecutors to avoid admitting any or all guilt in the matter, or with administrative matters, they may choose to pay fines or other administrative penalties or voluntarily come into compliance when appropriately notified by a regulatory agency or other governmental body with relevant authority in the matter (U.S. EPA, 2024a). Another defining feature of criminal provisions in environmental statutes may be the possibility of prison time for offenders (Ozymy and Jarrell Ozymy, 2021). Outside the possibility of incarceration, environmental criminals may face fines, restitution to the state to clean up or remediate pollution, restitution for the harm caused by a violation, or other forms of supervision, such as probation, home confinement, community corrections, or community service (Ozymy, Menard and Jarrell, 2021).

While administrative and civil enforcement actions targeted at returning violators to compliance evolved through the 1970s, criminal enforcement structures did not become commonplace until the 1980s (Rosbe and Gulley, 1984; Ozymy and Jarrell Ozymy, 2021). This period represented a broader global movement supporting stronger punishments for serious violations of environmental laws (Pendleton, 1997). This change ultimately entailed institutionalising resources for policing environmental crimes, as well as hiring prosecutors and specialised support staff to prosecute environmental crimes (U.S. Department of Justice, 2015). An early public example was the adoption of Resolution 77 (28) in 1978 by the Council of Europe, which called for the necessity of criminal law to protect the environment in cases of serious transgressions (Vercher, 1990). The evolution of criminal penalties and support staff for environmental crime investigation and prosecution began in the early 1980s in the United States. The Canadian Environmental Protection Act, passed in 1988, provided significant penalties for environmental crimes. Germany amended its penal code in 1980 to set the stage for a more consistent system of criminal law to protect the environment. The Spanish Constitution of 1978 includes language in Article 45 for 'criminal or administrative sanctions' for violations of environmental law (Vercher, 1990).

To use the United States as an example of the evolution of a criminal enforcement process, the U.S. Environmental Protection Agency (EPA), the principal agency tasked with overseeing enforcement of federal environmental laws, created an Office of Enforcement in 1981 and hired full-time criminal investigators the following year (U.S. Department of Justice, 2015). The difference in organisational culture compared to traditional regulatory enforcement agencies is apparent, as the current EPA Criminal Investigation Division (EPA-CID), tasked with environmental crime investigations, refers to itself as 'America's Environmental Crime Fighters' in their official publications, centring their image as the 'Nation's environmental police' focused on deterring and punishing environmental crimes, rather than bringing violators back into compliance (Suarez, 2003; U.S. EPA, 2024e).

The US EPA is tasked with investigating environmental crimes but works with prosecutors in the federal Department of Justice (DOJ) to pursue criminal charges against offenders if such action is warranted (Mintz, 2006). The DOJ founded the Environmental Crimes Section in 1982 to centralise resources and expertise for the prosecution of environmental crimes. Criminal provisions were added to major environmental statutes that provided enhanced penalties for felonies, particularly 'knowing violations' that involve intent, beginning with hazardous waste laws in 1984, water pollution in 1987, air pollution in 1990, and so forth across environmental media (Starr, 1991; Galactos, 1995; Lazarus, 1994; Ozymy, Menard and Jarrell, 2021). Criminal enforcement agents and prosecutors work together, often in a taskforce setting involving state, local, or other federal officials to build cases against defendants that may ultimately lead to prosecutors convening a grand jury, filing a criminal information in a district court, or possibly deferring prosecution to state-level officials (Mintz, 2004, 2006).

There has traditionally been a lack of empirical and theoretical research on environmental criminal enforcement, which is somewhat understandable, given the 1980s represented the nascent development of these organisations. Early legal work tried to centre criminal enforcement within the broader checks and balances of the federal system (Starr, 1991; Lazarus, 1994; Galactos, 1995). Later research began to focus on the internal, organisational dynamics of enforcement agencies, their values, and their prerogatives (Mintz, 2004; 2006). Early empirical work examining the outcomes of prosecutions came in the early 2000s (Brickey, 2001, 2008). The 2000s saw additional studies that compiled extensive data and information on environmental crime (Burns and Lynch, 2004) and began to examine novel aspects of environmental crime and law enforcement, such as its representation in the media (Jarrell, 2009), relationship to crime victims (Cassell, 2005; Cassell and Joffee, 2011), and its relationship to environmental justice (Stretesky and Lynch, 1999). Later studies examined the broader deterrent effect that criminal enforcement may have on environmental crime (Paternoster, 2010; Billiet and Rousseau, 2014; Ozymy and Jarrell, 2021a, 2021g), as well as predicting criminal enforcement outcomes (Ozymy and Jarrell, 2021f).

More recent research has begun to examine criminal enforcement at the sub-national level and to examine broader outcomes across environmental media. Cochran et al. (2018) examined sentencing gaps for environmental offenders at the state level. Crow, O'Conner Shelley and Stretesky (2013) explored wildlife crimes in the US State of Florida. Periconi (2009) showed the state of environmental crime prosecutions in the US State of New York. Lynch (2019) more recently explored environmental crimes at the county level in the US State of Georgia. Recent regional studies of the United States have explored criminal enforcement in the Pacific Northwest (Ozymy and Jarrell, 2021h), Southern region (Ozymy and Jarrell, 2021i), and the Midwest (Ozymy and Jarrell, 2021j).

Examining criminal enforcement across various environmental media, Ozymy and Jarrell (2021b) explored the history of the US Clean Water Act, Ozymy and Jarrell Ozymy (2021) examined historical charging and sentencing patterns in the US Clean Air Act, Superfund (Ozymy and Jarrell, 2020a), pesticide crimes (Ozymy and Jarrell, 2021c), toxic substances crimes (Ozymy and Jarrell, 2021d), and hazardous waste crimes (Ozymy and Jarrell, 2021e). Recent work has also focused on environmental victimisation and its role in environmental crime enforcement for both humans and non-human animal victims (Ozymy and Jarrell, 2020b; Ozymy and Jarrell, 2021k). All of these studies have done well to work with limited data to explore the geography of environmental crime prosecutions, but much more empirical work is needed both inside and outside the United States.

Conclusion

Environmental law focuses on protecting the health and welfare of humans, non-human animals and the natural environment. Most transgressions of environmental law are remedied through administrative or civil methods that return violators to compliance. Serious violations, particularly those that involve intent, merit criminal prosecution (Ozymy, 2022). There is increasing research and scholarship on these matters, particularly with the growing international interest in embedding ecocentric principles and concepts into legal processes (i.e., valuing nature for its own sake), legislative reforms that extend new legal rights to non-human entities such as rivers, mountains, dolphins and apes (i.e., rights of Nature laws), renewed interest in forms of restorative and reparative justice (which emphasise repairing the harm), and global attention on ecocide as a potential international crime (under the auspices of the International Criminal Court).

MELISSA JARRELL OZYMY AND JOSHUA OZYMY

Further reading

Bjällås, Ulf. (2010). Experiences of Sweden's environmental courts. *Journal of Court Innovation*, 3(Winter), 179–183.

Lynch, Michael J., Barrett, Kimberly L., Stretesky, Paul B., and Long, Michael. (2016). The weak probability of punishment for environmental offenses and deterrence of environmental offenders: A discussion based on USEPA criminal cases, 1983–2013. *Deviant Behavior*, 37, 1096–1109.

Ozymy, Joshua, Menard, Bryan, and Jarrell, Melissa L. (2021). Persistence or partisanship: Exploring the relationship between presidential administrations and criminal enforcement by the U.S. Environmental Protection Agency,

1983–2019. *Public Administration Review*, 81, 49–63.
Pendleton, Michael R. (1997). Beyond the threshold: The criminalization of logging. *Society & Natural Resources*, 10, 191–193.
Tegner Anker, Helle, Fauchald, Kristian Ole, Nilsson, Annika, and Suvantola, Leila. (2009). The role of courts in environmental law: A Nordic comparative study. *Nordic Environmental Law Journal*, 1, 18.
U.S. Department of Justice. (2015). *Historical Development of Environmental Criminal Law*. https://www.justice.gov/enrd/about-division/historical-development-environmental-criminal-law
U.S. EPA. (2024). *Basic Information on Enforcement*. https://www.epa.gov/enforcement/basic-information-enforcement
U.S. EPA. (2024). *Enforcement and Compliance History Online (ECHO)*. https://echo.epa.gov/
U.S. EPA. (2024). *Summary of Criminal Prosecutions Database*. https://cfpub.epa.gov/compliance/criminal_prosecution/index.cfm?
Vercher, Antonio. (1990). The use of criminal law for the protection of the environment in Europe: Council of European Resolution 77 (28). *Northwestern Journal of International Law & Business*, 10, 442–459.

References

Barton, David T. (1991). Corporate officer liability under RCRA: Stringent but not strict. *Brigham Young University Law Review*, 4(3), 1548–1550.
Billiet, Carole M., and Rousseau, Sandra. (2014). How real is the threat of imprisonment for environmental crime? *European Journal of Law and Economics*, 37, 183–188.
Brickey, Kathleen F. (2001). Charging practices in hazardous waste crime prosecutions. *Ohio State Law Journal*, 62(1), 1077–1124.
Brickey, Kathleen F. (2008). *Environmental Crime: Law, Policy, Prosecution*. Aspen Publishers.
Burns, Ronald G., and Lynch, Michael J. (2004). *The Sourcebook on Environmental Crime*. LFB Publishers.
Carson, Rachel. (1962). *Silent Spring*. Houghton Mifflin.
Cassell, Paul G. (2005). Recognizing victims in the federal rules of criminal procedure: Amendments in light of the Crime Victims' Rights Act. *Brigham Young University Law Review*, 835, 835–925.
Cassell, Paul G., and Joffee, Steven. (2011). The crime victims' expanding role in a system of public prosecution: A response to the critics of the Crime Victims' Rights Act. *Northwestern University Law Review*, 105, 164–183.
Cochran, Joshua C., Lynch, Michael J., Toman, Elisa L., and Shields, Ryan T. (2018). Court sentencing patterns for environmental crimes: Is there a 'green' gap in punishment? *Journal of Quantitative Criminology*, 35, 37–66.
Crow, Matthew S., O'Conner Shelley, Tara, and Stretesky, Paul B. (2013). Camouflage-collar crime: An examination of wildlife crime and characteristics in Florida. *Deviant Behavior*, 34, 635–652.
Devaney, Earl E. (1994). *The Exercise of Investigative Discretion*. https://www.law.uh.edu/faculty/thester/courses/Environmental-Practicum-2017/Devaney%20Invest%20Discretion%20Memo.pdf
Fisher, Elizabeth, and Preston, Brian (eds). (2022). *An Environmental Court in Action: Function, Doctrine and Process*. Hart.
Galactos, Theodora. (1995). The United States Department of Justice Environmental Crimes Section: A case study of inter-branch and intrabranch conflict over Congressional oversight and the exercise of prosecutorial discretion. 64 *Fordham Law Review* at 590.
Griefe, Matthew J., Stretesky, Paul B., O'Conner Shelley, Tara, and Pogrebin, Matthew. (2017). Corporate environmental crime and environmental justice. *Criminal Justice Policy Review*, 28, 327–346.
Hamilton, Mark. (2021). *Environmental Crime and Restorative Justice: Justice as Meaningful Involvement*. Palgrave Macmillan.
Jarrell, Melissa L. (2009). Environmental crime and injustice: Media coverage of a landmark environmental crime case. *Southwest Journal of Criminal Justice*, 6, 25–44.
Lazarus, Richard J. (1994). Assimilating environmental protection into legal rules and the problem with environmental crime. *Loyola Law Review*, 27, 867–875.
Lynch, Michael J. (2017). The sentencing/punishment of federal environmental/green offenders, 2000–2013. *Deviant Behavior*, 38, 991–995.
Lynch, Michael J. (2019). County-level environmental crime enforcement: A case study of environmental/green crimes in Fulton County, Georgia, 1998–2014. *Deviant Behavior*, 40, 1090–1104.
Lynch, Michael J., Barrett, Kimberly L., Stretesky, Paul B., and Long, Michael. (2016). The weak probability of punishment for environmental offenses and deterrence of environmental offenders: A discussion based on USEPA criminal cases, 1983–2013. *Deviant Behavior*, 37, 1096–1109.
Mintz, Joel A. (2004). Treading water: A preliminary assessment of EPA enforcement during the Bush II administration. *Environmental Law Reporter*, 34, 10912.
Mintz, Joel A. (2006). Some thoughts on the interdisciplinary aspects of environmental

enforcement. *Environmental Law Reporter*, 36, 10495–10505.
Ozymy, Joshua. (2022). The persistence of vision. *The Environmental Forum*, May/June, 27–33.
Ozymy, Joshua, and Jarrell, Melissa L. (2020a). Failure to notify: Exploring charging and sentencing patterns in Superfund criminal prosecutions. *Environmental Law Reporter*, 50, 10723–10733.
Ozymy, Joshua, and Jarrell, Melissa L. (2020b). Exploring the role of victims in federal environmental crime prosecutions. *Willamette Law Review*, 57(1), 101–137.
Ozymy, Joshua, and Jarrell, Melissa L. (2021a). Does the criminal enforcement of federal environmental law reduce crime? The case of the Resource Conservation and Recovery Act. *Environmental and Earth Law Journal*, 11, 65–88.
Ozymy, Joshua, and Jarrell, Melissa L. (2021b). Illegal discharge: Exploring the history of the criminal enforcement of the U.S. Clean Water Act. *Fordham Environmental Law Review*, 32, 195–230.
Ozymy, Joshua, and Jarrell, Melissa L. (2021c). Mislabeled: Exploring the history of charging and sentencing patterns in FIFRA criminal prosecutions, 1983–2019. *Drake Journal of Agricultural Law*, 25(3), 369–401.
Ozymy, Joshua, and Jarrell, Melissa L. (2021d). The toxic crusaders: Exploring the history of the criminal enforcement of the Toxic Substances Control Act. *Mitchell Hamline Law Journal of Public Policy & Practice*, 42(2), 182–217.
Ozymy, Joshua, and Jarrell, Melissa L. (2021e). The toxic offenders: Charging and sentencing patterns in criminal prosecutions. *Texas Environmental Law Journal*, 51(1), 1–26.
Ozymy, Joshua, and Jarrell, Melissa L. (2021f). Predicting the U.S. Environmental Protection Agency's criminal enforcement outcomes, 1983–2019. *Environmental Politics*, 30(7), 1237–1258.
Ozymy, Joshua, and Jarrell, Melissa L. (2021g). Sub-optimal deterrence and criminal sanctioning under the U.S. Clean Water Act. *University of Denver Water Law Review*, 24(2), 218–229.
Ozymy, Joshua, and Jarrell, Melissa L. (2021h). Pungent sound: Analyzing the criminal enforcement of environmental law in the Pacific Northwest. *Manitoba Law Journal*, 44(6), 75–105.
Ozymy, Joshua, and Jarrell, Melissa L. (2021i). Southern harm: Analyzing the criminal enforcement of environmental law in the Southern United States, 1983–2019. *William & Mary Environmental Law and Policy Review*, 46, 115–148.
Ozymy, Joshua, and Jarrell, Melissa L. (2021j). A knowing violation: Exploring the history of the criminal enforcement of environmental law in the Midwestern United States. *Chicago-Kent Journal of Environmental and Energy Law*, 10(2), 60–84.
Ozymy, Joshua, and Jarrell, Melissa L. (2021k). Exploring the role of non-human animal victims in federal environmental crime prosecutions. *Animal Law Review*, 27, 35–56.
Ozymy, Joshua, and Jarrell Ozymy, Melissa L. (2021). Exploring charging and sentencing patterns in U.S. Clean Air Act criminal prosecutions. *Natural Resources Journal*, 61, 225–248.
Ozymy, Joshua, and Jarrell Ozymy, Melissa. (2022). The green police: Criminal enforcement and the prospects for deterrence in the era of climate change. *Environmental Law Reporter*, 52(7), 10526–10538.
Ozymy, Joshua, Menard, Bryan, and Jarrell, Melissa L. (2021). Persistence or partisanship: Exploring the relationship between presidential administrations and criminal enforcement by the U.S. Environmental Protection Agency, 1983–2019. *Public Administration Review*, 81, 49–63.
Pali, Brunilda, Forsyth, Miranda, and Tepper, Felicity (eds). (2022). *The Palgrave Handbook of Environmental Restorative Justice*. Palgrave Macmillan.
Paternoster, Raymond. (2010). How much do we really know about criminal deterrence? *Journal of Criminal Law & Criminology*, 100, 765–768.
Pendleton, Michael R. (1997). Beyond the threshold: The criminalization of logging. *Society & Natural Resources*, 10, 191–193.
Periconi, James J. (2009). The state of environmental crime prosecutions in New York. *Natural Resources and Environment*, 23, 15–19.
Ringquist, Evan J., and Emmert, Craig E. (1999). Judicial policymaking in published and unpublished decisions: The case of environmental civil litigation. *Political Research Quarterly*, 52, 12–13.
Rosbe, William L., and Gulley, Robert L. (1984). The hazardous and solid waste amendments of 1984: A dramatic overhaul of the way America manages its hazardous waste. *Environmental Law Reporter* at 10458–10463.
Starr, Judson W. (1991). Turbulent times at Justice and EPA: The origins of environmental criminal prosecutions and the work that remains. *George Washington Law Review*, 59, 900–902.
Stretesky, Paul B., and Lynch, Michael J. (1999). Corporate environmental violence and racism. *Crime, Law and Social Change*, 30, 163–180.
Suarez, John Peter. (2003). Management review of the Office of Criminal Enforcement. *Forensics and Training*, 7. https://www.epa.gov/sites/production/files/documents/oceft-review03.pdf
Uhlmann, David M. (2014). Prosecutorial discretion and environmental crime. *Harvard Environmental Law Review*, 38, 159–216.
Uhlmann, David M. (2019). Prosecutorial discretion and environmental crime redux: Charging trends, aggravating factors, and individual

outcome data for 2005–2014. *Michigan Journal of Environmental & Energy Law*, 8, 312.
U.S. Department of Justice. (2015). *Historical Development of Environmental Criminal Law*. https://www.justice.gov/enrd/about-division/historical-development-environmental-criminal-law
U.S. EPA. (2021). *Using All Appropriate Injunctive Relief Tools in Civil Enforcement Settlements*. https://www.epa.gov/enforcement/using-all-appropriate-injunctive-relief-tools-civil-enforcement-settlements
U.S. EPA. (2024a). *Basic Information on Enforcement*. https://www.epa.gov/enforcement/basic-information-enforcement
U.S. EPA. (2024b). *Guidance on Use of Penalty Policies in Administrative Litigation*. https://www.epa.gov/enforcement/guidance-use-penalty-policies-administrative-litigation
U.S. EPA. (2024c). *Securing Mitigation as Injunctive Relief in Certain Civil Enforcement Settlements*. https://www.epa.gov/enforcement/securing-mitigation-injunctive-relief-certain-civil-enforcement-settlements-2nd-edition
U.S. EPA. (2024d). *Supplemental Environmental Projects (SEPs)*. https://www.epa.gov/enforcement/supplemental-environmental-projects-seps
U.S. EPA. (2024e). *U.S. Environmental Protection Agency Criminal Enforcement Program: America's Environmental Crime Fighters*. https://www.epa.gov/sites/production/files/documents/oceftbrochure.pdf
Vercher, Antonio. (1990). The use of criminal law for the protection of the environment in Europe: Council of European Resolution 77 (28). *Northwestern Journal of International Law & Business*, 10, 442–459.
Voigt, Christina, and Makuch, Zen (eds). (2018). *Courts and the Environment*. Edward Elgar Publishing.
Wright, Mark. (2022). *Responding to Environmental Crimes: Lessons from New Zealand*. Palgrave Macmillan.

MELISSA JARRELL OZYMY AND JOSHUA OZYMY

48. Environmental law enforcement

Introduction

Transnational environmental law enforcement is challenging for several reasons. Environmental regulation is often highly complex and subject to change, and the criminal actors involved may be powerful economic entities. Competences vary between administrative enforcement agencies, organised from the local to the national level, and also include the police, customs, and the public prosecution service. Agencies often lack sufficient numbers of specialised staff and adequate equipment. Although administrative penalties such as fines are regularly imposed, criminal cases may take years and often end with settlements or limited financial penalties for legal persons, and prison sentences remain rare and light. Many environmental crimes are transnational and substantial legal and practical barriers hinder effective cross-border law enforcement cooperation. However, global law enforcement attention has increased, particularly regarding environmental crimes involving organised crime groups, and enforcement agency networks have developed many new initiatives to improve cross-border cooperation.

After the Second World War, countries in the Global North started to adopt a wide range of legislation and ever stricter regulations with the aim of protecting the environment. These efforts caused a transfer of, for instance, pollution and waste problems to the Global South, requiring governments there to also establish and tighten environmental legislation. Nowadays very few activities that cause harm to the environment remain unregulated, although for economic reasons many laws allow environmental harm within certain thresholds (e.g., rules pertaining to air and water pollution). Whether prohibited or regulated, adequate enforcement and applying meaningful penalties are nonetheless essential. For several reasons, environmental law enforcement is a challenging task for the public actors involved.

Over the past few decades, green criminologists have pointed to the fact that environmental law enforcement suffers from a lack of political priority and thus of sufficient numbers of properly trained and equipped staff, to enable the effective detection, investigation, prosecution and sentencing of environmental criminals (Akella & Cannon, 2009; Wellsmith, 2011; Sollund et al., 2016; Nurse, 2022). A second main problem is that although causing harm to the environment may be fully prohibited in some cases (such as dumping hazardous waste from synthetic drug laboratories into the countryside), environmental law to a large degree aims to *regulate* legitimate economic activities and is highly technical, complicated and sector specific (Eurojust, 2014; Spapens, 2014; Billiet et al., 2020). Third, and consequently, environmental law enforcement calls for multi-agency cooperation between different public and private actors, which is difficult to organise (Spapens, 2014; Mehlbaum & Spapens, 2017; Spapens & Mehlbaum, 2019; Billiet et al., 2020). Finally, environmental crimes are often cross-border crimes, which call for law enforcement cooperation on different levels, which presents specific challenges, particularly when a case requires cooperation between countries in the Global North and Global South (Spapens, 2014; Spapens & Huisman, 2016; Spapens & Mehlbaum, 2019). This entry discusses these four major challenges and possible improvements.

Closing gaps in the enforcement chain

Adequate enforcement concerns the entire chain of actors involved and their capabilities. When an environmental crime remains undetected, investigation is impossible. Inspectors at administrative enforcement agencies and police detectives may be effective in collecting evidence on the ground, but when public prosecutors and courts fail to follow up, their work will have limited added value to protecting the environment. However, adequate enforcement starts with awareness at the political and policy levels that decide upon investigative priorities and which resources to allocate to the environmental enforcement chain.

Environmental rule violations regularly cause public concern, particularly when green crimes cause pollution, affect human health and well-being and seriously damage the environment. Such issues may be put on the agenda by local interest groups, NGOs (non-government organisations), journalists, politicians, scientists, and other actors.

However, this may not directly result in stricter enforcement actions and increasing awareness therefore requires a sustained process. One reason is that damaging effects may be local or the sum of small-scale violations and thereby less visible. Second, damaging effects often emerge over time and may be difficult to separate from other legitimate activities that cause damage to the environment. Third, although events such as spills and fires may cause immediate damage and injury and involve direct responses by enforcement agencies, such mishaps can easily be framed as accidents, even when caused or aggravated by environmental rule violations. Finally, when perpetrators are large corporations, politicians and policymakers will balance economic interests and jobs against environmental interests and may choose to give perpetrators the opportunity to improve their conduct and repair the damage, instead of imposing harsh sanctions.

These factors all help to explain why environmental law enforcement usually suffers from a lack of political priority, and thus adequate staff numbers and resources, which is noted widely in green criminological literature. Furthermore, environmental crimes are often committed in rural and sometimes remote areas, where law enforcement is less present or unable to arrive at crime scenes quickly, particularly in the Global South where travel distances may be large (Mawby & Yarwood, 2016; Ungar, 2018; Ceccato & Abraham, 2022).

Environmental crimes often do not produce visible victims and are therefore under-reported with enforcement agencies. Humans may for instance not be aware of being victims of environmental rule violations (e.g., pollution-related health matters) (Pemberton, 2014). Non-human victims of course do not report at all. Consequently, enforcement agencies must actively detect rule violations themselves or rely on the help of other actors, including the general public. An example of the latter is a successful cell phone app developed in Romania, through which people could report sightings of timber transports, thus enabling the authorities to perform real-time checks of whether the shipment had been notified and whether the truck was equipped with a mandatory GPS-tracking device (Spapens & Mehlbaum, 2019). In recent years new technical detection methods have become available, such as using DNA and spectrometric analysis, surveillance drones, and satellites (Stoett & Omrow, 2021). However, intelligence-led analyses and on-the-ground inspection remain necessary to successfully detect environmental crimes (Spapens, 2014; Gibbs, 2016; Mayer, 2019; Stoett & Omrow, 2021).

Investigating environmental crime is complex, particularly when suspected perpetrators are corporate actors (Spapens, 2014). Environmental regulations are often detailed, technically complex, and fall under the responsibility of different enforcement agencies. Consequently, successful enforcement requires specialised knowledge of different business activities and applicable legislation, as well as of the *modi operandi* of perpetrators. The difference between a valuable CITES-protected bird and a more common species may just be a red spot on its head, for example (van Uhm & Spapens, 2020). However, the police and the public prosecution service often lack specialised staff (Bisschop, 2012; Meško & Eman, 2020). Inspection agencies (such as health and safety agencies and environmental protection agencies) usually do have the necessary knowledge but are less experienced with gathering and presenting evidence that will hold up in a criminal case. Their orientation is generally forward-looking, in terms of ending regulatory offences and repairing the damage, whereas prosecuting and punishing perpetrators requires a backward-looking perspective (see also Sahramäki, 2016). In some cases, public prosecutors choose not to focus on environmental legislation but instead on common crimes such as document fraud and money laundering, although the latter may be more complicated in cases of crimes of omission (Huisman & van Erp, 2013). Another strategy may be to focus on relatively small and easy to prove rule violations, to justify extra inspections to be carried out by administrative bodies and inspection agencies. Criminal conviction may also jeopardise (future) operating permits. In the Netherlands, for example, environmental licences are subject to screening and may be denied to legal (e.g., corporations) and natural persons when authorities conclude there is a high risk that operating permits will be misused to facilitate criminal activities (Spapens, Peters & Vandaele, 2015).

Criminological research notes that only a small percentage of known environmental crimes lead to court cases (Akella & Cannon, 2009; Wellsmith, 2011; Sahramäki, 2016; Cochran et al., 2018). In developing countries, this may be associated with corruption problems (Wellsmith, 2011). In the Global North, investigators and prosecutors may also experience pressure, particularly from local and sometimes national governments, when economic interests are at stake. Well-respected board members of large companies are often well connected to politicians and authorities varying from the local and regional to national levels, and may for instance try to halt investigation. Public–private partnerships, in which for instance municipalities are co-owners with a private operator, mean that suspected rule violations can be particularly sensitive. Furthermore, when confronted with criminal investigation, large corporations immediately hire high-end law firms that will use every procedural trick in the book to frustrate investigations, and often threaten potential witnesses with damage claims (Spapens, 2014). All of this may put public prosecutors and enforcement agency staff under enormous pressure.

Specialised public prosecutors and judges may contribute to successfully responding to environmental crimes. The European Network of Prosecutors for the Environment (ENPE) now comprises members from 31 countries, including Latin American and North African states. In Latin America, specialised units have been established in 13 countries, of which some also train prosecutors in environmental law (Ungar, 2018). White (2013, 2022) points to the added value of specialised environmental courts, which for instance have been established in New South Wales in Australia. As of 2015, six Latin American countries had established separate courts or court branches for environmental cases (Ungar, 2018).

Nevertheless, criminal prosecution in environmental crime cases remains problematic, and sentences are usually low, and in cases of corporate crime often limited to financial penalties (Billiet & Rousseau, 2014; Eurojust, 2014). Natural persons, particularly at the management level, are prosecuted mostly when authorities decide to pursue cases to send a signal to society, or to enable administrative enforcement agencies to take action. In other situations, corporations will usually settle cases out of court when chances of conviction are deemed relatively high. Billiet and colleagues (2020) also pointed at trade-offs between remedial and punitive sanctions, in which the latter will be dropped or moderated in favour of the former.

Court actors may be less familiar with harms associated with environmental crimes and less willing to pursue incarceration or other severe punishments for such crimes, with the exception of wildlife and animal offenders (Billiet & Rousseau, 2014). However, practical issues may also play a role. In the Netherlands, for example, suspects of environmental rule violations are not subjected to pre-trial detention, and therefore courts do not schedule such cases with high priority, leading to delays of several years, which judges take into account when imposing their sentences. Of course, punishing perpetrators is not an end in itself, and environmental rule violations may be disrupted in a number of ways. Corporate offenders are usually more concerned about their image and reputation, and the deterrent effect of 'naming and shaming' may be far higher than being convicted (van Wingerde, 2012).

Complexities in enforcing environmental legislation

Environmental legislation covers a wide range of activities, and perpetrators differ from individuals to criminal groups and corporate offenders. As most activities are regulated, legal persons are involved in most types of environmental crimes. These may be legitimate corporations which commit rule violations within the context of their regular business activities, as well as criminal groups which establish (shell) companies specifically to facilitate environmental crimes. Environmental legislation is usually sector specific, for instance mining, waste shipments and waste treatment, air, water and sound pollution, and trade in protected wildlife (Ungar, 2018).

Sometimes legislation is simple. For example, there is not much to discuss when a person is caught illegally dumping waste on public grounds or poaching protected wildlife. However, when corporate activities become more complex, so are the environmental rules that must be complied with (Spapens, 2014). Operating a chemical plant, for example, requires many permits, based on different (environmental) laws. Technical standards, for instance on thresholds of pollution, are usually included in lower-level regulations and in a company's specific operating licences, and both may be adapted from time to time. Operators usually have profound understanding of their business processes and accompanying regulations, as well as how to use these to their advantage (Sahramäki et al., 2017; van Uhm & Spapens, 2020; Lavorgna & Sajeva, 2021).

In practice, the complexity of regulations offers many loopholes that malicious operators can exploit. Furthermore, regulators have not always focused on enforceability when drawing up legislation, or it does not contain requirements to criminalise violations. One example is the Convention on the Trade in Endangered Species (CITES), which does not apply to captive bred wildlife, whereas it is extremely difficult to distinguish from fauna that has been caught in the wild (van Uhm, 2016; Wyatt, 2022). Another is the Basel Convention on the Control of Transboundary Movements of Hazardous Wastes and their Disposal, which lacks a clear definition of waste (Brownell, 2011). In addition, countries that have ratified these conventions have implemented specific provisions slightly differently in their national legislation. This for instance applies to implementation of the EU Waste Shipment Regulation, which allows perpetrators the opportunity to choose to operate in countries where specific articles have been interpreted rather leniently (Mehlbaum & Spapens, 2017).

Legislation is further complicated by the fact that environmental regulations may be included in different areas of law: criminal; civil (non-criminal disputes); administrative (covering state agencies); and commercial (covering other natural resource use). Regulations may be drawn up and enforced at the national level, but particularly in operating licences, regional and local authorities may set specific requirements (Ungar, 2018).

The need for multi-agency cooperation

Environmental law enforcement involves different agencies. Administrative enforcement agencies, customs, the tax authority, the police and the public prosecution service may all be drawn in to handle cases, depending on a country's legal system, the type of environmental crime, the severity of the impact of the crime, whether human injuries occur, the type of perpetrator, the level of criminal intent, and other variables. In response, Interpol has developed a programme to support individual countries to establish multi-agency taskforces called *National Environmental Security Taskforces* or NESTs. Their objective is to bring together expertise from various law enforcement agencies (Stewart, 2014; White, 2016; Stoett & Omrow, 2021). Depending on the risks and types of economic activities, local, regional or national administrative agencies may be competent to issue permits and be responsible for first-line inspection and enforcement, although the latter may also be (partly) delegated to other agencies, for instance the fire department for checking environmental safety regulations, or health inspectors in cases of shipments of live (protected) animals.

Although administrative enforcement agencies have a range of tools at their disposal, varying from issuing formal warnings and imposing financial penalties, to shutting down business activities, their main concern is to stop environmental rule violations and to have the damage repaired, and not primarily to punish offenders. The customs service hold responsibility for checking incoming and outgoing shipments of goods, including wildlife and wildlife products and waste (Mehlbaum & Spapens, 2017). Criminal law enforcement agencies have the advantage of being able to employ different investigation methods, including covert ones such as wiretapping and surveillance. However, few countries have specialised environmental law investigation teams, and generally trained police officers may be less familiar with complex environmental regulations, or have less affinity with environmental crimes (Spapens, 2014).

Environmental law enforcement therefore greatly benefits from multi-agency cooperation, for instance in joint investigation teams, in which knowledge about environmental legislation, specific business processes, and species of flora and fauna, usually present in administrative enforcement agencies and customs, is combined with investigative expertise available from the police, ideally guided by public prosecutors who specialise in environmental law and economic offences. Yet, for practical and judicial reasons, such cooperation is challenging (Spapens, 2014; Sahramäki, 2016).

For instance, multi-agency cooperation requires national legislation on information exchange. Instead of full-fledged joint investigation, enforcement agencies may also 'work apart together' in coordinated efforts. Administrative enforcement agencies, for instance, cannot apply covert investigation methods, and acquiring hard proof of environmental offences is therefore time-consuming, unless calamities occur. The police may therefore use their investigative tools to perform a small-scale criminal investigation aiming at a conviction. A conviction often allows administrative enforcement agencies to impose a stricter inspection regime, or other measures that are far more effective than a conviction as such. Performing joint inspections, for instance of goods shipments or factories, may also be of added value. During such inspections, each agency performs checks based on its own legal competences, and exchange information when for instance a criminal offence has been noted. Public servants are usually required to report knowledge of a criminal offence to the competent authority, usually the public prosecution service. Finally, cooperation with NGOs, which may possess specific expertise, may be helpful during inspection or investigation (Billiet et al., 2020; White, 2021).

Cross-border law enforcement cooperation

Environmental crime is in many ways cross-border crime. For example, illegal activities may be transnational in their effect, such as the pollution of air and water. Second, the 'business process' of environmental criminal acts may be international in scope, such as the trafficking of hazardous waste and wildlife. Third, members of criminal groups responsible for illegal activity may be operating in two or more countries. Finally, cross-border environmental cybercrime may occur, for example fraud in emission trading schemes. In each of these cases, cross-border police cooperation may be necessary to tackle the problem (Spapens, 2014). Effective cooperation, however, is often far from simple.

Cross-border law enforcement cooperation comprises both operational and non-operational cooperation. The first refers to inspection and investigation, in order to collect indications or evidence of rule violations. Non-operational cooperation covers supporting activities, such as joint training of police officers, the exchange of good practices and techniques, and network-building.

Operational law enforcement cooperation

Territorial sovereignty remains a leading principle in operational law enforcement cooperation (Spapens & Mehlbaum, 2019). Only in very specific and limited circumstances will states tolerate (independent) activities of foreign law enforcement agencies on their territory. Instead, cooperation is based upon a system of request when it concerns collection of information and evidence, although information may also be exchanged spontaneously. Regarding criminal law enforcement cooperation, and to a lesser extent customs cooperation, there exists a legal framework to enable cooperation, as well as a supporting formalised or informal infrastructure to facilitate exchange of requests for mutual legal assistance and cooperation, provided for instance by Interpol, Europol and the World Customs Organization. However, such a legal framework is largely missing when it comes to operational cross-border cooperation between administrative enforcement agencies, and these must rely on case-by-case arrangements, which are slow to materialise because these need to comply with meta legislation, such as human rights conventions and data protection laws.

Criminal law enforcement cooperation depends on a patchwork of multilateral and bilateral conventions, which state requirements for drawing up requests for mutual legal assistance and which type of assistance, for instance information, interrogation of suspects, house searches and application of special investigation methods. The police may exchange information directly via Interpol, as do customs via the Environet platform, or through their networks of liaisons. Such information may, however, not be used before the court unless this is authorised by the public prosecution service or the Ministry of Justice, and restrictions may apply to non-democratic states or countries that execute the death penalty.

Finally, hardly any arrangements exist for 'diagonal' cooperation, particularly between criminal law and administrative enforcement agencies, and here, similar barriers apply. In some cases, so-called 'U-turns' have been taken, in other words the exchange of information via police channels, and passing it on to administrative enforcement agencies based on national legislation. However, in the EU the GDPR (General Data Protection Regulation) has virtually closed such escape routes. There remains a 'grey zone' of 'informal' exchange of information, but the downside is that it cannot be officially used as a starting point for investigation or in the courts, whereas such exchange is also vulnerable to liability complaints.

Non-operational cooperation

Institutions such as Interpol, the World Customs Organization, and informal networks such as INECE (International Network for Environmental Compliance and Enforcement) and IMPEL (EU Network for the Implementation and Enforcement of Environmental Law) have taken many initiatives to improve the quality of both administrative and criminal law enforcement cooperation, for instance by organising seminars, providing training and technical support abroad, drawing up manuals, building networks and establishing contact points, as well as basing liaison officers in for instance the Global South. Such networks may also engage in promoting operational actions, such as the Demeter operations by the World Customs Organization, in which participating countries simultaneously inspect waste shipments during a specific period of time, exchange information and allow foreign staff to be present during inspections in order to learn from each other's expertise. Interpol has promoted on the ground multi-agency cooperation in NESTs and experimented with these in projects such as Project Leaf (illegal logging) and Project Scale (illegal fisheries) (Stewart, 2014; Stoett & Omrow, 2021). Environmental police officers (EnviCrimeNet), public prosecutors (ENPE) and judges (EUFJE) also have their own informal networks, which have on occasion organised joint seminars.

Cross-border law enforcement cooperation with states where law enforcement is weak

Transnational environmental crime, particularly wildlife and illicit waste trafficking and dumping, often involves states in the Global South where political corruption is a problem, leaving the country vulnerable to powerful actors internally as well as from the Global North. Simultaneously, environmental enforcement agencies in these countries will usually be understaffed and ill-equipped. Criminal law enforcement, in particular, will be reluctant to cooperate for fear that information on ongoing investigations may be disclosed to suspects, and expect that those prosecuted and convicted will be able to escape punishment anyway. Enforcement agencies in the Global North may sometimes prefer to cooperate with NGOs who have people on the ground in developing countries, but this may present a substantial risk to their safety and poses problems with using the collected information in court cases.

Conclusion

This entry has discussed many difficulties that confront environmental law enforcement. On a positive note, attention to environmental issues is growing in general, and many dedicated staff currently address environmental crimes. At the same time effective environmental law enforcement remains a 'wicked problem' and much can be improved, in terms of multi-agency and cross-border cooperation, legislation, and most importantly, sufficient numbers of well-trained and equipped personnel.

TOINE SPAPENS

Further reading

Billiet, C., Boogers, S., Dimec, K., Weissová, K., Nési, F., Wüst, A., van Die, E., & Girón Conde, L. (2020). *Sanctioning Environmental Crime (WG4) Final Report: Key Observations and Recommendations.* LIFE-ENPE Project.

Mehlbaum, S., & Spapens, T. (2017). *Enforcing the EU-WSR: Challenges of Cross-Border Cooperation.* Project BlockWaste.

Spapens, T., & Huisman, W. (2016). Tackling cross-border environmental crime: A 'wicked problem'. In T. Spapens, R. White, & W. Huisman (Eds.), *Environmental Crime in Transnational Context* (pp. 27–42). Routledge.

Stoett, P., & Omrow, D. (2021). *Spheres of Transnational Ecoviolence: Environmental*

Crime, Human Security, and Justice. Palgrave Macmillan.
Walters, R., & Westerhuis, D. (2013). Green crime and the role of environmental courts. *Crime, Law & Social Change*, 59, 279–290.
White, R. (2016). Building NESTs to combat environmental crime networks. *Trends in Organized Crime*, 19, 88–105.

References

Akella, A., & Cannon, J. (2009). Strengthening the weakest links: Strategies for improving the enforcement of environmental laws globally. In R. White (Ed.), *Environmental Crime: A Reader* (pp. 528–567). Willan Publishing.
Billiet, C., & Rousseau, S. (2014). How real is the threat of imprisonment for environmental crime? *European Journal of Law and Economics*, 37, 183–198.
Billiet, C., Boogers, S., Dimec, K., Weissová, K., Nési, F., Wüst, A., van Die, E., & Girón Conde, L. (2020). *Sanctioning Environmental Crime (WG4) Final Report: Key Observations and Recommendations*. LIFE-ENPE Project.
Bisschop, L. (2012). Is it all going to waste? Illegal transports of e-waste in a European trade hub. *Crime, Law & Social Change*, 58, 221–249.
Brownell, E. (2011). Negotiating the new economic order of waste. *Environmental History*, 16(2), 262–289.
Ceccato, V. & Abraham, J. (2022). *Crime and Safety in Rural Areas: Lessons from Research*. Springer.
Cochran, J., Lynch, M., Toman, E., & Shields, R. (2018). Court sentencing patterns for environmental crimes: Is there a 'green' gap in punishment? *Journal of Quantitative Criminology*, 34, 37–66.
Eurojust (2014). *Strategic Project on Environmental Crime*. Eurojust.
Gibbs, C. (2016). Addressing transnational environmental crime. In T. Spapens, R. White, & W. Huisman (Eds.), *Environmental Crime in Transnational Context* (pp. 85–100). Routledge.
Huisman, W., & van Erp, J. (2013). Opportunities for environmental crime. *British Journal of Criminology*, 53, 1178–1200.
Lavorgna, A., & Sajevo, M. (2021). Studying illegal online trades in plants: Market characteristics, organisational and behavioural aspects, and policing challenges. *European Journal on Criminal Policy and Research*, 27, 451–470.
Mawby, R., & Yarwood, R. (Eds.) (2016). *Rural Policing and Policing the Rural: A Constable Countryside?* Routledge.
Mayer, C. (2019). *Combating Wildlife Crime in South Africa*. Springer.
Mehlbaum, S., & Spapens, T. (2017). *Enforcing the EU-WSR: Challenges of Cross-Border Cooperation*. Project BlockWaste.
Meško, G., & Eman, K. (2020). Policing water crimes. In K. Eman, G. Meško, L. Segato, & M. Migliorini (Eds.), *Water, Governance, and Crime Issues* (pp. 75–91). Springer Nature Switzerland.
Nurse, A. (2022). Green criminology, policing and protecting the environment. In J. Gacek & R. Jochelson (Eds.), *Green Criminology and the Law* (pp. 39–60). Palgrave Macmillan.
Pemberton, A. (2014). Environmental victims and criminal justice: Proceed with caution. In T. Spapens, R. White, & M. Kluin (Eds.), *Environmental Crime and its Victims* (pp. 63–86). Ashgate.
Sahramäki, I. (2016). Enforcement and professional constructions of environmental crime in Finland. In G. Potter, A. Nurse, & M. Hall (Eds.), *The Geography of Environmental Crime* (pp. 189–216). Palgrave Macmillan.
Sahramäki, I., Favarin, S., Mehlbaum, S., Savona, E., Spapens, T., & Kankaanranta, T. (2017). Wasting opportunities: Prevention of illicit cross-border waste trafficking. *European Journal of Policing Studies*, 5(2), 1–61.
Sollund, R., Stefes, C., & Germani, A. (Eds., 2016). *Fighting Environmental Crime in Europe and Beyond: The Role of the EU and its Member States*. Palgrave Macmillan.
Spapens, T. (2014). Invisible victims: The problem of policing environmental crime. In T. Spapens, R. White, & M. Kluin (Eds.), *Environmental Crime and its Victims: Perspectives within Green Criminology* (pp. 221–236). Ashgate.
Spapens, T., & Huisman, W. (2016). Tackling cross-border environmental crime: A 'wicked problem'. In T. Spapens, R. White, & W. Huisman (Eds.), *Environmental Crime in Transnational Context* (pp. 27–42). Routledge.
Spapens, T., & Mehlbaum, S. (2019). Policing and prosecution of transnational environmental crime. In V. Mitsilegas, S. Hufnagel, & A. Moiseienko (Eds.), *Research Handbook on Transnational Crime* (pp. 171–182). Edward Elgar Publishing.
Spapens, T., Peters, M., & Van Daele, D. (2015). *Administrative Measures to Prevent and Tackle Crime*. Eleven International Publishing.
Stewart, D. (2014). Project LEAF and Interpol's work on illegal logging and forest crime. In T. Spapens, R. White, & M. Kluin (Eds.), *Environmental Crime and Its Victims:*

Perspectives within Green Criminology (pp. 237–247). Ashgate.
Stoett, P., & Omrow, D. (2021). *Spheres of Transnational Ecoviolence: Environmental Crime, Human Security, and Justice*. Palgrave Macmillan.
Ungar, M. (2018). Introduction: The evolution of environmental enforcement. In M. Ungar (Ed.), *The 21st Century Fight for the Amazon* (pp. 1–20). Palgrave Macmillan.
van Uhm, D. (2016). *Uncovering the Illegal Wildlife Trade: In the World of Poachers, Smugglers and Traders*. Springer.
van Uhm, D., & Spapens, T. (2020). Illegal trade in protected birds in the Netherlands: Three criminological perspectives. In P. van Duyne, D. Siegel, G. Antonopoulos, J. Harvey, & K. von Lampe (Eds.), *Criminal Defiance in Europe and Beyond: From Organised Crime to Crime–Terror Nexus* (pp. 217–243). Eleven International Publishing.
van Wingerde, K. (2012). *De afschrikking voorbij*. Wolf Legal Publishers.
Wellsmith, M. (2011). Wildlife crime: The problem of enforcement. *European Journal on Criminal Policy and Research*, 17, 125–148.
White, R. (2013). Environmental crime and problem-solving courts. *Crime, Law and Social Change*, 59, 267–278.
White, R. (2016). Building NESTs to combat environmental crime networks. *Trends in Organized Crime*, 19, 88–105.
White, R. (2021). United Nations initiatives in preventing environmental crime. In H. Kury & S. Redo (Eds.), *Crime Prevention and Justice in 2030* (pp. 253–274). Springer Nature Switzerland.
White, R. (2022). Environmental crime, ecological expertise and specialist environment courts. In J. Gacek & R. Jochelson (Eds.), *Green Criminlogy and the Law* (pp. 61–83). Palgrave Macmillan.
Wyatt, T. (2022). *Wildlife Trafficking: A Deconstruction of the Crime, the Victims, and the Offenders* (2nd ed.). Palgrave Macmillan.

49. Environmental restorative justice

Introduction

Environmental restorative justice is the application of the principles and processes of restorative justice to environmental concerns. Predominantly, this has involved the use of conferencing, as a facilitated dialogue and interaction between stakeholders, following environmental offending either as a diversion from prosecution or embedded in the prosecution process and considered in sentencing. Evolution of thought surrounding environmental restorative justice sees its usefulness also in a proactive manner at the application, approval, and implementation stages of major projects; for environmental harm arising from sanctioned activity; and as permeating the entire regulatory spectrum. While some may talk in terms of the principles of restorative justice (Zehr 2015: 43, 83–88), others talk in terms of values (Braithwaite 2000), signposts (Zehr 2015: 51), accounts (Braithwaite 1999), guiding questions (Zehr 2015: 49), central tenets (Hamilton 2021: 88–92), or key attributes (Forsyth et al. 2021: 20, 29–36). Each has at their cores the notion that restorative justice processes are inclusive and aim to repair the harm that has been caused by crime or conflict, or more broadly, decision-making. Traditionally in an environmental context, restorative justice processes have been used following offending in two different ways. First, as a diversion from prosecution (the so-called front-end model). Second, embedded within the prosecution process itself (the so-called back-end model). These models conceive 'environmental offending' quite broadly to encompass pollution, planning breaches and offending against Aboriginal cultural heritage. What all of these variants of offending have in common is the fact that the very unlawfulness is a result of not having obtained, or having breached, a permit, approval, licence, or consent.

Drawing inspiration from green criminology, there has been recent exploration of the potential of restorative justice in the context of sanctioned (i.e., lawful) activity which negatively affects the environment (Hamilton 2022a). Some have suggested that rather than waiting for harm to arise before deploying restorative justice, its processes could be used in a 'pro-active' way 'throughout the application, approval and implementation process for major projects, … to enhance public participation and improve environmental outcomes' (Wilson 2016: 252). Others, in what promises to be the new frontier of environmental restorative justice, envision environmental restorative justice permeating 'the entire regulatory spectrum … [fostering] a cultural commitment to thinking restoratively *at all stages* of regulatory processes' (Forsyth et al. 2021: 17, 29).

Having introduced environmental restorative justice, the remainder of this entry will flesh out some central features. Namely:

- the *principles of environmental restorative justice*;
- the *practice of environmental restorative justice*;
- *proactive* (environmental) *restorative justice*;
- environmental restorative justice in the context of *lawful but awful activity*; and
- environmental restorative justice permeation through the *entire regulatory spectrum*.

As discussed, there are several key dimensions of environmental restorative justice that warrant sustained attention and future study.

Principles of environmental restorative justice

The principles of environmental restorative justice are captured by Hamilton's (2021) central tenets. First, 'crime [and conflict are] … a violation of people and relationships' (Hamilton 2021: 88); 'humans are profoundly relational. There is a fundamental need to be in good relationship with others' because 'humans are communal' (Pranis 2011: 64–65). Such violation dictates that 'responses to crime [and conflict] should be inclusive' (second central tenet) (Hamilton 2021: 89), because '[i]nterrelationships imply mutual obligations and responsibilities' (Zehr 2015: 29), requiring 'the active involvement of stakeholders' (Hamilton 2021: 90). If responses to crime and conflict are to be inclusive (second central tenet), dictated by the fact that crime and conflict are a violation of people and relationships (first central tenet), then it follows that 'responses to crime [and conflict] should heal and put things right' (third central tenet) (Hamilton 2021: 90). The exact responses to heal and put things right will be highlighted when the front-end and back-end models of environmental restorative justice are explored shortly.

Forsyth et al. (2021) capture the principles of environmental restorative justice in their 'key attributes'. Environmental restorative justice is '[f]undamentally oriented towards *healing*, often of multiple harms, including relational and physical harm to humans/more-than-humans, inclusive of nature'; is '[b]ased on requiring direct (not delegated) *participation* of those with power to take responsibility and make changes, and those who have suffered harm (inclusive of more-than-humans)'; is '[b]ased on *storytelling* and *dialogue*'; is '[d]ependent on *identifiable harm, identifiable victims* and *identifiable individuals, groups or institutions who take responsibility for harm*'; and, is '[g]eared towards ensuring *accountability* of those who have created harm to those who have suffered harm, to achieve relational justice' (Forsyth et al. 2021: 20; emphasis original).

Together these summary outlines describe the conceptual framework within which varied practical expressions of core environmental restorative justice principles are concretely manifested.

Practice(s) of environmental restorative justice

There is a plethora of restorative justice processes which have been deployed around the world following crime. The United Nations Office on Drugs and Crime ('UNODC') (2020: 24) categorises the three main categories of processes as victim–offender mediation (also known as victim–offender conciliation), restorative conferencing, and circles. According to UNODC, victim–offender mediation is the most common restorative justice process and features a facilitated discussion between victim and offender. Restorative conferences (such as family group conferences and community conferences) are differentiated from victim–offender mediation by the presence of a wider number of 'stakeholders' – 'other persons affected by the offence, such as family members, friends, community representatives, and, depending on the model, the police or other professionals, are brought together by an impartial third party who acts as a facilitator of the conference' (UNODC 2020: 27). Circles are generally used in the context of Indigenous offending and 'can be used to facilitate the sentencing process' (UNODC 2020: 30), often with the involvement of Indigenous Elders. While there is no particular magic attached to the name given to the use of restorative justice processes in an environmental context, one of the common descriptions is 'restorative justice conferencing'. As will be revealed, such conferencing can involve victims, offenders, and other relevant stakeholders, under the guidance of an independent facilitator.

Before exploring the front-end and back-end models of environmental restorative justice conferencing, it is worth exploring three features of environmental offending which make it different from mainstream offending (for want of a better phrase) and provide challenges for the use of restorative justice conferencing in that context. First, the victims of environmental offending are diverse – 'humans (currently living and future generations), communities (Indigenous and non-Indigenous), the environment (and its constituent parts – flora, fauna, and ecosystems) and commercial operators' (Hamilton 2021: 22). Each victim may have different needs, and the fact that some victims cannot talk (either because they are non-human, or because they will be human but are not born yet) means that they will need some sort of representation at conferencing through a human guardian or representative. This then leads to a consideration of who the best representative may be.

Second, perpetrators of environmental crime can be human, but predominantly are organisational offenders (such as corporations and government entities such as a council or utility provider) (Hamilton 2019: Figure 5). In terms of organisational offenders, this means establishing whether the organisation is suitable for attendance at conferencing, and if so, who is the best person to represent the organisation.

Third, even though environmental crime may be deliberate, it may also be accidental or negligent (Hamilton 2019: Figure 3). This may have implications for the 'blameworthiness' of an offender and therefore their desire to attend conferencing. All of these considerations must be at the forefront of any decision to hold an environmental restorative justice conference and may place additional responsibilities/burdens on a facilitator.

Front-end model of environmental restorative justice conferencing

Conferences are used in the front-end model to *divert* matters away from prosecution. Typically, this model entails a five-step process, designated as commencement/invitation, adjournment, conference, outcome fulfilment, and withdrawal (Hamilton 2022b: 597–600). The five steps are based on Environment Canterbury's (New Zealand) 'Alternative Environmental Justice' Scheme and may not be identical for all such schemes. Other New Zealand front-end model schemes include those by Environment Southland and West Coast Regional Council. Stage one sees the prosecutorial authority file a prosecution with the relevant court while simultaneously assessing whether the offender is suitable for conferencing. Where the offender is deemed suitable, an invitation will be extended to participate in conferencing. Where the conference is to proceed, stage two involves the prosecution seeking an adjournment of proceedings so that the conference can occur. The conference itself is stage three and will see the bringing together of stakeholders (offender, victims (or representatives), support people, community members, the prosecutor) before an independent facilitator. The conference provides the opportunity for stakeholder dialogue and interaction in an effort to devise outcomes to repair the harm that has been occasioned by the offending. The fourth stage allows the fulfilment of the outcome agreement by the offender. Examples of some of the outcomes decided at conferencing come from New Zealand through conferencing held as part of Environment Canterbury's 'Alternative Environmental Justice' Scheme. Outcomes include an offender agreeing to run a training programme for others in the industry, the making of donations to a wetland planning project and to stream care groups, a farmer presentation to Federated Farmers of New Zealand groups about his offending, remedies, and how to avoid such offending (McLachlan 2014: 23), payment to plant willows for river protection, and payment for the implementation of a native planting trial to see how the native plants stand up against willow (Environment Canterbury Regional Council 2017). The fifth stage of the front-end model involves the prosecutor seeking the leave of the court to withdraw the charges and hence effectively ending the prosecution. For the leave to be granted the prosecution must demonstrate to the court that it 'followed a principled and robust process' leading to the conclusion that the prosecution is no longer in the public interest (*Canterbury Regional Council v Bathurst Coal Limited* [2019] NZDC 14416, [25]; for an exploration of the public interest, see Crown Law Office 2013).

Back-end model of environmental restorative justice conferencing

Conferences in the back-end model are *embedded* in the prosecution process, meaning that the fact of the conferencing occurring, and the outcomes derived at conferencing, can be considered by the court when sentencing an offender. Typically, this model entails a five-step process, designated as commencement, establishment/determination, suitability, conference, and sentencing (Hamilton 2022b: 600–601). Stage one sees the prosecutorial authority file a prosecution with the relevant court. Stage two is concerned with the determination of the facts surrounding the offending, and the ascertaining of guilt which will invariably come in the form of a guilty plea if the matter is to progress to a conference. The assessment of the suitability of a conference is a part of stage three and generally requires voluntary participation by an identified victim, and non-coerced participation of an offender who accepts responsibility for their offending (UNODC 2006: 8). Contrition and remorse have been proffered as indicia of an offender's acceptance of responsibility for offending (Al-Alosi and Hamilton 2019; 2021). Stage four sees the proceedings adjourned and the conference held. In some jurisdictions there are express legislative provisions which permit the use of restorative justice conferencing, while in other jurisdictions the power to adjourn proceedings and to consider conferencing in sentencing is an exercise of judicial discretion to case manage proceedings (Hamilton 2022c). The conference provides the opportunity for victim and offender voice, interaction, and input (Hamilton 2021: 157–159), culminating in an outcome agreement designed to repair the harm that has been occasioned by the offending. Outcomes can include various donations, strengthening of relationships between offenders and victims, commitments to avoid future offending, apology, and various projects (McDonald 2008: 43; Hamilton 2021: 135–137, 147, 150). Following the conference, the matter is returned to court for sentencing, which comprises stage five of the process.

For an overview of the use of the back-end model of environmental restorative justice, readers are directed to the cases of *Garrett v Williams* (2007) 151 LGERA 92; [2007] NSWLEC 96, *Chief Executive, Office of Environment and Heritage v Clarence Valley Council* (2018) 236 LGERA 291; [2018] NSWLEC 205, and *Canterbury Regional Council v Interflow (NZ) Limited* [2015] NZDC 3323, and the academic exploration thereof (McDonald 2008; Preston 2011; Sugrue 2015; Pain et al. 2016; Ashton and Etherington 2018; Pain 2018; Smith 2019).

Proactive restorative justice

Wilson's conceptualisation of 'proactive' restorative justice is concerned with the front-end use of restorative justice 'throughout the application, approval and implementation process for major projects, … to enhance public participation and improve environmental outcomes' (Wilson 2016: 252), rather than confining conferencing to the back end when offending has occurred. Wilson envisages four restorative justice principles which will aid the use of restorative justice for major projects, those being constructive dialogue, knowledge sharing, allocation of benefits to local or Indigenous communities, and focus on preventing future harm.

Hamilton draws on Wilson's conceptualisation to suggest the use of environmental restorative justice in the context of sanctioned activity (that is, the lawful but awful, drawing the phrase from Passas 2005). Such work is also inspired by the focus of green criminology on environmental harm, recognising the fact that a lot (if not the majority) of environmental harm (including climate change) comes from sanctioned activity. In the context of lawful but awful activity, Hamilton sees the use of restorative justice at the pre-operation stage of a project 'as a means of delineating the expected environmental harm and explaining why such environmental harms are unavoidable, as a forum to explore some of the benefits to bestow on the local community through the activity or project, and, to establish a social licence to operate' (Hamilton 2022a: 379). It is assumed that the design process has led to these projects having the lowest possible impact on the environment. Where design changes can result in better environmental outcomes, this can be discussed at the proactive restorative justice conference.

In what promises to be the new frontier of environmental restorative justice, Forsyth et al. envision environmental restorative justice permeating 'the entire regulatory spectrum … [fostering] a cultural commitment to thinking restoratively *at all stages* of regulatory processes' (Forsyth et al. 2021: 17, 29; emphasis original). Such a 'conceptualisation … seeks to forge a new vision in which humans pursue a harmonious, restorative relationship towards nature and with each other' (Forsyth et al. 2021: 36). Only time will tell how this new frontier of environmental restorative justice manifests in practice and what concrete benefits it will bring.

Conclusion

Environmental restorative justice involves a democratisation of justice engagement through the inclusion of both human and non-human interests and stakeholders (via advocates and experts). A key aspect of environmental restorative justice is repairing harm and providing for good environmental outcomes. Once confined to the aftermath of environmental offending, either as a diversion from prosecution or embedded in prosecution, restorative justice is being increasingly considered in the aftermath of environmental harm caused by lawful but awful activities. Restorative justice is also being considered in the application, approval, and implementation stages of development, and indeed throughout the entire regulatory spectrum, to enhance public participation and environmental outcomes, and to foster restorative relationships among humans and nature.

MARK HAMILTON

Further reading

Al-Alosi, H., & Hamilton, M. (2019). The Ingredients of Success for Effective Restorative Justice Conferencing in an Environmental Offending Context. *University of New South Wales Law Journal 42*(4), 1460–1488.

Al-Alosi, H., & Hamilton, M. (2021). The Potential of Restorative Justice in Achieving Acceptance of Responsibility in the Context of

Environmental Crimes. *University of New South Wales Law Journal 44*(2), 487–512.
Forsyth, M., Cleland, D., Tepper, F., Hollingworth, D., Soares, M., Nairn, A., & Wilkinson, C. (2021). A Future Agenda for Environmental Restorative Justice? *The International Journal of Restorative Justice 4*(1), 17–40.
Hamilton, M. (2019). *Restorative Justice Conferencing in Response to Pollution Offending: A Vehicle for the Achievement of Justice as Meaningful Involvement* (PhD Dissertation). UNSW.
Hamilton, M. (2021). *Environmental Crime and Restorative Justice: Justice as Meaningful Involvement.* Cham: Palgrave Macmillan.
Hamilton, M. (2022a). Restorative Justice Conferencing: A Vehicle for Repairing Harm Emanating from Lawful but Awful Activity. In J. Gacek & R. Jochelson (Eds.), *Green Criminology and the Law* (pp. 361–386). Cham: Palgrave Macmillan.
Hamilton, M. (2022b). Restorative Justice Conferencing in a New Zealand Environmental Offending Context: Two Models. In B. Pali & M. Forsyth (Eds.), *The Palgrave Handbook of Environmental Restorative Justice* (pp. 593–616). Cham: Palgrave Macmillan.
Wilson, C. (2016). Proactive Restorative Justice: A Set of Principles for Enhancing Public Participation. *Environmental Planning Law Journal 33*(3), 252–263.
Zehr, H. (2015). *The Little Book of Restorative Justice: Revised and Updated.* New York: Good Books.

References

Al-Alosi, H., & Hamilton, M. (2019). The Ingredients of Success for Effective Restorative Justice Conferencing in an Environmental Offending Context. *University of New South Wales Law Journal 42*(4), 1460–1488.
Al-Alosi, H., & Hamilton, M. (2021). The Potential of Restorative Justice in Achieving Acceptance of Responsibility in the Context of Environmental Crimes. *University of New South Wales Law Journal 44*(2), 487–512.
Ashton, S., & Etherington, S. (2018). Chief Executive, Office of Environment and Heritage v Clarence Valley Council. *Newcastle Law Review 13*, 86–91.
Braithwaite, J. (1999). Restorative Justice: Assessing Optimistic and Pessimistic Accounts. *Crime and Justice 25*, 1–127.
Braithwaite, J. (2000). Restorative Justice and Social Justice. *Saskatchewan Law Review 63*(1), 185–194.
Canterbury Regional Council v Bathurst Coal Limited [2019] NZDC 14416.
Canterbury Regional Council v Interflow (NZ) Limited [2015] NZDC 3323.
Chief Executive, Office of Environment and Heritage v Clarence Valley Council (2018) 236 LGERA 291; [2018] NSWLEC 205.
Crown Law Office (2013). *Solicitor-General's Prosecution Guidelines* (as at 1 July).
Environment Canterbury Regional Council (2017). 'Illegal Clearing of Land' (Media Release, 6 April). https://www.ecan.govt.nz/get-involved/news-and-events/2017/illegal-clearing-of-land/.
Forsyth, M., Cleland, D., Tepper, F., Hollingworth, D., Soares, M., Nairn, A., & Wilkinson, C. (2021). A Future Agenda for Environmental Restorative Justice? *The International Journal of Restorative Justice 4*(1), 17–40.
Garrett v Williams (2007) 151 LGERA 92; [2007] NSWLEC 96.
Hamilton, M. (2019). *Restorative Justice Conferencing in Response to Pollution Offending: A Vehicle for the Achievement of Justice as Meaningful Involvement* (PhD Dissertation). UNSW.
Hamilton, M. (2021). *Environmental Crime and Restorative Justice: Justice as Meaningful Involvement.* Cham: Palgrave Macmillan.
Hamilton, M. (2022a). Restorative Justice Conferencing: A Vehicle for Repairing Harm Emanating from Lawful but Awful Activity. In J. Gacek & R. Jochelson (Eds.), *Green Criminology and the Law* (pp. 361–386). Cham: Palgrave Macmillan.
Hamilton, M. (2022b). Restorative Justice Conferencing in a New Zealand Environmental Offending Context: Two Models. In B. Pali & M. Forsyth (Eds.), *The Palgrave Handbook of Environmental Restorative Justice* (pp. 593–616). Cham: Palgrave Macmillan.
Hamilton, M. (2022c). Restorative Justice Conferencing in an Environmental Offending Context: The Role of Legislation. *Asia Pacific Journal of Environmental Law 25*(1), 51–76.
McDonald, J. M. (2008). Restorative Justice Process in Case Law. *Alternative Law Journal 33*(1), 41–44.
McLachlan, M. (2014). Environmental Justice in Canterbury. *Public Sector 37*(4), 22–23.
Pain, Hon Justice N. (2018). Encouraging Restorative Justice in Environmental Crime. *Newcastle Law Review 13*, 29–52.
Pain, Hon Justice N., Pepper, Hon Justice R., McCreath, M., & Zorzetto, J. (2016). Restorative

Justice for Environmental Crime: An Antipodean Experience. *Australian Environment Review 31*(8), 286–295.

Passas, N. (2005). Lawful but Awful: 'Legal Corporate Crimes'. *Journal of Socio-Economics 34*(6), 771–786.

Pranis, K. (2011). Restorative Values. In G. Johnstone & D. W. Van Ness (Eds.), *Handbook of Restorative Justice* (pp. 59–74). Abingdon: Routledge.

Preston, Hon Justice B. J. (2011). *The Use of Restorative Justice for Environmental Crime*. Paper Presentation, EPA Victoria Seminar on Restorative Environmental Justice, Melbourne, 22 March.

Smith, D. (2019). Case Note: Chief Executive, Office of Environment and Heritage v Clarence Valley Council. *Australian Environment Review 34*(1), 16–18.

Sugrue, V. (2015). What Happens when Values Are Put to Work? A Reflection in One Outcome from a Restorative Justice Conference in the Criminal Division of the District Court: Environment Warranted Judge Jurisdiction. *Resource Management Journal*, 19–22.

UNODC (2006). *Handbook on Restorative Justice Programmes*. Vienna: United Nations Office on Drugs and Crime.

UNODC (2020). *Handbook on Restorative Justice Programmes*. Vienna: United Nations.

Wilson, C. (2016). Proactive Restorative Justice: A Set of Principles for Enhancing Public Participation. *Environmental Planning Law Journal 33*(3), 252–263.

Zehr, H. (2015). *The Little Book of Restorative Justice: Revised and Updated*. New York: Good Books.

MARK HAMILTON

50. Non-speciesist criminology

Introduction

Non-speciesist criminologies adopt a species justice perspective in examining harms and crimes perpetrated against non-human animals. The terms 'non-human animals', 'animals', 'animals other than humans' and 'animals other than human animals' are used interchangeably throughout this entry. This is to problematise the human/animal binary and to reinforce the fact that humans are themselves animals. Non-speciesist criminology is grounded in a critique of conventional criminology, which routinely neglects the harming of animals or examines such harming through a speciesist lens. In delineating a non-speciesist criminology, this entry will begin by conceptualising 'speciesism', revealing that this phenomenon is deeply entrenched within systems of language and thought. The entry will then move on to consider the pervasive speciesism within criminological inquiry before turning to early and contemporary endeavours to develop a non-speciesist criminology that acknowledges the inherent rights and interests of animals. Following this, some core concepts within non-speciesist criminology are examined – including species justice, utilitarianism, animal rights, the ecofeminist care tradition, and the animal welfare–rights spectrum. The entry will then shift from theory to practice in considering some key issues deemed worthy of non-speciesist criminological attention and will finally reflect on some ways forward for a non-speciesist criminology.

Understanding speciesism

In pursuing a non-speciesist criminology, it is important to first interrogate the phenomenon of speciesism, which is pervasive not only within criminological inquiry but within language and culture more broadly. Whilst speciesist attitudes are discoverable throughout much of history, the term 'speciesism' itself did not enter the public lexicon until the 1970s (Ryder, 2009). It was coined by Richard R. Ryder in 1970 and popularised by Peter Singer in 1975 (Ryder, 2009; Singer, 2015 [1975]). These thinkers drew parallels between speciesism, sexism, and racism, viewing these as forms of discrimination based on physical markers (Albersmeier, 2021). Where sexism involves the discriminatory view that men are superior to women, and racism holds that white people are superior to people of colour, speciesism can be broadly defined as discrimination against non-human animals based on the assumed superiority of the human species. The term derives from the biological categorisation, and subsequent hierarchisation, of living entities into discrete classes or species membership.

Speciesist attitudes, which are deeply embedded in global capitalist (White, 2016) and patriarchal (Adams, 1996) structures, elevate humans over other species of animals, and reduce non-human animals to their instrumental value to humans. As White (2016: 179) attests, 'the dominant ideology of speciesism enables humans to exploit non-human animals as commodities to be eaten, displayed, hunted and dissected for human benefit'. Where Ryder and Singer posit speciesism as parallel to sexism and racism, vegetarian and vegan ecofeminists argue that speciesism is intricately interwoven with sexism, racism, and other forms of oppression (Donovan, 1990; Adams, 1996). Indeed, ecofeminists have revealed that speciesism is deeply entrenched within language, culture, and thought – underlying these structures are dualisms that valorise humans over animals, men over women, culture over nature, mind over body, subject over object, self over other, and reason over emotion (Donovan, 1990; Adams, 1996). Adams (1996), for example, argues the boundary used to separate humans from other animals is both gendered and racialised in that it derives from a racist patriarchy. Non-speciesist criminologists such as Beirne (2007, 2020) have further illustrated how speciesism and sexism coalesce in everyday language. Pejorative descriptions of women as 'bitches', 'cows', 'cougars' and 'pieces of meat' relegate both women and animals to the Other and reinforce the dominance of humans (typically taken to be white, heterosexual, middle- to upper-class, able-bodied men).

Whilst there have been notable efforts to overcome speciesist language, these have at times inadvertently reinforced speciesism. Take for example the term 'non-human animal'. This term challenges speciesist language by problematising the binary opposition between 'human' and 'animal', affirming that humans are themselves, after all, animals. However, Cazaux (1998: 373 points out that using the term 'non-human animals' is akin to describing women as 'non-male humans', as both terms are reliant on negation. There have been attempts to rectify this with terminology such as 'animals other than human animals' and the accompanying acronym 'aothas' (see Cazaux, 1999). But despite their merits, these terms still define animals in a negative relation to humans and have a somewhat homogenising effect, in that a diverse multitude of animal species are collapsed into the one term, all the while humans are allotted their own category that is distinguished from other animals. Beirne (1999) and Sollund (2008) approach the issue by initially juxtaposing 'humans' with 'non-human animals', before shifting to 'animals' on subsequent mentions. Beirne (1999) maintains that the jarring impact of the terminological shift can promote more respectful relations between human and non-human inhabitants of the planet.

Speciesist criminology

Given how pervasive speciesism is, it is not surprising that considerations of non-human animals in criminological inquiry have been fraught with it. It is not that non-human animals have been omitted entirely from conventional criminology; rather, criminological speciesism has routinely valorised humans whilst subordinating and objectifying animals. One need only look to some historical examples to illustrate this. In medieval Europe, there are documented instances in which non-human animals were put on trial, found guilty, and punished for engaging in criminal acts (Beirne, 1995; Cazaux, 1999). These judicial practices derive from biblical scripture, such as the Book of Exodus, which dictates that 'if an ox gore a man or woman that they die, then the ox shall be surely stoned' (cited in Beirne, 1995: 6). However, finding an animal guilty of crime was not due to animals being thought of as having the agency required for criminal intent. Instead, the true crime that animals were guilty of was repudiating the divine hierarchy of humans over animals (Cazaux, 1999). Within medieval records, non-human animals were further labelled as accomplices or reincarnations of the devil, with the devil purportedly acting upon animals to carry out evil (Cazaux, 1999). The positing of non-human animals as passive vessels, and their portrayal as objects rather than subjects, is further symptomatic of speciesism.

The link between animality and criminality can also be found in accounts of nineteenth-century biological positivists who sought to establish 'similarities between the higher species of animals and some of the lower races of humans' (Beirne, 1995: 8). Drawing on social Darwinism, Lombroso (2006 [1876]) developed the typology of the 'born' or 'atavistic' criminal: an evolutionary 'throwback' to a 'primitive' version of humanity with animal resemblance. Lombroso's typology – along with other forms of scientific racism popular at the time – is further illustrative of the overlap between racism and speciesism.

More contemporary considerations of non-human animals have also been dominated by speciesism, with animals featuring primarily as 'objects of human agency' (Beirne, 1995: 16) – that is, as property, weapons, and predictors and/or signifiers of inter-human violence (Beirne, 1995). The term 'livestock' – which is used to describe farm animals such as cows, pigs, chickens, and sheep – is a clear example of the commodification and objectification of animals, with animals being characterised as human property. Harms committed against non-human animals are, in many cases, deemed acceptable if they are perpetrated by the animal's human 'owner' or are otherwise labelled as 'property damage'. Abducted farm animals are not viewed as kidnapped; their abduction is considered 'livestock theft', with the human 'owners' posited as victims rather than the non-human animals themselves. Indeed, harms perpetrated against non-human animals are largely seen as minor property offences rather than 'real' crimes (Beirne, 2007).

Criminological speciesism has been further perpetuated through studies of animals used as tools for harming humans. Such research considers topics ranging from the utilisation of guard dogs to the weaponisation of pain inflicted on companion animals (colloquially referred to as 'pets') in the context of family, domestic, and intimate partner violence (Beirne, 1995). With a few exceptions (see Flynn, 2000; Taylor & Fraser, 2019), research on family violence and domestic abuse involving the mistreatment of companion animals predominantly focuses on how animal cruelty affects human family members rather than the animals themselves. Any harm that is inflicted on companion animals, in other words, is seen as collateral damage. The abuse that animals themselves suffer is not the focus; what is at stake is the psychological and emotional abuse suffered by human victims who have an emotional bond with the animal who is harmed (Beirne, 1995).

Violence against animals has further been studied in relation to serial murderers and rapists Beirne, 1995, 2007). However, again, such considerations have been predominately speciesist, with violence against non-human animals seen as a precursor to inter-human violence (Beirne, 1995, 2007). It is not violence against animals that is of primary concern but, rather, the potential that such violence could demonstrate pre-assaultive or pre-homicidal tendencies towards humans (Beirne, 2007). Indeed, the refusal to acknowledge animals as anything more than objects and appendages to humans within criminology illuminates a blatant speciesism in dire need of remedy. The next section considers noteworthy efforts to overcome speciesism within the space of green criminology.

Towards a non-speciesist criminology

Non-speciesist criminologies, which gained traction in the 1990s, move away from the speciesism entrenched within conventional criminology to examine harms and crimes committed against non-human animals. It must be noted, however, that there were some early attempts to repudiate criminological speciesism from the discipline's inception. As early as 1766, Beccaria (who is regarded as the founder of modern criminology), implored humans 'be just with all the beings that surround you. Remember that even the smallest creatures, crushed by arrogant and cruel man, are endowed with a little ray of life' (cited in Beirne, 1999: 130). In 1789, Bentham further condemned the 'insensibility of ancient jurists' for relegating animals to 'the class of things' and remarked that 'the day may come when the rest of the animal creation may acquire those rights which never could have been withholden from them but by the hand of tyranny' (cited in Beirne, 1999: 130). Despite these early efforts, mainstream criminology has largely either neglected the harming of animals or has examined such harming through a speciesist lens.

More critical strands of green criminology challenge speciesism by positing animal abuse as an important criminological issue. To illustrate, a 1998 special issue of *Theoretical Criminology* featured two articles that placed animal abuse on the green criminological agenda (Benton, 1998; Agnew, 1998). Benton (1998) analyses the notions of rights and justice for non-human animals on a 'shared planet'. Meanwhile, Agnew (1998) formulates a psycho-social framework for understanding animal abuse. These articles testify to a growing recognition that criminology needs to move beyond an exclusive focus on humans as the dominant subjects of criminology to assume a non-speciesist analysis of harms and crimes perpetrated against non-human animals. Indeed, the harms-based approach espoused by critical green criminologists (as opposed to the narrow legalistic definition assumed in more conventional criminology) provides fertile ground to consider the abuse of non-human animals. A critical harms-based approach is crucial, as many harms inflicted on animals – for example, the production and consumption of animals and animal-based products – are socially sanctioned and are carried out on an everyday basis (see Sollund, 2008).

Germinal efforts to establish non-speciesist criminologies can be traced to the work of Beirne (1995, 1999, 2007, 2021) and Cazaux (1998, 1999, 2007). Their respective green criminological research has done much to illuminate and to ultimately challenge the speciesist assumptions entrenched within mainstream criminological discourse and to pave the way for non-speciesist criminologies that consider the harming of animals as a subject worthy of consideration. Some of the earliest non-speciesist criminological work asserts the need to examine animal abuse from a non-anthropocentric and non-speciesist perspective. Where speciesist considerations of animal abuse consider the harming of animals as important only in relation to its impact on humans, a *non*-speciesist perspective acknowledges that non-human animals are living, sentient beings, with their own value and interests (Cazaux & Beirne, 2001). From the perspective of a non-speciesist criminology, animal abuse is important not because of its potential impacts on, and consequences for, humans but on its detrimental impact on animals themselves.

Green criminology and species justice

More recently, the study of harms and crimes against non-human animals – along with those that occur on environmental and ecological levels – has become widely recognised as one of the three major foci of green criminology (White, 2013; Brisman & South, 2018). Taken together, environmental justice, species justice, and ecological justice make up what White (2013) refers to as an eco-justice perspective. The species justice approach assumes a critical stance towards speciesism and posits non-human animals as its central point of analysis (White, 2013; Brisman & South, 2018). It further adopts a biocentric perspective with humans posited as just one among many species of animals inhabiting the Earth, and as no more or less important than any other species (Brisman & South, 2018). Species justice calls for the recognition of the rights and interests of non-human species, just as the rights and interests of humans are recognised. This involves challenging anthropocentric perspectives that prioritise human interests over the well-being of other species and advocating a more inclusive approach to justice. This can include legal protections for non-human animals, the criminalisation of animal harms, and heightened ethical concern for the interests of non-human animals in one's everyday actions – for example, in the consumption of animals and animal-based products.

Within green criminology, species justice is approached from three key philosophical perspectives: utilitarianism; animal rights; and an ecofeminist ethic of care (Brisman & South, 2018). The utilitarian perspective, which is associated with the work of Singer (2015 [1975]), is based on maximising pleasure and minimising suffering. The animal rights perspective, which is associated with the work of Regan (2004 [1983]), argues for the ethical treatment of animals based on their intrinsic value and natural rights. Finally, the ecofeminist position, which is associated with the work of Adams (1996) and Donovan (1990), views the oppression of women and non-human animals as interconnected and advocates an ethic of relationality, love, and care.

Two further positions have been identified in the theorisation and treatment of non-human animals: the animal welfare and animal rights approaches (White, 2013; Pedersen & White, 2021). Rather than seeing these perspectives as oppositional, they are best understood as existing at either end of a spectrum. The animal welfare approach assumes a reformist stance towards the ethical treatment of animals. It accepts the existence and legitimacy of animal-based agribusiness, along with the commodification and consumption of animals; however, it demands that these practices are carried out in a 'humane' manner – for example, through the oxymoronic notion of 'humane slaughter' (Pedersen & White, 2021; White, 2013). The welfare perspective calls for widescale interventions and reforms to ensure that non-human animals are not subjected to any 'unnecessary' suffering, but it does not challenge the exploitation of non-human animals by humans (White, 2013).

At the other end of the spectrum, the rights-based approach assumes an abolitionist stance, calling for the end of animal exploitation – including the use of non-human animals as food and resources. This approach contends that animals have inherent value and should be legally recognised as the bearers of rights that are worthy of protection. Whilst there is growing support for the welfare approach within public consciousness, the rights-based approach, despite its merits, is viewed by the general public as radical and antagonistic or as going 'too far' in challenging the status quo (Pedersen & White, 2021).

From theory to practice: non-speciesist criminological issues

There are multiple issues that can be examined from a non-speciesist criminological perspective. Cazaux (1998, 1999) suggests there is scope to examine topics such as animal abuse, animal welfare legislation, the use of animals in law enforcement (e.g., police dogs and horses), and the therapeutic use of animals for offender rehabilitation in correctional settings. Meanwhile, Beirne (1999, 2007) rejects the speciesist language used to consider harms inflicted on non-human animals and configures non-speciesist frameworks for examining different forms of animal abuse. This, for example, involves a rejection of the term 'bestiality', which is used to describe sexually violent acts perpetrated by humans against non-human animals. Beirne (1999, 2007) instead opts for the terms 'interspecies sexual assault' and 'animal sexual assault' to acknowledge the immense harm it causes non-human animals. He further utilises the term 'theriocide' to refer to the killing of animals by humans (Beirne, 2004). Theriocide encapsulates diverse human actions that lead to the killing of animals – whether they be intentional or unintentional, legal or illegal, socially acceptable or unacceptable, and that occur on micro, meso or macro levels (Beirne,

2004). Indeed, it is Beirne's view that properly naming the killing of non-human animals by humans challenges the privileging of human over animal life. More recently, Beirne (2021) has taken non-speciesist criminology in a novel direction by considering the human-to-animal transmission of pathogens in the context of COVID-19.

The topic of animal abuse, ranging from extreme to routine, has received a continued focus within non-speciesist adaptations of green criminology (Beirne, 1995, 1999, 2007; Cazaux, 1998, 1999; Taylor & Fitzgerald, 2018; White, 2013, 2016). This includes the systematic and institutionalised exploitation and (ab)use of animals within advanced capitalist societies – otherwise referred to as the animal-industrial complex (Fitzgerald & Taylor, 2014; Taylor & Fitzgerald, 2018). As Sollund (2008) and White (2013) point out, many harms inflicted on non-human animals – for example, factory farming, fur farming, and the use of animals in research – are socially sanctioned and are routine features of industrial agribusiness. Meanwhile, Flynn and Hall (2017) extend non-speciesist considerations of animals into the realm of victimology. In so doing, they propose a non-human animal victimology that studies the nature, prevalence, characteristics, impacts and justice responses to non-human victims. White (2018) also offers valuable insight into non-human victimology by considering non-human victims (e.g., trees, rivers, and animals) as victims of environmental crime.

Conclusion

Given that speciesism is not only rampant in criminology but is also entrenched within everyday systems of language and thought, it is crucial that a non-speciesist criminology does not take an 'add animals and stir' approach. As revealed earlier, it is not that animals other than human have been omitted from criminological inquiry altogether but, rather, that their treatment has been contaminated by speciesism. There are different ways that a non-speciesist criminology can be configured. According to Cazaux (1999: 113), a non-speciesist criminology must 'take into account recent findings concerning the physical and emotional life of animals and the specific characteristics of human–animal interactions'. Taylor and Fitzgerald (2018), on the other hand, argue that non-speciesist considerations of animal (ab)use in green criminology ought to be informed by work undertaken in critical animal studies and ecofeminism.

Whilst there are a multitude of promising avenues being pursued in the development of a non-speciesist criminology, there is much work yet to do. The non-speciesist efforts of green criminologists are deserving of deeper and more sustained attention from both critical and mainstream perspectives. It is not until then that the routine exploitation and (ab)use of animals will be acknowledged as legitimate harms in and of themselves and adequate legal protections can be afforded to animals, potentially involving the criminalisation of harms perpetrated against animals other than humans. The time is now due for humans to acknowledge the widespread and routine harms inflicted on non-human animals, and to appreciate other animals as having value outside their instrumental use for humans.

CASSIE PEDERSEN

Further reading

Beirne, P. (1999). For a non-speciesist criminology: Animal abuse as an object of study. *Criminology*, *37*(1), 117–147. https://doi.org/10.1111/j.1745-9125.1999.tb00481.x

Cazaux, G. (1999). Beauty and the beast: Animal abuse from a non-speciesist criminological perspective. *Crime, Law and Social Change*, *31*, 105–126. https://doi.org/10.1023/A:1008347609286

Sollund, R. (2008). Causes for speciesism: Difference, distance and denial. In R. Sollund (Ed.), *Global harms: Ecological crime and speciesism* (pp. 109–129). Nova Science Publishers.

Taylor, N., & Fitzgerald, A. (2018). Understanding animal (ab)use: Green criminological contributions, missed opportunities and a way forward. *Theoretical Criminology*, *22*(3), 402–425. https://doi.org/10.1177/1362480618787173

White, R. (2016). Inter-species violence: Humans and the harming of animals. In J. Stubbs & S. Tomsen (Eds.), *Australian violence: Crime, criminal justice and beyond* (pp. 176–193). Federation Press.

References

Adams, C. J. (1996). Caring about suffering: A feminist exploration. In J. Donovan & C. J. Adams (Eds.), *Beyond animal rights: A feminist caring ethic for the treatment of animals* (pp. 170–196). Continuum.

Agnew, R. (1998). The causes of animal abuse: A social-psychological analysis. *Theoretical*

Criminology, *2*(2), 177–209. https://doi.org/10.1177/1362480698002002003
Albersmeier, F. (2021). Speciesism and speciescentrism. *Ethical Theory and Moral Practice*, *24*, 511–527. https://doi.org/10.1007/s10677-021-10168-6
Beirne, P. (1995). The use and abuse of animals in criminology: A brief history and current review. *Social Justice*, *22*(1), 5–31. https://www.jstor.org/stable/29766862
Beirne, P. (1999). For a non-speciesist criminology: Animal abuse as an object of study. *Criminology*, *37*(1), 117–147. https://doi.org/10.1111/j.1745-9125.1999.tb00481.x
Beirne, P. (2004). Theriocide: Naming animal killing. *International Journal for Crime, Justice and Social Democracy*, *3*(2), 49–66. https://doi.org/10.5204/ijcjsd.v3i2.174
Beirne, P. (2007). Animal rights, animal abuse and green criminology. In P. Beirne & N. South (Eds.), *Issues in green criminology: Confronting harms against environments, humanity and other animals* (pp. 55–83). Willan Publishing.
Beirne, P. (2020). Animals, women, and terms of abuse: Towards a cultural etymology of con(e)y, cunny, cunt and c*nt. *Critical Criminology*, *28*, 327–349. https://doi.org/10.1007/s10612-019-09460-w
Beirne, P. (2021). Wildlife trade and COVID-19: Towards a criminology of anthropogenic pathogen spillover. *The British Journal of Criminology*, *61*(3), 607–626. https://doi.org/10.1093/bjc/azaa084
Benton, T. (1998). Rights and justice on a shared planet: More rights or new relations? *Theoretical Criminology*, *2*(2), 149–175. https://doi.org/10.1177/1362480698002002002
Brisman, A., & South, N. (2018). Green criminology and environmental crimes and harms. *Sociology Compass*, *13*(1), 1–12. https://doi.org/10.1111/soc4.12650
Cazaux, G. (1998). Legitimating the entry of 'the animals issue' into (critical) criminology. *Humanity and Society*, *22*(4), 365–385. https://doi.org/10.1177/016059769802200403
Cazaux, G. (1999). Beauty and the beast: Animal abuse from a non-speciesist criminological perspective. *Crime, Law and Social Change*, *31*, 105–126. https://doi.org/10.1023/A:1008347609286
Cazaux, G. (2007). Labelling animals: Non-speciesist criminology and techniques to identify other animals. In P. Beirne & N. South (Eds.), *Issues in green criminology: Confronting harms against environments, humanity and other animals* (pp. 87–113). Willan Publishing.
Cazaux, G., & Beirne, P. (2001). Animal abuse. In E. McLaughlin & J. Muncie (Eds.), *Sage dictionary of criminology* (pp. 8–10). Sage.
Donovan, J. (1990). Animal rights and feminist theory. *Signs*, *15*(2), 350–375. http://www.jstor.org/stable/3174490
Fitzgerald, A.J. & Taylor, N. (2014). The cultural hegemony of meat and the animal industrial complex. In N. Taylor & R. Twine (Eds.), *The rise of critical animal studies: From the margins to the centre* (pp. 165–182). Routledge.
Flynn, C. P. (2000). Women's best friend: Pet abuse and the role of companion animals in the lives of battered women. *Violence Against Women*, *6*(2), 162–177. https://doi.org/10.1177/10778010022181778
Flynn, M., & Hall, M. (2017). The case for a victimology of nonhuman animal harms. *Contemporary Justice Review*, *20*(3), 299–318. https://doi.org/10.1080/10282580.2017.1348898
Lombroso, C. (2006 [1876]). *Criminal man*. Duke University Press.
Pedersen, C., & White, R. (2021). Discourses of discord: Animal activism and moral judgement. *International Criminology*, *1*(3), 178–192. https://doi.org/10.1007/s43576-021-00027-w
Regan, T. (2004 [1983]). *The case for animal rights*. University of California Press.
Ryder, R. (2009). Speciesism. In M. Bekoff (Ed.), *Encyclopedia of animal rights and animal welfare* (2nd ed.) (pp. 527–528). Greenwood Press.
Singer, P. (2015 [1975]). *Animal liberation: A new ethics for our treatment of animals*. HarperCollins.
Sollund, R. (2008). Causes for speciesism: Difference, distance and denial. In R. Sollund (Ed.), *Global harms: Ecological crime and speciesism* (pp. 109–129). Nova Science Publishers.
Taylor, N., & Fitzgerald, A. (2018). Understanding animal (ab)use: Green criminological contributions, missed opportunities and a way forward. *Theoretical Criminology*, *22*(3), 402–425. https://doi.org/10.1177/1362480618787173
Taylor, N., & Fraser, H. (2019). *Companion animals and domestic violence: Rescuing me, rescuing you*. Palgrave Macmillan.
White, R. (2013). *Environmental harm: An eco-justice perspective*. Policy Press.
White, R. (2016). Inter-species violence: Humans and the harming of animals. In J. Stubbs & S. Tomsen (Eds.), *Australian violence: Crime, criminal justice and beyond* (pp. 176–193). Federation Press.
White, R. (2018). Green victimology and non-human victims. *International Review of Victimology*, *24*(2), 239–255. https://doi.org/10.1177/0269758017745615

CASSIE PEDERSEN

51. Preventing illegal fishing

Introduction

Illegal, unreported and unregulated (IUU) fishing is the term given to particular kinds of fishing activity that in some way contravene national or international laws (DAFF, 2019). This activity has numerous environmental impacts, such as depleting fish stocks (especially of vulnerable species) and causing damage to ecosystems. It also impacts both socially and economically, such as through disrupting the livelihood of lawful fishers, removing a source of protein for those who rely on fish for consumption, and diminishing amenity and activity for tourism and recreation. Left unchecked, IUU fishing can create irreversible harms. IUU is largely concealed, with illegal catches easily intermingled with lawful catches, making prevention, detection and thus penalisation difficult. Nevertheless, various laws, treaties and monitoring programmes combined with technological and other surveillance tactics seek to offer some level of traceability and deterrence.

IUU fishing and its impacts

Illegal, unreported and unregulated (IUU) fishing refers to three types of harmful activities. *Illegal* fishing occurs in violation of fishery laws, such as those setting size and take limits; *unreported* fishing is where fishing activity and catches are not reported to national authorities or regional fisheries management organisations; and *unregulated* fishing is fishing activity from vessels with no national flag or flying the flag of a country not regulated to do so in a particular fishery (AFMA, 2023).

IUU has numerous harmful environmental impacts. The ecologist Garrett Hardin (1968) coined the phrase 'the tragedy of the commons' (later changed to 'the tragedy of the unmanaged commons') to refer to the depletion of shared resources for individual gain, in the absence of effective rules, regulations and sustainable resource management. That is, if people make their own economically rational decisions without some formal intervention – for example, international treaties and law enforcement measures – then a resource will be depleted.

This illicit activity also impacts socially and economically – affecting livelihoods, food sources and local industries. An array of associated criminal activities including pollution offences, theft, fraud, quarantine violation, tax evasion and violent crime including murder also occurs (Putt and Nelson, 2008, UNODC, 2022; White, 2023). A systemic review by Temple et al. (2022) also flagged an array of environmental impacts, brought about by overfishing for instance. It is vital, therefore, that crime prevention measures be implemented to limit the likelihood of offending and the harms which it causes.

White (2008) identifies five types of illegal fishing: (i) commercial fishing with catches over quota; (ii) recreational fishing which could be unlicensed or with excess catches; (iii) Indigenous fishing which is undertaken in foreign waters or without a permit; (iv) large-scale illegal fishing which over-exploits a particular species; and (v) specialist illegal fishing which targets endangered species for private collections or for medicinal purposes.

Supply and demand economics dictate that as marine faunal resources become scarcer, they become more valuable, and thus more attractive to those intent on capitalising through targeting of endangered species. IUU is largely concealed, with illegal catches often taking place on the high seas, which are then easily intermingled with lawful catches, making detection and thus penalty difficult (see for example High Seas Task Force, 2006). Nevertheless, there are a variety of methods currently being employed to prevent and stop these activities. Before considering these, it is important to distinguish between 'legal' and 'illegal' activities, so as to acknowledge that each may include environmentally harmful aspects.

Crime versus harm

An action with environmental, social and economically harmful consequences might not necessarily be deemed illegal, and thus criminal – that is, no laws prohibit the action – but it can nevertheless be harmful. Crime is, after all, a social construct, and the notion of crime can exclude serious harms (Dorling et al., 2008; see also Canning and Tombs, 2021; White 2023) and still offend against the greater public interest.

An example of this is Japanese whaling in the Great Southern Ocean (Hurst, 2020).

Whilst the International Whaling Commission (IWC) has placed a moratorium on commercial whaling (IWC, 2024), until 2020 Japan routinely hunted for whales, arguing that it was engaging in this activity for scientific conservation research. The International Court of Justice rejected this argument, determining this was not an exemption from the International Convention for the Regulation of Whaling (Poorhashemi and Zarei, 2021). Opponents of the whaling programme argued that Japan's rationale was a surreptitious way of providing sought-after whale meat for high-end restaurants in Japan (Kolmaš, 2021).

In the absence of formal direct preventative actions and enforcement of international conservation law on the high seas (international waters), organisations such as Greenpeace and Sea Shepherd actively engaged with Japanese whaling vessels, often resulting in confrontations with the central goal being to disrupt (Moffa, 2012). The dangerous nature of this activity culminated in the 2010 sinking of the Sea Shepherd vessel *Ady Gil* in the Southern Ocean after being rammed by a Japanese whaling ship (Associated Press, 2010; Anton, 2010).

Another example of harm versus crime relates to Indigenous fishing practices. In Australia, since the *Mabo* judgment provided native title to First Nations peoples, native title holders are permitted under the Native Title Act 1993 (Cth) to be exempt from laws which restrict the ability to hunt, fish and gather – such as, for instance, the taking of undersized abalone. This, though, presents challenges for (often starkly under-resourced) fisheries enforcement officers when organised criminality involving First Nations peoples occurs (see for example Rule, 2024). Controversial, too, is the spearing and drowning of dugongs (a vulnerable marine animal) and killing of marine turtles (recognised as a species of conservation concern internationally), both justified as a cultural practice by some Indigenous people. Exercising native title rights has seen some First Nations people prosecuted under inconsistent state laws, although the High Court ruled in 2013 in *Kapany v Dietman* that state and territory fisheries management legislation does not extinguish native title rights (Founten and Byrne, 2013). However, this has become a contested policy space with native title rights being a defence to state/territory criminal proceedings, particularly the need to prove that the stocks were taken for customary not commercial purposes (Pain and Pick, 2020). Meanwhile in the Faroe Islands, the killing of sea mammals such as white-sided dolphins is legal although regulated. The tradition of *grindadráp* sees animals herded towards the shore where they are then slaughtered en masse, turning the sea bright red. In the context of long-standing traditional cultural practices, persuasion and education are, amongst other measures, thus necessary preventative actions (Sutton et al., 2021).

Fishing and the law

Oceans are regulated internationally under the 1994 United Nations Law of the Sea Convention (LOSC) (UNCLOS, 1994). Within the context of LOSC a 'state' refers to a country which is party to the convention not a subnational breakdown of a federated nation. For instance, it refers to Australia (federal government) not individual states such as New South Wales or Victoria. There exists a complex web of overlapping jurisdictions, with the prevailing principle that a flag state has jurisdiction over ships which fly its flag (LOSC article 91). Up to the end of the 12 nautical miles of territorial sea, a coastal state has sovereignty over the seabed, water column and airspace whilst beyond that limit they enjoy sovereign rights.

The LOSC brought approximately 90 per cent of commercial fisheries in what was the high seas under the control of coastal states through 200 nautical mile exclusive economic zones (EEZ). Although there is an obligation on states to maximise the exploitation of fisheries resources over which they have sovereign rights (LOSC article 62), state practice over time has moved towards conservation. Such conservation measures are not subject to compulsory dispute resolution measures. One significant issue has been a state's ability to enforce their sovereign rights within the EEZ (for more see Barrett, 1998).

Generally speaking, on the high seas under the LOSC, the flag state of a vessel has primary jurisdiction over the actions of vessels which fly its flag. As a consequence, this results in 'doughnut' arrangements with areas of the high seas subject primarily to the jurisdiction of the flag state. Upon the high seas other states can only assert jurisdiction if the particular vessel has transited to or from its ports. Unlike non-living resources under the seabed, there was no United Nations agency to manage fishing stocks on the high seas – with them regarded as 'the commons' available for all. Initially this was not problematic, as those regions were too distant for commercial operators to economically exploit. However, with advances in technology, fish stocks have become increasingly accessible and thus regulation was required. The Conservation and Management of Straddling Fish Stocks and Highly Migratory Fish Stocks (Fish Stocks Agreement) came into force in late 2001. The aim of the agreement was to ensure the long-term conservation and viability of straddling and highly migratory fish stocks through enhanced precautionary management. An enhanced role was created for coastal and port states to operate concurrently with that of flag states. The Fish Stocks Agreement promotes regional agreements for the conservation of fisheries such as that in the South Pacific. Enforcement mainly takes place by denying 'blacklisted' ships – describing vessels which have been added to a 'refusal of access' list or on a 'letters of warning' list (AMSA, 2024) – the right to port.

The establishment of the South Pacific Regional Fisheries Management Organisation (SPRFMO) in 2012 was a significant development. SPRFMO (2024) is an intergovernmental organisation charged with ensuring the long-term conservation and sustainability of fisheries in the Southern Ocean (high seas), an area stretching from the east coast of Australia to the west coast of South America and south of 10° north and north of 60° south. An important aspect of this arrangement is the large membership which not only includes countries from the region but also major fishing states such as China, Russia and South Korea. Another agreement, supported by the European Union, is the Cape Town Agreement, which aligns with the United Nations Sustainability Development Goal 14: it offers a global standard for vessel safety and seeks to ameliorate issues of IUU, forced labour, and pollution from vessels.

Offenders and offending

Illegal fishing is a worldwide criminal behaviour, perpetrated by motivated individuals, corporate entities, organised criminal networks and nation states (Putt and Nelson, 2008; UNODC, 2022), with more or less accessible targets but an almost complete absence (especially on the high seas) of capable guardianship. It varies greatly depending on scale and participants.

Recreational fishers

The illegal activities of recreational fishers, although individually small in scale, can cumulatively be impactful. Such offending includes exceeding a regulated bag limit, keeping undersized fish or protected species, use of illegal fishing gear, and fishing in protected waters such as in marine sanctuaries or inland waterways (see for example DPIR, 2022).

Offending might result from oversight or ignorance. Alternatively, it might be premeditated, involving actions such as arranging for a refrigerated van to be located onshore whereby the risk of being caught over-limit on the boat can be minimised or through the creation of a fake bottom in the boat to prevent catches. Illegal diving can be disguised with the use of rebreathers to hide bubbles appearing on the water surface, fishing at night without lights, using global positioning systems, working in teams masquerading as recreational fishers, and hiding catches such as abalone in clothing (Putt and Nelson, 2008; Petrossian, 2019).

Organised crime

Illegal fishing in Australia is believed to be small scale and opportunistic, but organised criminal activity exists particularly with high-value stocks such as abalone, rock lobster and shark fins. In addition to specific fishing-related illegal activity by large-scale illegal commercial activities – such as under-reporting a catch, mixing illegally caught fish with legal catches and exceeding quotas – commercial businesses may also be involved in money laundering activities and selling catches directly to the hospitality sector on a cash basis (Putt and Nelson, 2008). In an Australian context, a concern exists amongst key stakeholders that the fishing sector is vulnerable to infiltration from organised crime groups (Putt and Anderson, 2007). This, though, is a transnational issue, with a wealth of research produced in recent years indicating the prevalence of organised crime involvement in IUU such as in Indonesian waters (for example Yuliantiningsih et al., 2022) and has global impacts on a sustainable ocean economy (see for example Witbooi et al., 2020).

Some evidence points to growth in the participation of organised crime groups in 'the systematic harvesting, processing, and distribution of abalone and rock lobster and use of the sector to launder money and manufacture drugs at aquaculture facilities' in Australia (Putt and Nelson, 2008, p. 1). The Global Initiative Against Transnational Organized Crime also indicates that organised crime is significantly involved in illegally acquired abalone in South Africa (de Greef and Haysom, 2022).

Results of a meta-analysis conducted by Mackay, Hardesty and Wilcox (2020) found that, whilst there exists a narrative in the literature of a link between organised crime and illegal fishing, there is a dearth of evidence to support this (note, however, the extensive work of the United Nations Office on Drugs and Crime, for example UNODC, 2022). Further, they found that three distinct business models operate – harvesting; moving cargo; provision of a venue – but that 'integrated criminal activities where multiple business models are operating simultaneously are uncommon' (Mackay et al., 2020, p. 5), and that whilst forced labour and workers' rights violations are common, less so are drugs and weapons smuggling offending related to IUU fishing.

Flags of convenience

Under the LOSC (article 92) flag states are granted exclusive jurisdiction on the high seas over vessels which fly their flag: in essence representing a legal fiction where sovereignty of the flag state prevails. In Britain, the Privy Council (*Chung Chi Cheung v R* [1939] AC 167) was clear that flag state jurisdictions can only be overridden in exceptional cases which are directly authorised by the LOSC or other international treaties. Article 91 of the LOSC allows states to grant permission for ships which have 'a genuine link' to fly their flag; however, the United States Supreme Court (*Lauritzen v Larsen* 345 US 571 (1953)) found that it is not up to individual states to determine unilaterally that no genuine link exists. When there is a questionable link, it is known as a flag of convenience (FOC): many fleet owners register their ships in developing countries (for example Panama, Liberia and the Bahamas) which have little to do with where they operate.

An investigative journalism endeavour (Al Jazeera, 2012) assessed the activities of South Korean fishing trawlers operating illegally inside the coastal EEZ off Sierra Leone. With over 500 kilometres of coastline, Sierra Leone has a heavy reliance on fishing – for its GDP and employment, but also as a source of protein for citizens. However, this is significantly impacted by foreign fleets operating within the EEZ, combined with poor governance, corrupt officials, and lacklustre enforcement practices and infrastructure (International Trade Administration, 2021).

Approximately 15 per cent of large-scale commercial fishing vessels fly an FOC or are listed as 'flag unknown', and indeed many vessels engaging in IUU are specifically designed for this purpose (approximately 14%) and the FOC system is an inexpensive and often deliberate mechanism for rules of the seas to be avoided and for profits to be made. Seventy-five per cent of large-scale fishing vessels flying an FOC come from Belize, Honduras, Panama, and St Vincent and the Grenadines (Gianni and Simpson, 2005; see also EJF, 2020). The infrastructure in place to support fishing fleets on the high seas is 'well-organised and largely unregulated' (Gianni and Simpson, 2005, p. 4), and includes refrigerated vessels and refuelling vessels to allow catches to continue uninterrupted (Gianni and Simpson, 2005, sections 3 and 4).

Key drivers of IUU

A key driver of IUU is supply and demand economics: that is, scarcity leads to higher potential profits, and thus already over-exploited species are targeted and supplied to both licit and illicit markets. This is enabled by opportunity: certain targeted species are concentrated in a small number of fisheries, such as marine national parks along the Great Barrier Reef off the north-eastern Australian coastline (Zahnow, 2021).

The key factors are economic (overcapacity caused by an imbalance between fishing capacities and opportunities, ineffective management and provision of subsidies); institutional (such as gaps in legal frameworks of the sea; use of FOC; insufficient monitoring, control and surveillance); and social (such as poverty) (Le Gallic and Cox, 2006; Meere and Lack, 2008). Increasing demand for seafood in developed states also adds pressure and profitability for both legal and illegal markets to fish more.

Impacts of IUU fishing

The effects of illegal fishing are social, economic and ecological and felt by individuals, communities, fish species, and the environment itself.

Social and economic impacts

With marine species providing an important source of protein in the diet of many people, especially in coastal developing countries, IUU can lead to a food crisis when people can no longer fish because of depleted fish stocks and there is limited access to arable land for food production. IUU creates other life-threatening impacts too, such as abandonment of crew in foreign ports, forced labour, violations of work health and safety, and the lack of lifesaving equipment on some vessels (Gianni and Simpson, 2005).

After the collapse of the central government in Somalia in 1991, local communities established their own coastal patrols to 'protect' their traditional fishing grounds from foreign vessels which were depleting the stocks upon which they relied. An unintended consequence of this activity was that these fishing 'policing' operations proved so profitable that they morphed into general piracy activity off the Horn of Africa (Fergusson, 2013; Bahadur, 2011).

The depletion of fish also impacts on employment opportunities for those who earn income from auctioning, processing and retailing fish, leading to higher levels of indebtedness and a perpetuation of poverty and inequality for both those directly and indirectly involved in the sector (Meere and Lack, 2008). Declines in revenue will also have regional and national impacts on a country's GDP: a case study from the east coast of the Malaysian Peninsula indicates economic losses from non-payment of landing fees, licensing fees, taxes and levies, as well as loss of income and purchasing power. Added to this is the additional resource strain on law enforcement to combat the problem of IUU (Meere and Lack, 2008).

The lure of profit from IUU can lead some to engage in risky, indeed deadly, practices. For instance, an Indonesian fishing boat caught in a cyclone in 2022 capsized off the north-west coast of Australia, with nine of the 12-member crew missing, presumed drowned. This crew, with no boating experience, were fishing – after two years of COVID-19 lockdown and unemployment – illegally in the Australian EEZ for *trepang* (sea cucumber) to gain much needed income (Barker, Barry and Prihantari, 2022).

Ecological and environmental impacts

A key cause of the rapid depletion of various fisheries is the use of technology such as sonar to discover fish stocks underwater, and helicopters, fixed-wing aircraft and satellites for those on or close to the surface. The use of bottom and pelagic trawling, gillnets and longlines can result in enormous catches, which are then processed on factory ships, but that can be extremely ecologically destructive (MSC, 2024). Two key ecological issues are consequential: first is the bycatch of non-target species, which might include animals such as dolphins; and second is the damage done to the seabed through trawling and the resulting ecological disruption.

The attraction of bigger catches has led to the complete collapse of some fisheries. The Grand Banks fishery, off the north-east coast of Newfoundland, Canada, was once a plentiful source of Atlantic cod but was overfished to the point that an indefinite moratorium on fishing this species was adopted in 1992 (Rose, 2010; Brodie, Walsh and Maddock Parsons, 2010). The ecological impacts of fisheries collapses are magnified with the depletion of predatory species.

A particularly targeted and vulnerable species is the Patagonian toothfish (and the related Antarctic toothfish), sometimes marketed as Chilean Sea Bass or Miro, that was fished almost to the point of collapse in the Southern Ocean until the mid 2000s. However, with increased government and non-government patrols, along with significant media awareness, the extent of IUU fishing of these species reduced (Gianni and Simpson, 2005, section 2). An Australian policing operation in 2003 detected illegal fishing of the Patagonian toothfish by the Uruguayan registered vessel *Viarsa 1* within the Australian EEZ of Heard Island: this saw one of the longest 'hot pursuits' ever seen, extending to the East African coast (southwest of Cape Town), some 3,900 nautical miles over a three-week period. *Viarsa 1* entered the pack ice of the Antarctic coast and Australia then controversially continued its hot pursuit through electronic rather than visual monitoring. Ultimately the vessel was intercepted with the assistance of South African and British vessels (see Knecht, 2006; Clare, 2010).

Shark-finning is the process by which fins (considered a food delicacy in some countries) are cut from a live shark. Whilst sometimes the fins are a byproduct, often the fins are retained but the rest of the shark is discarded back into the ocean where it slowly dies. Ecologically, as an apex predator species, ocean ecosystems are significantly disrupted and unbalanced by such practices (Haase, 2022). The United Nations International Plan of Action for the Conservation and Management of Sharks was developed in 1999 (FAO, 1999); the United States' Shark Conservation Act (2009) mandates that sharks must be brought ashore with fins intact; but in other jurisdictions no provisions are present (Shark Research Institute, n.d.). Whilst the process itself is illegal in Australia, the trade is not (AMCS, 2024).

Law enforcement and crime prevention responses

Whilst there exist laws of the sea which are intended to regulate fishing practices, ongoing law enforcement and the implementation of crime prevention measures face numerous challenges.

Social action to prevent IUU includes school-based education programmes which instil awareness of environmental harm; and community-orientated strategies designed to encourage community engagement as protectors of nature, and that include 'Fish Watch' schemes and reporting hotlines. Situational crime prevention measures meant to minimise impacts on fisheries include offering advice on the boundaries of marine parks, regular patrols, and use of technology such as satellites to undertake surveillance of popular fishing locations (Sutton et al., 2021).

Sutton et al. (2021) offer a useful summary of an array of tactics and techniques aimed at arresting crimes such as IUU. In addition to situational crime prevention approaches, the 'CRAVED theft model' can assist in analysing and thus addressing the motivating factors of such offending. 'Crime script analysis' and the 'market reduction approach', too, can be employed to identify necessary steps leading to practical prevention campaigns. Various methods have been proposed by criminologists and law enforcement bodies to counter IUU activities.

Policing EEZs

Policing of an EEZ is left very much to the coastal state with associated sovereign rights; however, increasingly there is cooperation among nations (Rothwell and Stephens, 2016). For instance, countries of the South Pacific have mutual recognition treaties which allow enforcement of fisheries management arrangements across the different EEZs, utilising the natural interoperability of Australian-provided Pacific and Guardian-class patrol boats (Karcher et al., 2020; Department of Defence, 2020).

By contrast, a lack of offshore resources is acute in Africa where many nations cannot adequately police their EEZs. For this reason, non-government organisations such as Sea Shepherd have been invited to actively collaborate with African nations to assist in the enforcement of laws pertaining to illegal fishing. For example, a novel partnership has developed between Sea Shepherd and enforcement agencies of countries such as Tuvalu (Island Business, 2023). Sea Shepherd provide a blue water vessel capable of interdicting the large commercial vessels: law enforcement then sends a boarding party to the fishing vessel (Weinman, 2023; Korten, 2024). However, the legality of such partnerships is unclear as the Sea Shepherd vessels are generally flagged in the Netherlands and do not possess sovereign immunity (LOSC articles 95, 96 and 111).

Although not directly involved in the policing of illegal fishing, Interpol plays an important role through their global fisheries enforcement team, primarily in intelligence coordination and building capacity amongst member countries. Such action includes shoring up the transparency of supply chains to enable the catch-to-market tracing of stock (Interpol, 2018). For instance, in 2014 Operation Spindrift was conducted, targeting the transnational trade in abalone through enhanced information and intelligence exchange. The lessons learnt from this operation saw recommendations for improved reporting, monitoring and operational procedures. In a similar vein, the United Nations Office on Drugs and Crime produces resources and information kits on how best to combat organised illegal fishing (see, for example, Wyatt, 2022).

Monitoring programmes

Although not every fishing vessel can be monitored, both government and not-for profit organisations engage in monitoring programmes to deter IUU. For instance, the Seaford Import Monitoring Program is an initiative of the United States Government which dictates reporting and record-keeping for certain seafood products (AJIL, 2022).

The World Wildlife Fund (WWF) is an example of a not-for-profit organisation which engages in an array of monitoring, such as using satellite data to reveal locations of illegal activity and web-based software to track the movement of catches between ports and countries. WWF, in recognising the remoteness of offending in the high seas beyond EEZs, is involved in a partnership project which installs electronic monitoring on tuna vessels to capture real-time estimates of catches (Crispino, 2020).

Certification and labelling

Various eco-certification and labelling schemes exist to maintain a watching brief on the provenance of fishing catches. These include the United Nations Food and Agriculture Organization's International Plan of Action on IUU Fishing, which has been adopted by regional fishery management organisations including in the Antarctic. A not-for-profit organisation which coordinates a certification and labelling programme for traceable and sustainable seafood is the Marine Stewardship Council (Longo et al., 2021).

Conclusion

Sutton et al. (2021) argue that a holistic crime prevention approach is essential: that is, one strategy in isolation will not be effective in prevention or control of illegal fishing practices. IUU is socially, economically and environmentally harmful. Crime prevention and enforcement responses are challenging owing to the dynamics and complexity of the offending. Nevertheless, various legal and regulatory measures combined with crime prevention and enforcement strategies seek to offer some level of traceability and deterrence.

ALISTAIR HARKNESS, MATTHEW BOX AND KYLE MULROONEY

Further reading

Canning, V. and Tombs, S. (2021). *From social harm to zemiology: A critical introduction.* Abingdon: Routledge.

Dorling, D., Gordon, D., Hillyard, P., Patazis, C., Pemberton, S. and Tombs, S. (2008). *Criminal obsessions: Why harm matters more than crime* (2nd ed.). London: Centre for Crime and Justice Studies, King's College London. Retrieved from https://www.crimeandjustice.org.uk/sites/crimeandjustice.org.uk/files/Criminal%20obsessions.pdf

Mackay, M., Hardesty, B.D. and Wilcox, C. (2020). The intersection between illegal fishing, crimes at sea, and social well-being. *Frontiers in Marine Science*, *7*, 1–9. https://doi.org/10.3389/fmars.2020.589000

Rothwell, D. and Stephens, T. (2016). *The international law of the sea* (2nd ed.). Oxford: Hart Publishing.

UNODC (United Nations Office on Drugs and Crime). (2022). *Stretching the fishnet: Identifying crime in the fisheries value chain.* Vienna: UNODC. Retrieved from https://www.unodc.org/res/environment-climate/resources_html/Stretching_the_Fishnet.pdf

White, R. (2023). *Advanced introduction to applied green criminology.* Cheltenham, UK and Northampton, MA, USA: Edward Elgar Publishing.

References

AFMA (Australian Fisheries Management Authority). (2023). *IUU fishing.* Canberra: Australian Government. Retrieved from https://www.afma.gov.au/fisheries-management/international-fisheries-management/iuu-fishing

AJIL. (2022). President Biden signs national security memorandum on combating illegal, unreported, and unregulated fishing and associated labor abuses. *American Journal of International Law*, *116*(4), 858–863. doi:10.1017/ajil.2022.65

Al Jazeera. (2012). *Pirate fishing: People & power.* Retrieved from https://www.youtube.com/watch?v=oKQ0rf06Jw4 (Part 1) and https://www.youtube.com/watch?v=FcXCvY6hnEE (Part 2).

AMCS (Australian Marine Conservation Society). (2024). If shark finning is illegal, how come Australia is still part of the shark fin trade? Retrieved from https://www.marineconservation

.org.au/shark-finning-is-illegal-but-australia-part-of-shark-fin-trade/

AMSA (Australian Maritime Safety Authority). (2024). *Refusal of access list and letters of warning list*. Canberra: Australian Government. Retrieved from https://www.amsa.gov.au/vessels-operators/port-state-control/refusal-access-list-and-letters-warning-list

Anton, D. (2010, 20 April). Protecting whales by hue and cry: Is there a role for non-state actors in the enforcement of international law? *ANU College of Law Research Paper No. 10-08*. Retrieved from https://papers.ssrn.com/sol3/papers.cfm?abstract_id=1593305

Associated Press. (2010, 18 November). *Ady Gil* and Japanese whaler both blamed for collision. *The Guardian*. Retrieved from https://www.theguardian.com/environment/2010/nov/18/ady-gil-whaler-blamed-collision

Bahadur, J. (2011). *Deadly waters: The hidden world of Somalia's pirates*. London: Profile Books.

Barker, A., Barry, H. and Prihantari, A. (2022, 23 August). Desperate Indonesian fishermen are risking their lives to sneak into rough Australian waters and plunder sea treasures. *ABC News*. Retrieved from https://www.abc.net.au/news/2022–08–23/why-indonesian-fishermen-sneak-into-australian-waters/101321960.

Barrett, M. (1998). Illegal fishing in zones subject to national jurisdiction. *James Cook University Law Review*, *5*, 1–26, Retrieved from https://www.austlii.edu.au/au/journals/JCULawRw/1998/1.pdf

Brodie, W.B., Walsh, S.J. and Maddock Parsons, D. (2010). An evaluation of the collapse and recovery of the yellowtail flounder (Limanda ferruginea) stock on the Grand Bank. *ICES Journal of Marine Science*, *67*(9), 1887–1895.

Canning, V. and Tombs, S. (2021). *From social harm to zemiology: A critical introduction*. Abingdon: Routledge.

Clare, A. (2010). The quest to combat the illegal fishing of 'white gold' in the Southern Ocean. *Australian Journal of Maritime and Ocean Affairs*, *2*(3), 69–81.

Crispino, M. (2020, 28 January). *Setting the line on transparency in tuna fishing*. Washington, DC: World Wildlife Fund. Retrieved from https://www.worldwildlife.org/stories/setting-the-line-on-transparency-in-tuna-fishing

DAFF (Department of Agriculture, Fisheries and Forestry). (2019). *Overview: Illegal, unreported and unregulated (IUU) fishing*. Canberra: Australian Government. Retrieved from https://www.agriculture.gov.au/agriculture-land/fisheries/iuu/overview_illegal_unreported_and_unregulated_iuu_fishing

de Greef, K. and Haysom, S. (2022, February). *Disrupting abalone harms: Illicit flows of H. midae from South Africa to East Asia*. Geneva: Global Initiative Against Transnational Organized Crime.

Department of Defence. (2020). *Department of Defence Annual Report 2019–20*. Retrieved from https://www.transparency.gov.au/publications/defence/department-of-defence/department-of-defence-annual-report-2019-20/defence-at-a-glance/letter-of-transmittal

Dorling, D., Gordon, D., Hillyard, P., Patazis, C., Pemberton, S. and Tombs, S. (2008). *Criminal obsessions: Why harm matters more than crime* (2nd ed.). London: Centre for Crime and Justice Studies, King's College London. Retrieved from https://www.crimeandjustice.org.uk/sites/crimeandjustice.org.uk/files/Criminal%20obsessions.pdf

DPIR (Department of Primary Industries and Regions). (2022). *Illegal fishing activities*. Adelaide: Government of South Australia. Retrieved from https://pir.sa.gov.au/recreational_fishing/reporting/report_illegal_fishing_activities

EJF (Environmental Justice Foundation). (2020). *Off the hook: How flags of convenience let illegal fishing go unpunished*. London: Environmental Justice Foundation. Retrieved from https://ejfoundation.org/resources/downloads/EJF-report-FoC-flags-of-convenience-2020.pdf

Fergusson, J. (2013). *The world's most dangerous place: Inside the outlaw state of Somalia*. London: Transworld Publishers.

FAO (Food and Agriculture Organization of the United Nations). (1999). *The International Plan of Action for the Conservation and Management of Sharks*. Rome: United Nations Food and Agriculture Organization.

Founten, L. and Byrne, E. (2013). High Court native title decision: Abalone fishermen Owen and Daniel Karpany allowed to keep undersize catch. *ABC News*. Retrieved from https://www.abc.net.au/news/2013–11–06/native-title-abalone-owen-daniel-karpany-undersize/5072466.

Gianni, M. and Simpson, W. (2005). *The changing nature of high seas fishing: How flags of convenience provide cover for illegal, unreported and unregulated fishing*. Australian Department of Agriculture, Fisheries and Forestry, International Transport Workers' Federation, and WWF International. Retrieved from https://www.agriculture.gov.au/sites/default/files/sitecollectiondocuments/fisheries/iuu/iuu_flags_of_convenience.pdf

Haase, A. (2022). Soup minus shark: How the shark finning industry continues to cause transboundary environmental harm. Student Theses 2015–Present, 123. Retrieved from https://research.library.fordham.edu/environ_2015/123

Hardin, G. (1968). The tragedy of the commons. *Science*, *162*(3859), 1243–1248.

High Seas Task Force. (2006). *Closing the net: Stopping illegal fishing on the high seas*. Final report of the Ministerially led Task Force on IUU fishing on the high seas. Retrieved from https://www.oecd.org/sd-roundtable/papersandpublications/39375276.pdf

Hurst, D. (2020, 3 April). Japanese whaling is down but not out. *The Interpreter*. The Lowy Institute. Retrieved from https://www.lowyinstitute.org/the-interpreter/japanese-whaling-down-not-out

International Trade Administration. (2021). *Sierra Leone – Country Commercial Guide: Agriculture Sector*. Retrieved from https://www.trade.gov/country-commercial-guides/sierra-leone-agriculture-sector

Interpol. (2018, February). *International law enforcement cooperation in the fisheries sector: A guide for law enforcement practitioners*. Interpol. Retrieved from https://www.interpol.int/en/content/download/5147/file/GuideIntErLawEnforcementCoop-entier-WEB-2019–04.pdf.

Island Business. (2023, 11 May). Tuvalu joins forces with Sea Shepherd Global to combat illegal fishing. *Island Business*. Retrieved from https://islandsbusiness.com/news-break/tuvalu-fisheries-1/

IWC (International Whaling Commission). (2024). Commercial whaling. Retrieved from https://iwc.int/management-and-conservation/whaling/commercial

Karcher, D.B., Fache, E., Breckwoldt, A., Govan, H., Elías Ilosvay, X.E., Kam King, J.K., Riera, L. and Sabinot, C. (2020). Trends in South Pacific fisheries management. *Marine Policy*, *118*, 104021. https://doi.org/10.1016/j.marpol.2020.104021

Knecht, B. (2006). *A true story of pirates and the perfect fish*. Sydney: Allen & Unwin.

Kolmaš, M. (2021). International pressure and Japanese withdrawal from the International Whaling Commission: When shaming fails. *Australian Journal of International Affairs*, *75*(2), 197–216. doi:10.1080/10357718.2020.1799936

Korten, T. (2024, 23 January). Sea Shepherd's sea change. *Outside*. Retrieved from https://www.outsideonline.com/outdoor-adventure/environment/sea-shepherd/

Le Gallic, B. and Cox, A. (2006). An economic analysis of illegal, unreported and unregulated (IUU) fishing: Key drivers and possible solutions. *Marine Policy*, *30*, 689–695. doi:10.1016/j.marpol.2005.09.008

Longo, C.S., Buckley, L., Good, S.D., Gorham, T.M., Koerner, L., Lees, S., Liow, S.Y., Oloruntuyi, O., Schley, D., Rice, J. and Currey, R.J.C. (2021). A perspective on the role of eco-certification in eliminating illegal, unreported and unregulated fishing. *Frontiers in Ecology and Evolution*, *9*, 1–19. doi:10.3389/fevo.2021.637228

Mackay, M., Hardesty, B.D. and Wilcox, C. (2020). The intersection between illegal fishing, crimes at sea, and social well-being. *Frontiers in Marine Science*, *7*, 1–9. https://doi.org/10.3389/fmars.2020.589000

Meere, F. and Lack, M. (2008, November). *Assessment of impacts of illegal, unreported and unregulated (IUU) fishing in the Asia-Pacific*. Singapore: Asia-Pacific Economic Cooperation (APEC). Retrieved from https://www.apec.org/docs/default-source/Publications/2008/11/Assessment-of-Impacts-of-Illegal-Unreported-and-Unregulated-IUU-Fishing-in-the-AsiaPacific/08_fwg_IUU_fishing_assessmt.pdf

Moffa, A.L.I. (2012). Two competing models of activism, one goal: A case study of anti-whaling campaigns in the Southern Ocean. *Yale Journal of International Law*, *37*(1), 201–214.

MSC (Marine Stewardship Council). (2024). *Fishing methods and gear types*. London: Marine Stewardship Council. Retrieved from https://www.msc.org/what-we-are-doing/our-approach/fishing-methods-and-gear-types

Pain, N. and Pick, G. (2020). Balancing competing interests in the criminal justice system: Aboriginal fishing rights in coastal New South Wales. *University of New South Wales Law Journal*, *43*(4), 1383–1404.

Petrossian, G.A. (2019). *The last fish swimming: The global crime of illegal fishing*. Santa Barbara, CA: Praeger.

Poorhashemi, A. and Zarei, S. (2021). Legal analysis of the Judgment of the International Court of Justice on the Whaling in the Antarctic (Australia v. Japan: New Zealand Intervening). *CIFILE Journal of International Law*, *2*(3), 14–20. doi:10.30489/cifj.2020.240844.1022

Putt, J. and Anderson, K. (2007). *A national study of crime in the Australian fishing industry*. Research and Public Policy Series No. 76. Canberra: Australian Institute of Criminology. Retrieved from https://www.aic.gov.au/sites/default/files/2020-05/rpp076.pdf

Putt, J. and Nelson, D. (2008). *Crime in the Australian fishing industry*. Trends & Issues in Crime and Criminal Justice No. 366. Canberra: Australian Institute of Criminology. Retrieved from https://www.aic.gov.au/publications/tandi/tandi366

Rose, A. (2010). *Who killed the Grand Banks? The untold story behind the decimation of one of the world's greatest natural resources*. Mississauga, ON: John Wiley and Sons Canada.

Rothwell, D. and Stephens, T. (2016). *The international law of the sea* (2nd ed.). Oxford: Hart Publishing.

Rule, A. (2024, 20 April). How a broken system is set to wipe out a species. *Herald Sun*. Retrieved from https://www.heraldsun.com.au/news/opinion/andrew-rule/andrew-rule-how-a-broken

-system-is-set-to-wipe-out-a-species/news-story/257696b1465585e6f603805c9b9be56c

Shark Conservation Act of 2009 (SCA) (H.R. 81, S. 850).

Shark Research Institute. (n.d.). Shark finning legislation: A patchwork of protections at best. Retrieved from https://www.sharks.org/shark-finning-legislation

SPRFMO (South Pacific Regional Fisheries Management Organisation). (2024). Welcome to the South Pacific Regional Fisheries Management Organisation. Retrieved from https://www.sprfmo.int/

Sutton, A., Cherney, A., White, R. and Clancey, G. (2021). *Crime prevention: Principles, perspective and practices* (3rd ed.). Cambridge: Cambridge University Press.

Temple, A.J., Skerritt, D.J., Howarth, P.E.C., Peace, J. and Mangi, S.C. (2022). Illegal, unregulated and unreported fishing impacts: A systematic review of evidence and proposed future agenda. *Marine Policy*, *139*, 10533.

UNCLOS (1994). Retrieved from https://www.un.org/depts/los/convention_agreements/texts/unclos/unclos_e.pdf.

UNODC (United Nations Office on Drugs and Crime). (2022). *Stretching the fishnet: Identifying crime in the fisheries value chain.* Vienna: UNODC. Retrieved from https://www.unodc.org/res/environment-climate/resources_html/Stretching_the_Fishnet.pdf

Weinman, S. (2023, 22 May). Sea Shepherd on anti-poacher patrol in Tuvalu. *Divernet.* Retrieved from https://divernet.com/scuba-news/sea-shepherd-on-anti-poacher-patrol-in-tuvalu/

White, R. (2008). *Environmental harm and crime prevention.* Trends & Issues in Crime and Criminal Justice No. 360. Canberra: Australian Institute of Criminology. Retrieved from https://www.aic.gov.au/publications/tandi/tandi360

White, R. (2023). *Advanced introduction to applied green criminology.* Cheltenham, UK and Northampton, MA, USA: Edward Elgar Publishing.

Witbooi, E., Ali, K.D., Santosa, M.A., Hurley, G. … and Salas, O. (2020). Organized crime in the fisheries sector threatens a sustainable ocean economy. *Nature*, *588*, 48–56. https://doi.org/10.1038/s41586-020-2913-5

Wyatt, T. (2022). Transnational collaborations. In T. Wyatt, (ed.), *Wildlife trafficking: Critical criminological perspectives.* Cham: Palgrave Macmillan. Retrieved from https://doi.org/10.1007/978–3-030–83753–2_7.

Yuliantiningsih, A., Hartiwiningsih, Suherman, A.M. and Latifah, E. (2022). From illegal, unreported and unregulated fishing to transnational organised crime in fishery from an Indonesian perspective. In E.Y.J. Lee (Ed.) *ASEAN International Law* (pp. 481–502). Singapore: Springer. Retrieved from https://doi.org/10.1007/978–981–16–3195–5_27.

Zahnow, R. (2021). Risky places: Risky facilities – Illegal fishing in the natural environment. Video presentation to the Safeplaces Network, KTH Royal Institute of Technology in Stockholm. Retrieved from https://play.kth.se/media/Risky+PlacesA+Risky+facilities+-+Illegal+fishing+in+the+natural+environment+by+Dr.+Renee+Zahnow/0_z4pqod4h